CIMA

STRATEGIC

PAPER E3

STRATEGIC MANAGEMENT

TUDY TEXT

Our text is designed to help you study **effectively** and **efficiently**.

In this edition we:

- **Highlight** the **most important elements** in the syllabus and the **key skills** you will need

- **Signpost** how each chapter links to the syllabus and the learning outcomes

- Use **overview and summary diagrams** to develop understanding of interrelations between topics

- Provide **exam alerts** explaining how what you're learning may be tested

- **Include examples** and **questions** to help you apply what you've learnt

- **Emphasise key points** in **section summaries**

- **Test your knowledge** of what you've studied in **quick quizzes**

- **Examine your understanding** in our **practice question bank**

SUITABLE FOR EXAMS IN 2017 AND 2018

PUBLISHED NOVEMBER 2016

Third edition 2016

ISBN 9781 5097 0682 2
e-ISBN 9781 5097 0726 3

British Library Cataloguing-in-Publication Data
A catalogue record for this book
is available from the British Library

Published by

BPP Learning Media Ltd
BPP House, Aldine Place
London W12 8AA

www.bpp.com/learningmedia

Printed in the United Kingdom

Your learning materials, published by BPP Learning Media Ltd, are printed on paper sourced from sustainable, managed forests.

A note about copyright

Dear Customer

What does the little © mean and why does it matter?

Your market-leading BPP books, course materials and e-learning materials do not write and update themselves. People write them on their own behalf or as employees of an organisation that invests in this activity. Copyright law protects their livelihoods. It does so by creating rights over the use of the content.

Breach of copyright is a form of theft – as well as being a criminal offence in some jurisdictions, it is potentially a serious breach of professional ethics.

With current technology, things might seem a bit hazy but, basically, without the express permission of BPP Learning Media:

- Photocopying our materials is a breach of copyright
- Scanning, ripcasting or conversion of our digital materials into different file formats, uploading them to Facebook or emailing them to your friends is a breach of copyright

You can, of course, sell your books, in the form in which you have bought them – once you have finished with them. (Is this fair to your fellow students? We update for a reason.) Please note the e-products are sold on a single user licence basis: we do not supply 'unlock' codes to people who have bought them secondhand.

And what about outside the UK? BPP Learning Media strives to make our materials available at prices students can afford by local printing arrangements, pricing policies and partnerships which are clearly listed on our website. A tiny minority ignore this and indulge in criminal activity by illegally photocopying our material or supporting organisations that do. If they act illegally and unethically in one area, can you really trust them?

Contents

Review form

How our Study Text can help you pass

Streamlined studying	• We show you the best ways to study efficiently • Our Text has been designed to ensure you can easily and quickly navigate through it • The different features in our Text emphasise important knowledge and techniques
Exam expertise	• **Studying E3** on page xiii introduces the key themes of the syllabus and summarises how to pass • We highlight throughout our Text how topics may be tested and what you may have to do in the exam • We help you see the complete picture of the syllabus, so that you can answer questions that range across the whole syllabus • Our Text covers the syllabus content – no more, no less
Regular review	• We frequently summarise the key knowledge you need • We test what you've learnt by providing questions and quizzes throughout our Text

Our other products

BPP Learning Media also offers these products for the Objective Text exams and the integrated case study (ICS) exams:

i-Pass	Providing computer-based testing in a variety of formats, ideal for self-assessment
Exam Practice Kit	Providing helpful guidance on how to pass the objective test and more question practice
Passcards	Summarising what you should know in visual, easy to remember, form
ICS Workbook	Providing help with exam skills and question practice for the integrated case study exam

You can purchase these products by visiting www.bpp.com/learning-media

Online Learning with BPP

BPP's online learning study modes provide flexibility and convenience, allowing you to study effectively, at a pace that suits you, where and when you choose.

Online Classroom Live	Through live interactive online sessions it provides you with the traditional structure and support of classroom learning, but with the convenience of attending classes wherever you are
Online Classroom	Through pre-recorded online lectures it provides you with the classroom experience via the web with the tutor guidance & support you'd expect from a face to face classroom

You can find out more by visiting www.bpp.com/cima

Features in our Study Text

Chapter Overview Diagrams illustrate the connections between the topic areas you are about to cover

 Section Introductions explain how the section fits into the chapter

 Key Terms are the core vocabulary you need to learn

KEY TERM

 Key Points are points that you have to know, ideas or calculations that will be the foundations of your answers

KEY POINT

 Exam Alerts show you how subjects are likely to be tested

 Exam Skills are the key skills you will need to demonstrate in the exam, linked to question requirements

 Formulae To Learn are formulae you must remember in the exam

LEARN

 Exam Formulae are formulae you will be given in the exam

EXAM

 Examples show how theory is put into practice

 Questions give you the practice you need to test your understanding of what you've learnt

 Case Studies link what you've learnt with the real-world business environment

CASE STUDY

 Links show how the syllabus overlaps with other parts of the qualification, including Knowledge Brought Forward that you need to remember from previous exams

 Website References link to material that will enhance your understanding of what you're studying

 Further Reading will give you a wider perspective on the subjects you're covering

 Section Summary Diagrams allow you to review each section

Streamlined studying

What you should do	In order to
Read the Chapter and Section Introductions and look at the Chapter Overview Diagram	See why topics need to be studied and map your way through the chapter
Go quickly through the explanations	Gain the depth of knowledge and understanding that you'll need
Highlight the Key Points, Key Terms and Formulae To Learn	Make sure you know the basics that you can't do without in the exam
Focus on the Exam Skills and Exam Alerts	Know how you'll be tested and what you'll have to do
Work through the Examples and Case Studies	See how what you've learnt applies in practice
Prepare Answers to the Questions	See if you can apply what you've learnt in practice
Review the Chapter Summary Diagrams	Remind you of, and reinforce, what you've learnt
Answer the Quick Quiz	Find out if there are any gaps in your knowledge
Answer the Question(s) in the Practice Question Bank	Practise what you've learnt in depth

Should I take notes?

Brief notes may help you remember what you're learning. You should use the notes format that's most helpful to you (lists, diagrams, mind maps).

Further help

BPP Learning Media's *Learning to Learn Accountancy* provides lots more helpful guidance on studying. It is designed to be used both at the outset of your CIMA studies and throughout the process of learning accountancy. It can help you **focus your studies on the subject and exam**, enabling you to **acquire knowledge**, **practise and revise efficiently and effectively**.

Syllabus and learning outcomes

Paper E3 Strategic Management

The syllabus comprises:

Topic and Study Weighting

		%
A	Interacting with the organisation's environment	20
B	Evaluating strategic position and strategic options	30
C	Leading change	20
D	Implementing strategy	15
E	The role of information systems in organisational strategy	15

Learning Outcomes		
Lead	**Component**	**Syllabus content**
A Interacting with the organisation's environment		
1 Evaluate the influence of key external factors on an organisation's strategy	(a) Evaluate the influence and impact of the external environment on an organisation and its strategy	(i) Different organisational environments (including profit and not-for-profit organisations)
		(ii) The key environmental drivers of organisational change and their prioritisation
	(b) Recommend approaches to business/government relations and to relations with society	(i) Non-market strategy and forms of corporate political activity
	(c) Discuss the drivers of external demands for environmental sustainability and corporate social responsibility and the organisation's response	(i) External demands for sustainability and responsible business practices and ways to respond to these
	(d) Recommend how to build and manage strategic relationships with stakeholders (including suppliers, customers, owners, government and the wider society)	(i) Stakeholder management (stakeholders to include internal stakeholders, government and regulatory agencies, non-governmental organisations and civil society, industry associations, customers and suppliers)
		(ii) Building strategic alliances with stakeholders

Learning Outcomes		
Lead	**Component**	**Syllabus content**
		(iii) The customer portfolio: customer analysis and behaviour, including the marketing audit and customer profitability analysis as well as customer retention, relationship management and loyalty
		(iv) Strategic supply chain management
		(v) Implications of interactions with the external environment for Chartered Management Accountants
2 Evaluate ethical issues arising from the organisation's interaction with its environment	(a) Evaluate ethical issues and their resolution within a range of organisational contexts	(i) Business ethics and the CIMA Code of Ethics for Professional Accountants (Parts A and B) in the context of the implementation of strategic plans
B **Evaluating strategic position and strategic options**		
1 Evaluate the process of strategy formulation	(a) Evaluate the processes of strategic analysis and strategic options generation	(i) Vision and mission statements and their use in orientating the organisation's strategy
		(ii) The process of strategy formulation
		(iii) Strategic options generations (eg using Ansoff's product/market matrix and Porter's generic strategies)
		(iv) Scenario planning and long-range planning as tools in strategic decision making
		(v) Value drivers (including intangibles) of business and the data need to describe and measure them
		(vi) Game theory approaches to strategic planning and decision making
		(vii) Real options as a tool for strategic analysis

Learning Outcomes			
Lead	**Component**		**Syllabus content**
			(viii) Acquisition, divestment, rationalisation and relocation strategies in the context of strategic planning
	(b)	Recommend strategic options	(i) The identification and evaluation of strategic options, including the application of the suitability, acceptability and feasibility framework
	(c)	Discuss the role and responsibilities of directors in the strategy formulation and implementation process	(i) The role and responsibilities of the board of directors and senior managers in making strategic decisions (including issues of due diligence, fiduciary responsibilities and corporate social responsibility)
			(ii) The role of the Chartered Management Accountant in the strategy development process
2 Evaluate tools and techniques used in strategy formulation	(a)	Evaluate strategic analysis tools	(i) Audit of key resources and capabilities needed for strategy implementation
			(ii) Forecasting and the various techniques used: trend analysis, system modelling, in-depth consultation with expects (eg the Delphi method)
	(b)	Recommend how to manage the product portfolio of an organisation to support the organisation's strategic goals	(i) Management of the product portfolio
	(c)	Produce an organisation's Value Chain	(i) Value Chain analysis
C Leading change			
1 Advise on the important aspects of organisational change	(a)	Evaluate the key aspects of organisation change on organisations	(i) The impact of change on organisational culture (including the cultural web and McKinsey's 7S model)
	(b)	Evaluate the role of leadership in managing the change process and building and managing effective teams	(i) Team building, collaboration, group formation and shared knowledge and accountability

Learning Outcomes		
Lead	**Component**	**Syllabus content**
2 Evaluate tools and methods for successfully implementing a change programme	(a) Evaluate tools, techniques and strategies for managing and leading the change process	(i) The importance of managing critical periods of adaptive, evolutionary, reconstructive and revolutionary change
		(ii) Tools, techniques and models associated with organisational change
		(iii) Approaches, styles and strategies of change management
3 Recommend change leadership processes in support of strategy implementation	(a) Evaluate the role of the change leader in supporting strategy implementation	(i) Change leadership and its role in the successful implementation of strategy
		(ii) The role of the change leader in effective strategic communication
	(b) Recommend appropriate leadership styles within a range of organisational change contexts	(i) The advantages and disadvantages of management styles on the successful implementation of strategy
		(ii) Executive mentoring and coaching to promote effective change leadership
D Implementing strategy		
1 Evaluate the tools and techniques of strategy implementation	(a) Evaluate alternative models of strategic performance measurement in a range of business context	(i) Alternative strategic business unit (SBU) performance measures, including shareholder value analysis (SVA) and economic value added (EVA)
		(ii) Alternative models of measuring strategic performance (eg the Balanced Scorecard and the performance pyramid as strategic evaluation tools)

Learning Outcomes		
Lead	**Component**	**Syllabus content**
	(b) Recommend solutions to problems in strategic performance measurement	(i) Setting appropriate strategic targets through the use of a range of non-financial measures of strategic performance and their interaction with financial ones
		(ii) Evaluation of strategic targets through the development of critical success factors (CSFs)
		(iii) Linking CSFs to Key Performance Indicators (KPIs) and corporate strategy, and their use as a basis for defining an organisation's information needs
		(iv) Effective communication of strategic performance targets, including the need to drive strategic performance through stretch targets and promotional of exceptional performance
		(v) The role of the Chartered Management Accountant in the process of strategic performance evaluation
E **The role of information systems in organisational strategy**		
1 Evaluate the information system requirements for successful strategic implementation	(a) Evaluate the information systems required to sustain the organisation	(i) The purpose and contents of information systems strategies
		(ii) The classifications of knowledge
		(iii) Learning organisations
	(b) Advise managers on the development of strategies for knowledge management	(i) Knowledge management systems and knowledge-based organisations
		(ii) The need for information systems strategy to be complementary to the corporate and individual business unit strategies

Learning Outcomes		
Lead	**Component**	**Syllabus content**
2 Evaluate the opportunities for the use of IT and IS for the organisation, including Big Data	(a) Evaluate the impact of IT/IS on an organisation and its strategy	(i) The impact of IT, including the internet, on an organisation (utilising frameworks such as Porter's Five Forces and the Value Chain)
	(b) Evaluate the strategic and competitive impact of information systems, including the potential contribution of Big Data	(i) Competing through exploiting information, rather than technology (eg use of databases to identify potential customers or market segments, and the collection, analysis, storage and management of data)
		(ii) Aligning information systems with business strategy (eg strategic important of information systems; information systems or competitive advantage; information systems for competitive necessity)
		(iii) Contemporary developments in the commercial use of the internet (eg e-business, virtual organisations and Web 2.0, Big Data, social media and other forms of digital marketing)
		(iv) The role of Big Data and Digitisation in knowledge-based organisations

Studying E3

1 What E3's about

1.1 Business Strategy and the organisation's environment

Business strategy reflects an organisation's goals and the way it seeks to organise its resources in the long term, to achieve competitive advantage in its environment, and to meet market and stakeholder expectations.

E3 looks at how organisations **design** and **implement** strategy. In Chapter 1 we look at how business strategies are developed, and we identify different approaches to strategy development. We also highlight the role that management accountants can play in strategy development – particularly in relation to strategic management accounting.

In Chapter 2, we look at the **goals and objectives** of organisations, and how **stakeholders** affect those goals and objectives. Strategy is developed in a situational context, so it is important to understand how an organisation's external environment and its stakeholders can affect strategy development. It is also important to recognise the range of objectives an organisation may have, and we reflect this by looking at themes of **corporate social responsibility** and sustainability.

Although strategy development is a process, it is one which is affected by a significant degree of **uncertainty**. The external environment in which organisations exist is a major source of uncertainty, and can also be a driver for change. In Chapter 3 we look at some of the ways businesses can analyse their environments and also how they can address uncertainty with those environments in their **strategic decision-making process**.

1.2 Internal capabilities

Alongside the external context in which it operates, the internal resources and capabilities of an organisation also help shape the strategic options which are available to it. In Chapter 4 we look at some of the key aspects of an organisation's current position – including its **resources**, **value chain** and **product portfolio**.

1.3 Strategic options

By drawing together external and internal factors, organisations can identify appropriate strategies which they can pursue to exploit their core competences and achieve their strategic objectives.

Chapter 5 of this Text is concerned with the **strategic choices** organisations make. The most important issues here are how they **compete**, and what methods they employ to **grow**. With respect to growth, we consider both the **directions** (products and markets) and the **methods** of growth – organic growth, acquisitions or strategic alliances.

We also highlight that an organisation should make strategic choices on the basis of three key factors: **suitability, feasibility** and **acceptability**. In this context, it is important to remember how management accountants can apply decision techniques to assist strategic decision making.

1.4 Information systems

Information and **information systems** play an increasingly important role in shaping and supporting the business strategies of contemporary organisations.

On the one hand, the management **information** produced by an organisation's information systems can be crucial in enabling managers to plan and control activities, and to make strategic decisions. However, information and knowledge can also be the source of competitive advantage in their own right.

Equally, technological developments are increasingly influencing business strategies in their own right, most notably through the growth of **e-business** and **e-commerce**.

Chapter 6 looks primarily at the importance of information systems in supporting business strategy, while Chapter 7 examines how organisations can use and manage data, information and knowledge to help them compete. In this context, it is important to recognise the impact which the **internet** has had on the information which is available to businesses – for example as a result of **Web 2.0 technologies**, **social media** and **Big Data**.

1.5 Strategic marketing

Technology and the use of databases can help organisations compete by identifying potentially profitable customers and market segments. In Chapter 8 we turn to look more specifically at the way organisations **attract and retain customers**, and we highlight the importance of organisations analysing the profitability of their customers (**customer profitability analysis**).

1.6 Change management

We have already identified the importance of options and choices in business strategy. However, once an organisation has made a strategic choice it will have to implement that strategy. Implementing strategy involves a number of tools and techniques associated with change management, and we look at these in Chapters 9 and 10.

We have already highlighted in Chapter 3 some of the factors that may **trigger change**, so the primary focus of Chapter 9 is the **process of change** itself.

It is important to recognise that organisations can face different **types of change**, and the styles needed to manage change will vary according to the type of change, and the **context** in which the change is taking place.

In both Chapters 9 and 10 we look at the different **styles and strategies for managing change**, but our main focus in Chapter 10 is the vital importance of effective **leadership** and **communication** in implementing change.

1.7 Implementing strategy

In order for an organisation to know whether its strategy has been successful it needs to be able to **measure performance** (Chapters 11 and 12). These are areas where the management accountant's role will be vital. However, it is important that performance measurement systems consider non-financial performance as well as financial performance. Frameworks such as the balanced scorecard and the performance pyramid illustrate how financial and non-financial measures can be combined.

2   What's required

At the heart of E3 is the ability to **apply your knowledge** to **analyse and resolve practical problems**, so that you can make sensible recommendations or provide valuable advice to managers in an organisation. Particularly in the context of the integrated case study scenario, the examiner is not simply looking for you to display your knowledge of the syllabus topics, but to be able to apply that knowledge to a specific context highlighted by the question scenario.

Key skills which will be tested are your ability to **analyse** information, **evaluate** it and make **sensible recommendations** based on that analysis and evaluation.

The aspects of business strategy you discuss in your answer must follow from the **content and context** of the scenario. You may also have to use appropriate numerical techniques to quantify a strategic choice or an issue facing an organisation.

Any advice you give, or recommendations you make, must not only be **relevant** to deal with the issues identified in the question, but must also be **appropriate** for the organisation described in the scenario. For example, a strategy which may be appropriate for a small, not for profit organisation may not be appropriate for a large, multinational corporation.

3 How to pass

3.1 Study the whole syllabus

You need to be comfortable with **all areas of the syllabus**, as questions in the **objective test exam** will cover all syllabus areas. **Wider reading** will help you understand the strategic issues organisations face, which will be particularly useful in the integrated case study exam.

3.2 Lots of question practice

You can **develop application skills** by attempting questions in the Practice Question Bank. While these might not be in the format that you will experience in your exam, doing the full question will help you to answer the exam questions. In the integrated case study exam you will have to answer questions that combine E3 syllabus areas with F3 and P3. However, by answering questions on E3 now you will develop the technical knowledge and skills you will need to draw on to answer those questions.

You should also practise OT exam standard questions, which you will find in the BPP Exam Practice Kit.

4 Brought forward knowledge

The examiner may test knowledge or techniques you've learnt at lower levels. As E3 is at the top of the Enterprise pillar, the content of Papers E1 and E2 will be significant.

CIMA provide the following syllabus overview:

'E3 builds on the insights gained from E1 and E2 about how organisations effectively implement their strategies by aligning their structures, people, processes, projects and relationships. E3 aims to develop the skills and abilities of the strategic leaders of organisations, enabling them to create the vision and direction for the growth and long-term sustainable success of the organisation.'

A number of areas of material from the Operational and Managerial level papers (particularly P1 and P2, as well as E1 and E2) could also be relevant in E3, including:

- Product and pricing decisions
- Managing costs for competitive advantage
- Budgeting and management control
- Organisational structure in management control
- Performance management and control

Remember, however, that brought forward knowledge will only be useful if it is **applied at a strategic level**. Hence for example you are unlikely to be asked to prepare a budget in E3, but you may have to discuss how effective budgets are as control mechanisms.

5 The Integrated Case Study and links with F3 and P3

The Integrated Case Study exam is based on the expectation that students are developing a pool of knowledge, and can appropriately apply their knowledge from any syllabus when faced with a problem. As such, CIMA expects you to make links between the strategic level papers, and not to view the three subjects (E3, F3 and P3) in isolation.

- **Strategic management decisions** will have an **impact** on the **financial objectives**, sources of finance chosen, the investment decisions, the risks the organisation faces and the controls necessary to counter those risks.

- Strategic management decisions will also be constrained by an **organisation's risk management strategy** and its attitude to risk.

- Strategic management can have an impact on the information systems in an organisation, and so the **risks and controls associated with information systems** need to be considered.

- At the same time, **investment choices** will be **constrained** by the finance available and the financial objectives of an organisation. Equally, the possible **costs**, **benefits** and **risks** attached to a strategic choice all need to be subject to a **financial evaluation**.

- **Performance measurement** techniques such as ratio analysis may be useful in any paper. The **effectiveness of management accounting systems**, particularly the information provided and how useful they are as control mechanisms, could also be relevant to any of the strategic level papers.

6 What the examiner means

The table below has been prepared by CIMA to help you interpret the syllabus and learning outcomes and the meaning of questions.

You will see that there are 5 levels of Learning objective, ranging from Knowledge to Evaluation, reflecting the level of skill you will be expected to demonstrate. CIMA Certificate subjects only use levels 1 to 3, but in CIMA's Professional qualification the entire hierarchy will be used.

At the start of each chapter in your Study Text is a topic list relating the coverage in the chapter to the level of skill you may be called on to demonstrate in the exam.

Learning objectives	Verbs used	Definition
1 Knowledge		
What are you expected to know	• List	• Make a list of
	• State	• Express, fully or clearly, the details of/facts of
	• Define	• Give the exact meaning of
2 Comprehension		
What you are expected to understand	• Describe	• Communicate the key features of
	• Distinguish	• Highlight the differences between
	• Explain	• Make clear or intelligible/state the meaning or purpose of
	• Identify	
	• Illustrate	• Recognise, establish or select after consideration
		• Use an example to describe or explain something
3 Application		
How you are expected to apply your knowledge	• Apply	• Put to practical use
	• Calculate/ compute	• Ascertain or reckon mathematically
		• Prove with certainty or to exhibit by practical means
	• Demonstrate	
	• Prepare	• Make or get ready for use
	• Reconcile	• Make or prove consistent/compatible
	• Solve	• Find an answer to
	• Tabulate	• Arrange in a table
4 Analysis		
How you are expected to analyse the detail of what you have learned	• Analyse	• Examine in detail the structure of
	• Categorise	• Place into a defined class or division
	• Compare and contrast	• Show the similarities and/or differences between
		• Build up or compile
	• Construct	• Examine in detail by argument
	• Discuss	• Translate into intelligible or familiar terms
	• Interpret	• Place in order of priority or sequence for action
	• Prioritise	• Create or bring into existence
	• Produce	
5 Evaluation		
How you are expected to use your learning to evaluate, make decisions or recommendations	• Advise	• Counsel, inform or notify
	• Evaluate	• Appraise or assess the value of
	• Recommend	• Propose a course of action

Competency Framework

CIMA has developed a competency framework detailing the skills, abilities and competencies that finance professionals need. The CIMA syllabus has been developed to match the competency mix as it develops over the three levels of the professional qualification. The importance of the various competencies at the strategic level is shown below.

Assessment

The CIMA assessment is a two-tier structure with objective tests for each subject and an integrated case study at each level.

Objective test

The objective tests are computer based and can be taken on demand. The student exam preparation section on the CIMA website (www.cimaglobal.com) has additional information and tools to help you become familiar with the test style. Make sure you check back regularly as more information may be added.

Integrated case study

Candidates must pass or receive exemptions from the three objective tests at each level, before attempting the integrated case study exam for that level.

The integrated case studies are available four times a year.

The integrated case study exams combine the knowledge and learning from all the pillars. They will be set in the context of a preseen fictional organisation based on a real industry.

The focus from a E3 perspective will be in evaluating whether an organisation is developing an appropriate strategy, and ensuring that strategy is implemented effectively.

INTERACTING WITH THE ORGANISATION'S ENVIRONMENT

Part A

FUNDAMENTALS OF STRATEGIC MANAGEMENT

 This chapter provides an overview of the key approaches to corporate strategy theory, and the way organisations formulate their corporate strategies.

We begin by looking at some of the general principles and practice of business strategy, before comparing some different approaches to strategic planning.

We then examine the role of the management accountant in the strategy development process, particularly in relation to strategic management accounting.

The chapter finishes with a discussion of the role of directors and senior managers in the strategic process.

This chapter builds on knowledge gained in Paper E2 where you first saw different approaches to strategy (for example, prescriptive versus emergent approaches).

Although we can identify these different generic approaches to strategy, there are still a number of interpretations about how an organisation can best implement its strategy. Ultimately, an organisation's strategy needs to be seen in the context of its history and culture, its competitive environment and its resources, and we look at the influence of these factors in Chapters 3 and 4 later in this Study Text.

Topic list	Learning outcomes	Syllabus references	Ability required
1 Strategic management	B1(a)	B1(a) (ii)	Evaluate
2 Strategic planning: the rational model	B1(a)	B1(a) (ii)	Evaluate
3 Less formal strategic planning	B1(a)	B1(a) (ii)	Evaluate
4 Environmental complexity and organisations	B1(a)	B1(a) (ii)	Evaluate
5 Resource-based strategy	B1(a)	B1(a) (ii)	Evaluate
6 Management accountants and strategy development	B1(c)	B1(c) (ii)	Discuss
7 Directors' strategic roles and responsibilities	B1(c)	B1(c) (i)	Discuss

Chapter Overview

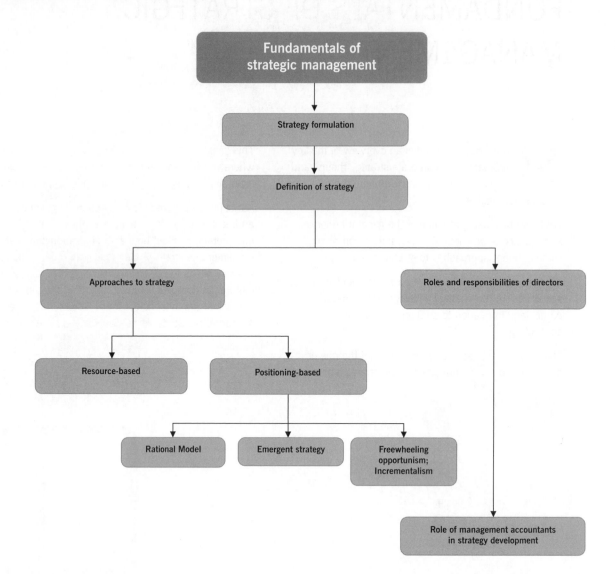

1 Strategic management

Introduction

The E3 syllabus explores the ways in which organisations design and implement their strategies, and looks at the factors which affect those strategies. However, before we move on to examine these issues, we consider why organisations need to develop strategies.

All organisations need to plan if they are going to maintain their direction and scope over the long term. If they do not plan, they are liable to drift and lose their competitive advantage in a changing environment.

KEY POINT

Strategic decisions relate to the scope of a firm's activities, the long-term direction of the organisation, and allocation of resources.

Managing business strategy involves the entire cycle of **planning and control**, at a **strategic** level.

- Strategic analysis
- Strategic choice
- Implementation of chosen strategies
- Review and control

KEY TERM

PLANNING is the 'establishment of objectives and the formulation, evaluation and selection of the policies, strategies, tactics and action required to achieve them. Planning comprises long-term/strategic planning, and short-term/operational planning'.   *(CIMA Official Terminology)*

How does this relate to the management of business strategy?

KEY TERMS

A STRATEGY is a 'course of action, including the specification of resources required, to achieve a specific objective'.

A STRATEGIC PLAN is a 'statement of long-term goals along with a definition of the strategies and policies which will ensure achievement of these goals'.   *(CIMA Official Terminology)*

In their text *Exploring Corporate Strategy,* Johnson, Scholes and Whittington (2008) define strategy as follows:

'**Strategy** is the **direction and scope** of an organisation over the **long term** which **achieves advantage** in a **changing environment** through its configuration of **resources and competences** with the aim of fulfilling **stakeholder expectations**.'

We can take the highlighted phrases out of this definition, and expand them to indicate that there is general agreement on what constitutes the key elements of strategy.

Phrase	Comment
Direction and scope	Strategy gives at least an **initial deliberate direction**, range of **activities** and **future** for the company to aim at, even if environmental circumstances conspire to send it off course and demand management action.
Long term	Strategy is the **long-term direction** of an organisation.
	This long-term direction can include both **planned** strategy, and more **incremental, emergent** patterns of strategy. (We look at these different approaches to strategy later in this chapter.)

Phrase	Comment
Achieves advantage	Strategy affects the overall wellbeing of the organisation, and its position against competitors.
	For commercial organisations, strategy is ultimately a means to achieve **a sustainable competitive advantage** against its competitors.
Changing environment	As we explore further in Chapter 3, organisations are inextricably linked with their environments, and strategy can help organisations to cope with **changes** and **complexity** in those environments.
	An organisation needs to match its activities to its **capabilities** and the **environment** in which it operates.
Configuration of resources and competences	Strategies require **processes** to guide the **effective utilisation** of resources and competences in order to achieve competitive advantage.
	Strategies also require integration across functional and operational boundaries, and need to be supported by operational decisions.
Stakeholder expectations	Stakeholders (in particular **shareholders**) have their own interests in the organisation. Should the pursuit of shareholder wealth be the main concern of management? What about **customers'** expectations and satisfying market demand? And what about the organisations' **employees**?

To develop a business strategy, an organisation has to decide the following:

- What it is **good at**
- How the market might **change**
- How **customer satisfaction** can be delivered
- What might **constrain** realisation of the plan
- What should be done to **minimise risk**
- What **actions** should be put in place

We return to this point in more detail in Chapter 5 (in relation to choosing a generic strategy), but another way of defining 'strategy' might be:

- Deciding **how** to compete (eg in terms of cost, or quality)

- Deciding **where** to compete (which geographical markets, and which market segments to compete in)

Exam skills

There is often no single 'right' or 'wrong' strategy an organisation can use in a situation, although some strategies will be more suitable than others. A good strategy will enable an organisation to use its resources and capabilities successfully in circumstances it cannot confidently predict.

Remember this as you tackle the integrated case study scenarios in the exam – and always make sure that any strategies you suggest address the circumstances and **context** highlighted by the scenario.

The context of strategy is very important. For example, **small businesses** tend to have limited resources and face strong competition. **Large multinationals** will have more resources, but have to make decisions about structure, resource allocation, and which markets to compete in.

Public sector and **not for profit organisations** are influenced by ideology, politics and a range of stakeholders.

1.1 Approaches to strategic planning

It is also important to recognise that firms can take different approaches to strategic planning, meaning that they prioritise different elements of strategic analysis.

There are three main approaches to strategic planning:

(a) **Accounting-led**: An organisation adopting an accounting-led approach starts by looking at its key stakeholders and their objectives (eg to increase pre-tax profits by x% per year, and earnings per share by y% per year). The organisation then develops plans which are designed to achieve those objectives.

However, critics argue that such an approach to strategic planning is flawed because it doesn't take sufficient account of market conditions and the external environment.

(b) **Position-based approach**: By contrast, an organisation adopting a position-based approach analyses its environment (eg markets and competitors; using PEST analysis and Porter's five forces) before setting its objectives and strategy. In this way, the organisation can try to ensure its strategic plans provide a good 'fit' with its environment.

Importantly, the external focus of the position-based approach should help organisations be aware of changes in their environments. Moreover, if an organisation is able to predict changes in advance of them happening, this could help the organisation plan how to deal with those changes rather than simply having to react to them.

(We look in more detail at the environment and uncertainty in Chapter 3 of this Study Text.)

(c) **Resource-based approach**: Critics of the position-based approach argue that the extent of the changes in the environment make it very difficult for organisations to predict the future with any certainty. Therefore, rather than trying to focus on a 'fit' with the environment, organisations should focus their strategy on their own core competences and capabilities – what they are good at.

However, the potential flaw with this approach is that it is too inward-looking. For example, there would be little use in an organisation being good at something if there is no longer a market demand for it. Equally, environmental changes may mean that the organisation's core competences are no longer a source of competitive advantage (for example, due to the emergence of new technologies or substitute products).

We discuss resources, competences and capabilities in more detail in Chapter 4 of this Study Text.

Section summary

Organisations need strategies to establish their direction and scope in the long term, and to determine the resources and competences needed to achieve their desired courses of action.

2 Strategic planning: the rational model

Introduction

The **rational model** is a comprehensive approach to strategy. It suggests a logical sequence which involves analysing the current situation, generating choices (relating to competitors, products and markets) and implementing the chosen strategies.

2.1 The rational model

The rational model provides a useful way of summarising the strategic planning process.

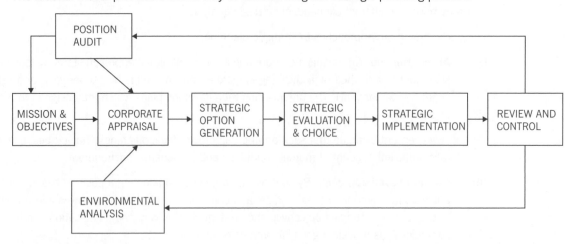

Strategic planning can be divided into three related stages: strategic **analysis**, strategic **choice** and strategic **implementation**.

However, Johnson, Scholes and Whittington argue that the three elements of analysis, choice and implementation do not necessarily follow a linear process as the rational model suggests. Instead, they argue that the elements are interlinked and feed back on each other. For example, when an organisation starts to implement a strategy, it may discover things about its environment or capabilities that may in turn help it with future strategic analysis and choices. In this respect, Johnson, Scholes and Whittington stress the **interdependence** and **integration** of the three elements of analysis, choice and implementation in strategic management.

Equally, Johnson, Scholes and Whittington also note that strategic management is not a 'neat and tidy path' and often not 'tidy' in practice. Nonetheless, the general idea of the rational model, and the three aspects of strategic analysis, choice and implementation can still provide us with a useful framework in which to look at strategic planning within organisations.

In effect, the structure of this Study Text loosely follows the structure of the rational model:

Mission and objectives – Chapter 2
Environmental analysis – Chapter 3
Position audit (resource and capabilities) – Chapter 4
Options generation and evaluation – Chapter 5
Strategic implementation (marketing, IT/IS, change management) – Chapters 6 to 10
Review and control (performance measurement/management) – Chapters 11 and 12

2.1.1 Strategic analysis

Strategic analysis can be viewed as understanding the **strategic position** of any organisation.

Michael Porter, one of the key writers on business strategy, highlights the importance of understanding the strategic position of an organisation when he argues that 'the essence of formulating competitive strategy is relating a company to its environment'.

We can break down the strategic analysis stage of strategic planning into a series of steps:

	Stage	Comment	Key tools, models, techniques
Step 1	Mission and/or vision	Mission denotes values, the business's rationale for existing; vision refers to where the organisation intends to be in a few years' time	• Mission statement
Step 2	Goals	Interpret the mission to different stakeholders	• Stakeholder analysis
Step 3	Objectives	Quantified embodiments of mission	• Measures such as profitability, timescale, deadlines
Step 4	Environmental analysis	Identify opportunities and threats	• PEST analysis • Porter's five forces analysis; 'diamond' (competitive advantage of nations) • Scenario building
Step 5	Position audit or situation analysis	Identify strengths and weaknesses Firm's current resources, products, customers, systems, structure, results, efficiency, effectiveness	• Resource audit • Distinctive competence • Value chain • Product life cycle • BCG matrix • Marketing audit
Step 6	Corporate appraisal	Combines Steps 4 and 5	• SWOT analysis charts
Step 7	Gap analysis	Compares outcomes of Step 6 with Step 3	• Gap analysis

2.1.2 Strategic choice

Stage	Comment	Key tools, models, techniques
Strategic options generation	Come up with new ideas to help fill the 'gaps' identified in gap analysis: • How to compete (competitive advantage) • Where to compete • Method of growth	• Value chain analysis • Scenario building • Porter's generic strategic choices • Ansoff's growth vector matrix • Acquisition vs organic growth
Strategic options evaluation	Normally, each strategy has to be evaluated on the basis of: • Suitability • Acceptability • Feasibility	• Stakeholder analysis • Risk analysis • Decision-making tools such as decision trees, matrices, ranking and scoring methods • Financial measures (eg ROCE, DCF, NPV)

Strategy selection involves choosing between the alternative strategies.

The **competitive strategies** are the generic strategies for competitive advantage an organisation will pursue. They determine **how an organisation generates competitive advantage**: for example, by cost leadership or differentiation.

Product-market strategies (which markets you should enter or leave) determine **where you compete** and the direction of growth.

Institutional strategies (ie relationships with other organisations) determine the **method of growth**.

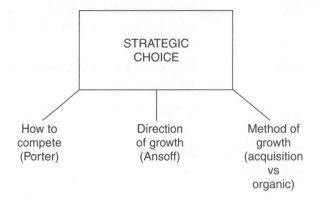

2.1.3 Strategy implementation

Strategy implementation is the **conversion** of the strategy into detailed plans or objectives for operating units. In this respect, strategic implementation is a vital part of the strategic planning process, because a strategy can only start delivering benefit to an organisation once it has been put into practice.

The planning of implementation has several aspects.

- **Resource** planning (eg financial; HRM)
- **Operations** planning
- **Organisation** structure and control systems

Change is often a critical component of strategy implementation, because organisations have to change in order to achieve their chosen strategies.

2.1.4 Review and control

Ultimately, the success of any strategy comes from the results it delivers. However, it is equally important for an organisation to monitor and evaluate its progress towards its strategic objectives.

This not only highlights the need for performance measurement (eg KPIs; comparing actual results to targets) but, equally importantly, it also highlights the need to set budgets and targets in the first place in order to provide a benchmark to compare actual performance against.

Exam skills

An organisation's ability to successfully deliver its strategy is likely to depend on departments and individuals within the organisation all having goals which are congruent with that overall strategy. This highlights the importance of individuals' and departments' objectives being consistent with those of the organisation as a whole.

If an organisation in a case study question appears not to be performing as well as might be expected, one issue to look out for may be whether there are clashes between department objectives or performance measures, and overall objectives. For example, if a department's performance is being judged using ROCE this might deter department managers from investing in new capital, although that capital investment might be necessary for the longer-term growth and success of the business.

2.2 Levels of strategy

Corporate strategy is the highest level of strategy in an organisation, identifying the strategy for the organisation as a whole. For example, this might include setting the overall objectives for the organisation and identifying its corporate values, whether to enter a new industry or market, or to leave an existing industry/market.

Business strategy relates to how an organisation approaches a particular market, or the activity of a particular business unit. For example, this might include the way a business unit adapts to customer requirements or competitors' actions, and how it manages unique competences to compete successfully in specific markets.

While corporate strategy relates to an organisation as a whole, business strategy focuses **on strategic business units** (SBUs).

Operational and functional strategies involve decisions which are made at operational level and affect the day to day operation of the business. These decisions include marketing strategy, HR strategy, IT/IS strategy and so forth. The contributions of these different functions determine the success of the strategy.

This again reinforces the importance of **strategy implementation** within strategic management. A strategic plan is ultimately only likely to be successful if it is delivered effectively at an operational level.

The idea of different levels of strategy can be represented by the Anthony hierarchy. We look at the Anthony hierarchy in relation to the information required for organisational decision making and control in Chapter 6 of this Study Text.

Section summary

The **rational model** describes a highly structured approach to strategic planning. An organisation identifies its objectives, analyses its current position, develops its strategic options and then selects a strategy to implement.

3 Less formal strategic planning

Introduction

The rational model can be seen as a formal approach to strategy. This approach has identifiable advantages, but it also has problems. In an attempt to address these problems, alternative models of strategic planning have been developed, including **freewheeling opportunism, incrementalism** and **emergent strategies**. The management accountant's role differs in each case.

3.1 Advantages of formal planning

The following table lists the advantages of a formal system of strategic planning.

Advantages	Comments
Identifies risks	Strategic planning helps in managing these risks.
Forces managers to think	Strategic planning can encourage creativity and initiative by tapping the ideas of the management team.
Forces decision making	Companies cannot remain static – they have to cope with changes in the environment. A strategic plan draws attention to the need to change and adapt, not just to 'stand still' and survive.

Advantages	Comments
Better control	Management control can be exercised better if targets are explicit.
Enforces consistency at all levels	Long-term, medium-term and short-term objectives, plans and controls can be made consistent with one another. Otherwise, strategies can be rendered ineffective by budgeting systems and performance measures which have no strategic content.
Co-ordinates activities of different business functions	The management writer, Peter Drucker, has argued that an entrepreneur who builds a long-lasting business has 'a theory of the business' which informs their business decisions. In large organisations, that theory of the business has to become public knowledge, as decisions cannot be taken only by one person.

3.2 Criticisms of strategic planning in practice (Mintzberg)

The idea that strategy making can be reduced to planning processes has come under attack from Henry Mintzberg in his book *The Rise and Fall of Strategic Planning.* Mintzberg argues there are a number of problems with formal planning processes.

Problem	Comments
Practical failure	Empirical studies have not proved that formal planning processes contribute to success. Companies which adopt long-range views and planning techniques do not consistently outperform those which do not.
Routine and regular	Strategic planning occurs often in an annual cycle. But a firm cannot allow itself to wait every year for the budget planning process to address its problems.
Reduces initiative	Formal planning discourages strategic thinking. Once a plan is locked in place, people are unwilling to question it, or to take alternative actions to improve a situation, because they feel that, if they do, they will have to defend themselves for acting 'outside the plan' – regardless of any benefits which result from their actions.
Internal politics	The assumption of 'objectivity' in evaluation ignores political battles between different managers and departments.
Exaggerates power	Managers are not all-knowing, and there are limits to the extent to which they can control the behaviour of the organisation.

3.3 General limitations of planning models

Plans are made so that sensible attempts may be made to guide and control future developments. All planning methods are limited in their ability to help in doing this, simply because of the **difficulty in trying to predict the future** with any degree of certainty.

(a)   It is very common to assume that **the future will resemble the past**. Unfortunately, discontinuities or shocks occur and these are, by definition, impossible to predict with accuracy.

(b)   All models require **assumptions** to be made. This has two important implications:

    (i)   The assumptions used should be tailored to the industry and organisation in question. For example, industry price inflation rates may be different from the national rate.

    (ii)   The further into the future one looks, the less likely it is that assumptions will **remain valid**. Predictions of more distant future events become less reliable. For some industries with extremely distant time horizons, forecasting on any basis may be quite impractical. However, one of the characteristics of strategic planning is that it looks at the **long-term** direction an organisation might take.

BPP
LEARNING MEDIA

3.3.1 Difficulties with long-term planning

One of the key difficulties in strategic (long-term) planning comes from trying to accurately forecast what will happen in the long term.

The fact that strategic planners are dealing with a long time period could, in itself, be a problem.

However, their difficulties are likely to be increased further by the **complexity and dynamism of the environment**, and **the rapidity of change** within the environment.

Equally, it can be difficult to predict how the relationships between different variables in the environment will develop.

Managers also face difficulties in balancing **long-term** planning objectives and **short-term** pressures. Although managers might set long-term plans, they will also be under pressure to deliver short-term results – particularly in listed companies.

One of the criticisms of long-term plans is that they are **too rigid**, and do not give companies the flexibility to react to unforeseen short-term opportunities or unexpected short-term crises.

Exam skills

One of the difficulties which strategic planners face is the pressure to deliver strategies which are acceptable to different stakeholder groups with different (possibly contradictory) objectives.

This highlights the importance of **stakeholder management**, which we look at in more detail in Chapter 2 of this Study Text. Stakeholder management is an important element of strategic management, and when discussing or recommending a proposed strategy it is important that you consider how acceptable that strategy might be to different stakeholder groups.

3.4 Structural determinism

KEY TERM

STRUCTURAL DETERMINISM is the notion that an organisation's response to an environmental shock or influence will depend on what type of structure it (the organisation) is.

We also need to acknowledge the concept of structural determinism when considering the relationships between an organisation and its environment.

We have already noted that one of the potential problems of prescriptive approaches to strategy is that they cannot predict or control external environmental factors. However, this problem is complicated further by the fact that an **organisation's response to an environmental shock will depend on what type of structure the organisation is**.

As an analogy, if you put clay into a hot oven, the clay will harden, but if you put ice into a hot oven, the ice will melt. Although the environmental conditions are the same in both cases, they generate very different responses. The same is true for organisations: where the same environmental conditions can generate different strategic responses in different organisations, depending on their individual internal characteristics.

For example, during the 2008–9 recession in the UK, Marks & Spencer – whose competitive strategy places importance on quality rather than low cost – was forced to make job cuts and to close some of its food stores. However, at the same time, low-cost food retailers such as Aldi and Lidl reported increased sales as cash-conscious customers looked to buy their groceries as cheaply as possible.

Structural determinism has two important implications for strategy makers.

(a)   It is inappropriate for all organisations to pursue a single approach for strategic success because organisations are different. A strategy needs to be adapted to the specific circumstances of the organisation.

(b)   Strategists need to look inside the organisation as well as at the environment. They need to understand the behaviour of the organisation as much as the environment.

Exam skills

The first bullet point about structural determinism could have important implications for your integrated case study exam.

Since strategies need to be adapted to the specific circumstances of an organisation, make sure that any strategies you recommend are appropriate to the organisation and context described in the case study scenario.

3.5 No strategic planning: 'freewheeling opportunism'

The **freewheeling opportunism approach** suggests firms should not bother with strategic plans but should exploit opportunities as they arise.

The opportunist approach means that an organisation can **seize opportunities** quickly (rather than getting slowed down by formal planning processes), but the lack of planning may also mean the organisation **fails to identify possible opportunities** which might be available.

Advantages

(a)   Good opportunities are not lost through spending time completing formal planning processes.

(b)   A freewheeling opportunistic approach would **adapt to change** more quickly (eg if there were a very steep rise in the price of a key material input, the opportunist firm would look to find any alternative material as quickly as possible).

(c)   It might encourage a more **flexible, creative attitude**.

Disadvantages

(a)   **No co-ordinating framework** for the organisation, so that some potentially valuable opportunities get missed.

(b)   It emphasises the **profit motive** to the exclusion of all other considerations.

(c)   The firm ends up **reacting** all the time rather than acting purposively.

3.5.1 Management accounting and freewheeling opportunism

A **freewheeling opportunism** approach abandons the careful routine of planning, and instead seizes such opportunities that arise. Not all 'opportunities' will work out, and there may be problems sustaining this policy.

The management accountant's role will be **investigative**.

(a)   What are the financial characteristics of the proposed strategy? For example, in an acquisition, what is the effect on **cash flow**?

(b)   How does the proposed strategy affect the firm's **risk profile**?

(c)   What **new markets** will the firm be entering by pursuing this strategy? If so, what is the likely response of competitors?

3.6 Incrementalism

Herbert Simon suggested that managers often have to adopt a solution which is reasonable, if not ideal. Managers are limited by **time**, by the **information** they have and by their own skills, habits and perceptions of reality.

This has the following implications:

(a) Strategic managers do not evaluate all the possible options but choose between relatively few alternatives. Managers can only handle a limited number of options at any one time. (This restriction in the number of options managers are able to choose from is known as **bounded rationality**.)

(b) Strategy making tends to involve small-scale extensions of past policy – **incrementalism** – rather than radical shifts.

KEY POINT

Incrementalism is an approach to strategy and decision making highlighting small and slow changes rather than one-off changes in direction. The danger is that such small-scale adjustments may not be enough to move with customers and their needs, leading to **strategic drift**.

We discuss issues around the speed and extent of change in more detail later, in the chapters on change management.

Quinn coined the term **logical incrementalism** to mean that strategies might not be formulated by planning, but using an incremental process with an underlying logic. Top managers guide internal activities (as with the rational approach) while at the same time responding to external events, and develop their conscious strategies this way.

CASE STUDY

Tesco.com and Webvan

Tesco.com, the online shopping operation set up by the UK supermarket giant, is a good example of successful incrementalism. In 1996, Tesco decided to test the potential for online grocery shopping with a website based on a single store at Osterley in West London. Over the next two years the business model was refined and the crucial decision to impose a delivery charge was made. This had the beneficial effect of leading customers to place fewer, larger orders so as to obtain the greatest benefit from the flat-rate charge.

Tesco's online business has grown successfully since its launch, and in its 2014 Annual Report Tesco noted that its online business had grown to become a 'market-leading, profitable grocery home shopping business that … generates £2.5 billion of sales in the UK'. As such, the online business has now become a key platform in Tesco's multichannel strategy.

Initially, the goods delivered to customers through the online service were picked and packed from its existing stores. However, where customer demand is very high Tesco has complemented the in-store picking model with a number of specialised dotcom-only stores which provide customers with the total food range (which none of Tesco's customer-facing stores can do).

Tesco's approach was markedly different from that of Webvan which set out to completely remodel the US grocery retailing industry in 1997. It aimed to create a chain of highly automated warehouses in order to increase worker productivity, and it offered free delivery regardless of location.

Unfortunately, Webvan was never really in control of its costs and it was estimated that the company lost US$130 on every order. The distribution networks used by traditional supermarket companies mean that they use fully loaded lorries to bring products to a supermarket store close to the consumer, resulting in relatively low transportation costs. But Webvan had much higher transportation costs for its home delivery system – despite its decision to offer free delivery to all customers.

By July 2001, the company was declared insolvent after losing US$1.2bn.

Herbert Simon's ideas about the constraints which affect managers' decisions highlight that ultimately it is the actions of the **people** in an organisation (the directors, managers and employees) that actually deliver a strategy. This contrasts with ideas in prescriptive strategy which treat strategy as if it is something objective, imposed upon an organisation.

Critics of the prescriptive approach are very damning in this respect. They argue it is quite inappropriate to simply think of an organisation's behaviour as being a set of deliberate choices from a menu of alternatives. Instead the strategies an organisation chooses, and the ways they are implemented, will be guided by the people and processes already working there.

Therefore it is important to consider the human resource based implications of strategy, and to highlight the importance of **motivation**, **politics** and **culture** in organisations. As we discuss later in this Study Text, it is also important to consider the **impact of change and uncertainty** as new strategies are introduced.

3.7 Emergent strategies

Whereas the rational model describes a top-down process which is clearly defined from the outset, Henry Mintzberg argues that strategy is better viewed as an emergent process.

An emergent strategy is one whose **final objective is unclear** at the outset, and whose **elements develop** during its life as the strategy proceeds.

Moreover, emergent strategies can emerge 'bottom up'; they can result from a number of *ad hoc* **choices** within an organisation, possibly made lower down the business, not just by senior management.

KEY POINT

An **emergent strategy** is one developed out of a pattern of behaviour rather than being consciously imposed in advance by senior management. There is a high degree of experimentation to find the most productive route.

Timescale: Emergent strategies usually **take longer to develop than planned strategies**, because they evolve rather than being formally planned in one go.

Emergent strategies can sometimes be seen as **survival-based theories of strategy**. In order to survive and prosper in an environment which is shifting and changing an organisation has to be 'fitter' than its competitors: only the fittest will survive.

In which case, there is little point having a prescriptive strategy which has to be regularly changed; it is better for an organisation to change and develop as the market changes, letting its strategy emerge in the process.

The diagram below can help to explain the contrast between prescriptive (planned) and emergent strategy.

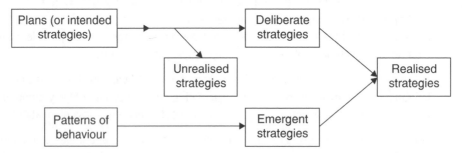

There are dangers in following an emergent strategy as it may involve **risks**, or it may **interfere** with other strategies. It will also need to be **managed** if it commits the organisation to using resources.

The diagram above also highlights the important distinction between **realised** and **unrealised** strategies. Plans may be unworkable for a variety of reasons: resources may be inadequate, important stakeholders may oppose them, and so on.

You have probably encountered examples in everyday life where an intended strategy is not realised. For example, how many times have organisations promised you 'excellent customer service' or 'first rate service'? Has the service you have actually received matched those promises?

The intended plan may have been to offer 'excellent customer service', but what is realised often falls short of what is intended.

3.7.1 Crafting strategy

Mintzberg uses the metaphor of **crafting strategy** to help understand the idea.

CASE STUDY

Honda

Honda is now one of the leading manufacturers of motorbikes. The company is credited with identifying and targeting an untapped market for small 50cc bikes in the US, which enabled it to expand, trounce European competition and severely damage indigenous US bike manufacturers. By 1965, Honda had 63% of the US market, but this actually occurred by accident.

On entering the US market, Honda had wanted to compete with the larger European and US bikes of 250ccs and over. These bikes had a defined market, and were sold through dedicated motorbike dealerships. Disaster struck when Honda's larger machines developed faults – they had not been designed for the hard wear and tear imposed by US motorcyclists. Honda had to recall the larger machines.

Honda had made little effort to sell its small 50 cc motorbikes – its staff rode them on errands around Los Angeles. Sports goods shops, ordinary bicycle and department stores had expressed an interest, but Honda did not want to confuse its image in its 'target' market of men who bought the larger bikes.

The faults in Honda's larger machines meant that, reluctantly, Honda had to sell the small 50cc bikes just to raise money. They proved very popular with people who would never have bought motorbikes before. Eventually the company adopted this new market with enthusiasm with the slogan: 'You meet the nicest people on a Honda'. The strategy had emerged, against managers' conscious intentions, but they eventually responded to the new situation.

How to craft strategy

Mintzberg mentions the following essential activities in strategic management.

(a)   Manage stability.

(b)   Detect discontinuity. Environments do not change regularly, nor are they always turbulent. Some changes are more important than others.

(c)   Know the business. This has to include an awareness and understanding of operations.

(d)   Manage patterns. Detect emerging patterns and help them take shape if appropriate.

(e)   Reconcile change and continuity. Avoid concentrating on one or the other.

Following these, **crafting strategy** might involve the following roles for the management accountant.

(a)   **Managing stability**. Standard management accounting information in stable environments enables the business to **control its activities** and use its resources effectively.

(b)   **Detecting discontinuity**. Management accountants are probably not the best source of information for detecting **environmental change**. Concerns such as the failure of a major customer may be picked up through receivables' age analysis.

(c)   **Know the business**

    (i)   Management accounting information can model the operations of the business in financial terms.

    (ii)   Many of a business's **critical success factors**, such as customer confidence, are not easily susceptible to management accounting analysis.

(d)   **Managing patterns**. The management accounting system must enable 'patterns' to be detected. All this would suggest an aggregation of financial and non-financial information in a **relational database**, with a variety of tools and techniques (eg graphical systems).

(e)   **Reconciling change and continuity**. The inflexibility of management accounting information makes it inappropriate for this purpose.

3.8 Learning in strategy

Another important aspect of emergent strategy is the value of learning strategy development. Proponents of learning-based strategy, such as Peter Senge, emphasise that managers should be prepared to use **trial and error**, and to **learn from mistakes** on the way to developing their optimal strategy.

Some advocates of the emergent approach also argue that the **creation and dissipation of new ideas** throughout an organisation are the most important aspects of strategy development.

This learning approach to strategy is very different to the focus of the prescriptive model: rather than being clearly defined in advance, an organisation's strategy emerges as a result of **trial and error**, and **experimentation**. Here again, the rational model and the prescriptive approach do not fully reflect the strategic process.

However, while emergent strategies highlight some weaknesses in prescriptive strategies, we must not overlook the fact that there are also some concerns about the emergent strategic process. Emergent strategies seem to overlook the **role of the corporate centre**.

This is unrealistic, though. Directors and board members will not simply let companies operate without any targets or direction. Management **will** have a vision of where they want the organisation to be, and they are likely to have some plans for how to get there, what resources are required and so on.

3.9 Is a compromise approach needed?

While critics of the rational model and its prescriptive approach to strategy argue that there is no room for flexibility or learning in the strategy formulation process, critics of the emergent approach argue that letting a strategy evolve means there is no overall control over the strategy. Therefore, perhaps the best way to develop strategy is through a way that combines elements of both approaches.

So far we have presented the prescriptive and emergent approaches to strategy as two conflicting approaches. However, in his classic text *The Mind of the Strategist*, Kenichi Ohmae argues that what is important is not what approach to strategy an organisation takes, but that everyone in the organisation shares the same vision and goals, and pulls in the same direction to achieve those goals.

Ohmae makes an analogy with an orchestra making music. The score (the printed music on the page) is equivalent to the strategic plan. It sets out what the composer intended, plus any subsequent arrangements or edits that have been made.

The conductor represents the senior management of the organisation; controlling speeds, dynamics and phrasing, and making sure that the orchestra's playing is co-ordinated.

The orchestra represents the organisation itself. Each musician has their own role to play (as indicated by the score), guided by the conductor and playing in harmony with their fellow musicians.

Finally, there is an element of the unexpected. Even though orchestras rehearse in advance of a performance, they can never know how a performance will turn out until it happens. Moreover, some truly great performances have come about when everything did not go exactly as planned, but everyone pulled together and adapted or improvised successfully.

This analogy illustrates that both formal, rational approaches and emergent strategy have a role to play in an organisation's success. An organisation needs a plan to underpin its success. But the real strategic story lies in how the strategy unfolds on top of that plan, and how the organisation reacts and adapts to what is going on around it and within it.

Exam skills

In this Text, we have compared and contrasted the rational approach to strategy and the less formal, emergent approaches. The E3 syllabus expects you to be able to evaluate the process of strategy formulation so you may need to assess whether an organisation would be better served by having a formal (rational model) approach or an emergent approach, given the context provided in a case study scenario. It is important that you understand the advantages and disadvantages of each approach so that you can assess which circumstances they would be most appropriate for.

Section summary

There is a basic distinction to be made between **prescriptive** and **emergent** theories of strategy. The emergent process does not identify final strategic objectives in advance, and so is more adaptable than a prescriptive approach. It also recognises the important role people play in actually designing and delivering strategies, and the importance of learning and innovation as outputs from strategy.

4 Environmental complexity and organisations

Introduction

A business can be seen as a self-organising, complex entity that responds to its dynamic and complex environment in ways determined and promoted by its pattern of human relationships.

The classical, rational view of strategy treats organisations as being as **automatic and machine-like** as possible, but alternative (and more recent) views recognise the challenge presented to this approach by a **dynamic and complex environment**.

Ralph Stacey discerns a further layer of complication in the way that organisations work, which he explores in terms of **chaos theory**. He proposes a radical theory of how strategy emerges, based on a view of the organisation as a **self-organising complex process**.

Stacey suggests that modern thinking about complexity can offer us a useful insight into the way organisations actually work, and how they move towards learning, innovation and adaptation in a complex and unstable global environment.

The interaction between an organisation and its environment has the potential for significant disruption. Stacey argues that the complexity and instability of the business environment means that organisations are operating in unpredictable circumstances. Consequently, there is no value in setting a prescriptive strategy. The reality is so complex that the **linear assumptions** between **cause** and **effect** cannot be justified.

The classical approach to theory – for example, the world of models such as Porter's five forces – assumes that the environment is in a stable equilibrium, and so works in a regular, orderly and predictable way. But Stacey argues this is too simplistic, and to understand how companies actually work we need to understand complexity in a way which the classical, rational model does not allow. Given this, strategy should be allowed to emerge and adapt to the changes in the environment, rather than being prescribed.

Uncertainty-based theories of strategy ultimately derive from **chaos theory** and mathematical modelling, which are most obviously used in weather forecasting. The key point behind chaos theory is that although a system – the weather (or the business environment) – is not completely random and does follow some patterns, it is not totally predictable either.

The sheer number of influences in the environment as a whole mean that small 'triggers' can sometimes lead to major changes later on – changes which could not have been predicted when the initial 'trigger' occurred.

The importance of this for business strategists is that, because organisations are **operating in an unpredictable environment**, strategy becomes virtually impossible to model because the future cannot be known with any certainty.

One other characteristic of chaotic systems is that they **oscillate between steady states and states of flux**, and at the end of a period of turbulence a new order will emerge. The combination of these periods of turbulence and the inherent complexity of the environment have led Stacey to suggest that many businesses – particularly those in rapidly growing industries, or those where innovation is vital to success – are inherently unstable. They are operating in the chaotic region between stability and instability. Consequently, their business strategies have to emerge, rather than being subjected to the constraints of prescriptive strategy.

4.1 Complex adaptive systems

Below the level of the collective response, it should be remembered that organisations rely heavily on the individual **people** they contain. Those people interact according to common rules that are laid down in various ways.

- The formal organisation structure
- The organisation's culture
- The informal organisation
- Legal presumptions
- Cultural norms of the industry/national origin

Stacey sees the behaviour of the organisation as taking place both at the level of its people, and the collective level, simultaneously. He suggests that organisations that are capable of learning and adapting do so because, as systems, they are operating in the chaotic region between stability and instability.

Importance of management

Stacey pays considerable attention to the **position of the manager** in all this, and particularly the manager or managers at the **strategic apex**. Management has a very important role to play. Managers are in a position to see how things are going and to interact with many more other agents than most members of the organisation.

In this context, Stacey highlights the difference between **ordinary management** and **extraordinary management**.

Ordinary management is just what most of us would mean by that term: it is bureaucratic, procedural, hierarchical, rational and largely consists of controlling resources and operations in order to achieve the objects of a stated plan.

Extraordinary management, on the other hand, is about the emergence of new paradigms from a free-form process of persuasion, intuition and group-based organisational learning. It exists alongside ordinary management and is the means by which the problems and anomalies that ordinary management finds it difficult to deal with are integrated and resolved.

Section summary

Stacey argues that organisations operate in the chaotic region between **stability** and **instability**. This makes it difficult to predict the future with any certainty, but also highlights the importance of the strategic manager role in guiding organisations through **states of flux**.

5 Resource-based strategy

Introduction

All the approaches to strategy we have looked at so far show how organisations respond to their competitive environment (the position-based approach to strategy). However, organisations can base their strategy around exploiting their own resources and competences: the resource-based approach to strategy.

All the approaches to strategy we have discussed so far are examples of the **position-based approach** to strategy. This is because they seek to develop competitive advantage in a way that responds to the **nature of the competitive environment**: the firm positions its offering in response to the opportunities or threats it discerns.

Resource-based approaches to strategy offer a fundamentally different approach. In the resource-based approach, rather than being developed in response to the external competitive environment, strategy is developed by looking at what makes a firm unique, and using an understanding of these unique competences to determine what to produce and what markets to produce for.

Resource-based strategy was developed in response to two problems with the positioning method.

(a)   Many environments are too complex and dynamic to permit continuing effective analysis and response.

(b)   Once an opportunity is discerned and an offering made, it is very easy for competitors to make similar offerings, thus rapidly eroding competitive advantage.

The resource-based view is that sustainable competitive advantage is only attained as a result of the possession of distinctive resources. These may be physical **assets or resources**, such as the effective monopolisation of diamonds by De Beers, or, more typically in today's service economies, they may be capabilities or **competences**.

Competences develop in a variety of ways. Here are some examples:

*   **Experience** in making and marketing a product or service
*   The talents and potential of **individuals** in the organisation
*   The **quality of co-ordination**

5.1 Resources and competences

Johnson, Scholes and Whittington in *Exploring Corporate Strategy* provide a clear and specific set of terms which you can use when discussing resources and competences.

KEY TERMS

STRATEGIC CAPABILITY is the adequacy and suitability of the resources and competences of an organisation for it to survive and prosper.

TANGIBLE RESOURCES are the physical assets of an organisation, such as plant, labour and finance.

INTANGIBLE RESOURCES are non-physical assets such as information, reputation and knowledge.

COMPETENCES are the activities and processes through which an organisation deploys its resources effectively.

THRESHOLD CAPABILITIES are essential for the organisation to be able to compete in a given market.

THRESHOLD RESOURCES and THRESHOLD COMPETENCES are needed to meet customers' minimum requirements and therefore for the organisation to continue to exist.

UNIQUE RESOURCES and CORE COMPETENCES underpin competitive advantage and are difficult for competitors to imitate or obtain.

This analysis requires some discussion.

(a)   Note the way that Johnson, Scholes and Whittington use the word **capabilities** to denote a useful overall category that contains both resources and competences.

(b)   Look carefully at the definitions of **tangible** and **intangible resources**. These are not the tangible and intangible **assets** you are familiar with as an accountant: the inclusion of labour and finance under tangible resources, for example, demonstrates this.

(c)   **Competences**. A connected point is the definition of **competences**; make sure you appreciate the difference between a **competence** and an **intangible resource**. We might say that the relationship between the two is that a competence might well create, use or exploit an intangible resource (or a tangible one, for that matter). Thus, information is an **intangible resource**; the ability to make good use of it is a **competence**.

(d)   **Capabilities**. We have said that capabilities consist of **resources** and **competences**. As you can see, this means that Johnson, Scholes and Whittington effectively give a choice of definition for **threshold resources** and **threshold competences**. Each has its own specific definition but, since each qualifies as a **threshold capability**, we could, presumably, also use that definition.

(e)   Johnson, Scholes and Whittington do not provide a term to mean **unique resources** and **core competences** taken together as a class: we might speculate that **unique capabilities** or **core capabilities** could be used in this way, but it would probably be unwise to do this in your exam.

An important point to note here is that **resources are not productive on their own**. Therefore, organisational capability – an organisation's capacity to successfully deploy its resources to achieve a desired end result – is vital as a basis for achieving competitive advantage. These organisational capabilities could be in a range of different areas:

- Corporate functions (financial control; multinational co-ordination)
- Research and development
- Product design
- Operations (operational efficiency; continuous improvement; flexibility)
- Marketing
- Sales and distribution

 We consider resources and capabilities in more detail in Chapter 4 in relation to the resource audit, and the context of evaluating the resources and capabilities needed for strategy implementation.

As such, it is important not simply to look at an organisation's resources and capabilities in isolation, but also to assess whether they are appropriate for the strategy being proposed, and whether they will help the strategy to be implemented successfully.

CASE STUDY

Case Study: Huawei smartphones

Although sales of smartphones have been increasing in recent years, not all phone makers have shared this success.

In the three months to July 2012, Nokia made losses of £1.1 billion as it battled to remain competitive in a smartphone market dominated by Apple and Samsung, which between them had over 50% of global market share.

Nokia was once the world's leading mobile phone maker, but in the second quarter of 2012 it sold 4 million Windows phones, which was only a fraction of Apple's sales of approximately 30 million iPhones or Samsung's 50 million smartphones.

However, another big winner has emerged in the smartphone market: Huawei Technologies. Although Huawei was only the seventh largest smartphone maker in 2011, by the fourth quarter of 2012 it had become the third-largest smartphone maker, although its sales were still much lower than Samsung's or Apple's.

Huawei was founded in 1987, and quickly became a high-tech success story in China by selling telecom products to phone companies, routinely beating rivals such as Alcatel-Lucent Ericsson and Cisco Systems with good-enough products and great prices. Huawei only began making mobile phones in the mid-2000s. However, the Shenzhen-based company's inexpensive, often unbranded models gained market share in China, the Middle East and Africa.

Huawei kept this low-cost approach as it became serious about smartphones during 2009. It didn't try to build its own software operating system (like Apple and Microsoft) but used Android instead. Furthermore, unlike Samsung and Motorola, it didn't try to differentiate from Google's mobile software with its own tweaks. It simply installed Android on its hardware and then began to distribute it.

Huawei sold 27 million smartphones in 2012 (an increase of 74% compared to 2011), partly as a result of gaining a larger market share of the US market. In 2013, sales again increased by over 70%, to a total of 46.7 million units sold.

Prior to 2012, Huawei sold handsets costing less than US$200 to providers such as MetroPCS and Cricket that offer pay as you go plans, mostly to lower-income consumers.

In November 2011, it landed a deal with a top-tier US provider when AT&T started selling Huawei's Impulse phone for $29. And in July 2012, T-Mobile announced that Huawei would be building two models in the mobile phone operator's MyTouch line of handsets.

'We essentially made the market for affordable smartphones,' says William Plummer, Huawei's US Vice-President for external affairs. 'We're in a good position because we've established ourselves as a trusted partner to carriers.'

However, succeeding in smartphones is vital for Huawei if it wants to remain a fast-growing company. Its US$23 billion a year telecom equipment business grew only 3.5% in 2011, before tumbling due to the slowdown in China's economy in 2012.

The company reorganised in 2011 to create a separate Huawei Devices unit to drive what executives say is the company's best growth opportunity. The division also makes laptop modems and other functional devices.

Huawei's growth rate may even make it a plausible challenger to Samsung in smartphone sales, according to Horace Dediu of equity research firm, Asymco. Dediu argues that Samsung has prospered largely because of vertical integration: it makes many of the chips and screens that go into its devices. Yet he doubts Samsung has built up enough brand loyalty to withstand a much cheaper alternative, not least because Samsung itself was only the fourth or fifth largest supplier just a few years ago.

So, as smartphones evolve from novelty technology into just another gadget, Huawei will be well positioned to benefit. Although their phones may not be as sophisticated as those of some competitors, they are inexpensive and, as one research analyst commented, 'Their devices don't have to have jet packs to do 90% of what most people need.'

Moreover, by 2013, sales of handsets in mature regions (US; Western Europe) began to slow, with emerging markets – in particular India and China – providing the engine for growth. This again would seem to favour manufacturers of cheaper handsets, compared to Samsung or Apple.

Analysis by the technology research firm, Gartner, showed that Samsung's share of the global mobile phone market fell from 31.1% in the fourth quarter of 2012 to 29.5% in the fourth quarter of 2013. Gartner attributed this dip to the saturated high-end markets in the developed regions (US; Western Europe) which had previously been the engines for growth in the global market. Over the same period, Apple also saw its market share drop from 20.9% to 17.8% while Huawei's share increased from 4.2% to 5.7%.

In response to changing patterns in demand across the global market, Gartner said it expected an increasing number of manufacturers to refocus their product portfolios on lower-end devices.

Based on: Burrows, P. (2012) 'The New Smartphone Powerhouse: Huawei', 19 July, www.businessweek.com

Latham, C. (2012) 'Nokia loses £1.1 bn as rivals steal limelight', 20 July, www.metro.co.uk.

Gartner (2014) Market Share Analysis: Mobile Phones, Worldwide, 4Q13 and 2013, 12 February, www.gartner.com

Reuters (2014) Smartphone sales growth to slow this year – Gartner, 13 February, www.reuters.com

5.2 Core competences – Hamel and Prahalad

Hamel and Prahalad suggest that an important aspect of strategic management is the determination of the competences a company will require **in the future** in order to be able to provide new benefits to customers. They say a **core competence** must have the following qualities.

(a)   It must make a **disproportionate** contribution to the **value** the customer perceives, or to the efficiency with which that value is delivered.

(b)   It must be '**competitively unique**', which means one of three things: actually unique; superior to competitors; or capable of dramatic improvement.

(c)   It must be **extendable**, in that it must allow for the development of an array of new products and services.

In many cases, a company might choose to combine competences.

Bear in mind that **relying on a competence is no substitute for a strategy**. However, a core competence can form a basis for a strategy. Here it is important to reiterate that a core competence must be difficult to imitate if it is to confer lasting competitive advantage. In particular, skills that can be bought in are unlikely to form the basis of core competences, since competitors would be able to buy them in just as easily. Core competences are more about what the organisation is than about what it does. So it is possible to regard a strong brand as a kind of core competence: it is a unique resource that confers a distinct competitive advantage.

Section summary

In essence, approaches to strategy can either be **position-based** or **resource-based**. The resource-based approach to strategy starts from a consideration of strengths and weaknesses and highlights the importance of developing core competences as a basis of competitive advantage.

6 Management accountants and strategy development

Introduction

Although we have focused on the process of developing strategy, it is important to think how a management accountant can contribute to this process; for example, by providing information which is relevant for strategic decision making.

6.1 The role of the management accountant

Before we look specifically at the role of the management accountant in strategy development, let us briefly consider what a management accountant does more generally, using CIMA's Official Terminology.

KEY TERM

CHARTERED MANAGEMENT ACCOUNTANTS: 'Help organisations establish viable strategies and convert them into profit (in a commercial context) or into value-for-money (in a not-for-profit context). To achieve this they work as an integral part of multi-skilled management teams in carrying out the:

- Formulation of policy and setting of corporate objectives

- Formulation of strategic plans derived from corporate objectives

- Formulation of shorter-term operational plans

- Acquisition and use of finance

- Design of systems, recording of events and transactions and management of information systems

- Generation, communication and interpretation of financial and non-financial information, for management and other stakeholders

- Provision of specific information and analysis on which decisions are based

- Monitoring performance against plans and other benchmarks, and initiating responsive action for performance improvement

- Derivation of performance measures and benchmarks, financial and non-financial, quantitative and qualitative for monitoring and control

- Improvement of business systems and processes through risk management and internal audit review'.

(CIMA Official Terminology)

In the context of developing business strategy, perhaps the most important of these job roles is the provision of information and analysis on which decisions are based.

Whereas, historically, the main focus of management accounting was on financial control (particularly cost control), it now also has an increasing focus on **business support** and **decision support**. In effect, the management accountant can act as an internal consultant to the operational managers within an organisation – providing them with insight and advice into their planning, budgeting and performance management. And a key aspect of the management accountant's role as a business partner is to work closely with the business to improve decision making and to enhance the business's ability to create value.

6.1.1 The importance of decision making in organisations

This change in the focus of the management accountant's role also reflects an increasing recognition that high-quality decision making is becoming critical to superior business performance. In its research paper *'Improving decision making in organisations: The opportunity to transform finance'* CIMA highlights that: 'Decision making is becoming the basis of competitive advantage and value creation. If markets give all organisations access to similar resources globally, and competition causes many routine business processes to converge on world-class standards, the quality of decision making could become the key differentator' in determining an organisation's performance relative to its competitors.

Management accountants are well placed to work with both operational managers and senior management to improve decision making, because they can provide the metrics and analysis to support the decision-making process. Moreover, as business partners, management accountants should be uniquely placed to use a combination of financial expertise and understanding of the business in order to inform decision making.

As CIMA's research paper notes, when discussing finance's role in evaluating strategic choices: 'Management accountants can facilitate unbiased, fact based decision making that is aligned with ethical standards, [as well as] providing consistent quantitative and qualitative analysis of the situation and proposals.'

However, their ability to do this also depends on reliable and timely financial and management information being available.

6.1.2 Future uncertainty

Although we have highlighted the management accountant's role in providing management information which enables **strategic planning** and **control decisions** to be made, it is also worth emphasising the **uncertainty** in much strategic planning.

(a)   Strategic plans may cover a **long period** into the future.

(b)   Many strategic plans involve big changes and **new ventures**, such as capacity expansion decisions and decisions to develop into new product areas and new markets.

Inevitably, management accounting information for strategic planning will be based on incomplete data and will use **forecasts** and **estimates**.

(a)   It follows that strategic management accounting information is unlikely to give clear guidelines for management decisions and should incorporate some **risk and uncertainty analysis** (eg sensitivity analysis).

(b)   For longer-term plans, discounted cash flow techniques ought to be used in financial evaluation.

(c)   The management accountant will be involved in:

- Project evaluation
- Managing cash and operational matters
- Reviewing the outcome of the project (post-implementation review)

6.1.3 External and competitor orientation

Much management accounting information has been devised for internal consumption.

However, it is important to balance this with a consideration of external factors.

- Strategic management involves **environmental considerations**.
- A strategy is pursued in relation to **competitors**.

6.2 The challenge for management accountants

The challenge lies in providing more relevant information for decision making. Traditional management accounting systems may not always provide this.

(a)   **Historical costs** are not necessarily the best guide to decision making. One of the criticisms of management accounting in a strategic context is that management accounting information is biased towards the **past rather than the future**.

(b)   **Strategic issues** are not easily detected by management accounting systems.

(c)   **Financial models** of some sophistication are needed to enable management accountants to provide useful information.

In other words, to support strategic decisions, management accounting itself needs to become more strategic.

6.3 What is strategic management accounting?

KEY TERM

STRATEGIC MANAGEMENT ACCOUNTING is a 'form of management accounting in which emphasis is placed on information which relates to factors external to the entity, as well as non-financial information and internally generated information'.   *(CIMA Official Terminology)*

Ward suggests that the role of the strategic management accountant can be analysed as follows.

(a)   **Financial analysis** indicates the **current position** of a business and its financial performance in comparison with competitors, as well as breaking it down into product and customer profitability analyses. (The concepts of product profitability and customer profitability are discussed in relation to marketing later in this Study Text.)

(b)   **Financial planning** quantifies the goals and objectives of the business, normally in a budget.

(c)   **Financial control**. Financial information is an essential part of the feedback mechanism comparing planned with actual performance.

However, although Ward focuses on the financial information which could be provided by a strategic management accountant, it is also important to remember the contribution of non-financial information to strategic management accounting; for example, in relation to a product or business unit's market share.

We can also appreciate something of the context of strategic management accounting by reminding ourselves what strategy itself is:

'Strategy is the direction and scope of an organisation over the long term which achieves advantage in a changing environment, through its configuration of resources and competences with the aim of fulfilling stakeholder expectations.'   *(Johnson, Scholes and Whittington)*

The references to the **environment** and to **stakeholders** are important here, because they highlight that strategy has an **external focus** as well as an internal one.

6.3.1 External orientation

The important fact which distinguishes strategic management accounting from other management accounting activities is its **external orientation**, towards customers and competitors, suppliers and other stakeholders. For example, whereas a traditional management accountant would report on an organisation's own revenues, the strategic management accountant would report on market share or trends in market size and growth.

(a)   **Competitive advantage is relative**. Understanding competitors is therefore of prime importance. For example, knowledge of competitors' costs, as well as a firm's own costs, could help inform strategic choices: a firm would be unwise to pursue a cost leadership strategy without first analysing its costs in relation to the cost structures of other firms in the industry.

(b)   **Customers** determine if a firm has competitive advantage.

6.3.2 Future orientation

Another criticism of traditional management accounts is that they are **backward-looking**. Decision making is a forward- and outward-looking process.

Strategic management accountants will use **relevant costs** and revenues (ie **incremental** costs and revenues and **opportunity** costs) for decision making.

KEY TERM

RELEVANT COSTS AND REVENUES are 'costs and revenues appropriate to a specific management decision. These are represented by future cash flows whose magnitude will vary depending upon the outcome of the management decision made.'   *(CIMA Official Terminology)*

6.3.3 Goal congruence

Business strategy involves the activities of many different functions, including marketing, production and human resource management. The strategic management accounting system will require the **inputs of many areas of the business**.

(a) Strategic management accounting translates the consequences of different strategies into a **common accounting language for comparison**.

(b) It **relates business operations to financial performance** and, therefore, helps ensure that business activities are focused on shareholders' needs for profit.

It **helps to ensure goal congruence**, again by translating business activities into the common language of finance.

KEY TERM

GOAL CONGRUENCE. 'In a control system, the state which leads individuals or groups to take actions which are in their self-interest and also in the best interest of the entity. Goal incongruence exists when the interests of individuals or of groups associated with an entity are not in harmony.'

(CIMA Official Terminology)

6.4 What information could strategic management accounting provide?

In general terms, strategic management accountants could expect to help an organisation through providing information which supports more effective strategic planning, better decision making, and improved control over an organisation's performance.

However, bearing in mind the need for **goal congruence**, **external orientation** and **future orientation**, some more specific **examples** of how strategic management accounting information could be useful to an organisation are provided below.

(a) **Competitor analysis**. Analysing competitors' costs and the activities competitors carry out. How do competitors' costs compare with ours? Are competitors vulnerable because of their cost structure or their product/service portfolio (or are we vulnerable because of our cost structure or our product/service portfolio)?

Analysing competitors' costs and performance also highlights the potential importance of **benchmarking**.

(b) **Financial effect of competitor response**. How might competitors respond to an initiative (eg to reduce prices; to introduce new products/services)? What might the impact of the competitor response be?

(c) **Product profitability**. A firm should want to know what profits or losses are being made by each of its products, and why.

(d) **Portfolio analysis**. What are the firm's key products or SBUs – in terms of their contribution to revenue or profit? What strategies should be adopted for different products/business units (eg in relation to their relative market share and market growth; per BCG matrix)?

(e) **Customer profitability**. Some customers or groups of customers are worth more than others. Which customers are most important/profitable to us? Why are some groups of customers more profitable than others?

(f) **Pricing decisions**. How is customer demand for a product/service likely to vary at different prices? How will this affect profits and cash flows? How does the proposed price fit with the organisation's overall generic strategy? How does it compare to competitors' prices?

(g) **Product–market decisions**. What are the potential costs and benefits of launching new products and/or entering new markets? Should the organisation launch the products, or enter the markets? Alternatively, should the organisation discontinue a product or leave a market which does not seem to be performing well?

(h)   **Capacity expansion**. Should the firm expand its capacity, and if so by how much?

(i)   **Brand valuation**. What are the costs and benefits of investing in building brands?

(j)   **Shareholder wealth**. Future profitability determines the value of a business.

Exam skills

Most strategic decisions are unique, so the information needed to support them is likely to be specifically tailored to the decision in hand. This is also true for the integrated case study you will face in your exam. Make sure any strategic decisions you recommend are supported by the detail given in the scenario.

6.5 Success factors for a strategic management accounting system (SMAS)

Strategic management accounting has to bridge a gap between financial reporting on the one hand and the uncertainties of the future on the other. We can now go on to identify the success factors of a strategic management accounting system (SMAS). It should:

- Aid strategic decisions
- Close the communication gap between accountants and managers
- Identify the type of decision
- Offer appropriate financial performance indicators
- Distinguish between economic and managerial performance
- Provide relevant information
- Separate committed from discretionary costs
- Distinguish discretionary from engineered costs
- Use standard costs strategically
- Allow for changes over time

These are now discussed in more detail.

6.5.1 Aid strategic decisions

As part of a strategic management system, the SMAS will provide one-off information to support and evaluate particular strategic decisions and information for strategic management, in order to monitor strategies and the firm's overall competitive position. Changes in the external environment and competitor responses should be easily incorporated into the system.

6.5.2 Close the communication gap

The SMAS converts financial data into information for strategic decision making. Financial data is off-putting to many people. Consequently, the originator of such information should make sure that it is tailored.

- Ask the recipient how he or she would like the **format** of the report
- Provide only the **relevant** supporting financial data
- Identify the **key assumptions** on which the information is prepared

6.5.3 Identify the types of decision

Ward states that, despite the one-off nature of many strategic decisions, it is possible to identify the following types of financial decision.

(a)   **Changing the balance of resource allocation** between different business areas, for example by increasing spending in one area.

(b)   **Entering a new business area** (eg new product development, new markets). Some account will have to be taken of the timescale in which the strategy is expected to consume resources, as benefits may be some time in coming.

(c)   **Exit decisions** which come in two forms.

    (i)   **Closing down** part of the business and selling off the assets

    (ii)   Selling the business as a **going concern**

To support such decisions, the SMAS should:

- Incorporate **future cash flows** rather than historic costs
- Include only those items which will be **changed** by the particular decision

6.5.4 Offer suitable financial performance indicators

Two general points can be made.

(a)   **Financial data is not enough**. Customers drive a business, and competitors can ruin it, so performance measures which ignore key variables of customer satisfaction or competitor activity ignore critical strategic issues.

(b)   **The financial information must suit the competitive strategies**. A report complaining about the expense of an advertising campaign ignores the fact that failing to advertise could lead to loss of market share.

6.5.5 Distinguish economic from managerial performance

A business's **overall economic performance** results from both controllable and uncontrollable factors.

(a)   **Risk**. Shareholders may be happy with the risk, if it is balanced by suitable return, but a manager may be unhappy if their career is at risk from pursuing a strategy whose success is outside their control.

(b)   **Performance**. Judging a manager's contribution on the basis of the overall economic performance of the business may not reflect their contribution at all. Managers should therefore be judged on their contribution in areas over which they have control.

6.5.6 Provide relevant information

Relevant financial information should be provided, which presents strategic decisions from the organisation's viewpoint. Specific, tailored reports should support individual decisions and activities, perhaps with **profitability analyses** for each market segment.

6.5.7 Separate committed from discretionary costs

Ignore sunk costs. This has a number of ramifications for the making of business strategies.

- A cost may be **committed** even though it has not actually been incurred.
- **Discretionary costs** are those over which the decision maker still has choice.

6.5.8 Distinguish between discretionary and engineered costs

Engineered costs are those which derive from a relatively predictable relationship between input materials and output units of production.

6.5.9 Use standard costs strategically

Standard costs consist of a physical usage element (eg volume of materials) and a price element. The split between the **price** and **usage** elements is indicative.

- The extent to which the firm is **vulnerable** to suppliers raising prices
- The possible impact of **trade-offs** between, say, labour and materials

Trade-offs. If the relationships between the input material and output quantities are known, or variable, then standard costing can show the financial effects of different mixes.

(a)   For example, if there is a trade-off between labour and raw materials, changes in the relative costs of these factors can indicate a suitable mix: more expensive labour would result in less of a valued raw material being used.

(b)   If the price of a raw material escalates suddenly, the standard costing system can be amended with the new price, and a new mix analysis calculated which takes it into account.

Absorbing indirect/fixed overheads into products can lead to poor pricing decisions, in the short term.

If a factory is working at 60% capacity utilisation, this could lead to higher indirect costs being absorbed per unit. This information, if wrongly interpreted, could be used to suggest a price rise, rather than a reduction to encourage more sales and hence an increased utilisation of capacity.

Section summary

The management accountant can play a valuable role in the process of planning and developing strategy; for example, by providing information which is relevant for strategic decision making, such as product profitability and the value of market share.

7   Directors' strategic roles and responsibilities

Introduction

There is an ethical dimension to many aspects of business strategy, including mission and objectives, organisations' dealings with their stakeholders, relationships with governments and society, and evaluating different strategic options.

However, one of the most important examples of ethics can be found in the role of directors, who act as agents to run an organisation on behalf of its owners – often the shareholders.

The fundamentals of ethics, corporate governance and corporate social responsibility are covered in Paper E1.

However, the examiners for the integrated case study assume that you are familiar with this material and can apply it as necessary to the case study scenario. If you are not comfortable that you could incorporate ethical or CSR issues into an answer make sure you revise this material from your earlier studies.

In most businesses, a small number of key strategic decisions can make the difference between superior long-term performance and ordinary results – and these decisions frequently affect the whole organisation and its stakeholders. Consequently, there is a great deal of responsibility attached to these decisions, making it appropriate that they are taken by very senior management – usually the directors of a business.

In this section, we consider directors' roles and responsibilities to an organisation in relation to making strategic decisions and formulating strategies, and within the wider context of corporate governance.

7.1 Corporate governance

KEY TERM

CORPORATE GOVERNANCE is 'the system by which organisations are directed and controlled' (Cadbury Report).

However, it is important to distinguish between the purpose and the objectives of corporate governance.

The main **purpose** of corporate governance is to monitor the parties within an organisation who control and use the organisation's resources on behalf of its owners.

The main **objective** of corporate governance is to contribute to improved accountability and performance in creating long-term value for the owners (long-term shareholder value).

Exam skills

If you recall our definition of strategy from the start of this chapter, we suggested that strategy helps define the direction an organisation takes to achieve competitive advantage in the long term.

In this respect, the objective of corporate governance – to contribute to improved ... performance in creating long-term shareholder value – can also be seen as supporting an organisation's strategic objectives.

Consequently, it could be important to consider the impact of an organisation's governance structures, as well as its corporate strategies, on its current and future performance.

Although governance is mostly discussed in relation to large quoted companies, it is an issue for all corporate bodies, whether they are commercial or not for profit.

There are a number of key elements in corporate governance:

(a)   The management and **reduction of risk** is a fundamental issue in all definitions of good governance; whether explicitly stated or merely implied.

(b)   The notion that overall **performance is enhanced by good supervision and management** within set best practice guidelines underpins most definitions of good corporate governance.

(c)   Good governance provides a **framework** for an organisation to pursue its strategy in an **ethical and effective** way from the perspective of **all stakeholder groups** affected, and offers safeguards against misuse of resources, physical or intellectual.

(d)   Good governance is not just about externally established codes; it also requires a willingness to **apply the spirit** as well as the letter of the law.

(e)   **Accountability** is generally a major theme in all governance frameworks.

Good corporate governance involves managing risk and internal control, being **accountable to shareholders** and other stakeholders, and conducting business in an ethical and effective way.

Directors' accountability to 'other stakeholders' beyond 'shareholders' not only highlights the importance of stakeholder management but also highlights the link between stakeholder management, ethics and corporate social responsibility, which we examine in Chapter 2 of this Text.

In addition, the idea of accountability highlights the importance of performance and performance management which are key aspects of the E3 syllabus. A company's performance has to be measured to assess how well it (and its directors and managers) is performing against the strategic objectives which have been set.

We look at performance measurement and performance management in more detail in Chapters 11 and 12 of this Text.

7.1.1 Key aspects of governance

The UK Corporate Governance Code (2014) identifies five key areas of governance:

(a) **Leadership** – Every company should have an effective board which is responsible for the long-term success of the company. The board should include non-executive directors, and there should be a clear **division of responsibility** between the Chairman (responsible for running the board) and the CEO (responsible for running the company).

  The roles of Chairman and Chief Executive are the two leading management roles in a company. As such, there needs to be a clear division of responsibilities between the two so that there is a balance of power, and no one person has unfettered powers of decision making in the company.

(b) **Effectiveness** – The board and its committees should have an appropriate balance of skills, experience, independence and knowledge.

(c) **Accountability** – The board should present a balanced and understandable assessment of the company's current position and its future prospects. (The directors are responsible for producing a company's accounts, and they must publish a statement of this responsibility in the company's annual report.)

  The board should conduct a review of the effectiveness of the risk management and internal controls within the company at least once a year.

(d) **Remuneration** – There should be a formal and transparent procedure for developing a company's policy on executive remuneration, and no director should be involved in deciding their own remuneration.

(e) **Relationship with shareholders** – The board collectively has responsibility for ensuring that a satisfactory dialogue takes place with shareholders, based on a mutual understanding of objectives.

However, while corporate governance plays a beneficial role in risk management and control within organisations, it could still have some less favourable implications in relation to business strategy:

(a) Governance increases **shareholders' power** and prioritises shareholders' interests, potentially at the expense of other stakeholder groups.

(b) The increased scrutiny to which results are exposed (particularly in listed companies) may encourage a focus on short-termism and **short-term results** rather than long-term plans.

(c) The increased emphasis on risk management and risk reduction may make directors feel that they should accept lower risk (and lower return) projects in favour of ones which might generate higher returns (but which might also carry higher risk).

7.2 Role of the board of directors

Scope of role

The King Report provides a good summary of the role of the **board of directors**.

  'To define the purpose of the company and the values by which the company will perform its daily existence and to identify the stakeholders relevant to the business of the company. The board must then develop a strategy combining all three factors and ensure management implements that strategy.'

This highlights that the board is responsible for **taking strategic decisions** and major policy decisions, and also ensuring that these decisions are properly implemented by an organisation.

If the board is to act effectively, its role must be defined carefully. The Cadbury Report suggests that the board should have a formal schedule of matters specifically reserved to it for decision. Some would be decisions such as **mergers and takeovers** that are fundamental to the business and hence should not be taken just by executive managers.

Other decisions would include **acquisitions and disposals of assets of the company** or its subsidiaries that are material to the company and **investments**, **capital projects**, **bank borrowing** facilities, **loans** and their repayment, and foreign currency transactions, all above a certain size (to be determined by the board).

Other tasks the board of directors should perform include:

- Monitoring the Chief Executive Officer

- Monitoring risks and control systems

- Monitoring the human capital aspects of the company in regard to succession, morale, training, remuneration and so on

- Ensuring that there is effective communication of its strategic plans, both internally and externally

Whether an organisation has a prescriptive or emergent approach to strategy, the board of directors still has the key role in controlling its strategy. Although emergent strategies may develop from within the business rather than being imposed by senior management, the directors still have to ensure that the strategy is delivering value and wealth to the business, and the business is not simply being allowed to drift.

Changing the scope of the role

Directors have traditionally had quite clear ideas about what their responsibilities are in the strategic development process, and what managers' responsibilities are.

These can be summarised as follows:

The board of directors' traditional role in strategy development

	Formulate	Approve	Implement	Monitor
Board		X		X
Management	X		X	

However, recently directors have been expressing a desire to have a greater input into companies' growth plans.

Directors increase shareholder value by challenging the CEO to grow revenues, by asking questions about the current position, and by challenging the strategic plan. However, directors often have experience and capabilities which could be useful in formulating business strategy.

In this case, organisations can benefit if the board is involved not only in approving and monitoring their business strategies, but also in offering concrete advice to the management team about strategic formulation.

Equally, where directors have experience of strategic implementation, they can also use this to assist the management team.

Contemporary current directors are often highly qualified business professionals, and so they can use their experience to help grow revenues and profits by increasing their role in strategy formulation.

7.3 Attributes of directors

In order to carry out effective scrutiny, directors need to have **relevant expertise** in industry, company, functional area and governance. The board as a whole needs to contain a **mix of expertise** and a **balance** between **executive management** and independent non-executive directors. The King Report stresses the importance of also having a good **demographic balance**.

New and existing directors should also have **appropriate training** to develop the knowledge and skills required.

7.4 Responsibilities of directors

The directors of a commercial enterprise are **collectively responsible** for the conduct of its affairs. There is a **chain of authority and accountability** that runs hierarchically up and down the organisation. Junior managers are accountable to more senior ones and so on up the chain until the board of directors is reached. The question then arises: to whom are the directors accountable for the activities of the company as a whole?

As a matter of principle we can say that in any type of organisation there should be some external entity on whose behalf the managers at the strategic apex act and to whom they are accountable. In the case of an incorporated business in which ownership is separated from control, the answer is that the directors are ultimately accountable to the **shareholders** collectively, according to the internal rules of the company.

7.4.1 Fiduciary responsibility and due diligence

The essence of external accountability is that **organisations are not autonomous**: that is to say, they do not exist to serve their own purposes or those of their senior managers or directors.

They exist to serve some external purpose and their managers have a duty to run them in a way that serves that purpose, whether it be to relieve distress (a charity), to keep the peace and manage the economy (a government), to promote the interests of its members (a trade union) or to make a profit (a business).

Directors and managers have a **fiduciary responsibility** (or duty of faithful service) in this respect and their behaviour must always reflect it.

In addition to the requirement to **act in good faith**, directors are expected not to be negligent or reckless and to bring a reasonable degree of competence to the discharge of their duties. There is thus a requirement to act with **due diligence**, a phrase you may be more familiar with in connection with business acquisitions; there, the phrase describes just one aspect of the directors' duty of care.

Due diligence – The care a reasonable person should take before entering into an agreement or a transaction with another party.

Due diligence and acquisitions

When taking decisions about what course of action or strategy to pursue, directors need adequate, relevant and reliable information on which to base their decisions. However, in relation to key strategic decisions (such as whether or not to acquire another company), one party to the transaction may have more, or better, information than the other.

This problem is exacerbated by the fact that frequently there is an incentive for the party with greater information to use its superior position to gain an unfair advantage in a transaction. For example, if an acquisition target presents an optimistic forecast of its level of future earnings, this could lead to the purchase price for the company (and therefore the sale proceeds earned by its shareholders) being greater than if a less optimistic forecast had been presented.

However, the directors of the company making the acquisition need to ensure they do not pay an excessively high price for the acquisition. With any acquisition or merger, shareholder value must be protected as far as possible, and thus it is essential to perform some level of due diligence. For example, it will be very important that management forecasts are evaluated critically to ensure they do not appear to be over- or understated.

Although the company hoping to make the acquisition will be able to review the statutory audited financial statements of the target company, these may not be sufficient to narrow the information gap between the purchasers and vendors, because the financial statements are prepared for a different purpose. A greater, and more specific, level of assurance is therefore likely to be required for acquisitions, mergers or joint ventures.

Fiduciary responsibility

Directors must try to act in a way which is most likely to promote the success of the company for the benefit of the shareholders. This needs to consider a number of statutory factors, including the long-term consequence of decisions, the firm's reputation and the interests of other stakeholders, such as employees and the community.

In the UK, the Companies Act (2006) identifies that, among other things, directors have a duty:

- To promote the success of the company
- To exercise reasonable care, skill and diligence
- To avoid conflicts of interest or of duties
- To declare their interests in proposed transactions or arrangements
- Not to accept benefits from third parties

This duty to 'promote the success of the company' could have important implications in the context of business strategy:

(a)   Directors need to consider the consequences of any strategic decisions for both the long and the short term.

(b)   Directors need to consider how different stakeholder groups can affect the company's success; for example, the company's relationships with its employees, suppliers, customers, the local community and the environment. Once again, this highlights the importance of **stakeholder management** as a key element of business strategy.

7.4.2 The objectives of commercial organisations

We implied above that the objective of a commercial organisation is to make a profit. It is possible to argue that **wider objectives** should be acknowledged and that the interests of people other than the owners should be served. This is the **stakeholder view** and is discussed later in this Study Text. Nevertheless, whatever an organisation's objectives may be, it is the duty of its managers to seek to attain them. Many senior figures in the world of business have given the impression that the organisations they run exist to serve their own personal purposes. This is not the case and managers at all levels must be aware of this.

7.4.3 Personal motivation and corruption

We must emphasise that managers need not be actually corrupt in order to fail in their fiduciary duty. The CEO who sets in motion a takeover bid that will enhance their prestige; the head of department who 'empire builds'; and the IT manager who buys an unnecessarily sophisticated system are all failing in their fiduciary duty even though they may receive no material benefit themselves.

 Section summary

The board of directors should be responsible for taking the policy and strategic decisions in an organisation, and they should ensure that good corporate governance is maintained within the organisation.

 Further reading

Although this Study Text is designed to provide you with comprehensive coverage of the material you need for your E3 exam, if you wish to do some further reading around areas of corporate strategy, we recommend the following texts:

Johnson, G., Whittington, R. & Scholes, K. (2011) *Exploring Strategy* (9th edition), Harlow, FT/Prentice Hall.

Lynch, R. (2012) *Strategic Management* (6th edition), Harlow, Pearson.

Chapter Summary

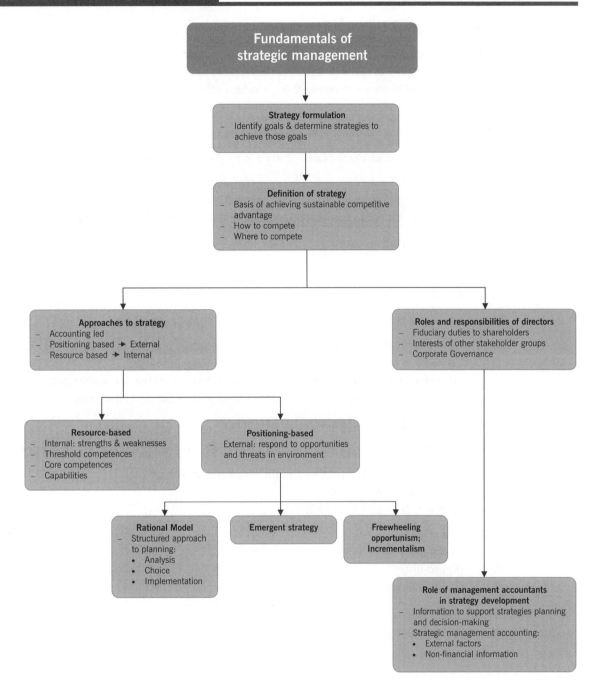

Fundamentals of strategic management

Strategy formulation
- Identify goals & determine strategies to achieve those goals

Definition of strategy
- Basis of achieving sustainable competitive advantage
- How to compete
- Where to compete

Approaches to strategy
- Accounting led
- Positioning based ➔ External
- Resource based ➔ Internal

Roles and responsibilities of directors
- Fiduciary duties to shareholders
- Interests of other stakeholder groups
- Corporate Governance

Resource-based
- Internal: strengths & weaknesses
- Threshold competences
- Core competences
- Capabilities

Positioning-based
- External: respond to opportunities and threats in environment

Rational Model
- Structured approach to planning:
  - Analysis
  - Choice
  - Implementation

Emergent strategy

Freewheeling opportunism; Incrementalism

Role of management accountants in strategy development
- Information to support strategies planning and decision-making
- Strategic management accounting:
  - External factors
  - Non-financial information

Quick Quiz

1   What is a strategy?

2   AZ Co is an electronics company based in a European country, and it uses a rational model approach to strategic planning. AZ is currently looking to expand abroad into other European countries. The European electronics market is known to be dynamic, and to contain a number of fast-moving, innovative companies.

Which of the following statements about AZ Co is/are true?

(i)   Its approach to strategic planning will allow it to adapt quickly to deal with unexpected changes in the market.

(ii)   Its approach to strategic planning will allow AZ to develop a picture of the opportunities and threats the European market presents before it decides to enter the market.

A   Neither of them
B   (i) only
C   (ii) only
D   Both (i) and (ii)

3   Which one of the following statements about emergent strategy is **not** true?

A   Final objectives are unclear at the outset of the strategy process.
B   Elements of the strategy are developed as the strategy proceeds.
C   Emergent strategies are deliberately imposed on an organisation by senior management.
D   Emergent strategies usually take longer to develop than planned strategies.

4   What is the basic principle of resource-based strategy?

5   Which of the following types of information are relevant to strategic management accounting?

(i)   Information about competitors and the external environment
(ii)   Non-financial information
(iii) Internally generated information

A   (i) and (ii)
B   (i) and (iii)
C   (ii) and (iii)
D   (i), (ii) and (iii)

Answers to Quick Quiz

1   A strategy is a course of action, including the specification of resources required, to achieve a specific objective.

2   C   (ii) only.

Part of the strategic analysis stage of the rational model is an environmental analysis – identifying the opportunities and threats in an environment. However, one of the perceived problems of the rational model approach to strategy is that its rigidity prevents companies from responding quickly to unforeseen opportunities or threats, or other changes.

3   C   Emergent strategies are developed out of patterns of behaviour throughout an organisation, rather than being imposed in advance by senior management.

4   Competitive advantage can only be sustained by the possession of distinctive resources or competences.

5   D   (i), (ii) and (iii).

Strategic management accounting is a 'form of management accounting in which emphasis is placed on information which relates to factors external to the entity, as well as non-financial information and internally generated information'.

Now try these questions from the Practice Question Bank	Number	Level	Marks	Time
	1.1 – 1.5	Intermediate	n/a	10 mins
	1.6	Examination	20	36 mins

CORPORATE OBJECTIVES AND STAKEHOLDERS

 In this chapter we begin to look at the factors which shape an organisation's strategy and its objectives. An organisation's **mission** and **vision** (Section 1) describe its underlying purpose and values, and what it wants to achieve in the future.

Many organisations, especially public sector ones, have to juggle a number of conflicting objectives, and so developing a mission may be difficult. Businesses (Section 2) generally pursue some kind of **financial objectives**, although a number of measures can be used to monitor performance.

Often trade-offs have to be made between different goals and objectives. **Short-term versus long-term perspectives** also affect business performance (Section 3).

Various groups of **stakeholders** (Section 4) have their own expectations of the organisation. Conflicts between the expectations of different stakeholder groups often arise.

The relationships that an organisation develops with governments, regulators and society at large can all affect its performance. Therefore organisations need to consider **non-market factors** as well as market factors when developing their strategies (Section 5).

The **ethical stance** taken by an organisation (Section 6) can also affect the strategy it develops.

The theme of **social responsibility and sustainability** (Section 7) is the question of how far a business is accountable to the wider community for the effects of its operations. However, sustainability also highlights the importance of **business sustainability**, as well as environmental sustainability.

Topic list	Learning outcomes	Syllabus references	Ability required
1 Mission, vision, goals and strategy	B1(a)	B1(a) (i)	Evaluate
2 Business goals and objectives	B1(a)	B1(a) (i)	Evaluate
3 The short term and the long term	–	–	–
4 Managing relationships with stakeholders	A1(d)	A1(d) (i); (ii)	Recommend
5 Corporate political activity	A1(b)	A1(b) (i)	Recommend
6 Business ethics	A2(a)	A2(a) (i)	Evaluate
7 Corporate social responsibility and sustainability	A1(c)	A1(c) (i)	Discuss
8 Not for profit organisations	–	–	–

Chapter Overview

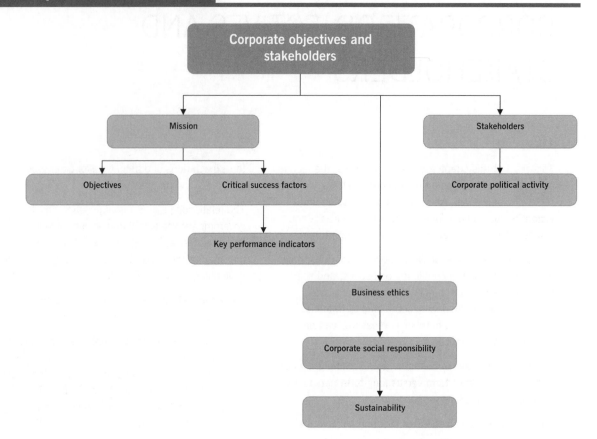

1 Mission, vision, goals and strategy

Introduction

Strategies are developed in order to achieve desired outcomes. These desired outcomes are inherent in the organisation's mission and vision. **Mission** describes an organisation's basic purpose, and what it is trying to achieve. As such it can guide strategic decisions and helps to identify the organisation's values. **Vision** is oriented towards the future, and can help give the organisation a sense of direction.

In Chapter 1, we identified that strategic planning was the process by which an organisation evaluated the strategies it wanted to pursue in order to achieve its strategic objectives.

However, an organisation's mission and vision underpin the development of an organisation's objectives and therefore provide a starting point for the strategic planning process.

1.1 Mission

An organisation's mission identifies the overriding purpose of the organisation, and what the organisation is trying to achieve. Mission is sometimes described in relation to the questions of '**What is the organisation for**?' or '**What business are we in**?'.

In this, and at a very high level, the mission helps strategic managers identify the factors which are central to their strategy.

The Ashridge College model of mission **links business strategy to culture and ethics** by including four separate elements in an expanded definition of **mission**.

(a)   **Purpose**. Why does the company exist? Who does it exist for?

   (i)   To create wealth for shareholders, who take priority over all other stakeholders?
   (ii)   To satisfy the needs of all stakeholders, including employees, for example?
   (iii)   To reach some higher goal such as the advancement of society?

(b)   **Values** are the beliefs and moral principles that underlie the organisation's culture.

(c)   **Strategy** provides the commercial logic for the company (the **nature** of the organisation's business), and so addresses the following questions: 'What is our business? Or, what should it be?' 'What are our elements of sustainable competitive advantage?'

   When answering these questions, the mission should look at them from the **customer's perspective**. So, for example, a company which produces study materials for professional exams might say 'We are in the business of producing high quality books that help our readers pass their exams.' The competitive advantage will come from the quality of the books and the extent to which they help their readers pass their exams.

(d)   **Policies and standards of behaviour** provide guidance on how the organisation's business should be conducted. For example, a service industry that wishes to be the best in its market must aim for standards of service, in all its operations, which are at least as good as those found in its competitors.

1.2 The importance of mission for corporate strategy

There are several reasons why a business should give serious consideration to establishing a clear concept of its corporate mission.

(a)   Values are acknowledged as integral elements of consumers' buying decisions; this is shown by the attention paid to them in advertising, brand building and market research. Customers ask not only 'What do you sell?' but also 'What do you stand for?'.

(b)   Studies into organisational behaviour show that people are motivated by many things other than money: employees are likely to be both more productive and more satisfied with their work when they feel that what they are doing has significance beyond the mere pursuit of a living.

(c)   Some writers believe there is an empirical relationship between strong corporate values and profitability.

1.3 Mission statements

KEY TERMS

A MISSION STATEMENT is a published statement, apparently of the entity's fundamental objective(s). This may or may not summarise the true mission of the entity.   *(CIMA Official Terminology)*

A MISSION is an entity's 'fundamental objectives ... expressed in general terms.'
(CIMA Official Terminology)

In essence, a mission statement describes an organisation's basic purpose and what it is trying to achieve. There is no standard format, but the four elements in the Ashridge model of mission offer a good basis for writing a mission statement. Mission statements are likely to have some of the following characteristics:

(a)   Stating the purpose of the organisation
(b)   Stating the business areas in which the organisation intends to operate
(c)   Providing a general statement of the organisation's culture
(d)   Acting as a guide to develop the direction of the entity's strategy and its goals/objectives

The authors of the Ashridge model make another important point. Mission statements contain only **statements** of purpose and strategy, but in order for an organisation to develop a 'sense of mission' that 'mission' must be exhibited in the performance standards and values of the organisation.

Richard Lynch (in his text, *Strategic Management*) provides the following criteria by which to judge the effectiveness of a corporate mission statement:

(a)   Is it specific enough to impact upon individuals' behaviour throughout the business?

(b)   Does it reflect the distinctive advantage of the organisation and recognise its strengths and weaknesses?

(c)   Is it realistic and attainable?

(d)   Is it flexible to the demands of a changing environment?

CASE STUDY

The following are the mission statements for some well-known companies:

Coca-Cola   –   'To refresh the world ... To inspire moments of optimism and happiness ... To create value and make a difference.'

Google   –   'To organise the world's information and make it universally accessible and useful.'

Starbucks   –   'Our mission: to inspire and nurture the human spirit – one person, one cup and one neighbourhood at a time.'

eBay   –   'To provide a global trading platform where practically anyone can trade practically anything.'

Microsoft   –   'To help people and businesses throughout the world realise their potential.'

Although a number of successful companies have mission statements, critics raise the following criticisms of mission statements:

(a)   They are often **public relations** exercises rather than an accurate portrayal of the organisation's actual values.

(b)   They can often be full of **generalisations** which are impossible to tie down to specific strategic implications, and practical objectives.

(c)   They may be ignored by the people responsible for formulating or implementing strategy.

(d)   Mission statements have little value in uniting behaviours and values in the organisation if employees are either not aware of them or misunderstand them.

(e)   They become obsolete, as they fail to evolve over time to reflect changes in the organisation, or in its markets or the external environment.

However, there are no fixed rules about how long an organisation should keep the same mission statement. Therefore a company's mission statement could be periodically reviewed to ensure it still accurately reflects the company's position and its environment.

1.4 Mission and planning

The mission statement can play an important role in the strategic planning process.

(a)   **Inspires and informs planning**. Plans should further the organisation's goals and be consistent with its values. In this way, the mission statement provides a focus for consistent strategic planning decisions.

(b)   **Screening**. Mission acts as a yardstick by which plans are judged.

(c)   Mission also affects the **implementation** of a planned strategy in terms of the ways in which an organisation carries out its business, and through the culture of the organisation. A mission statement can help to develop a corporate culture in an organisation by communicating the organisation's core values. A mission statement can also often help to establish an ethics framework.

1.5 Vision

Like mission, an organisation's vision also relates to its overall goals, but crucially it refers to the desired future state of the organisation. Whereas an organisation's mission statement should help to answer questions surrounding what it is for (its purpose), its vision should address questions of 'What do we want to achieve?' or 'Where is the organisation going?'.

Vision statements should express the organisation's aspirations, with a view to mobilising the motivation and energy of its employees in order to realise those aspirations. However, vision can also give a general sense of direction to an organisation, which provides a framework to develop specific objectives and the detail of the organisation's strategy.

In some organisations, the vision statement is combined with the mission statement, but many organisations choose to keep the two statements separate in order to emphasise the intent highlighted in the vision statement.

CASE STUDY

The following examples illustrate vision and mission statements for three very different organisations.

Cincinnati Children's Hospital Medical Centre: a not for profit hospital and research centre

Vision – Cincinnati Children's Hospital Medical Centre will be the leader in improving child health.

Mission Statement – Cincinnati Children's Hospital Medical Centre will improve child health and transform delivery of care through fully integrated, globally recognised research, education and innovation.

For patients from our community, the nation and the world, the care we provide today and in the future will achieve the best:

- Medical and quality of life outcomes
- Patient and family experiences
- Value

Pertamina: a state-owned Indonesian energy company

Vision – To be a world-class national energy company.

Mission – To carry out integrated business in oil, gas, renewable and new energy based on strong commercial principles.

Mitsui & Co. Ltd: a Japanese conglomerate (keiretsu) – including chemical, construction, engineering, insurance and banking companies.

Vision – Aim to become a global business enabler that can meet the needs of our customers throughout the world.

Mission – Strive to contribute to the creation of a future where the aspirations of the people can be fulfilled.

Section summary

Mission guides strategic decisions and provides value and direction. Mission statements are formal documents that state an organisation's mission. They can play an important role in the strategic planning process, but have also been criticised for being overgeneralised, ignored in practice, static/obsolete, and little more than PR.

2 Business goals and objectives

Introduction

Goals and **objectives** derive from mission and support it. For a business, a primary corporate objective will be the return offered to shareholders, however this is measured. There may be other primary objectives and there will certainly be supporting objectives for costs, innovation, markets, products and so on.

2.1 Goals, objectives and targets

An understanding of an organisation's mission is invaluable for setting and controlling the overall **functioning and progress** of the organisation.

However, mission statements themselves are open-ended and are not stated in quantifiable terms, such as profits and revenues. Equally, they are not time bound.

Therefore mission statements can only be seen as a general indicator of an organisation's strategy. In order to start implementing the strategy and managing performance, an organisation needs to develop some more specific and measurable objectives and targets.

Most people's work is defined in terms of specific and immediate **things to be achieved**. If these things are related in some way to the wider purpose of the organisation, this will help the organisation to function more effectively than if these tasks are not aligned to the organisation's overall purpose.

Loosely speaking, these 'things to be achieved' are the goals, objectives and targets of the various departments, functions and individuals that make up the organisation. In effective organisations **goal congruence** will be achieved, such that these disparate goals, objectives and targets will be **consistent** with one another and will **operate together** to support progress with the mission.

However, while mission statements are high-level, open-ended statements about a firm's purpose or strategy, **strategic objectives** translate the mission into more **specific milestones and targets** for the business strategy to follow and achieve.

2.1.1 A hierarchy of objectives

A simple model of the relationship between the various goals, objectives and targets is a **pyramid** analogous to the traditional organisational hierarchy. At the top is the **overall mission**; this is supported by a **small number of wide-ranging goals**, which may correspond to overall departmental or functional responsibilities. Each of these goals is supported in turn by **more detailed, subordinate goals** that correspond, perhaps, to the responsibilities of the senior managers in the function concerned. This pattern is continued downwards until we reach the work targets of individual members of the organisation.

As we work our way down this pyramid of goals we will find that they will typically become **more detailed** and will relate to **shorter time frames**. So, the mission might be very general and specify no timescale at all, but an individual worker is likely to have very specific things to achieve every day, or even every few minutes.

Note that this description is very basic and that the structure of objectives in a modern organisation may be much more complex than this, with the pursuit of some goals involving input from several functions. Also, some goals may be defined in very general terms, so as not to stifle innovation, co-operation and informal ways of performing tasks.

An important feature of any structure of goals is that there should be **goal congruence**; that is to say, goals that are related to one another should be **mutually supportive**. This is because goals and objectives drive actions, so if goals aren't congruent then the actions of one area of a business will end up conflicting with those of another area of the business.

Goals can be related in several ways:

*   **Hierarchically**, as in the pyramid structure outlined above

*   **Functionally**, as when colleagues collaborate on a project

*   **Logistically**, as when resources must be shared or used in sequence

*   In **wider organisational senses**, as when senior executives make decisions about their operational priorities

A good example of the last category is the tension between long- and short-term priorities in such matters as the need to contain costs while at the same time increasing productivity by investing in improved plant.

The words 'goal', 'objective' and 'target' are used somewhat imprecisely and, to some extent, interchangeably. The suggestions we make below about the usage of these words are only tentative and you should read as widely as you can in order to make your own mind up about how to employ them.

KEY TERMS

A GOAL is often a longer-term overall aspiration: Henry Mintzberg defines **goals** as 'the intentions behind decisions or actions, the states of mind that drive individuals or collectives of individuals called organisations to do what they do.' Goals may be difficult to quantify and it may not be very helpful to attempt to do so. An example of a goal might be to raise productivity in a manufacturing department.

OBJECTIVES are often quite specific and well defined, though they can also embody comprehensive purposes.

TARGETS are generally expressed in concrete numerical terms and are therefore easily used to measure progress and performance.

2.1.2 Management by objectives

The contrast between objectives and mission statements can be highlighted by the fact that objectives should be 'SMART'.

Specific   **M**easurable   **A**chievable   **R**elevant   **T**ime-related

Relevant is sometimes replaced with **realistic**; but 'realistic' and 'achievable' could be seen as meaning similar things. An objective is relevant if it is appropriate to an organisation's mission.

There are other variants: 'achievable' may be replaced with 'attainable', which has an almost identical meaning. Achievable is also sometimes replaced with 'Agreed'; denoting that objectives should be agreed with those responsible for achieving them. However, note that whichever version you prefer, a SMART objective corresponds very closely with our description of the way the word **target** is commonly used.

(a)   **S**pecific: An objective must be a clear statement, and must be easy to understand. Whereas mission statements tend to be vague, objectives must be specific.

(b)   **M**easurable: Again, in contrast to mission statements, objectives must be measurable so that performance against the objectives can be assessed. Measuring performance against objectives is a key element of control in organisations.

(c)   **A**chievable: If the objectives set are not achievable, people will not bother trying to achieve them, so there is little point setting them.

(d)   **R**elevant: An objective is relevant if it relates to an organisation's mission, and will help it fulfil that mission. (This reiterates the link between an organisation's mission and its objectives.)

(e)   **T**ime-related: Whereas mission statements tend to be open-ended, an organisation needs to define a specific time period in which objectives should be achieved. Again, this is very important for enabling management to judge whether or not the objective has been achieved. For example, if an organisation has an objective 'To increase sales revenue by 5%', how will managers know the time period over which this sales increase is expected? However, if the objective is 'To increase sales revenue by 5% per year' the time frame is clearly identified.

Functions of objectives

(a)   **Planning**: Objectives define what the plan is about.

(b)   **Responsibility**: Objectives define the responsibilities of managers and departments.

(c)   **Integration**: Objectives should support one another and be consistent; this integrates the efforts of different departments.

(d)   **Motivation**: The first step in motivation is knowing what is to be done. Objectives must be created for all areas of performance.

(e)   **Evaluation**: Performance is assessed against objectives and control exercised.

2.2 Primary and secondary objectives

Some objectives are more important than others. In the hierarchy of objectives, there is a **primary corporate objective** and other **secondary objectives** which should combine to ensure the achievement of the overall corporate objective.

For example, if a company sets itself an objective of growth in profits as its primary aim, it will then have to develop strategies by which this primary objective can be achieved. An objective must then be set for each individual strategy. Secondary objectives might then be concerned with sales growth, continual technological innovation, customer service, product quality, efficient resource management or reducing the company's reliance on debt capital.

Corporate objectives should relate to the business as a whole and can be both **financial** and **non-financial**:

- Profitability
- Market share
- Growth
- Cash flow
- Asset base

- Customer satisfaction
- The quality of the firm's products
- Human resources
- New product development
- Social responsibility

Equally, when setting corporate objectives, it is important that an organisation considers the needs of all of its **stakeholders**, to try to ensure that these are met wherever possible. (We discuss stakeholders and stakeholder management in more detail later in this chapter.)

CASE STUDY

Jaguar Land Rover

In its 2013/14 Annual Report, Jaguar Land Rover summarised its objectives and strategy as follows:

'The Company has a multifaceted strategy to position itself as a leading manufacturer of premium vehicles offering high-quality products tailored to specific markets, and to profitably grow its strong, globally recognised brands. The Company invests substantially to develop new products in new and existing segments with new powertrains(*) and technologies to meet customer aspirations and regulatory requirements. Complementing this, the Company invests in manufacturing capacity in the United Kingdom and internationally to meet customer demand.'

> ** The 'powertrain' in a motor vehicle describes the main components (like the engine, transmission, drive shaft and wheels) that generate power and deliver it to a road surface.*

The focus on 'premium' and high quality is important here, because it shows how Jaguar Land Rover is looking to differentiate itself from the budget and mid-range vehicles.

The Annual Report then goes on to identify five objectives, which Jaguar Land Rover believes are the key steps it needs to take to achieve this strategy:

(1) *Grow the business through new products and market expansion* – Jaguar focuses on producing products in the premium performance car and all-terrain vehicle market segments, and aims to grow the business by diversifying its product ranges within those segments. For example, the Range Rover Evoque is designed for the market segment for smaller, lighter and more 'urban' off-road vehicles, complementing the more mature, existing markets for Range Rover, Freelander and Discovery.

Alongside this product development, the company is also looking to 'expand its global footprint'. On the one hand, this market development has seen Jaguar Land Rover increasing its marketing and dealership network in emerging markets such as China where, by 31 March 2014, it had 170 dealerships. On the other hand, the company is progressing with new manufacturing facilities, assembly points and suppliers in selected markets. This includes a manufacturing and assembly joint venture in China with Chery Automobile Company Limited, an assembly facility in India, operated by Tata Motors, and a manufacturing facility in Brazil.

(2) *Invest in manufacturing* – Over the long term, Jaguar has a capital spending target of between 10 and 12% of revenue, which is in line with other premium automotive manufacturers. However, in the short and medium term, Jaguar expects capital spending to be higher to allow it to take advantage of the growth opportunities presented.

(3) *Invest in R&D, technology and people* – The company aims to maintain and improve its competitive position by developing technologically advanced vehicles, particularly with regard to economy and emissions aspects. Jaguar undertakes extensive in-house research and development (R&D), particularly through two advanced engineering and design centres, which centralise capabilities in product design and engineering. However, the company is also involved in a number of advanced research consortia which bring together leading manufacturers, suppliers and academic specialists.

The company recognises that its workforce is key to its success, and it recruits talent from many sources, as well as engaging in a number of collaborations.

(4) *Transform the business structure to deliver sustainable returns* – The company undertakes a range of internal and external benchmarking activities which help to identify cost improvement opportunities for components and systems. This includes sharing components across different designs and models of car in order to reduce engineering costs and to gain economies of scale. The company is also looking to enhance global sourcing and to take advantage of lower-cost bases in countries such as India and China.

(5) *Continuing quality improvement and focus on putting the customer first* – Superior vehicle quality is a key element of Jaguar's competitive advantage, and it has implemented a range of programmes (both internally and at suppliers' operations) designed to improve the quality of its products, enhance customer satisfaction and reduce future warranty costs.

Robust procedures are in place in the supply chain to ensure quality control of outsourced components, and products purchased from approved suppliers undergo a supplier quality improvement process.

Downstream in the supply chain, the extensive sales and service network enables high quality and timely customer services. Through close co-ordination, supported by IT systems, Jaguar monitors the quality performance of its vehicles and implements corrections on an ongoing basis to minimise any inconvenience to its customers.

www.jaguarlandrover.com

2.3 Time horizons: long- and short-term objectives

Objectives may be long or short term. A company that is suffering from a recession in its core industries and making losses in the short term might continue to have a long-term primary objective of achieving a growth in profits, but in the short term its primary objective might be survival.

We return to this topic in Section 3 of this chapter.

2.4 Financial objectives

For commercial businesses, the primary objective is concerned with **delivering value to shareholders**.

(a) A satisfactory return for a company must be sufficient to **reward shareholders adequately** in the long run for the risks they take. The reward will take the form of **profits**, which can lead to **dividends** or to **increases in the market value** of the shares.

(b) The size of return which is adequate for ordinary shareholders will vary according to the risk involved.

There are different ways of expressing a financial objective in quantitative terms. Financial objectives would include the following:

- Profitability
- Return on investment (ROI) or return on capital employed
- Share price, earnings per share, dividends
- Growth

We consider in more detail how organisations measure their performance later in this Text.

Growth

There are some difficulties in accepting growth as an overall objective.

(a) **Growth of what?** In the long run, some elements must be expected to grow faster than others because of the dynamics of the business environment.

BPP
LEARNING MEDIA

(b)   In the long run, growth might lead to **diseconomies of scale** so that inefficiencies will occur.

Smaller companies will usually have a greater potential for significant rates of growth, especially in new industries, and growth will be a prime objective. Larger companies grow to achieve a size which will enable them to compete with other multinationals in world markets.

2.5 Multiple objectives

A firm might identify several financial objectives.

- Scope for growth and enhanced **corporate wealth**
- Maintaining a policy of paying attractive but not overgenerous **dividends**
- Maintaining an acceptable **gearing ratio**

Although we have been focusing primarily on the objectives of commercial organisations (which seek to make a profit and create wealth for their shareholders) it is important to remember that for public sector and not for profit organisations making a profit is not their primary objective. The lack of an overriding profit motive, and the range of different stakeholders they need to satisfy, can increase the difficulty of setting objectives for these organisations.

We will discuss not for profit organisations in more detail in Section 8 of this chapter.

2.6 Subsidiary or secondary objectives

Whatever primary objective or objectives are set, **subsidiary objectives** will then be developed beneath them.

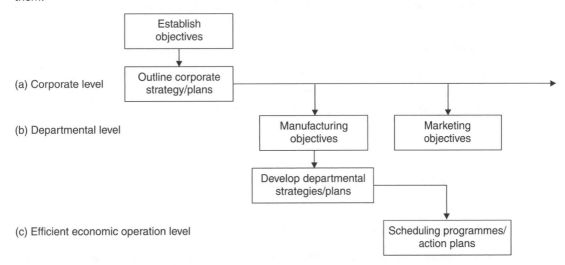

The overall objectives of the organisation will indicate different requirements for different functions.

In this respect it is important to appreciate the structure of goals or objectives in an organisation:

Strategic (corporate) **objectives**:   Set the overall long-term objectives for the business as a whole.

Tactical objectives: The 'middle tier' of objectives; designed to plan and control individual functions within the organisation. Tactical objectives are then implemented by setting operational objectives.

Operational objectives: Day to day performance targets to ensure that the organisation's operations are carried out efficiently or effectively.

2.6.1 Unit objectives

Unit objectives relate either to strategic business units or functions of the business.

(a)   Private sector objectives

      (i)   Increasing the number of customers by 10%

      (ii)   Reducing the number of rejects by 50%

      (iii)   Producing monthly reports more quickly, within five working days of the end of each month

(b)   Public sector objectives

      (i)   Responding more quickly to emergency calls

      (ii)   Reducing the length of time a patient has to wait for an operation

2.6.2 Goals for markets and marketing

Goals for **markets** will involve the following type of decisions.

(a)   **Market leadership**. Whether the organisation wants to be the market leader, or number two in the market, what rate of growth it desires and so on

(b)   **Coverage**. Whether the product range needs to be expanded

(c)   **Positioning**. Whether there should be an objective to shift position in the market – eg from producing low-cost for the mass market to higher-cost specialist products

(d)   **Expansion**. Whether there should be an objective of broadening the product range or extending the organisation's markets

2.6.3 Goals for products and services

Labour productivity objectives are often quantified as targets to reduce unit costs **and increase output per employee** by a certain percentage each year.

Capital productivity is measured less often, but it can denote how efficiently a firm is using its equipment.

Quality objectives might be measured in low rejects (eg through quality targets set under 'Six Sigma' methodologies). In some environments, targets may be set for service delivery, such as speed in answering the telephone, customer satisfaction and service quality.

Goals for products include **technology**.

2.7 Ranking objectives and trade-offs

Where there are multiple objectives a problem of ranking can arise.

(a)   **There is never enough time or resources** to achieve all the desired objectives.

(b)   **There are degrees of accomplishment**. For example, if there is an objective to achieve a 10% annual growth in earnings per share, an achievement of 9% could be described as a near-success. When it comes to ranking objectives, a target ROI of, say, 25% might be given greater priority than an EPS growth of 10%, but a lower priority than an EPS growth of, say, 15%.

When there are several key objectives, some might be achieved only at the expense of others. For example, attempts to achieve a good cash flow or good product quality, or to improve market share, might call for some sacrifice of short-term profits.

For example, there might be a choice between the following two options.

Option A   15% sales growth, 10% profit growth, a $2 million negative cash flow and reduced product quality and customer satisfaction.

Option B   8% sales growth, 5% profit growth, a $500,000 surplus cash flow, and maintenance of high product quality/customer satisfaction.

If the firm chose option B in preference to option A, it would be trading off sales growth and profit growth for better cash flow, product quality and customer satisfaction. It may feel that the long-term effect of reduced quality would negate the benefits under Option A.

One of the tasks of strategic management is to ensure **goal congruence**. Some objectives may not be in line with each other, and different **stakeholders** have different sets of priorities.

2.7.1 Dealing with conflict between different types of goals

(a)   **Rational evaluation** according to financial criteria.

(b)   **Bargaining**. Managers with different goals will compete and form alliances with other managers to achieve their goals.

(c)   **Satisficing**. Organisations do not aim to maximise performance in one area if this leads to poor performance elsewhere. Rather they will accept satisfactory, as opposed to excellent, performance in a number of areas.

(d)   **Sequential attention**. Goals are dealt with one by one in sequence.

(e)   **Priority setting**. Certain goals are prioritised over others. This is determined by senior managers, but there are quite complicated systems to link goals and strategies according to certain criteria.

(f)   **Exercise of power**.

2.8 Critical success factors (CSFs)

The **critical success factor** approach is an alternative to the pyramid structure of objectives. It aims to identify a small number of performance areas in which satisfactory results will derive successful competitive performance overall.

KEY TERM

CRITICAL SUCCESS FACTORS (CSFs) are 'Elements of the organisational activity which are central to its future success. Critical success factors may change over time, and may include items such as product quality, employee attitudes, manufacturing flexibility and brand awareness'. *(CIMA Official Terminology)*

Johnson, Scholes and Whittington describe a six-stage process for using CSFs.

(a)   **Identify the CSFs** for the process under review. (Try to restrict the number of CSFs to six or less.)

(b)   **Identify the underlying competences** required to gain a competitive advantage in each of the CSFs.

(c)   Ensure the list of competences is sufficient to generate competitive advantage.

(d)   **Develop performance standards** – key performance indicators (KPIs).

(e)   Ensure these standards cannot be matched by competitors. (If they can be matched by competitors they will not form the basis of competitive advantage.)

(f)   **Monitor competitors** and assess the impact on the CSFs of any response competitors may make.

2.8.1 Mission, CSFs and key performance indicators (KPIs)

Earlier, we introduced the idea of a hierarchy in which an organisation's goals help support its mission. We could suggest a parallel here in which the CSFs and KPIs are crucial for enabling an organisation to achieve its mission.

Vision and mission	The organisation's vision is a **statement of its aspirations** or what it wants to be in the future. The organisation's mission expresses its **fundamental objectives**; what it wants to achieve.
CSFs	The CSFs are the **building blocks** which will enable an organisation to implement its mission and thereby achieve future success.
KPIs	KPIs are the **measures** which indicate whether or not the CSFs are being achieved.
	For example, if a CSF has been identified as 'We need new products to satisfy market needs', possible KPIs to measure how well this is being achieved could be: 'Number of new products introduced in a period' or 'Proportion of revenue generated from new products'.

We look at CSFs and KPIs again in the context of performance management in Chapter 11, later in this Study Text.

In Chapter 11 we also consider multidimensional performance measurement systems, such as the balanced scorecard. The balanced scorecard seeks to translate an organisation's mission and strategy into operational level objectives and measures. As such, the scorecard reinforces the vital role which operational performance plays in enabling an organisation to achieve its strategic goals, and also highlights the importance of ensuring that an organisation's operational goals are properly aligned to its strategic goals.

Section summary

Goals and **objectives** derive from, and support, the mission. The relationship can be modelled as a pyramid with the mission at the top. Where there are lots of objectives, problems of ranking and trade-offs can occur. Critical success factors and key performance indicators can be used as an alternative to the pyramid structure of objectives.

3 The short term and the long term

Introduction

Objectives are set for varying time horizons. There is a trade-off between long-term and short-term objectives when they are in conflict, or its resources are scarce. For example, capital expenditure projects may be postponed or abandoned in order to protect short-term cash flow and profits.

KEY TERM

SHORT-TERMISM is 'bias towards paying particular attention to short-term performance with a corresponding relative disregard to the long run'.

(CIMA Official Terminology)

3.1 Long-term and short-term objectives

Objectives may be long term or short term.

(a)   For example, a company's primary objective might be to increase its earnings per share from 30c to 50c in the next five years. Strategies for achieving this objective might be selected to include the following.

      (i)   Increasing profitability in the next 12 months by cutting expenditure

      (ii)   Increasing export sales over the next 3 years

      (iii)   Developing a successful new product for the domestic market within 5 years

(b)   Secondary objectives might then be reassessed to include the following.

      (i)   The objective of improving manpower productivity by 10% within 12 months

      (ii)   Improving customer service in export markets with the objective of doubling the number of overseas sales outlets in selected countries within the next 3 years

      (iii)   Investing more in product–market R&D, with the objective of bringing at least 3 new products to market within 5 years

Targets cannot be set without an awareness of what is realistic. Quantified targets for achieving the primary objective, and targets for secondary objectives, must therefore emerge from a realistic 'position audit'.

3.2 Trade-offs between short- and long-term objectives

Just as there may have to be a trade-off between different objectives, so too might there be a need to make trade-offs between short- and long-term objectives. This is referred to as **S/L trade-off**.

Decisions which involve the **sacrifice of longer-term objectives** include the following.

(a)   Postponing or abandoning capital expenditure projects, which would eventually contribute to growth and profits, in order to protect short-term cash flow and profits.

(b)   Cutting R&D expenditure to save operating costs, and so reducing the prospects for future product development. Ultimately, cost leadership as a whole is a short-term strategy.

(c)   Reducing quality control, to save operating costs (but also adversely affecting reputation and goodwill).

(d)   Reducing the level of customer service, to save operating costs (but sacrificing goodwill).

(e)   Cutting training costs or recruitment (so the company might be faced with skills shortages).

Section summary

Objectives may be short or long term and there may be a **trade-off** between the two. This occurs when they are in conflict or resources are scarce.

4   Managing relationships with stakeholders

Introduction

Stakeholders' interests can have an influence on an organisation's mission, objectives and strategy. However, the variety of different stakeholder groups an organisation may have – each with very different interests and requirements – means that the organisation may have to manage the conflicting interests of different stakeholder groups.

Stakeholder mapping (Mendelow's matrix) is discussed in Paper E2, and is a very useful way of identifying the key stakeholders who have an interest in an organisation's activities, and the power to influence them. However, learning outcomes for E3 also require you to be able to 'Recommend how to ... manage strategic relationships with stakeholders', so we will briefly revisit Mendelow's stakeholder in this chapter.

KEY TERM

STAKEHOLDERS are 'Those persons and organisations that have an interest in the strategy of the organisation. Stakeholders normally include shareholders, customers, staff and the local community.'

(CIMA Official Terminology)

Since, by definition, stakeholders have an interest in an organisation (and its mission and strategy) then it is very important that the organisation bears the interests of its stakeholders in mind when it is developing its mission, objectives and strategy.

For many organisations, developing a mission statement and then developing strategic objectives is a very difficult process, because it involves making decisions about the needs and interests of different groups of stakeholders – both inside and outside the organisation.

An organisation must take the needs of its stakeholders into account when formulating its mission and objectives, but if the needs of different stakeholders conflict the organisation will need to prioritise the interests of its key stakeholders (based on their level of power and interest in the organisation).

Exam skills

The learning outcomes for E3 identify that you should be prepared to recommend how organisations can build and manage strategic relationships with the following stakeholder groups: internal stakeholders (managers; employees); suppliers; customers; owners (shareholders); government and regulatory agencies; non-governmental organisations and civil society; and industry associations.

4.1 Stakeholders and their interests

Organisations have a variety of stakeholders, and each stakeholder group is likely to have its own interests.

Internal stakeholders	Interests to defend	Response risk if interests are not recognised
Managers; employees	• Jobs/careers • Pay/remuneration • Promotion/career development • Benefits • Job satisfaction	• Pursuit of individual goals rather than shareholder interests • Industrial action • Negative power to impede implementation of strategies • Resignation
Connected stakeholders	**Interests to defend**	**Response risk if interests are not recognised**
Shareholders (corporate strategy)	• Increase in shareholder wealth, measured by profitability, P/E ratios, market capitalisation, dividends and yield • Risk	• Sell shares (eg to predator) or vote against management (eg at AGM)
Bankers (cash flows)	• Security of loan • Adherence to loan agreements	• Denial of credit • Higher interest charges • Receivership
Suppliers (purchase strategy)	• Profitable sales • Payment for goods • Long-term relationship	• Refusal of credit; increased costs • Stop supplying/end relationship • Legal action (eg for unpaid debts)
Customers (product market strategy)	• Goods as promised • Future benefits	• Buy elsewhere • Damage reputation (eg bad publicity) • Legal action
External stakeholders	**Interests to defend**	**Response risk if interests are not recognised**
Government and regulatory agencies (*)	• Jobs, training, tax • Investment and infrastructure • Aggregate demand • National competitiveness; protect emerging industries • Compliance with legislation	• Tax increases • Regulation • Legal action • Tariffs
Interest/pressure groups (**)	• Protecting the environment • Human rights • Other	• Publicity • Direct action • Sabotage • Pressure on government
Industry associations and trade unions	• Member rights	• Legal action • Direct action
Non-governmental organisations (***)	• Human rights	• Legal action

Notes

* As well as considering the interests and influence of national governments and regulators, organisations may need to consider supranational organisations (such as the EU and the World Trade Organization).

** Braithwaite and Drahos refer to the idea of '**Mass publics**' – large groups of citizens who express a common concern about an issue.

*** Braithwaite and Drahos also refer to the idea of **Civil society**. Civil society includes, among others, non-governmental organisations, charities, trades unions, social and religious groups, environmental groups, professional associations, academic institutions, consumer groups, sports and social clubs, and the media.

Civil society is also sometimes referred to as the '**third sector**' of society – on the basis that it is distinct from government and business.

When considering stakeholder groups which could have an interest in a strategy, organisations should consider these groups from 'civil society' as well as the potentially more obvious internal and connected stakeholders.

4.2 Internal stakeholders

In Section 4.1, we identified a range of stakeholders and what they might want from an organisation. However, an organisation should also consider what it wants and needs from its stakeholders, and the role that stakeholders have in shaping its strategy and performance.

This interaction can be particularly important in relation to internal stakeholders – employees and managers – not least because they play a key role in the operational implementation of the organisation's strategy.

Equally, the relationship between an organisation and its internal stakeholders highlights that, while stakeholders can influence an organisation's strategy and performance, the organisation's performance can also have an important impact on its stakeholders. For example, how is the organisation's performance likely to affect bonuses payable to managers and staff?

In the context of stakeholder management, it is also important for organisations to consider how they can align the interests of their staff and managers with those of the organisation – to ensure congruence between the individual's objectives and the objectives of the organisation, and to motivate employees and managers to perform better in pursuit of the organisation's objectives.

Motivation for employees to perform well comes in a variety of guises. Some will work harder and better for more money, whereas others prefer benefits or promotion. Bonuses could be used as an incentive to achieve target returns or profit, and share options can be granted as a means of linking potential reward to the growth in the share price of the organisation. Aside from monetary reward, other employees might rank the environment in which they work as being important for their wellbeing and productivity.

4.3 Stakeholder conflicts

When considering stakeholders, organisations need to be aware of two important differences in stakeholder focus:

Economic or social focus   Some stakeholders' interests are primarily economic (for example, shareholders are interested in profitability, employees about salaries) while other stakeholders will care more about social issues (such as social responsibility and environmental protection).

Local or national focus   Often, the interests of local stakeholder groups may be different from national (or international) groups. Think, for example, of the debate about whether to build a third runway at Heathrow airport. Local residents are concerned about increased noise, pollution and traffic, but at a national level politicians have highlighted the economic benefits of expansion.

We discuss the relationships between organisations and their suppliers in more detail in the context of supply chain management in Chapter 4 of this Study Text.

Also, we look at an organisation's relationships with its customers in more detail in the context of marketing and customer relationship management in Chapter 8 of this Study Text.

Conflict is likely between different stakeholder groups due to the divergence of their interests. This is further complicated when individuals are members of more than one stakeholder group and when members of the same stakeholder group do not share the same principal interest. Both cases are illustrated by considering a workforce, some of whose members are also shareholders and some of whom are not.

Exam skills

Different stakeholder groups are likely to have a range of responses to possible business strategies. In the integrated case study, if you are asked to evaluate a strategy, you should always think what impact it will have on the key stakeholders.

However, you should also consider the different types of responsibility an organisation has to its stakeholders. For example:

Economic – to generate an acceptable rate of return to shareholders

Legal – to comply with relevant rules and regulations

Socially responsible – to be a good corporate citizen, and to make a positive contribution to the local community

Question 2.1	Stakeholder influences

Learning outcome A1(d)

Ticket and Budget International is a large multinational firm of accountants. The firm provides audit services, tax services and consultancy services for its many clients. The firm has a strong Technical Department which designs standardised audit procedures. The firm has just employed a marketing manager. The marketing manager regards an audit as a 'product', part of the entire marketing mix including price (audit fees), place (usually on the client's premises) and promotion (advertising in professional journals). The marketing manager is held in high regard by the firm's senior partner. The marketing director and the senior partner have unveiled a new strategic plan, drawn up in conditions of secrecy, which involves a tie-up with an advertising agency. The firm will be a 'one-stop shop' for business services and advice to management on any subject. Each client, or 'customer', will have a dedicated team of auditors, consultants and advertising executives. Obviously, a member of staff will be a member of a number of different teams.

The firm has recently settled a number of expensive law suits for negligence (which it has, of course, 'contested vigorously') out of court, without admitting liability. The Technical Department is conducting a thorough review of the firm's audit procedures.

In the light of what we have covered in this section, what do you think will be the organisational and stakeholder influences on the proposed strategy?

So, different stakeholders will have their own views as to strategy. As some stakeholders have **negative power**, in other words power to impede or disrupt the decision, their likely response might be considered.

4.4 Pressure groups

The members of **pressure groups** come together to promote an issue or cause.

Stakeholders may be unable to exercise any power over an organisation, whether as consumers, employees or members of the public at large. In these circumstances, individuals may seek to influence an organisation by joining a **pressure group**.

Pressure groups arise for two reasons:

- Political representatives fail to air important concerns.
- Different groups in society have different interests.

Pressure groups have an interest in matters of public policy, but do not aspire to control the machinery of government. There are many thousands of groups ranging from major umbrella groups to small, purely local groups, often established for a specific purpose.

(a) **Cause** groups (or **promotional** groups) promote a distinct cause or issue (eg Greenpeace and Friends of the Earth).

(b) **Interest groups** (or **defensive** or **sectional** groups) defend the wider interests of groups in society such as workers (unions), business firms (eg the CBI in the UK) or consumers (eg the AA or the RAC defending the interests of motorists in the UK).

Some of these groups have other activities than trying to influence government and might regard political activity as only one of their many roles. Some of the major charities, such as Oxfam, do good work and also try to influence government policy. A group can have one of two sorts of relationship with government.

(a) **Insider groups** are regularly consulted by government as a matter of routine in areas of policy. In fact, some insider groups **expect** to be consulted. Note that insider groups do not necessarily support the government of the day. The British Medical Association, for example, although not always supporting government policy on the NHS, is still regularly consulted.

(b) **Outsider groups** do not have a direct link to government. Some of their activities are to **promote interest** in their cause outside government (eg in the media) so that the issue is raised in the public arena and to **gain credibility** in the eyes of the public and thereby recognition of their importance by the Government, so that their pronouncements are taken seriously.

The role of pressure groups is controversial.

(a) Some argue that the existence of a pressure group means that **power** is **diffused widely**, and that they are an informal check on ever-increasing power of the State. They also help protect minorities.

(b) Others argue that some pressure groups (eg business interests) are far **more influential** than others (eg some supporters of rail transport believe that 'the road lobby' has undue influence on UK transport policy) and that this is anti-democratic.

Pressure groups may either encourage or try to discourage a policy. For example, this might be trying to encourage equal opportunities in the workplace, or discouraging the use of fracking (hydraulic fracturing) as means of oil and gas extraction.

4.5 Interest groups

The main pressure groups reflecting economic interests are:

(a) **Businesses**: Employers' organisations. These can be supplemented by smaller, more specified trade associations in particular industries, which group together to promote common interests (eg newspapers to oppose tax on the press).

(b) **Professional associations** are people who do the same type of job or use similar skills, such as accountants and doctors. Professional associations are generally involved in setting standards of skill and enforcing adherence to good practice (for example, through disciplinary schemes) on the part of their members.

(c) **Trade unions** are similar to professional associations, in that they represent people who work.

(d)   **Consumers' associations** represent people as consumers; in other words, campaigning for the interests of consumers on issues such as product pricing, safety, quality and information. Consumer associations have campaigned for labelling on food, for example.

4.6 Management of stakeholders

Mendelow's stakeholder mapping helps the organisation to establish its priorities and manage stakeholder expectations, by looking at the relative levels of **interest** and **power** different stakeholder groups have in relation to the organisation.

Stakeholder power can come from a number of different sources. For example:

(a)   **Position** power within an organisation (eg directors)

(b)   **Resource** power – eg a supplier may have high power if it supplies a vital input into a manufacturing process

(c)   **Expert** power – eg skilled staff may have a high level of power if their skills are critical to a business and difficult to replace

Level of interest

	Low	High
Low	A	B
High	C	D

Power

A   Stakeholders in this quadrant of Mendelow's matrix have low interest and low power, therefore only **minimal effort** should be given to their needs.

B   Stakeholders in this quadrant have important views, but little ability to influence strategy, therefore they should be **kept informed** only.

C   An organisation should treat stakeholders in this quadrant with care because while they are often passive they are capable of moving to segment D. Therefore it is important to **keep them satisfied**.

D   These are **key players**, eg a major customer, so the strategy must be **acceptable** to them at least. Equally, powerful stakeholder groups must have confidence in the management team of an organisation. **Regular communication** with these stakeholder groups can be a good way to help achieve this.

An important part of managing the relationship between an organisation and its stakeholders is ensuring that powerful stakeholder groups have confidence in the organisation's management team. The issues of effectiveness and dialogue which we considered in Chapter 1 in relation to corporate governance could also be relevant here:

Effectiveness – If the board and its committees have an appropriate balance of skills, experience and knowledge this should increase stakeholder confidence in it. The same applies to the organisation's senior management team.

Relationship with stakeholders – The organisation should ensure that a satisfactory dialogue takes place with the main stakeholder groups. For example, it should hold frequent face to face meetings with the key players or keep satisfied groups, and should establish a communication process, such as question and answer sessions, with the other two groups.

An organisation needs to ensure that it understands, acknowledges and manages the expectations of its key stakeholders, and regular communication with the stakeholders should help to achieve this.

Exam skills

A single stakeholder map is unlikely to be appropriate for all circumstances. Stakeholders may move from quadrant to quadrant when different potential future strategies are concerned; for example, different groups may have varying degrees of power over different potential strategies. As a result, stakeholder analysis has to be carried out in the context of each specific strategic decision being considered.

The firm can make strategic gains from managing stakeholder relationships. Studies have revealed the following:

(a) There is a correlation between **employee** and **customer loyalty** (eg reduced staff turnover in service firms generally results in more repeat business).

(b) **Continuity** and **stability** in relationships with employees, customers and suppliers are important in enabling organisations to respond to certain types of change, necessary for business as a sustained activity.

Responsibilities towards customers are mainly those of providing a product or service of a quality that customers expect, and of dealing honestly and fairly with them.

Responsibilities towards suppliers are expressed mainly in terms of trading relationships.

(a) The organisation's size could give it considerable power as a buyer. One ethical guideline might be that the organisation should not use its power unscrupulously. 'Fair trade' organisations illustrate the principle of large buyers giving a fair deal to their (much smaller) suppliers.

(b) Suppliers might rely on receiving prompt payment in accordance with the terms of trade negotiated with their customers.

(c) All information obtained from suppliers and potential suppliers should be kept confidential.

Successful stakeholder management presents the organisation with the opportunity of creating positive, productive and long-lasting relationships. However, if the situation is mismanaged, the organisation may damage these relationships creating threats such as resource withdrawal and reputational damage.

Such opportunities and threats should be analysed in terms of:

(a) **Impact**. How seriously will the performance of the company be affected by the interests/actions of the stakeholders?

(b) **Direction**. Is the primary effect moving from the company to the stakeholder (such as pollution to the local community) or from the stakeholder to the company (such as government levies on pollution)?

(c) **Timescale**. When will the company be affected by the demands/actions of the stakeholders?

(d) **Ability to resolve**. Does the company have the capability and resources to deal with stakeholder demands?

Macmillian and Jones suggest that management should consider the following decisions when determining their approach to stakeholder management.

(a) Do they deal directly or indirectly with stakeholders?
(b) Do they take an offensive or defensive approach?
(c) Do they accommodate, negotiate, manipulate or resist stakeholder claims?
(d) Do they take a single course of action, or a combination of the approaches above?

4.6.1 Resolving conflicting objectives

Additionally, Cyert and March suggest that management should consider the following four ways of resolving conflicting objectives between different stakeholder groups.

(a)   **Satisficing**. Using negotiations between key stakeholder groups to reach a **compromise** which is acceptable to all of them.

(b)   **Sequential attention**. Instead of considering the needs of all stakeholders simultaneously, management should focus on the needs of different stakeholder groups in turn, and with the understanding that once a group has had their needs addressed they will then have to 'wait their turn' while the needs of other stakeholder groups are addressed.

(c)   **Side payments**. If a stakeholder group's primary objectives cannot be met, management should ensure that the group is compensated in some other way; either through a policy concession, or – literally – a payment. For example, if local residents have argued against a new factory being built (due to concerns about the impact the factory will have on their neighbourhood) the factory company could look to appease the local community by offering to fund local projects (eg schools, sports clubs).

(d)   **Exercise of power**. If it appears that there is no other way of resolving conflicting views, a senior figure could force through a decision by virtue of the power they possess.

Exam skills

If you are faced with a stakeholder question in the case study exam, you must ensure you apply your knowledge specifically to the context given in the requirement. You will not earn marks by simply repeating everything you know about stakeholder management. Too often students assume that a question about stakeholder management automatically requires them to begin by explaining or describing Mendelow's matrix in general terms.

However, this is not the case! Even if you are asked to analyse stakeholders into the various categories of the matrix, the most important part of your answer is likely to be explaining **why** you believe each group has the level of power or interest in the issue at hand which you have ascribed to it. Simply explaining the model (or drawing it) will earn you very few, if any, marks.

4.7 Measuring stakeholder satisfaction

Measuring the satisfaction of stakeholder interests is likely to be difficult, since many of their expectations relate to **qualitative** rather than **quantitative** matters. It is, for example, difficult to measure good corporate citizenship. On the other hand, some stakeholder groups do have fairly specific interests, and it is relatively easy to measure whether these have been satisfied or not. Here are some examples of possible measures:

Stakeholder group	Measure
Employees	Staff turnover; pay and benefits relative to market rate; job vacancies
Government	Pollution measures; energy efficiency; promptness of filing annual returns; amount of tax paid; number of people employed
Distributors	Share of joint promotions paid for; rate of stock-outs

4.8 Stakeholder alliances

So far, we have looked at stakeholder management predominantly in the context of how stakeholders' power and interest (and what they want from an organisation) will influence that organisation's strategy and objectives.

However, it is also important to consider what an organisation wants or needs from its stakeholders, and how the organisation could work with its stakeholders to meet those needs and to improve its performance. Some stakeholders (for example, key suppliers) could become important allies for an organisation in helping it achieve its goals and objectives.

As such, Mendelow's matrix could be used to identify not only the key stakeholders which an organisation has to keep satisfied but also the ones who could be its most important allies (due to the high levels of power and interest they have).

However, a strategic alliance will only work if it benefits both parties. Therefore, when considering potential allies, an organisation has to consider not only the allies' power and interest, but also how the allies could benefit from the alliance.

For example, most of the personal computers produced by Dell have some sort of Microsoft software installed on them, meaning that Microsoft has a major impact on Dell.

However, the two companies also work together in a global alliance to develop integrated solutions that offer improved IT efficiency and enhanced business capability.

The arrangement benefits both companies because it promotes innovation and improves the functionality of their products, thereby providing their mutual customers with the latest in value-added products and services and delivering them the most complete IT solution possible.

Section summary

Organisations have many **stakeholders**. Conflict between stakeholder groups is likely due to the wide range of specific interests and requirements held by each group. Firms can make strategic gains by managing stakeholder relationships to create positive, productive and long-lasting relationships with key stakeholder groups.

5 Corporate political activity

Introduction

The range of different stakeholders who have an interest in an organisation suggests that competitive advantage is dependent not only on products and markets, but also on a firm's relationships with the non-market environment: for example, with governments, regulators and non-government organisations.

5.1 Corporate political activity

How an organisation responds to external pressures and the external environment is one of the key aspects of strategic management. PEST analysis highlights how these external factors can be summarised.

The 'P' in PEST analysis (political) also suggests that governments can play a key **role in influencing an organisation's strategy** or business activities.

Governments, by definition, have a degree of **legitimate power** in a country and so can establish and enforce the **institutional environment** in which firms operate. In this respect, governments are a potential resource or threat to every firm and industry in society.

For example, government initiatives can create changes in industry cost structure by providing direct subsidies, imposing minimum wage laws, introducing tax policies, or introducing quality standards for industrial products. In this respect, governments can play a key role in shaping business strategy.

However, there is a danger that we might think that firms are simply passive players in this political environment and have to accept the institutional environment which their national government creates. This is not the case, though.

Mainstream business theory considers business organisations pursuing economic goals, and in this context political factors are viewed as a constraint for a firm's activities. However, **political factors can also be considered as resources for a firm**. Although laws and regulations do affect a firm's competitive environment, firms can also try to influence political decision making.

Under these circumstances, corporate political activity can be seen as part of an organisation's strategy to generate and sustain profits. Moreover, the relationship between business and government should be seen as a 'two-way' process (as illustrated in the diagram below), rather than just government imposing legislation and regulation on businesses.

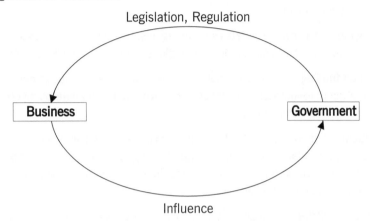

KEY TERM

CORPORATE POLITICAL ACTIVITY can be seen as 'every deliberate attempt of a firm to influence government political decision-making'.   (Getz)

Keim and Baysinger offer an alternative definition which indicates more clearly why corporate political activity is relevant to business strategy. For them, corporate political activity is 'managerial decisions that represent an integrated set of activities within a firm, intended to produce public policy outcomes favourable to the firm's economic survival and continued success'.

This second definition highlights the role corporate political activity can play in securing competitive advantage over competitors. This definition also alludes to the way that corporate political activity – as a way of promoting or maintaining the competitiveness of the firm – can play an **integral part of corporate competitive strategy**.

In this respect, for a business strategy to be effective, its components must be integrated and tailored to the firm's market and non-market environments, as well as to its competencies.

5.1.1 The non-market environment

Political behaviour, in general, relates to the acquisition and use of power in relation to other entities. However, note that business political behaviour takes place in the **political** (or **non-market) environment** of a firm, as opposed to its **economic** (or **market) environment**. It is important that firms recognise that **competitive advantage** can be built (or lost) in the non-market environment as well as in the market environment. For example, a firm's ability to work with regulators, or its ability to foresee relevant government actions, could contribute to its competitive advantage.

In the political environment, a firm interacts with a set of actors, such as governments (including politicians and officials), interest groups, non-government organisations and the public. However, whereas the economic environment consists of the supply and demand of goods and services, the political environment provides the supply and demand of public policies.

Also, whereas the activities in the economic environment are typically voluntary (a consumer chooses whether or not to buy a good or service), in the political environment they may be either **voluntary** (for example, if a firm co-operates with government officials) or **involuntary** (for example, when government regulates an activity).

5.1.2 Types of corporate political activity

Since the 1980s, in developed countries, firms have increasingly established public affairs offices and employed specialists in public relations in order to monitor and manage their political environment.

Alongside this, firms have used different types of political activity in order to influence public policy decision making.

Such activities include:

Lobbying – Senior representatives of an organisation, or else a professional lobbyist employed by the organisation, contact political decision makers in order to try to shape their views and their policies.

Election funding – Businesses make contributions either directly to candidates or else to political parties, in an attempt to increase the chances of a favourable candidate being elected, and then to influence subsequent legislative voting.

Petitions – Petitions to political decision makers are a conventional corporate response to increased government regulation or foreign competition. Typically, firms use petitions to inform policy-makers or emergent or realised threats to their competitiveness, with a view to influencing the policy-makers to take action to sustain competitiveness.

Coalition building – Coalition is a tactic to improve collective power. Coalitions may be temporary (for example, a coalition may form to respond to a specific piece of legislation) or may be more permanent (for example, a trade association). Coalition building typically involves collective action – for example, sending a petition to a government.

5.1.3 Stakeholder alliances and corporate political activity

In our discussion of stakeholders earlier, we highlighted how organisations could benefit from working together in an alliance.

However, the idea of stakeholder alliances isn't restricted to relationships between commercial organisations, and they could equally benefit from 'non-market' stakeholder alliances as well as commercial ones. For example, if a government is looking to attract investment to a region to help create jobs, a company could suggest opening a new factory in the region in exchange for tax reliefs or other incentives for doing so.

5.1.4 Levels of corporate political activity

Corporate political activity varies according to the context in which it takes place:

- Institutional level
- Industry level
- Firm level

Institutional level – This is the level which affects all the firms operating in a national economy. So, for example, it includes all the laws and statutes of a country. At this level, the institutional environment can affect national competitive advantage. (Note the link here to the ideas in Porter's diamond.)

Industry level – We can illustrate the distinction between industry and firm level by suggesting that the benefits from corporate political activity may be either **collective** or **selective**.

Corporate political strategies may be considered collective in that the results of political activities may benefit more than one individual firm: for example, introducing trade barriers, quotas, subsidies or

product quality standards which may act as barriers to entry for potential new entrants into an industry as a whole.

Firms can also use corporate political activity to try to get extra funding or loans. For example, the car industry was very badly affected by the recession in 2009 and car plants in the UK argued they needed government help to ensure they could survive the recession. The UK Government set aside over £2 billion in support for the car industry, mostly in the form of loan guarantees, as well as direct aid to car makers.

In the 2009 budget in the UK, the Chancellor of the Exchequer announced that motorists trading in an old car (more than 10 years old) and buying a brand new car would get a £2,000 discount off their new car for a limited period. (The scrappage scheme only ran between 2009 and 2010.)

This measure was seen as a stimulus to the car industry, but also as a response to the pressure the car industry had been putting on the Chancellor.

Firm level – Selective benefits, by contrast, accrue only to those who participate in the activity. Selective benefits could be gained, for example, by having access to decision makers which competitors do not have.

In this respect, the pattern of political behaviour is likely to vary between large and small firms. In general, large firms are more politically active than small firms, because they have the resources required for potentially costly political manoeuvring. Moreover, large firms are likely to have more political bargaining power to influence political decision making than small firms.

However, the different levels at which corporate political activity can take place also has important implications, especially for large, diversified firms containing various business divisions which may experience different (and conflicting) political goals. In this case, each of the divisions will face different political and regulatory concerns.

5.1.5 Corporate political activity and ethics

We have noted that corporate political activity involves organisations trying to influence politicians. However, if you need to advise about any such activity in your E3 exam, remember that any actions you suggest should meet with the standards of ethics required by the CIMA Code of Ethics for Professional Accountants. For example, it is not appropriate for organisations to offer bribes to politicians in order to secure publicly funded business.

Exam skills

We cannot overstate how important it is that any actions you recommend in your answers to the integrated case study comply with CIMA's Code of Ethics. If you suggest unethical political responses in any part of your answer, you will score poorly for that part of your answer, even if you make a number of other valid points.

Section summary

The relationships a firm maintains with government, regulators, non-government organisations and society at large can all affect its performance and competitive advantage. Therefore, organisations need to consider non-market factors and forces when formulating their strategies and objectives.

6 Business ethics

Introduction

Modern society is very concerned to define for itself what is and what is not 'acceptable'. This has forced businesses to become more aware of their activities and take measures to demonstrate that they are ethical organisations.

KEY TERM

BUSINESS ETHICS can be defined as the standards of behaviour in the conduct of business.

In their text *Business Ethics*, Crane and Matten summarise the subject of business ethics as 'the study of business situations, activities and decisions where issues of right and wrong are addressed'.

6.1 Fundamental ethical principles

CIMA has developed a 'Code of Ethics' for CIMA members (including students) which dictates that a professional accountant shall comply with five fundamental principles (Section 100.5 of the Code):

(a) **Integrity**: acting honestly, straightforwardly and truthfully in all professional and business relationships.

The principle of integrity implies that professional accountants should not be associated with any information which they believe contains a materially false or misleading statement, or which is incomplete and therefore misleading as a result of the omissions from it. In addition, professional accountants should not be associated with information or statements which have been 'furnished recklessly'.

(b) **Objectivity**: not allowing bias, conflict of interest, or the undue influence of others to override professional or business judgements.

(c) **Professional competence and due care**: maintaining professional knowledge and skill at the level required to ensure that a client or employer receives competent professional services, based on current applicable technical and professional standards.

This principle highlights that professional accountants must keep themselves up to date with current business or professional developments, hence the need for **continuing professional development**.

This principle also implies that staff working under the authority of a professional accountant must receive appropriate training and supervision.

(d) **Confidentiality**: respecting the confidentiality of information acquired through professional and business relationships, and not disclosing any such information to third parties without proper and specific authority, unless there is a legal or professional duty to do so.

Confidentiality also requires an accountant not to use any information acquired through professional or business relationships for their own personal advantage or for the advantage of any third parties.

(e) **Professional behaviour**: complying with relevant laws and regulations in order to avoid any action that would discredit the profession. Similarly, any marketing activities should not bring the professional into disrepute.

The principle of 'professional behaviour' also requires accountants to treat all people they deal with in a professional capacity with courtesy and consideration.

6.1.1 Threats to the fundamental ethical principles

CIMA's Code of Ethics identifies five categories of threat which could compromise the accountant's ability to comply with one or more of the fundamental ethical principles:

(a) **Self-interest threat**: the threat that a financial or other interest (eg concern about job security) will inappropriately influence the professional accountant's judgement or behaviour. In other words, this relates to the threat of a conflict of interest.

(b) **Self-review threat**: the threat that a professional accountant will not appropriately evaluate the results of a previous judgement made by themselves, or by another individual within their organisation, but will rely on that judgement as part of a service they are currently providing.

(c) **Advocacy threat**: occurs if a professional accountant is promoting a client or employer's position or opinion to the extent that the accountant's subsequent objectivity is compromised.

(d) **Familiarity threat**: if the accountant develops too close a relationship with a client or employer (for example, through length of service) the accountant could become too sympathetic to the interests of the client or employer such that their professional judgement becomes compromised.

(e) **Intimidation threat**: when an accountant is deterred from acting objectively by actual or perceived threats, including attempts to exercise undue influence over the accountant.

6.1.2 Safeguards

Safeguards are actions of other measures designed to eliminate threats or reduce them to an acceptable level.

There are two broad categories of safeguard:

(a) **Safeguards created by the profession, legislation or regulation**. These include:

(i) Education, training and experience requirements for entry into the profession

(ii) Requirements for continuing professional development

(iii) Corporate governance regulation

(iv) Professional standards

(v) Professional monitoring and disciplinary procedures

(vi) External review by a legally empowered third party (eg an auditor) of the reports, returns and information produced by a professional accountant

(b) **Safeguards in the work environment**. These include complaint systems within employing organisations which enable colleagues, employers and members of the public to draw attention to unprofessional or unethical behaviour. For example, employing organisations often have whistle-blowing or grievance procedures to help protect employees against threats.

Similarly, a professional accountant has an explicit duty to report breaches of ethical requirements.

CIMA's Code of Ethics adopts a 'threats and safeguards' approach to resolving ethical issues. This means that if an accountant perceives one or more of the fundamental ethical principles to be under threat (and the threat is significant), the accountant should take action to remove or mitigate the threat.

6.1.3 Resolving ethical conflicts

If one or more of the five fundamental principles is threatened, then the accountant faces an **ethical dilemma**. For example, such a situation would arise if an accountant is asked to act contrary to the law or professional standards, or to issue a report which materially misrepresents. The Code of Ethics stresses that a professional accountant must actively respond to such circumstances, and must not simply remain silent.

Similarly, the Code identifies that a professional accountant may be required to **resolve a conflict** in relation to compliance with the fundamental ethical principles. For example, the accountant may face a conflict between responsibility to their employer, and their obligations to the Code's fundamental principles.

The Code recommends the following as an approach for resolving ethical conflicts.

(a)   Establish the relevant facts.

(b)   Establish the ethical issues involved.

(c)   Identify the fundamental ethical principles related to the matter in question.

(d)   Follow established internal procedures.

(e)   Investigate alternative courses of action, and consider the consequences of each possible course of action.

(f)   Once they have considered the relevant factors, the professional accountant should then determine the appropriate course of action, weighing the consequences of each possible course of action.

(g)   If the matter remains unresolved, the accountant may wish to **consult with other appropriate people** within their firm or employing organisation for help in resolving it. For example, the accountant could discuss the matter with their line manager and then, if necessary, also raise it with the people charged with governance of the organisation, such as the directors or the audit committee.

(h)   If a significant issue cannot be resolved, the accountant should then consider obtaining **professional advice** from the relevant professional body (such as CIMA, via the ethics helpline) or from **legal advisers**. The accountant can generally obtain guidance on ethical issues without breaching the fundamental principle of confidentiality if a matter is discussed with a relevant professional body on an anonymous basis.

(i)   Ultimately, if the accountant remains unable to resolve the matter creating the conflict, the accountant may need to reconsider their position in their organisation. In the worst-case scenario, they may have to **resign from their current role** or their current employment.

Exam skills

CIMA's Code of Ethics is an explicit part of the E3 syllabus. Students should be prepared for questions that deal either with the general principles of the Code, or that require a more detailed knowledge and application of the Code, in order to analyse how a scenario fits with the Code or what actions might be required in a given scenario.

For example, in a case study scenario, you might be asked to analyse the threats a management accountant faces, and then to recommend safeguards which could eliminate, or reduce, those threats.

WEBLINK – CIMA Code of Ethics:

http://www.cimaglobal.com/Professionalism/Ethics/CIMA-code-of-ethics-for-professional-accountants/

6.2 Ethics in organisations

Organisations are coming under increasing pressure to adopt an ethical approach towards:

- **Stakeholders** (employees, customers, competitors, suppliers and society as a whole)
- **Environmental issues** (such as pollution and recycling)
- **The disadvantaged**
- Dealings with **unethical companies or countries**

This pressure may come from:

- **Government**
- UK and European **legislation**
- **Treaty obligations** (such as the Kyoto protocol)
- **Consumers**
- **Employers**
- **Pressure groups**

To be effective, a code of ethics will have to be incorporated into the entire culture of the organisation. Its ethical views can therefore directly impact on the mission statement and strategy adopted by the organisation.

 Governance and ethical issues are covered in more detail in the 'Risk and Internal Control' section of Paper P3 – *Risk Management*.

6.3 Ethics and strategy

As well as presenting possible threats to a management accountant, ethics and ethical issues can have a role in strategy more generally.

For example, strong ethical policies – that go beyond simply upholding the law – can add value to a brand. Conversely, failing to act ethically can cause social, economic and environmental damage, and in doing so can undermine an organisation's long-term reputation and prospects.

In this respect, a social and environmentally ethical approach can assist an organisation's ability to thrive in the long run, and ethical behaviour can help contribute to **sustainable competitive advantage**.

The collapse of Enron (as a result of a massive fraud) clearly showed how unethical behaviour led to a failure to create a sustainable business model. It is also possible to argue that some other corporate failures – such as Lehman Brothers, Bear Stearns and Northern Rock – came about as a result of the organisations focusing too much on trying to pursue high short-term gains, and in doing so jeopardising their longer-term survival.

These examples highlight the importance of organisations not only understanding the **risks** they are taking in their business, but also focusing on long-term sustainability as well as short-term profitability.

Such considerations can be directly relevant in the context of strategic options. For example, how might a consideration of ethical behaviour affect an investment decision? In simple terms, if a project generates a positive net present value it is likely to be accepted. If, however, the project involves exploiting cheap labour (or even child labour) it should not be accepted by an organisation; either on ethical grounds, or because of the potential risk to its reputation (and therefore future sales) if its labour practices become more widely known.

Consequently, it is important that ethics are embedded in an organisation's business model, organisational strategy and decision-making processes. Moreover, ethical issues are particularly important when considered alongside aspects of sustainability, which we are going to consider in more detail shortly.

 Section summary

Organisations are coming under increasing pressure to adopt an ethical approach to stakeholders, the environment, the disadvantaged, and their dealings with unethical companies or countries. To be effective, a code of ethics must be incorporated into the entire culture of the organisation.

7 Corporate social responsibility and sustainability

Introduction

Some people argue that a business has a **social responsibility** for the cost of its activities, while others argue that businesses already contribute enough to society via the taxes on their profits.

The **sustainability** of business activity is becoming a major concern as business moves into the 21st century. This considers both environmental and social pressures. The '**triple bottom line**' refers to a whole new way of measuring business performance using not only economic prosperity, but also environmental quality and social equality.

7.1 Corporate social responsibility

If it is accepted that businesses do not bear the total **social cost** of their activities, it could be suggested that **corporate social responsibility** might be a way of recognising this.

KEY TERMS

SOCIAL COST. 'Tangible and intangible costs and losses sustained by third parties or the general public as a result of economic activity, for example pollution by industrial effluent'.

SOCIAL RESPONSIBILITY ACCOUNTING. 'Identification, measurement and reporting of the social costs and benefits resulting from economic activities.'   (CIMA Official Terminology)

Businesses, particularly large ones, are subject to increasing expectations that they will exercise **social responsibility**. This is an ill-defined concept, but appears to focus on the provision of specific benefits to society in general, such as charitable donations, the creation or preservation of employment, and spending on environmental improvement or maintenance. A great deal of the pressure is created by the activity of minority action groups and is aimed at businesses because they are perceived to possess extensive resources. The momentum of such arguments is now so great that the notion of social responsibility has become almost inextricably confused with the matter of ethics. It is important to remember the distinction.

Social responsibility and ethical behaviour are not the same thing although they are related. Business ethics is concerned with the standards of behaviour in the conduct of business.

KEY TERM

CORPORATE SOCIAL RESPONSIBILITY **(CSR)** is an organisation's obligation to maximise positive stakeholder benefits while minimising the negative effects of its actions.

Johnson, Scholes and Whittington point out that CSR is concerned with how an organisation exceeds its minimum obligations to stakeholders specified through regulation.

Importantly, CSR includes **economic** and **legal issues**, as well as **ethical ones**: reflecting the whole range of stakeholders who have an interest in an organisation. In this respect, CSR requires an organisation to go beyond simply adhering to minimum ethical standards. Ethics concerns issues such as justice, fairness and honesty, which are fundamental, unchanging values that have implications for business.

CSR is more closely associated with contemporary business issues, and concerns organisations giving something back to society, and being good citizens. Therefore, in contrast to ethics, CSR is socially mediated and likely to be specific to the time and culture in which it is considered. For example, CSR could include:

- Staff development via training and education
- Equal opportunities statements
- Written anti-discrimination policies
- Commitment to reporting on CSR
- Policies for restricting the use of child labour by suppliers
- Policies on fair trade
- Commitment to the protection of the local community

We can suggest that companies achieve society's expectation that they are good corporate citizens through their **philanthropic responsibilities**. These might include: making charitable donations; supporting local schools, arts or sports projects; or even building educational or leisure facilities in the local communities where they operate.

However, an important point to note about philanthropic responsibilities is that, while local communities may hope that companies contribute to their wellbeing, it does not make the companies unethical if they do not. Philanthropic responsibilities may be desired by society, but companies are not obliged to make such contributions, and they should not be considered unethical just because they do not make them.

A business managed with the sole objective of maximising shareholder wealth can be run in just as ethical a fashion as one in which far wider stakeholder responsibility is assumed. On the other hand, however, there is no doubt that many large businesses have behaved irresponsibly in the past and some continue to do so.

7.1.1 Pyramid of corporate social responsibility (CSR)

Carroll and Buchholtz (in *Business and Society: Ethics and Stakeholder Management*) argue that there are four main kinds of CSR:

Economic responsibilities – Companies have economic responsibilities to **shareholders** (who want a good return on their investments), to **employees** (who want fair employment conditions) and **customers** (who want good-quality products at a fair price). Businesses are set up to be properly functioning economic units and so this economic responsibility forms the basis of all other responsibilities. Companies should act in a way which enables them to maintain a strong competitive position, and to be as profitable and efficient as possible.

Legal responsibilities – Since laws codify society's moral views, obeying relevant international, national or local regulations must be the foundation of an organisation's compliance with its social responsibilities. It is important for an organisation to be a **law-abiding corporate citizen**. This responsibility includes providing goods and services which meet minimum legal requirements, as well as complying with any laws and regulations which affect its internal operations and processes.

Ethical responsibilities – An organisation should act in a **fair and just way** even if the law does not compel them to do so. Ethical responsibilities are the fundamental underlying principles that guide social (and corporate) behaviour, and good corporate citizenship can be defined as doing what is expected ethically or morally. Therefore, ethical responsibilities underpin the way that organisations fulfil their corporate social responsibilities.

Philanthropic responsibilities – These are behaviours and actions that are **desired** rather than being required of companies. Philanthropic responsibilities include making charitable donations, contributions to local communities, and providing employees with the chances to improve their own lives. For example, Bill Gates, the Chairman of Microsoft, is noted for his philanthropic gestures, and has established the Bill & Melinda Gates Foundation which works to help people lead healthy and productive lives, and to break free from poverty.

However, Carroll and Buchholtz also go on to suggest that the four categories of CSR should be depicted as a pyramid. A company's economic responsibilities (to be profitable) represent the foundation on which the pyramid is built and the underlying driver of an organisation's behaviour while, at the top of the pyramid, philanthropic responsibilities are discretionary rather than required.

Social responsiveness

As well as categorising the different kinds of responsibility, Carroll (in his paper *A three-dimensional conceptual model of corporate social performance*) identified the different ways organisations can respond to social responsibility and social issues:

Reaction – An organisation denies any responsibility for social issues, and either ignores calls for it to act in response to them, or rejects them.

Defence – An organisation accepts a basic responsibility for social issues, but does only the minimum required to defend its current position.

Accommodation – An organisation accepts responsibility for social issues, and does what is asked of it by the stakeholder groups affected.

Proaction – An organisation makes considerable effort to address social issues; actively addressing specific concerns, and anticipating future issues. For example, a company which discovers a possible fault in a product and recalls the product without being forced to, and before any injury or damage is caused, acts in a proactive way.

7.1.2 CSR stances

Carroll's notion of social responsiveness highlights that the different stances organisations take to social responsibility will be reflected in how they manage such responsibilities.

In addition to Carroll's classification of the different types of social response, Johnson, Scholes and Whittington identify four CSR stances, which reflect a progressively more inclusive list of stakeholder interests:

- Laissez-faire
- Enlightened self-interest (long-term shareholder interest)
- Multiple stakeholder obligations
- Shaper of society

Laissez-faire stance

Organisations which adopt a laissez-faire stance take the view that an organisation's only responsibilities are the **short-term interests of shareholders**, and to make a profit, pay taxes and provide jobs.

Organisations adopting this view believe that it is the Government's role to prescribe, through legislation and regulation, the constraints which are placed on businesses in their pursuit of economic efficiency. Laissez-faire organisations will meet these minimum obligations but no more.

Enlightened self-interest (long-term shareholder interest)

The rationale behind the 'enlightened self-interest' stance is that there can be a long-term benefit to shareholders from well-managed relationships with other stakeholders. Therefore, the justification for social action is that it makes good business sense.

There are two reasons why an organisation might take a wider view of ethical responsibilities when considering the longer-term interest of shareholders.

(a) The organisation's **corporate image** may be enhanced by an assumption of wider responsibilities. The cost of undertaking such responsibilities may be justified as essentially promotional expenditure.

(b) The responsible exercise of corporate power may prevent a build-up of social and political **pressure for legal regulation**. Freedom of action may be preserved and the burden of regulation lightened by acceptance of ethical responsibilities.

For example, in 2012 in the UK, following a downturn in its profits, the supermarket giant Tesco sought to reinvent its business to persuade people that it wasn't simply a money-making machine, but also had 'a softer side'. To this end, the Chief Executive at the time (Philip Clarke) said 'We will do more to ensure that Tesco is valued and trusted in local communities all around the world for doing the right thing' – although critics were quick to point out that this was the same company which had been squeezing farmers and other suppliers for years to extract the best price it could for its customers.

Multiple stakeholder obligations

Organisations adopting this stance accept the **legitimacy of the expectations of stakeholders other than shareholders** and build those expectations into the organisation's stated purposes. Such organisations recognise that without appropriate relationships with groups such as suppliers, employers and customers, they would not be able to function.

However, organisations adopting a 'multiple stakeholder obligations' stance also argue that performance should not be measured simply through the financial bottom line. They argue that the key to long-term survival is dependent on social and environmental performance as well as economic (financial) performance, and therefore it is important to take account of the views of stakeholders with interests relating to social and environmental matters.

Shaper of society

Shapers of society regard financial considerations as being of secondary importance to changing society or social norms. For such organisations, ensuring that society benefits from their actions is more important than financial and other stakeholder interests.

7.1.3 Against CSR

However, although organisations are paying increasing attention to CSR, it has not been universally accepted. Milton Friedman argued against it along the following lines.

(a)   Businesses do not have responsibilities, only people have responsibilities. Managers in charge of corporations are responsible to the owners of the business, by whom they are employed.

(b)   These employers may have charity as their aim, but 'generally [their aim] will be to make as much money as possible while conforming to the basic rules of the society, both those embodied in law and those embodied in ethical custom'.

(c)   If the statement that a manager has social responsibilities is to have any meaning, 'it must mean that he is to act in some way that is not in the interest of his employers'.

(d)   If managers do this they are, generally speaking, spending the owners' money for purposes other than those they have authorised; sometimes it is the money of customers or suppliers that is spent and, on occasion, the money of employees. By doing this, the manager is, in effect, both raising taxes and deciding how they should be spent, which are functions of government, not of business. There are two objections to this:

   (i)   Managers have not been democratically elected (or selected in any other way) to exercise government power.

   (ii)   Managers are not experts in government policy and cannot foresee the detailed effect of such social responsibility spending.

Friedman argues that the social responsibility model is politically collectivist in nature and deplores the possibility that collectivism should be extended any further than absolutely necessary in a free society.

A second argument against the assumption of CSR is that the **maximisation of wealth is the best way that society can benefit from a business's activities**.

(a)   Maximising wealth has the effect of increasing the tax revenues available to the State to disburse on socially desirable objectives.

(b)   Maximising shareholder value has a 'trickle down' effect on other disadvantaged members of society.

(c)   Many company shares are owned by pension funds, whose ultimate beneficiaries may not be the wealthy anyway.

7.1.4 Arguments in favour of CSR

Despite Friedman's arguments against it, there are a number of reasons why CSR can be strategically beneficial for businesses:

Customer expectations – There is an increasing expectation from consumers and other stakeholders that businesses will act in a more socially responsible manner. For example, from the food they eat, to the coffee they drink and the clothes they wear, consumers are becoming more aware of the origins of the everyday things they buy, and they want to buy products that are responsibly sourced.

Given that one of the key success factors for a business is the ability to offer customers what they want, then offering products and services which are deemed to be socially responsible could help boost sales.

In this respect, CSR could provide opportunities to enter new markets or develop new products; for example, in the way that Toyota developed the 'Prius' hybrid car.

Brand name – Being seen as socially responsible can help enhance a business's reputation and therefore its brand. Customers may prefer to deal with a business they feel is socially responsible rather than with one which is not. Therefore, CSR could actually be a source of differentiation for a business.

Lower environmental costs – If firms improve the efficiency of their energy usage, for example, then as well as making lower emissions they will also have lower cost bases. If firms can achieve a lower cost base through the efficient use of resources, this could help them create (or improve) their competitive advantage.

More generally, firms could also find it is less costly to regulate their own activities voluntarily than ignoring social responsibility in the short term and then having to comply with statutory regulations (in the form of taxes or fines, for example) which may be imposed on them later.

Trading opportunities – If firms are perceived as not being socially responsible, they may find it harder to attract trading partners, or support from nations and local communities where they might want to invest.

Access to staff – Similarly, the way firms are perceived to treat their employees may affect their ability to attract staff. For example, firms that are perceived to offer good working conditions are likely to be able to appeal to a higher calibre of staff than firms which are perceived to offer unfavourable working conditions. In turn, a firm which is able to attract (and retain) high-quality staff may be able to generate competitive advantage over a firm which is less able to recruit good-quality staff.

Investment and funding – A firm's reputation may also affect its ability to attract finance, particularly from ethical investors. For example, obtaining a listing on the FTSE4Good (index of companies that meet globally recognised corporate responsibility standards) is likely to help a firm attract finance from ethical investors.

Sustainable business – Taken collectively, the arguments in favour of CSR suggest that a socially responsible business is likely to be able to operate for longer in society than a less responsible one. In turn, if the business can expect more years of cash flows in the future, it might be reasonable to expect the value of the company to be higher than that of one whose future is perceived to be less secure.

7.1.5 Stakeholder theory and the stakeholder view

The notion of CSR highlights that, when making business decisions, firms need to consider the implications of those decisions on a range of different stakeholders – not just their shareholders.

This idea is captured more generally through the notion of stakeholder theory. Stakeholder theory highlights that the extent of the impact firms have on society is so significant that firms need to **be accountable to many more groups in society (stakeholder groups) than just their shareholders**.

The shareholder-based view of the firm argues that a firm's primary objective is to meet the needs of its owners (shareholders) and to generate value for them.

However, stakeholder theory argues that there is a much wider range of parties (stakeholders) who have legitimate interests in a firm, and who can affect it or are affected by it. Consequently, a firm's management needs to give due consideration to the interests of those groups. As we have identified earlier in this chapter, potential stakeholder groups in a firm include employees, customers, suppliers, banks and other finance providers, local communities, government or government bodies, trade unions, and environmental agencies – as well as shareholders.

Consequently, the logic of stakeholder theory suggests that, instead of viewing business as a way of creating value solely for shareholders, we should see business as a way of **creating value for the much wider range of stakeholders**. Therefore, a firm's strategy and its strategic decisions should not be evaluated purely in terms of their ability to generate value for shareholders, but also in relation to how they address the needs and requirements of other stakeholder groups – for example, managing relationships with customers and suppliers, and maintaining employee motivation.

In the stakeholder model, business decisions also need to consider the following sorts of question: If this course of action is taken, for whom does it create value and for whom does it destroy value? Who benefits from the decision and who is harmed by it? Once again, this emphasises that business decisions cannot be based purely on the basis of the value they generate for shareholders.

For example, a company may affect an entire community by closing a major production plant or factory, enforcing long-term unemployment on a large proportion of the local workforce. Similarly, a company may damage people's quality of life by polluting the environment, or it may use its purchasing power or market share to impose unequal contracts on suppliers and customers alike. The importance of CSR in cases such as these comes from making the company consider whether it is acting as a good corporate citizen before making any decisions.

Another argument points out that corporations exist within society and are dependent on it for the resources they use. Some of these resources are obtained by direct contracts with suppliers but others are not, being provided by government expenditure. Examples are such items as transport infrastructure, technical research and education for the workforce. Clearly, corporations contribute to the taxes that pay for these, but the relationship is rather tenuous and the tax burden can be minimised by careful management. The implication is that corporations should recognise, and pay for, the facilities that society provides by means of socially responsible policies and actions.

Henry Mintzberg (in *Power In and Around Organisations*) suggests that simply viewing organisations as vehicles for shareholder investment is inadequate.

(a)   In practice, he says, organisations are rarely controlled effectively by shareholders. Most shareholders are passive investors.

(b)   Large corporations can manipulate markets. Social responsibility, forced or voluntary, is a way of recognising this.

(c)   Moreover, as mentioned above, businesses do receive a significant amount of government support. The public pays for roads, infrastructure, education and health, all of which benefit businesses. Although businesses pay tax, the public ultimately pays, perhaps through higher prices.

(d)   Strategic decisions by businesses always have wider social consequences. In other words, says Mintzberg, the firm produces two kinds of outputs: **goods and services** and the **social consequences of its activities** (eg pollution).

7.1.6 The social audit

Firms sometimes carry out **social audits**. This generally involves:

*   Recognising a firm's rationale for engaging in socially responsible activity
*   Identifying programmes which are congruent with the mission of the company
*   Setting objectives and priorities related to this programme
*   Specifying the nature and range of resources required
*   Evaluating company involvement in such programmes (past, present and future)

Whether or not a social audit is used depends on the degree to which social responsibility is part of the **corporate philosophy**. A cultural awareness must be achieved within an organisation in order to implement environmental policy, which requires board and staff support.

In the US, social audits on environmental issues have increased since the Exxon Valdez catastrophe in which millions of gallons of crude oil were released into Alaskan waters. The **Valdez principles** were drafted by the Coalition for Environmentally Responsible Economics to focus attention on environmental concerns and corporate responsibility.

- Eliminate pollutants and hazardous waste

- Conserve non-renewable resources

- Market environmentally safe products and services

- Prepare for accidents and restore damaged environments

- Provide protection for employees who report environmental hazards

- Companies should appoint an environmentalist to the board of directors, name an executive for environmental affairs and develop an environmental audit of global operations

There are many contrasting views about the responsibilities of the corporation.

(a)   If the company creates a social problem, it must fix it (eg Exxon, or more recently BP clearing up the massive oil spill which resulted from the explosion on the Deepwater Horizon oil rig in the US Gulf of Mexico in April 2010).

(b)   Companies already discharge their social responsibility, simply by increasing their profits and thereby contributing more in taxes. If a company was expected to divert more resources to solve society's problems, this would represent a double tax.

(c)   The multinational corporation has the resources to fight poverty, illiteracy, malnutrition, illness and so on. This approach disregards who actually creates the problems.

7.2 Environmental and green concerns

Business activities, in general, were formerly regarded as problems for the environmental movement, but the two are now increasingly complementary. There has been an increase in the use of the green approach to market products. 'Dolphin friendly' tuna and paper products from managed forests are two such examples.

Environmental impacts on business may be direct.

- Changes affecting costs or resource availability
- Impact on demand
- Effect on power balances between competitors in a market

They may also be **indirect**. Pressure for better environmental performance is coming from many quarters.

(a)   **Green pressure groups** have increased their membership and influence dramatically.

(b)   **Employees** are increasing pressure on the businesses in which they work for a number of reasons – partly for their own safety, partly in order to improve the public image of the company.

(c)   **Legislation** is increasing almost by the day. Growing pressure from the green or green-influenced vote has led to mainstream political parties taking these issues into their programmes, and most countries now have laws to cover land use planning, smoke emission, water pollution and the destruction of animals and natural habitats.

(d)   **Environmental risk screening** has become increasingly important. Companies in the future will become responsible for the environmental impact of their activities.

7.3 Environmental issues and strategic planning

Physical environmental conditions are important for strategic planning.

(a)   **Resource inputs**. Managing physical resources successfully (eg oil companies, mining companies) is a good source of profits.

(b)   **Logistics**. The physical environment presents logistical problems or opportunities to organisations. Proximity to road and rail links can be a reason for siting a warehouse in a particular area.

(c)   **Government**. The physical environment is under the control of other organisations.

    (i)   Local authority town planning departments can influence where a building and necessary infrastructure can be sited.

    (ii)   Governments can set regulations about some of the organisation's environmental interactions.

(d)   **Disasters**. In some countries, the physical environment can pose a major 'threat' to organisations.

Issues relating to the effect of an organisation's activities on the physical environment have come to the fore in recent years.

7.3.1 Impact of green issues on business

Possible issues to consider are:

- **Consumer demand** for products which appear to be environmentally friendly
- Demand for **less pollution** from industry
- Greater **regulation** by government and the EU (eg recycling targets)
- Demand that **businesses be charged** with the external cost of their activities
- Possible requirements to conduct **environmental audits**
- Opportunities to develop **products and technologies** which are environmentally friendly
- Taxes (eg landfill tax)

However, as with so many other areas of business, while some people advocate 'green claims' others are more cynical about them.

(a)   **Marketing**. Some critics argue that companies such as The Body Shop have exploited environmental friendliness as a marketing tool.

(b)   **Publicity**. Perhaps companies have more to fear from the impact of bad publicity (relating to their environmental practices) than they have to benefit from positive ecological messages, as such. Public relations is a vital competitive weapon.

(c)   **Lifestyles**. There may be a limit to which consumers are prepared to alter their lifestyles for the sake of ecological correctness. For example, how much more will consumers be prepared to pay to buy organic products compared with non-organic ones?

(d)   Consumers may be **imperfectly educated** about green issues. (For example, much recycled paper has simply been replaced by paper produced from trees from properly managed (ie sustainably developed) forests.) In short, some companies may have to 'educate' consumers as to the relative ecological impact of their products.

7.3.2 Renewable and non-renewable resources

KEY TERM

SUSTAINABILITY involves developing strategies so that the company only uses resources at a rate that allows them to be replenished such that the needs of the current generation can be met without compromising the needs of future generations. At the same time, emissions of waste are confined to levels that do not exceed the capacity of the environment to absorb them.

Sustainability means that resources consumed are **replaced** in some way: for every tree cut down another is planted. Some resources, however, are inherently non-renewable: for example, oil will eventually run out.

(a)   Metals can be recycled. Some car manufacturers are building cars with recyclable components.

(b)   An argument is that as the price of resources rises, market forces will operate to make more efficient use of them or to develop alternatives. When oil becomes too expensive, solar power will become economic.

Motor manufacturers are looking to a future without oil. Hydrogen power is one option, using **fuel cell** technology. Electric cars are another option.

John Elkington, Chairman of the think tank SustainAbility Ltd, has said that **sustainability** now embraces not only environmental and economic questions, but also social and ethical dimensions. He writes about the **triple bottom line** (TBL), which highlights that businesses now face the challenge of delivering simultaneously:

- Economic prosperity
- Environmental quality
- Social equity

However, a full consideration of sustainability in company reports is hampered by several difficulties.

- Lack of a standard methodology
- Accountants/auditors lack environmental expertise
- Difficulties in determining environmental costs
- Identification and valuation of potential liabilities is problematic

Elkington considers there to be three main forms of capital that businesses need to value.

- **Economic capital** (physical, financial and human skills and knowledge)
- **Natural capital** (replaceable and irreplaceable)
- **Social capital** (the ability of people to work together)

Environmental and social accounting is still embryonic, but Elkington believes that it will eventually develop our ability to see whether or not a particular company or industry is 'moving in the right direction'.

7.4 The triple bottom line (TBL) and sustainability

Elkington's concept of the TBL emphasises that, although firms can be capable of socially and environmentally responsible action, many will only take such action if accounting conventions are changed to record and monitor the entire impact of business activities and not just the financial (profit) benefits. If such a change is made, firms may be able to improve their sustainability record without the need for excessive government regulation.

There are potentially a number of ways poor environmental behaviour can affect a firm: it could result in fines (for pollution or damages), increased liability to environmental taxes, loss in value of land, destruction of brand values, loss of sales, consumer boycotts, inability to secure finance, loss of insurance cover, contingent liabilities, law suits, and damage to corporate image.

TBL

The TBL is sometimes summarised as People, Planet, and Profit. It consists of:

(a)   **Social justice**: fair and beneficial business practices towards labour and the community and the region in which a corporation conducts its business. A TBL company conceives a reciprocal social structure in which the wellbeing of corporate, labour and other stakeholder interests are interdependent.

(b)   **Environmental quality**: a TBL company endeavours to benefit the natural order as much as possible, or at the least do no harm and curtail environmental impact. In this way, the company tries to reduce its ecological footprint by, among other things, carefully managing its consumption of energy and non-renewable resources, and by reducing manufacturing waste, as well as rendering waste less toxic before disposing of it in a safe and legal manner.

(c)   **Economic prosperity**: the economic benefit enjoyed by the host society. It is the lasting economic impact the organisation has on its economic environment. Importantly, however, this is not as narrow as the internal profit made by a company or organisation.

For many years, sustainability has been seen from an environmental perspective, but now the social side of sustainability is gaining increasing importance.

Issues such as the health and safety of workers, and paying workers a fair wage, are becoming increasingly important. For example, while Apple's iPhones and iPads are becoming 'must-have' consumer items in Western countries, a number of concerns have been raised about the working conditions of the employees in China who are making them; with allegations of excessive working hours, draconian workplace rules, and workers even being urged to sign an 'anti-suicide' pledge after a series of employee deaths in 2010.

Although health and safety measures do not necessarily add value to a company on their own, they can help to protect a company against the cost of accidents which might otherwise occur.

Moreover, if a company has poor health and safety controls this might result in, among other things, increased sick leave for staff and possible compensation claims for any work-related injuries, as well as higher insurance costs to reflect the higher perceived risks within the company.

Equally, the issue of social responsibility in relation to consumers has also been highlighted in recent years. The tobacco industry and the food and drink industry have received criticism in relation to the potential harm their products may cause to consumers.

Ultimately, if consumers cease to buy a product because they are concerned about the consequences of its consumption, that product will not be sustainable because it will not generate any sales. For example, concerns about the high level of sugar in the 'Sunny D' orange drink forced Procter & Gamble to withdraw the drink's original formulation from the market.

CASE STUDY

In 2010, BP suffered its first annual loss for nearly 20 years, following the catastrophic explosion at the Deepwater Horizon oil rig in the Gulf of Mexico which will cost it at least £25 billion. Some analysts think the total cost to shareholders could exceed £40 billion over the next 10 years from 2010 to 2020.

2010 was one of the most damaging years in BP's history as the devastating explosion, which killed 11 workers and triggered the biggest offshore oil spill in history, shattered the company's reputation.

In February 2011, BP's chief executive said he was determined to see BP 'emerge from this episode as a company that is safer, stronger, more sustainable, more trusted and also more valuable ... 2011 will be a year of recovery and consolidation as we implement the changes we have identified to reduce operational risk and meet our commitments arising from the spill. But it will also be a year in which we have the opportunity to reset the company, adjusting the shape of our business, and focus on growing value for shareholders.'

Meanwhile, however, the White House oil commission into the fatal blowout on the drilling rig in April 2010 concluded that it was 'an avoidable disaster caused in part by a series of cost-cutting decisions made by BP and its partners'.

The commission's report argued that 'systemic management failure' at BP, Halliburton and Transocean (the other companies involved with the rig) was ultimately to blame for the blowout, and many of the poor decisions taken on the drilling rig were made in order to save time and money.

'Whether purposeful or not, many of the decisions that BP, Halliburton, and Transocean made that increased the risk of the blow-out clearly saved those companies significant time (and money)', the report stated.

Moreover, investors claimed that BP executives and directors breached their fiduciary duties to the company by ignoring safety and maintenance for years before the well exploded on 20 April 2010. The investors' lawyers argued that, despite warnings about the safety of the well, BP continued to systematically cut budgets.

The investors (who had filed a claim against BP claiming diminished share value) claimed that in addition to the tragic loss of life which resulted from the blowout, the disaster is anticipated to cost the company billions of dollars in damages, permanent reputational harm and intense government scrutiny.

The claimants argued that, despite existing concerns raised by federal safety regulators, BP had cut operational costs by 15% in 2009 alone (the year before the disaster). In their opinion, 'This reduction in budgets and manpower further undermined the company's ability to operate safely, as personnel were stretched even thinner, and resources that should have been devoted to maintenance, monitoring and addressing crucial safety failures in every aspect of the company's operations were diverted.'

[*Extracted from*: BP press release, www.bp.com, 1 February 2011; and 'BP's Pursuit of Cost-Cutting Led to Gulf Spill, Lawyers Say', www.bloomberg.com, 5 February 2011]

Conversely, some companies do realise the important of responding positively to environmental issues in order to protect and sustain their brand, and they can use sustainability issues to help maintain public trust in the brand.

For example, Toyota responded to environmental trends by successfully launching the Prius hybrid car, which supplements normal fuel usage with an electric-powered engine. The battery-powered electric engine starts the car, and operates it at low speeds. At higher speeds, the car switches automatically to a conventional engine and fuel. However, this combination saves on fuel compared with conventional cars and causes less pollution.

Equally, environmental and social responsibility can provide marketing opportunities for companies, and companies can even achieve competitive advantage by addressing and accommodating their customers' ethical concerns. For example, Innocent drinks has built its business on CSR ideals.

CASE STUDY

Innocent Drinks has based its business model on 'leaving things a little bit better than we found them'. The company combines a belief in product purity with eco-humanist values. It sees its ethical stance as affecting five main areas.

- **Keeping things natural** – using 100% natural ingredients and only making food that has a positive health benefit, and which is therefore free of additives, concentrates and flavourings. Innocent's sustainability strategy is underpinned by a desire to achieve a balance between nutrition and environmental impact.

- **Sustainable ingredients** – favouring suppliers that look after their environment and their workers, as certified by independent environmental and social organisations. Innocent pays a premium for fruit with the highest ethical accreditations, such as those from the Rainforest Alliance. Employees and independent auditors check standards on the farms Innocent uses.

- **Sustainable packaging** – using recycled, or renewable, material as much as possible, using the least possible amount of material per pack, using material with a low carbon footprint, using material with a widely available sustainable waste management option.

- **Sustainable production** – working with suppliers to improve water and energy efficiency, to reduce waste produced, and to increase recycling levels. Importantly, Innocent also acknowledges that the need to reduce carbon emissions and climate change is directly relevant to its business. Its current sources of banana, mango, strawberry and pineapple all fall within areas that will be significantly affected by climate change, giving Innocent a strong commercial imperative to reduce carbon emissions.

- **Sharing profits (Sustainable legacy)** – donating a minimum of 10% of profits each year to charity, mostly to the Innocent Foundation, funding rural development projects in countries where fruit comes from, promoting sustainability and best use of these community projects.

Given that firms are more likely to embrace sustainability if it brings them a financial benefit, it is important to note that introducing better environmental management systems can create 'win–win'

situations. For example, if introducing environmental management systems can allow a company to continue to produce the same amount of product by using less resources, and generating less waste, this is both economically efficient and also beneficial from an environmental and ecological perspective. In this context, the cost savings, more efficient resource usage, and waste minimisation can be substantial. For example, by 2005, DuPont used 7% less energy than it did in 1990, despite producing 30% more goods – thereby saving $2 billion.

7.4.1 Sustainability and strategy

The challenge that sustainability presents for decision makers in organisations comes from having to incorporate longer-term (sustainability) issues alongside short-term issues. If organisations focus too much on short-term issues at the expense of the longer-term this could undermine their **long-term reputation and prospects**.

Although the challenges facing organisations will vary according to their specific circumstances, the following summarises some possible issues to consider in relation to sustainability and the triple bottom line.

Environmental quality

- Resource usage (scope for using renewable rather than finite resources)
- Risks of contamination
- Levels of waste
- Carbon dioxide emissions
- Scope to use locally sourced inputs to reduce carbon footprint involved in transporting raw materials in
- Relations with authorities (especially if there are any legal requirements, such as planning permission for a new factory)

Social dimension

- Being seen as an attractive employer (which, in turn, can affect: ability to recruit high-quality staff, retain staff and staff know-how, and employee motivation)
- Quality of working conditions (in own company, and across the supply chain)
- Labour practices (labour/management relations, health and safety, training, diversity and opportunities (eg equal opportunities)
- Data protection and privacy
- Risk of accidents (and subsequent litigation against the company)
- Human rights (non-discrimination against minorities; use of child labour or forced labour; disciplinary practices; freedom for staff to belong to a union or other association)
- Relations with society: contribution to local community
- Integrity and image: not being involved with bribery and corruption, or anti-competitive prices (eg price fixing)
- Product responsibility: ensuring product's health and safety for customers, honesty in advertising and communications with consumers

Economic issues

- Business relations (security of business, relationship with banks and shareholders)
- Supplier and customer structure: quality of relationships with suppliers and customers
- Market position
- Brand name: risk to reputation and sales from negative publicity

Ethical consumerism

In relation to the sustainability of their sales, firms should also remember that, in most cases, consumers have a choice whether or not to buy their products. Individual consumers can make purchasing decisions based not only on personal interests but also on the interests of society and the environment. For example, they may boycott companies whose products are made by sweatshops or child labour, choosing wherever possible fair trade products. Moreover, some customers are prepared to pay more for products that are environmentally or socially responsible (fair trade, organic etc) compared with cheaper, less responsibly sourced products.

However, if firms are going to portray themselves as ethical or socially responsible, for this to have any meaningful benefit, they must be genuinely committed to ethical principles, rather than just treating them as an 'ethical veneer'.

CASE STUDY

On its website (www.starbucks.com), the coffee house Starbucks tells us that, over the years, it has received input from a broad range of stakeholders that has helped the company create a holistic approach to sourcing its coffee responsibly. Starbucks is committed to continuously improving economic transparency, promoting responsible labour practices, reducing environmental impacts, and ensuring the long-term supply of its high-quality coffee. While it accepts there is much more to do, it believes it has already made a measurable impact in coffee-growing communities where it does business.

Starbucks's approach is grounded in 'Coffee and Farmer Equity' (C.A.F.E.) Practices, its comprehensive set of social, economic, environmental and quality guidelines. Farms and mills are evaluated with approximately 200 performance indicators by third-party verification organisations, overseen by Scientific Certification Systems.

Starbucks complements purchases of C.A.F.E. Practices-verified coffee with third-party certified coffees grown and produced in ways that contribute to environmental preservation and/or sound production standards, including Fair Trade certified coffee and certified organic coffee.

However, alongside this commendable approach, critics present a somewhat less favourable impression of Starbucks.

Ethiopian coffee is widely recognised as one of the world's finest crops, and the coffee plantations in Ethiopia are hugely important for the future development of the country. Since 2005, the Ethiopian Government has tried to support the country's farmers by trade-marking their coffee in the US market. The trademark campaign is intended to protect the product and raise the price which farmers earn for their coffee, thereby generating additional revenue for the national economy.

However, to the surprise of media commentators, the major opponent (of the trade-marking) has not been a bulk-buyer with a purely economic interest in Ethiopian coffee, but the world's largest premium coffee franchise, Starbucks.

The reason for the commentators' surprise was the apparent contradiction with Starbucks's policy of helping local farming communities. Moreover, once Starbucks's position in this matter became public knowledge, its reputation as an ethically minded company was damaged, and it was portrayed as a modern-day colonialist exploiting one of the world's poorest countries.

In October 2012 Starbucks's reputation was further damaged by a tax scandal when it emerged that, despite telling its investors that it was profitable, the UK results for 2011 recorded a loss of £33 million. It achieved this by paying fees to other parts of its global business, such as brand royalty payments. This allowed the company to effectively make a loss therefore exempting itself from paying corporation tax in the UK.

The company was accused of paying only £8.4 million in corporation tax since arriving in the UK 14 years earlier, and none at all in the 3 years to 2011.

Starbucks insisted that it was fully tax compliant, but the public reaction and the concerns of its customers and employees encouraged the company to 'reconsider its tax status'. However, the damage may have already been done, as branding experts suggest the Starbucks name had become 'tarnished' since details of the tax scandal came to light.

7.4.2 Short- or long-term focus

Our discussions of triple bottom line and corporate responsibility should have highlighted a key point about sustainability in a business context: that sustainability refers to the social, economic and environmental concerns of a business that aims to thrive in the **long term**. From a strategic perspective, there is little point in a business being profitable in the short term if it alienates customers, suppliers and/or staff in the process. By doing so, the firm will weaken its chances of being profitable in the longer term.

In this respect, the idea of business sustainability can be seen as central to corporate strategy. Organisations need to use their resources and capabilities to develop a **sustainable competitive advantage**; and an organisation's ability to create and sustain this competitive advantage over its rivals is likely to be critical to its long-term success.

Equally, a sustainable business needs an understanding of the changing business landscape and external environment in which it operates so that it can respond and adapt to the opportunities and threats presented by the environment. In this respect, the idea of sustainability should be seen as a strategic issue for almost every business – for example, in relation to risk mitigation, strategic innovation and the development of new skills and capabilities.

Crucially, however, the concept of sustainability should encourage an organisation to consider long-term orientation in business decisions, rather than purely focusing on short-term (financial) information and metrics.

Short-term metrics may push managers towards making decisions that deliver short-term performance at the expense of long-term value creation. Equally, a focus on creating value for shareholders in the short term may result in a failure to make the necessary strategic investments to ensure future profitability.

By contrast, an increased focus on business sustainability will support decisions aimed at attracting human capital, establishing more reliable supply chains, and engaging in product and process innovation, even if those decisions do not necessarily maximise short-term financial performance and profitability.

However, this focus on the longer term can pose problems for the corporate decision maker or the management accountant. **Corporate reporting and performance measurement is often biased towards the short term**. The fact that companies report their results on a yearly basis, and may be under pressure from shareholders and market analysts to deliver results, means they may be forced into measures which boost profits in the short term, but may create problems in the longer term and in doing so may threaten sustainability.

7.5 Legal requirements and social responsibility

While some of the pressure on organisations to become more socially responsible has come from stakeholder expectations, (including investors and the media who are paying closer attention to companies' social and environmental performance), many businesses now also face a **legal requirement** to report on social and environmental matters in their annual reports.

7.5.1 Business review

In the UK, the Companies Act 2006 requires company directors to report on environmental issues in a 'Business review' as part of their directors' report. (From October 2013, quoted companies have to produce a 'Strategic report' which replaces the 'Business review'.)

The Companies Act states that companies, in particular, quoted companies, have to ensure that to the extent necessary for an understanding of 'the development and performance of the company's business during the financial year, and the position of the company's business at the end of that year' the business review should include:

(a)   The main trends and factors likely to affect the future development, performance and position of the company's business

(b)   Information about:

    (i)   **Environmental matters** (including the impact of the company's business on the environment)

    (ii)   The **company's employees**

    (iii)   **Social and community issues**, including information about any company policies in relation to those matters and the effectiveness of those policies

    (iv)   Persons with whom the company has contractual or other arrangements which are essential to the business of the company

Category (iv) could be very broad, and might include key suppliers and customers, as well as any partners in a joint venture or other contractual agreement (eg licence holders and agents). The aim of category (iv) is not to require companies to list all their suppliers (or customers) but to highlight any key relationships which are critical to the business and so could influence its performance and the value it generates for its owners (for example, reliance on a key supplier which is particularly important to the company's business).

7.5.2 Company employees

The Companies Act 2006 (Strategic Report and Directors' Report) Regulations 2013 require that, in addition to general reporting on their employees, quoted companies report specifically on the number of men and women on their board, in executive committees and the organisation as a whole.

These regulations also expand the requirements surrounding social and community issues to include specific consideration of human rights.

7.5.3 Greenhouse gas emissions

In conjunction with the general requirement for companies to include information about environmental matters in their business reviews, the Companies Act 2006 (Strategic Report and Directors' Reports) Regulations 2013 require that quoted companies have to report their annual greenhouse gas emissions in the directors' report.

Mandatory reporting is seen as a vital first step in getting companies to reduce their greenhouse gas emissions. By measuring and reporting greenhouse gas emissions, companies can begin to set targets and put in place management initiatives to reduce emissions in the future. (The requirement covers all greenhouse gases, not just carbon dioxide emissions.)

Commentators have suggested that by helping businesses to understand their carbon emissions, carbon reporting will help them identify opportunities to reduce costs, improve their reputation and potentially manage longer-term business risks.

However, the legislation also has important performance measurement and performance management implications for companies.

The Companies Act Regulations apply to all emission sources for which the reporting company is responsible, not just those sources in the UK. This means that multinational companies will have to have data collection systems for gathering information from global operations, as well as a set of global emissions factors to measure performance against.

Perhaps equally importantly, the legislation could encourage companies to make energy efficiency part of their business strategy and, for example, when evaluating a new strategic option, to consider the energy implications of that option rather than focusing solely on financial or commercial factors.

7.5.4 Implications of the increased importance of environmental issues

The increased focus on environmental issues and environmental performance also means that companies should introduce procedures to try to prevent non-compliance with environmental laws and regulations, and to avoid the fines or penalties which accompany such non-compliance.

In this respect, companies should consider:

(a)   Monitoring legal requirements and ensuring that operating procedures are designed to comply with these requirements

(b)   Implementing an appropriate system of internal controls and regularly reviewing the controls over environmental risks

(c)   Developing and operating a code of practice for environmental issues, such as accidental spills and the disposal of waste, especially hazardous waste

Environmental information

A company's internal reporting system also needs to record information about environmental issues, and should be capable of providing sufficient information to enable the financial impact of any environmental issues to be estimated with a reasonable degree of reliability.

In addition, it will be important to maintain regular communication between those responsible for environmental issues in a company and the accounting staff, so that the financial implications of any environmental issues are understood, and any necessary action can be taken promptly.

Environmental issues and the supply chain

Environmental issues are not confined within the normal financial reporting boundaries of an organisation. For example, supermarkets' concerns over supply chain issues are driving significant changes in supplier companies. To avoid a supplier's reputation being seriously damaged by sourcing products in a way which harms the environment, suppliers are manufacturing products sustainably and from sustainable sources.

Exam skills

In your exam, you may be asked to analyse or evaluate the appropriateness of a strategic option which an organisation is considering. When doing so, as well as looking at the short-term financial implications of the proposal, it may be necessary to consider how sustainable the proposal is.

Equally, you may be asked to evaluate how well a proposal fits with an organisation's objectives. Again, when considering objectives, you should be prepared to consider objectives relating to sustainability and social responsibility, as well as more narrowly defined financial or commercial objectives.

WEBLINK – CIMA article on sustainability and incorporating ethics into strategy:

http://www.cimaglobal.com/Research--Insight/Incorporating-ethics-into-strategy-second-edition/

CIMA's research article (from 2010) concluded that having strong ethical principles can add significant value to a brand, whereas failing to have such principles can undermine a company's long-term prospects, as well as causing social, economic and environmental damage.

CIMA's research suggests that companies which demonstrate high ethical standards often find that these standards translate into bottom-line benefits.

However, CIMA's report also highlighted that companies need good-quality **management information** about social, environmental and ethical performance if they are going to monitor the environmental and social impacts of their operations.

Equally, the report warned that company reporting on sustainability needs to provide hard evidence of the actions companies are taking to address the negative effects of their operations. In this respect, it is not sufficient for companies simply to pay lip service to the 'green agenda'.

WEBLINK – CIMA article on corporate sustainability practices:

http://www.cimaglobal.com/sustainabilityevolution

In a second report (also from 2010), produced in conjunction with the Chartered Accountants of Canada and the American Institute of CPAs, CIMA examined the drivers of business sustainability, the elements which are most important to embedding it within organisations, and the level of the finance function's involvement in corporate sustainability initiatives.

Drivers of business sustainability

- **Regulatory requirements** – The report found that compliance with regulatory requirements remains the most common driver for business sustainability.

- **Managing reputational risk** – Companies, particularly large companies, are concerned about the potential damage to their reputation and brand if they do not act in a sustainable manner.

- **Cost-cutting and efficiency** – Using resources in a more sustainable manner (for example, becoming more energy efficient) can help to reduce costs. In CIMA's survey this was identified as the second most important driver of business sustainability (after regulatory requirements) for small companies.

The report identified that ten elements are integral to embedding sustainability within organisations, and noted that finance and accounting functions can play an important role in a number of them.

Strategy and oversight

- Board and senior management commitment
- Understanding and analysing the key sustainability drivers for the organisation
- Integrating the key sustainability drivers into the organisation's strategy

Execution and alignment

- Ensuring that sustainability is the responsibility of everyone in the organisation (and not just of a specific department)

- Breaking down sustainability targets and objectives for the organisation as a whole into targets and objectives which are meaningful for individual subsidiaries, divisions and departments

- Ensuring that processes are in place to enable sustainability issues to be taken into account, clearly and consistently, in day to day decision making

- Extensive and effective sustainability training

Performance and reporting

- Including sustainability targets and objectives in performance appraisal
- Champions to promote sustainability and celebrate success
- Monitoring and reporting sustainability performance

One of the key messages here is that sustainability is becoming an increasingly integral part of business strategy and, therefore, companies need to consider sustainability issues when developing and implementing strategic plans.

Section summary

Corporate social responsibility is an organisation's obligation to maximise shareholder benefits while minimising the negative effects of its actions. It is not the same as ethical behaviour although the two are related. Social audits are sometimes carried out by firms that have social responsibility built into their corporate philosophy.

The issues of environmental and social sustainability are becoming increasingly important in strategic decision making.

8 Not for profit organisations

Introduction

Not for profit organisations have their own objectives, generally concerned with **efficient use of resources** in the light of specified targets.

8.1 Voluntary and not for profit sectors

Although most people would know one if they saw it, there is a surprising problem in clearly defining what counts as a **not for profit (NFP) organisation**. Local authority services, for example, would not be setting objectives in order to arrive at a profit for shareholders, but nowadays they are being increasingly required to apply the same disciplines and processes as companies which are oriented towards straightforward profit goals.

KEY TERM

Bois proposes that a NOT FOR PROFIT ORGANISATION be defined as: '... an organisation whose attainment of its prime goal is not assessed by economic measures. However, in pursuit of that goal it may undertake profit-making activities.'

This may involve a number of different kinds of organisation with, for example, differing legal status – charities, trade unions and government departments providing services such as education, health, leisure or public utilities such as water and road maintenance.

Business strategy issues are just as relevant to an NFP organisation as they are to a business operating with a profit motive. The tasks of setting objectives, developing strategies and controls for their implementation can all help in improving the performance of charities and NFP organisations. While the basic principles are appropriate for this sector, differences in how they can be applied should not be forgotten.

8.2 Objectives

Objectives will not be based on profit achievement but rather on achieving a **particular response** from various target markets. This has implications for reporting of results. The organisation will need to be open and honest in showing how it has managed its budget and allocated funds raised. **Efficiency and effectiveness** are particularly important in the use of donated funds, but there is a danger that resource efficiency becomes more important than the service effectiveness.

Listed below are some possible objectives for an NFP organisation.

(a)   Surplus maximisation (equivalent to profit maximisation)
(b)   Revenue maximisation (as for a commercial business)
(c)   Usage maximisation (as in leisure centre swimming pool usage)
(d)   Usage targeting (matching the capacity available, as in a hospital service)
(e)   Full/partial cost recovery (minimising subsidy)
(f)   Budget maximisation (maximising what is offered)
(g)   Producer satisfaction maximisation (satisfying the wants of staff and volunteers)
(h)   Client satisfaction maximisation (the police generating the support of the public)

There are a number of different **stakeholder groups** and **audiences** which NFP organisations may serve.

(a)   A **target public** is a group of individuals who have an interest or concern about the charity.
(b)   Those benefiting from the organisation's activities are known as the **client public**.
(c)   Relationships are also vital with **donors and volunteers** from the general public.
(d)   There may also be a need to lobby **local and national government** and businesses for support.

The objective-setting process must **balance** the interests and concerns of these audiences, which may result in a range of objectives, rather than a single overriding one. In order to allow for this balance to be achieved, NFPs may allow wide **participation** in the objective-setting process, or, indeed, may have it enforced upon them by, for example, legal requirements for consultation with interested parties, or constitutional provision for a range of constituencies to be heard.

NFP objective-setting has other complications:

(a) Providers of funds have potentially greater influence than members or beneficiaries and may have different objectives.

(b) There is no overall profit motive. There is often a conflict between delivering a profit or achieving social responsibilities.

(c) Priorities may change rapidly as circumstances change, as for instance when a natural disaster occurs or a government changes.

(d) All the factors above make it easier for powerful insiders to pursue their personal objectives for power or recognition.

Charities and NFP organisations often deal more with **services and ideas** than products.

(a) **Appearance** needs to be businesslike rather than appearing extravagant.

(b) **Process** is increasingly important, for example, the use of direct debit to pay for council tax reduces administration costs, leaving more budget for community services.

(c) **People** need to offer good service and be caring in their dealings with their clients.

(d) **Distribution channels** are often shorter with fewer intermediaries than in the profit-making sector. Wholesalers and distributors available to business organisations do not exist in most non-business contexts.

(e) **Promotion is usually dominated by personal selling**. Advertising is often limited to public service announcements due to limited budgets. Direct marketing is growing due to the ease of developing databases. Sponsorship, competitions and special events are also widely used.

(f) **Pricing** is probably the most different element in this sector. Financial price is often not a relevant concept. Rather, opportunity cost, where an individual is persuaded of the value of donating time or funds, is more relevant.

Controlling activities is complicated by the difficulty of judging whether **non-quantitative objectives** have been met. For example, assessing whether the charity has improved the situation of client publics is difficult to research. Statistics related to product mix, financial resources, size of budgets, number of employees, number of volunteers, number of customers serviced and number and location of facilities are all useful for this task.

Section summary

Not-for-profit organisations do not have profit as their primary motive, but are increasingly required to apply the same disciplines and processes as a profit-oriented company. Business strategy is equally relevant to these organisations to help them improve performance; however, the differing objectives set by such organisations mean that the concepts will be applied differently.

Further reading

Although this Study Text is designed to provide you with comprehensive coverage of the material you need for your E3 exam, if you wish to do some further reading around the areas of business strategy covered in this chapter we recommend the following texts:

Johnson, G., Whittington, R. & Scholes, K. (2011) *Exploring Strategy* (9th edition), Harlow, FT/Prentice Hall.

Lynch, R. (2011) *Strategic Management* (6th edition), Harlow, Pearson.

Chapter Summary

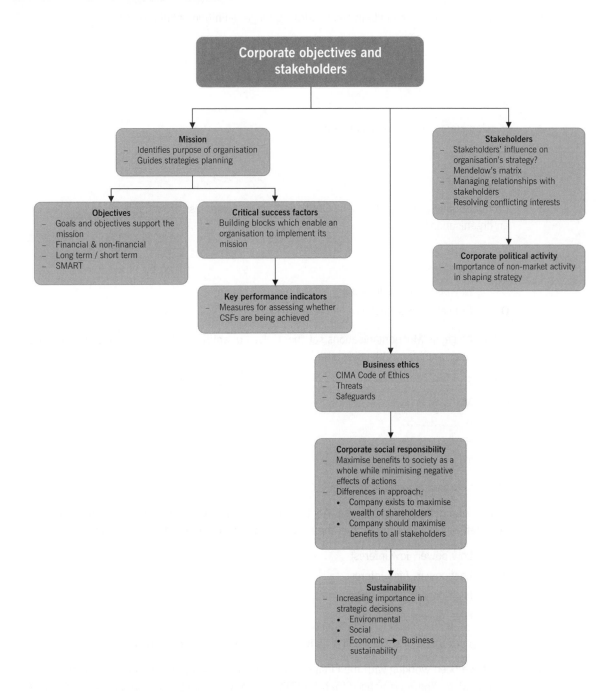

Quick Quiz

1   What are the four elements in the Ashridge College definition of 'mission'?

P ....

S ....

P ....

V ....

2   Mission statements have a standard format.

☐ True

☐ False

3   Product quality, manufacturing flexibility and brand awareness are most likely to be .... for an organisation?

A   Objectives

B   Performance targets

C   Key performance indicators

D   Critical success factors

4   Fill in the gaps: 'Most organisations set themselves quantified (1) .... in order to enact the corporate (2) .... Many objectives are:

(3)   S ....

(4)   M ....

(5)   A ....

(6)   R ....

(7)   T ....

5   What is corporate social responsibility?

6   As part of a restructuring exercise, AB Co will have to make some of its staff redundant. How should AB Co's staff be classified in terms of their levels of power and interest in relation to this decision?

A   Low power; low interest

B   Low power; high interest

C   High power; low interest

D   High power; high interest

7   How do questions of sustainability tie in with the long-/short-term debate?

8   You have been working with the Finance Director preparing a presentation for your company's shareholders. You have noticed that the FD's presentation makes the company's performance look significantly more favourable than it actually is, because the FD has excluded the results from a poorly performing division from the presentation.

When you mentioned this omission to the FD, he replied that he was already aware of it, and he had deliberately chosen to exclude the division's results.

Which fundamental ethical principle is being threatened here?

Answers to Quick Quiz

1   Purpose

Strategy

Policies and standards of behaviour

Values

2   False. Although the four elements of the Ashridge model are a good basis, there is no standard format for a mission statement.

3   D   Critical success factors

Critical success factors (CSFs) 'are those factors on which the strategy is fundamentally dependent for its success', and at which an organisation must excel to outperform its competitors.

Key performance indicators (KPIs) and performance targets could be used to measure how well an organisation is achieving its CSFs. However, KPIs and targets must be measurable. Similarly, in order to be SMART, objectives must be measurable.

4   (1) objectives (2) mission (3) specific (4) measurable (5) attainable (6) results-oriented (or realistic) (7) time bounded

5   Corporate social responsibility is an organisation's obligation to maximise positive stakeholder benefits while minimising the negative effects of its actions.

6   B   The staff will have a high level of interest in the decision (because it directly affects them) but it is likely that they will only have a low level of power to be able to influence it; not least because they don't appear to be able to prevent the redundancies from occurring.

7   Issues of sustainability challenge an organisation to look at the longer-term consequences of its actions rather than just the short-term financial impact. Some decisions that are taken from an ecological sustainability standpoint may have an impact on short-term performance (such as the decision to invest in a new recycling process) but the longer-term consequences should also be considered in the investment decision.

8   Integrity.

The FD appears to be deliberately presenting incomplete information in order to make the company's performance look better than it is (which is misleading to the shareholders).

Answers to Question

2.1 Stakeholder influences

Accountants have divided loyalties – to their firm, and to their profession.

The Technical Department will almost certainly resist such a change, as the proposals devalue audit to being one of many business services to management. An audit is undertaken for the benefit of shareholders, not the company management. The Technical Department (the firm's technostructure) is also powerful as enforcement of the standards it will suggest should reduce professional negligence costs. The technostructure will thus exert a powerful influence over the strategy and business practices. External influences include professional associations which have a technostructural influence on the profession as a whole. The marketing manager may also be misled as to the degree to which customers want a 'one-stop shop' for accounting and advertising services. Perhaps he is overestimating the power of this factor in the external coalition.

Now try these questions from the Practice Question Bank	Number	Level	Marks	Time
	2.1–2.5	Intermediate	n/a	10 mins
	2.6	Examination	25	45 mins

THE ENVIRONMENT AND UNCERTAINTY

An organisation needs to use the information it gathers about its strategic position to inform its strategic options (Sections 1 and 2).

Gap analysis (Section 3) allows an organisation to compare its expected performance against its objectives. However, the effectiveness of gap analysis depends on an organisation's ability to forecast its performance in the future (Section 4).

Often information about the environment is uncertain, and can be incomplete or even ambiguous. This makes strategic decision making a complicated process.

You also need to remember that environmental changes, in any given situations, can have an impact on corporate appraisal, particularly in relation to the opportunities and threats facing an organisation.

A number of the topics covered in this chapter (for example, scenario planning, foresight and game theory) are ways organisations try to include some of the uncertainty they face in their strategic planning (Sections 6, 7 and 8).

Despite this uncertainty, gathering strategic intelligence (Section 9) remains a very important part of strategic planning.

Topic list	Learning outcomes	Syllabus references	Ability required
1 The external environment	A1(a)	A1(a) (ii)	Evaluate
2 The environment as a driver for change	A1(a)	A1(a) (ii)	Evaluate
3 Environmental information and analysis	B1(a)	B1(a) (vii)	Evaluate
4 Gap analysis	B1(a); B2(a)	–	Evaluate
5 Forecasting	B1(a); B2(a)	B2(a) (ii)	Evaluate
6 Scenario planning	B1(a)	B1(a) (iv)	Evaluate
7 Foresight	B1(a)	B1(a) (iv)	Evaluate
8 Game theory	B1(a)	B1(a) (vi)	Evaluate
9 Strategic intelligence	–	–	–

Chapter Overview

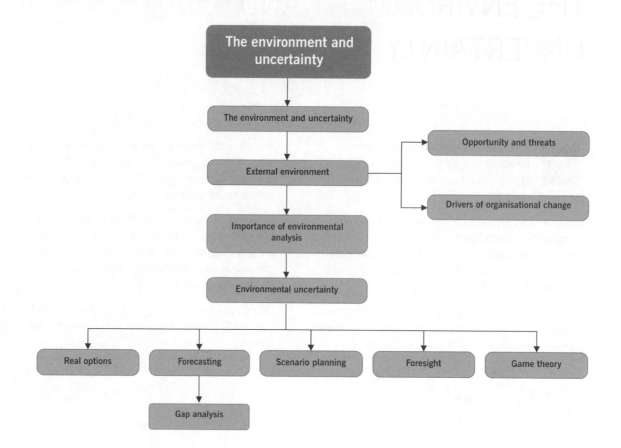

1   The external environment

Introduction

An important part of developing a strategy is analysing an organisation's position in relation to its external environment, in order to ensure that the proposed strategy fits with the environment. PEST analysis forms a useful framework for analysing the macro-environment in which an organisation operates.

The environment within which organisations operate influences what they do, and their ability to survive and grow. Strategic decision makers and planners must take account of potential environmental impacts in order to produce plans that are realistic and achievable. The external environment is also the source of opportunities and threats for an organisation, so environmental analysis is important for an organisation to enable it to take advantage of **opportunities** which arise, and minimise the potential **threats** it faces.

Where an organisation undertakes international or even global operations, it is particularly important to understand that there may be important differences between the environments present in the various regions and countries involved.

(This recognition of the influence of the environment on organisations underpins the **position-based approach** to strategy which we discussed in Chapter 1 of this Study Text.)

An organisation's environment includes everything outside the organisation's boundaries, which can be summarised in the diagram below.

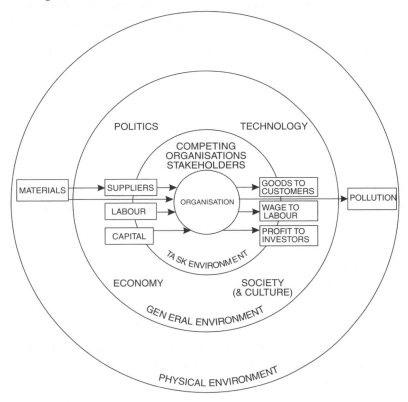

KEY TERMS

The GENERAL ENVIRONMENT (or macro-environment) covers all the political/legal, economic, social/cultural and technological (**PEST**) forces which affect not only individual organisations but also the other actors in the micro-environment.

The TASK ENVIRONMENT (or micro-environment) relates to the factors in an organisation's immediate environment, which affect its ability to operate effectively in its chosen markets, such as customers, competitors, customers, distributors and suppliers.

BPP
LEARNING MEDIA

1.1 PEST analysis

Management can use the PEST framework to analyse the macro-environment and to identify the opportunities and threats which could affect the organisation. The mnemonic 'PEST' stands for political, economic, social and technological; but increasing public concern for the natural environment, corporate social responsibility and sustainability in recent years has led to the inclusion of a second 'E' in the mnemonic, standing for 'environment'. Equally, if legal matters (eg employment law, anti-discrimination policies, consumer protection; health and safety law) are given their own heading, the mnemonic becomes expanded to 'PESTEL'.

Nonetheless, it is important to recognise that not all environmental factors will fit neatly into a single category: instead, they may interact and take effect in complex ways. For example, government policy could also affect economic factors.

Political/Legal – government policies affect national economies and governments are responsible for creating and maintaining a stable framework in which business can be carried out. Government policies can also be important in relation to:

- Physical infrastructure (eg transport, broadband networks)
- Social infrastructure (education, welfare, law enforcement, equal opportunities)
- Tax
- Trade regulations

Political stability in a country can also affect the macro-economic environment in which a business operates. For example, a **change of government** in a country might prove to be a significant factor in an organisation's decision about whether or not to undertake business in that country.

Economic – a business can be affected by national and international economic factors, such as:

- Inflation
- Interest rates
- Exchange rates
- Unemployment levels
- Business cycles and trends in national income
- International trade (and balance of payments)

Social factors – **demographics** (eg birth and death rates, average age, ethnicity) and **cultural** factors are important for understanding the market, and developing marketing strategies. They can also be important in developing an organisation's HR policies.

Other important social factors include:

- Income distribution
- Levels of education
- Attitudes to work and leisure
- Attitudes to consumption, and lifestyle choices

Technological – developments in technology affect all aspects of business, through reducing costs, improving quality, and leading to innovation and new product development. Technological developments can result in new:

- Products and services
- Methods of producing or providing products and service (which, in turn, could lead to changes in an organisation's cost base)
- Sales channels (such as e-commerce) and media for communication (eg internet; social media)
- Ways to analyse markets (eg database systems to enable data mining)
- Organisation structures to exploit technology (eg remote working; greater integration across the supply chain)

The level of government spending on research, and government attitudes to research, can affect the level of new product development in a country.

Technological factors are also important to the extent that they encourage innovation in a country or an industry. On the one hand, technology provides opportunities (through the development of new products and services) but it could also present a threat by making existing products obsolete.

Exam skills

The **E2** syllabus required you to be able to **discuss** different competitive environments and the key external characteristics of those environments.

However, in **E3**, the focus will be on your ability to **apply** different models in order to **evaluate** the impact of the external environment on strategic decisions. So, in the strategic level case study, you might need to analyse the extent to which political, economic, social or technological factors in the environment represent opportunities or threats to an organisation and, therefore, how they might shape its strategic decisions.

Analysing PEST (or PESTEL) factors could also be a useful way of identifying drivers for change in an organisation's external environment. We discuss the environment as a driver for organisational change in more detail later in this chapter.

1.2 LoNGPEST analysis

It is important to recognise that environmental factors can operate at local, national and global levels. (This recognition of the global level could be particularly important to multinational companies, assessing the opportunities and threats which are present in different countries.)

Once an organisation has identified the environmental factors which could have an impact on it, it then also needs to consider the level of that impact – in the organisation's home region only (local); across the organisation's home country (national); or across a number of countries (global). Identifying the extent of a factor's influence on the organisation could be particularly important when considering which opportunities or threats are priorities for the organisation to deal with.

In effect, a LoNGPEST analysis framework could be seen as a grid as follows:

	Political	**Economic**	**Social**	**Technological**
Local				
National				
Global				

It is debatable whether technological factors will have a local or national impact in the same way that social factors might, for example. In this respect, it might be more appropriate to consider technological factors as affecting all three levels (local, national and global) together.

1.3 Limitations of PEST analysis

Although PEST analysis can help an organisation to understand its environment, and the opportunities and threats in it, there could still be drawbacks to using it:

(a) External factors are dynamic, and can change frequently and rapidly (for example, due to advances in technology). As such, the factors identified in a PEST analysis could quickly become obsolete, meaning they have little value for any future strategic planning.

(b) Alternatively, if an organisation keeps updating its PEST analysis – to reflect changes in the external environment – this means the analysis will become a time-consuming and costly exercise.

(c) Often the output from PEST analysis becomes little more than a list of environmental factors that can affect an organisation or a project. However, unless these factors are prioritised – in terms of their potential impact and the likelihood of them occurring – the value of the environmental analysis in terms of helping an organisation identify the **key opportunities** and **threats** it faces is reduced.

(d) Equally, there is no guarantee that the organisation will identify all the environmental factors that could affect it. This is another illustration of the problem of **bounded rationality** we mentioned in Chapter 1. Although strategic planners will take account of the environmental factors they are aware of, there are likely to be some factors which they are not aware of.

(e) On a related point, although PEST analysis can provide useful information to assist strategic planning, the strategic options that an organisation can actually pursue successfully are determined not only by the opportunities and threats in the external environment but also by its own internal resources, competences and capabilities.

As organisations begin to recognise the limitations of PEST analysis, some have started to look at other possible ways of understanding their environments. One of these ways is **foresight** – through which strategic managers try to predict future environmental changes, analyse the potential consequences of those changes, and make plans to respond to them effectively. Moreover, rather than relying on a single method for predicting future environmental changes, foresight can encompass a range of techniques, including scenario planning, visioning and the Delphi method.

We will discuss foresight and scenario planning in more detail later in this chapter (Sections 6 and 7).

1.4 Porter's five forces

As well as analysing the opportunities and threats presented by the macro-environment, organisations need to monitor their more immediate environment (the micro-environment).

Porter's five forces model suggests that five competitive forces influence the state of competition in an industry and, therefore, collectively determine the level of profit which can be sustained in the industry as a whole:

- The threat of new entrants to the industry
- The threat of substitute products or services
- The bargaining power of customers
- The bargaining power of suppliers
- The rivalry among current competitors in the industry

Source: adapted from Porter (Competitive Strategy)

Threat of new entrants to the industry

The threat of new entrants is limited by **barriers to entry**:

(a)   **Economies of scale**. Increased scale leads to lower costs. New entrants must start on a large scale or they will suffer cost disadvantages compared with established producers.

(b)   **Product differentiation**. Existing brand images and customer loyalty make it difficult for new competitors to enter the market.

(c)   **Capital requirements**. High or risky capital investment requirements create strong barriers to entry.

(d)   **Switching costs**. Costs incurred by a customer when switching from one supplier's product to another supplier's product. High switching costs are likely to make a customer more loyal to their existing supplier.

(e)   **Access to distribution channels**. These carry the manufacturer's product to the end-buyer. New distribution channels are hard to set up and existing channels hard to access.

(f)   **Access to resources** eg patent rights, experience and know-how, and government subsidies.

(g)   **Expected retaliation** eg through a price war which, in turn, reduces profit margins. If a potential entrant expects the existing competitors to retaliate fiercely to its entry, this may act as a deterrent from entering the market at all.

The threat of substitute products or services

A substitute product is a good/service provided by **another industry** which satisfies the same customer needs. An industry which has few substitutes will be more able to sustain a high profit than an industry with many substitutes.

Bargaining power of customers

The bargaining power of customers depends on:

*   How much the **customer buys**
*   How **critical** the product is to the customer's own business
*   Whether the products are **standard items** (easily copied) or specialised
*   The **customer's own profitability**
*   Customer's **ability to bypass** the supplier or take over the supplier
*   The **skills** of the customer's **purchasing staff**, or price awareness of customers
*   The importance of **product quality** to the customer

If customers have high bargaining power this will restrict the industry's ability to sustain high profits.

Bargaining power of suppliers

The bargaining power of suppliers depends on:

- The **number** of **suppliers** (one or two dominant can charge monopoly or oligopoly prices)
- The threat of **new entrants** or substitute products to the **supplier's industry**
- The **number** of **customers** in the industry
- The scope for **substitution**
- Whether **switching costs** for customers would be high
- Whether the supplier has a **differentiated product** which buyers need to obtain

Competitive rivalry among existing firms

The intensity of competitive rivalry within an industry will affect the profitability of the industry as a whole. Rivalry levels are affected by:

- **Market growth** – rivalry is intensified in markets where growth is low.
- Ability of customers to **switch** (eg Coke and Pepsi).
- **Market structure** – markets in which a number of competitors are roughly the same size are likely to have more intensive rivalry than, for example, a monopoly market.
- Level of output **capacity** required to obtain reductions in unit costs.
- **Cost structure** – if fixed costs are high, firms may be tempted to compete on price. In the short term, any contribution to profit (to help cover fixed costs) is better than none at all.
- **Uncertainty** about competitors' strategy. There is a tendency to respond to uncertainty by formulating a more competitive strategy.
- **Exit barriers** which make it difficult to leave the industry. If it is hard for existing suppliers to leave the industry, they will stay and compete, thereby intensifying competition.

High levels of rivalry are likely to suppress the level of sustainable profits in the industry.

Role of government

Although Porter only identified five forces which he felt determine the level of profitability in an industry, some commentators suggest that the role of **government needs to be added as a sixth force**. For example, if governments offer subsidies to certain firms or industries, this could allow them to reduce the price of their goods or services yet still earn a sustainable profit.

1.5 Limitations of Porter's five forces model

Although Porter's model can provide some valuable insights into the level of profits which can be sustained in an industry, it does still have some potential drawbacks and limitations.

We have already identified the fact that Porter ignores the impact which governments can have in determining the profitability of an industry. However, critics have identified other possible limitations:

Collaboration rather than competition – One of the underlying ideas behind Porter's model is that firms are constantly competing against each other, and the intensity of this competition helps to determine the profitability of an industry. The model assumes that companies try to achieve competitive advantages over their rivals in the market, as well as over suppliers and customers. However, such an approach does not accurately reflect the logic of strategic alliances or supply chain networks where the focus is primarily on collaboration rather than competition.

Industry-based rather than firm-based – The model focuses on the wider environment (and profitability) of an industry. However, by doing so it ignores the extent to which the competences and capabilities of individual firms can determine their profitability within an industry. Even though an industry as a whole may be profitable, an individual firm may not be if it doesn't have the competences or capabilities to be successful in that industry. Similarly, an individual firm could earn better margins than its competitors in an industry if it can deal more effectively with key forces, or if it can develop some distinctive competences which provide it with a sustainable competitive advantage in relation to its competitors.

Dynamic industries – The model suggests a static picture of the competition in an industry, and therefore understates the role of innovation. For example, the development of new products or processes could significantly change the competitive forces, and therefore the level of profit which could be earned.

Definining the industry – Another potential problem in applying the model comes from defining the market or industry being analysed. For a large organisation, or one operating in a complex environment, this could be extremely difficult.

BPP's provision of accountancy tuition is a good example of this point. The market for training potential chartered accountants (ICAEW students in the UK) is subject to considerable customer bargaining power – due to the large accountancy firms which dominate the market, and pay for their students to attend courses. CIMA and ACCA courses, on the other hand, are subject to greater rivalry from existing competitors – because universities and colleges offer these courses as well as other commercial training providers.

In the context of a five forces analysis, though, does BPP have a single market (accountancy training) or does it have different markets, according to the different qualifications?

This issue around market definition identifies a wider problem with Porter's model. It is best used for analysing simple market structures, because analysis of the different forces can get very difficult in more complex industries where there may be lots of interrelated segments or product groups.

1.6 Competitor analysis

Although understanding that the overall intensity of the competitive rivalry in an industry is important – since it is one of the five factors which can determine the profitability of an industry – it is also important for an organisation to analyse individual competitors to understand their goals and strategies, their strengths and weaknesses, and how they are likely to respond to the organisation's own strategies.

In order to be successful, a company must provide consumers with some greater value or satisfaction than its competitors do. However, in order that it can know how to position its products or services more strongly in the minds of consumers, the organisation needs to analyse its competitors.

Competitor analysis helps an organisation understand its **competitive advantages/disadvantages compared with its competitors**. It can also provide an organisation with **insights into its competitors' strategies**. In doing so, competitor analysis helps the organisation **develop its own strategies** to achieve (or sustain) competitive advantage over its competitors.

However, as well as looking at competitors' **current** strategies and objectives, competitor analysis can help a firm try to forecast competitors' **future** strategies and decisions. Again, such insight might be useful to the firm in **shaping its own strategies** for the future.

KEY TERM

COMPETITOR ANALYSIS is the 'identification and quantification of the relative strengths and weaknesses (compared with competitors or potential competitors), which could be of significance in the development of a successful competitive strategy'.   *(CIMA Official Terminology)*

One of the first questions an organisation needs to ask is: Who are the competitors?

Once it has established this, an organisation should then look at the following key factors when undertaking competitor analysis.

(a) **Objectives**. What are the competitor's current goals or strategic objectives? How well is it achieving them? Are its goals likely to change in the future?

(b) **Strategy**. How is the competitor firm competing (eg cost leadership or differentiation)? In what markets is the firm competing?

(c) **Assumptions**. What assumptions does the competitor hold about the industry and its own performance (eg trends in the market, products and consumers)?

(d) **Resources and competences**. What are the competitor's key strengths and weaknesses? What resources, competences and capabilities does it have, or not have?

(e) **Competitor response profile**. How is the competitor likely to respond to any strategic initiatives the organisation introduces? Will its response be the same across all products/markets, or might it react more aggressively in some markets than others?

Key questions in the competitor response profile will also include: Is the competitor satisfied with its current position? What strategic changes might the competitor initiate itself? Where is the competitor vulnerable? What will provoke the greatest and most effective retaliation by the competitor?

1.6.1 Competitor reaction and response

Once an organisation has analysed its competitors, it can then begin to assess their likely response to its strategies or tactics.

We can identify four types of competitor response.

(a) **Laid-back**: competitor does not respond, even though it has seen and recognised your move.

(b) **Selective**: competitor only responds to certain types of attack. However, unlike 'Unpredictable' competitors, they tend to be consistent in their responses; so, if they respond to price discounting on one occasion they will do so on all occasions.

(c) **Retaliatory** (or 'Tiger'): competitor reacts and responds aggressively to any attack.

(d) **Unpredictable** (or 'Stochastic'): impossible to predict how competitor will react. Sometimes they will react aggressively, other times they will not respond at all.

2   The environment as a driver for change

Introduction

The external environment is the source of opportunities and threats for an organisation. In order to respond effectively to those opportunities and threats, the organisation may need to make changes to its current products, markets or processes. In this way, the environment can act as a trigger for change in organisations.

The external environment is the source of opportunities and threats for an organisation, and environmental analysis should help an organisation anticipate opportunities and threats within a timescale which allows it to take advantage of the **opportunities** which arise, and respond to the potential **threats** it faces.

However, events in the external environment can also act as triggers for change in an organisation, and **PEST** (or LoNGPEST) analysis and **Porter's five forces** model could both be useful ways of identifying potential external triggers for change for an organisation.

In this respect, triggers relating to general, macro-environmental factors (PEST factors) can be classified as **indirect triggers**. By contrast, triggers which relate to an organisation's immediate competitive environment (Porter's five forces) can be classified as **direct triggers**.

The exact triggers for change will depend on the context of an organisation and its industry, but the following could all act as change triggers:

Indirect triggers

(a) Changes in the economic cycle (for example, an economic downturn, or recovery from recession into a period of economic growth; either domestically or internationally)

(b) New laws or regulations affecting an industry; or changes in government legislation more generally

(c) Changes in customer expectations and tastes; responding to customer pressure (for example, car manufacturers moving towards producing more environmentally friendly cars in response to customer concerns about carbon emissions and pollution)

(d)   Changes in product or process technology (for example, the impact of faster communications and digital downloads on the music and film entertainment industries)

(e)   Changes in communications media, in particular the growth of e-business and e-commerce

Direct triggers

(a)   Arrival of new entrants into the market, or mergers/acquisitions between existing competitors in the industry

(b)   Changes in level or intensity of competition (prompting a need to gain or protect market share)

(c)   Changes in supply chain or distribution networks

More generally, organisations and their managers are faced with highly dynamic and ever more complex operating environments, and this dynamism and complexity creates pressure for change.

Industries and products change, along with the markets they serve, and organisations have to change and adapt. Such changes, together with the need to introduce innovations within ever-diminishing timescales (as a result of shortening product life cycles), places change management towards the top of the core competences required by an organisation if it is to be successful.

Change triggers can be national or even international. For example, throughout Europe, as countries join the Eurozone or have to conform with directives on working time and working practices, organisations operating within those countries have to adapt to the changing commercial environments they face.

Globalisation

Reductions in transportation, information and communication costs, new technologies and e-business, and the growth of new trading blocs such as the 'Tiger' economies of South-East Asia mean that the geography of world trade has changed dramatically since the 1960s.

Organisations (particularly in developed, Western countries) have had to plan how to respond to the increasing competitive pressures which result from the growth of rivals based in locations with lower cost bases.

Globalisation also opens up opportunities for organisations to shift production internationally, or to sell to customers in a number of countries. Such changes could have a significant impact on how a company manages its supply chain.

Natural environment

The increased importance of social responsibility and sustainability indicates that the potential impact of businesses on the natural environment is becoming increasingly recognised. The potential exhaustion of supplies of natural resources; concern about levels of waste and pollution being created; and the threat of climate change and global warming will force organisations to change their behaviour sooner or later.

Organisations are now increasingly keen to show they are responsible corporate citizens, so changes may be introduced sooner so that they can demonstrate their corporate social responsibility.

Changing workplace structures

Historically, the traditional organisation structure has seen businesses staffed by a core, permanent workforce.

However, this model is changing to one where an increasing number of organisations are using a mix of core and peripheral workforces (for example, using home workers) and outsourcing their labour requirements for certain services.

Despite these changes, social and demographic issues will continue to affect the workplace. For example, how will organisations deal with equal opportunities legislation which could affect recruitment decisions on the grounds of gender or age?

Continuing impact of advanced communications technologies

Since the 1980s, most of the developed economies in the world have been riding the 'third wave' of an industrial revolution which is bringing changes as profound as those that followed the earlier two waves of steam power and the internal combustion engine.

Advanced communications technologies have created new industries, new products and new lifestyles and have enabled the fragmentation of firms into 'virtual businesses' such that activities that were once all conducted in-house are now being factored out around the globe. The new technologies have also brought new organisational structures, and have led to organisations having enriched information about individuals and groups of customers. However, these technologies have also raised new concerns about privacy and surveillance.

2.1 Prioritising drivers of change

As we mentioned in the previous section, the exact triggers for change in any scenario will depend on the context of an organisation and its industry. However, once the strategic planners in an organisation have identified the opportunities and threats facing the organisation they also have to prioritise them.

One useful way of prioritising change triggers – and strategic uncertainties more generally – is in relation to their impact and immediacy.

The **impact** (importance) of a strategic uncertainty is related to:

- The extent to which it involves trends or events that will impact the organisation

- The importance to the organisation of the business units or products affected by the uncertainty/trigger

- The number of business units or products potentially affected by the uncertainty; ie the **scale** of the impact on the organisation

The **immediacy** or **urgency** of a strategic uncertainty is related to:

- The likelihood (**risk**) of a trend or event occurring – if an event only has a low probability of occurring it may not be worth acting upon

- The time frame of the trends or events (eg does the event need an immediate response?)

- The time which will be available in which to react to the event, compared with the time which will be required to develop and implement an appropriate strategy to respond to that event

The order of priority for responding to environmental triggers can then be determined in relation to the relative impact (importance) and immediacy (urgency) of the different triggers. This can be illustrated in the **importance/urgency matrix** as follows:

Strategic importance

	Low	High
High	Lower priority	**Highest priority** (major issues)
Low	Other issues (lowest priority)	High priority (but not as high as major issues)

(Urgency)

Aaker and McLoughlin's impact analysis matrix suggests that an organisation should then respond to strategic uncertainties on the basis of their urgency and importance as follows:

Strategic importance

	Low	High
High	Monitor and analyse	Analyse in detail and develop a strategy to deal with the uncertainties
Low	Monitor	Monitor, analyse and consider contingent strategies

(Urgency — left axis)

Impact analysis matrix (Based on Aaker and McLoughlin)

The ideas of 'strategic importance' and 'urgency' in Aaker and McLoughlin's matrix are similar to those of the likelihood/consequences matrix which is covered in Paper P3 in relation to risk mapping and risk response. This matrix is included below for reference.

Consequences

	Low	High
Low	**Accept or absorb** Risks are not significant. Keep under review, but costs of dealing with risks unlikely to be worth the benefits.	**Transfer** Insure risk or implement contingency plans. Reduction of severity of risk will minimise insurance premiums.
High	**Reduce or manage** Take some action, eg self-insurance to deal with frequency of losses.	**Avoid or control** Take immediate action to reduce severity and frequency of losses, eg insurance, charging higher prices to customers or ultimately abandoning activities.

(Likelihood — left axis)

Likelihood/consequences matrix

Exam skills

Useful elements to consider when considering which issues to prioritise are: timescale (short term vs long term); scale of impact (significant vs not significant) and level of risk (high risk vs low risk).

Note that a short-term problem (for example, short-term cash flow problems) can still have a significant impact and be a high risk. Anything fundamental to the survival of the business has, by definition, high strategic importance.

Section summary

Once it has identified the opportunities and threats present in its environment, an organisation has to decide how to respond to them, and which of them need to be given the highest priority. The organisation's response to opportunities and threats could then act as a trigger for organisational change.

3 Environmental information and analysis

Introduction

An organisation's response to its environment is influenced by environmental complexity and its dynamism. These factors also affect an organisation's ability to make long-term forecasts and plans about the future with any certainty.

3.1 Environmental fit

The position-based approach to strategy seeks to achieve an environmental fit, between an organisation and its environment. However, as critics of the position-based approach point out, strategies are developed in conditions of uncertainty and partial ignorance. The environment is a major cause of such 'ignorance'.

(a) It contains **opportunities and threats** which may influence the organisation's activities and may even threaten its existence.

(b) The environment is sometimes so **varied** that many organisations will find it difficult to discern its effects on them. (Note the link here back to the ideas of 'chaos' and 'complexity' which we discussed in Chapter 1.)

(c) Firms can conduct **audits** to identify which of the many different sorts of environmental factors (PEST; Porter's five forces) have had a significant influence.

(d) Environmental conditions change. Consequently it is important that organisations have an ongoing process of **environmental scanning** to look for emerging opportunities and threats in the environment. In this respect, environmental analysis will be a key part of an emergent approach to strategy.

The role of the management accountant

In Chapter 1 we noted that, in strategic management accounting, emphasis is placed on information relating to factors which are external to an organisation – environmental consideration, market analysis, competitor analysis and customer analysis. In this respect, the quality of the information provided by the strategic management accountant is likely to be very important – not only in enabling an organisation to improve its understanding of its environment, but also in making effective decisions in a context of uncertainty and complexity.

3.2 Complexity and dynamism

Johnson, Scholes and Whittington (in *Exploring Corporate Strategy*) contrast the concepts of environmental **complexity** (how many influences there are and the interrelationships between them) and environmental **dynamism** (the rate of change).

Together, complexity and dynamism create **uncertainty**.

KEY TERM

UNCERTAINTY is 'the inability to predict the outcome from an activity due to a lack of information about the required input/output relationships or about the environment within which the activity takes place'.

(CIMA Official Terminology)

3.3 Environmental analysis and uncertainty

One way of identifying the environmental factors which have significant influences on an organisation's development, or its performance in the past, is by conducting an **audit of environmental influences**.

Strategic decisions are made in partial ignorance, as we have seen, because the environment is **uncertain**. As we mentioned earlier, uncertainty arises from the **complexity and dynamism** of the environment.

(a)   **Complexity** arises from:

   (i)   The **variety of influences** faced by the organisation. The more open an organisation is, the greater the variety of influences. The greater the number of markets the organisation operates in, the greater the number of influences to which it is subject.

   (ii)   The amount of **knowledge** necessary. All businesses need to have knowledge of the tax system, for example, but only pharmaceutical businesses need to know about mandatory testing procedures for new drugs.

   (iii)   The **interconnectedness** of environmental influences. Importing and exporting companies are sensitive to exchange rates, which themselves are sensitive to interest rates. Interest rates then influence a company's borrowing costs.

(b)   **Dynamism**. Stable environments are unchanging. Dynamic environments are in a state of change. The computer market is a dynamic market because of the rate of technological change, for example. Shortening product life cycles are a feature of dynamic environments but, as product life cycles become shorter, it becomes harder for businesses not only to predict future sales accurately but also to recoup investments in major research and development (R&D) projects.

Question 3.1	Contrasting environment

Learning outcome A1(a)

Analyse the environments of the two situations below according to the criteria given above.

(a)   A new product has just been introduced to a market segment. It is proving popular. As it is based on a unique technology, barriers to entry are high. The product will not be sold outside this market segment.

(b)   A group of scientists has recently been guaranteed, by an EU research sponsoring body, funds for the next ten years to investigate new technologies in the construction industry, such as 'smart materials' (which respond automatically to weather and light conditions). This is a multidisciplinary project with possible benefits for the construction industry. A number of building firms have also guaranteed funds.

The implication is that the type of business strategy adopted, and indeed the approach to making business strategy, will depend on the type of environment the firm inhabits.

3.4 Impact of uncertainty

If an organisation is operating in a highly uncertain environment, this will affect its strategy.

(a)   **The planning horizon will be shortened** because the uncertainty will mean that management will not dare plan too far ahead.

(b)   **Strategies may be more conservative** because management are unlikely to risk anything new. However, the counter argument to this is that management may want to try something new, because the uncertainty could mean that the existing strategies will no longer work.

(c) **Emergent strategies may be encouraged**, instead of planned strategies. Advocates of emergent strategies argue they are more appropriate to periods of uncertainty because of their adaptability to changing circumstances.

(d) **Increased information requirements**. Management will require more regular information to allow them to monitor and assess the changing conditions. Uncertainty will make forecasting harder, so management will need more information to gauge their strategic position.

(e) **Firms may follow multiple strategies**. Firms may respond to risk and uncertainty by trying to develop a number of alternative options. For example, in the current climate of uncertainty surrounding oil reserves and production, oil firms may try to develop multiple sources of oil around the world, to avoid being dependent on a particular region or a particular extraction technology.

It is worth considering the links between the ideas of uncertainty and developing multiple strategy options and the techniques of real options and investment appraisal covered in Paper P2, *Advanced Management Accounting*. The real options behaviours we look at in Section 3.5 below are modelled on the behaviours of investors in derivative markets.

3.5 Real options

Options theory can be applied to strategic decisions. There are three common types of 'real option' which are relevant to strategic projects: the option to make follow-on investments, the option to abandon a project, and the option to wait.

(a) The **option to make follow-on investments**

Traditional net present value (NPV) analysis means that an organisation will invest in a project if it makes a positive return on the initial investment for that project. However, there may be occasions when that initial project does not make a positive return by itself but it opens up other potential projects which the organisation can then take advantage of.

If these subsequent projects make a positive return, and the organisation can only invest in them by undertaking the initial project, then the organisation should invest in the initial project – although conventional NPV analysis suggests it shouldn't. In this respect, NPV is not a sufficient basis for making the investment decision, and to make an informed choice managers have to consider the value of keeping their options open.

Example: follow-on investments as options

Cornseed Publishing is a publisher of study guides in a sector of the professional training market. Over the last ten years, it has built up a share of approximately 30% of its target market. The directors of the company are now considering a project which would involve producing its study guides as electronic downloads, to be called *Online Guides*. The new *Online Guides* would not simply duplicate the material in the study guides as they would include some interactive features. However, it is thought that in the future the *Online Guides* might be developed into a more innovative, fully interactive format – provisionally called *Online Tutor* – which provides students with online tutorials and seminars, and allows them to ask questions to an online tutor. The *Online Tutor* product offering would take much more time and would require greater software know-how than is currently available.

The initial *Online Guides* project would involve employing additional staff to develop the material required for the new format. Cornseed think that their competitors are also considering similar projects.

However, one of the directors has questioned whether the project is worthwhile. It has been calculated, using the NPV method, that the *Online Guides* project as proposed has a negative NPV of $50,000. The director has challenged why Cornseed should invest in a project with a negative NPV. He argues *Online Guides* which are not fully interactive are not likely to be a success. 'Just because our competitors are putting money into them doesn't mean we should make the same mistake.'

However, another director has pointed out that if the initial *Online Guides* project does not go ahead, Cornseed may be missing out on the opportunity to develop *Online Tutor.* This second director argues that developing the *Online Guides* will provide Cornseed with the expertise and competences which will help it pursue the follow-on option (*Online Tutor*).

The *Online Tutor* is expected to be very profitable.

Cornseed should consider the value of the follow-on investment in *Online Tutor* when evaluating the *Online Guides* project.

(b)   The **option to abandon a project**

Many strategic projects involve a significant capital investment up front. If the subsequent revenue streams from the project are highly uncertain, the option to abandon the project if things go wrong would be very valuable to an organisation. This may be particularly important for projects involving new products where their acceptance by the market is uncertain.

(c)   The **option to wait** before making an investment

An organisation may opt to 'wait and see' before making a decision in the expectation of gaining more relevant information which will help inform its decision. This is not simply an excuse for doing nothing. Rather, a firm's decision making could be improved by waiting and taking advantage of new information when it becomes available.

In this case, managers need to balance the potential benefits of waiting and taking advantage of the new information, with the cost of potential cash inflows forgone.

For example, an option to wait may be particularly valuable for a mining company, which can delay the decision to start mining a deposit until the market price of the commodity is favourable.

In each of these three instances (follow on; abandon; wait) the option can be valued using the Black-Scholes model. The resulting option value can then be added to the initial NPV of the project, allowing a more informed decision to be made about whether to undertake the project or not.

Real options could also be used in the following situations:

Input mix options: For example, a utility company may have the option to build a new coal-fired power station or one that burns either coal or gas. The dual fuel station costs more to build. Simply applying a discounted cash flow (DCF) analysis might suggest that the coal-fired station is preferable since it can be constructed more cheaply. However, the dual plan provides more flexibility, and gives management the ability to select which fuel to use as the relative prices of coal and gas vary. Therefore the value of this operating option should be taken into account in the initial decision.

Output mix options: Whereas the previous example looks at flexibility in the inputs to a process, this one looks at flexibility in product outputs. These options are particularly valuable in industries where goods are bought in small batches, or demand is very volatile; for example, a clothing manufacturer's ability to stop producing one line of garments that has become unfashionable to quickly being able to produce a popular new style of garment. Although a production facility which allows this flexibility may be more expensive than a simpler facility, the flexibility may be a valuable benefit.

3.5.1 Other issues to consider

Level of uncertainty	If there is a very high degree of uncertainty surrounding a project, the more valuable the option will be, but equally the higher the cost of the option.
Duration of the option	The length of the option will affect its value to a business. A longer option will be more valuable than a shorter one, because it provides more opportunity for evaluating different outcomes.
Interest rates	The value of an 'option to wait' will be higher when interest rates are high, because the firm benefits more from delaying its initial investment expenditure.

3.6 Forecasts

Forecasting attempts to reduce the uncertainty managers face by predicting future events and quantifying their impact. In **simple/static conditions the past is a relatively good guide** to the future.

In **dynamic/complex conditions**, though, this is not the case.

- **Future developments**: the past is not a reliable guide.

- Techniques such as **scenario building** are useful as they can propose a number of possible futures.

- **Complex environments** require techniques to reduce the effects of complexity on organisational structure and decision making.

Some firms aim to deal with planning in complex environments by techniques such as **scenario building** (which we will consider in Section 6 of this chapter).

One way organisations can use forecasting is in analysing the **planning gap**.

Section summary

The inherent uncertainty in the environment means that strategic decisions are often made in partial ignorance. This uncertainty may also encourage organisations to adopt emergent strategies rather than prescriptive strategies.

4 Gap analysis

Introduction

Gap analysis quantifies the size of the gap between the objective for the planning period and the forecast based on the extrapolation of the current situation, and current prospects.

Once they have analysed an organisation's current position, strategic planners need to think about the extent to which new strategies are needed to enable the organisation to achieve its objectives. One technique whereby this can be done is **gap analysis**.

KEY TERM

GAP ANALYSIS is a 'comparison between an entity's ultimate objective and the expected performance from projects, both planned and under way, identifying means by which identified difference or gap might be filled'.   *(CIMA Official Terminology)*

KEY POINT

The **planning gap** is **not** the gap between the current position of the organisation and the desired future position. Rather, it is the gap between the position forecast from continuing with current activities, and the desired future position.

Gap analysis is based on two questions.

(a)   What are the organisation's targets for achievement over the planning period?

(b)   What would the organisation be expected to achieve if it 'did nothing' – ie it did not develop any new strategies, but simply carried on in the current way with the same products and selling to the same markets?

This difference is the gap. **New strategies will then have to be developed which will close this gap**, in order for an organisation to be able to achieve its targets over the planning period.

'Gap analysis' is a generic term and can be used to refer to more than one basis for analysis.

*   *CIMA Official Terminology* describes an analysis of existing and potential sales.

*   The term is more commonly used in connection with plans for eliminating a future gap in overall performance.

We examine these two versions below, before suggesting some other possible uses of the gap analysis idea.

4.1 A forecast or projection based on existing performance: F_0 forecasts

This is a **forecast** of the company's future results assuming that it **does nothing**. For example, if the company sells ten products in eight markets, produces them on a certain quantity and type of machinery in one factory, has a gearing structure of 30% and so on, a forecast will be prepared, covering the corporate planning period, on the assumption that none of these items are changed.

Argenti identified four stages in the preparation of such a forecast.

(a)   **Review** past results and analyse:

    (i)   Revenues into units of sale and price
    (ii)   Costs into variable, fixed and semi-variable

(b)   A **projection** into the future for each major item of revenue and cost should be made up to the end of the planning period.

(c)   **Consider any other factors** which might significantly affect the projections. Examples are:

    (i)   Internal factors such as machine breakdown and strikes
    (ii)   External PEST factors, such as new technology and changes in the law

(d)   The forecast is then finalised. The forecast allows the company no new products or markets and no other new strategies: but the purpose of the forecast and gap analysis is to determine the size of the task facing the company if it wishes to achieve its target profits.

4.1.1 Errors in the forecast

A forecast cannot be expected to guarantee **accuracy** and there must inevitably be some **latitude for error**:

(a)   By estimating **likely variations**. For example, 'in 201X the forecast profit is $5 million with possible variations of plus or minus $2 million'.

(b)   By providing a **probability distribution** for profits. For example, 'in 201X there is a 20% chance that profits will exceed $7 million, a 50% chance that they will exceed $5 million and an 80% chance that they will exceed $2.5 million. Minimum profits in 201X will be $2 million.'

4.2 Analysing an existing gap in sales

The diagram below is adapted from the *CIMA Official Terminology*.

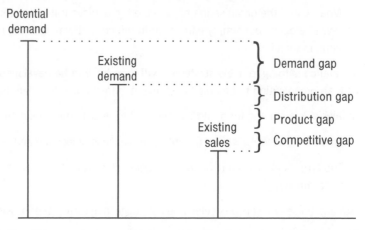

The **demand gap** is the difference between total market potential and current demand from users.

The **distribution gap**, **product gap** and **competitive gap** together make up the difference between current demand and actual sales achieved.

(a)   The **distribution gap** arises from lack of access to, or utilisation of, distribution channels.

(b)   The **product gap** arises from product failure or deliberate product decisions.

(c)   The **competitive gap** arises from failures of pricing or promotion.

This analysis is based on the 4 Ps of the **marketing mix**. The marketing mix illustrates how an organisation needs to align **product**, **price**, **place** and **promotion** in order to market a product successfully.

4.3 The profit gap

The **profit gap** is the difference between the target profits and the forecast profit from current operations (F_0 in the figure below).

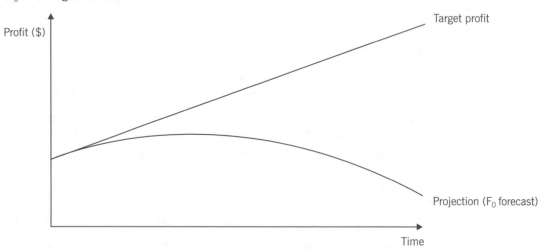

4.3.1 Filling the gap

An organisation has two broad types of strategy it can use to try to fill the gap.

(a)   **Improved efficiency**. Here an organisation seeks to boost profits by reducing costs or increasing output with the same level of inputs as a result of increased efficiency (an **efficiency drive**).

(b)   **Growth**. If an organisation is unable to close the gap through an efficiency drive, it will then have to consider an expansion strategy: looking to develop **new products** or expanding into **new markets**, or both. The organisation could even consider acquiring another company as a means of achieving the growth required.

In the diagram below, we have illustrated how a combination of efficiency savings and new strategic initiatives can be used to fill the gap. However, it is possible that, even when all an organisation's planned strategic initiatives have been included, a 'gap' may still remain. In such a case, additional new strategies would be needed to close the gap.

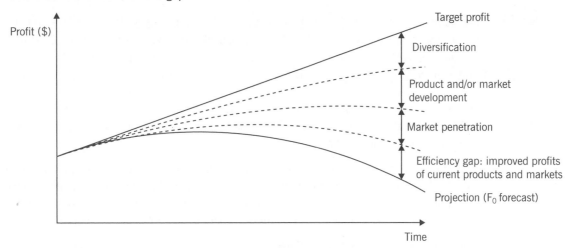

 The idea of using new products and/or new markets as sources of growth forms the basis of Ansoff's product–market matrix. We discuss Ansoff's matrix in the context of strategic choices (in Chapter 5 of this Study Text) but it is worth noting the potential link between gap analysis and the matrix. Once an organisation has identified that it has a gap, it then needs to develop potential strategies to fill the gap. Market penetration, product development, market development and diversification are all potential strategies it could consider, depending on its current strategic position and the environment in which it is operating.

Although gap analysis can be a very useful strategic tool, there could also be some problems with it.

(a)   The financial propositions may be susceptible to **inflation** – there is no easy way of dealing with this problem.

(b)   More serious, however, is risk: remember that in many cases a higher return can equate to a higher risk. In seeking to develop strategies to give a higher return the firm may, unwittingly, be raising its **risk profile**.

(c)   In addition, gap analysis tends to give an impression that there are no restrictions on an organisation's ability to implement strategies designed to fill the gap. However, in reality this may not be the case. For example, there could be a number of different powerful **stakeholder groups**, with differing objectives, which could mean that the organisation has to adopt some kind of compromise, rather than simply selecting a strategy purely on the basis of its ability to fill the gap.

 ## Section summary

Gap analysis allows an organisation to compare its expected performance against its objectives. However, the effectiveness of gap analysis depends on the organisation's ability to forecast its performance in the future.

5 Forecasting

Introduction

Forecasting is an essential part of the process of strategic management. Methods include the use of statistical techniques based on extrapolation; modelling; and expert jury opinion. Sometimes individual judgement is used. The weakness of all these methods is that they are based on the assumption that the future will tend to resemble the past.

Forecasting attempts to reduce the uncertainty managers face, by predicting what is likely to happen in the future. Almost every form of decision making and planning activity undertaken by organisations will involve some kind of forecasting.

Forecasting can be carried out using both quantitative and qualitative techniques. **Quantitative** (statistical) techniques use historical data as a basis for predicting the future. **Qualitative** techniques make much more use of judgement about changing conditions, and are more appropriate when the past should not be used as a guide for the future (for example, due to environmental uncertainty).

Some definitions can usefully be outlined at this stage.

KEY TERMS

A FORECAST is 'a prediction of future events and their quantification for planning purposes'.

A PROJECTION is an 'expected future trend pattern obtained by extrapolation. It is principally concerned with quantitative factors, whereas a forecast includes judgements.'   (*CIMA Official Terminology*)

EXTRAPOLATION is the technique of determining a projection by statistical means.

Forecasts and financial analysis are covered in more detail in the syllabus for F3 – Financial Strategy.

As you know, a variety of techniques can be used in connection with forecasting, including DCF, expected values and sensitivity analysis. Different techniques are appropriate according to the **degree of uncertainty** perceived in the relevant forecast.

(a)   We are used to employing an **NPV** approach when the amount and timing of future cash flows are assumed to be known with something **approaching certainty**.

(b)   Projects that are **repeated several times** lend themselves to the use of **expected values** and **decision trees**.

(c)   **Modelling** and **sensitivity analysis** are appropriate when there is **less confidence** about the range and distribution of potential outcomes: such techniques are employed in conjunction with decision rules that reflect the degree of risk aversion of the decision makers.

(d)   It is important to remember that **certainty cannot be attained in any forecast**. Major, rapid changes, such as the collapse of the dot.com bubble, cannot be known in advance. This is perhaps the realm where **scenario planning** makes its greatest contribution.

It is also important to appreciate the implications that forecast error or uncertainty could have on decision making.

Managers can develop a reasonably reliable forecast of the future when the business environment is stable and predictable, but it is much harder to forecast successfully when the business environment is unstable or unpredictable. For example, how can a manager accurately forecast sales if there is uncertainty about whether new entrants will join the market or not? (The potential entrant may decide not to join, in which case the market will stay the same; or the new firm may decide to join. And if the entrant joins the market, will it do so in its own right – thereby creating an extra player in the market – or will it do so by acquiring an existing player?)

While gap analysis and rational planning approaches may be appropriate to a stable and predictable environment, they cope less well with an uncertain environment. Businesses will need to use alternative approaches to cope with uncertainty, for example scenario planning (which we consider later in this chapter).

5.1 Statistical projections

Statistical forecasts take past data and endeavour to direct it to the future, by **assuming** that **patterns or relationships which held in the past will continue to do so**. Many statistical techniques aim to reduce the uncertainty managers face. In **simple/static conditions the past is a relatively good guide** to the future.

Statistical forecasting techniques for static conditions

(a)   **Trend analysis**. Data from past events is collected and analysed with a view to identifying a pattern, or trend, in that data, and using that trend to gain an idea of what may happen in the future.

   Time series analysis is a type of trend analysis. Data for a number of months/years is obtained and analysed. The aim of time series analysis is to identify:

   (i)   Seasonal and other cyclical fluctuations
   (ii)   Long-term underlying trends

   For example, the UK's monthly unemployment statistics show a **headline figure** and the **underlying trend**.

(b)   **Regression analysis** is a quantitative technique to check any underlying **correlations** between two variables (eg sales of ice cream and the weather). Remember that the relationship between two variables may **only hold between certain values**. (You would expect ice cream consumption to rise as the temperature becomes hotter, but there is a maximum number of ice creams an individual can consume in a day, no matter how hot it is.)

(c)   **Econometrics** is the study of economic variables and their interrelationships, using computer models. Short- or medium-term econometric models might be used for forecasting.

   (i)   **Leading indicators** are indicators which change **before** market demand changes. For example, a sudden increase in the birth rate would be an indicator of future demand for children's clothes. Similarly, a fall in retail sales would be an indicator to manufacturers that demand from retailers for their products will soon fall.

   (ii)   A firm needs the ability to **predict the span of time between a change in the indicator and a change in market demand**. Change in an indicator is especially useful for demand forecasting when they reach their highest or lowest points (when an increase turns into a decline or *vice versa*).

Organisations can use complex computer programs to try to model economic systems, and to capture the complex interactions between the various economic and non-economic drivers in the organisation's environment. However, one of the key challenges in any such modelling exercise comes from identifying all the variables which need to be included, and understanding how they relate to each other.

5.1.1 Problems with statistical projections

(a)   **Past relationships do not necessarily hold for the future**.

(b)   Data can be misinterpreted, and **relationships assumed where none exist**. For example, sales of ice cream rise in the summer, and sales of umbrellas fall – the link is the weather, not any correlation between them.

(c)   Forecasts do not account for special events (eg wars), the likely response of competitors and so on.

(d)   The variation and depth of business cycles fluctuate.

(e)   In practice, statistical forecasters **underestimate uncertainty**.

(f)   Projections can reflect bias as outlined below.

Bias in forecasts and projections

A business forecast can become biased in two different ways.

(a) By inputting inappropriate assumptions:

     (i) Having too narrow a focus so that it doesn't foresee the occurrences of future events and their relevance to the forecast

     (ii) By consistently under- or overestimating the impact of future events

     (iii) Relying too heavily on selected past events to build forecasts rather than looking at all past events

     (iv) Over- or underestimating an activity's revenue-earning potential, or its associated costs

(b) Through deliberate actions within the process:

     (i) The tendency to interpret information so that it supports a given belief

     (ii) Having to manipulate figures so that they achieve a particular outcome (eg a manager increasing the forecast for their department to prevent subsequent budget allocations being cut)

     (iii) Compensation adjustments – for example, under-forecasting in the second half of a forecast period to compensate for over-forecasting in the first half

5.2 Judgemental forecasts

In contrast to statistical projections and forecasts, judgemental (or intuitive) forecasts place much greater emphasis on judgement, opinions and intuition.

Exam skills

A note about terminology: Judgemental forecasting methods incorporate intuitive judgements and estimates.

As such, they are sometimes referred to as **intuitive** forecasting methods, rather than **judgemental** forecasting methods. In this Text, we refer to them as 'judgemental' but an exam question could equally refer to them as 'intuitive' forecasting methods.

Judgemental forecasting methods include think tanks, the Delphi method, scenario planning and brainstorming.

Judgemental forecasts are often used for the long term, covering several decades. However, because of the limitations of short-term forecasting they are used for the short term too. Effectively, they are based on **hunches or educated guesses**. Sometimes these prove surprisingly accurate but, obviously, at other times they are wide of the mark.

(a) **Individual forecasting**. A company might forecast sales on the basis of the judgement of one or more executives.

     (i) **Advantages** are that it is cheap and suitable if demand is stable or relatively simple.

     (ii) The **disadvantage** is that it is influenced most heavily by **most recent** experience rather than trend.

(b) **Genius forecasting**

     An individual with expert judgement might be asked for advice. This could be the case with the fashion industry. Although demand might be hard to quantify, an ability to understand the mind of the customer will, nevertheless, be very useful.

(c) In practice, forecasts might be prepared by an interested individual who has read the papers, say, and has promoted an item for management attention.

5.3 Consensus forecasts

5.3.1 Jury forecasts

A panel of experts and/or executives prepare their own forecasts and a consensus forecast emerges from the panel.

(a)   **Advantages**. Expert opinions are sought and obtained.

(b)   **Disadvantages**. The jury might **dilute** the best. The **group dynamics** would interfere with the decision, as each expert might differ and, in a face to face situation, the more forceful or confident personalities would most likely impose their will and win the argument.

5.3.2 Think tank

A group of experts are encouraged, in a relatively unstructured atmosphere, to speculate about future development in particular areas, and to identify possible courses of action.

(a)   **Advantages**. Provides a useful way of generating ideas and assessing their feasibility. The group nature of the activity allows views to be shaped and encourages a consensus view.

The independence of group members, and the unstructured nature of the group, without a prescribed leader, enables free discussion and argument to take place.

(b)   **Disadvantages**. There can be a danger that think tanks (as groups of experts) may think their remit goes beyond simply forecasting and they may start planning, as sometimes happens with large organisations, including governments. However, it is important to remember that think tank proposals do not necessarily represent company, or government, policy.

5.3.3 Delphi method

This was developed to overcome problems relying on **known** experts or personalities in the jury.

(a)   Participants remain **anonymous**, known only to the organiser.

(b)   Participants respond to a **questionnaire** containing tightly defined questions. The Delphi technique **retains anonymity**. The results are collated and statistically analysed, and are returned by the organiser to each expert. The experts respond again, having seen the opinions of the other experts.

(c)   The Delphi technique is **time consuming**.

(d)   In practice, it seems to be the case that experts are **universally optimistic**.

5.3.4 Brainstorming

A group of people from across an organisation generate ideas without any initial evaluation or criticism of those ideas. Only after the list of ideas is complete is each suggestion evaluated.

(a)   The lack of any initial evaluation means that everybody's ideas are heard and listed. Brainstorming differs from many other forecasting methods because it invites ideas from across all levels of an organisation; it doesn't simply rely on experts' opinions.

(b)   The initial suggestions can then provoke other, follow-up ideas. The evaluation stage which follows the initial idea generation allows ideas to be developed and modified.

5.3.5 Derived demand

The concept of derived demand in economics describes the demand for a good or service which results from it being used in the production of another good or service. So, for example, the demand for bricks will be influenced by the demand for houses (which are built using bricks).

More generally, the demand for labour can also be seen as a derived demand – influenced by the demand for the goods and services which workers in an economy produce, and the overall strength of the economy.

In relation to forecasting, an organisation might assess future demand for its goods and services by analysing the aspects of economic activity and the environment which will affect demand for the 'end product' goods and services from which demand for its own goods and services is derived.

However, in practice, derived demand analysis is very complex and costly to apply, because of the large number of factors which affect demand for goods and services.

5.4 Statistical versus judgemental forecasts

David Mercer identifies the relative advantages and disadvantages of each method.

Use of forecasts	Statistical	Judgement
Changes in established patterns	Past data is no guide	Can be predicted but could be ignored
Using available data	Not all past data is used	Personal bias and preferences obscure data
Objectivity	Based on specific criteria for selection	Personal propensity to optimism/pessimism
Uncertainty	Underestimated	Underestimated, with a tendency for overoptimism
Cost	Inexpensive	Expensive

It is important to recognise that judgemental forecasting is **speculative**. However, speculation may be necessary to identify changing patterns in data, or weak signals reflecting or foreshadowing social changes.

5.5 Market forecasts and sales forecasts

Market forecasts and sales forecasts complement each other. The market forecast should be carried out first of all and should cover a longer period of time.

KEY TERM

MARKET FORECAST. This is a forecast for the market as a whole. It is mainly involved in the assessment of environmental factors, outside the organisation's control, which will affect the demand for its products/services.

(a)   Components of a market forecast:

(i)   The **economic review** (national economy, government policy, covering forecasts on investment, population, gross national product, and so on)

(ii)   **Specific market research** (to obtain data about specific markets and forecasts concerning total market demand)

(iii) Evaluation of **total market demand** for the firm's and similar products (for example, profitability and market potential)

(b)   **Sales forecasts** are estimates of sales (in volume, value and profit terms) of a product in a future period at a given marketing mix.

5.5.1 Research into potential sales

KEY TERM

SALES POTENTIAL is an estimate of the part of the market that is within the possible reach of a product.

Factors governing sales potential

- The price of the product
- The amount of money spent on sales promotion
- How essential the product is to consumers

- Whether it is a durable commodity whose purchase can be postponed
- The overall size of the possible market
- Competition (or potential competition) in the market

Whether sales potential is worth exploiting will depend on the cost which must be incurred to realise the potential.

5.6 Example

Market research has led a company to the opinion that the sales potential of product X is as follows.

	Sales value	Contribution earned before selling costs deducted	Cost of selling
either	$100,000	$40,000	$10,000
or	$100,000	$44,000	$15,000

In this example, it would not be worth spending an extra $5,000 on selling in order to realise an extra sales potential of $10,000, because the net effect would be a loss of $(5,000 – 4,000) = $1,000.

Section summary

A forecast is a prediction of future events and their quantification for planning purposes. Be aware, however, that forecasts are susceptible to uncertainty and bias.

6 Scenario planning

Introduction

Most organisations are faced with great environmental complexity. Scenario planning is a technique to help enable them to allow for different possibilities, and be aware of the range of plausible alternatives.

When forecasting, organisations are effectively trying to predict what will happen in the future. By contrast, scenario planning aims to develop a range of alternative futures, so that an organisation can think about how it could develop or adapt its strategy to respond to the challenges it would face if one or more of those futures materialised.

According to Johnson, Scholes and Whittington, scenario planning involves:

- Building plausible views about how the business environment of an organisation might develop in the future ...

- ... based on sets of key drivers for change about which there is a high level of uncertainty

As with other areas of strategic management, we have to distinguish between the decision-making process and the content of the decision itself. For example, it is quite possible that a decision to launch a new product could have been taken as a result of any number of strategic decision processes, such as rational planning, visionary decision making and incrementalism.

KEY TERM

A SCENARIO is 'an internally consistent view of what the future might turn out to be'.

In addition to their usefulness in providing some guidance in strategic planning, scenarios are valuable in that preparing and updating them forces the managers at the strategic apex to **look carefully at the business environment** and to monitor developments within it. This can be particularly important (and useful) in the context of rapidly changing environments.

6.1 Macro scenarios

Macro scenarios use macro-economic or political factors, creating alternative views of the future environment (eg global economic growth, political changes, interest rates). Macro scenarios were developed because the activities of oil and resource companies (which are global and at one time were heavily influenced by political factors) needed techniques to deal with uncertainties.

6.1.1 Steps in scenario planning

There is no single way to construct a scenario. However, the ten steps which Schoemaker describes are a good illustration of how a scenario could be created.

 Define the scope. The scope should be defined with reference to time frame involved, products considered and markets considered.

 Identify the major stakeholders that drive change or affect the industry (within the scope of the scenario identified in Step 1).

 Identify the basic trends that affect the industry and the business environment.

 Identify the key areas of uncertainty and their drivers. Uncertainties in scenario planning should be viewed as future possibilities. They could be based upon the political/legal, economic, social/cultural and technological (PEST) factors identified through environmental analysis, and also an organisation's own competences and capabilities.

 Construct initial scenarios based on the key areas of uncertainty. The scenarios should be created by shaping the key areas of uncertainty (Step 4) into coherent themes.

 Check for consistency and plausibility. In other words, re-examine the scenarios to assess whether they make sense. For scenario planning to be useful, the scenarios presented must be able to happen, and in the timescale identified by the scope of the scenario.

 Develop learning scenarios. At this stage, the initial frameworks identified in Step 5 should be expanded into full descriptions of the scenario as if it were actually occurring.

At this point, **senior management should become involved** in the process, and should start considering the implications of each scenario in terms of the potential impacts they could have on the business.

 Identify research needs. Understand what additional information is required to fill in any gaps in the scenario, and obtain that information to improve the coverage as initially given by the scenario.

 Develop quantitative models. This stage builds on Step 7, to put together business models to forecast the effects of different scenarios on an organisation's activities and future profitability/cash flow.

 Use scenarios to formulate competitive strategy. The value of the scenario planning process is that it assists an organisation's decision making in times of uncertainty. The process should help to highlight the key areas of uncertainty which face an organisation and, in this final stage, management should develop strategic courses of action which they can apply to each of the scenarios to deal with the uncertainties they may face.

6.1.2 Using scenarios

As well as identifying the ten steps which could be followed to create a scenario, Schoemaker describes a four-step approach for using scenarios. This approach could be useful for an organisation looking at its strategic options.

(1)   Develop scenarios through examining the external environment and identifying key trends and uncertainties.

(2)   Conduct industry analysis and develop strategies for each scenario, to enable the organisation to fit with those scenarios.

(3)   Compare the organisation's present competences and capabilities with the future needs identified in the alternative scenarios, and strengthen the organisation's key competences and capabilities to withstand or benefit from each of the scenarios.

(4)   As the future unfolds, and key uncertainties in the environment begin to resolve themselves, adopt the appropriate strategic option.

6.2 Industry scenarios

Porter believes that the most appropriate use for scenario analysis is if it is restricted to an industry. An **industry scenario** is an internally consistent view of an **industry's** future structure. Different competitive strategies may be appropriate to different scenarios.

The **entire range**, not the most **likely** 'future', is used to design a competitive strategy. The process is as follows.

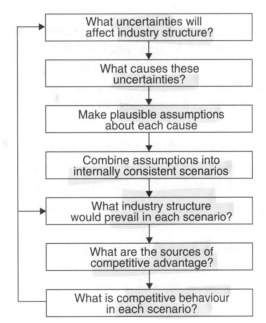

6.2.1 Using scenarios to formulate competitive strategy

(a) A strategy built in response to only **one scenario is risky**, whereas one supposed to cope with them **all might be expensive**.

(b) The way firms use different scenarios can reflect the way they make decisions about competitive strategy.

Approach	Comment
Assume the most probable	This choice puts too much faith in the scenario process and guesswork. A less probable scenario may be one whose failure to occur would have the worst consequences for the firm.
Hope for the best	A firm designs a strategy based on the scenario most attractive to the firm: wishful thinking.
Hedge	The firm chooses the strategy that produces satisfactory results under all scenarios. Hedging, however, is not optimal. The low risk is paid for by a low reward.
Flexibility	A firm taking this approach plays a 'wait and see' game. It is safer, but sacrifices first-mover advantages.
Influence	A firm will try to influence the future, for example, by influencing demand for related products in order that its favoured scenario will be realised in events as they unfold, or even by attempting to influence government and regulatory bodies.

6.3 Evaluating scenario planning

It is unusual for scenario planning to create an accurate prediction of what actually happens. Also, managers are often criticised for identifying trends and uncertainties from their own cultural perspectives rather than adopting a more 'universalist' perspective.

These limitations mean it could be tempting to dismiss scenario planning as a worthless exercise. Moreover, critics argue that it is unacceptably costly, due to the resources and time required to develop the scenarios.

However, scenario planning does have some valuable benefits.

(a) It **identifies the key uncertainties** to which an organisation is exposed, allowing it to plan for how to deal with them and to know what warning signs to look for as time goes on.

(b) It forces management to look externally at the wider business environment (and potential change triggers in it) rather than focusing purely on the internal operations of an organisation.

(c) It may provide managers with useful insights into the future of their industry which can then help shape their strategy.

    (i) It helps the organisation become more future oriented.

    (ii) It may help the organisation to expect surprises, because it has already started to try to anticipate uncertainties.

We could argue that the purpose of the scenarios is not forecasting but **competence building**, with the competence being the organisation's ability to manage the future strategically.

Developing the scenarios can also encourage communication between different managers and departments in an organisation, and this improved communication could, by itself, be beneficial to the organisation.

Note, although we have mainly described scenario planning in terms of medium to long timescales, it could also be useful in the shorter run. Encouraging managers to consider responses to the question of 'What if such and such happens' is still an important part of strategic management because it increases the organisation's ability to respond flexibly to circumstances. For example, short-term scenario planning

could be useful for an airline company or a tour operator in response to the question 'What if there is an outbreak of pandemic influenza, such as Swine flu?'.

6.4 Scenario planning and the rational model

The rational model, and prescriptive approaches to strategy, assume there is a degree of predictability and control in the strategy process.

In other words, **a forecast** is a prediction of relevant environmental trends, and a plan is the organisation's way to **control** its own behaviour in the future.

But scenario planning takes a rather different approach to strategic planning. It suggests there is an inherent ambiguity and uncertainty in the future. Such an approach suggests that a successful strategy can only be developed by acknowledging this uncertainty.

Importantly, this approach also suggests that planning for the future should not be treated as a one-off activity, but should be an ongoing learning proposition.

By looking at a number of **alternative** futures, scenario planning **does not pretend to predict** one of them – it is of more benefit to **management learning processes** to take a variety of perspectives into account.

This is one of the key benefits of scenario planning. By identifying a range of possible scenarios and outcomes, scenario planning can help management respond to real situations when they arise. In this way, however, scenario planning fits more comfortably with an emergent, flexible approach to strategy than the more prescriptive, rational model.

Scenario planning also encourages managers to challenge their assumptions and the ways they think about their organisations.

6.5 Long-range planning

In our definition of 'strategy' in Chapter 1 of this Study Text, we noted that strategy relates to the long-term direction of an organisation. This also identifies the potential importance of long-range planning to enable the organisation to address questions such as:

- Where is the organisation heading, and how will it get there?
- What must be done in the long run to enable the organisation to achieve its goals and objectives?

The purpose of long-range planning is to evaluate where an organisation currently is and where it hopes to be at some point in the future, and then to develop strategies or plans to move the organisation closer to its goals. Equally, long-range planning could involve environmental analysis – for example, assessing competitors, and identifying an organisation's weaknesses and threats so that plans can be made to address those weaknesses.

Long-range plans usually relate to goals that are expected to be met five or more years in the future.

6.5.1 Types of approach

In this context, it would be useful to note that there are two types of approach organisations could take to develop their strategic plans.

Goals-based approaches – focus on where the organisation wants to be in the future (its **vision**), and how it plans to get there

Issues-based approaches – focus on the issues facing an organisation, and then develop strategies to address those issues (for example, funding requirements, competitor activity, or the impact of changes in the economic environment)

6.5.2 Mission, objectives and planning

The goals-based approach to strategic planning highlights that the development of effective long-range plans is central to the process of strategic management.

The rational model also illustrates this. The sequence of the model illustrates the need to define an organisation's mission and objectives; assess the relationship between an organisation and its environment; and then identify, evaluate and implement strategic alternatives which enable the organisation to fulfil its mission and objectives.

One of the key outputs of long-range planning is the development of **corporate-level strategies**. Importantly, though, since corporate plans (such as expanding internationally, or developing new products) may take years to complete, measuring their success can often be difficult. Traditional financial measures – such as profitability – may not be practical in evaluating corporate-level strategic plans.

Equally, it is important that individual strategic decisions are consistent with, or 'fit' with, the context of an organisation's long-range plans. Therefore, the long-range plans can provide a context for evaluating individual strategic options.

Exam skills

We have mentioned the impact of environmental uncertainty on strategy a number of times in this chapter.

This highlights one of the limitations of the rational model and the prescriptive approach to strategic planning: this approach assumes a degree of order and predictability often not present in the real world.

In the exam, if you have to consider the effectiveness of an organisation's strategy, try to establish whether the organisation has a prescriptive or emergent approach to strategy. Then consider, is this suitable to the environment in which it is operating?

Section summary

Scenario planning is one of the techniques an organisation can use to help it cope with uncertainty. Scenario planning helps identify the key uncertainties to which an organisation is exposed, and can therefore help the organisation plan how to deal with some of those uncertainties.

7 Foresight

Introduction

Whereas scenario planning allows an organisation to identify the uncertainties to which it could be exposed, foresight is a process of identifying possible ways in which the future could develop.

Scenario planning, jury forecasts and the Delphi method are all ways management can attempt to get **insights into the future**, and therefore prepare itself to deal with the opportunities and threats the future holds for it.

The business environment is said to be changing at a faster pace than ever before. A number of factors – including technological change, changing lifestyles and consumer tastes, the rise of international competitors from developing countries, and regulatory upheavals – are presenting challenges to the competitive advantage of the existing dominant companies in an industry.

These changes present a challenge to business managers, in that successful management no longer simply involves reviewing current results, but also requires **visioning** the opportunities and threats that may lie ahead, to develop an organisation's strategic vision. Competitive advantage no longer simply

comes from the way an organisation manages its tangible resources, but from the way it reinvents its business model before circumstances force it to do so.

In this context, senior managers must develop 'vision' and '**foresight**'. Foresight can be described as the art and science of anticipating the future. However, unlike forecasting, foresight does not attempt to predict the future, but rather to identify a range of possible outcomes based on an understanding and analysis of current trends.

Foresight can be particularly useful in relation to research and development, and in identifying new technologies which could have major long-term benefits for society in the future.

In this respect, we can identify **five key benefits** an organisation could gain as a result of developing foresight. Irvine and Martin in their book *Research Foresight: Creating the Future* refer to these five benefits as the '**five Cs**':

- **Communication**: Foresight will involve a wide range of people from different departments or divisions across an organisation (as well as, possibly, external people such as industry experts). By bringing together different groups of people, foresight will help to improve communication and sharing of ideas across an organisation.

- **Concentration** on the longer term: A commitment to foresight will help to ensure that an organisation is consistently looking to the future, and is well prepared to deal with any threats or opportunities that may arise.

- **Co-ordination**: Enabling different groups and departments within an organisation to co-ordinate their development plans, and harmonising any future research and development activities.

- **Consensus**: Creating a consensus about the organisation's priorities and plans should be in order to address the issues which have been identified. (As such, 'consensus' is linked to 'co-ordination'.)

- **Commitment**: Ensuring that people are committed to making the changes which will help an organisation deal with the issues which have been identified; for example, by ensuring that people are committed to delivering the technological developments or innovations required to take advantage of opportunities or to respond to threats.

KEY POINT

Do not confuse 'foresight' with 'forecasting'. The two are very different concepts.

Futurists argue that the future is continuous with the present, so by analysing the present we can learn a great deal about what might happen in the future.

A foresight project can be divided into four stages:

- **Monitoring** – identifying relevant current trends
- **Analysis** – understanding the drivers of change
- **Projection** – anticipating the future
- **Transformation** – drawing implications for the business based on the projected futures (in terms of new product or new business development, and in terms of strategic management)

An organisation can use a number of techniques to improve its foresight. These include:

(a) **Scenario planning** – We have already discussed scenario planning as a way of generating a range of possible futures derived from the current environment and the uncertainties contained within it.

(b) **Issues analysis** – Potentially significant events are analysed in terms of their likelihood and impact. In effect, issues analysis provides a means of developing an impact analysis matrix (as we discussed in Section 2.1 earlier in this chapter) and thereby helping managers to identify and prioritise the key risks they need to consider (ie those with a high probability of occurring and which will have a significant impact if they do occur).

(c) **Delphi technique** – A number of experts are asked to independently and anonymously give their opinions and insights on a particular trend and how it may develop. These initial results are summarised and the summary is returned to the experts, who are then asked to respond again once they have seen the responses of the group. The process is repeated until a consensus is achieved.

(d) **Cross-impact analysis** – A basic limitation of many forecasting methods (including the Delphi technique) is that they produce only isolated forecasts. In other words, events and trends are projected one by one, without explicit reference to their possible influence on each other. However, most events and developments are connected to each other in some way, and so the interdependencies between them need to be considered to develop more consistent and accurate foresight. Cross-impact analysis addresses these interdependencies.

Cross-impact analysis involves recording events on a matrix, and at each matrix intersection questioning what impact the event in the row occurring would have on the likelihood of the event in the column occurring. In this way, cross-impact analysis provides a more systematic way of examining a range of possible future events and outcomes.

(e) **Morphological analysis** – All the attributes of a product or strategy are listed as column headings in a table and then as many variations of each attribute as possible are listed in each column. In effect, a matrix of components is created. One entry from each column is then chosen to create a new mixture of components. This new mixture could represent a new product or strategy.

Morphological analysis can be used to identify a range of opportunities for an organisation which would not otherwise be obvious. Also, if an organisation carries out a morphological analysis on its competitors it may be able to identify any new products or strategies they might be considering.

(f) **Relevance trees** – Relevance trees start by identifying future goals or outcomes, and then seek to identify the circumstances, events, actions, technologies etc which will be required to meet those needs or objectives. By comparing its current position to the path which is needed to achieve the desired outcome, an organisation can identify what changes or developments will be needed in order for it to achieve that outcome.

(g) **Visioning** – Visioning requires an organisation's management to develop an image of a possible or desirable future state. This image may initially be quite vague, but then needs to be developed into a more definite goal, accompanied by a strategic plan for how to achieve that goal. However, for visioning to be useful for an organisation, the image or goal articulated has to be a realistic, achievable and preferable alternative to the current state.

(h) **Opportunity mapping** – An opportunity map is a qualitative and experience-based analysis aimed at identifying gaps in the current user experience of an organisation's product portfolio. Opportunity maps allow an organisation to discover the desired qualities of its products, which may, in turn, prompt it to change its priorities and strategies in order to provide those desired qualities.

(i) **Trend extrapolation** – This is a projection technique based on the assumption that certain social, economic or technological trends or patterns identified in the past will manifest themselves in the future and that one can forecast future trends by observing how certain patterns have changed in the past and projecting or extrapolating those changes into the future.

(j) **Role playing** – This is another technique where alternative options are generated by a group, but unlike the Delphi technique it does not use experts. A group of people are given a description of a hypothetical future situation, and told to act as they think they would if that situation was actually happening. Analysing their actions can give useful insights into what might happen if that hypothetical situation actually occurred.

However, one of the disadvantages of foresight is that it **relies on the future being shaped by actions that can be imagined now**. It cannot take account of sudden one-off events which could dramatically change the business environment. For example, a person at the start of the 20th century may not have been able to foresee that by the end of that century the world would be shaped by (among other things) television, computers, aeroplanes, the rise and the decline of communism, and atomic energy and weapons. Nevertheless, foresight can help organisations plan for the uncertainties which they will inevitably face in the future.

Section summary

Foresight is a process of identifying a range of possible outcomes which could develop, based on an understanding and analysis of current trends.

8 Game theory

Introduction

Scenario planning and foresight both highlight the inherent uncertainty in trying to predict the future.

One particular aspect of this uncertainty comes from how competitors will react to any new strategy an organisation introduces.

KEY TERM

GAME THEORY is the study of the ways in which the strategic interactions among rational players produce **strategic outcomes** which were not intended by any of the players.

8.1 Game theory approach to strategy

Game-based approaches to strategy treat **strategy as an interaction** between an organisation and its competitors. To this end, an organisation cannot simply develop its strategy by analysing its current position in the environment, and looking at its internal resources. Instead, it also needs to look at its competitors, identify their strengths and weaknesses and examine how their responses to a strategy could affect the effectiveness of that strategy. Anticipating competitors' moves is a crucial part of strategic thinking: gauging competitors' likely reactions to a strategy greatly improves an organisation's ability to choose a strategy that will be successful.

We can illustrate this with a simple example.

Example: soft drinks market

Firms A and B are the two market leaders in the soft drinks market in a country, and between them they hold virtually 100% of the market share. Firm A is considering launching a major advertising campaign, because its marketing director believes this will not only increase its own sales and profit, but also reduce those of its rival (B).

However, the marketing director in Firm A has not considered B's response. B has become aware of A's campaign, and is now considering launching a campaign of its own to restore its market share.

At the moment, both A and B make profits of $250m per year. Firm A is thinking of spending $25m on its campaign, because it wants a major campaign to generate a significant increase in revenue. The anticipated increase of revenue resulting from the campaign is $75m.

Because A and B essentially share the market, A's revenue increase is expected to come from customers who switch to it from B (ie overall market sales will remain largely the same despite the advertising campaign). Therefore, alongside A's revenue increase of $75m, B will suffer a revenue reduction of $75m.

Consequently, at the end of A's initial campaign, and in the short term, B will have suffered a reduction in profit of $75m, while A will have enjoyed an increase in profit of $50m ($75m revenue less $25m marketing costs). This is a **'win–lose'** situation, because A has 'won' while B has 'lost'.

However, B then runs a rival campaign, also costing $25m, and which also generates $75m additional revenue. Following the logic from before, this is now a **'lose–win'** situation because A has 'lost' and B has 'won'.

Let us look at the impact these campaigns have on A and B's profits, and the overall profits earned by the soft drink industry.

Option	A's profit	B's profit	Industry profit
Currently (no advertising)	$250m	$250m	$500m
A advertises	$300m	$175m	$475m
B then launches counter advert	$225m	$225m	$450m

After the advertising campaigns **both firms are worse off** than they were before, and the industry profit has reduced by the cumulative cost of the advertising campaigns. So, overall the advertising campaign has created a **'lose–lose'** situation.

The figures show that although one firm can gain in the **short run** from a competitive strategy, in the **long run** both firms are likely to be better off by working together and not advertising, rather than competing with each other.

One of the assumptions of game theory is that the firms do not have any collusive agreements and do not know what the other is going to do. So A and B must select their strategies based solely on the outcome which they think is best for them, regardless of the decision made by their rival.

Under these circumstances, both firms will choose to advertise. Individually, they hope to increase their profits by advertising; however, collectively this course of action causes them each to lose $25m (ie profits fall from $250m each to $225m each).

(Note, however, that this example assumes that there is no increase in the overall size of the market following the advertising campaigns. In practice, this may not be the case as the advertising campaigns might encourage additional people to start drinking soft drinks, although they had previously bought neither Firm A's nor Firm B's drinks.)

Game theory illustrates the key problem of **interdependent decision making** which organisations face. Organisations need to consider the possible responses of their competitors when making strategic decisions or introducing new strategies.

Moreover, game theory suggests that it may benefit firms to **co-operate** and **negotiate** with others in the search for optimal solutions rather than simply working alone and **competing** with all the other players in the market. In order to create a **'win–win'** scenario, firms are likely to have to compromise and co-operate rather than always seeking to compete with each other.

In this context of networks and co-operation being preferable to constant competition, game theory can help explain the reasoning behind **strategic alliances**. Game theory also supports the cartel arrangement which the OPEC nations have established to control the production and price of oil.

CASE STUDY

GlaxoSmithKline's strategy for the developing world

In 2009, GlaxoSmithKline (GSK), the world's second biggest pharmaceutical company, announced plans to radically shift its attitude in relation to providing cheap drugs to millions of people in the developing world.

In a major change of strategy, Andrew Witty, GSK's Chief Executive, announced that the company would reduce prices on all medicines in the poorest countries, give back profits to be spent on hospitals and clinics and – most ground-breaking of all – share knowledge about potential drugs that are currently protected by patents.

Witty said he believed drug companies have an obligation to help the poor get treatment, and he challenged other pharmaceutical giants to follow GSK's lead.

Pressure on the industry had been growing as drug companies had been repeatedly criticised for failing to drop their prices for HIV drugs while millions died in Africa and Asia. Campaigners criticised the drug companies for defending the patents, which allow them to maintain high prices.

Campaigners had also been critical of the way drug companies attempted to crush competition from generic manufacturers, which undercut them dramatically in countries where patents did not apply.

However, the moves which Witty announced go a long way to addressing these concerns, and marked a significant change to the way GSK does business in the developing world.

Witty said that GSK will:

- Cut its prices for all drugs in the 50 least developed countries to no more than 25% of the levels in the UK and US – and less if possible – and make drugs more affordable in middle-income countries such as Brazil and India

- Put any chemicals or processes over which it has intellectual property rights that are relevant to finding drugs for neglected diseases into a 'patent pool', so they can be explored by other researchers

- Reinvest 20% of any profits it makes in the least developed countries in hospitals, clinics and staff

The extent of these changes was expected to stun not only critics of drug companies but also other pharmaceutical companies, which risked being left exposed.

Witty accepted that his stance may not win him friends in other drug companies, but he invited them to join him in an attempt to make a significant difference to the health of people in poor countries.

Witty explained that the changes reflected his desire that GSK finds solutions for developing and developed countries alike. However, he also said he was aware that the move might raise concerns among GSK's shareholders.

'I think the shareholders understand [the need to help the developing countries as well as the richer, developed countries] and it's my job to make sure I can explain it. I think we can. I think it's absolutely the kind of thing large global companies need to be demonstrating, that they've got a more balanced view of the world than short-term returns.'

The move on intellectual property, until that time regarded as the sacred cow of the pharmaceutical industry, was seen as the most radical of his proposals. 'I think it's the first time anybody's really come out and said we're prepared to start talking to people about pooling our patents to try to facilitate innovation in areas where, so far, there hasn't been much progress,' Witty said.

However, he also acknowledged that the issue of how the other major pharmaceutical companies responded was a similarly important question.

(Based on an article by Sarah Boseley in guardian.co.uk, 13 February 2009. *Drug giant GlaxoSmithKline pledges cheap medicine for world's poor.*)

The value of game theory is that it highlights that both competition and co-operation can exist in an industry. An important part of an organisation's strategy is how it interacts with the other players in an industry in this respect.

Although both scenario planning and foresight aim to assist an organisation in designing its future strategies, their effectiveness will depend in part on the organisation's current strategic intelligence.

Specifically, game theory highlights the importance of **competitor analysis**, and of having an insight into competitors' strategies.

Three key purposes of competitor analysis are to:

- Gain an insight into competitors' strategies and to forecast competitors' future strategies and decisions

- Predict competitors' likely reactions to a firm's own strategic decisions

- Determine how competitors' behaviour can be influenced to make it more favourable for the firm

The second of these, in particular, has a significant overlap with the ideas of game theory.

However, critics of game theory argue that its value to strategic management is limited because it focuses on only a small fraction of the strategy process. For example, it does not provide any insight into the development

of the competitive resources or capabilities of an organisation. Equally, it does not provide any useful guidance as to how to actually **implement** whatever co-operative strategies may have been negotiated.

Section summary

Game theory illustrates that an organisation cannot develop its strategy without considering the possible reactions of its competitors. Competitor reaction may mean that the outcomes of a strategy are very different to what was initially intended.

9 Strategic intelligence

Introduction

An organisation should plan to obtain **strategic intelligence** as a basis for future strategies. Internal and external databases should be maintained and the data they contain assessed and applied.

If a key task of strategic management is to ensure environmental fit, managers need a willingness and an ability to understand the environment and to anticipate future trends.

- A separate strategic planning department collects data on trends.
- The marketing department identifies customer needs.
- The R&D department identifies new technology.
- The production department suggests process innovation.

Arguably, as strategy is about the whole organisation, there are dangers in restricting the gathering of strategic information to functional departments. The whole firm needs to be aware of **strategic intelligence**.

Earlier in this chapter, we discussed PEST analysis and Porter's five forces model. These are very useful models for environmental analysis which, in turn, could help an organisation improve its knowledge of its business environment.

9.1 Creating strategic intelligence

KEY TERM

STRATEGIC INTELLIGENCE, according to Donald Marchand, is defined as 'what a company needs to know about its business environment to enable it to anticipate change and design appropriate strategies that will create business value for customers and be profitable in new markets and new industries in the future'.

A model of the process of creating strategic intelligence is outlined below.

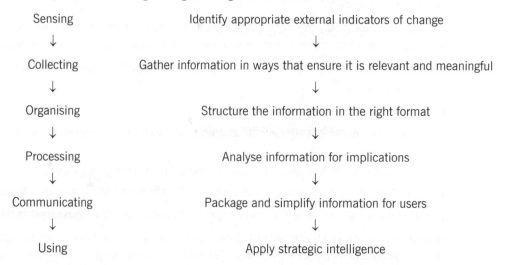

Key dimensions of strategic intelligence

Information culture	What is the role of information in the organisation? Is it only distributed on a 'need to know basis' or do people have to give specific reasons for secrecy?
Future orientation	Is the focus on specific decisions and trade-offs, or a general attitude of enquiry?
The structure of information flows	Is communication vertical, up and down the hierarchy, or lateral?
Processing strategic intelligence	Are 'professional' strategists delegated to this task or is it everybody's concern?
Scope	Is strategic intelligence dealt with by senior management only, or is intelligence built throughout the organisation?
Time horizon	Short-termist or oriented towards the long term?
The role of IT	Is the firm developing sophisticated knowledge management systems to capture the information?
Organisational 'memory'	In other words, do managers keep in mind the lessons of past successes or failures?

There are many **sources** of strategic intelligence.

(a)   **Internal sources** or sources relatively close to the company.

    (i)   The **sales force** deals with customers, and so is in a position to obtain customer and competitor information.

    (ii)   Many companies conduct **market research**. Although generally this deals with specific issues, it can indicate general environmental concerns (eg consumers' worries).

    (iii)   The **management information system** may generate information about the environment, although its main focus is internal.

(b)   **External sources** of environmental data are varied.

    (i)   **Media**. Newspapers, periodicals and television offer environmental information.

    (ii)   Sometimes, more detailed country information is needed than that supplied by the press. **Export consultants** might specialise in dealing with particular countries, and so can be a valuable source of information. The **Economist Intelligence Unit** offers reports into particular countries.

    (iii)   Academic or **trade journals** might give information about a wide variety of relevant issues to a particular industry.

    (iv)   **Trade associations** also offer industry information.

    (v)   The Government can be a source of statistical data relating to money supply, the trade balance and so forth, which is often summarised in newspapers. In the UK, the Department for Business, Innovation and Skills also publishes **Overseas Trade**, concentrating on export opportunities for UK firms. Official statistical sources also include government censuses, and demographic and expenditure surveys.

    (vi)   Sources of technological environmental information can include the national patents office (because patents for new products are registered with the patent office).

(vii)   Stockbrokers produce investment reports for the clients which involve analysis into particular industries.

(viii)   Specialist consultancy firms provide information (eg CACI provides demographical and market information for UK and Europe).

(ix)   The **internet** (for example, 'current awareness services' where subscribers can register particular key words related to their industry with media vendors and then receive automatic emails of articles and announcements that include those key words as tags). However, the websites of rival firms may also give an insight into their mission, objectives, strategy and financial performance.

(x)   **Annual reports** of competitors, suppliers or firms in a potential target market can also provide useful information.

9.2 Database information

A **management information system** or **database** should provide managers with a useful flow of relevant information which is easy to use and easy to access. Information is an important corporate resource. Managed and used effectively, it can provide considerable competitive advantage and so it is a worthwhile investment. Large-scale databases are created and stored on **computer systems**, using **database application packages** such as **Microsoft Access**.

Knowledge management (KM) is becoming an increasingly important issue in contemporary business. We look in more detail at KM and related topics, such as data warehousing and data mining, later in this Study Text.

It is now possible to access large volumes of generally available information through databases held by public bodies and businesses.

(a)   Some **newspapers** offer free or paid-for access on the web to both current and archived editions, with facilities available to search for information on particular companies or issues.

(b)   Public databases are also available for inspection. **Dun & Bradstreet** provides general business information. **Nielsen** operates online information regarding products and market share.

(c)   Developments in information technology allow businesses to have access to the databases of **external organisations**. Reuters, for example, provides an online information system about money market interest rates and foreign exchange rates to firms involved in money market and foreign exchange dealings, and also to the treasury departments of a large number of companies. The growing adoption of technology at **point of sale** provides a potentially invaluable source of data to both retailer and manufacturer.

Legislation and regulation exists to protect consumers from misuse of **personal details** held on computer, unsolicited mail and invasion of privacy.

For example, in the UK, the Data Protection Act (1998) regulates how personal information should be used, and means that companies can only access personal data in relation to the use for which it was originally registered.

9.2.1 Environmental data

Areas of environmental data that ought to be included in a database for strategic planners are:

(a)   **Competitive data**. This would include information derived from an application of Porter's five forces analysis.

(b)   **Economic data**. Details of past growth and predictions of future growth in GDP and disposable income, the pattern of interest rates, predictions of the rate of inflation, unemployment levels and tax rates, developments in international trade and so on.

(c)   **Political data**. The influence that the Government is having on the industry.

(d)   **Legal data**. The likely implications of recent legislation, legislation likely to be introduced in the future and its implications.

(e)   **Social data**. Changing habits, attitudes, cultures and educational standards of the population as a whole, and customers in particular.

(f)   **Technological data**. Technological changes that have occurred or will occur, and the implications that these will have for the organisation.

(g)   **Geographical data**. Data about individual regions or countries, each of them potentially segments of the market with their own unique characteristics.

(h)   **Energy suppliers' data**. Energy sources, availability and price of sources of supply generally.

(i)   **Data about stakeholders in the business**. Employees, management and shareholders, the influence of each group, and what each group wants from the organisation.

In other words, data which covers the key elements of the general and market environment should be included in a database for strategic and marketing planners.

As well as obtaining data from its own internal database system, an organisation can obtain it from an **external database** operated by another organisation.

9.2.2 A word of caution

Most external databases are online databases, which are very large computer files of information, supplied by **database providers** and managed by **host** companies whose business revenue is generated through charges made to **users**.

Information sources have to be used with caution. The internet, in particular, has made data more available: but this data is often unchecked and unmediated. For example, Wikipedia can often be a source of useful information, but the fact that it can be edited by any of its readers means that the reliability of its data cannot always be guaranteed.

9.3 Market research

One of the key aspects of the research a firm should undertake about its environment before considering a strategic action is market research.

Market research will help establish:

(a)   The size of a potential market (and the potential revenues which could be earned from it)

(b)   Potential bases of segmentation in the market (for example, by age, income or cultural differences; or by frequency and type of purchase, such as frequent vs infrequent purchasers, or industrial vs personal customers)

(c)   Who the main competitors are, and what products or services they are offering

9.3.1 Customer behaviour

In relation to customer needs and expectations, it is also important to understand why buyers purchase particular goods or services.

Such an understanding could be useful for two different reasons.

(a) It could help an organisation to identify the **critical success factors** (CSFs) required to satisfy those customers successfully. This, in turn, should help an organisation establish whether it has the core competences required to meet those CSFs (for example, to be able to produce goods more cheaply than competitors, or produce goods which are smaller, more lightweight, more reliable, more energy efficient etc).

(b) It could help an organisation design its advertising messages so that they highlight those aspects of the product or service which are most important to the customer's buying decision. For example, when choosing which washing powder to buy, some people will choose according to which removes stains best; others may choose according to which leaves their white clothes 'whitest'; while others may choose according to the price of the powder.

This very short example is also interesting because it raises the idea that within a single product class (washing powder) a manufacturer may offer several different products or brands, each aimed at a different specific benefit which customers value.

Section summary

An organisation needs strategic intelligence about its environment to allow it to anticipate changes and to design strategies that will allow it to respond effectively to those changes.

Chapter Summary

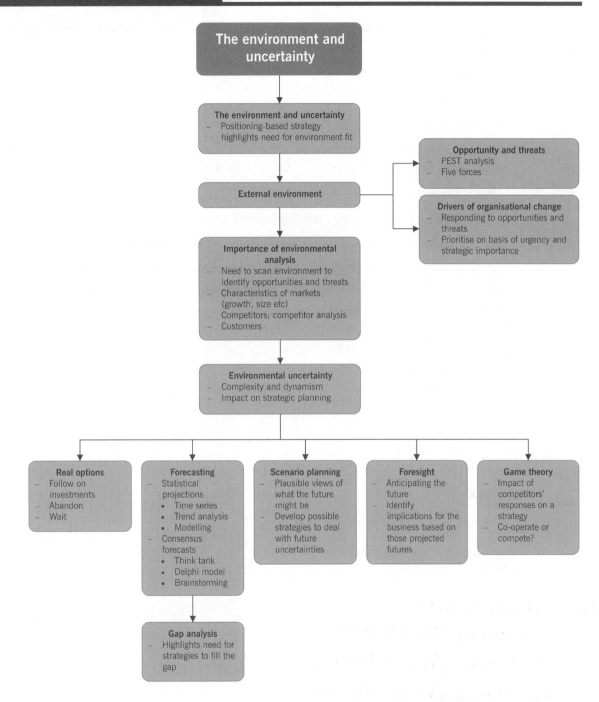

The environment and uncertainty

The environment and uncertainty
- Positioning-based strategy highlights need for environment fit

External environment

Opportunity and threats
- PEST analysis
- Five forces

Drivers of organisational change
- Responding to opportunities and threats
- Prioritise on basis of urgency and strategic importance

Importance of environmental analysis
- Need to scan environment to identify opportunities and threats
- Characteristics of markets (growth, size etc)
- Competitors; competitor analysis
- Customers

Environmental uncertainty
- Complexity and dynamism
- Impact on strategic planning

Real options
- Follow on investments
- Abandon
- Wait

Forecasting
- Statistical projections
  - Time series
  - Trend analysis
  - Modelling
- Consensus forecasts
  - Think tank
  - Delphi model
  - Brainstorming

Scenario planning
- Plausible views of what the future might be
- Develop possible strategies to deal with future uncertainties

Foresight
- Anticipating the future
- Identify implications for the business based on those projected futures

Game theory
- Impact of competitors' responses on a strategy
- Co-operate or compete?

Gap analysis
- Highlights need for strategies to fill the gap

Quick Quiz

1   The planning gap is the gap between the current position of the organisation and the forecast desired position.

☐ True

☑ False

2   Fill in the gaps.

According to Aaker and McLoughlin's impact analysis matrix, organisations should respond to strategic uncertainties on the basis of their .... and ....

3   What is foresight?

4   What are the ten steps in scenario planning (according to Schoemaker)?

5   List three common types of real options that could be relevant to strategic projects.

6   An organisation follows a strategy which it thinks will be beneficial to it, but because of the response of its competitors the strategy turns out to be detrimental to both the organisation and the industry as a whole.

Which one of the following does this demonstrate best:

A: Emergent strategy
B: Game theory
C: Gap analysis
D: Delphi technique

5. option to wait
option to abandon
option to follow on

4. 1. Define scope
2. Identify stakeholders
3. Identify basic trends
4. Identify key areas of

Answers to Quick Quiz

1   False. It is the gap between the forecast position from continuing with current activities, and the desired future position.

2   Urgency and strategic importance

   Aaker and McLoughlin's impact analysis matrix suggests that an organisation should respond to strategic uncertainties on the basis of their urgency and their strategic importance.

3   Foresight is the art and science of anticipating the future. It is a process of identifying a range of possible outcomes which could develop, based on an understanding and analysis of current trends.

4   Step 1   Define the scope
   Step 2   Identify the major stakeholders
   Step 3   Identify basic trends
   Step 4   Identify key areas of uncertainty
   Step 5   Construct initial scenarios
   Step 6   Check for consistency and plausibility
   Step 7   Develop learning scenarios
   Step 8   Identify research needs
   Step 9   Develop quantitative models
   Step 10   Use scenarios to formulate competitive strategy

5   Option to make follow-on investments
   Option to abandon a project
   Option to wait

6   B   Game theory.

   Game theory illustrates the way that strategic interactions between competitors produce outcomes that were not intended by any of the players.

Answer to Question

3.1 Contrasting environment

(a)   The environment is simple, as the product is only being sold in one market. The environment is dynamic, as the product is still at the introduction stage and demand might be predicted to increase dramatically.

(b)   The environment is complex, but stable. The knowledge required is uncertain, but funds are guaranteed for ten years.

Now try these questions from the Practice Question Bank	Number	Level	Marks	Time
	3.1 – 3.5	Intermediate	n/a	10 mins
	3.6	Examination	20	36 mins

STRATEGIC POSITION AND STRATEGIC OPTIONS

Part B

RESOURCES AND CAPABILITIES

In the previous chapter we looked at the external environment in which organisations operate. By contrast, in this chapter, we examine some of the key aspects of organisations' own (internal) resources and capabilities.

The quantity and quality of the **resources and capabilities** an organisation possesses (Section 1) represent a strength or weakness for the organisation.

In the context of developing its strategic position, **value drivers** (Section 2) are particularly important for an organisation, because they help it develop and sustain a competitive advantage.

Value chain analysis (Section 3) identifies how an entity adds value to the resources it obtains, and how it deploys these resources to satisfy customers.

Supply chain management (Section 4) extends this idea to demonstrate the possible gains available through developing strong relationships with all parties who add value to the finished product/service.

In Section 5, we look at the concepts of the **product portfolio** and the **product life cycle**. Analysing its current portfolio may encourage an organisation to develop new products, and we look at innovation and new products in Section 6.

An organisation's resources and competences are difficult to assess in isolation, so some form of comparison is needed. **Benchmarking** (Section 7) can be used to compare an organisation's performance or processes against competitors or against 'best in class' organisations. Such an exercise could highlight areas where improvements can be made.

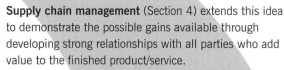

4

Topic list	Learning outcomes	Syllabus references	Ability required
1 Strategic resources and capabilities	B2(a)	B2(a) (i)	Evaluate
2 Value drivers	B1(a)	B1(a) (v)	Evaluate
3 Converting resources: the value chain	B2(c)	B2(c) (i)	Produce
4 The supply chain and supply chain management	A1(d)	A1(d) (iv)	Recommend
5 Outputs: the product portfolio	B2(b)	B2(b) (i)	Recommend
6 New products and innovation	B2(a)	B2(a) (i)	Evaluate
7 Benchmarking	B2(a)	B2(a) (i)	Evaluate

Chapter Overview

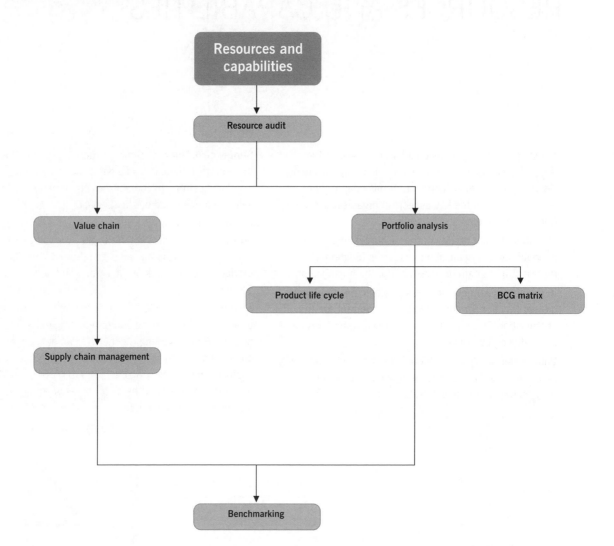

1 Strategic resources and capabilities

Introduction

Although it is important that organisations identify opportunities and threats in the external environment and develop strategies to respond to them, an organisation's ability to compete effectively is also determined by its own internal resources and capabilities.

In the previous chapter, we looked at the way the external environment influences strategies, through the opportunities and threats which it presents to organisations.

Once an organisation has analysed its external environment, it can then establish an appropriate strategy to achieve a good **strategic fit** with that environment. This is the essence of the **position-based approach** to strategy: organisations seek to develop competitive advantage in a way that responds to the nature of the competitive environment, and position their strategy in response to the opportunities or threats they discern in the environment.

However, an organisation's internal competences and capabilities also affect its ability to deliver value to customers and achieve competitive advantage in an industry. **Resource-based approaches** to strategy focus on these internal characteristics of an organisation.

In resource-based approaches, rather than being developed in response to the external competitive environment, strategy is developed by looking at what makes an organisation unique, and using an understanding of these unique competences to determine what to produce and what markets to produce for. The resource-based view is based on the idea that sustainable competitive advantage can only be attained as a result of possessing **distinctive resources** (either tangible or intangible).

The resource-based approach also suggests that strategic advantage begins with a few key elements that the organisation must concentrate on – its **core competences**, those things that it does better than its rivals.

In Chapter 1, we highlighted the contrast between a position-based approach to strategy and a resource-based approach. The ideas we examine in this chapter are particularly important in relation to the resource-based approach, in which an organisation analyses its own internal resources and competences and then adopts a strategy which helps it exploit those resources and competences.

1.1 Position audit

KEY TERM

POSITION AUDIT is 'part of the planning process which examines the current state of the entity in respect of:

- Resources of tangible and intangible assets and finance
- Products, brands and markets
- Operating systems such as production and distribution
- Internal organisation
- Current results
- Returns to stockholders'   (*CIMA Official Terminology*)

The rest of this chapter is concerned with how this vital task may be successfully carried out.

The elements of the position audit are:

- Resource audit
- Analysis of limiting factors
- Identification of threshold resources/competences
- Identification of unique resources/core competences

Remember we looked at threshold and core competences, and the distinction between them, in Chapter 1.

1.2 Resource audit

As the name suggests, a resource audit identifies the resources available to an organisation. By determining what resources they already have, organisations can identify what additional resources are required to pursue their chosen strategy.

The **Ms model** categorises the limiting factors as follows.

Resource	Example
Machinery	Age, condition, and utilisation rate of assets. Technologically up to date? Cost. Quality of outputs?
Make-up	Culture and structure of organisation. Other intangibles such as: patents; goodwill; brands.
Management	Skills, experience and vision of senior management. Loyalty. Career progression. Structure.
Management information	Ability to generate and disseminate ideas accurately and on a timely basis. Innovation. Information systems. Availability of information to support strategic decision making.
Markets	Markets (and market segments) the organisation operates in. Position of the organisation and its products/services in those markets.
Materials	Relationships with suppliers. Quality and reliability of inputs. Waste. New materials. Cost. Availability. Future provision.
Men and women	Human resources: Number of staff. Skills. Wage costs (as a proportion of total costs). Efficiency. Labour turnover. Staff morale. Industrial relations.
Methods	How are activities carried out? Capital-intensive or labour-intensive. Outsourcing. JIT.
Money	What is the organisation's cash position? Credit and turnover periods? Cash surpluses/ deficits? Short-term and long-term finance. Gearing levels. Investment plans.

Resources are of little or no value to an organisation unless they are organised into systems. A resource audit considers how well (or badly) resources have been utilised, and the efficiency and effectiveness of the organisation's systems in meeting stakeholders' needs (eg in meeting customer needs profitably). This also includes the quality and timeliness of information available to managers.

Johnson, Scholes and Whittington highlight this point in their text *Exploring Strategy* when they note:

'There would be no point in having state-of-the-art equipment if it were not used effectively. The efficiency and effectiveness of physical or financial resources, or the people in an organisation, depend, not just on their existence, but on the systems and processes by which they are managed, the relationships and co-operation between people, their adaptability, their innovatory capacity, the relationship with customers and suppliers, and the experience and learning about what works well and what does not.'

1.3 Competitive resources

In his text *Strategic Management*, Richard Lynch provides a checklist which could be used as a framework for analysing whether an organisation's internal 'resources' can be construed as strengths or weaknesses.

Aspect of resources	Questions to ask
Market share	How does the company's market share compare to competitors?
	Are there any particular areas in which the company dominates or has a strong market share?
	How does the level and quality of the company's marketing activity compare to competitors'?
Market growth	Is the company involved in growth markets, or is it involved primarily in mature/declining markets?
Product quality	Do the company's products and services offer good value for money for customers?
	Does the company have a good quality record in relation to the price of its goods or services? How many customer complaints does it receive?
Leadership	How effective is the company leadership?
	Is it risk taking or risk averse?
	Is it ethical?
Purpose and objectives	Are the company's purpose and objectives clearly stated?
	Are the objectives known to the people responsible for delivering them?
	Is performance against key objectives measured?
Management and workers	Does the company have a good industrial relations record?
	How does staff turnover compare to competitors'?
	How does the quality or experience of management resource compare to competitors'?
Financial position	Is the company financially sound or are its financial resources stretched?
	What has its profit record and earnings per share record been over the past few years?
	Are there any 'difficult' shareholders?
Profit performance	How does the company's profit record compare to competitors'?
	How do products and distribution costs compare to competitors'?
	Could production and distribution costs be reduced?
Investment practice	How much does the company invest in capital investment?
	How does this compare to the level of competitors' investment?
R&D; Innovation	How important are research and development, and innovation in the industry? How does the company's record in these areas compare to competitors'?
	Does the company support innovation and knowledge management?

1.4 Strategic capability

An organisation's ability to survive and prosper, and to deliver future value, depends on its strategic capability. This can be defined as the **adequacy and suitability of the resources and competences the organisation has**, and which are necessary for its future success.

So, when evaluating an organisation's strategic capability, the following questions are important.

(a)   Does the organisation have a **suitable business model** to deliver future success, based on an understanding of the sources of competitive advantage that contribute to profitability and growth across the value system of the organisation?

(b)   Does it have the **people, processes and resources** it needs to be able to deliver this success?

When considering resources and competences, it is important to remember that companies often need to acquire assets or competences from outside their own controllable resources and competence-building activities in order to enhance the value they create.

These 'external' resources can include:

- Integrated supply chains
- Networks of firms
- Longer-term alliances
- Acquisition of, or merger with, another company

Equally, a resource for a firm could include **access** to supplies and/or distribution networks, so resource management is not simply a matter of ownership and control.

1.4.1 Dynamic capabilities

So far, when looking at resources and competences, we have tended to view them as long-term phenomena since, for example, resources will be more valuable if they can be counted upon to last for a long time, or because it might take an organisation a long time to develop its core competences.

However, if managers focus on internal resources alone, there is a danger they will overlook the importance of the external environment on their strategy. This could be a particular problem during periods of environmental uncertainty and change.

Critics of resource-based approaches to strategy argue that, while the resource-based view can help to explain how firms achieve competitive advantage in a static environment, it does not explain how and why firms can achieve and sustain competitive advantage in situations of rapid and unpredictable change.

Therefore, we could suggest that the traditional resource-based view (of resources and competences) needs to be extended to acknowledge that, in order to sustain competitive advantage, firms may need to renew – or upgrade – their competences in line with the changing business environment. This ability to achieve new forms of competitive advantage, by developing and changing competences to meet the needs of rapidly changing environments, is known as **dynamic capability**.

In this context, the distinction between resources, competences and capabilities which we identified earlier is important because it enables us to develop a hierarchical order that we can use to analyse a firm's ability to create and sustain a competitive advantage.

Resources form the base of the hierarchy, the 'zero-order' element. They are the foundation of the firm, and need to be in place before a firm can develop any higher capabilities. However, by themselves resources cannot be a source of sustainable competitive advantage.

Competences or capabilities are the 'first-order' and represent the ability to deploy resources to attain a desired goal. In this way, capabilities are likely to result in improved performance. However, this improved performance will be manifest at an operational level – for example through the performance of business processes – rather than at a strategic level.

Core competences or core capabilities are 'second-order', and consist of those resources and capabilities that are strategically important to a firm's competitive advantage at any given point. However, these core capabilities may not necessarily continue to confer a sustainable competitive advantage if (or when) the environment changes. Depending on the nature and extent of the change, capabilities might either become irrelevant or possibly even become 'core rigidities'. (That is, a potential downside of core capabilities is that they inhibit innovation, because managers prefer instead to concentrate on using resources in the current way, rather than combining them in different ways or repurposing them for new use, such as producing new product lines.)

Therefore 'third-order' dynamic capabilities emphasise a firm's constant pursuit of the renewal, reconfiguration and re-creation of resources, capabilities and core capabilities in order to address the changing environment. This ability to adapt to changes in markets or the environment sooner and more astutely than competitors is at the heart of dynamic capabilities, and is also a source of sustained competitive advantage.

CASE STUDY

GlaxoSmithKline and dynamic capabilities

Since the 1950s, a key resource for large pharmaceutical companies has been patented drugs with regulatory approval. This resource stock has been continually refreshed through research and development (R&D) activity which has involved testing large numbers of prototype drugs for their effectiveness in treating different illnesses.

Pharmaceutical companies built up learning dynamic capabilities through establishing and developing teams of specialist researchers, and other groups who were skilled in the extensive phases of the testing required to gain regulatory approval for new drugs.

At the end of the 20th century, a series of mergers and acquisitions led to consolidation in the industry, for example with GlaxoWellcome merging with SmithKline (which had previously merged with Beecham) to form GSK in 2000.

However, GSK has also acquired some much smaller firms, many of whom have never sold any products, and who operate with quite different technologies and sciences bases; for example, biotechnology firms. This is because biotechnology is now seen as the main driver of innovation in the pharmaceutical sector, and the big pharmaceutical companies are seeking closer relations with the highly innovative biotech industry.

For example, GSK's acquisition of Corixa in 2005, despite being partially driven by the financial potential of Corixa's Monophosphoryl Lipid A (MPL) (which was contained in many of GSK's candidate vaccines including its potential blockbuster Cervarix), also dramatically expanded GSK's already lucrative vaccine platform, providing it with much-needed additional expertise in the field.

Similarly, in 2007, GSK bolstered its biopharmaceuticals portfolio with the purchase of the UK-based speciality antibody company, Domantis. The acquisition cost £230 million, but Domantis has become a key part of GSK's Biopharmaceuticals Centre of Excellence for Drug Discovery, and helped catapult GSK into the arena of next-generation antibody drugs by more than doubling the number of projects it has in this area.

More recently, GSK has also divested (or outsourced) activities traditionally performed in-house. Pharmaceutical giants were not immune to the global economic downturn, and they were forced to adopt cost-saving strategies in the same way as organisations in other industries were. However, GSK looked towards more sophisticated approaches than simply cutting jobs and shelving expensive projects.

GSK assigned a group of its scientists and product patents to a standalone company dealing specifically with pain relief. Fourteen of GSK's leading researchers, along with the rights to a number of patents for experimental analgesic medicines, moved into a start-up company formed in October 2010: Convergence Pharmaceuticals.

This arrangement was specifically engineered to reduce the overhead costs involved with R&D, while simultaneously allowing GSK to benefit from any breakthroughs that Convergence might develop and go on to market.

So, Glaxo's original learning processes of R&D have subsequently been augmented by three different phases of reconfiguring its capabilities. The first phase (of mega-mergers) involved similar firms combining; the second phase consisted of the acquisition of innovative biotech companies; and the third, most recent, phase consisted of restructuring and outsourcing activities.

This sequence of phases is evidence of GSK's regenerative dynamic capabilities, triggered by performance problems caused by the declining value of the existing resource base as the patents on existing products expired. GSK's existing R&D capabilities were insufficient in themselves to maintain, or expand, the stock of resources. The move into biotechnology acquisitions was triggered by the realisation that the pipeline of new drugs was drying up, as well as the fact that pharmaceutical companies are operating in an increasingly challenging environment, with high competitive rivalry, price sensitivity among healthcare providers, and stricter ethical standards.

1.5 Limiting factors

Every organisation operates under resource **constraints**.

KEY TERM

A LIMITING FACTOR or **key factor** is 'anything which limits the activity of an entity. An entity seeks to optimise the benefit it obtains from the limiting factor.

Examples are a shortage of supply of a resource or a restriction on sales demand at a particular price'.

(CIMA Official Terminology)

Examples of limiting factors are:

- A shortage of production capacity
- A limited number of key personnel, such as salespeople with technical knowledge
- A restricted distribution network
- Too few managers with knowledge about finance, or overseas markets
- Inadequate research design resources to develop new products or services
- A poor system of strategic intelligence
- Lack of money
- A lack of adequately trained staff

Once the limiting factor has been identified, the planners should:

- In the short term, make best use of the resources available
- Try to reduce the limitation in the long term

1.6 Resource use

Resource use is both the **efficiency** with which resources are used, and the **effectiveness** of their use in achieving the planning objectives of the business. Resources can be a source of competitive advantage when used efficiently and effectively.

KEY TERMS

EFFICIENCY relates to how well resources have been utilised, irrespective of the purpose for which they have been employed.

EFFECTIVENESS relates to whether the resources have been deployed in the best possible way.

1.7 Competences and critical success factors (CSFs)

So far in this section, we have been discussing organisations' resources and competences and the extent to which they could be strengths or weaknesses for an organisation. However, it is also important to think about the relationship between competences and critical success factors (CSFs). (We will discuss CSFs in more detail in Chapters 6 and 11.)

BPP
LEARNING MEDIA

An organisation's **competences** relate to its skills and abilities which enable it to deploy its resources effectively; in other words, what it is good at.

CSFs are the activities it **needs** to excel at in order to satisfy the needs and demands of its customers; in other words, what it needs to be good at in order to be successful.

Therefore, when assessing an organisation's competences and capabilities, it is important to do so in the context of its CSFs. A key question for strategic managers to consider is whether an organisation's competences help it to achieve its CSFs. For example, if the customers in a restaurant value the speed of service they receive in a restaurant, then the fact that the restaurant provides its customers with a very high level of service is not a source of competitive advantage – particularly if the focus on quality and attention to detail actually slows down the service.

Equally, another important consideration is whether an organisation's competences and capabilities need to be changed to enable it to deliver against its CSFs more effectively. For example, in the illustration in the previous paragraph, the restaurant's competitive position could be strengthened by finding ways of serving its customers more quickly.

Section summary

Resource-based approaches to strategy focus on the way an organisation can use its own internal resources, competences and capabilities as the basis for competitive advantage. However, this also highlights the importance of analysing an organisation's resources and capabilities to assess whether they represent strengths or weaknesses for the current strategic position.

Limiting factors are anything which limit the activity of an entity. Resources should be used as effectively and efficiently as possible in order to make the best use of them. Firms should aim to reduce the limitation in the long run.

2   Value drivers

Introduction

Value drivers are factors which affect the value of a business, and so organisations need to identify their key value drivers and then put strategies in place to try to maximise the value of the organisation.

In general terms, value drivers are the crucial organisational capabilities which create value (revenues, profits) for an organisation and help it generate competitive advantage. An organisation will need to identify its value drivers, and then put strategies in place for each of them, to help ensure that it creates, or sustains, its competitive advantage.

More specifically, the shareholder value approach (as set out by Rappaport) argues that the value of a company is dependent on seven drivers of value. In effect, these drivers enable management to estimate the value of an investment, by discounting forecast cash flows by the cost of capital.

We will look at the shareholder value approach and Rappaport's drivers of value in more detail in Chapter 12 later in this Study Text, in the context of performance measurement and performance management, more generally.

2.1 Creating shareholder value

A company's overall aim is to create value for its shareholders. This is achieved by selecting a business strategy which it believes will be successful, with that strategy being derived from an analysis of external forces (opportunities and threats) and of the company's internal resources and competences.

However, that strategy also needs to link to those factors that drive value in the business. Rappaport identified seven value drivers:

(a) Increase sales growth
(b) Increase operating profit margin
(c) Reduce cash tax rate
(d) Reduce incremental investment in capital expenditure
(e) Reduce investment in working capital
(f) Increase time period of competitive advantage
(g) Reduce cost of capital

The first five drivers can be used to prepare cash flow forecasts for a suitable period. The length of this period should be defined according to the likely period of a company's competitive advantage (driver (f)). Discounting these cash flows at the cost of capital (driver (g)) leads to the value of the business's operations.

Identifying the value drivers in a company is also important when deciding what **performance measures are the most meaningful to measure**. One way to ensure that a company uses meaningful performance metrics is to link those metrics to value drivers. For example, a metric of 'new product sales' could be useful to measure how well a company is achieving sales growth.

In this respect, the drivers should not all be treated equally. Different drivers will be more important than others in different businesses. For example, for a hotel business, with a high fixed cost base, the most important driver is sales, meaning that occupancy rates are a key performance measure for them. By contrast, for a bank lending to corporate customers, profits are driven by the margin between the rate at which the bank borrows and that at which it lends. That margin is usually slim, so for the bank, more value will be created by improving interest margins and reducing operating costs than by increasing the volume of business.

2.2 Value drivers and business strategy

Value creation does not occur, and costs do not arise, evenly across an organisation, so managers need a firm grasp of the key cost and value drivers affecting their operations. Some of these cost and value drivers may be located outside the organisation, elsewhere in the **value system** (or value network), so the ability to influence suppliers and distributors may also be crucial to an organisation's success.

More generally, the choice of **generic strategy** interacts with cost and value: strict control of cost is obviously fundamental to cost leadership, while differentiation will inevitably have cost implications associated with such matters as brand communications, product quality and customer service.

Similarly, the structure of costs and value creation is likely to **change over time** as, for example, illustrated by the cost and profit aspects of the **product life cycle**.

2.3 Value drivers and intangibles

Importantly, a number of the drivers which can create value for an organisation are intangible. For example, the following attributes within a business could all create value for it:

- Superior management
- Employees' skills and knowledge
- Brand and reputation
- Intellectual property
- Network relationships and linkages
- Quality management
- First-mover advantage

For a high-quality restaurant – with a reputation for good food and offering customers a positive dining experience – key value drivers might include: the skill of the chefs and the quality of the cooking; the quality of the waiting staff; and the ambience of the restaurant.

For a professional services firm (eg accountants; lawyers; and management consultants) key value drivers might include: highly skilled staff, and the quality of the relationships developed with clients.

In both of these cases, the value drivers are **non-financial** and, therefore, the performance metrics needed to measure how well the organisation is performing against them will also need to be non-financial.

We discuss performance measurement systems in more detail in Chapter 11 later in this Study Text, but the need to monitor non-financial performance (as well as financial performance) is central to multidimensional performance measurement systems such as the balanced scorecard and the performance pyramid.

Section summary

Value drivers are the key elements of a business which generate value and underpin its competitive advantage.

3 Converting resources: the value chain

Introduction

The **value chain** models all the activities of a business and the linkages between them. It shows how value is created, how costs are caused and how competitive advantage can be gained.

The **value chain**, developed by Michael Porter, offers a bird's eye view of the firm and what it does. Competitive advantage, says Porter, arises out of the way in which firms organise and perform **activities**. Businesses are made up of value-creating activities. It is important to consider the structure of an organisation in terms of these activities.

KEY TERMS

The VALUE CHAIN is the 'sequence of business activities by which, in the perspective of the **end-user**, value is added to the products or services produced by an entity'.   (*CIMA Official Terminology*)

ACTIVITIES are the means by which a firm creates value in its products. (They are sometimes referred to as **value activities**.)

Activities incur costs and, in combination with other activities, provide a product or service which earns revenue.

3.1 Example of the value chain

A **restaurant's** activities are buying, cooking and serving food. The customer is prepared to **pay more than the cost of** the resources (food, wages etc). The ultimate value created is the amount customers are willing to pay above the cost of carrying out value activities. A firm is profitable if the value to customers exceeds the cost of activities.

(a) Customers **purchase value**, which they measure by comparing a firm's products and services with those of competitors.

(b) The business **creates value** by carrying out its activities either more efficiently than other businesses, or combining them in such a way as to provide a unique product or service.

Question 4.1 Creating value

Learning outcome B2(c)

Outline different ways in which the restaurant can 'create' value.

Porter (in *Competitive Advantage*) grouped the various activities of an organisation into a value chain:

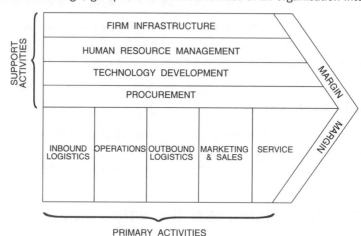

The **margin** is the excess the customer is prepared to **pay** over the **cost** to the firm of obtaining resource inputs and providing value activities. In this respect the chain highlights the underlying business logic that a firm's activities should be designed to **create a margin** by producing outputs which have a greater sale price (or value to customers) than the cost of the inputs.

3.2 Activities

Primary activities are directly related to production, sales, marketing, delivery and service.

	Comment
Inbound logistics	Receiving, handling, storing and distributing inputs to the production system (warehousing, transport, inventory control etc).
Operations	Convert resource inputs (people and materials) into a final product. Testing and packaging of the product.
Outbound logistics	Storing the product and distributing it to customers.
Marketing and sales	Informing customers about the product, persuading and enabling them to buy it (advertising, promotion, selling etc).
After-sales service	Installing, repairing and upgrading products, providing spare parts, providing training and so on.

Support activities provide purchased inputs, human resources, technology and infrastructural functions to **support the primary activities**.

Activity	Comment
Procurement	Acquire the resource inputs to the primary activities (eg purchase of materials, subcomponents equipment).
Technology development	Product design, improving processes and/or resource utilisation.
Human resource management	Recruiting, training, developing and rewarding people.
Firm infrastructure	Planning, finance, quality control: Porter believes these are crucially important to an organisation's strategic capability in all primary activities.

Linkages connect the activities of the value chain.

(a)   **Activities in the value chain affect one another**. For example, more costly product design or better quality production might reduce the need for after-sales service.

(b)   **Linkages require co-ordination**. For example, just-in-time (JIT) requires smooth functioning of operations, outbound logistics and service activities such as installation.

Exam skills

The value chain provides a rational framework for carrying out analysis so is potentially useful in exam questions. At this level you should not expect to earn marks simply by reproducing the value chain in a generic form, but rather you should expect to have to apply it to a scenario situation.

Nonetheless, the syllabus requires you to be able to 'produce an organisation's value chain' so it is important you have a good understanding of the different activities included within it.

The value chain helps managers identify the activities which create value for an entity's customers. In doing so it can also help managers identify the key processes and areas in which the entity has to perform successfully to secure a competitive advantage.

These key areas could be seen as the entity's CSFs. It is important to note the potential link between this area of the syllabus and CSFs, performance targets and key performance indicators as elements of performance management (discussed in Chapter 11 of this Study Text).

Similarly, identifying the key processes can also have important implications for an organisation's information requirements – because managers will need information about how the organisation is performing in those key areas. We look at the relationship between CSFs and information requirements in more detail in Chapter 6 of this Study Text.

3.3 Value system

Activities that add value do not stop at the organisation's **boundaries**. For example, when a restaurant serves a meal, the quality of the meat and vegetable ingredients is determined by the farmer who supplies them. The farmer has added value. The farmer's ability is as important to the customer's ultimate satisfaction as the skills of the chef. A firm's value chain is connected to what Porter calls a **value system**.

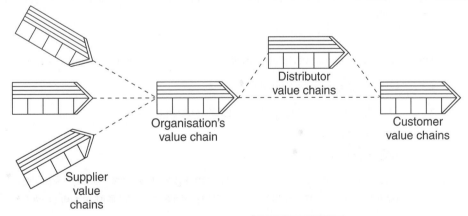

It may be possible to capture the benefit of some of the value generated both upstream and downstream in the value system. An obvious way to do this is by **vertical integration** through the acquisition of supplies and customers.

It is possible for large and powerful companies to exercise less formal power over suppliers and customers by using their **bargaining power** to achieve favourable purchase and selling prices.

A more subtle advantage is gained by fostering good relationships that can promote **innovation** and the **creation of knowledge**. Businesses are increasingly looking to work together in **partnerships** with other members of their value system.

3.4 Using the value chain

A firm can secure competitive advantage by:

- Inventing new or better ways to perform activities.
- Combining activities in new or better ways.
- Managing linkages in its own value chain to increase efficiency and reduce cost.
- Managing the linkages in the value system. This links to the ideas of **supply chain management**.

The **value system** offers the potential to improve efficiency and reduce cost through negotiation, bargaining, collaboration and vertical integration. Vertical integration offers the chance to increase profitability by **migrating** to the part of the value system that has the most potential for adding value.

Note also that Information Technology (IT) can transform an organisation's value chain, and a number of improvements in organisations' value chains have been the result of developments in IT.

We review the strategic significance of IT, including its impact on the value chain, in Chapter 6 of this Study Text.

Question 4.2	Value chain and value system

Learning outcomes B2(c); E2(a)

Sana Sounds is a small record company. Representatives from Sana Sounds scour music clubs for new bands to promote. Once a band has signed a contract (with Sana Sounds) it makes a recording. The recording process is subcontracted to one of a number of recording studio firms which Sana Sounds uses regularly. (At the moment Sana Sounds is not large enough to invest in its own equipment and studios.) Sana Sounds also subcontracts the production of CDs to a number of manufacturing companies. Sana Sounds then distributes the disks to selected stores, and engages in any promotional activities required.

What would you say were the activities in Sana Sounds' current value chain?

Also, stop and think how the development of MP3 technology might permit Sana Sounds to re-engineer its value chain.

The value chain is an important analytical tool because it helps management to:

- See the business as a whole

- Identify potential sources of competitive advantage

- Suggest strategies

- Analyse competitors

- Implement activities such as benchmarking, outsourcing, business process re-engineering, performance measurement, and activity-based costing and management

3.5 The value chain and management accounting

There is a clear link between the concept of value activities that cut across departments and the principles of activity-based costing.

A summary of the failure of traditional costing systems, and a contrast based on the value chain, is outlined in the table below.

	Traditional costing system	Value chain cost analysis: an alternative
Focus	Manufacturing operations	Customers Value perceptions
Cost objects	Products Functions Expense heads	Value-creating activities Product attributes
Organisational focus	Cost and responsibility centres	Strategic business units (SBUs) Value-creating activities
Linkages	1 Largely ignored 2 Cost allocations and transfer prices used to reflect interdependencies	Recognised and maximised
Cost drivers	Simple volume measures	Strategic decisions
Accuracy	Manufacturing operations	Low precision Indicative answers

Example

The practical application of value chain cost analysis can be seen with the following illustration which relates each element to the example of a supermarket's operations.

	Value chain cost analysis	Practical example
Focus	Customers	The supermarket is heavily focused on customers as the key source of value. Specific customers are targeted through marketing campaigns and 'customer delight' is sought. Competition forces retailers to invest more in customer service, systems and price.
Cost objects	Value-creating activities and profit attributes	Activities which promote customer loyalty and bigger spend are investigated and developed. For example, giving a 10% discount to new mothers could increase sales and profit margin above the cost of the discount. Self-scanning technology increases sales in stores.
Linkages	Recognised and maximised	Supplier and customer relationships are nurtured. Suppliers are ranked for their ability to meet the supermarket's demand and customers are constantly reminded via in-store promotions of the supermarket's commitment to giving them value.
Cost drivers	Strategic decisions	These are prompted either by competitor activity (eg price cuts) or new business initiatives such as investment in new technology and development of overseas markets. Target rates of return are required, often also measured in terms of the required sales uplift and related margin to justify an activity.
Accuracy	Indicative answers	Details of sales and margin by product are collected and individual customer spends are analysed. Customer surveys and level of customer complaints may highlight weak areas of the business.

In this context, we should also acknowledge how the value chain could be useful when developing **key performance indicators (KPIs)**. KPIs should monitor how well a business is performing against its **CSFs**, and these CSFs, in turn, should be linked to the key processes that deliver the organisation's strategy. So, the value chain should highlight the activities whose performance should be measured in the KPIs.

3.5.1 How the value chain drives costs

What might influence the costs of the value chain?

(a) **Structural cost drivers** are major strategic choices made by the firm which determine its underlying cost base.

    (i)   **Scale** of operations, capacity etc, giving rise to economies or diseconomies of scale

    (ii)   **Scope**: to what extent is the firm vertically integrated?

    (iii) **Experience**: has the firm climbed the learning curve?

    (iv) **Technology** used in the value chain

    (v)   **Complexity** and breadth of product range

(b) **Management** influences how well a firm manages the value chain operationally.

    (i)   Capacity utilisation

    (ii)   Product and process design

    (iii) Learning opportunities offered by continuous improvement programmes

    (iv) How well external linkages (eg liaison with suppliers) are exploited

Firms might create a more **outward-looking focus** in their costing systems as follows.

(a) Most products are a collection of benefits, which is why customers buy them. The provision of customer benefits is the real cost driver of the business. It should be possible to work backwards from these benefits to the underlying costs.

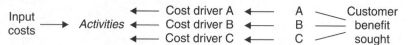

(b) For different products, it should be possible to identify the customer's perception of the value of the benefit and the cost of providing it.

For the accountant, problems with this approach are:

- A lack of precision in the data
- The subjectivity in deciding what customers value as a benefit

3.6 Limitations of the value chain

(a) It was originally designed for use in a manufacturing context, so can be difficult to apply to **service businesses**.

(b) The value system is difficult to apply to **network organisations**.

(c) Making the best use of the value chain idea is dependent on adopting at least some part of **activity-based costing** to establish the costs of value activities. This can be time consuming and expensive.

(d) The costs of the analysis may exceed the potential benefits.

(e) The value chain takes little account of the increasing role of IT in business. In response to this criticism Porter and Millar revisited the model and stressed the importance of using technology to increase linkages.

3.7 Alternative approaches

Stabell and Fjeldstad address the first two limitations listed above by proposing **new lists of primary activities** that relate better to service and network organisations respectively.

In their model, Stabell and Fjeldstad refer to the idea of a **value shop** rather than value chain.

3.7.1 The value shop and service organisations

The value shop model is based on the idea that an organisation needs to use its resources to address customers' issues or to solve their problems, so it can perhaps be seen most clearly in relation to a professional practice such as a firm of accountants or lawyers, or in medical services. **Expertise is the principal asset**, and is built by experience.

Primary activities include:

(a) **Problem-finding and acquisition**: Recording, reviewing and formulating the problem to be solved, and choosing an overall approach to solving the problem. Marketing effort could be required here as well as professional expertise.

(b) **Problem solving**: More extensive professional expertise must be deployed to identify and evaluate potential solutions to the issue at hand.

(c) **Choice between solutions**: A preferred solution is chosen (in consultation with the client) from alternative solutions which have been identified.

(d) **Solution implementation**: This activity involves communicating, organising and implementing the chosen solution.

(e) **Control and feedback**: Measuring and evaluating the extent to which the solution has solved the initial problem, to ensure the effectiveness of the solution.

The **secondary activities** in the value shop are the same as those in Porter's value chain.

An organisation which can be viewed as a value shop will:

(a) Use a variety of skills, expertise, disciplines and specialties

(b) Be able to cope with unique situations

(c) Perform repetitive and cyclical activities (Whereas Porter's value chain is essentially linear, the primary activities in the value shop are arranged as a circle to reflect the process of identifying and evaluating (and possibly rejecting) different solutions before reaching a conclusion.)

(d) Co-ordinate across different activities

(e) Rely on reputation-based referrals

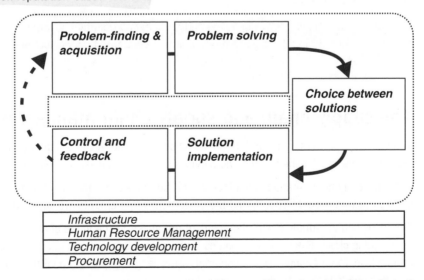

The value shop (after Stabell and Fjeldstad)

3.8 Strategic value analysis

One of the benefits of value chain analysis for managers is that it enables them to understand how the processes they manage add value for the customer. In turn, they can then help identify where the amount of value added can be increased, or else costs lowered, with a view to enhancing the competitive position of their organisation.

However, gaining and sustaining a competitive advantage requires an organisation to understand the entire value delivery system, not just the portion of the value system in which it participates. For example, the upstream value chain (suppliers) and the downstream value chain (distributors, retailers) are a crucial part of a manufacturer's value system.

Moreover, the upstream and downstream portions of the value system also have profit margins that will be important when identifying a company's cost/differentiation positioning, since the end-user consumer ultimately pays for the profit margins along the entire value chain.

Strategic value analysis (SVA) highlights the need to analyse business issues and opportunities across the entire value chain for an industry. Such analysis is critical for multi-stage industries because change in one stage will almost inevitably have an impact on other businesses all along the chain.

SVA prompts companies to ask four key questions:

(a) Are there any new or emerging players in the industry (in any portion of the value chain) that may be more successful than existing players?

(b) Are these companies positioned in the value chain differently from existing players? (In particular, are companies emerging which specialise in single activities within the value chain, eg marketing or logistics, rather than trying to cover all activities?)

(c) Are new market prices emerging across segments of the value chain?

(d) If we used these market prices as transfer prices within our company, would it fundamentally change the way any of the operating units behave?

SVA is particularly relevant to vertically integrated companies, because it encourages them to consider whether it would be more profitable for them to **outsource** certain functions or activities rather than continuing to perform them all in-house.

In such a context, the decisions an organisation takes around which activities to produce in-house, and which to outsource, coupled with the way in which it manages its relationships with its outsource partners could, in themselves, help contribute to its strategic capability and competitive advantage.

Section summary

The value chain shows how value is created and how competitive advantage can be gained. Value-adding activities do not stop at the organisation's boundaries, and a firm's value chain is connected to others in a value system.

4 The supply chain and supply chain management

KEY TERM

The SUPPLY CHAIN is the network of organisations involved in the different activities required to transform raw materials into finished goods and services in order to satisfy the requirements of the end customer.

In turn, supply chain management focuses on the interaction and collaborations required throughout the supply chain in order to ensure that the customers' requirements are satisfied adequately.

The ideas behind supply chain management are linked to the value chain and the value system. By establishing **closer links** with companies in the supply chain, firms can obtain best value for money and reduce inventory holdings. The adversarial, arms' length relationship with a supplier is replaced by one which is characterised by closer co-operation.

Supply chain linkage is demonstrated in the diagram on the next page.

4.1 Supply chain model

The supply chain is the network of organisations involved in the different processes and activities necessary to transform raw materials into finished goods and services in order to produce value for the end customer.

There are three main themes to supply chains and supply chain management:

(a) **Responsiveness**: The combination of shortening product life cycles and increasing customer expectations mean firms must be able to supply their customers quickly. Increased integration – for example, electronic data interchanges (EDI) – can be very useful here, allowing orders to be transmitted quickly and accurately.

(b) **Reliability**: Deliveries through the supply chain must be reliable, in terms of timeliness, quality and quantity. Reliability will be greatly assisted by **transparency** in the supply chain: so that upstream firms can see orders placed by customers and deliveries coming from downstream suppliers.

(c) **Relationships**: The need for responsiveness and reliability means that the members of the supply chain need to develop a mutual understanding and trust of each other. In this respect, the supply chain needs to be seen as a network based on collaboration and common interest, instead of the traditional dichotomy of the buyer/seller relationship.

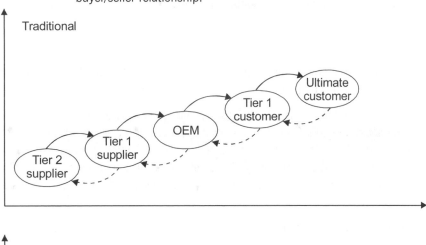

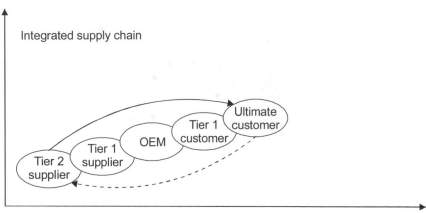

Historically, businesses in the supply chain operated relatively independently of one another to create value for an ultimate customer. Independence was maintained by buffers of material, capacity and lead times. This is represented in the 'Traditional' model shown above.

Market and competitive demands are now **compressing lead times** and businesses are reducing inventories and excess capacity. Linkages between businesses in the supply chain must therefore become tighter. This is shown in the 'Integrated supply chain' model.

Monczka (who developed this supply chain model) further claims that in the future **whole supply chains** will compete, not just individual firms. This will continue to have a great impact upon distribution methods.

In order to deliver their strategies successfully, organisations will need to build and maintain strategic relationships with their suppliers. Therefore, as we identified in Chapter 2, suppliers could be key stakeholders for an organisation. In turn, this could also mean that, for some organisations, supply chain management in itself becomes an important strategic capability.

4.2 'Push' vs 'Pull' models of supply chain processes

All the processes in a supply chain can be classified into one of two categories: 'pull' processes and 'push' processes.

Pull processes are carried out in response to a customer order (in other words, they operate in a 'build to order' context). Push processes are carried out in advance of a customer order, in anticipation of those orders based on a forecast, so they represent a 'make for stock' (inventory) environment.

Crucially, push processes operate in a context of uncertainty, because customer demand is not known. By contrast, pull processes operate in an environment in which customer demand is known. However, they may still be constrained by inventory and capacity decisions which were made during the push phase.

4.2.1 The push model

In a supply chain based on the push model an organisation produces goods according to schedules based on historical sales patterns.

A push-based supply chain is slow to respond to changes in demand, which can result in over-stocking, bottlenecks and delays, unacceptable service levels and product obsolescence. Where there are several links in the distribution chain, the system's inability to respond to variations in consumption leads to the establishment of buffer inventory at each stage of distribution. Poor co-ordination can lead to large fluctuations in the levels of buffer inventory, even where actual consumption patterns vary only marginally.

Features of a push system

- Forecasts of sales drive production and replenishment
- Long-term forecasts
- Inventory pushed to next channel level, often with the aid of trade promotions
- Inability to meet changing demand patterns
- Potential product obsolescence
- Excessive inventory and low service levels
- Bull whip effect

4.2.2 The pull model

Driven by e-commerce to empower clients, many companies are moving to a customer-driven **pull model**, where production and distribution are **demand driven**. The consumer requests the product and 'pulls' it through the delivery channel. There is an emphasis on the supply chain **delivering value to customers** who are actively involved in product and service specifications.

This new business model is less product-centric and more directly focused on the individual consumer. To succeed in the business environment, companies have recognised that there is an ongoing **shift in the balance of power** in the commerce model, from suppliers to customers.

Features of a pull system

- Demand drives production and replenishment
- Centralisation of demand information and of replenishment decision making
- Reduced product obsolescence
- Expanded ability to meet changing demand patterns
- Lower inventories and higher service levels
- Reduced bull whip effect

Push-based systems rely less on sophisticated IS support, since high inventory levels are used to cope with variations in customer demand. Pull-based systems, such as **JIT**, need accurate and quick information on actual demand to move inventory and schedule production in the chain: therefore, they require integrated internal systems and linkages throughout the supply chain.

In reality, most supply chains will include a **combination of both push and pull** processes. The interface between push-based stages and pull-based stages is known as the push-pull boundary.

Dell's build-to-order supply chain can be seen as an example of this. Dell carries an inventory of standard components, and inventory levels of these components are determined by forecasting general demand ('push'). Final assembly then occurs in response to specific customer orders ('pull'). However, a key goal in supply chain management is identifying an appropriate 'push-pull' boundary such that the supply chain matches supply and demand effectively. For Dell, the 'push-pull' boundary would occur at the beginning of the assembly line, where standard components start being used to build a customised PC in response to a customer order.

CASE STUDY

Case study: Zara

As a chain of fashion stores, Zara operates in an industry in which customer demand is rapidly changing and fickle. However, Zara has been able to grow successfully by employing a strategy that combines affordable prices with being highly responsive to changing trends.

Across the apparel industry as a whole, 'design to sales' cycle times have traditionally averaged more than six months. However, Zara has achieved cycle times of four to six weeks. This speed allows Zara to introduce new designs every week and to change 75% of its merchandise display every three to four weeks. As a result, the clothes on display in Zara's shops match customer preferences much more closely than the clothes in competitors' shops do. Consequently, Zara sells most of its products at full price, rather than having to apply markdowns to clear old stock.

Zara manufactures its clothes using a combination of flexible and quick suppliers in Europe and low-cost suppliers in Asia. This model contrasts with the majority of clothing manufacturers which have moved most of their manufacturing to Asia. About 40% of the manufacturing capacity is owned by Zara's parent company (Inditex), with the remainder outsourced.

Products with highly uncertain demand Zara sources from its European suppliers, whereas those with more predictable demand are sourced from Asian suppliers.

More than 40% of Zara's purchases of finished goods, and most of its in-house production, occur after a sales season starts. This compares with less than 20% production after the start of a sales season for a typical clothes retailer. This responsiveness, and the postponement of decisions until after seasonal trends are known, allows Zara to reduce inventories and reduce the risk of error in forecasting demand.

In addition, Zara has invested heavily in information technology to ensure that the latest sales data is available to drive replenishment and production decisions.

(Based on a case study in Chopra, S. & Meindl, P. (2012), *Supply Chain Management*)

4.2.3 Drivers of supply chain performance

The contrast between 'push' and 'pull' processes also identifies a key balancing act at the heart of supply chain management: that is, achieving the balance between **responsiveness** and **efficiency** which best supports a company's competitive strategy. For example, holding high levels of inventory should enable a company to be very responsive to changes in customer demand, but will it be efficient? The goal for a company in relation to supply chain performance is to ensure that they achieve the desired level of responsiveness (to customer demand) at the lowest possible cost.

Chopra and Meindl, in their text *Supply Chain Management*, argue that in order to understand how a company can improve its supply chain performance in terms of responsiveness and efficiency, we first need to examine the drivers of supply chain performance in that company. These drivers, as categorised by Chopra and Meindl, are:

(a) **Facilities** – The actual physical locations in the supply chain network where a product is produced or stored; in effect, property, plant and equipment. Decisions regarding the location, capacity, flexibility and role of different facilities can have a significant impact on performance.

(b) **Inventory** – All raw materials, work in progress, and finished goods within a supply chain. Changing inventory policies can dramatically alter the supply chain's responsiveness and efficiency. As we noted above, a company can make itself responsive by stocking large amounts of inventory and satisfying customer demand from stock, but the high inventory levels reduce efficiency. Such a strategy could be particularly dangerous in the clothing industry, for example, where frequent changes in trend lead to inventory losing value quickly.

(c) **Transportation** – Moving inventory from one point to another in the supply chain. The mode of transport used can have a large impact on responsiveness and efficiency. For example, an online retailer could use a specialist logistics company (such as FedEx) to deliver a product to a customer rather than using the standard postal service. Using a faster mode of transportation makes the supply chain more responsive, but also less efficient, given the relatively higher costs of using the logistics company compared with the traditional postal service.

(d) **Information** – Consists of data and analysis about facilities, inventory, transportation, costs, prices and customers throughout the supply chain. Information is potentially the most important driver of all in the supply chain because it affects each of the other drivers. For example, Zara's supply chain system relies on accurate and timely information about trends in customer demand.

Crucially, information presents management with the opportunity to make supply chains more responsive **and** more efficient.

(e) **Sourcing** – Choosing who will carry out a particular supply chain activity, such as production, storage or transportation. One of the key choices that affects the responsiveness and efficiency of a supply chain is whether to outsource activities or to retain them in-house. Companies can improve efficiency by outsourcing production to contract manufacturers in foreign countries where labour and other operating costs are cheaper. However, responsiveness may suffer as a result of the long distances involved in shipping products to their markets. Similarly, as we saw in the case example earlier, Zara keeps responsive capacity in-house so that it can respond quickly to orders as they arrive.

Note, however, that sourcing does not only relate to production. Online retailers have outsourced next-day package delivery to specialist package carriers because it is too expensive to the retailers to develop next-day delivery capabilities on their own.

(f) **Pricing** – Deciding how much a company will charge for the goods and services it makes available through the supply chain. Pricing affects the behaviour of customers, thereby affecting supply chain performance. For example, if a logistics company varies the prices it charges based on the lead time provided by the customer, it is likely that customers who value efficiency will order early, but customers who value responsiveness will wait until just before they need a product transported to order it.

The table below summarises the differences between responsive and efficient supply chains.

	Responsive supply chains	Efficient supply chains
Primary goal	Respond quickly to changes in demand	Supply demand at the lowest cost
Product design strategy	Create modularity, so that product differentiation comes as late in the product process as possible	Maximise performance at a minimum product cost
Pricing strategy	Higher margins because price is not a prime consideration for customers	Lower margins, because price is a key driver for customers
Manufacturing strategy	Maintain capacity flexibility to buffer against uncertainty in demand and/or supply	Lower costs through high utilisation
Inventory strategy	Maintain buffer inventory to deal with uncertainty in demand and/or supply	Minimise inventory to lower cost
Lead-time strategy	Reduce aggressively, even if the costs of doing so are significant	Reduce where possible, but not at the expense of increasing costs
Supplier strategy	Select suppliers based on speed, flexibility, reliability and quality	Select suppliers based on cost and quality

(Table adapted from Chopra, S. & Meindl, P. (2012), *Supply Chain Management* (5th edition))

Although we have identified the drivers of performance individually, it is also important to realise that they do not act independently of each other. Rather they all interact to determine supply chain performance. Consequently, it is crucial that entities choose supply chain strategies in which the balance between responsiveness and efficiency fits with their overall competitive strategy. For example, a retailer whose strategy is based on a low-cost model for a wide variety of mass-consumption goods is likely to emphasise the elements of efficiency in their supply chain.

In addition, although we have highlighted the contrasts between responsiveness and efficiency in a supply chain, in reality, entities will try to structure their supply chain in a way that maximises responsiveness **and** efficiency.

4.3 Supply chain management

KEY TERM

SUPPLY CHAIN MANAGEMENT. 'The planning and management of all activities involved in sourcing and procurement, conversion, and all logistics management activities. Importantly, it also includes co-ordination and collaboration with channel partners, which can be suppliers, intermediaries, third-party service providers and customers.'   *(The Council of Supply Chain Management Professionals)*

A key element of the definition above is its emphasis on the **inter-organisational** element of supply chain management. Effective supply chain management focuses on interactions and collaborations with **suppliers** and **customers** to ensure that the end customer's requirements are satisfied adequately. All activities in the supply chain should be undertaken with the customer's needs (or requirements) in mind; and, to this end, all supply chains ultimately exist to ensure that a customer's needs are satisfied.

4.3.1 Supply chain management and competitive advantage

Supply chain activities – procurement, inventory management, production, warehousing, transportation, customer service, order management – have all been part of business operations for many years. However, it is only more recently that companies have started to focus on logistics and supply chain management as a potential source of competitive advantage.

Earlier in the chapter we discussed the idea of capabilities and dynamic capabilities. Here, we could argue that supply chain management can now be seen as a capability for an organisation. For example, Seven-Eleven Japan is a company that has used excellent supply chain design, planning and operation to drive growth and profitability. Seven-Eleven has a very responsive replenishment system which, coupled with an excellent information system, ensures that products are available at each of its convenience stores to match customer needs. The responsiveness of Seven-Eleven's system allows it to change the merchandising mix at each store by time of day, to match precisely with customer demand.

Similarly, Amazon is consistently rated as one of the top e-commerce companies in the world. However, critical to Amazon's ongoing business success is maintaining the customer's trust that their orders will be delivered on time and with no errors. Amazon's supply chain and its warehouses are crucial to its performance in this respect.

In *Supply Chain Management*, Chopra and Meindl highlight the importance of the supply chain for organisations when they state: 'Supply chain design, planning, and operation decisions play a significant role in the success or failure of a firm. To stay competitive, supply chains must adapt to changing technology and customer expectations'.

For example, in the 1990s, stores such as Borders and HMV dominated the sales of books and music by implementing a superstore concept. Compared to small independent local retailers, they were able to offer a much greater range of titles to customers, and at a lower cost by aggregating operations in large stores. This allowed the large retailers to achieve higher inventory turns than local retailers, and at higher operating margins. However, the large retailers' business model was itself under attack with the growth of online markets – in particular Amazon, which offered greater variety than Borders and HMV and was able to sell at lower cost by selling online and stock its inventories in a few distribution centres. The inability of Borders, in particular, to adapt its supply chain to compete with Amazon led to its rapid decline.

4.3.2 Elements of supply chain management

Supply chain management is a means by which the firm aims to manage the chain from input resources to the consumer. It involves:

(a) Reduction in the number of suppliers.

(b) Reduction in customers served, in some cases, to focus on customers of high potential value.

(c) Price and inventory co-ordination. Firms co-ordinate their price and inventory policies to avoid problems and bottlenecks caused by short-term surges in demand, such as promotions.

(d) Linked computer systems – EDI saves on paperwork and warehousing expense. The internet and XML allow businesses to have a more automated procurement policy (e-procurement). Technology now also enables firms to track the status of purchases from order to dispatch and delivery.

(e) Early supplier involvement in product development and component design.

(f) Logistics design. Hewlett-Packard restructured its distribution system by enabling certain product components to be added at the distribution warehouse rather than at the central factory, for example user manuals which are specific to the market (ie user manuals in French would be added at the French distribution centre).

(g) Joint problem solving.

(h) Supplier representative on site.

KEY POINT

> The aim is to co-ordinate the whole chain, from raw material suppliers to end customers. The chain should be considered as a **network** rather than a **pipeline** – a network of vendors support a network of customers, with third parties such as transport firms helping to link the companies.

Service level agreements

Given the importance of companies collaborating and working together within the supply chain, it is also important for companies to be able to measure and manage the performance of key partners within the supply chain (for example, to control the number of late or incomplete deliveries).

A key issue will be whether upstream suppliers are delivering the agreed quantity and quality of goods or services on time. However, in order to measure whether the suppliers are meeting such requirements, the requirements first have to be established.

This highlights the importance of establishing service level agreements between organisations and their suppliers.

A service level agreement should include:

(a)   An explanation of the service the supplier has agreed to provide (and details of any information the company has agreed to provide the supplier)

(b)   The benchmarks being used to measure performance, details of how they are measured/calculated, and the implications for failing to meet them

(c)   Procedures for dealing with any complaints arising from the actual level of performance provided, and details of expected response times for responding to any queries or complaints raised

(d)   Procedures for cancelling the contract between the parties

Once a service level agreement is in place, both parties have a structure against which to measure their performance in the relationship, and to assess whether a satisfactory level of performance is being achieved.

4.3.3 Lean supply chain

We looked earlier at the contrast between 'push' and 'pull' approaches to the supply chain, and we can note the similarities between 'pull' and 'lean' supply chains. The objective of developing a lean supply chain is to completely remove waste from the process in order to achieve a competitive advantage.

Advantages	Counter arguments
Reduced cost	Focuses on reducing cost rather than improving quality. Too much cost reduction may actually worsen quality.
Improved quality (and lower costs of reworking and quality problems)	
Reduced inventories	There may be insufficient slack in the system to deal with fluctuations in damage.
Shorter lead times	Lean supply chain consists of a series of preferred supplier relationships. These may be akin to monopolies, so good for firms involved but not for the consumer, because the market operates most efficiently under perfect competition.

CASE STUDY

Li & Fung – which began life as a Hong Kong based export trading company, but has now evolved into a multinational trading, retailing and distribution group – takes the following approach to its manufacturing supply chain.

'Say we get an order from a European retailer to produce 10,000 garments. It's not a simple matter of our Korean office sourcing Korean products or our Indonesian office sourcing Indonesian products. For the customer we might decide to buy yarn from a Korean producer but have it woven and dyed in Taiwan. So we pick the yarn and ship it to Taiwan. The Japanese have the best zippers and buttons, but they manufacture them mostly in China. Okay, so we go to YKK, a big Japanese zipper manufacturer and we order the right zippers from their Chinese plants. Then we determine that, because of quotas and labour conditions, the best place to make the garments is Thailand. So we ship everything there. And because the customer needs quick delivery, we may divide the order across five factories in Thailand. Effectively, we are customising the value chain to best meet the customer's needs.

'Five weeks after we have received the order, 10,000 garments arrive on the shelves in Europe, all looking like they came from one factory with colours, for example, perfectly matched. Just think about the logistics and the co-ordination.

'This is a new type of value added, a truly global product that has never been seen before. The label may say "Made in Thailand", but it's not a Thai product. We dissect the manufacturing process and look for the best solution to each step. We're not asking which country can do the best job overall. Instead, we're pulling apart the value chain and optimising each step – and we're doing it globally … . A classic supply-chain manager in retailing is Marks & Spencer. They don't own any factories, but they have a huge team that goes into the factories and works with the management.'

In turn, Li & Fung itself has evolved from being a sourcing agent to becoming a global supply chain manager by being an innovator in the development of supply chain management.

Through its practice and research in this area, Li & Fung has derived the following **seven principles** which constitute the pillars of its supply chain management methodology.

(a)   Be customer-centric and market demand driven

(b)   Focus on one's own core competency and outsource non-core activities, in order to develop a positioning in the supply chain

(c)   Develop a close risk- and profit-sharing relationship with business partners

(d)   Design, implement, evaluate and continuously improve the workflow, physical flow, information flow and cash flow in the supply chain

(e)   Adopt information technology to optimise the operation of the supply chain

(f)   Shorten production lead time and delivery cycles

(g)   Lower costs in sourcing, warehousing and transportation

4.4 The importance of context

Managing the supply chain **varies from company to company**. A company such as Unilever will provide the same margarine to both Tesco and Sainsbury's. The way in which the product is delivered, transactions are processed and other parts of the relationship are managed will be different since both supermarket chains have their own ways of operating. The focus will need to be on customer interaction, account management, after-sales service and order processing.

A supplier that 'knows' what his customers want does not have to guess or wait until the customer places an order. It will be able to better plan its own delivery systems. The **internet** has allowed customers and suppliers to acquire more up to date information about forecast needs and delivery schedules than ever before.

The greatest changes in supply chain management have taken place in the implementation of **software applications**. Managers today have a wider choice of systems with quick implementation times – important in a competitive market where a new supply chain system is required. Supply chains at local, regional and global level are often managed simultaneously, via a standardised infrastructure that nevertheless allows for local adaptation where this is important.

As well as tactical issues, what might be the underlying strategic concerns?

(a)   Close partnerships are needed with suppliers whose components are essential for the business unit.

(b)   A firm should choose suppliers with a distinctive competence similar to its own. A firm selling 'cheap and cheerful' goods will want suppliers which are able to supply 'cheap and cheerful' subcomponents.

Problems with the **partnership approach** to supply chain management are that:

- Each partner needs to remain competitive in the long term
- There is a possible **loss of flexibility**
- The **relative bargaining power** may make partnership unnecessary
- Arguments about sharing profits may arise

4.5 The scope of supply chain management

The scope of decision making for supply chain professionals has expanded from trying to optimise performance within a division or business unit, then throughout the entity, and now across the entire supply chain – which includes trading partners both **upstream** (eg raw material suppliers and wholesalers) and **downstream** (eg distributors and customers). This reflects the goal of supply chain management, which is to maximise the total profitability of the supply chain.

The recognition of the importance of upstream and downstream processes reinforces the importance of **supplier relationship management** (the upstream interactions between an entity and its suppliers) and **customer relationship management** (the downstream interactions between an entity and its customers).

Chopra and Meindl summarise these different components of supply chain management as a table.

Supplier relationship management	Internal supply chain management	Customer relationship management
• Sourcing	• Strategic planning	• Marketing
• Negotiating contracts	• Demand planning	• Price
• Buying	• Supply planning	• Selling
• Design collaboration	• Fulfilment	• Call centre
• Supply collaboration	• After-sales service (eg setting inventory levels for spare parts)	• Order management

4.5.1 Supplier relationship management

Supplier resources and capabilities are likely to be a critical constraint of supply chain planning. Equally, however, effective collaboration with suppliers can have huge benefits across the supply chain. For example, once an agreement for supply has been established, the entity and the supplier can improve supply chain performance by collaborating on forecasts, production plans and inventory levels (supply collaboration).

There is perhaps even greater benefit to be gained from collaborating with suppliers on the design of products which have positive supply chain characteristics such as, for example, ease of manufacturing, or commonality across several end products (that is, where a single part can be used in a number of different end products, reducing the amount of different parts which need to be held in inventory).

4.5.2 Internal supply chain management

As its name suggests, internal supply chain management focuses on operations internal to an entity and includes all the processes that are involved in planning for, and fulfilling, a customer order. 'Supply planning' lies at the heart of this process. It uses the demand forecasts generated by demand planning, and the resources made available by strategic planning, to produce an optimal plan to meet this demand with the resources available.

4.5.3 Customer relationship management (CRM)

We discuss customer relationship management (CRM) in more detail in the context of strategic marketing in Chapter 8 of this Study Text, but the aim of the CRM process within supply chain management is to generate customer demand and to facilitate the transmission and tracking of customer orders. Weaknesses in this process could lead to poor customer experiences because orders are not processed and executed effectively. However, weaknesses in CRM could also result in lost opportunities to gather information about customer demand, and the factors which influence customer demand.

Including the customer in the supply chain also identifies the role that customers can play in the value creation process. Many retailers now use self-service checkouts, while Ikea's customers create their own value by assembling their furniture at home. However, a more significant way in which customers can create value is through being involved in the product design process ('co-creation'). For example, consumer product manufacturers, including Lego and Nike, have now established online design studios where customers can customise their own products to meet their specific needs.

4.6 Information and supply chain management

So far in this section we have focused mainly on the supply chain as a mechanism for providing goods and services to a customer. However, as Chopra and Meindl remind us, the flow of information through the supply chain is equally important to its efficient operation: 'A supply chain is dynamic and involves the constant flow of **information**, **product and funds** between different stages'.

The following two short examples illustrate this.

CASE STUDY

Case examples: Information, product and funds flows within the supply chain

(i)   Consider first the example of a customer walking into a supermarket to purchase detergent.

       The supply chain begins with the customer and their need for detergent. The next stage of this supply chain is the supermarket store that the customer visits in order to buy the detergent.

       The supermarket replenishes its shelves using inventory which may have been supplied from one of the supermarket's own warehouses, or else by a distributor. In turn, the distributor is stocked by the manufacturer of the detergent.

       The manufacturing plant (where the detergent is produced) receives raw material from a variety of suppliers, which may themselves have been supplied by lower-tier suppliers. For example, the manufacturer receives packaging material from a plastic producer, which may in turn receive the raw materials it needs to manufacture the plastic packaging from other suppliers.

       In this example, the supermarket provides the product, as well as pricing and availability information, to the customer. The customer transfers funds to the supermarket. The supermarket store conveys point of sales data as well as replenishment orders to the warehouse (or the distributor). In turn, the warehouse (or the distributor) provides fresh stocks of the detergent to replenish the store, and the supermarket transfers funds to the distributor to pay for the inventory which has been replenished.

(ii)   When a customer purchases a computer online from Dell, the supply chain includes (among other elements): the customer, Dell's website, Dell's assembly plant, and all of Dell's suppliers and their suppliers.

Dell's website provides the customer with information regarding pricing, product variety and product availability. Having made a product choice, the customer enters their order information, and pays for the product. The customer may later return to the website to check up on the status of their order.

In turn, stages further up the supply chain use the customer information in order to fulfil the request; for example, by supplying the components necessary to assemble the computer.

Having good information helps an entity to utilise its supply chain assets more effectively and to co-ordinate supply chain flows in order to increase responsiveness and reduce costs. For example, Seven-Eleven Japan uses information to improve product availability while decreasing inventories; and airlines routinely use information to decide how many seats to offer at a discount price while leaving sufficient seats for business customers making reservations at the last minute who are willing to pay a higher price.

As Chopra and Meindl note, having 'the right information can help a supply chain better meet customer needs at lower cost. The appropriate investment in information technology improves visibility of transactions and co-ordinaton of decisions across the supply chain.'

We consider information strategy in more detail in Chapter 6 of this Study Text but it is worth noting here some of the ways IT can help managers share and analyse information in the supply chain.

(a) **EDI** – Enabling instantaneous, paperless purchase orders with suppliers.

(b) **Enterprise resource planning (ERP) systems** – Integrating an entity's systems and thereby helping managers co-ordinate production, resources, procurement, inventory, customer orders and sales.

(c) **Radio frequency identification (RFID)** – RFID tags attached to materials or inventory enable an entity to track the movement of inventory between locations more accurately, and to get an exact count of incoming items and items in storage.

(d) **Supply chain management (SCM) software** – Whereas ERP systems show an entity what is currently going on, SCM systems help a company decide what it should plan to do in the future.

We must add one word of caution, however. While good information can clearly help an entity improve both responsiveness and efficiency, this does not automatically mean that simply having **more** information is always better. As more information is shared across a supply chain, the complexity and cost of the infrastructure required and the follow-up analysis increase. However, the marginal value provided by information may diminish as more and more information becomes available.

Hence, entities need to achieve a balance between providing sufficient information so that supply chain activities can be planned and controlled effectively, but without producing unnecessarily complex and detailed information.

4.7 Choosing suppliers

Although there are a few occasions when an organisation has no choice about which supplier to buy goods and services from, in most cases there is a degree of choice, so vendor selection becomes a critical sourcing decision.

How many suppliers will the entity have for a particular activity? (If the entity uses only a small number of suppliers, they could have a high degree of bargaining power over the entity; but if too many are used, and the orders placed with each are small, there is little chance of economies of scale.)

How will it choose its suppliers? Managers need to consider the performance objectives which are most important. An organisation's choice of supplier should take account of factors such as:

(a) The **price** the supplier is charging (relative to other potential suppliers).

(b) Whether the supplier can deliver the required **quality** of product or service.

(c) Whether the supplier has the capacity to deliver the required **quantity** of product.

(d)   Whether the supplier has sufficient spare capacity to increase the quantity if necessary, or deal with special orders at short notice; and whether they are willing to do so (ie **flexibility**).

(e)   How **quickly** the supplier will be able to deliver orders.

(f)   How **reliable** the supplier is at fulfilling orders; on time, in the correct quantity, and to the desired standard of quality.

(g)   Levels of **customer service** and how the supplier handles returns or other problems. (If the organisation is buying a complex product (for example, some software) it should also consider what level of technical support is available if required.)

(h)   Where the supplier is **located**. For multinational companies, there is also a question of whether different suppliers will be needed in different parts of the world.

(i)   The **number of suppliers** the organisation wants to use. Using a small number of suppliers may allow the organisation to benefit from bulk purchase discounts, but could increase the suppliers' bargaining power in relation to the company.

(j)   The credit period and **credit terms** offered.

(k)   Whether the supplier is **financially secure**.

(l)   The **relative size** of the supplier to the company (which will affect the strength of the bargaining power between the organisation and the supplier). However, while using a small supplier may give the organisation more bargaining power over the supplier, it may mean that the supplier is less able to fulfil large orders, or it could be less financially secure.

When choosing suppliers, an organisation should try to select suppliers with distinctive competences that are similar to its own. For example, a company selling high volume, low price products will want suppliers which are able to supply large quantities of low price components.

In Chapter 2 we highlighted the increasing importance of CSR for organisations. Questions of social responsibility can often arise in relation to supply chains: for example, is an organisation treating its suppliers fairly and paying them a fair price for the goods and services they provide? Equally, however, there could be questions around the social responsibility of companies upstream in the supply chain. For example, is a company buying goods from an upstream supplier which provides poor working conditions for its staff? Should the company continue to use that supplier, or should it switch to an alternative supplier?

4.8 E-procurement

The procurement process covers all the activities needed to obtain goods or services from a supplier. However, as with many other areas of business, developments in IT have enabled elements of the procurement process to be automated. **E-procurement** is the purchase of supplies and services through the internet and other information and networking systems, such as EDI. It is typically operated through a secure website, possibly using a paperless system based around a purchasing card.

In turn, e-procurement can be broken down into three components, reflecting the stages of the purchasing process:

E-sourcing is the use of electronic methods for identifying new suppliers.

E-purchasing relates to the process of product selection and ordering.

E-payment is, for example, the generation of electronic invoices and the use of electronic funds transfers to pay for products or services.

Traditionally, e-procurement has been seen as a simple process, from identifying a requirement to purchase something, to placing an electronic purchase order with a supplier, and then paying for the order through an electronic bank payment system such as BACS.

Today, the transactional process is considered to be only part of the e-procurement function as a whole. It includes purchasing, transportation, goods receipt and warehousing before the goods are used. A properly implemented system can connect companies and their business processes directly with suppliers, while managing all interactions between them. This includes management of correspondence, bids, questions and answers, previous pricing, and multiple emails sent to multiple participants.

It focuses on the complete purchasing mix, or the 'five rights of purchasing', which are that goods and services must be delivered:

- At the right **time**
- In the right **quantity**
- At the right **quality**
- At the right **price**
- From the right **vendor**

4.8.1 Methods of e-procurement

Typically, e-procurement websites allow authorised and registered users to log in using a password. The supplying organisation will set up its website so that it recognises the purchaser once they have logged in and presents a list of items that the purchaser regularly buys. This saves searching for the items required and also avoids the need to key in the purchaser's name, address and delivery details. Depending on the approach, buyers or sellers may specify prices or invite bids. Transactions can then be initiated and completed. Once the purchases are made, the purchasing organisation will periodically be billed by the supplier. Ongoing purchases may qualify customers for volume discounts or special offers.

4.8.2 Benefits of e-procurement

Cost reduction	Might include process efficiencies, reduction in the actual cost of goods and services, and reduced purchasing agent overheads.
Reduced inventory levels	Because orders are cheaper to place and process, organisations can afford to place orders more frequently, and can therefore hold lower levels of inventory.
Control	The ability to control parts inventories more effectively. E-procurement also provides greater financial transparency and accountability over the procurement process.
Wider choice of supplier	In theory, resources can be sourced from suppliers anywhere in the world, perhaps at much lower prices than could be obtained if an organisation only considered local suppliers. In this respect, one of the key stages in e-procurement is **e-sourcing**: using electronic methods to find new suppliers and establish contacts with them.
Quicker ordering	The **e-purchasing** element of e-procurement is very important here. E-purchasing allows organisations to select standard items from electronic catalogues and then automatically send electronic purchase orders to the supplier via an extranet.
Intangible benefits	Staff are able to concentrate on their prime function and there is financial transparency and accountability.
Benefits to suppliers	Reduction in ordering and processing costs, reduced paperwork, improved cash flow and reduced cost of credit control.

4.8.3 Risks of e-procurement

(a) **Control**. If anyone can order goods from anywhere, there is a risk that unauthorised purchases will be made. There is also an increased likelihood that purchases will be made from suppliers which cannot deliver the required quality (or cannot deliver at all!).

(b) **Organisational risk**. In moving to an e-procurement tool, an adopting company will make a substantial investment in the software, but for any number of reasons the implementation may

never be successful. Users may not adapt to it well. Suppliers may reject the technology or new process. Technical issues may stall the implementation. Also, managing the internal processes around the changeover is challenging.

(c) **Data security**. Putting a company's spending online means dealing with the security issues that come with any internet-related deployment. This brings up questions such as: Who has access to our data? Where is it stored? How is it protected? What happens if we change providers? Do we get our data back? Do they sell spending data to our competitors?

(d) **Management loses spending control**. There is a perceived risk that moving to e-procurement will put spending decisions in the wrong hands internally and management will lose decision-making control over who spends how much on what.

(e) **Supply chain problems**. Moving to e-sourcing speeds up the sourcing process dramatically, but the increased efficiency and speed can also destabilise the rest of a supply chain if it is not able to step up its performance to meet the increased speed in the purchasing link of the chain.

Section summary

By establishing closer links with companies in the supply chain, firms can obtain best value for money and reduce inventory holdings. Supply chain management is a means by which firms aim to manage the chain from input resources through to the final customer.

5 Outputs: the product portfolio

Introduction

Many firms make a number of different products or services. Each product or service has its own financial, marketing and risk characteristics. The combination of products or services influences the attractiveness and profitability of the firm.

5.1 The product life cycle

The **product life cycle** concept holds that products have a life cycle, and that a product demonstrates different characteristics of profit and investment at each stage in its life cycle. The life cycle concept is a model, not a prediction. (Not all products pass through each stage of the life cycle.) It enables a firm to examine its portfolio of goods and services as a whole.

The profitability and sales of a product can be expected to change over time. The **product life cycle** is an attempt to recognise distinct stages in a product's sales history. Marketing managers distinguish between different aspects of the product.

(a) **Product class**: This is a broad category of product, such as cars, washing machines and newspapers – also referred to as the **generic product**.

(b) **Product form**: Within a product class products take different forms, for example five-door hatchback cars and two-seater sports cars.

(c) **Brand**: The particular type of the product form (eg Ford Focus).

The product life cycle applies in differing degrees to each of the three cases. A product class (eg cars) may have a long maturity stage, and a particular make or brand (eg Rolls-Royce) **might** have an erratic life cycle or not. However, product forms tend to conform to the classic life cycle pattern.

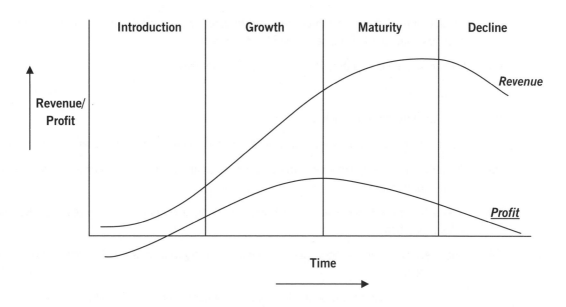

5.1.1 Introduction

(a)   Sales growth is slow to begin with, and sales are low.

(b)   Unit costs are high due to low output and costly promotions.

(c)   Marketing costs are high in order to get the product recognised by customers and to encourage them to try it.

(d)   The product is loss-making (or generates only very low profit) due to the low sales and high distribution and promotion expenses. Similarly, the product will have negative cash flows.

(e)   Firms focus their marketing on those buyers who are most ready to buy ('innovators' or 'early adopters').

(f)   Product range is limited, and firms usually produce basic versions of a product to begin with.

(g)   Product risk is high, because it is new and has not yet been accepted by the market.

(h)   The product has few, if any, competitors (either because they have not yet developed a rival product, or because they are not willing to take similar risks in launching it yet).

Pricing strategy will be influenced by price elasticity of demand. If demand is likely to be inelastic, **price skimming** is appropriate. If demand is expected to be elastic and/or gaining market share is an important objective, **penetration pricing** is likely to be appropriate.

5.1.2 Growth

(a)   If the new product gains market acceptance, sales will eventually rise more sharply and the product will start to make profits.

(b)   Capital investments are needed to fulfil levels of demand, meaning cash flows remain lower than profit. However, cash flows increase as sales increase and the market becomes profitable.

(c)   Competitors are attracted with similar products but, as sales and production rise, unit costs fall (eg due to economies of scale).

(d)   Sales for the market as a whole increase.

(e)   Need to add additional features to differentiate from competitors as buyers become more sophisticated. Product complexity is likely to rise. Alternatively, a firm may choose to lower price and compete on price grounds.

(f)   Continued marketing expenditure required to differentiate the firm's product from competitors' offerings. New market segments may be developed.

(g)   Growth sustained by attracting new types of customers.

5.1.3 Maturity

(a)   Sales growth rate slows down.

(b)   Sales increasingly result from repeat or replacement purchases, rather than new customers.

(c)   Slowdown in sales growth leads to overcapacity (market saturation), as many producers have many products to sell.

(d)   Overcapacity leads to greater competition – marking down prices, and increasing advertising and sales promotions.

(e)   Price becomes more sensitive, as firms compete to try to increase their share of a relatively fixed-size market.

(f)   Producers increase their product development budgets to try to find better versions of a current product.

(g)   Producers may also look to capitalise on existing brand names by launching spin-off products, or they may modify a product (eg by improving quality, features and performance) in order to attract new users or to inspire greater usage.

(h)   Successful products evolve to meet changing consumer needs and demands.

(i)   Companies also try to develop the market – to find new users and new market segments for products and brands.

(j)   Increased competition leads to a decrease in profit. (Maximum profit is reached during this stage, but profits will start to fall as supply exceeds demand.)

(k)   Some of the weaker competitors leave the market.

(l)   Environmental analysis is important. Firms need to detect or anticipate changes in the market so that they can be ready to undertake modifications in their product–market strategies to prolong their product's life cycle.

(m)   Similarly, firms need defensive strategies to protect their current positions from competitors.

5.1.4 Decline

(a)   Sales fall (eg due to technological advances or shifts in consumer tastes meaning that the product becomes superceded).

(b)   Prices fall as firms try to maintain customer numbers from a diminishing customer base.

(c)   As sales – and profit – decline, some firms withdraw from the market.

(d)   The remaining firms may try to reposition or reinvigorate their products/brands in the hope of moving it back into the growth stage of their life cycles, or to find a profitable niche in the market.

(e)   Some producers may rationalise their produce offerings (eg withdrawing from some market segments, and cutting the advertising budget).

(f)   Investment is kept to a minimum.

Television sets

CASE STUDY

Over time, the design and specification of television sets has changed. Black and white screens have been superseded by colour; cathode ray tubes have been superseded by flat screen and plasma screens; and manufacturers have developed home cinema systems.

However, the switch to online distribution methods of video content is also now having significant implications for the television set industry, and there are already indications that viewer habits are changing.

Online TV, mobile phone TV and free TV catch-up services offered by the major channels, and other platforms on which to view them (eg tablets), give viewers much greater choice and flexibility allowing them to watch programmes at their own convenience.

To prevent decline, the TV industry has had to adapt to cope with the changes and internet-enabled television has emerged. 3D televisions have also been developed to differentiate television from internet viewing and to capitalise on the changes in the cinema industry.

5.1.5 The relevance of the product life cycle to strategic planning

In reviewing outputs, planners should assess products in three ways in order to determine an appropriate strategy.

(a)   The **stage of its life cycle** that any product has reached. For example, in the growth stage, a firm's strategy might focus on trying to differentiate its product from competitors', and it might have to incur high marketing costs to achieve this. However, for a mature product, the focus will be on controlling costs.

(b)   The **product's remaining life**, ie how much longer it will contribute to profits.

(c)   How **urgent is the need to innovate**, to develop new and improved products?

A product's stage in its life cycle can also affect the suitability of different performance measures. Traditional performance measures (such as return on capital employed and return on investment (ROI)) are most applicable for the mature phase, but are less useful in the introduction or growth phases when the focus is on investing for future success.

Firms should also consider the range of products (or services) they offer, and what stages they are at in their life cycles. For example, mature products (which generate positive cash flows) could help fund the development of new products. This idea of creating a portfolio of products is expanded further in the BCG matrix.

5.1.6 Difficulties of the product life cycle concept

(a)   **Recognition**. How can managers recognise where a product is in its life cycle?

(b)   **Not always true**. Some products have no maturity phase, and go straight from growth to decline. Some never decline if marketed competitively.

(c)   **Descriptive not predictive**. Managers cannot use the life cycle to predict future sales, because the model describes general trends, rather than having any value for detailed predictions.

(d)   **Changeable**. Strategic decisions can change or extend a product's life cycle.

(e)   **Competition varies** in different industries. The financial markets are an example of markets where there is a tendency for competitors to copy the leader very quickly, so that competition has built up well **ahead** of demand.

(f)   **Focus on the product**. Sometimes a customer group or market is a better unit of strategic analysis than a single product. A product may be at different stages of its life cycle in different **markets**.

(g)   **Lack of clarity** about 'the product'. For example, for a car manufacturer, is its 'product' a car in general terms, a type of car (eg petrol vs diesel car) or a specific brand or model of car?

(h)   **Single product only**. The model only looks at a single product at a time. It does not consider the connections between that product and other products in a company's product portfolio. For

example, are some products which are mature necessary in order to attract customers who will then buy products which are in their growth stage?

5.1.7 The industry life cycle concept

In the same way we can identify a product life cycle, it may also be possible to discern an **industry life cycle**, which will have wider implications for the nature of competition and competitive advantage.

An industry is a group of firms producing the same product or products that are close substitutes for one another. So, the stages of the industry life cycle do not relate just to products, but to aspects such as the number of competitors in the industry, the number of customers, and the level of profits which firms can sustain.

This cycle reflects changes in demand and the spread of technical knowledge among producers. Innovation creates the new industry, and this is normally product innovation. Later, innovation shifts to processes in order to maintain margins. The overall progress of the industry life cycle is illustrated below.

	Introduction	Growth	Maturity	Decline
Products	Basic, no standards established	Better, more sophisticated, differentiated	Superior, standardised	Varied quality but fairly undifferentiated
Competitors	None to few	Many entrants Little concentration in industry	Competition increases, weaker players leave	Few remain. Competition may be on price
Buyers	Early adopters, innovators	More customers attracted	Mass market, brand switching common	Enthusiasts, traditionalists, sophisticates
Profits	Negative	Increasing as sales increase rapidly	High, but beginning to decline	Falling, as sales and prices have fallen
Objectives and strategy	Build product awareness Dominate market, build quality	Try to maximise market share React to competitors with marketing spend	Maximise profit while defending market share Cost reductions sought	Control costs Possibly harvest or divest

Notice the last row in the table: objectives and strategy. This is important because it highlights that the most suitable strategy for a firm to adopt is likely to depend on the stage of the industry in its life cycle.

5.1.8 Life cycles and marketing strategy

Kotler and Keller (in *Marketing Management*) also highlight that a firm should analyse its industry's – or a product's – position in its life cycle when formulating a marketing strategy.

	Introduction	Growth	Maturity	Decline
Marketing objectives	Create product awareness and get customers to try the product	Maximise market share	Maximise profit while defending market share	Reduce expenditure, and 'milk' the brand
Product	Offer a basic product	Offer product extensions, service, warranties	Diversify brands and models	Phase out weak items
Price	Cost-plus pricing	Penetration pricing (to increase sales volume and market share)	Price to match or beat competitors	Cut price
Distribution	Build selective distribution channels	Build intensive distribution (increase the number of markets in which the product is available, and the number of potential customers it is available to)	Build more intensive distribution	Go selective: phase out unprofitable outlets
Advertising	Build product awareness among early adopters	Build awareness and interest in the mass market	Emphasise brand differences and benefits	Reduce advertising, and focus on retaining hard-core loyals
Sales promotion	Use sales promotions to entice customers to try the product	Reduce to take advantage of heavy consumer demand	Increase to encourage brand switching	Reduce to minimal level

5.2 Portfolio planning

Portfolio analysis examines the current status of the organisation's products and their markets. Portfolio analysis is the first stage of **portfolio planning**, which aims to create a balance among the organisation's market offerings in order to maximise competitive advantage.

Four **major strategies** can be pursued with respect to products, market segments and, indeed, SBUs.

(a) **Build**. A build strategy forgoes short-term earnings and profits in order to increase market share. This could be achieved either through organic growth, or through external growth (acquisition; strategic alliances etc).

(b) **Hold**. A hold strategy seeks to maintain the current position, defending it from the threat of would-be 'attackers' as necessary.

(c) **Harvest**. A harvesting strategy seeks short-term earning and profits at the expense of long-term development.

(d) **Divest**. Disposal of a poorly performing business unit or product. Divestment stems the flow of cash to a poorly performing area of the business and releases resources for use elsewhere.

5.2.1 The Boston classification (BCG matrix)

The **Boston classification** (BCG matrix) classifies products or business units in terms of their capacity for growth within the market and the market's capacity for growth as a whole. A firm should have a balanced **portfolio of products or business units**. The GE Business Screen and the Shell matrix are similar tools.

The Boston Consulting Group **(BCG) matrix** assesses a company's products in terms of potential cash generation and cash expenditure requirements. Products or SBUs are categorised in terms of **market growth rate** and a firm's **relative market share**.

KEY TERMS

RELATIVE MARKET SHARE: 'One entity's sales of a product or service in a specified market compared to the total sales earned by the largest entity offering that product or service.'

(a) The rate of **market growth** depends on market conditions, and new markets often grow explosively while mature ones grow hardly at all. As a guide, 10% is often used as a dividing line between high and low growth. High market growth rate can indicate good opportunities for profitable operations. However, intense competition in a high growth market can erode profit, while a market which is growing slowly, but with high barriers to entry, can be very profitable.

(b) **Relative market share** is assessed as a ratio: it is a firm's market share compared with the market share of the **largest competitor**. A relative market share greater than one indicates that the product or SBU is the market leader, and this is used as the dividing line between high and low relative market share. Therefore, only market leaders (with a relative market share greater than one) should be said to have a high relative market share.

The BCG matrix uses market share to estimate costs associated with given products. This is used as there is a connection between lower costs and higher market share. However, **correlation does not necessarily prove causation**: just because a firm is large doesn't necessarily mean its costs are lower than a smaller firm's would be.

(c) Note that there is an unspoken assumption that the **market** itself is easily defined. This may not be the case and it is likely that much thought will have to be given to this problem, even if only to decide whether the analysis should be in terms of brand, generic product or product form.

(d) Be aware also that the **matrix ignores potential links between products**. However, it is important to consider such links: for example, if a firm stops producing one product will it have a knock-on effect on, say, other products?

| | *Relative market share* | |
	High	*Low*
High *Market growth*	Stars	Question marks
Low	Cash cows	Dogs

The product portfolio should be balanced, with cash cows providing finance for stars and question marks; and a minimum of dogs.

(a) **Stars**. In the short term, these require capital expenditure in excess of the cash they generate, in order to maintain their market position, and to defend their position against competitors' attack strategies, but they promise high returns in the future. Strategy: **build**.

(b) In due course, stars will become **cash cows**. Cash cows need very little capital expenditure (because opportunities for growth are low) and generate high levels of cash income. However, apparently mature products can be invigorated, possibly by competitors, who could come to dominate the market. Cash cows can be used to finance the stars or question marks which are in their development stage. Strategies: **hold**, or **harvest** if weak.

(c)   **Question marks**. Do the products justify considerable capital expenditure in the hope of increasing their market share, or will they be squeezed out of the expanding market by rival products? Question marks have the potential to become stars if they are successfully developed. However, if their development is not successful, they may end up consuming a great deal of investment and management time but ending up as 'problem adults' rather than stars as had been intended. Strategies: **build, harvest or divest**.

(d)   **Dogs**. They may be ex-cash cows that have fallen on hard times. Although they will show only a modest net cash outflow, or even a modest net cash inflow, they are cash traps which tie up funds and provide a poor ROI. However, they may have a useful role, either to complete a product range or to keep competitors out. There are also many smaller niche businesses in a market that are difficult to consolidate that would count as dogs but which are quite successful. Strategies: **divest** or **hold**.

Although developed for use with a product portfolio, the BCG matrix is also used in diversified conglomerates to assess the strategic position of subsidiary **SBUs**. This is an important point to note: the BCG matrix can be applied either to a **product portfolio** or a **business portfolio**.

The BCG matrix offers management a simple and convenient way of looking at a diverse range of businesses and products, within a single overall portfolio. In doing so, it encourages management to look at the portfolio as a whole rather than simply assessing the needs and performance of each unit independently. For example, the portfolio would allow a group of companies to consider the cash flow requirements of the group as a whole rather than focusing on individual units in isolation.

Also, the matrix should help management with long-term strategic planning: for example, by highlighting the need for new question marks or stars to be developed, to eventually replace the current crop of cash cows. In this respect, the matrix may also highlight the need for a firm to consider acquisitions if its portfolio is currently unbalanced, and only offers limited opportunities for growth and development.

However, critics argue the axes are too simplistic.

(a)   A high market share is assumed to indicate competitive strength but this is not necessarily true.

(b)   A strong brand may yield competitive strength despite a relatively low market share.

(c)   High market growth is deemed to indicate an attractive industry. But fast-growing industries are likely to require significant investment, so they may not be attractive to a firm with limited available capital.

(d)   The requirement that firms have a high relative market share is justified by the ability of large producers to benefit from scale economies and experience effects, and thereby to assist in surviving price pressure in late life cycle markets. However, following a **differentiation** strategy or a **niche** strategy allows a firm to prosper even with a small relative share.

(e)   The approach sees the board as working on behalf of shareholders as a super-investor seeking to balance the demands of cash returns now with future growth to make the firm's equity attractive. This overlooks other synergies from combining businesses together in the same portfolio, such as cross-selling, supply and demand integration, and knowledge spreading.

  Question 4.3   Juicy drinks

Learning outcome B2(b)

The marketing manager of Juicy Drinks Co has invited you in for a chat. Juicy Drinks Co provides fruit juices to a number of supermarket chains, which sell them under their own label.

'We've got a large number of products, of course. Our freshly squeezed orange juice is doing fine – it sells in huge quantities. Although margins are low, we have sufficient economies of scale to do very nicely in this market. We've got advanced production and bottling equipment and long-term contracts with some major growers. No problems there. We also sell freshly squeezed pomegranate juice: customers loved it in

the tests, but producing the stuff at the right price is a major hassle: all the seeds get in the way. We hope it will be a winner, once we get the production right and start converting customers to it. After all, the market for exotic fruit juices generally is expanding fast.'

What sort of products, according to the Boston classification, are described here?

5.2.2 The General Electric Business Screen (GEBS)

The approach of the GE Business Screen (GEBS) is similar to that of the BCG matrix. The GEBS includes a broader range of company and market factors. This matrix **classifies products (or businesses)** according to **industry attractiveness** and **company strengths**. The approach aims to consider a variety of factors which contribute to both these variables.

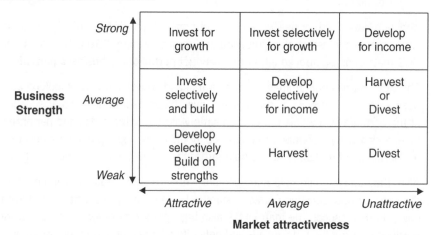

	Strong	Invest for growth	Invest selectively for growth	Develop for income
Business Strength	Average	Invest selectively and build	Develop selectively for income	Harvest or Divest
	Weak	Develop selectively Build on strengths	Harvest	Divest
		Attractive	Average	Unattractive

Market attractiveness

The broader approach of the GE matrix attempts to match competences within the company to conditions within the marketplace. Difficulties associated with measurement and classification mean that again the results must be interpreted with care.

5.2.3 The Shell directional policy matrix

There have been several other matrices designed as guides to strategy. The **Shell directional policy matrix** is similar to the GEBS in that its classifications depend upon **managerial judgement** rather than numerical scores, as in the BCG matrix. Its axes are **competitive capability** and **prospects for sector profitability**. Clearly, these measures are very similar to those used in the GEBS.

Prospects for sector profitability

		Unattractive	Average	Attractive
	Weak	Disinvest	Phased withdrawal	Double or quit
Enterprise's competitive capabilities	Average	Phased withdrawal	Custodial Growth	Try harder
	Strong	Cash generation	Growth Leader	Leader

(a)   **Double or quit** – SBUs in this sector have the potential to be major sources of profit in the future, but the corporate parent has to take a gamble on them fulfilling their potential. However, if the parent is not prepared to invest in the SBU, then it should withdraw from it.

(b)   **Growth** – Grow the market by focusing just enough resources here (for example to support product innovations, R&D).

(c)   **Custodial** – SBUs in this category resemble cash cows in the BCG matrix. The parent needs to 'milk' units in this category, but should not commit any more resources to them.

(d)   **Try harder** – The corporate parent needs to try harder to exploit the prospects offered by these SBUs. Although they are competing satisfactorily at the moment, they could be vulnerable over a longer period of time, and need additional resources to strengthen their capabilities.

(e)   **Cash generator** – This category resembles the cash cow quadrant of the BCG matrix even more closely; generating strong cash flows and earning satisfactory profits. The cash generated by SBUs in this category should be used to fund expansion elsewhere in a group.

(f)   **Phased withdrawal** – SBUs with a weak competitive position and with little scope for generating cash should gradually be phased out. Cash and investment should be moved away from these SBUs, and invested in ones with greater potential.

(g)   **Divest** – A corporate parent should look to divest SBUs which are loss-making or have uncertain cash flows, and whose performance is unlikely to improve in the future. The parent should liquidate or move these assets.

(h)   **Leader** – These SBUs should receive top priority within the group, and should be the primary focus for resources and investment.

5.2.4 Problems with portfolio planning

In addition to the questionable assumptions that the market is easy to define and that low cost is a result of experience, there are other important criticisms of the portfolio matrix approach.

(a)   Its recommendations are oversimplistic and ignore **innovation**.

(b)   It ignores links between products. A successful product can be damaged if a less successful one is discontinued or starved of funds. **Completeness of range** is important to both consumers and distributors.

(c)   It considers the position of the market leader but **ignores other rivals** that may be growing more effectively.

Also, it is difficult to put into practice as it gives no guidance on:

(a)   How the market position of the products should be **improved** – ie how much extra or less market share to go for

(b)   What the **mix** of question marks, stars and cash cows ought to be

(c)   How a policy of developing question marks into stars and stars into cash cows can be implemented in **practice**

5.3 Direct product profitability

Management accountants may be asked to review the profitability of a product or product line. This can be done using direct product profitability analysis.

5.3.1 Direct product profitability (DPP)

Direct product profitability (DPP) is a technique to analyse the profit on each individual product line, to arrive at relative profitability of different products.

KEY TERM

DIRECT PRODUCT PROFITABILITY is a measure 'used primarily within the retail sector, (and) involves the attribution of both the purchase price and other indirect costs (for example distribution, warehousing and retailing) to each product line. Thus a net profit, as opposed to a gross profit, can be identified for each product. The cost attribution process utilises a variety of measures (for example warehousing space and transport time) to reflect the resource consumption of individual products.'   (*CIMA Official Terminology*)

DPP arose from the need for manufacturers to encourage retailers to place new products onto their shelves. Supermarkets analyse the direct profitability of every branded and non-branded product they sell. This helps them decide on what ranges to present in store and provides a focus for individual marketing initiatives. The profitability of entire commodity groups is presented after taking account of factors in addition to cost, such as supplier discounts and wastage levels.

DPP is calculated by determining the sales revenue from a product (less any discounts or refunds given) and then deducting the costs incurred by stocking that product. These costs will be:

*   The purchase price charged by the supplier (less any discounts)
*   The costs of ordering the product
*   The costs of storing the product
*   Transport costs incurred in getting the product to its point of sale
*   Wastage and obsolescence

It is useful to analyse how DPP can be used in practice. In the following example, we can take the limiting factor to be shelf space.

	Product		
	X	*Y*	*Z*
Selling price	£1.50	£1.25	£1.30
Purchase cost	£1.00	£0.80	£1.00
Gross profit	£0.50	£0.45	£0.30
Gross profit % of sales price	33%	36%	23%
Shelf space per unit	15 cm^2	9 cm^2	12 cm^2
Gross profit per cm^2	3.3p	5p	2.5p

This would imply that Y was the most profitable for the retailer: however, this ignores stock turnover. In other words, if sales volumes of Y are higher than for X or Z, the product makes a higher profit in total. Let us add sales volumes into the calculation and estimate how much shelf space the product takes up.

	Product		
	X	*Y*	*Z*
Gross profit per product	£0.50	£0.45	£0.30
Total shelf space	750 cm^2	600 cm^2	1,200 cm^2
Weekly sales volume	30	20	60
Gross profit per cm^2 per week	$\dfrac{50p \times 30}{750} = 2p$	$\dfrac{45p \times 20}{600} = 1.5p$	$\dfrac{30p \times 60}{1,200} = 1.5p$

This analysis, based on sales volume, suggests that for the retailer X is the better bet. Why might this be so?

(a)   **Inventory turnover**. The manufacturer of X might offer to replenish the shelves twice a week, thereby halving the amount of space needed to support the same sales volume. This increases the profit per unit of scarce resource.

(b)   **Product size**, as indicated, is a reason why the unit profit might differ. This is why packaging decisions can, from the retailer's viewpoint, affect a product's attractiveness.

This example demonstrates the importance of obtaining sufficient information before a meaningful analysis can be carried out. Simple information on cm^2 occupied per unit was insufficient. Sales volumes,

total shelf space required and probably in some cases additional direct costs (such as handling and administration) all need to be taken into account.

DPP can also be useful in a **marketing context**. There are two broad approaches to marketing: one is that products are the source of an organisation's profits, the other is that customers are the source of profits. (We look at marketing in more detail in a later chapter of this Study Text.)

DPP can be useful in the first of these approaches to marketing, because it suggests that the way to commercial success is to make (and sell) more of the products which generate the highest product profitability.

However, DPP analysis might also lead companies to try alternative ways of increasing product profitability: for example, by reducing the costs of stocking the product by reducing the size of product packaging.

Alternatively, manufacturers may directly reduce retailers' costs in selling their product by offering point of sale support. For example, a frozen food manufacturer may provide a retailer with a refrigerator unit in which to store their products in the shop. This will increase the DPP of that supplier's products compared to rival products for which the supermarket may have to provide its own refrigeration units and so may influence which supplier the supermarket buys its products from.

Problems with DPP

(a)   Brand expenditure can be spread over a number of different products, making accurate allocation difficult.

(b)   DPP focuses internally on product characteristics, but in doing so ignores the needs of the customers.

(c)   **Cross-subsidisation** is a feature of many product strategies. An example is provided by computer games.

(i)   The hardware (eg the games console) may be priced relatively cheaply to:

- Deter competitors (raising entry barriers)
- Encourage customers to buy

(ii)   The software, or games which are run, will be priced relatively expensively, to recoup some of the cost. Also, barriers to entry will exist as the manufacturer will own patents, have exclusive distribution deals etc, and there will be a switching cost, of course.

However, DPP overlooks these interrelations between products.

Section summary

The **product life cycle** shows that, generally, products pass through four stages: introduction, growth, maturity and decline. Portfolio planning aims to create a balance among the firm's products in order to maximise competitive advantage. Matrices such as the Boston classification (BCG matrix), the GE Business Screen, and the Shell matrix can assist firms in achieving a balanced portfolio of products.

6 New products and innovation

Introduction

Innovation can be a major source of competitive advantage but brings a burden of cost and uncertainty. To avoid waste, there should be a programme of assessment for major product development.

6.1 Innovation

This section looks at how an organisation can develop its capacity for new products. This idea is developed further in Chapter 5, where we assess how product development can be used as a strategy for growth.

However, more generally, an organisation's ability to develop new ideas and combine existing ones to create new sources of value could also be an important strategic capability. For example, if a number of the products in the organisation's portfolio have reached the mature phase of their life cycle, or are starting to decline, the organisation will need to develop new products to replace them.

In this section, we look at innovation as an internal activity and as a source of organic growth. Alternatively, however, an organisation whose products are maturing might look to acquire another company with a capability for innovation or with a number of products which are at an earlier stage in their life cycle.

6.1.1 Innovation and competitive advantage

For many organisations, product innovation and being the **first mover** may be a major source of competitive advantage.

(a)   A reputation for innovation will attract **early adopters**, though it depends in part on promotional effort.

(b)   Customers may find they are locked in to innovative suppliers by unacceptable **costs of switching** to competitors.

(c)   The **learning** (or experience) **curve** effect may bring cost advantages.

(d)   The first mover may be able to **define the industry standard**.

(e)   A **price skimming** strategy can bring early profits that will be denied to later entrants.

(f)   Legal protection, such as patents, for intellectual property may bring important revenue advantages. This is particularly important in the pharmaceutical industry.

However, the first mover also has particular problems:

- Gaining regulatory approval where required
- Uncertain demand
- High levels of R&D costs
- Lower cost imitators
- Costs of introduction such as training sales staff and educating customers

Profit Impact of Market Strategy data indicate that there is a **negative correlation** between **profitability** and a high level of expenditure on **R&D**, perhaps because of the costs associated with these problems.

6.1.2 Technology and the value chain

Porter points out, in his text *Competitive Advantage*, that 'every value activity uses some technology to combine purchased inputs and human resources to produce some output'. He discusses the varied role of IT and emphasises the importance of administrative or office technology. The significance of this for strategy lies in the area of core competences. Just as R&D is as much concerned with processes as with products, so improvement in the linkages of the value chain will enhance competitive advantage.

6.2 New product strategies

The development of new products might be considered an important aspect of a firm's competitive and marketing strategies.

(a)   New and innovative products can lower **entry barriers** to existing industries and markets, if new technology is involved.

(b)   The interests of the company are best met with a balanced product portfolio. Managers must plan when to introduce new products, how best to extend the life of mature ones and when to abandon those in decline.

A strategic issue managers must consider is their approach to new product development.

(a)   Features of a **Leader strategy**:

- An innovative strategy is taken to gain competitive advantage
- Heavy **R&D** emphasis
- Shortened likely length of product life cycles
- Reduced potential profitability due to high **R&D costs**

(b)   Features of a **Follower strategy**:

- Lower costs

- Less emphasis on **R&D**

- Sacrifices early rewards of innovation but avoids its risks

- May have to license certain technologies from a leader

- Can be a **more profitable strategy** especially when the follower can learn from the leader's mistakes

A matrix of new product strategies and new market strategies can be set out as follows.

| | *Product* | | |
	No technological change	*Improved technology*	*New technology*
Market unchanged	–	*Reformulation* A new balance between price/quality has to be formulated	*Replacement* The new technology replaces the old
Market strengthened (ie new demand from same customers)	*Remerchandising* The product is sold in a new way – eg by repackaging	*Improved product* Sales growth to existing customers sought on the strength of product improvements	*Product line extension* The new product is added to the existing product line to increase total demand
New market	*New use* By finding a new use for the existing product, new customers are found	*Market extension* New customers sought on the strength of product improvements	*Diversification*

6.3 Research and development (R&D)

Research may be **pure**, **applied** or **development**. It may be intended to improve **products** or **processes**. New product development should be controlled by requiring strategic approval at key points of development.

R&D should support the organisation's strategy and be closely co-ordinated with marketing.

6.4 Product and process research

There are two categories of R&D.

PRODUCT RESEARCH is based on creating new products and developing existing ones.

KEY TERMS

PROCESS RESEARCH is based on improving the way, or efficiency with which, those products or services are made or delivered.

Product research – new product development

The product development process must be carefully controlled. New products are a major source of competitive advantage but are expensive to bring to market. A screening process is necessary to ensure that resources are concentrated on projects with a high probability of success and not wasted on those that have poor prospects.

Idea generation and **strategy formulation** are also important features of new product development.

(a) To be effective, **idea generation** requires a system to promote and reward creativity and innovative ideas. Cooper suggests a four-point plan.

    (i) Nominate one manager to be the **focal point for ideas**.
    (ii) That manager establishes where ideas may **arise**.
    (iii) Those sources are **encouraged**.
    (iv) The ideas they produce are **captured**.

(b) **Strategy formulation**. A business should have a detailed new product strategy, specifying goals, priorities, funding and methods. This is a top management responsibility.

Product research is not confined to dealing with new products. It has an important role in connection with **existing products**.

(a) **Value engineering** may be used to continue the development of existing products so that they use cheaper components or processes without compromising the perceived value of the market offer.

(b) As products near the end of their **life cycle**, it may be possible to develop them for launch in a different market, or simply to extend their lives.

(c) Where products are replaced by new versions it may be advantageous to ensure new products are **backwards compatible** with the installed base. This is an important consideration in software engineering, for example.

6.5 Process research

Process research looks at how the goods/services are produced and has the following aspects.

(a) **Processes** are crucial in service industries (eg fast food), where processes are part of the services sold.

(b) **Productivity**. Efficient processes save money and time.

(c) **Planning**. If you know how long certain stages in a project are likely to take, you can plan the most efficient sequence.

(d) **Quality management** for enhanced quality.

Advances in process research are much harder to imitate than product developments. Competitors can purchase and **reverse engineer** new products but, with good physical security in place, they will find it much harder to imitate new processes.

The strategic role of R&D. R&D should support the organisation's chosen strategy. For example, if a strategy of **differentiation** has been adopted, it would be inappropriate to research ways of minimising costs. If the company has a competence in R&D, this may form the basis for a strategy of product innovation. Conversely, where product life cycles are short, as in consumer electronics, product development is fundamental to strategy.

Customer needs, as identified by marketers, should be a vital input to new product developments.

The R&D department might identify possible changes to product specifications so that a variety of marketing mixes can be tried out and screened.

6.6 Problems with R&D

(a) **Organisational**. Problems of authority relationships and integration arise with the management of R&D. The function will have to liaise closely with marketing and with production, as well as with senior management responsible for corporate planning: its role is both strategic and technical.

(b) **Financial**. R&D is by nature not easily planned in advance, and financial performance targets are not easily set. Budgeting for long-term, complex development projects with uncertain returns can be a nightmare for management accountants.

(c) **Evaluation and control**. Pure research or even applied research may not have an obvious payoff in the short term. Evaluation could be based on successful application of new ideas, such as patents obtained and the commercial viability of new products.

(d) **Staff problems**. Research staff are usually highly qualified and profession-oriented, with consequences for the style of supervision and level of remuneration offered to them.

(e) **Cultural problems**. Encouraging innovation means trial and error, flexibility, tolerance of mistakes in the interests of experimentation, high incentives etc. If this is merely a subculture in an essentially bureaucratic organisation, it will not only be difficult to sustain, but will also become a source of immense 'political' conflict. The R&D department may have an 'academic' or university atmosphere, as opposed to a commercial one.

6.6.1 Drivers for innovation

Market pull: Marketers suggest that the best way to competitive advantage is to find out what the market wants and give it to them.

Technology push: Unfortunately, market pull innovation tends merely to produce better versions of products that already exist. A more fruitful approach may be 'product orientation'. The world is full of products that no one asked for, including post-it notes and mobile phones that are also cameras. This approach we might call **technology push**.

Collaboration: Perhaps the best approach would be a combination of the two, where technologists try to solve customers' problems and marketers try to find applications for new and emerging technologies. Many new developments are the result of **collaboration between suppliers and customers**.

CASE STUDY

Procter & Gamble – Open innovation

Historically, companies have looked for their own staff to provide them with their sources of innovation and new products. However, why should a company restrict the generation of new ideas to its own staff? There are many external sources – for example, scientists, engineers, universities and other companies – who could all have the know-how and technical expertise to contribute to new product development.

As with many mature organisations, in 2000 Procter & Gamble's R&D productivity was flat, while innovation costs were increasing faster than sales growth. Therefore, the CEO at the time challenged the company to stop spending more and more on R&D for diminishing returns, and reinvent Procter & Gamble's innovation business model. Put simply, the company's existing 'invent it yourself' approach was not capable of sustaining sales growth.

This prompted Procter & Gamble (P&G) to recognise the potential of the pools of expertise and ideas, and the opportunities for innovation which existed outside the company, and it sought to make use of them through its Connect+Develop programme.

The CEO set the business a target of acquiring 50% of its innovations from **outside** the company.

P&G practises 'open innovation', which is a means of accessing externally developed intellectual property and, at the same time, allowing its own internally developed assets and know-how to be used by others. So, for P&G, innovation has become a two-way process.

Through Connect+Develop, P&G actively seeks to collaborate with external partners to generate and develop new product ideas. P&G employs about 7,500 researchers, but the logic was that for every one P&G researcher there were another 200 scientists or engineers elsewhere in the world who were just as good. This meant that there were a further 1.5 million scientists out there who did not work for P&G. The logic of the Connect+Develop programme was that P&G's R&D programme should use ideas from the full 1,507,500.

By identifying promising ideas from this pool throughout the world, P&G could then apply its R&D, manufacturing, marketing and purchasing capabilities to them to create better and cheaper products, faster than it could otherwise have done.

This attempt to 'un-source' ideas appears to be working. By 2006, more than 35% of P&G's new products had elements that originate from outside the company, and 45% of the initiatives in their product development portfolio had key elements that were discovered externally. At the same time, R&D productivity within P&G had increased by nearly 60%.

By 2014, P&G's open innovation strategy had enabled it to establish over 2,000 successful agreements with innovation partners around the world.

Section summary

Innovation can lead to competitive advantage, but it is very expensive and results are not guaranteed. Research may be pure, applied or development and may be intended to improve products or processes.

---

7 Benchmarking

Benchmarking enables a firm to meet industry standards by copying others, but it is perhaps less valuable as a source of innovation.

KEY TERM

BENCHMARKING is the 'establishment, through data gathering, of targets and comparators, through whose use relative levels of performance (and particularly areas of underperformance) can be identified. By the adoption of identified best practices it is hoped that performance will improve'.

(CIMA Official Terminology)

Benchmarking provides management with a means of identifying how well areas of an organisation are performing, with a view to improving the performance of those areas which are currently underperforming. In this respect, benchmarking could be an important performance management tool. Benchmarking also relies on the availability of data for the areas of performance which an organisation wants to compare. We discuss information systems (as the potential sources of such data) in Chapter 6 of this Study Text.

7.1 Types of benchmarking

(a) **Internal benchmarking**. This involves comparing one operating unit or function with similar ones within the same organisation. This is easier to do than comparing performance with that of external organisations, but it is unlikely to lead to innovative or best practice solutions.

(b) **Competitive benchmarking**. Performance information is gathered about direct competitors. From a strategic perspective, the value of competitor benchmarking is that if an organisation can match a

competitor's performance in an area which was previously a core competence for the competitor, that area is no longer a source of competitive advantage for the competitor.

However, at a practical level, the biggest problem with competitor benchmarking would be in obtaining information about the competitor. In particular, a competitor is unlikely to disclose information about a process or area of performance which it knows relates to an area of competitive advantage for it.

(c)   **Functional benchmarking**. This involves comparing the performance of internal functions with that of the best external practitioners, regardless of their industry. (This type of benchmarking is also known as operational benchmarking or generic benchmarking.)

(d)   **Process (or activity) benchmarking**. This involves comparing work processes to similar processes in other organisations which are not competitors but which have innovative or best practice processes (for example, comparing the processes for serving customers in banks and supermarkets).

Through process benchmarking, an organisation can try to find new, innovative ways to create competitive advantage, as well as solving threshold problems. And, because the comparator is not a competitor, there is likely to be less resistance to sharing information than would be the case in relation to competitive benchmarking.

7.2 Undertaking a benchmarking exercise

Benchmarking can be divided into eight stages.

Obtain management support

Senior management commitment to the benchmarking process is only genuinely available when senior managers have a full appreciation of the objectives of the project, its benefits and its costs. Senior management can change their minds when it becomes apparent that they did not anticipate the actual levels of cost or inconvenience a project may bring. For the project to be a success it is essential that senior management endorse it.

Determine the areas to be benchmarked and set objectives

Determine areas to benchmark by identifying the **critical business processes** or those which are the main drivers of revenues and costs.

Set objectives. Note that here, the objectives will not be in the form of aspirations for improvement to specific processes and practices, but more in the nature of stating the extent and depth of the enquiry.

Understand processes and identify key performance measures

Understand processes. Before any key performance measures can be set, the benchmarking team will need to understand the processes which drive them. This will require discussion with **key stakeholders** plus observation and documentation of the way work is carried out.

Identify key performance measures. Once the team understand the processes, then they can identify key performance measures for the processes (for example, the length of time between receiving a customer order and dispatching the goods ordered).

Choose organisations to benchmark against

This can either be done **internally** (comparing one division against another) or through **external** competitive benchmarking (comparing performance with rival companies). Firms often want to compare their performance against the '**best in class**' external performer. However, they have to be realistic about whether that 'best in class' performer will be willing to share performance information with them.

Measure performance

Measure own and others' performance. Negotiation should take place to establish who does the measurement. Ideally, a joint team made up of people from both the organisations being benchmarked should do it, but there may be issues of confidentiality or convenience that mean each organisation does its own measuring.

Compare performance and discuss results

Raw data must be carefully analysed if appropriate conclusions are to be drawn.

Discuss results with management and staff. The **stakeholders** concerned are likely both to have useful comments and to be anxious about the possibility of adverse reflection upon them. It is important to remember that the purpose of benchmarking is not to apportion blame for poor performance, but to act as an opportunity to improve performance.

Improvement programmes

Design and implement improvement programmes. It may be possible to import complete systems or it may be appropriate to combine various elements of best practice. Sometimes, improvements require extensive **reorganisation** and **restructuring**, and may sometimes also involve **outsourcing**.

In many cases, there is likely to be a requirement for **training**. Improvements in administrative systems often call for investment in new equipment, particularly in IT systems.

Monitor improvements

The continuing effectiveness of improvements must be monitored. At the same time, it must be understood that **improvement is a continuous process rather than a one-off change** and so further adjustments (and follow-up benchmarking exercises) may be beneficial.

Johnson, Scholes and Whittington set out questions that should be asked when carrying out a benchmarking exercise as part of a wider strategic review.

- **Why** are these products or services provided at all?
- Why are they provided **in that particular way**?
- What are the examples of **best practice** elsewhere?
- How should activities be **reshaped** in the light of these comparisons?

They see three levels of benchmarking.

Level of benchmarking	Through	Examples of measures
Resources	Resource audit	Quantity of resources • Revenue/employee • Capital intensity Quality of resources • Qualifications of employees • Age of machinery • Uniqueness (eg patents)
Competences in separate activities	Analysing activities	Sales calls per salesperson Output per employee Materials wastage
Competences in linked activities	Analysing overall performances	Market share Profitability Productivity

When selecting an appropriate **benchmark basis**, companies should ask themselves the following questions.

(a)   Is it possible and easy to obtain reliable competitor information?

(b)   Is there any wide discrepancy between different internal divisions?

(c)   Can similar processes be identified in non-competing environments and are these non-competing companies willing to co-operate?

(d)   Is best practice operating in a similar environmental setting?

(e)   What is our timescale?

(f)   Do the chosen companies have similar objectives and strategies?

7.3 Advantages of benchmarking

Benchmarking has the following advantages.

(a)   **Position audit**. Benchmarking can assess a firm's existing position, and provide a basis for establishing standards of performance.

(b)   The comparisons are **carried out by the managers** who have to live with any changes implemented as a result of the exercise.

(c)   Benchmarking **focuses** on improvement and sets targets which are challenging but achievable.

(d)   The sharing of information can be a **spur to innovation**.

(e)   The result should be **improved performance**, particularly in cost control and delivering value.

(f)   Benchmarking can provide an organisation with an early warning if its performance begins to slip compared with the organisations against which it is being benchmarked.

7.4 Dangers of benchmarking

Many companies have gained significant benefits from benchmarking but there may also be dangers.

(a) It concentrates on **doing things right** rather than **doing the right thing**: the difference between **efficiency** and **effectiveness**. A process can be efficient but its output may not be useful. Other measures (such as amending the value chain) may be a better way of securing competitive advantage.

(b) The benchmark may be **yesterday's solution to tomorrow's problem**. For example, a cross-channel ferry company might benchmark its activities (eg speed of turnaround at Dover and Calais, cleanliness on ship) against another ferry company, whereas the real competitor is the Channel Tunnel.

(c) It is a **catching-up exercise rather than the development of anything distinctive**. After the benchmarking exercise, the competitor might improve performance in a different way.

(d) It depends on **accurate** information about comparator companies.

(e) It is **not cost-free** and can divert **management attention**. The benchmark measures have to be collated, turned into a report and then discussed. This takes time and effort, but at the end of it management may just feel they are being overloaded with information.

(f) It can become a hindrance and even a threat: **sharing information** with other companies can be a burden and a security risk.

(g) It may reduce managerial motivation, if the performance of the managers' areas is compared unfavourably to rival organisations. For benchmarking to be useful, the ultimate outcome of the benchmarking exercise should not be the measures themselves but improvements in the underlying processes which drive performance.

Section summary

Benchmarking enables a firm to identify relative levels of performance and best practice. Performance levels can then be improved by implementing the best practice identified by the benchmarking process.

Chapter Summary

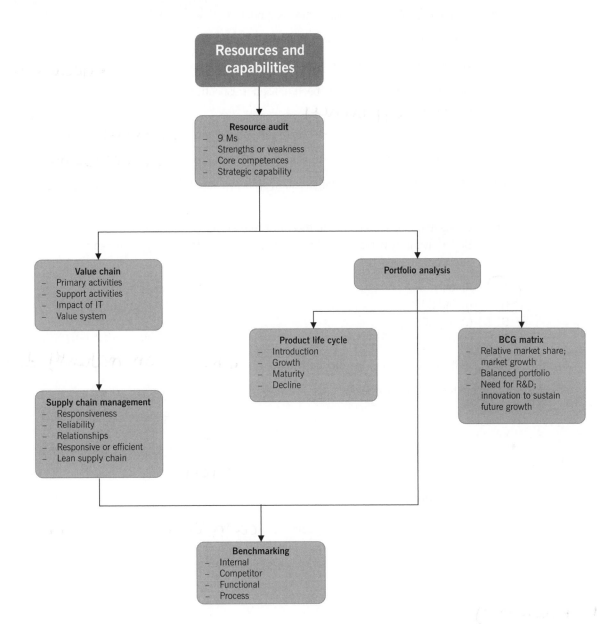

Quick Quiz

1   What are the nine 'Ms' categorised in the Ms model?

2   Which of these describes 'efficiency', and which 'effectiveness'?

(a)   Whether the resources have been deployed in the best possible way *effectiveness*

(b)   How well the resources have been utilised irrespective of the purpose for which they have been employed *efficiency*

3   Is logistics a primary or secondary activity in the value chain? *primary*

4   In Porter's value chain model, who is value ultimately created for? *end consumer*

5   Which of the following are characteristics of responsive supply chains as opposed to efficient supply chains?

(i)   Goods are supplied in order to meet demand at the lowest cost.
(ii)   Buffer inventory is maintained in order to deal with uncertainty in demand.
(iii)   Suppliers are selected on the basis of cost and quality.

A   (ii) only
B   (i) and (ii)
C   (i) and (iii)
D   (ii) and (iii)

6   What are the four stages of the product life cycle? *intro, growth, maturity, decline*

7   Complete the BCG matrix below.

	Relative market share	
	High	Low
High	Star	?
Low	Cash cow	Dog

Market growth

1. Machinery
   Management info
   Management
   Make-up
   Men & women
   Materials
   Methods
   Money
   Markets

Answers to Quick Quiz

1 Machinery; Make-up; Management; Management Information; Markets; Materials; Men and women; Methods; Money

2 (a) Effectiveness
 (b) Efficiency

3 Primary

4 The end-user consumer. The value chain expresses the way value is added to the products or services produced by an entity from the perspective of the end-user consumer (not from the perspective of the organisation).

5 A (ii) only

Responsive supply chains maintain buffer inventory to deal with uncertainty in demand and/or supply, whereas efficient supply chains look to minimise inventory in order to lower costs.

The primary goal of **efficient** supply chains is to supply demand at the lowest cost, but responsive supply chains seek to respond quickly to changes in demand.

Suppliers in responsive supply chains are selected on the basis of speed, flexibility, reliability and quality. Selecting suppliers on the basis of cost and quality is characteristic of efficient supply chains, not responsive ones.

6 Introduction, growth, maturity, decline.

7

Relative market share

Market growth		High	Low
	High	Stars	Question marks
	Low	Cash cows	Dogs

Answers to Questions

4.1 Creating value

Here are some ideas for organising the activities of buying, cooking and serving food in a way that customers will value.

(a) It can become more efficient, by automating production, as in fast food chains.

(b) The chef can develop commercial relationships with growers, so they can obtain the best quality fresh produce.

(c) The chef can specialise in a particular type of cuisine (eg Nepalese, Korean).

(d) The restaurant can be sumptuously decorated for those customers who value 'atmosphere' and a sense of occasion, in addition to good food.

(e) The restaurant can serve a particular type of customer (eg celebrities).

4.2 Value chain and value system

Sana Sounds is involved in the record industry from start to finish. Although recording and CD manufacture are contracted out to external suppliers, this makes no difference to the fact that these activities are part of Sana Sounds' own value chain. Sana Sounds earns its money by managing the whole set of activities. If the company grows then perhaps it will acquire its own recording studios.

Note the subsidiary point (in the 'Stop and think ...') that changes in technology are offering new opportunities in the way music is distributed. Consumers can now download tracks from the internet rather than having to buy physical discs.

4.3 Juicy drinks

(a) Orange juice is a cash cow.
(b) Pomegranate juice is a question mark, which the company wants to turn into a star.

Now try these questions from the Practice Question Bank	Number	Level	Marks	Time
	4.1 – 4.5	Intermediate	n/a	10 mins
	4.6	Examination	17	30 mins

IDENTIFYING AND EVALUATING STRATEGIC OPTIONS

After looking at the context in which strategic planning decisions are made, and the internal and external factors which affect strategic decisions, we now look at the range of strategic options which organisations can choose from.

There are three key aspects to these options: **how** to compete; **where** to compete (direction of growth); and **method** of growth.

The choice of how to compete relates to the generic competitive strategies which a firm can choose – identified by Porter as cost leadership or differentiation.

An organisation's choice about where to compete relates to the mix of products and markets it serves – as illustrated by Ansoff's product-market matrix.

Choices around the method of growth relate to whether an organisation looks to grow organically or externally. External growth could be through acquisition, or some kind of strategic alliance.

Given the increasingly global nature of business, international expansion can also be an important consideration within any discussions of growth.

However, as well as growth strategies, organisations need to know when to dispose of underperforming assets or to rationalise divisions whose costs are too high.

When evaluating any strategic options, the three key factors to consider are the suitability, acceptability and feasibility of the options.

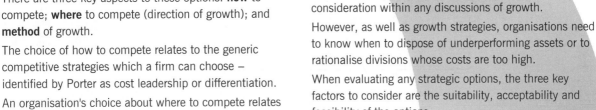

5

Topic list	Learning outcomes	Syllabus references	Ability required
1 Assessing strategic position	B1(a)	B1(a) (ii)	Evaluate
2 Generic competitive strategies	B1(a)	B1(a) (iii)	Evaluate
3 Product-market strategy: direction of growth	B1(a)	B1(a) (iii)	Evaluate
4 Methods of growth	B1(a)	B1(a) (viii)	Evaluate
5 Organic growth	B1(a)	B1(a) (viii)	Evaluate
6 Mergers and acquisitions	B1(a)	B1(a) (viii)	Evaluate
7 Joint ventures and strategic alliances	B1(a)	B1(a) (viii)	Evaluate
8 Divestment and rationalisation	B1(a)	B1(a) (viii)	Evaluate
9 The public and not for profit sectors	B1(a)	–	Evaluate
10 Evaluating strategic options	B1(b)	B1(b) (i)	Recommend
11 Risk and cost behaviour	B1(b)	B1(b) (i)	Recommend
12 Decision techniques	B1(b)	B1(b) (i)	Recommend

Chapter Overview

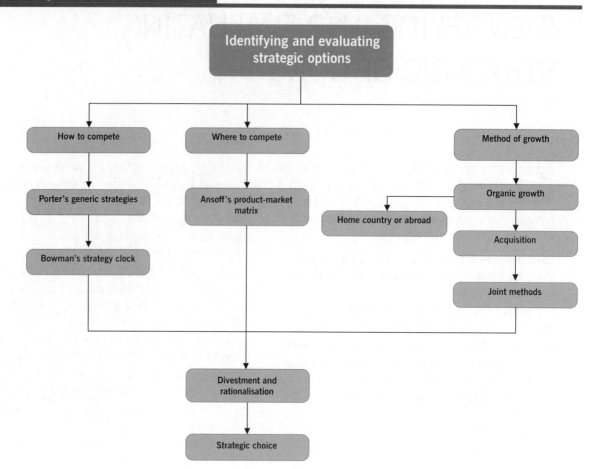

1   Assessing strategic position

Introduction

Once an organisation has identified the **opportunities** and **threats** in its external environment and its internal **strengths** and **weaknesses**, it can analyse its current strategic position (SWOT analysis). It also then needs to choose what **strategies** to pursue in order to achieve its targets and objectives.

1.1 Corporate appraisal (SWOT analysis)

In Chapter 3 of this Study Text, we highlight the importance of organisations analysing their external environment, and then in Chapter 4 we focus on the importance of organisations' internal resources and capabilities to their strategic success.

However, the two elements – external environment and internal capabilities – need to be drawn together in order to understand an organisation's **current strategic position** before preparing its long-term plan and formulating its potential strategies. It is very important for an organisation to understand its current position –'Where are we now?' – before it can start to make strategic choices about its future.

One of the main ways of analysing an organisation's current position is to combine its strengths and weaknesses (based on its internal resources and capabilities) with the opportunities and threats it faces (from the external environment) in order to produce a **SWOT analysis**. Moreover, by combining environmental analysis with internal appraisal in this way, SWOT analysis provides a means of assessing an organisation's current and future strategic fit (or lack of fit) with its environment.

KEY POINT

Strengths and **weaknesses** relate to the organisation itself – its resources and its products/services. They are internal matters, and are specific to the individual organisation.

Opportunities and **threats** exist in the business market and the market in which the organisation operates. They are external matters.

Strategies should be developed to remove weaknesses or develop strengths and to exploit opportunities and counter threats. In this respect, SWOT analysis can be used to guide strategy formulation, through applying S, W, O and T to the **TOWS matrix**.

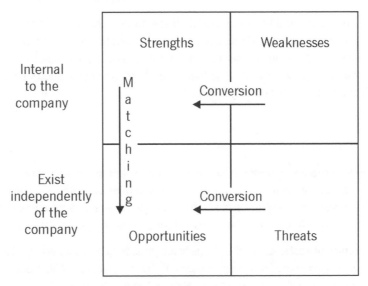

The organisation should try to **match** its strengths to the opportunities presented by the market.

It should also look to **convert** weaknesses into strengths in order to take advantage of some particular opportunity.

A third possible option is to attempt to **remedy weaknesses** so as to reduce exposure to threats and increase the ability to grasp opportunities. However, this course does not, in itself, lead to a sustainable strategy and is best regarded as a preliminary phase to matching or conversion.

Weirich (who developed the TOWS matrix) originally conceived the matrix as a way of highlighting the importance of organisations responding to the threats and opportunities presented by the environment. (In this respect it follows a positioning-based approach to strategy.) However, a further important element of Weirich's discussion was his categorisation of the basic types of strategic option available to organisations.

(a) **SO** strategies employ strengths to seize opportunities, and to develop strategic advantage in the marketplace.

(b) **ST** strategies employ strengths to counter or avoid threats.

(c) **WO** strategies address weaknesses so as to be able to exploit opportunities.

(d) **WT** strategies are defensive, aiming to avoid threats and the impact of weaknesses. However, depending on the strength of the threat, threats focusing on an existing weakness may necessitate rapid change in the organisation to respond to them.

In Chapter 3, we highlighted the environment as a source of drivers for change in an organisation. The basic types of strategic option illustrated by the TOWS matrix reinforce that point, since they are responding to opportunities or threats presented by the environment.

1.2 Strategic choices

When formulating a strategy, there are three overall types of strategic choice which organisations have to make.

(a) **Competitive strategies** are the strategies an organisation will pursue for competitive advantage. They determine **how** the organisation competes.

(b) **Product–market strategies** determine **where** you compete and the **direction of growth**.

(c) Institutional strategies determine the **method of growth** (eg organic growth or external growth).

Exam skills

It is very important that you appreciate these three categories of strategic choice. The scenarios you face in the integrated case study may require you to evelute one or more aspects of a strategic choice. If you are asked to advise an organisation about a proposed strategic choice, then you should be prepared to consider its implications for these three aspects of the organisation's strategy (how to compete, where to compete and the method of growth).

1.2.1 Horizontal boundaries

A firm's **horizontal boundaries** define the variety of products and services that it produces. The optimum horizontal boundary for a firm depends on **economies of scale**. In some industries, such as pharmaceuticals, company size is influenced by a preference for mergers ('bigger is better') and corporate giants emerge. A few large firms account for the vast proportion of industry sales.

Economies of scale occur when large-scale processes, such as production and distribution, have cost advantages over smaller-scale processes. Economies of scale affect both the size of firms and the structure of markets, and so consideration of them, and therefore where organisational boundaries should be, is vital in any business strategy decision about possible merger or expansion.

1.2.2 Vertical boundaries

The **vertical boundaries** of a firm define which activities the firm performs itself and which it purchases from independent firms. A number of firms now **outsource** activities which they feel are not part of their core competences.

The concept of vertical boundaries is allied to the concepts of the **value chain and value networks**. For example, a value chain might begin with the acquisition of raw materials and culminate in distribution and sale of the finished goods. In this case, a firm needs to decide how much of the value creation process it wants to control internally and how much of the value passes outside the firm.

We look at horizontal and vertical integration again later in the chapter in the context of **related diversification** as a product–market strategy.

1.2.3 Products and strategy

The right strategy depends on the type of product or service that the firm is producing.

(a)   **Search products**. These are products whose attributes the consumer can discern, evaluate and compare fairly easily, eg size and colour.

(b)   **Experience products**. These are products whose attributes cannot be discerned until the consumer has had experience of using the product – eg taste in the case of food.

(c)   **Credence products**. These are products whose important attributes cannot be evaluated by the consumer either because the product's attributes might vary over time (eg quality of service in a restaurant) or because the product's attributes cannot easily be evaluated (eg pet food).

Products may be categorised:

(a)   **Breakthrough products** offer either a radical performance advantage over competition or drastically lower prices, or ideally, may offer both.

(b)   **Improved products** are not radically different to their competition but are obviously superior in terms of better performance at a competitive price.

(c)   **Competitive products** show no obvious advantage over others, but derive their appeal from a particular compromise of cost and performance.

1.3 Strategic marketing issues

A **standard** product might satisfy the needs of all customers in the market. On the other hand, **variations** in a product's design might appeal more strongly to some prospective customers than others.

Customers differ in various respects – according to age, sex, income, geographical area, buying attitudes, buying habits etc. Each of these differences can be used to **segment** a market.

By creating a new market segment or entering a growing market segment a company can hope to achieve the following.

(a)   **Increase sales and profits**, by meeting customer needs in a number of different ways
(b)   Extend the **life cycle** of the product
(c)   Capture some of the overall **market share** from competitors
(d)   Survive in the face of competition

Section summary

A firm has to make strategic choices about **how** to compete, **where** to compete (products, markets), and **how to grow** (organically or externally).

2 Generic competitive strategies

Introduction

Porter suggests there are three generic strategies: **cost leadership**, **differentiation** and **focus**. These ideas have subsequently been extended into the idea of the **strategy clock**.

In any market where there are competitors, strategic and marketing decisions will often be taken in response to what a competitor has done.

Competitive advantage is anything which gives one organisation an edge over its rivals. Porter argues that a firm should adopt a competitive strategy which is intended to achieve some form of competitive advantage for the firm. A firm that possesses a **competitive advantage** will be able to make profit exceeding its cost of capital: in terms of economic theory, this is '**excess profit**' or '**economic rent**'. The existence of excess profit tends to be temporary because of the effect of the **five competitive forces**. When a company can continue to earn excess profit despite the effects of competition, it possesses a **sustainable competitive advantage**.

KEY TERM

COMPETITIVE STRATEGY means 'taking offensive or defensive actions to create a dependable position in an industry, to cope successfully with ... competitive forces and thereby yield a superior return on investment for the firm. Firms have discovered many different approaches to this end, and the best strategy for a given firm is ultimately a unique construction reflecting its particular circumstances'.   (Porter)

2.1 The choice of competitive strategy

Porter believes there are three **generic strategies** for competitive advantage. To be successful, Porter argues, a company must follow only one of the strategies. If they try to combine more than one they risk losing their competitive advantage and becoming '**stuck in the middle**'.

KEY TERMS

COST LEADERSHIP means being the lowest cost producer in the industry as a whole.

DIFFERENTIATION is the exploitation of a product or service which the **industry as a whole** believes to be unique.

Focus involves a restriction of activities to only part of the market (a segment) through:

- Providing goods and/or services at lower cost to that segment (**cost-focus**)
- Providing a differentiated product or service to that segment (**differentiation-focus**)

Cost leadership and differentiation are industry-wide strategies. Focus involves segmentation but involves pursuing, within the segment only, a strategy of cost leadership or differentiation.

2.1.1 Cost leadership

A cost leadership strategy seeks to achieve the position of lowest-cost producer in the **industry as a whole**.

By producing at the **lowest cost**, the manufacturer could either charge the same price as its competitors knowing that this would enable it to generate a greater profit per unit than them, or it could decide to charge a lower price than them. This might be particularly beneficial if the goods or services which the organisation sells are price sensitive.

How to achieve overall cost leadership:

- Establishing **economies of scale**

- Use the **latest**, **most efficient technology** to reduce costs and/or enhance productivity

- Exploit the **learning curve effect**

- **Get favourable access to sources of supply** and buy in bulk wherever possible (to obtain discounts for bulk purchases)

- **Minimise overhead costs**

- Reduce **direct costs** (for example, by using cheaper **raw materials**, or cheaper labour)

- **Relocate to cheaper areas** (possibly in a different country)

The airline industry provides some good examples of where companies have deliberately pursued cost leadership strategies: for example, South West Airlines in the US, and EasyJet and Ryanair in Europe.

 Value chain analysis, which we looked at in the previous chapter, could be very useful when considering which generic strategy to pursue. If a company wishes to pursue a cost leadership strategy, it will need to ensure that its costs are as low as possible across all the different activities in its value chain.

 Exam skills

Remember that Porter identified the importance of **cost** leadership (not **price** leadership) as one of the generic strategies. Although companies which are pursuing a cost leadership strategy might then choose to compete on price, the focus of Porter's model is on how companies can **produce** goods or services at a lower cost than their rivals, rather than selling price *per se*.

2.1.2 Differentiation

A differentiation strategy assumes that competitive advantage can be gained through **particular characteristics** of a firm's products or processes. Differentiation is often used to justify a firm charging a higher price for its products than its rivals do. This can allow the firm to earn higher margins than its rivals.

Products may be categorised as:

(a) **Breakthrough products**, which offer a radical performance advantage over existing products.

(b) **Improved products**, which are not radically different from their competition but are obviously superior in terms of better performance at a competitive price.

(c) **Competitive products**, which derive their appeal from a particular compromise of cost and performance. For example, cars are not all sold at rock-bottom prices, nor do they all provide immaculate comfort and performance. They compete with each other by trying to offer a more attractive compromise than rival models.

How to differentiate

- Build up a **brand image** (for example, as Levi has done in relation to jeans)
- Give the product **special features** to make it stand out
- Exploit other activities of the **value chain** such as **marketing** and sales or **service**
- Use **IT** to create new services or product features

CASE STUDY

Bang & Olufsen

The audio and television equipment manufacturer, Bang & Olufsen, has used a differentiation strategy, based on style, to distinguish its products from those of its competitors.

Bang & Olufsen has built an international reputation for performance, design excellence and quality, and has developed a very loyal customer base. Its sleek, tastefully discreet designs and high standards of production have earned it elite status in the market. For decades, these factors have formed the basis of Bang & Olufsen's advertising and marketing strategy, and the company has recognised that 'style' needs to be displayed distinctively in its retail outlets.

This has led to the creation of 'concept shops' where subtle images are projected onto walls and products are displayed in free-standing areas constructed from translucent walls.

The company's view is that one cannot sell Bang & Olufsen equipment when it is sandwiched amongst a densely packed range of electrical goods or domestic appliances. By contrast, the concept shop gives the right look and feel to make the most of the products.

Bang & Olufsen has focused on the importance of style and aesthetics rather than technology or low prices in buying decisions. It sells products on the basis of ambience as much as sound.

However, one of the key challenges Bang & Olufsen faces is to keep its brand (and strategy) relevant in a world where customers' audio-visual habits (eg listening to music via downloads and portable devices) are changing. At the same time, Bang & Olufsen needs to maintain its style distinction in the face of high-end equipment being produced, for example, by Samsung and Sony.

In response to this environmental context, Bang & Olufsen launched a new brand – B&O PLAY – in 2012, focusing on audio-video products which combine convenience with high-quality, contemporary design for the digital generation. Price points for B&O PLAY will also be lower than those typically seen from Bang & Olufsen.

At the launch of the new brand, Bang & Olufsen's CEO said, 'We are very excited about the range of products we will launch under this new brand. Through B&O PLAY we will bring core Bang & Olufsen values of design, performance and quality to a new audience.'

(Based on a case study in: Jobber, D. (2010), *Principles and Practice of Marketing* (6th edition), Maidenhead, McGraw-Hill)

B&O PLAY website: www.beoplay.com

Advantages and disadvantages of industry-wide strategies

Competitive force	Advantages		Disadvantages	
	Cost leadership	Differentiation	Cost leadership	Differentiation
New entrants	Economies of scale raise entry barriers	Brand loyalty and perceived uniqueness are entry barriers		
Substitutes	Firm is not as vulnerable to the threat of substitutes as its less cost-effective competitors	Customer loyalty is a weapon against substitutes		

Competitive force	Advantages		Disadvantages	
	Cost leadership	Differentiation	Cost leadership	Differentiation
Customers	Customers cannot drive down prices further than the next most efficient competitor	Customers have no comparable alternative Brand loyalty should lower price sensitivity and prevent price wars	Internally focused. Ignores customers' needs.	Customers may no longer need the differentiating factor Sooner or later, customers become price sensitive
Suppliers	Flexibility to deal with cost increases	Higher margins can offset vulnerability to supplier price rises	Increase in input costs can reduce price advantages	
Industry rivalry	Firm remains profitable when rivals collapse due to excessive price competition	Unique features reduce direct competition	Technological change will require capital investment, or make production cheaper for competitors Competitors learn via imitation Cost concerns ignore product design or marketing issues	Imitation narrows differentiation Differentiating factors may be undermined if rivals develop better technology

2.1.3 Focus (or niche) strategy

In a focus strategy, a firm concentrates its attention on one or more particular segments or niches of the market, and does not try to serve the entire market with a single product. For example, a firm could look to establish a niche based on: location, market segment and consumer type, product quality or product features.

Information technology (IT) can be useful in establishing the exact determining characteristics of the chosen niche, using existing customer records.

(a)   A **cost-focus strategy**: aim to be a cost leader for a particular segment. This type of strategy is often found in the printing, clothes manufacture and car repair industries.

(b)   A **differentiation-focus strategy**: pursue differentiation for a chosen segment. Luxury goods suppliers are the prime exponents of such a strategy. Ben and Jerry's ice cream is a good example of a product offering based on differentiation-focus.

CASE STUDY

Tyrrells

The crisp manufacturer, Tyrrells, successfully implemented a differentiation-focus strategy, by seizing an opportunity to produce better-quality potato crisps than those traditionally found in the supermarkets. Tyrrells has targeted its crisps at a market segment that would be prepared to pay a higher price for good quality produce.

Initially, one of the features of Tyrrells' strategy was to sell mainly through small retailers at the upper end of the grocery and catering markets – thereby avoiding direct competition with the market leader (Walker's crisps). However, following its acquisition by a private equity fund, Tyrrells crisps are now a fixture on most supermarket shelves in the UK, and the business has ambitions to expand internationally.

Nonetheless, Tyrrells still differentiates itself by cooking its potato crisps by hand using the finest home-grown potatoes. All the crisps are produced on the farm where the potatoes have been grown, so Tyrrells are in total control of the process 'from seed to crisp'. (The company was set up by a potato farmer, who saw crisp production as a way to add extra value to his basic product, potatoes.) This 'local-first' approach is a unique selling point for Tyrrells, supplemented by its production process – with the skin left on the potatoes, and the potatoes cooked in small batches.

- **Branding**. Tyrrells' marketing taps into the public's enthusiasm for 'authenticity' and 'provenance', and the packets emphasise the product as being 'hand-cooked English crisps'.

- **Quality**. Tyrrells' crisps are made from traditional varieties of potato and 'hand-fried' in small batches.

- **New product development.** The Tyrrells' product portfolio consists of 15 potato crisp varieties, and three varieties of 'furrowed' (crinkle cut) crisps. However, in addition to potato crisps, they now also produce a range of vegetable crisps – including beetroot, parsnip and sweet potato.

Porter suggests that a focus strategy can achieve competitive advantage when '**broad-scope**' businesses fall into one of two errors.

(a)   **Underperformance** occurs when a product does not fully meet the needs of a segment and offers the opportunity for a **differentiation-focus** player.

(b)   **Overperformance** gives a segment more than it really wants and provides an opportunity for a **cost-focus** player.

Advantages of a focus strategy

- A niche is more secure and a firm can insulate itself from competition.

- The firm does not spread itself too thinly and can specialise in one particular area of expertise.

- Because the segment is relatively small, this reduces the investment in marketing operations required, compared to a strategy which involves competing across the whole market.

Drawbacks of a focus strategy

- The firm sacrifices economies of scale which could be gained by serving a wider market.

- The segment may not be sufficiently large to enable sufficient returns to be earned in the long run to satisfy investors.

- Competitors can move into the segment, with increased resources (eg the Japanese moved into the US luxury car market, to compete with Mercedes and BMW).

- The needs of the segment may eventually become less distinct from the main market.

In effect, in order to be successful, a niche must be large enough in terms of potential buyers, and must have sufficient growth potential to generate returns for a firm, yet it must remain of negligible interest to major competitors so that they don't enter it.

2.2 Which strategy?

Although there is a risk with any of the generic strategies, Porter argues that a firm must pursue one of them. A **stuck in the middle** strategy is almost certain to make only low profits. 'This firm lacks the market share, capital investment and resolve to play the low-cost game, the industry-wide differentiation necessary to obviate the need for a low-cost position, or the focus to create differentiation or a low-cost position in a more limited sphere.'

Exam skills

If you are asked to recommend a generic strategy which an organisation should pursue, or advise whether a particular strategy might be appropriate for it, it is vital to consider how well that strategy would 'fit'

with the organisation's existing resources and culture. For example, if an organisation looks to provide high-quality services, a cost leadership strategy is unlikely to be suitable for it, because some of its competitors who provide lower-quality services are likely to have lower cost bases.

Question 5.1	Hermes

Learning outcomes B1(a)

The managing director of Hermes Telecommunications plc is interested in corporate strategy. Hermes has invested a great deal of money in establishing a network which competes with that of Telecom UK, a recently privatised utility. Initially, Hermes concentrated its efforts on business customers in the South-East of England, especially the City of London, where it offered a lower-cost service to that supplied by Telecom UK. Recently, Hermes has approached the residential market (ie domestic telephone users) offering a lower-cost service on long-distance calls. Technological developments have resulted in the possibility of a cheap mobile telecommunication network, using microwave radio links. The franchise for this service has been awarded to Gerbil phone, which is installing transmitters in town centres and stations etc.

What issues of competitive strategy have been raised in the above scenario, particularly in relation to Hermes Telecommunications plc?

2.3 Using the generic strategies

Porter's three generic strategies can help managers in their strategic planning in a number of different ways.

(a) **Encourage them to analyse competitors' positions**. For example, firms which are competing as cost leaders will need to analyse rivals' cost structures and value chains to identify if there are any areas where cost savings can be made. By contrast, firms which want to pursue differentiation strategies should undertake market research information to get an understanding of brand perceptions in the market.

(b) **Choose a competitive strategy**. This is the key point behind Porter's model: to be successful a firm needs to follow one of the generic strategies.

(c) **Analyse the risks of their present strategy**. Porter identifies that each generic strategy has some inherent risks. For example:

Differentiation

(i)   The brand loyalty underpinning differentiation may fail if the cost differential between the price difference with cost-leading products becomes too great.

(ii)   Buyers may value the differentiating factor less, and so may become more willing to buy generic products instead of differentiated products.

Cost leadership

(i)   Technological change could mean that existing low-cost technology becomes superseded by newer, cheaper technology.

(ii)   Inflation or exchange rates may destroy cost advantages.

Focus

(i)   The distinctions between segments narrow so that individual segments are no longer clearly identifiable.

(ii)   Segment collapses and leaves the firm with no other source of earnings.

The value of Porter's model is in reminding managers they need to focus on these threats and risks, and develop strategies to deal with them and to maintain their competitive advantage.

2.4 Limitations of Porter's model

In practice, it is rarely simple to draw hard and fast distinctions between the generic strategies as there are conceptual problems underlying them.

(a) **Problems with cost leadership**

    (i) **Internal focus**. Cost refers to internal measures, rather than the market demand. It can be used to gain market share: but it is the **market share that is important**, not cost leadership as such. Economies of scale are an effective way to achieve low costs, but they depend on high volumes. In turn, high volumes may depend on low prices which, in turn, require low costs. There is a circular argument here.

    (ii) **Only one firm**. If cost leadership applies across the whole industry, only one firm will pursue this strategy successfully. However, more than one firm might **aspire** to cost leadership, especially in dynamic markets where new technologies are frequently introduced. Firms competing across the industry as a whole might have different competence or advantages that confer cost leadership in different segments.

    (iii) **Higher margins can be used for differentiation**. Having low **costs** does not mean you have to charge lower prices or compete on **price**. A cost leader can choose to 'invest higher margins in R&D or marketing'. Being a cost leader arguably gives producers more freedom to choose other competitive strategies.

There is often confusion about what cost leadership actually means. In particular, cost leadership is often assumed to also mean low price. However, '**cost leadership**' and '**low price**' **are not necessarily the same thing**.

(b) **Problems with differentiation**. Porter assumes that a differentiated product will always be sold at a higher price.

    (i) However, a **differentiated product** may be sold at the same price as competing products in order to **increase market share**.

    (ii) **Choice of competitor**. Differentiation from whom? Who are the competitors? Do they serve other market segments? Do they compete on the same basis?

    (iii) **Source of differentiation**. This includes **all** aspects of the firm's offer, not only the product. For example, restaurants try to distinguish themselves from their competitors through their ambience and the quality of their service as well as by serving high-quality food.

Focus probably has fewer conceptual difficulties, as it ties in very neatly with ideas of market segmentation. In practice, most companies pursue this strategy to some extent, by designing products/ services to meet the needs of particular target markets.

'Stuck in the middle' is therefore what many companies actually pursue quite successfully. Any number of strategies can be pursued, with different approaches to **price** and the **perceived added value** (ie the differentiation factor) in the eyes of the customer.

In this way, Porter's model no longer reflects the full range of competitive strategies an organisation can choose from.

2.5 The strategy clock

The idea that firms can successfully pursue a number of strategies based on price and perceived added value has led to a reassessment of Porter's original arguments. Moreover, the emphasis on **price** and **added value** recognises the importance of the customer – in a competitive situation, rational customers will seek **value for money** in their purchases, and value for money is provided through the combination of **price** and **perceived product/service benefits**.

To this end, it is worth considering the strategy clock (developed by Bowman) as a successor to Porter's generic strategies. The **strategy clock identifies eight different strategies** a firm can take in terms of price and adding value.

The eight strategies on the clock represent different approaches to creating value for the customer, with the logic being that each customer will buy from the provider whose offering most closely matches their own view of the proper relationship between price and perceived benefits.

Each position on the clock has its own **critical success factor**, since each strategy is defined in market terms. Positions 1 and 2 will attract customers who are price conscious above all, with position 2 giving a little more emphasis to serviceability. These are typical approaches in commodity markets. By contrast, strategies 4 and 5 are relevant to consumers who require a customised product; for example, professional service firms have often used these strategies as a basis for competition.

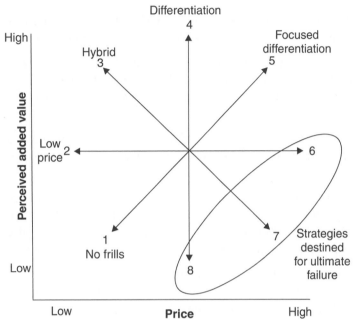

Bowman's strategy clock

2.5.1 No frills

A **no frills strategy** combines a low price with low perceived product/service benefits.

This type of strategy is appropriate for commodity-like products or for markets where customers are strongly price conscious. It is also suitable where customers' switching costs are low and where there is little opportunity for competition on product features.

A no frills strategy may be used for **market entry**, to **gain experience** and **build volume**. If the market leaders are competing on other bases, a no frills strategy may give new entrants a viable way of establishing themselves in the market before moving on to other strategies.

This was implemented by Japanese car manufacturers in the 1960s, and has also subsequently been seen in the airline industry, where companies such as EasyJet and Ryanair have successfully adopted a no frills approach.

2.5.2 Low price

A firm pursuing a **low price** strategy aims to **offer better value than its competitors**. It seeks to do this by offering the same perceived product or service benefits as its competitors, but at a lower price.

However, a potential drawback with such a strategy is that it **could lead to a price war**, if competitors lower their prices as well. A price war would reduce profit margins for all players in the market, and also lead to **lack of reinvestment** because the lower margins will reduce the amount of resources available.

Porter's generic strategy of **cost leadership** is appropriate to a firm adopting this strategy. However, low cost in itself is not the basis for a sustainable competitive advantage. The challenge which firms face is

how to reduce their costs to a level that competitors cannot match. If a firm can establish unique cost competences, then a low price strategy could afford it a sustainable competitive advantage.

CASE STUDY

Supermarket industry in the UK

The economic downturn in developed countries across the world in 2008-9 meant that consumers were being more careful about how they spent their cash. This caution affected a number of retail companies which saw their margins suffer as customer numbers fell away. However, while established retailers were suffering, discounters became much more popular, as cost-conscious shoppers started snapping up cut-price goods.

The growth of grocery discounters in Europe is not a new phenomenon, though. They have been steadily increasing market share since the early 1960s when the Albrecht family founded Aldi in Germany.

Chains such as Aldi and Lidl operate throughout Europe and, in total, discounters accounted for just below 18% of grocery spending across the continent in 2008. In Germany, where consumers are even more price conscious than in many other nations, discounter chains accounted for 43% of total food spend in 2007.

However, the growth of discount chains mirrored the economic downturn. From Dollar General in the US, to Uniqlo, the Japanese clothing chain, the conditions were near perfect for those promoting cost saving and low prices.

In the UK, discounters such as Aldi and Lidl, which had previously been kept at bay by supermarket chains Tesco and Sainsbury's, began enjoying an unprecedented growth spurt. And the supermarkets took note. Tesco, the UK's biggest retail chain, launched an aggressive price-cutting strategy – marketing itself as 'Britain's biggest discounter' – in an attempt to stem the flow of customers leaving it for cheaper rivals.

The supermarket industry research body, IDG, agreed that the discounters' growth was likely to be sustained throughout a recession. 'The historic perspective provides insight into key growth periods for discounters; namely times of economic uncertainty.'

However, discount supermarket chains have continued to increase their market share in the UK at the expense, the 'Big Four' supermarket chains (Tesco, Sainsbury's, Asda, Morrisons) since the recession has ended. Aldi achieved a record gain in market share – from 3.4% to 4.6% – for the 12 weeks to 30 March 2014 compared to the equivalent period a year earlier (2013), and Lidl also saw strong growth.

Alongside this, the upmarket food store Waitrose also enjoyed strong growth. However, the 'Big Four' all experienced a drop in market share.

The research panel, Kantar, which prepared the figures, noted that 'Amid a challenging market backdrop, individual retailer growth might be expected to be restricted. This is certainly not the case for Aldi, which achieved its highest ever growth rate of 35.3%.'

'Tesco, Sainsbury's, Asda and Morrisons have been dominant in the UK for some time. However, in recent years, supermarkets at both the discount and premium ends of the market have reported strong growth.'

Based on: 'Aldi, Lidl and Waitrose supermarkets increase market share', www.bbc.co.uk, 8 April 2014

Cost-cutters move into mainstream, *Financial Times*, 2 January 2009

Differentiation strategies

Strategies 3, 4 and 5 on the strategy clock are differentiation strategies. Each one represents a different trade-off between market share (with its cost advantages) and margin (with its direct impact on profit). Differentiation can be created in three ways:

- Product features
- Marketing, including powerful brand promotion
- Core competences

2.5.3 Hybrid strategy

A firm pursuing a hybrid strategy seeks both **differentiation** and a **lower price** than its competitors. The firm's cost base must be low enough to permit reduced prices and yet still retain high enough margins to be able to reinvest. Reinvestment is necessary to maintain differentiation.

Nonetheless, it could be argued that a firm which has a differentiated product should not need to have a lower price than its competitors, because differentiation should enable it to achieve prices that are equal to its competitors. Following this logic, we might question whether a hybrid strategy can be a successful competitive strategy or whether it will be a sub-optimal compromise between differentiation and low price.

If a hybrid strategy is merely a compromise strategy, then it is very likely it will be sub-optimal and therefore unsuccessful. However, there are circumstances where a hybrid strategy may be more advantageous than differentiation alone.

(a)   If it allows a firm to achieve much greater sales volumes than its competitors and, therefore, also better margins as a result of economies of scale which give it a low-cost base.

(b)   If differentiation rests on core competences, and costs can be reduced elsewhere. For example, Ikea builds differentiation on the basis of its product range and design logistics, store operations and marketing, but saves costs because customers are prepared to transport and build their products themselves.

(c)   If a low price approach is suited to a particular market segment.

(d)   Where it is used as a market entry strategy.

2.5.4 Broad differentiation

A broad differentiation strategy seeks to provide products or services that offer benefits which customers value and which are different from competitors' offerings.

The basic differentiation strategy comes in two variants:

- Offering better products or services than competitors at a higher price (**price premium**) to enhance margins

- Offering better products or services at the same price as competitors (**competitive price**) in order to build **market share**

If a firm wants to pursue a differentiation strategy it will need detailed and accurate **market intelligence** about **strategic customers**, and the **key competitors**. The **strategic customers** and their preferences and values must be clearly identified, as must the firm's competitors and their likely responses to its strategy.

The chosen basis for differentiation, which will probably need to be developed over time, should be inherently **difficult to imitate** so that it gives the firm a basis for a sustainable competitive advantage. One way a firm can create sustainable advantage is by creating **strategic lock-in** (establishing its product or service as the industry standards, like Microsoft Windows has done for computer operating systems).

A differentiation strategy can, however, still be **vulnerable to price-based competition**. There may be occasions when differentiation is not sufficient to affect customers' purchasing decisions in the face of lower prices. For example, in the recession which affected Western economies in 2008⊠9, a number of customers changed their shopping patterns from branded goods to own-label goods, or switched to discount retailers in an effort to curtail their spending. (Interestingly, this example also illustrates why a hybrid strategy can be so effective: allowing firms to offer superior products at lower prices than competitors.)

2.5.5 Focused differentiation

A firm pursuing a strategy of **focused differentiation** seeks a high price premium in return for a high degree of differentiation in a well-defined and probably quite restricted market segment (niche). Focused differentiation strategies are often used for premium products which are heavily branded.

However, focused differentiation raises some important issues.

(a)   A firm may have to choose between focused differentiation and broad differentiation (position 4 on the clock). A firm looking at international growth is likely to have to choose between building competitive advantage at a global level and with a global product (broad), and tailoring its products/services to specific markets (focus).

(b)   It is difficult to pursue focused differentiation for only part of an organisation: the less focused part, even if it is to some extent differentiated, can damage the brand values of the focused part.

(c)   In the public sector, stakeholders expecting universal provision will object to a focus on particular segments. For example, a dentist's surgery may feel it could generate increased revenue by focusing on cosmetic dentistry rather than traditional dental care. However, this would exclude patients who require traditional work on their teeth (such as fillings).

(d)   Focus is a common start-up strategy: expansion may prompt or require a gradual move to a less focused differentiation. Moving from focused to broad differentiation may require a lowering of price and, therefore, also cost, while still maintaining the differentiating features of a product or service.

(e)   Focus is aimed at a specific segment, but that segment or its requirements may not remain constant. For example, if a non-focused product is improved enough to become acceptable to this segment, the advantage of focus will be eroded. Alternatively, competitors may make even more focused offerings to sub-segments, again eroding the focuser's original advantage.

2.5.6 Failure strategies

Combinations 6, 7 and 8 on the strategy clock are likely to result in failure. A failure strategy is one which does not provide customers with perceived value for money – either with respect to product features, or price, or both.

Increased price/standard value

The logic here is to increase margins by increasing price while keeping costs (and, by inference, value) constant. However, unless the firm pursuing this strategy is a monopoly or is somehow protected by legislation or high barriers to entry, it is likely that such a strategy would cause it to lose market share, as customers switch to a competitor's product which offers the same value for a lower price.

One possible example of position 6 on the strategy clock is the way oil-producing countries increased the price of crude oil in 2007–8, by restricting supply in the face of excess demand. However, although there are significant barriers to entry, we can still see the potential problems with this strategy in terms of sustaining a competitive advantage because it has prompted people (and countries) to look at ways of reducing energy and fuel consumption, as well as stepping up their drive to discover alternative sources of energy.

Increased price/low value

Position 7 on the clock is even more likely to result in failure than option 6. A strategy which sees a firm increasing its prices while lowering the value it offers its customers would be expected to result in that firm losing all its customers to its competitors. Position 7 on the clock is only likely to be feasible in a monopoly situation.

Low value/standard price

Again, the logic here is to increase margins, effectively by cutting costs (reducing value) but keeping price the same. However, this strategy is again likely to lead to a loss of market share as customers become aware of the reduction in value, and switch their purchases to competitors whose products or services cost the same but offer greater value.

2.6 Overall limitations of the generic strategy approach

Problems in defining the 'industry' – Porter's model depends on clear notions of what the **industry** and **firm** in question are, in order to establish how competitive advantage derives from a firm's position in its industry. However, identifying the industry and the firm may not be clear, since many companies are part of larger organisations, and many 'industries' have boundaries that are hard to define. For example, what industry is a car manufacturer in? Cars, automotive (cars, lorries, buses), manufacturing, transportation?

Defining the strategic unit – As well as having difficulties in defining the industry, we can have difficulties in determining whether strategies should be pursued at **strategic business unit (SBU)** or **corporate level**, and in relation to exactly which category of products. For example, Procter & Gamble have a huge range of products and brands: are they to follow the same strategy with all of them? Similarly, the Volkswagen-Audi Group owns the Seat, Audi, Bentley and Skoda car marques.

Porter's theory states that if a firm has more than one competitive strategy this will dilute its competitive advantage. But does this mean that the Volkswagen-Audi's strategy for Skoda needs to be the same as for Bentley? Clearly not, and this is a major problem with Porter's theory.

It is impractical to suggest that a whole group should follow a single competitive strategy and so it seems more appropriate to suggest that the model should be applied at business unit level. Yet, if the theory is only applied at individual SBU level, then it could lead managers to overlook sources of competitive advantages which emerge from being part of a larger group – for example, economies of scale in procurement.

Another criticism which is sometimes made of Porter's model is that it doesn't look at how firms might use their competitive advantages and distinctive competences to **expand into new industries**, perhaps as the result of creative innovation. Porter only looks at how a firm might use its resources to develop strategy in its existing line of business. However, we could argue that this criticism isn't really valid. Although Porter doesn't talk about expansion into new industries, his model does not preclude it, and his arguments about following a competitive strategy would still ultimately need to be applied in the new industry.

2.7 The value chain and competitive strategy

The value chain can be used to design a competitive strategy, by deploying the various activities strategically. The examples below are based on two supermarket chains, one concentrating on low prices, the other differentiated on quality and service. See if you can tell which is which.

(a)

Firm infrastructure	Minimum corporate HQ				
Human resource management		De-skilled store- ops	Dismissal for checkout error		
Technology development	Computerised warehousing		Checkouts simple		
Procurement	Branded goods only – big discounts	Low cost sites			Use of concessions
	Bulk warehousing	1,000 lines only		Low price promotion	Nil
		Price points		Local focus	
		Basic store design			

INBOUND LOGISTICS   OPERATIONS   OUTBOUND LOGISTICS   MARKETING & SALES   SERVICE

(b)

	INBOUND LOGISTICS	OPERATIONS	OUTBOUND LOGISTICS	MARKETING & SALES	SERVICE
Firm infrastructure	Central control of operations and credit control				
Human resource management	Recruitment of mature staff	Client care training	Flexible staff to help with packing		
Technology development		Recipe research	Electronic point of sale	Consumer research & tests	Itemised bills
Procurement	Own label products	Prime retail positions		Adverts in quality magazines & poster sites	
	Dedicated refrigerated transport	In store food halls / Modern store design / Open front refrigerators / Tight control of sell-by dates	Collect by car service	No price discounts on food past sell-by dates	No quibble refunds

The two supermarkets represented are based on the following.

(a) The value chain in (a) is the 'discount' supermarket (perhaps similar to Lidl or Aldi in the UK) which sells on price, pursuing a cost leadership strategy. This can be seen in the limited product range and its low-cost sites.

(b) The value chain in (b) is for the supermarket which seeks to differentiate on quality and service (for example, Waitrose in the UK). Hence the 'no quibble' refunds, the use of prime retail sites, and customer care training.

You can probably think of other innovations, such as loyalty cards and internet shopping, which supermarkets have introduced to try to improve the quality and service they provide to their customers.

2.8 Pricing and strategy

As the strategy clock illustrates, the relationship between price and strategy is also important. Price is a key element of the marketing mix, and so it is important that an organisation's pricing strategy is consistent with the other elements of its strategy.

However, there are a number of different methodologies an organisation can use when deciding on the selling price for a product or service.

KEY TERMS

COMPETITIVE PRICING. Setting a price by reference to the prices of competitive products.

COST-PLUS PRICING. Determination of price by adding a mark-up, which may incorporate a desired return on investment, to a measure of the cost of the product/service.

MARKET-BASED PRICING. Setting a price based on the value of the product in the perception of the customer. Also known as perceived value pricing.

PENETRATION PRICING. Setting a low selling price in order to gain market share.

PREDATORY PRICING. Setting a low selling price in order to damage competitors. May involve dumping, ie selling a product in a foreign market at below cost, or below the domestic market price (subject to, for example, adjustments for taxation differences, transportation costs, specification differences).

PRICE SKIMMING. Setting a high price in order to maximise short-term profitability, often on the introduction of a novel product.

RANGE PRICING. The pricing of individual products such that their prices fit logically within a range of connected products offered by one supplier, and differentiated by a factor such as weight of pack or number of product attributes offered.

SELECTIVE PRICING. Setting different prices for the same product or service in different markets. Can be broken down as follows:

- **Category pricing**. Cosmetically modifying a product such that the variations allow it to sell in a number of price categories, as where a range of 'brands' are based on a common product.

- **Customer group pricing**. Modifying the price of a product or service so that different groups of consumers pay different prices.

- **Peak pricing**. Setting a price which varies according to level of demand.

- **Service level pricing**. Setting a price based on the particular level of service chosen from a range.

- **Time material pricing**. A form of cost plus pricing in which price is determined by reference to the cost of the labour and material inputs to the product/service.   *(CIMA Official Terminology)*

All profit-seeking organisations and many non-profit organisations face the task of **setting a price** on their products or services.

Price can be defined as a measure of the **value exchanged by the buyer for the value offered by the seller**. It might be expected, therefore, that the price would reflect the costs to the seller of producing the product and the benefit to the buyer of consuming it.

Unlike the other marketing mix elements, pricing decisions affect profits through their impact on **revenues** rather than costs. It also has an important role as a **competitive tool** to differentiate a product and an organisation and thereby exploit market opportunities.

Although pricing can be thought of as fulfilling a number of roles, in overall terms a price aims to produce the desired level of sales in order to meet the objectives of the business strategy.

Two broad categories of objectives may be specified for pricing decisions.

(a) **Maximising profits** is concerned with maximising the returns on assets or investments. This may be realised even with a comparatively small market share depending on the patterns of cost and demand.

(b) **Maintaining or increasing market share** involves increasing or maintaining the customer base which may require a different, more competitive approach to pricing, while the company with the largest market share may not necessarily earn the best profits.

2.9 Pricing and the customer

2.9.1 Price sensitivity

Price sensitivity will vary amongst purchasers. Those that can pass on the cost of purchases will be the least sensitive and will therefore respond more to other elements of perceived value.

(a) The family on holiday is likely to be very price sensitive when choosing an overnight stay.

(b) In industrial marketing the purchasing manager is likely to be more price sensitive than the engineer who will use the new equipment that is being sourced.

2.9.2 Price perception and quality connotations

Price perception is an important factor in the ways customers react to prices. For example, customers may react to a price increase by buying more. This could be for a variety of reasons.

(a)   They expect further price increases to follow (they are 'stocking up').

(b)   Many customers appear to judge quality by price:

    (i)   They assume the quality has increased, if there is a price rise.

    (ii)   The brand gains appeal as a status symbol, and therefore becomes desirable as a result of its high price.

2.9.3 Intermediaries' objectives

If an organisation distributes products or services to the market through independent **intermediaries**, the objectives of these intermediaries complicate the pricing decision. Such intermediaries are likely to deal with a range of suppliers and their aims concern their own profits rather than those of suppliers.

2.9.4 Multiple products and loss leaders

Most organisations sell a range of products. The management of the pricing function is likely to focus on the profit from the whole range rather than the profit on each single product. Take, for example, the use of **loss leaders** – a very low price for one product is intended to make consumers buy additional products in the range which carry higher profit margins.

2.9.5 Ethics

Ethical considerations are a further factor; for example, whether or not to exploit short-term shortages through higher prices.

An alternative aspect of ethics and social responsibility in pricing is ensuring that all suppliers are paid a fair price for what they produce. '**Fair Trade**' products illustrate this. And although they may be slightly more expensive than some rival products, the 'fair trade' aspect may be an important factor in leading consumers to buy them in preference to some cheaper alternatives.

2.10 New product pricing: market penetration and market skimming

There are three elements in the pricing decision for a new product.

- Getting the product **accepted**
- Maintaining a **market share** in the face of competition
- Making a **profit** from the product

2.10.1 Penetration

Market penetration pricing is a policy of low prices when the product is first launched in order to gain sufficient penetration into the market. It is, therefore, a policy of sacrificing short-term profits in the interests of long-term profits.

(a)   The firm wishes to **discourage rivals** from entering the market.

(b)   The firm wishes to **shorten the initial period of the product's life cycle**, in order to enter the growth and maturity stages as quickly as possible. (This would happen if there is high elasticity of demand for the product.)

2.10.2 Skimming

Market skimming. The aim of market skimming is to gain high unit profits very early on in the product's life.

(a)   The firm charges high prices when a product is first launched.

(b)   The firm spends heavily on advertising and sales promotion to win customers.

(c) As the product moves into the later stages of its life cycle (growth, maturity and decline) progressively lower prices will be charged. The profitable 'cream' is thus 'skimmed' off in progressive stages until sales can only be sustained at lower prices.

(d) The firm may lower its prices in order to attract more price-elastic segments of the market. However, these price reductions will be gradual. Alternatively, the entry of competitors into the market may make price reductions inevitable.

Introductory offers and temporary **discounts** may be used to attract an initial customer interest.

2.11 Other pricing decisions

Promotional prices are short-term price reductions or price offers which are intended to attract an increase in sales volume. (The increase is usually short term for the duration of the offer, which does not appear to create any substantial new customer loyalty.) Loss leaders and 'money-off' coupons are a form of promotional pricing.

A temporary **price cut** may be preferable to a permanent reduction because it can be ended without unduly offending customers and can be reinstated later to give a repeated boost to sales.

2.12 Pricing and the management accountant

The decision about pricing is one which involves both the accountant and the marketing manager.

Short-term pricing. Marketing management should have the responsibility for estimating the price–demand interrelationship for their organisation's products. The accountant should become involved in short-term pricing decisions because of cost.

(a) The sales-revenue maximising price for a product and the profit-maximising price might not be the same.

(b) Simple cost-volume-profit (CVP) analysis can be used to estimate the breakeven point of sales, and the sales volume needed to achieve a target profit figure.

(c) Many organisations use a **cost-plus** approach to pricing. Accounting figures are needed for cost in order to establish a floor for making a cost-plus pricing decision.

By analysing **product profitability**, the accountant also provides information for pricing control, because profit statements indicate whether prices have been high enough, given the sales demand, to provide a satisfactory return.

2.13 Price and competition

In classical economic theory, price is the major determinant of demand and brings together supply and demand to form an equilibrium market price. However, economic theory can only determine the optimal price structure under the two extreme market conditions.

(a) **Perfect competition**: many buyers and many sellers all dealing in an identical product. Neither producer nor user has any market power and both must accept the prevailing market price.

(b) **Monopoly**: one seller who dominates many buyers. The monopolist can use their market power to set a profit-maximising price.

However, in practice, most of UK industry can be described as an **oligopoly**: where relatively few competitive companies dominate the market.

2.13.1 Price leadership

Given that price competition can have disastrous consequences in conditions of oligopoly, it is not unusual to find that large corporations emerge as price leaders.

A price leader will have the dominant influence on price levels for a class of products. Price increases or decreases by the price leader provide a direction to market price patterns.

However, a danger with price leadership is that it might appear to limit the impact of competition. If firms actively collude to keep prices to a certain level, and to divide the 'spoils' between them, they are forming a cartel. Cartels are illegal under UK and European competition law.

Generally speaking, therefore, price cuts to increase market share will be matched by competitors in some way. If a rival firm cuts its prices in the expectation of increasing its market share, a firm has the following options.

(a) **Maintain its existing prices**. This would be done if the expectation is that only a small market share would be lost, so that it is more profitable to keep prices at their existing level. Eventually, the rival firm may drop out of the market or be forced to raise its prices.

(b) **Maintain prices but respond with a non-price counter-attack**. This is a more positive response, because the firm will be securing or justifying its current prices with a product change, advertising, or better back-up services, etc.

(c) **Reduce prices**. This should protect the firm's market share so that the main beneficiary from the price reduction will be the consumer.

(d) **Raise prices and respond with a non-price counter-attack**. A price increase would be based on a campaign to emphasise the quality difference between the rival products.

Predatory pricing is the use of price to drive a competitor out of business. It is a grey area, as competing on price is legitimate and economically efficient.

The intensely competitive supermarket sector in the UK and US provides a prime example of periodic price-cutting activity that can lead, in extreme cases, to all-out price 'wars' between the largest competitors. **Price competition** like this will undermine the value of the market that is being competed for. (Note the link here between price competition and game theory which we discussed earlier in this Study Text.)

When faced with price competition, firms might ask themselves the following questions.

- What is the minimum potential **sales loss** that justifies meeting a **lower competitive price**?
- What is the minimum potential **sales gain** that justifies **not following** a competitive price **increase**?
- What is the minimum potential **sales loss** that justifies **not following** a competitive price **decrease**?

2.14 Competitive pricing actions

Different competitive pricing actions can say a lot about a company's strategy and send signals to the market.

(a) **Reducing price below that of competitors** in order to win a contract gives certain messages.

   (i) The company is desperate for sales volume.
   (ii) It believes it is the lowest cost supplier.
   (iii) The target customer is strategically important.

(b) **Reducing price by the same amount as a competitor**, in order to win back business, demonstrates to that competitor that contracts cannot be won or lost on price considerations alone.

(c) **Substantial price reductions** and public announcements of new manufacturing facilities show the market that, despite price reductions, sales are set to expand and revenues will not decrease in the long term.

(d) A **quick negotiation of lower prices** without alerting the competition indicates a belief that a gain can be made through the short-term winning of a customer.

Section summary

Porter's **generic strategies** suggest that a firm generates competitive advantages by either being a **cost leader**, or **differentiating itself** from its competitors. Bowman has subsequently developed the concept of the **strategy clock** to show how firms can position their strategies on the basis of their **prices** and the **value** they provide to their customers.

Pricing strategy, and particularly the relationship between price and value, is an important element of an organisation's overall strategy. Price is a key element of the **marketing mix**.

3 Product–market strategy: direction of growth

Introduction

Product–market strategy looks at the mix of products and markets a firm can use to try to increase its sales. Ansoff demonstrates the choices available in the form of a matrix with four options:

- **Market penetration**: current products, current markets
- **Market development**: current products, new markets
- **Product development**: new products, current markets
- **Diversification**: new products, new markets

All of these can secure growth. **Diversification** is often perceived to be most **risky**. Although it can be justified by 'synergies' (common assets, expertise etc which can be applied in a number of different business areas), these are often more apparent than real.

KEY TERM

PRODUCT-MARKET MIX is a shorthand term for the **products/services** a firm sells (or a service which a public sector organisation provides) and the **markets** it sells them to.

3.1 Product–market mix: Ansoff's growth vector matrix

Ansoff drew up a **growth vector matrix**, describing how a combination of a firm's activities in current and new markets, with existing and new products, can lead to **growth**. Ansoff's original model was a four cell matrix based on product and market.

Ansoff's matrix

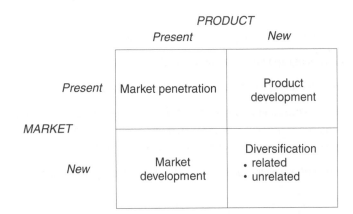

Lynch has produced an enhanced model that he calls the **market options matrix**. This adds the external options shown in this second diagram.

Lynch – Market options matrix

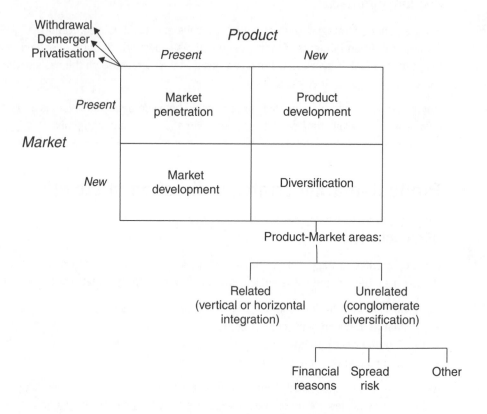

3.1.1 Current products and current markets: market penetration

The firm seeks to:

(a)   Maintain or increase its share of current markets with current products, eg through competitive pricing, advertising, sales promotions, quantity discounts (designed to increase purchases by existing customers)

(b)   Secure dominance of growth markets

(c)   Restructure a mature market by driving out competitors

(d)   Acquire a rival in the same market

(e)   Increase usage by existing customers (eg retailers' loyalty cards)

3.1.2 Current products and new markets: market development

(a)   **New geographical areas** and export markets

(b)   **New demographic segments** (eg different age groups)

(c)   **New distribution channels** to attract new customers (eg different age groups, industrial or domestic customers), accompanied by advertising in different media, and in different ways, to reflect the new customer segments being targeted

(d)   **Differential pricing policies** to attract different types of customer and create **new market segments**

3.1.3 New products and current markets: product development

Product development is the launch of new products to existing markets, either through the internal research and development (R&D) of a firm's own products, or possibly by acquiring the rights to produce someone else's product.

An example of firms looking to grow through product development is the mobile telephone manufacturers which are currently looking to develop and introduce fourth generation (4G) wireless infrastructure. 4G networks are based on wireless broadband technology called Long Term Evolution (LTE). LTE is expected to fuel the growth of the mobile internet because it should significantly increase download speeds on mobile handsets. For the manufacturers which secure contracts with leading operators to supply 4G networks, these contracts could provide a basis for future growth.

(a)   **Advantages of product development**

    (i)   Product development forces competitors to innovate.

    (ii)   Newcomers to the market might be discouraged.

(b)   The **drawbacks** include the expense, and the risk.

CASE STUDY

Product development in the music industry

Over time, recorded music has been distributed on LP records, cassette tapes, compact discs, and now digitally via downloads and online streaming.

However, the major record labels were slow to respond to demands for online music and faced an ongoing battle against illegal downloading and piracy.

Online music piracy could be seen as a response to the record labels' slow response to consumers' demands for how they want to listen to music.

Eventually record labels began to understand that the industry was changing and realised the only way for them to survive was to get onboard.

An early defence to online piracy involved offering in-store kiosks where customers could download music direct to their MP3 players, followed by a number of ways to exploit the web.

Web retailers such as iTunes allow users to browse huge back catalogues, but they expect the user to actually pay for each track they listen to. Other services include subscription-based website Napster that allows paying members to consume as much music as they want.

Another approach is ad-supported downloads, such as We7, where consumers can download songs for free, but each track is preceded by an advertisement. This has further been developed into streaming sites such as Spotify which also use the advertisement approach to provide free listening online. Spotify allows users to play music either track by track, listen to an album, or receive customised 'radio'. This is where the user selects one track and the programme will automatically play a series of tracks by similar artists that the user is likely to enjoy based on the track they have selected.

The internet-based method of obtaining music is now also starting to be overtaken by apps which are used directly on smartphones and tablets. App versions of Spotify and others provide yet further convenience to users and have increased the ease with which music can be listened to or bought instantly.

These changes have meant that artists now have to work a lot harder to earn a living. The huge decrease in recording royalties has been partly responsible for the current revival of live performance, the number of which has increased as artists attempt to maintain their income.

3.1.4 New products: new markets (diversification)

Diversification occurs when a company decides to make **new products for new markets**. It should have a clear idea about what it expects to gain from diversification.

(a)   **Growth.** New products and new markets should be selected which offer prospects for growth which the existing product–market mix does not.

(b)   **Investing surplus** funds not required for other expansion needs. (The funds could be returned to shareholders.)

3.2 Related diversification

KEY TERM

RELATED DIVERSIFICATION is 'development beyond the present product market, but still within the broad confines of the industry ... [It] ... therefore builds on the assets or activities which the firm has developed' (Johnson, Scholes and Whittington). It takes the form of vertical or horizontal integration.

Horizontal integration is development into activities which are competitive with or directly **complementary** to a company's present activities; for example, a newspaper company moving into magazine production. The firm's advantage lies in using its technical and technological competences. This form of integration is also called **concentric diversification**.

Vertical integration occurs when a company becomes its own:

(a)   **Supplier** of raw materials, components or services (**backward vertical integration**). For example, backward integration would occur where a milk producer acquires its own dairy farms rather than buying raw milk from independent farmers.

(b)   **Distributor** or sales agent (**forward vertical integration**), for example: where a manufacturer of synthetic yarn begins to produce shirts from the yarn instead of selling it to other shirt manufacturers.

Advantages of vertical integration

- A **secure supply of components** or **materials**, thus lower supplier bargaining power

- **Stronger relationships** with the 'final consumer' of the product (thereby reducing the bargaining power of consumers)

- Win a share of the **higher profits** at all stages of the **value chain**

- Avoiding costs of **intermediate transactions** (eg packaging of component parts required if bought in from an external supplier)

- Pursue a **differentiation strategy** more effectively (because a greater amount of the product is under the firm's control)

- Raise **barriers to entry**

- Improvements in **quality** and **innovation**

Disadvantages of vertical integration

(a)   **Overconcentration**. A firm places 'more eggs in the same end-market basket' (Ansoff). Such a policy is fairly inflexible, more sensitive to instabilities and increases the firm's dependence on a particular aspect of economic demand. For example, the flexibility to change suppliers is reduced if a firm is using an 'in-house' supplier.

(b)   The firm **fails to benefit from any economies of scale or technical advances** in the industry into which it has diversified. This is why, in the publishing industry, most printing is subcontracted to specialist printing firms, which can work machinery to capacity by undertaking work for many firms.

(c)   **Fixed costs**. Vertical integration increases the proportion of a firm's costs which are fixed. If a firm buys in inputs from an external supplier, the costs of those inputs are variable costs. If the input is produced internally, the firm has to bear all the fixed costs of production. The increase in fixed costs as a proportion of total costs increases the firm's **operating gearing** and the business risk associated with this.

(d)   **Inefficiency**. The internal relationship between buyer and seller can lead to inefficiencies, as the seller no longer faces the same level of competition as it would in an open market transaction. As a result, production costs could start to rise, and this cost inefficiency, in turn, could be passed through to the group's final product. This will mean that the price of the final product will either have to be higher than that of competitors' products, or – if the price is held the same as competitors' prices – the group will earn lower margins on its product than competitors do on theirs.

3.3 Unrelated diversification

KEY TERM

UNRELATED OR CONGLOMERATE DIVERSIFICATION 'is development beyond the present industry into products/markets which, at face value, may bear no close relation to the present product/market'.

Conglomerate diversification is now very unfashionable. However, it has been a key strategy for companies in Asia, particularly South Korea, where the diversified conglomerates known as *chaebol* have been very popular.

CASE STUDY

Hutchinson Whampao

Hutchinson Whampoa Limited is among the largest companies listed on the main board of the Hong Kong Stock Exchange. Flagship companies within the Hutchinson group include: Hutchinson Port Holdings, Hutchinson Whampoa Properties, A S Watson (health, beauty and lifestyle retailer), Cheung Kong Infrastructure, and Hutchinson Telecom.

The group has businesses spanning the globe, but its diverse array of holdings includes five different core businesses:

- Ports and related services
- Property and hotels
- Retail (in particular, health and beauty)
- Energy and infrastructure
- Telecommunications – including mobile phones and networks under the '3' brand

3.3.1 Advantages of conglomerate diversification

- Risk spreading by entering new products into new markets
- An improvement of the overall profitability and flexibility of the firm through synergy
- Escape from the present business
- Better access to capital markets
- Organisational learning by buying-in expertise
- Use surplus cash
- Exploit underutilised resources
- Obtain cash, or other financial advantages (such as accumulated tax losses)
- Use a company's image and reputation in one market to develop into another

3.3.2 Disadvantages of conglomerate diversification

- The dilution of shareholders' earnings.
- Lack of a common identity and purpose in a conglomerate organisation.
- Failure in one of the businesses will drag down the rest.

- Lack of management experience may reduce management's ability to run the new business properly.

- Increased risk: the business is either entering a new market or producing a new product. Because they are new, they carry an increased risk that the venture may not be successful – for example, have the needs of the customer been correctly identified? Will the organisation's culture be appropriate to the new market?

3.4 Trade-offs

Conglomerate diversification can lead to a wide range of organisational characteristics. Generally there will be trade-offs to be made between elements, such as those listed below.

- Economies of scale (increasing the utilisation of dedicated assets)
- Economies of scope (increasing the utilisation of general assets)
- Overhead cost structure and level
- Responsiveness to changing customer needs and wants
- Exploitation of resources and competences
- Organisational learning
- Competition reaction
- Management attention and capacity

3.5 Diversification and synergy

Synergy is the 2 + 2 = 5 effect, where a firm looks for **combined results** that reflect a better rate of return than would be achieved by the same resources used independently as separate operations. Synergy is used to justify diversification. Much of the benefit of synergy is derived from **economies of scale and scope**.

3.5.1 Obtaining synergy

(a) **Marketing synergy**: use of common marketing facilities such as distribution channels, sales staff and administration, and warehousing.

(b) **Operating synergy**: arises from the better use of operational facilities and personnel, bulk purchasing, a greater spread of fixed costs whereby the firm's competence can be transferred to making new products. For example, although there is very little in common between sausages and ice cream, both depend on a competence of refrigeration.

(c) **Investment synergy**: the joint use of plant, common raw material inputs, transfer of R&D from one product to another – ie from the wider use of a common investment in fixed assets, working capital or research.

(d) **Management synergy**: the advantage to be gained where management skills concerning current operations are easily transferred to new operations because of the similarity of problems in the two industries.

Question 5.2	Road transport

Learning outcome B1(a)

A large organisation in road transport operates nationwide in general haulage. This field has become very competitive and, with the recent downturn in trade, has become only marginally profitable. It has been suggested that the strategic structure of the company should be widened to include other aspects of physical distribution so that the maximum synergy would be obtained from that type of diversification.

Suggest two activities which might fit into the suggested new strategic structure, explaining each one briefly. Explain how each of these activities could be incorporated into the existing structure. State the advantages and disadvantages of such diversification.

3.6 Withdrawal

It might be the right decision to cease producing a product and/or to pull out of a market completely. This is a hard decision for managers to take if they have invested time and money or if the decision involves redundancies.

Exit barriers make this difficult.

- Cost barriers include redundancy costs and the difficulty of selling assets.
- Managers might fail to grasp opportunity costing.
- Political barriers include government attitudes.
- Marketing considerations may delay withdrawal.
- Managers hate to admit failure.
- People might wrongly assume that carrying on is a low risk strategy.

Reasons for exit

- The company's business may be in buying and selling firms.
- Resource limitations mean that less profitable businesses have to be abandoned.
- A company may be forced to quit, because of insolvency.
- Change of competitive strategy.
- Decline in attractiveness of the market.
- Funds can earn more elsewhere.

3.7 Guidelines for a product–market strategy

Johnson, Scholes and Whittington suggested the following principles and guidelines for product–market planning.

(a)   **The potential for improvement and growth**. It is one thing to eliminate unprofitable products but will there be sufficient growth potential among the products that remain in the product range?

(b)   **Cash generation**. New products require some initial capital expenditure. Retained profits are by far the most significant source of new funds for companies. A company investing in the medium to long term which does not have enough current income from existing products will go into liquidation, in spite of its future prospects.

Exam skills

In this context it might be useful to look at an organisation's product portfolio matrix (BCG matrix) as part of the preparation of a product–market strategy. Has the organisation got a balanced portfolio, with enough cash cows to fund present growth, and stars and question marks to sustain future growth?

(c)   **The timing decision for killing off existing products**. There are some situations where existing products should be kept going for a while longer, to provide or maintain a necessary platform for launching new models.

(d)   **The long-term rationale of a product or market development**.

(e)   **Diversification by acquisition**. It might pay to buy product ranges or brands in a takeover deal. If the product–market strategy includes a policy of diversification, then the products or services which the expanding company seeks to acquire should provide definite benefits.

3.7.1 Closing the profit gap and product–market strategy

The aim of product–market strategies is to **close the profit gap** that is found by gap analysis. A mixture of strategies may be needed to fill the gap between the current profit forecast (F_0 in the following diagram) and the target profit.

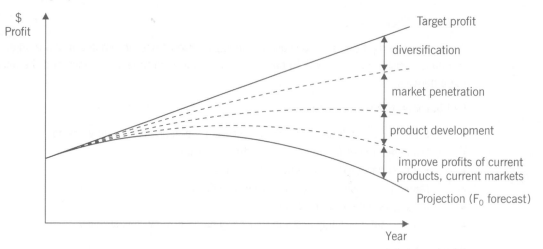

It is worth remembering that **divestment** is also a product–market option to close the profit gap, if the business being divested is making losses.

A related question is what do you do with spare capacity – go for market penetration, or expand into new markets? Many companies begin exporting into new overseas markets to use surplus capacity.

The strategies in Ansoff's matrix are not mutually exclusive. A firm can quite legitimately pursue a penetration strategy in some of its markets, while aiming to enter new markets.

However, remember that the strategies in Ansoff's matrix have different levels of **risk** attached to them.

3.8 Risk and return

An important factor managers need to consider when evaluating different product–market strategies is the level of risk attached to each.

Market penetration strategies are the least risky, because they make use of an organisation's existing resources and capabilities. However, market penetration is also likely to offer the lowest growth potential – particularly if an organisation's existing markets are approaching saturation level.

Market development – Because an organisation is expanding into a new market, as opposed to continuing in an existing market with which it is already familiar, market development typically involves a higher level of risk than market penetration. Equally, however, the scope for additional revenue from the new market may mean that market development offers greater scope for growth than market penetration does.

Product development – Similarly, because the organisation is introducing a new product, rather than trying to sell more of an established product, product development involves a higher level of risk than market penetration, but also offers greater scope for growth.

Diversification strategies present the highest levels of risk among the four product–market strategies, because they involve both product development and market development. Also, particularly in the case of unrelated diversification, they may extend beyond an organisation's existing competences and capabilities.

However, because diversification strategies give an organisation the opportunity to sell new products in new markets, they also have the potential to deliver the highest returns of the four product–market strategies.

3.8.1 Types of risk

If a firm is looking to implement product–market growth strategies it needs to be aware of the potential risks it will be facing.

Market risk

(a)   If a firm enters a new market, it will face competition from the existing firms in the market which will want to protect their market share.

(b)   The new entrant needs to understand the culture of the market and the needs of the customers if it is to be able to compete successfully.

(c)   The new entrant needs to persuade customers to buy from it in preference to the existing firms.

Product risk

(a)   If a firm is developing a new product, or a new production process, production costs may be increased to lack of experience.

(b)   There may be problems with quality and reliability to begin with, and these could severely damage the firm's reputation and its prospects in the market.

(c)   Because the firm is making a new product, it may have to develop new supply-chain relations, and the absence of an existing supply chain infrastructure could adversely affect cost and quality.

Managerial risk

(a)   The management team may not be able to run the new business effectively, especially if it is in a significantly different business area to its existing business.

(b)   There is a related risk here that if management devote too much time to the new business at the expense of the existing business, the performance of the existing business will suffer.

Financial risk

(a)   The cash flows from a new business are likely to be volatile.

(b)   The business may need to raise additional funds to support a new investment, but there is a risk the new venture will not be successful meaning that the new assets may have to be written off.

(c)   The need for funds to support the business may reduce the level of dividend paid to shareholders. The firm will need to reassure shareholders about the respective levels of risk and return, so that they support the new projects.

(d)   Equally, the company will need to try to reassure the markets that the projects will be successful, because uncertainty tends to lead to a fall in a company's share price.

3.9 Brand switching and competitive rivalry

A company may introduce measures to counteract **brand switching** by customers (and consequent loss of market share). One example is provided by the loyalty card schemes used by supermarkets to encourage repeat (and increased) spending by customers who may otherwise defect to the opposition.

Section summary

Ansoff's growth vector matrix identifies the four product–market strategies firms can use to try to increase sales: **market penetration; market development; product development; and diversification**. The degree of risk involved varies between strategies, with diversification being the most risky.

4 Methods of growth

Introduction

So far we have considered the basis on which firms might look to develop (for example, as cost leaders or differentiators) and the product–market strategies they might adopt in order to do so.

However, we now need to look at **how firms grow**. Do they develop internally, or do they look for external growth, through mergers and acquisitions or strategic alliances?

Once a firm has made its choice about which strategies it wants to pursue, it needs to choose an appropriate **mechanism** to deliver that strategy.

- Develop the business from scratch
- Acquire or merge with an already existing business
- Co-operate in some way with another firm

The main issues involved in choosing a method of growth are:

- **Resources**. Does a firm have enough resources and competences to go it alone, or does it have plenty of **resources** to invest?

- Two different businesses might have **complementary skills**.

- **Speed**. Does a firm need to **move fast**?

- A firm might wish to **retain control** of a product or process.

- **Cultural fit**. Combining businesses involves integrating **people and organisation culture**.

- **Risk**. A firm may either increase or reduce the level of risk to which it is subject. External growth often involves more risk than organic (internal) growth.

The type of relationships between two or more firms can display differing degrees of intensity.

- **Formal integration**: acquisition and merger
- **Formalised ownership/relationship**, such as a joint venture
- **Contractual relationships**, such as franchising

4.1 Expansion method

Lynch summarised possible expansion methods in an expansion method matrix that analysed them on two axes: **internal** vs **external** development, and **home country** vs **international** location.

(a) Internal development in the home country is simply organic growth.

(b) Internal development internationally:

    (i)   Exporting   (iv)   Multinational operation

    (ii)   Overseas office   (v)   Global operation

    (iii)   Overseas manufacture

(c)   External development in the home country or internationally:

   (i)   Merger   (iii)   Joint venture or alliance
   (ii)   Acquisition   (iv)   Franchising or licensing

Company

	Inside	Outside
Home country	Organic growth	Merger Acquisitions Joint venture Alliance Franchise Licence
International	Exporting Overseas office Overseas manufacture Multinational operation Global operation	Merger Acquisitions Joint venture Alliance Franchise Licence Contract manufacturing

Location

Lynch – Expansion method matrix

Section summary

A firm can either choose to grow internally or else it can link with another firm.

5 Organic growth

Introduction

Organic growth is a popular method of growth for many organisations. It is achieved through the development of an organisation's own internal resources, rather than combining with any other firms.

KEY TERM

ORGANIC GROWTH. Expansion of a firm's size, profits, activities achieved without taking over other firms.

Why might a firm pursue organic growth?

(a)   The **process of developing** a new product gives the firm the best understanding of the market and the product.

(b)   It might be the only sensible way to pursue **genuine technological innovations**.

(c)   There is **no suitable target for acquisition**.

(d)   The firm has **sufficient current resources** to comfortably plan, finance and deliver the growth itself.

(e)   The same **style of management** and **corporate culture** can be maintained.

(f)   There are no issues with trying to integrate the firm's **operating systems** with those of another firm.

(g)   May be less onerous on cash flow than an acquisition. Investment on internal growth can be funded in stages, but to make an acquisition a firm is likely to have to commit a large amount of funds in one go.

(h)   **Hidden or unforeseen losses** are less likely with organic growth. There are also no issues with having to **value a potential acquisition**.

If we assume that existing products have a finite life, a strategy of organic growth must include plans for **innovation**.

- It provides the organisation with a **distinctive competence**, and with the ability to maintain such a competence.

- It maintains the organisation's **competitive advantage** and market share.

There are two key triggers for innovation:

Market pull – new market opportunities may generate growth opportunities for firms.

Technology push – technological change provides new opportunities. Often technological change can migrate from one industry to another. If firms monitor technological changes in other industries they can sometimes identify opportunities for their own.

However, organic growth by innovation is not always a guarantee of success.

5.1 Potential disadvantages of organic growth

(a)   **Time**. It will take longer for a firm to grow organically, than by acquiring another firm. This may be a problem in an industry which is changing rapidly, and where an acquisition could allow the firm to 'buy-in' new skills and knowledge.

(b)   If the firm is looking to break into new markets, it may lack the **access** to key suppliers or customers which established players have.

(c)   The firm has to bear all the **risk** of any new product development or market entry strategies. By contrast, if, for example, the firm entered into a joint venture, this risk would be shared with the venture partner.

Capacity issues: critical mass and economies of scale

For some firms, organic growth must result in a target **critical mass** being achieved, in order to realise economies of scale. In an industry where fixed costs are high, and variable costs relatively small, significant reductions in unit costs can be attained by producing on a larger scale.

For example, suppose that in the widget-manufacturing industry the following costs are applicable.

Factory capacity (output in units pa)	Fixed costs	Unit variable costs
	$	$
10,000	400,000	5.00
50,000	800,000	4.80
200,000	1,600,000	4.60

Unit costs of producing at maximum capacity in each size of factory would be:

Capacity Units	Unit costs Fixed $	Unit costs Variable $	Total $	
10,000	40.0	5.0	45.00	Effect of
50,000	16.0	4.8	20.80	economies of
200,000	8.0	4.6	12.60	scale

If an organisation plans to achieve a certain capacity of output, it will not minimise its costs unless actual production volumes reach the capacity level. In the table above, the factory with 200,000 units capacity can achieve unit costs of $12.60 when operating at full capacity; but if actual production were only 50%, say, unit fixed costs would double to $16, and unit costs would be $20.60 (very nearly as high as in a factory with 50,000 units capacity operating at full capacity).

5.2 International expansion

There are two fundamental approaches to internationalising production: (i) cost or competence-led; and (ii) market-led.

Cost or competence-led location

In this approach, production decisions are taken on the basis of the technology to be adopted, the scale of production (how many units per year) and the inherent characteristics of the location.

Company choices are then determined by a desire to obtain the cheapest – or, rather, best value or most cost-effective – place to obtain supplies. The **cost reduction opportunities** must be sufficient to overcome any cost and inconvenience incurred in subsequently transporting goods to market.

With regard to location, **labour** is a major factor in terms of its cost, quality, productivity and its flexibility. This helps to explain why many clothing companies now use (cheap) labour in South-East Asian countries to manufacture garments which are subsequently exported for sale to Western Europe and America.

Market-led location

Alternatively, a company may choose to locate some of its production activities inside a particularly attractive market, in order to benefit from customer demand in that market.

Locating in a market could also enable a company to avoid trade barriers (such as tariffs or import quotas).

CASE STUDY

Case example: Automobile Production in Central and Eastern Europe

Central and Eastern Europe (CEE) has become an attractive destination for investments by global car manfacturers. In 2014, 3.6 million vehicles were produced in the region (whch incorporates the Czech Republic, Hungary, Poland, Romania, Slovakia and Slovenia). This equated to 21% of total EU production.

However, most of the factories which produce the vehicles were established through foreign direct investment (FDI). The CEE region has been able to attact FDI due to its attractive labour costs, educated workforce, and geographical proximity to Western Europe,

Production is dominated by Western European brands, in particular German ones – with Audi, Mercedes and Volkswagen all having factories there. However, the CEE region is also attrative for Asian manufacturers, such as Hyundai, Toyota and Suzuki.

Analysis by Coface (2015) found that the automotive sector employed over 850,000 workers in 2013 in the six countries analysed. Coface's analysis also found that the number of vehicles produced in the CEE had more than doubled in the period 2004-2014.

However, a large proportion of the demand for the vehicles comes from foreign consumers. Consequently, vehicle exports account for a significnt share of CEE's foreign trade. In Slovakia, for example, vehicle exports represent 25% of the country's total exports.

Historically, the Russian market has been a secondary source of export demand for CEE, but Russian demand has fallen in recent years. However, the fall in Russian demand has been compensated by increased demand for other export destinations and domestic CEE sales.

Domestic demand in CEE countries is benefitting from better prospects for local households, due to the improved labour market, subdued inflation, low oil prices, rising consumer confidence and attractive interest rates. The relatively high propensity to spend is resulting in more dynamic car sales in CEE economies. And customers are not only individuals but also companies expanding their fleets of passenger cars and commercial vehicles.

Nonetheless, the sector's overall performance is primarily dependent on its exports to Eurozone countries, which remains its main export market.

Demand for new vehicles has been affected in recent years by the global financial crisis and the double dip recession in the Eurozone (2007-2010). Faced with a decline in demand, coupled with weak

consumer and business confidence indicators, manufacturers tried to implement processes for reducing their costs. This created manufacturing opportunities for locations with attractive labour costs, such as the CEE countries.

> Based on: Coface Economic Publications (2015) *The CEE automotive sector is highly dependent on foreign investments but there are positive dynamics in domestic demand*

International expansion is a big undertaking and firms must know their reasons for it, and be sure that they have the resources to manage it, both strategically and operationally. The decision about which overseas market to enter should be based on assessment of **market attractiveness**, **competitive advantage**, and **risk**.

Some key decisions for international expansion

Firms must deal with three major issues.

- Whether to expand internationally at all
- Which markets to enter
- The mode(s) of entry

5.2.1 Porter's diamond

If a firm is considering investing in new production facilities in a foreign country – or more generally to expand internationally – the choice of which country to invest in is a key strategic decision. Porter's diamond is a useful model for analysing the factors which could make a country attractive (or not) as a place to invest for different industries.

The diamond identifies four key factors which determine the relative attractiveness of different countries, and also identifies why some industries within countries are more successful than others.

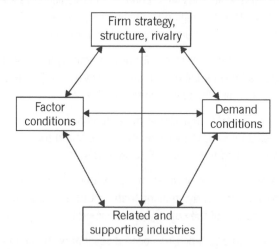

Each element of the diamond is capable of enhancing national competitive advantage. Conversely, a nation that enjoys competitive advantage will find its advantage diminishes if the elements cease to work positively.

Factor conditions are endowments to inputs of production (in effect, supply side factors). Porter distinguishes between:

(a)   **Basic factors**: natural resources, climate, unskilled labour. These are basic (threshold) requirements, but will not, by themselves, confer a sustainable competitive advantage.

(b)   **Advanced factors**: infrastructure and communications, higher education, and skilled employees (eg in skilled scientists or engineers to support high-tech industries). In contrast to basic factors, the presence of these advanced factors can help to promote competitive advantage.

Demand conditions: The domestic market determines how firms perceive, interpret and respond to buyer needs. A tough domestic market is likely to encourage competitiveness, as firms have to produce high-quality, innovative goods to meet the requirements of their domestic customers. The experience which a firm gains from supplying domestic customers will then allow it to compete successfully on a global scale.

Related and supporting industries: Competitive success in one industry is linked to success in related industries. (Notice there is a potential link here to ideas of value chains and value systems, which we looked at in Chapter 4 of this Study Text.)

Strong home suppliers make the industry more robust. Rivalry creates supplier specialisations. Clusters of related industries derive strength from their links.

Firm strategy, **structure and rivalry**: The way firms are created, organised and managed can affect a foreign company's decision to invest in a country.

Equally, cultural factors could be important – management structures, management styles and work ethics in the country need to fit with those of the investing company. Rivalry among existing firms leads to competitive strength, and spurs innovation.

Government policy: Porter also points out the importance of government policy in nurturing all four of the diamond factors by means of investing in infrastructure and higher education. The tax regime and attitudes to foreign investors could also affect an investment decision.

Chance events can also change the factors in the diamond unexpectedly. For example, civil unrest can make a country a much less attractive location.

Remember, however, that the four factors of the diamond are interrelated. Competitive advantage in an industry rarely comes from one single element of the diamond.

Porter also highlights that successful firms tend to have **linkages** between them, and this leads to **clustering**. Clustering helps to reinforce the factors in the diamond – for example, by providing a concentration of advanced factor conditions, and related/supporting industries (as with the high-tech electronics industry in Silicon Valley, California).

However, remember that the individual factors which determine the attractiveness of different locations change over time. So, for example, if a country fails to maintain its skill base or invest in new technologies and infrastructure, it will lose its competitive advantage over time.

5.2.2 Limitations of Porter's diamond model

Be aware, also, that Porter's diamond model is not without its critics.

Rugman and Collinson in their text, *International Business*, acknowledge that Porter's diamond is an important model, but nonetheless highlight some potential criticisms which can be made of it.

(a)   Porter developed the model based on export data from ten comparatively wealthy countries (Denmark, Germany, Italy, Japan, Singapore, South Korea, Sweden, Switzerland, UK and US). As such, it is unlikely to be universally applicable, and is only really relevant to developed countries.

(b)   Similarly, Porter's data was based on a narrow range of industry sectors (manufacturing, banking and management consultancy). This again questions its relevance to other sectors – in particular consumer service sectors, such as fast food restaurants.

(c)   Ultimately, it is **firms** rather than nations that compete in international markets and a firm's international abilities and competitiveness reflect **firm-specific advantages** as well as country-specific advantages. Not all firms from a country operating in the same industry are equally successful, suggesting that firm-specific advantages (in production, marketing, or human resource management for example) are more important than geographical location in determining their competitive advantage.

(d)   Porter's model focuses on the **'home base' concept**, in which a firm can only benefit from the location advantage of a single 'home' country. By doing so, the model does not adequately consider

the role and nature of **multinational companies**, which build upon both 'domestic' and 'foreign' diamonds to become globally competitive. Similarly, the model does not address the extent to which location advantages present in several countries may complement each other within a multinational company. Porter's model essentially views firms as being exporters from a 'home base' so his model does not take into account the organisational complexities of multinational firms.

5.2.3 Why expand overseas?

Firms may be pushed into international expansion by domestic adversity, or pulled into it by attractive opportunities abroad. More specifically, some of the reasons firms expand overseas are listed below. They can be classified as either **internal** or **external** factors.

(a) **Chance**. Firms may enter a particular country or countries by chance. A company executive may recognise an opportunity while on a foreign trip or the firm may receive chance orders or requests for information from potential foreign customers.

(b) **Life cycle**. Home sales may be in the mature or decline stages of the product life cycle. International expansion may allow sales growth since products are often in different stages of the product life cycle in different countries. For example, if a product is at the mature stage of its life cycle in a firm's home market, it could be beneficial to expand into an emerging market where the product may be at the introductory or growth stages of the life cycle.

(c) **Competition**. Intense competition in an overcrowded domestic market sometimes induces firms to seek markets overseas where rivalry is less keen.

(d) **Reduce dependence**. Many companies wish to diversify away from an overdependence on a single domestic market. Increased geographical diversification can help to **spread risk**.

(e) **Economies of scale**. Technological factors may be such that a large volume is needed either to cover the high costs of plant, equipment, R&D and personnel or to exploit a large potential for economies of scale and experience. For these reasons, firms in the aviation, ethical drugs, computer and automobile industries are often obliged to enter multiple countries.

(f) **Cheaper sources of raw materials**. Access to cheaper raw materials, or cheaper labour, could be a source of competitive advantage for an organisation, particularly if it is pursuing a cost leadership strategy.

(g) **Financial opportunities**. Many firms are attracted by favourable opportunities such as:

   (i)   The development of lucrative emerging markets (such as China and India)
   (ii)   Depreciation in their domestic currency values
   (iii)   Corporate tax benefits offered by particular countries
   (iv)   Lowering of import barriers abroad

5.2.4 Strategic and tactical issues

Before undertaking an international expansion, a company must consider both strategic and tactical issues involved.

(a) **Strategic issues**

   (i)   Does the strategic decision fit with the company's overall mission and objectives? Or will 'going international' cause a mismatch between objectives on the one hand and strategic and tactical decisions on the other?

   (ii)   Will the operation make a positive contribution to shareholders' wealth?

   (iii)   Does the organisation have (or can it raise) the resources necessary to exploit effectively the opportunities overseas?

(b)   **Tactical issues**

    (i)   How can the company get to understand customers' needs and preferences in foreign markets? Are the company's products appropriate to the target market?

    (ii)   The company's performance will reflect the local economic environment, as well as management's control of the business. So the company needs to understand the economic stability and prospects of the target country before investing in it.

    (iii)   Cultural issues. Does the company know how to conduct business abroad, and deal effectively with foreign nationals? For example, will there be language problems? Are there any local customs to be aware of?

    (iv)   Are there foreign regulations and associated hidden costs?

    (v)   Does the company have the necessary management skills and experience?

    (vi)   Have the foreign workers got the skills to do the work required? Will they be familiar with any technology used in production processes?

If you remember, in Chapter 1, we distinguished between resources and competences, and such a distinction could also be useful here. An important consideration for a company will be whether it has the core competences to expand internationally, not simply whether, for example, it has sufficient financial resources to do so.

Social responsibility

Before moving to a foreign country, an organisation should also consider whether there could be any **corporate social responsibility** (CSR) implications arising from such an expansion. For example, if local labour laws allow workers to be employed for low wages and in poor working conditions, does the organisation take advantage of this, or does it treat its workers better than it has to? Similarly, if pollution laws are not very strict, does the organisation comply with the minimum requirements or does it build more environmentally friendly facilities than it has to?

In both cases, the socially responsible course of action may not be the one which maximises profits. But the organisation needs to consider its reputation as a whole, and its CSR position as a whole. If it is seen to be exploiting workers in one country, this could damage its brand more widely.

5.2.5 Deciding which markets to enter

In making a decision as to which market(s) to enter the firm must start by establishing its objectives. Here are some examples.

(a)   What proportion of total sales will be overseas?

(b)   What are the longer-term objectives?

(c)   Will it enter one, a few, or many markets? In most cases it is better to start by selling in countries with which there is some familiarity and then expand into other countries gradually as experience is gained. Reasons to enter fewer countries at first include:

    (i)   Market entry and market control costs are high

    (ii)   Product and market communications modification costs are high

    (iii)   There is a large market and potential growth in the initial countries chosen

    (iv)   Dominant competitors can establish high barriers to entry

(d)   What types of country should it enter (in terms of environmental factors, economic development, language used, cultural similarities and so on)? Three major criteria should be:

    (i)   **Market attractiveness** – this concerns indicators such as GDP per head and forecast demand, as well as market accessibility.

    (ii)   **Competitive advantage** – this is principally dependent on prior experience in similar markets; language and cultural understanding.

(iii)   **Risk** – including an analysis of political stability, and the possibility of government intervention.

The matrix below (based on a model developed by Philip Kotler) can be used to bring together these three major criteria and assist managers in their decisions.

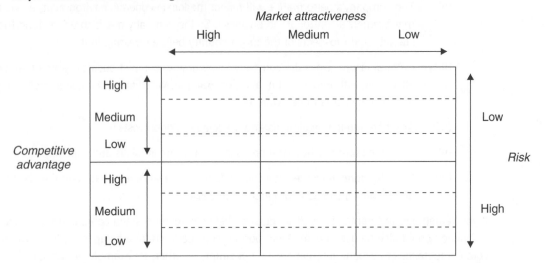

Kotler's market entry matrix

The best markets to enter are those located at the top left of the market entry matrix diagram. The worst are those in the bottom right corner. Obtaining the information needed to reach this decision requires detailed and often costly international marketing research and analysis. Making these decisions is not easy, and a fairly elaborate screening process will be instituted.

In international business there are several categories of risk.

(a)   **Political risk**. This relates to factors as diverse as wars, nationalisation, arguments between governments etc.

(b)   **Business risk**. This arises from the possibility that the business idea itself might be flawed. As with political risk, it is not unique to international marketing, but firms might be exposed to more sources of risk arising from failures to understand the market.

(c)   **Currency risk**. This arises out of the volatility of foreign exchange rates. Given that there is a possibility for speculation and that capital flows are free, such risks are increasing.

(d)   **Profit repatriation risk**. Government actions may make it hard to repatriate profits.

 The risks arising from international operations, such as cultural differences and differences between legal systems, are covered in more detail in Paper P3, *Risk Management*.

Market analysis

Firms need to analyse different markets before deciding which ones to enter. The following questions should be considered within such analysis:

(a)   **Submarkets** – What submarkets are there within the market; defined by different price points, or niches for example?

(b)   **Size and growth** – What are the size and growth characteristics of the market and submarkets within it? What are the driving forces behind trends in sales? What are the major trends in the market?

(c)   **Profitability** – How profitable is the market and its submarkets now, and how profitable are they likely to be in the future? How intense is the competition between existing firms? How severe are the threats from potential new entrants of substitute products? What is the bargaining power of suppliers and customers?

(d) **Cost structure** – What are the major cost components for various types of competitor, and how do they add value for customers?

(e) **Distribution channels** – What distribution channels are currently available? How are they changing?

(f) **Key success factors** – What are the key success factors, assets and competences needed to compete successfully? How are these likely to change in the future? Can the organisation neutralise competitors' assets and competences?

5.2.6 Involvement in international markets

If an organisation has decided to enter a foreign market, the way it does so is of crucial strategic importance. Broadly, three ways of entering foreign markets can be identified: **indirect exports**, **direct exports** and **overseas manufacture**. Foreign manufacturing can either be through wholly owned production or through a joint venture with an existing manufacturer in the country.

Choosing models of entry

The most suitable mode of entry varies:

(a) **Among firms in the same industry** (eg a new exporter as opposed to a long-established exporter)

(b) **According to the market** (eg some countries limit imports to protect domestic manufacturers whereas others promote free trade)

(c) **Over time** (eg as some countries become more, or less, hostile to direct inward investment by foreign companies)

A large number of considerations apply.

Consideration	Comment
The firm's marketing objectives	These relate to volume, timescale and coverage of market segments. Thus setting up an overseas production facility would be inappropriate if sales are expected to be low in volume.
The firm's size	A small firm is less likely than a large one to possess sufficient resources to set up and run a production facility overseas.
Mode availability	Some countries only allow a restricted level of imports, but will welcome a firm if it builds manufacturing facilities which provide jobs and limit the outflow of foreign exchange.
Mode quality	All modes may be possible in theory, but some are of questionable quality or practicality. The lack of suitably qualified distributors or agents would preclude the export, direct or indirect, of high-technology goods needing installation, maintenance and servicing by personnel with specialist technical skills.
Human resources requirements	When a firm is unable to recruit suitable staff either at home or overseas, indirect exporting or the use of agents based overseas may be the only realistic option.
Market feedback information	In some cases a firm can receive feedback information about the market and its marketing effort from its sales staff or distribution channels. In these circumstances direct export or joint ventures may be preferred to indirect export.
Risks	Firms might prefer the indirect export mode as assets are safer from expropriation.
Control needs	Production overseas by a wholly owned subsidiary gives a firm absolute control while indirect exporting offers only limited control over the marketing mix to the exporter.

5.2.7 Exporting

Goods are made at home but sold abroad. It is the easiest, cheapest and most commonly used route into a new foreign market.

Advantages of exporting

(a) Exporters can **concentrate production** in a single location, giving **economies of scale** and **consistency of product quality**.

(b) Firms lacking experience can try international marketing on a **small scale**.

(c) Firms can **test** their international marketing plans and strategies before risking investment in overseas operations.

(d) Exporting **minimises operating costs**, administrative overheads and personnel requirements.

Disadvantages of exporting

(a) **Distance**. The firm remains a long way from its customers. This could make it harder to develop relationships with the customer, or to research information about the customer (for example, their credit status).

(b) **Working capital**. The firm's working capital cycle could be extended due to the time taken to ship produce to the customer.

(c) Potential **foreign exchange risk**.

Indirect exports

Indirect exporting is where a firm's goods are sold abroad by other organisations which can offer greater market knowledge.

(a) **Export houses** are firms which facilitate exporting on behalf of the producer. Usually the producer has little control over the market and the marketing effort.

(b) **Specialist export management firms** perform the same functions as an in-house export department but are normally remunerated by way of commission.

(c) **UK buying offices of foreign stores and governments**.

(d) **Complementary exporting** ('piggy back exporting') occurs when one producing organisation (the carrier) uses its own established international marketing channels to market (either as distributor, or agent or merchant) the products of another producer (the rider) as well as its own.

Direct exports

Direct exporting occurs where the producing organisation itself performs the export tasks rather than using an intermediary. Sales are made directly to customers overseas who may be the wholesalers, retailers or final users.

(a) **Sales to final user**. Typical customers include industrial users, governments or mail order customers.

(b) Strictly speaking, an **overseas export agent** or distributor is an overseas firm hired to effect a sales contract between the principal (ie the exporter) and a customer. Agents do not take title to goods; they earn a commission (or profit).

(c) **Company branch offices abroad**. A firm can establish its own office in a foreign market for the purpose of marketing and distribution as this gives greater control.

5.2.8 Foreign (overseas) production

A firm can either choose to manufacture in a foreign country because it wants to **sell to that country**, or it may choose to relocate its production to a foreign country but **continue to sell in its 'home' market**.

The firm can either undertake the overseas production itself or it can use an overseas manufacturer.

Benefits of foreign manufacture

(a)   A **better understanding of customers** in the overseas market.

(b)   **Economies of scale** in large markets.

(c)   **Production costs are lower** in some countries than at home (for example, labour costs or costs of raw materials may be cheaper).

(d)   **Lower storage and transportation costs**, because the distance between production and market is reduced.

(e)   **Overcomes the effects of tariff and non-tariff barriers**. For example, governments might relax trading restrictions if the foreign investment is going to create jobs in their country.

(f)   Manufacture in the overseas market **may help win orders from the public sector**.

(g)   Removes foreign exchange risk if goods are sold in the same country as they are produced in.

If a firm wants to move its manufacturing operations to a foreign country, it can either establish its own plant in the country (foreign direct investment), or it can look to negotiate production contracts with existing producers in that country.

We have identified that one of the reasons a firm may move production overseas is to take advantage of lower production costs. However, it is possible that a firm can benefit from lower costs by relocating within its existing country. For example, there may be regional development incentives available for relocating to less affluent areas.

So a firm need not necessarily relocate overseas to benefit from lower costs.

Wholly owned overseas production

Production capacity can be built from scratch or, alternatively, an existing firm can be acquired.

(a)   **Acquisition** has all the benefits and drawbacks of acquiring a domestic company.

(b)   **Creating new capacity** can be beneficial if there are no likely candidates for takeover, or if acquisition is prohibited by the Government.

Advantages

(a)   The firm does **not have to share its profits** with partners of any kind.
(b)   The firm does **not have to share or delegate decision making**.
(c)   There are **none of the communication problems** that arise in joint ventures.
(d)   The firm is able to operate completely **integrated** international systems.
(e)   The firm gains a more **varied experience** from overseas production.

Disadvantages

(a)   **Significant initial investment** needed. The investment needed prevents some firms from setting up operations overseas.

(b)   Suitable **managers** may be **difficult to recruit** at home or abroad.

(c)   Some overseas **governments discourage**, and sometimes prohibit, **100% ownership** of an enterprise by a foreign company.

(d)   This mode of entry **forgoes the benefits of an overseas partner's market knowledge**, distribution system and other local expertise.

You should also note that if a firm is considering foreign direct investment it needs to conduct an investment appraisal on the project. Investment appraisals are covered in the syllabus for Paper P2 *Advanced Management Accounting*.

Contract manufacture

As an alternative to setting up a wholly owned production facility in a foreign country, a firm could set up a production contract with an existing manufacturer in that country. (This is sometimes known as a **turnkey operation**.)

This way, the firm can take advantage of the cheaper production costs in the foreign country without incurring the capital expenditure involved in setting up its own factory. And when the firm needs goods to be produced it can exercise its contract (ie turn its key) and get the foreign plant to produce the goods it needs.

Contract manufacture is suited to **countries** where the **small size of the market** discourages investment in plant and to firms whose main **strengths are in marketing** rather than production.

Advantages of contract manufacture

(a)   No need to invest in plant overseas
(b)   Lower risk of asset expropriation (because assets owned by the contractor)
(c)   Lower transport costs and lower production costs (from overseas production)

Disadvantages of contract manufacture

(a)   Suitable overseas producers cannot always be easily identified
(b)   The need to train the contractor's personnel
(c)   The contractor may eventually become a competitor
(d)   Quality control problems in manufacturing may arise

5.2.9 Outsourcing and off-shoring

Although outsourcing or off-shoring are not primarily growth strategies, they are business strategies which might relate to an organisation relocating some of its activities. A number of companies in developed countries have outsourced some of their operations to foreign countries where they can be performed more cheaply.

KEY TERMS

OUTSOURCING is the contracting out of specified operations or services to an external provider.

OFF-SHORING is a form of outsourcing in which the external provider is based in a different country to the organisation which is outsourcing its operations or services.

By removing some of an organisation's work, outsourcing allows an organisation to devote more time to the activities which it continues to perform in-house. Generally speaking, outsourcing is appropriate for peripheral activities, meaning an organisation has more time to concentrate on its core activities and competences.

A further advantage of outsourcing is that external suppliers may capture economies of scale and experience effects. This allows them to provide the function being outsourced at a lower cost than if the organisation had retained it in-house.

Getting the best out of outsourcing depends on **successful relationship management** rather than through the use of formal control systems.

Outsourcing of non-core activities is widely acknowledged as having the potential to achieve important cost savings.

Advantages

(a)   Can save on costs by making use of a specialist provider's **economies of scale**

(b)   Can **increase effectiveness** where the supplier deploys higher levels of expertise (eg in software development)

(c)   Allows the organisation to focus on its own **core activities** or core **competences**

(d)   Can deliver benefits and change more quickly than business process reorganisation in-house

(e)   Service level agreements mean that the company knows the level of service they can expect

(f)   **Cost control**; the creation of a 'customer/contractor' relationship introduces a focus on cost control which is sometimes lost when functions are performed internally

Disadvantages

(a)   There may be problems finding a single supplier which can manage complex processes in full. If more than one supplier has to be used for a single process then the economies of scale are likely to be reduced.

(b)   Firms may be **unwilling to outsource whole processes** due to the significance of those processes or the confidentiality of certain aspects of them. (This could be a particular problem if the contractor company is also working for competitors.) Again, if processes are fragmented in this way, the economies of scale may be reduced.

(c)   Outsourcing can lead to **loss of control** particularly in relation to **quality issues**. This occurs when agreed service levels are not met. The firm which is outsourcing activities now has to develop competences in relationship management (with the outsourced suppliers) in place of its competences in the processes it has outsourced.

(d)   Firms may be tied to **inflexible, long-term contracts**.

(e)   If there are specialist skills involved in the work, it may be difficult to switch to a new supplier if there are problems, or at the end of a contract period. This gives the external contractor significant bargaining power.

(f)   Firms may be unwilling to give up an area of threshold competence that may be difficult to reacquire. If they lose the competence, they will become dependent on suppliers; again, giving the supplier significant bargaining power.

The outsourcing decision needs to be treated with care. The advantages it delivers will largely be seen in the short term, but there could be longer-term disadvantages in relation to loss of control, quality or knowledge. Therefore both the short-term and longer-term implications need to be considered before an organisation chooses to outsource.

Joint ventures

Some governments discourage or even prohibit foreign firms setting up independent operations, so joint ventures are the only option. That said, a joint venture with an indigenous firm provides local knowledge, quickly.

5.3 Summary of entry strategies

The different entry strategies a firm could use for entering a foreign market can be summarised diagrammatically as below:

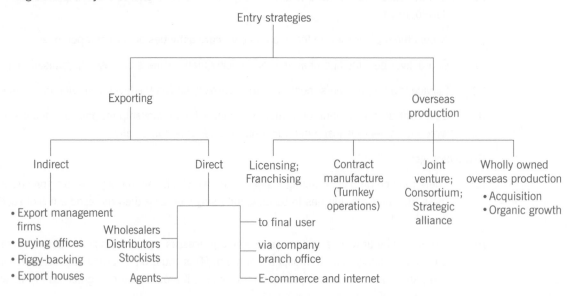

Section summary

Organic growth allows a firm to expand by developing its own resources rather than by combining with any other firms. A firm growing organically can **expand internationally**, but managing an international operation will require different resources and competences than managing an operation in a single country. Decisions about **which countries to enter**, and **how to enter them**, are key strategic decisions.

6 Mergers and acquisitions

Introduction

So far, we have looked predominantly at the issues related to a firm growing by itself. However, a firm can also grow by combining with other firms, through merger or acquisition. A **merger** is the integration of two or more businesses. An **acquisition** is where one business purchases another.

Many companies consider growth through acquisitions or mergers.

KEY TERMS

A MERGER is the joining of two separate companies to form a single company.

An ACQUISITION is the purchase of a controlling interest in another company.

It is important for a company to understand its reasons for acquisition and that these reasons are valid in terms of its strategic plan. The classic reasons for acquisition as a part of strategy are:

Reason	Effect on operations
Marketing advantages	New (or extended) product range Market presence Rationalise distribution and advertising Eliminate competition Combine adjoining markets
Production advantages	Economies of scale: synergies Acquire technology and skills Greater production capacity Safeguard future supplies Bulk purchase opportunities
Finance and management	Management team improve running of the business Cash resources Gain assets, including intellectual property Tax advantages (eg losses bought) Asset stripping Turnaround opportunities
Risk spreading	Diversification
Retain independence	
Overcome barriers to entry	
Outplay rivals	

Acquisitions provide a means of entering a market, or building up a market share, more quickly and/or at a lower cost than would be incurred if the company tried to develop its own resources. Corporate planners must, however, consider the level of **risk** involved. Acquiring companies in overseas markets is more risky, for a number of reasons, such as differences in culture and/or language, and differences in the way the foreign company is used to being managed.

The acquirer should attempt an evaluation of:

- Prospects of technological change in the industry
- Size and strength of competitors
- Reaction of competitors to an acquisition
- Likelihood of government intervention and legislation
- State of the industry and its long-term prospects
- Amount of synergy obtainable from the merger or acquisition
- Cultural fit between predator and target

Exam skills

Whatever the reason for the merger or acquisition, it is unlikely to be successful unless it offers the company opportunities that cannot be found within the company itself and unless the new subsidiary fits closely into the strategic plan outlined for future growth.

If you are asked to assess the appropriateness of an acquisition, you should also consider whether the company being acquired will gain any competitive advantage from the acquisition.

6.1 Better-off tests

Michael Porter suggests that one of the key issues behind acquisitions should be in realising synergies between the existing company and the new acquisition.

To this end, he suggests that potential acquisitions should be assessed against three tests:

(a) **Better-off test** – Will the company being acquired be better off after the acquisition? Will it gain competitive advantage from being in the Group?

(b) **Attractiveness test** – Is the target industry structurally attractive? (Porter originally developed his tests in relation to diversification, and so was looking at companies making acquisitions in unrelated industries. However, the point about 'attractiveness' could be applied more generally to look at target companies in foreign countries.)

(c) **Cost of entry** – The cost of the acquisition (or the cost of entering a new market) must not capitalise all future profits from that acquisition (or market). In other words, will the future cash flows from the acquisition be greater than the amounts paid to acquire it?

Porter also identified another key point in relation to successful acquisitions, which could be called the **parenting test**. Has the company making the acquisition got the necessary skills as a corporate parent to get the best value out of the company being acquired? For example, has it got any **experience of previous acquisitions**?

It is also important to remember that many acquisitions turn out not to be successful. Ashridge Management College suggests that as many as 70% of mergers and acquisitions fail to meet their objectives, and some even bankrupt the acquiring company. In many cases, managers have too little experience with the acquisition process, and they also make acquisitions for the wrong reasons.

Equally, acquisitions can fail because there isn't a good strategic fit between the company making the acquisition and the company being acquired.

6.2 The mechanics of acquiring companies

The financial issues involved in evaluating opportunities for mergers and acquisition are covered in more detail in Paper F3 – *Financial Strategy*.

As a management accountant you may be required to assess the value of an acquisition. A number of methods are available.

(a) **Price/earnings ratio**: the market's expectations of future earnings. If it is high, it indicates expectations of high growth in earnings per share (EPS) and/or low risk.

(b) **Accounting rate of return**, whereby the company will be valued by estimated future profits over return on capital.

(c) **Value of net assets** (including brands).

(d) **Dividend yield**.

(e) **Discounted cash flows**, if cash flows are generated by the acquisition. A suitable discount rate (eg the acquirer's cost of capital) should be applied.

(f) **Market prices**. Shareholders may prefer to hang on for a better bid.

6.2.1 Takeovers or mergers financed by a share exchange arrangement

Many acquisitions are paid for by **issuing new shares** in the acquiring company, which are then used to buy the shares of the company to be taken over in a 'share exchange' arrangement. An enlarged company might then have the financial 'muscle' and borrowing power to invest further, so as to gain access to markets previously closed to either company because they could not individually afford the investment.

6.2.2 Acquisitions and earnings per share (EPS)

Growth in EPS will only occur after an acquisition in certain circumstances:

(a) **Lower P/E ratio**: when the company being acquired is bought on a lower P/E ratio

(b)   **Higher P/E ratio**: when the company being acquired is bought on a higher P/E ratio, but there is profit growth to offset this

6.2.3 Debt finance

Another feature of takeover activities, in the US especially, but also in the UK, has been the **debt-financed takeover**. This is a takeover bid where most or all of the purchase finance is provided by a syndicate of banks for the acquisition. The acquiring company will become very highly geared and will normally sell off parts of the target company.

A **leveraged buyout** is a form of debt-financed takeover where the target company is bought up by a team of managers in the company.

6.3 Acquisitions and organic growth compared

Advantages of acquisition

Acquisitions are probably only desirable if organic growth alone cannot achieve the targets for growth that a company has set for itself.

(a)   Acquisitions can be made to enter new product or geographical areas, or to expand in existing markets, much more **quickly**.

(b)   **Can avoid barriers to entry**. If there are significant barriers to entry into a market (or if there is already intense competitive rivalry) then it might not be possible for a new entrant to join the market in its own right. However, acquiring an existing player in the market would enable a Group to join that market.

(c)   Acquisitions can be made **without cash**, if share exchange transactions are acceptable to the company.

(d)   When an acquisition is made to diversify into new product areas, the company will be **buying technical expertise, goodwill and customer contracts**.

Disadvantages (or risks) of acquisitions

(a)   **Cost**. They might be too expensive, and will involve high initial capital costs to acquire shareholdings in the target company. If the acquisition is resisted by the directors and shareholders of the target company this may force the offer price to be increased further.

(b)   There could also be **valuation issues**. The management team of the target company is likely to know more about its true value than the acquiring company, and so it could be difficult to arrive at a fair price for the sale.

(c)   **Customers** of the target company might consider switching to other suppliers for their goods.

(d)   **Incompatibility**. In general, the problems of assimilating new products, customers, suppliers, markets, employees and different systems of operating might create 'indigestion' and management overload in the acquiring company. One of the main reasons why acquisitions and mergers fail is because of the **lack of 'fit'** between the two companies.

(e)   **Post-acquisition costs**. Even if the acquisition goes ahead, there will be significant costs involved in integrating the acquired company's systems (production systems, IT systems etc) with those of the parent company.

(f)   **Lack of information**. Commentators have suggested that the 'acquisitions' market for companies is rarely efficient. This means that companies making an acquisition do not have perfect information about the company they are acquiring. This could mean that the price they pay for the acquisition is too high and/or the future value the company brings to the Group is lower than they had anticipated.

(g) **Cultural differences**. There may be clashes if the culture and management style of the acquired company is different to the acquiring one. There is potential for human relations problems to arise **after** the acquisition.

(h) **Rationalisation costs**. As the parent organisation looks to benefit from synergies after an acquisition, it often streamlines the workforce, leading to redundancy costs, and possibly also damaging morale among the workforce.

As previously stated, it is also worth considering the **stakeholders** in the acquisition process:

(a) Some acquisitions are driven by the personal goals of the acquiring company's **managers**. For example, some managers may want to make the acquisition and increase the size of the firm as a means of increasing their own status and power. Alternatively, other managers may view an acquisition as a means of preventing their own company being taken over, thereby making their job safer.

(b) **Corporate financiers and banks** also have a stake in the acquisitions process as they can charge fees for advice.

Takeovers often benefit the shareholders of the acquired company more than the acquirer. According to the Economist Intelligence Unit, there is a consensus that fewer than half of all acquisitions are successful. One of the reasons for failure is that firms rarely **take into account non-financial factors**.

(a) All acquirers conduct financial audits of target companies but many do not conduct anything approaching a **management audit**.

(b) Some major problems of implementation relate to **human resources and personnel issues** such as morale, performance assessment and **culture**. If key managers or personnel leave, the business will suffer.

Another common problem following a merger or acquisition is that the **post-acquisition phase is not properly managed**, so the two component companies are never properly integrated. In this way, the potential benefits of the deal cannot be fully realised.

Section summary

Mergers and acquisitions allow firms to grow by combining with others. A merger or acquisition can provide quicker growth than organic growth, but strategic planners must consider the levels of risk involved.

7 Joint ventures and strategic alliances

Introduction

There are other types of arrangement whereby businesses pool resources:

- **Joint ventures**, consortia and other alliances

- **Franchising**, where the franchiser provides expertise, a brand name etc, and the franchisee offers some of the capital

Short of mergers and takeovers, there are other ways by which companies can co-operate.

Consortia: Organisations co-operate on specific business prospects. Airbus is an example, a consortium including British Aerospace, Daimler, Aerospatiale and Casa.

Joint ventures: Two or more organisations set up a **new**, **separate organisation** in which they each hold an equity stake. This is very common in entering normally closed markets.

7.1 Joint ventures

KEY TERM

A JOINT VENTURE is a 'contractual arrangement whereby two or more parties undertake an economic activity which is subject to joint control'.

(CIMA Official Terminology)

Advantages of joint ventures

Like any acquisition, joint ventures provide a way of building scale quickly. Joint ventures are especially attractive to **smaller or risk-averse firms**, or where very expensive new technologies are being researched and developed because they allow **risks and capital commitment to be shared between the venture partners**. This could be particularly useful for expensive technology and research projects.

Other advantages are:

- Joint ventures permit coverage of a **larger number of countries** since each one requires less investment.

- A joint venture can reduce the risk of **government intervention**.

- Joint ventures can provide close **control** over operations.

- A joint venture with an indigenous firm provides **local knowledge**, and can also allow firms a **route into markets** they might otherwise struggle to enter.

- A joint venture can also be a **learning exercise**, as each party gains **access to the other's competences**.

- A joint venture is often an alternative to seeking to buy or build a wholly owned manufacturing operation abroad.

CASE STUDY

Telstra – Telkom Indonesia Joint Venture

In August 2014, the Australian telecommunications and information services company Telstra finalised a joint venture agreement with Telkom Indonesia (the largest telecommunication and network services provider in Indonesia) to provide Network Application and Services (NAS) support to Indonesian businesses, multinationals and Australian companies operating in Indonesia.

NAS support provides businesses with managed network and cloud-based communications services, and the joint venture will be able to offer an integrated end to end service which is unique in the Indonesian market. NAS will be bundled with Telkom's connectivity and sold through Telkom Indonesia and Telstra's enterprise sales team.

From Telstra's perspective, the joint venture (JV) accelerates Telstra's growth in the rapidly growing Indonesia market (South-East Asia's largest economy) and across the South-East Asian region more generally.

Announcing the venture, a Telstra executive said, 'We are looking forward to partnering with Telkom Indonesia, a well-respected market leader, which has a large enterprise and government customer base and the broadest reach of domestic connectivity in Indonesia. Indonesia is a fast growing NAS market and we believe the best way to make inroads is by partnering a well-recognised and respected local player.'

He continued by saying that the JV is also aligned to Telstra's strategy of supporting its business customers around the world. The venture forms part of Telstra's expansion plans for Asia, and Telstra is 'looking forward to giving our [business] customers local support, allowing them to focus on their business rather than managing information technology and telecommunication as a business cost.'

Telkom highlighted that the deal will enable it to bring proven NAS solutions to Indonesia to assist businesses to be more productive and competitive. Telkom's CEO also stated, 'We believe the JV ... will grow significantly not only because of the partnership with Telstra, but also considering Telkom's capabilities in network and data centre, as well as [its] strong position in the enterprise market segment which is the target market of NAS.'

Disadvantages of JVs

The major disadvantage of JVs is that there can be major **conflicts of interest**. Disagreements may arise over profit shares, amounts invested, the management of the JV, and the marketing strategy.

Other disadvantages are:

- The **profits** from the venture **have to be shared among the venture partners**, reducing the amount earned by each partner.

- The JV may **not be fully supported by its parent companies** because none of them feel they really own it.

- Partners can **gain confidential information** about each other which could subsequently be used competitively by one partner against the other.

- One partner may ultimately take over the joint venture.

7.2 Strategic alliances

Unlike a JV where two or more partners set up a new, separate entity, alliances occur where firms work together to enhance their competitive advantages, but do not create a new legal entity. For example, the 'One World' alliance brings together ten of the world's biggest airlines, including American Airlines, British Airways, Cathay Pacific and Qantas. The alliance allows them to offer an integrated service, including code-sharing, and the common use of passenger terminals.

Firms may enter **strategic alliances** with others for a variety of reasons.

(a)   They **share development costs** of a particular technology, and **share the risks** associated with developing them. Alliances can also be used to share risks more generally.

(b)   The regulatory environment prohibits takeovers (eg most major airlines are in strategic alliances because in most countries – including the US – there are limits to the level of control an 'outsider' can have over an airline). In this respect, an alliance could be a way of overcoming a barrier to entry into a market.

(c)   Alliances can facilitate entry into new markets on a global or regional basis. For example, BP's alliance with the Russian oil producer TNK gave BP access to Russian oil fields. In return, TNK benefited from BP's extensive resources and oil exploration skills.

(d)   **Complementary markets**, **technology** or **competences**. By working together, alliance partners may be able to exploit synergies between their different businesses.

(e)   Smaller firms can often work together in an alliance to act as **more effective competition to a dominant player** in the market than they could if they all acted independently.

(f)   **Knowledge**. An important potential benefit from alliances is the opportunity to get access to the knowledge and expertise of the partners involved.

Strategic alliances only go so far, as there may be disputes over control of strategic assets leading to a breakdown of trust and co-operation among the partners.

If a firm enters an alliance as a means of learning from, or gaining knowledge about, an alliance partner, this could also ultimately cause a problem. If the partners do not want others to learn from them, or if they feel there is an unfair exchange between the alliance partners, this could signal the end of the alliance. In a well-structured alliance, the risk, rewards and resource commitments are fairly apportioned among the alliance partners.

Nevertheless, it is worth noting that a number of **alliances end in takeover**, possibly after one of the organisations has gained knowledge from their partners. Firms entering an alliance need to be aware of this risk.

An additional issue which alliances face is that because the partners remain separate entities they may fail to achieve the level of integration (synergies) needed to deliver any significant competitive advantage or economies of scale.

Case example: General Motors and Peugeot Citroen

In February 2012, in an attempt to address increasing global competition in the automobile industry and a slow down in the European market, the American car manufacturer General Motors (GM) and the French manufacturer PSA Peugeot Citroen (PSA) announced a global alliance which the two companies said would save them $2bn annually within about five years (by combining purchasing) and would see them develop cars together.

The US and French carmakers said they would share vehicle platforms, components and modules, and create a global purchasing JV to buy commodities and parts that would have a combined purchasing power of $125bn a year. Additionally, the alliance is exploring areas for further co-operation, such as integrated logistics and transportation. GM's chief executive described the deal as 'a broad-scale global strategic alliance that will improve each company's competitiveness and will contribute to the long-term profitability in Europe particularly, but around the world as well'.

The alliance will give GM and PSA, which have joint sales of about 12 million units, global industry leadership in production of 'B' compact and 'D' upper-middle segment cars.

However, both companies stressed the alliance was not a merger, and said that it would not change either company's existing plans to rationalise their operations in Europe and to return them to sustainable profitability. At the time the alliance was announced, both PSA and GM's Opel unit were losing money and had more plants than they needed. GM and PSA said the cost synergies from the alliance would be split evenly between the two carmakers, which will continue to compete and sell cars under their own brands and on a competitive basis.

PSA's chief executive said that the alliance grew out of 'a growing realisation of very concrete synergies that exist between our companies'.

GM and PSA's alliance will initially focus on small and midsize cars, multipurpose vehicles and small sport utility vehicles (or crossovers). The two companies said they would also consider developing a new common platform for low-carbon vehicles.

However, while GM and PSA highlighted the potential benefits of the alliance, history showed that alliances between rival carmakers have a patchy track record. Daimler demerged from Chrysler in 2007 after an acrimonious partnership that lasted nine years, and Volkswagen and Suzuki went to arbitration after an alliance they concluded in 2009 ran into difficulties in 2011.

Commenting on GM and PSA's alliance, the head of European automotive research at Credit Suisse said 'The European auto industry is running out of options. This [alliance] is obviously worth the effort, but whether it's going to be successful, who knows?'

Such caution about the alliance appears to have been justified.

In October 2013, GM and PSA announced they were 'scaling back' their alliance, as GM sought greater control of its destiny in Europe and PSA pursued an investment by the Chinese automobile manufacturer, Dongfeng.

PSA said that the planned joint platform for sub-compact cars, at the heart of the alliance, was likely to be cancelled, and the expected level of synergies from the alliance may also need to be adjusted downwards. The company said that the joint purchasing organisation had only achieved savings of around 60 million euros in the first year – far less than the original target savings of $2 billion per year.

The slower than expected financial impact of the alliance put PSA under pressure to find new partners, as it was facing a cash shortage. One source suggested that Dongfeng might acquire a stake of around 20% in PSA.

However, if Dongfeng purchases a holding in PSA this may lead to GM pulling out of the alliance altogether. GM works with the rival SAIC Motor company in China, and any relationship between PSA and Dongfeng would be very sensitive because GM has high ambitions in China and different partners. From the outset, GM has had the option to terminate the alliance with PSA if there was a change in control of the French company.

GM also appeared to be increasingly committed to managing its own European turnaround independently, rather than through alliances. As such, GM is stepping up internal efforts to increase economies of scale by using its own vehicle platforms globally.

Based on: Reed. J. (2012), GM and Peugeot confirm alliance, *Financial Times*, 29 February, www.ft.com

Automotive News (2013), GM, Peugeot to scale back alliance, 23 October, www.autonews.com

7.2.1 Choosing alliance partners

Hooley *et al* suggest the following factors should be considered in choosing alliance partners.

Drivers	What benefits are offered by collaboration? What are the objectives of the alliance?
Partners	Which partners should be chosen? What competences and capabilities will the partners bring to the alliance? In a well-structured alliance, the partners will be selected such that the strengths of one partner complement the weaknesses of another partner.
Facilitators	Does the external environment favour a partnership?
Components	Activities and processes in the network.
Effectiveness	Does the previous history of alliances generate good results? Is the alliance just a temporary blip? For example, in the airline industry, there are many strategic alliances, but these arise in part because there are legal barriers to cross-border ownership.
Market orientation	Alliance partners are harder to control and may not have the same commitment to the end-user.

In addition, when considering an alliance it is also important that the alliance's targets/objectives, methods and resource commitments are clearly understood by all the alliance partners, and that the prospective partners are prepared to co-operate fully with the alliance. If they are not, the alliance could be doomed to failure from the outset.

Limitations of alliances

(a) **Core competence**. Each organisation should be able to focus on its core competence. Alliances do not enable it to create new competences.

(b) Because alliance partners remain separate entities, many **fail to achieve the integration or commitment** needed to gain any significant competitive advantage.

(c) **Strategic priorities**. If a key aspect of strategic delivery is handed over to a partner, the firm loses flexibility. A core competence may not be enough to provide a comprehensive customer benefit.

7.2.2 IS-based alliances

The cost of major IS-based methods of working, combined with their inherent communications capability, have made alliances based on IS a natural development. There are four common types.

(a) **Single industry partnerships**: For example, the 'Oneworld' alliance in the airline industry allows passengers to cross-book across all the member airlines' networks and it also introduced interline e-ticketing across all the member airlines' networks.

(b) **Multi-industry joint marketing partnerships**: Some industries are so closely linked with others that it makes sense to establish IS linking their offerings. A well-known example is holiday bookings, where a flight reservation over the internet is likely to lead to a seamless offer of hotel reservations and car hire.

(c)   **Supply chain partnerships**: As discussed in Chapter 4, greater and closer co-operation along the supply chain has led to the need for better and faster information flows. Electronic data interchange between customers and suppliers is one aspect of this improvement, perhaps seen most clearly in the car industry, where the big-name manufacturers effectively control the flow of inputs from their suppliers.

(d)   **IT supplier partnerships**: A slightly different kind of partnership is not uncommon in the IT industry itself, where physical products have their own major software content. The development of these products requires close co-operation between the hardware and software companies concerned.

7.3 Other arrangements

7.3.1 Licensing agreement

A **licensing agreement** is a commercial contract whereby the licenser gives something of value to the licensee in exchange for certain performances and payments.

(a)   The licenser may provide any of the following.

     (i)   Rights to produce a patented product or use a patented production process
     (ii)   Manufacturing know-how (unpatented)
     (iii)   Technical advice and assistance
     (iv)   Marketing advice and assistance
     (v)   Rights to use a trademark, brand etc

(b)   The licenser receives a royalty.

(c)   Production is higher with no investment.

(d)   The licensee might eventually become a competitor.

7.3.2 Agency agreement

Instead of opening its own sales distribution channel, a firm may grant agency agreements so that agents market and sell its products.

The agent receives a set of sample products, sales literature (eg brochures) and product training.

In return for selling the product, the agent receives a commission based on the number of sales they generate. Although the agent generates the sale, the firm still supplies the customer, so they can tell how many sales each agent has generated.

While agency agreements can be useful where customers like to compare between products (eg for financial services products) or where sales are enhanced by social networks (eg cosmetics, like Avon ladies), they can have some disadvantages.

There is a danger that an agent could mis-sell a product simply to gain a commission. However, the mis-selling could damage the underlying brand.

- The firm doesn't establish any relationships with its customers, so it misses out on customer feedback or the opportunity for relationship marketing.

- There is a risk that agents could desert the firm, taking their customers with them.

7.3.3 Subcontracting

Subcontracting is also a type of alliance. Co-operative arrangements also feature in supply chain management.

7.3.4 Franchising

Franchising is a method of expanding the business on less capital than would otherwise be possible. The franchisee pays a capital lump sum to enter the franchise and also bears some of the running costs of its outlet.

Franchisers include McDonald's, Holiday Inn, Kall Kwik Printing, Kentucky Fried Chicken, and The Body Shop.

The franchiser offers the franchisee:

- Use of the franchise name, and any goodwill associated with it
- Use of its business systems and support services (including central marketing support)
- Its product/service to sell, and relevant instructions for selling the product/service
- Management and staff training programmes

In return:

- The franchisee pays the franchiser for being granted these rights.

- The franchisee has responsibility for the day to day running, and for the ultimate profitability, of his own franchise.

- The franchisee supplies capital, personal involvement (staff, and human resources management) and local market knowledge. As well as reducing costs for the franchiser, this can allow barriers to entry to be overcome effectively.

7.3.5 Benefits of franchising

(a) **Reduces capital requirements**. Firms often franchise because they cannot readily raise the capital required to set up company-owned stores. John Y. Brown, former president of Kentucky Fried Chicken (KFC), maintained that it would have cost KFC $450 million to establish its first 2,700 stores, and this was a sum that was not available to the corporation in the early stages of its life.

(b) **Reduces managerial resources**. A firm may be able to raise the capital required for growth, but it may lack the managerial resources required to set up a network of company-owned stores. Recruiting and training managers and staff account for a significant percentage of the cost of growth of a firm.

Under a franchise agreement, the franchisees supply the staff required for the day to day running of the operation.

(c) **Improves return on promotional expenditure through speed of growth**. A retail firm's brand and brand image are crucial to the success of its stores. Companies often develop their brand through extensive advertising and promotion, but this only translates into sales if they have a number of stores that customers can visit after seeing their advertisements.

To reap the benefits of its national or regional advertising efforts, the company needs to attain the minimum efficient scale, in terms of number of stores, as quickly as possible.

Because franchising provides quicker access to capital and managerial resources, a firm can **expand more quickly through franchising than through opening company-owned stores**. Faster expansion through franchising, in turn, should allow companies to achieve a favourable return from their promotional campaigns.

(d) **Benefits of specialisation**. Because the franchisee and the franchiser both contribute different resources to the franchise, franchising provides an effective way of reducing costs: each party concentrates on their core areas, and increases their efficiency in those areas.

In general, franchisers are more cost efficient than franchisees in performing functions that decrease in cost with a substantial level of output. By contrast, franchisees are more efficient in performing functions which are more efficient on a smaller scale. For example, in the fast-food business, product development and national promotion are more efficiently handled on a large

scale (by the franchisor), whereas the production of food itself is handled better on a relatively smaller scale (by the franchisee).

(e)   **Low head office costs**. The franchiser only needs a small number of head office staff because there is a considerable delegation of operational responsibility to the franchisees. For example, in the fast-food business, the franchisees provide the staff who work in the restaurants, and so the franchisees incur the HR and payroll costs associated with that.

(f)   **Reduced supervision costs**. Company-owned retail stores are run by employee managers who may often perform poorly if they are not supervised. A company, therefore, has to supervise its store managers, and this will result in central overhead costs. However, under a franchise arrangement, because franchisees have invested capital in their own stores, and because their earnings come from the profits of those stores, they are motivated to work hard to maximise the success of the stores. Consequently, the franchiser will have much lower supervision costs.

(g)   **Risk management**. When opening new stores, a corporation does not know with certainty the business potential and the chances of success of different locations. Under a franchising arrangement, the franchiser can judge the profitability potential of different sites without incurring a significant business risk. If a particular store fails, the franchisee bears the brunt of the failure.

However, franchising also helps franchisees reduce their risks. Franchised stores typically open more quickly, and become profitable more quickly, than independent company-owned stores. The franchisee benefits from the franchisor's managerial experience and from the established brand name. In effect, when a franchisee enters a lease agreement with the franchisor, it is leasing managerial know-how and brand recognition, as well as the physical store it is operating.

7.3.6 Disadvantages of franchising (for the franchiser)

(a)   The **search for competent candidates** is both costly and time consuming where the franchiser requires many outlets (eg McDonald's in the UK).

(b)   **Reduced profits**, because part of the profit has to be paid to the franchisee.

(c)   Danger that poor franchisee performance can **harm the brand**. The franchiser has to monitor its franchisees to ensure they are all offering a consistent product or service (for example, that all McDonald's outlets prepare their meals to the same recipe, sell them for the same price, and serve them in restaurants that are clean and follow the correct branding guidelines).

(d)   Danger that franchisees can gain **confidential information** about the franchiser and subsequently set up as a competitor.

Section summary

Joint ventures and **strategic alliances** are ways firms can combine resources. This can allow them growth opportunities which would not have been available to them acting in isolation. **Franchising** can be a useful method of expanding a business with limited capital.

---

8   Divestment and rationalisation

Introduction

So far we have looked at growth and acquisition strategies. However, history has shown that not all growth strategies prove successful. In particular, companies which have pursued diversification strategies have subsequently decided to refocus on their core competences rather than trying to have a wider range of interests. In such situations, Groups need to divest the business units which no longer fit into their corporate portfolio.

Most strategies are designed to promote growth, but management should consider what rate of growth they want, whether they want to see any growth at all, or whether there should be a contraction of their business.

KEY TERM

DIVESTMENT is 'disposal of part of its activities by an entity'.   *(CIMA Official Terminology)*

Reasons for divestment are:

(a) To **rationalise** a business as a result of a strategic appraisal, perhaps as a result of portfolio analysis. For example, if a Group has a business unit (SBU) which is a 'dog' (in terms of the BCG matrix) and is unlikely to be generating positive net cash flow for the Group, the corporate parent may try to find a buyer for that SBU.

(b) To **satisfy investors**. Diversified conglomerates are unfashionable. Modern investment thinking is that investors prefer to provide their own portfolio diversification. So firms may divest business units which are not core to their business, and make their Groups into a more coherent investment for investors.

(c) To **focus on core competences**. If a Group is too widely diversified it is likely to include some operations that could be more effectively bought in than retained in-house. The Group should focus on those areas that it can do better than any outside sides: its core competences.

(d) To **improve control**. Similarly, if a Group is too diverse, it can be difficult for management to control, and to appraise the performance of individual divisions.

(e) To **allow market valuation to reflect growth and income prospects**. Where a low-growth, steady-income operation exists alongside a potentially high-growth new venture, the joint P/E is likely to be too high for the cash cow and too low for the star. The danger is that the two businesses are not split so that their share prices correctly reflect their value, and a predator will take over the whole operation at a discounted price. The predator will then split the business in two, allowing each part to settle at its own level, in effect doing what the business had failed to do itself.

(f) To sell off **subsidiary companies** at a profit, perhaps as an **exit route** after managing a turnaround. If the subsidiary was struggling it could have been acquired at a low price. If the Group then **turned it around** so that it became profitable, the Group could then sell it at a profit. In this way, the subsidiary could be seen as an investment by the Group, and the divestment allows the Group to realise its investment.

(g) To **raise funds** to invest elsewhere or to reduce debt. This may be particularly important if a Group is suffering cash flow shortages and needs to raise cash.

CASE STUDY

Divestment

In January 2010, the US confectionery, food and beverage company Kraft acquired the UK confectionery business, Cadbury, in a deal costing £11.5bn ($18.9bn).

Kraft (whose group companies include Oscar Meyer, Philadelphia, Jacobs, Maxwell House and Nabisco) said the deal would create a 'global confectionery leader'.

However, by contrast, in 2008 Cadbury had been involved in divestment activity – selling the drinks businesses which it had previously held in its portfolio.

In December 2008, it sold its Australian drinks arm, Schweppes Beverages, to Japan's biggest brewer, Asahi.

That sale completed Cadbury's exit from the drinks market, following the demerger of Dr Pepper Snapple Group earlier that year (May 2008).

Talking about the Schweppes sale, Cadbury Chief Executive, Todd Stitzer, said: 'The successful sale of Schweppes Australia will complete Cadbury's divestment of its beverage operations. As a result, Cadbury will focus solely on growing its chocolate, gum and candy portfolio in line with our strategy announced in June 2007.'

Market analysts also looked favourably on the sale. One commented, 'Strategically and financially, we think that this is an excellent deal for Cadbury. Their exit from soft drinks is now complete and they can focus exclusively on confectionery. They are exiting a 'so-so' asset for a price well ahead of our expectations.'

Methods of divestment

Methods of divestment are:

(a) **Sale as a going concern** to another business (in return for cash and/or shares). This option allows the business to continue, and so should allow staff to keep their jobs. It should also provide continuity for customers.

(b) **Assets are liquidated**: the business is closed and its assets are sold. This is likely to create job losses. While this option may be necessary if no buyer can be found, it can create negative publicity. For example, if the business being closed is part of a Group, it may raise questions about the group as a whole.

(c) **Demerger**

(d) **Management buyout** (MBO)

(e) **Management buy-in** (MBI)

8.1 Demergers

One term that describes divestment is **demerger**. This is sometimes referred to as **unbundling**. The main feature of a demerger is that one corporate entity becomes two or more separate entities. The newly separated businesses might have the same shareholders, but they will usually have different people on their board of directors. In other words, the supposed synergies are negative (a '2 + 2 = 3' effect, rather than a '2 + 2 = 5' effect).

8.2 Management buyout (MBO)

KEY TERM

A MANAGEMENT BUYOUT is 'purchase of a business from its existing owners by members of the management team, generally in association with a financing institution. Where a large proportion of the new finance required to purchase the business is raised by external borrowing, the buy-out is described as leveraged'.
(CIMA Official Terminology)

Typically, a better price can be obtained by selling a business as a unit, and there might well be many other firms interested in buying. In recent years there have been a large number of **MBOs**, whereby the subsidiary is sold off to its managers.

This option may appear attractive to managers because it gives them the chance to **control their own business**, with the absence of any head office constraints.

Moreover, it removes any concerns about **redundancy or imposed changes** if the business is sold to a new owner.

Finally, the management team should know the **business's potential**, and if they think it is profitable they should be well positioned to maximise that profitability.

However, the MBO option may also be attractive for the divesting company because it can present the MBO as being an opportunity for the business to **develop its own talent**.

The managers put in some of their own capital, but obtain the rest from venture capital organisations and hope to make a bigger success of the business than the company which is selling it off.

CASE STUDY

Green & Black's

When Craig Sams sold his organic chocolate company Green & Black's to Cadbury for £20m in 2005, he was anxious to emphasise that his ultra-ethical brand (the holder of the UK's first Fair Trade designation) was in good hands.

Following Cadbury's takeover by Kraft in 2010, it seems that Green & Black's is less than keen to remain in a Group headed by one of the globe's most ruthlessly efficient conglomerates. Green & Black's management are reportedly trying to engineer a buyout from Kraft's empire, with Mr Sams seemingly keen to take back the brand.

Green & Black's (which has an annual turnover of about £40m) claims it is struggling to maintain its 'entrepreneurial spirit' under Kraft (which has an annual turnover of £25bn). Reports suggest that the company was keen to return to being a separate company, with its managers incentivised by linking performance to compensation.

There are suggestions that the chocolate maker approached Kraft at the end of 2010 with an initial proposal to spin off the company via an MBO, but this approach seems to have been rejected by Kraft.

However, Green & Black's position highlights the potentially uneasy relationship between brands which start out as small-scale, highly ethical products and are eventually swallowed by multinational suitors.

There was already a degree of discontent within Green & Black's at being part of the Cadbury group, but the arrival of Kraft seems to have exacerbated this. Annual growth, which had been close to 70% in 2005, has fallen sharply and some staff within Green & Black's have been bemoaning the amount of time devoted to projects that seldom came off.

8.2.1 Strategic factors in a buyout decision

Particularly important questions are:

(a) Can the buyout team **raise the finance** to pay for the buyout? Buyouts are well favoured by venture capital organisations, which regard them as less risky than new start-up businesses.

(b) Can the bought-out operation generate enough **profits** to pay for the costs of the acquisition?

8.3 Management buy-in (MBI)

An MBI is similar to an MBO, but the new management team comes from outside the existing business, rather than being the current management team.

8.4 Cost rationalisation

Divestments occur when a Group wants to sell off part of its business. However, firms may also want to reduce their costs and overheads, without actually selling off any parts of the business.

This is particularly relevant in periods of economic downturn, when firms have to deal with tighter margins or falling sales.

Firms are likely to review all their spending more closely, and many will look to make job cuts to reduce their wage bills.

However, as a cautionary note, firms should try to take a balanced approach between short-term cost cutting and longer-term robustness. If firms cut back too much in the short term (for example, by not investing in their staff or in maintaining their infrastructure) this could weaken their competitive position in the longer term.

Many organisations which lay people off in recessionary times struggle to meet renewed business demand when the economy picks up. Moreover, those employers who treat their staff well during hard times will

benefit from having a committed workforce which will serve them well in the longer term. By contrast, simply making workers redundant can have serious negative impacts on morale and performance.

8.5 Product rationalisation

Product rationalisation entails reducing the number of products an organisation sells so that it focuses on the products which generate the greatest profit, and avoids having a product portfolio which is too large and expensive to maintain.

In Chapter 4, we looked at product portfolio analysis (BCG matrix) and product profitability – both of which could be useful in the context of deciding whether to reduce the number of products an organisation sells.

Also, although we are looking at product rationalisation here, a similar logic could be applied to looking at the profitability generated by different customers or groups of customers. We explore this idea in more detail in Chapter 8, in relation to customer profitability analysis.

For most firms, the majority of their revenue and profit comes from a small proportion of its products. In effect, this could be seen as an illustration of the Pareto principle (or '80/20' rule): that 80% (or more in some cases) of a firm's revenue and profit comes from 20% (or less) of its products. The remaining 80% of its products generate little value for the firm, which suggests they could be suitable candidates for divestment.

However, before divesting any products a firm should also consider the following points:

(a)   **Impact on total sales** – If a firm stops producing and selling a product, will sales transfer to other products, or will they be lost completely? Has the firm got alternative products which it can offer to customers in place of the ones being rationalised?

(b)   It is likely that at least a proportion of sales will not be transferred to other products, so if a firm wants to continue growing overall, it is important for it to assess whether any new products being developed, or the remaining products in its portfolio, can compensate for the loss of sales from the discontinued products.

(c)   **Joint purchases** – Although a product in itself may not be profitable, do customers buy it in conjunction with other, more profitable products? If customers have to find an alternative supply for the less profitable product, will they also buy the profitable product from that alternative supply?

(d)   **Production overhead costs** – If the number of products is reduced, but fixed costs remain the same, these fixed costs will have to be apportioned across a smaller range of products.

(e)   An important factor for a firm to consider is whether the production volume of the remaining products in the portfolio will be increased following the rationalisation. If it is, this will enable the fixed costs to be spread across this higher volume, which should minimise any increase in the unit costs of production. However, if volumes are not going to be increased, the firm may also need to find ways of reducing its fixed costs, to avoid a subsequent increase in unit costs.

(f)   **Increasing profitability** – Although a product may not be profitable in the way it is currently produced and sold, it may be possible to increase its profitability; for example, by simplifying the production process, or by packaging it more cheaply. If a firm can increase the profitability of a product, this could be preferable to removing the product from its portfolio.

8.6 Relocation strategies

In Section 5, above, we looked at some of the ways firms may relocate internationally as part of a growth strategy.

However, firms may also look to relocate within the same country, and this can often be as a means of saving costs. For example, in the UK a number of government and quasi-government bodies have relocated from London to Manchester because office costs and wages are much lower there.

Nonetheless, relocation strategies within a single country are not necessarily driven solely by the need to save costs.

There are a number of factors an organisation should consider when thinking about relocating:

- The savings that could be achieved through reduced accommodation costs (land, buildings, refurbishment, rent, rates etc) and staff costs

- Improved recruitment/retention of staff (if moving to an area of higher unemployment)

- Enhanced productivity (for example, if reduced accommodation costs allow new machinery and equipment to be purchased)

- Increase in operational efficiency (for example, by moving into purpose-built premises)

- Improved quality of service

- Improved working environment/quality of life

- Creation of a new corporate image, brand or new look

However, it is important that the relocation strategy reflects the business's needs, and the views of stakeholders, including staff and customers.

In some cases, a firm may need to relocate because it is expanding and needs to recruit additional staff. In this case, the choice of location will be influenced by 'positive' factors such as the availability of labour (with suitable qualifications), quality of life, amenities and transport links.

Nevertheless, economic factors still need to be considered alongside these non-economic ones – with accommodation costs and salary expectations still being important factors in the location decision.

It will also be important to consider the transitional costs which may be involved in the relocation.

These will include:

- Transfer of staff (relocation allowances)

- Redundancies (for staff who do not wish to relocate)

- Recruitment and training costs (for replacement staff in the new location)

- Productivity losses (over the period of the move and as new staff get established)

- Plant and equipment, fixtures and fittings for the new premises

- Telecommunications and IT infrastructure of the new premises

- Costs of parallel running (if new offices are run alongside existing offices during the period of the move)

Section summary

Although strategic planning often focuses on growth and expansion, management need to be aware that they can sometimes benefit from **disposing** (divesting) of part of their activities. This can often be true for diversified groups which need to refocus on their core activities.

Organisations can also make savings by relocating activities to new locations.

9 The public and not for profit sectors

Introduction

Public sector and **not for profit organisations** will find some commercial strategic management techniques useful, particularly in the fields of marketing and innovation.

9.1 The public sector

Just as business organisations' objectives are drawn up according to the priorities of their stakeholders, with owners having priority and managers great influence, so public sector organisations' objectives are set, in theory, for the benefit of the public in general and the defined client groups in particular. Nonetheless, public sector organisations still need strategic management – in theory – to ensure that appropriate value chains, processes and resources are in place to allow them to achieve their objectives. In practice, however, public sector organisations' objectives often become subjected to politicians' and civil servants' own personal and professional priorities.

Political forces, in particular, can introduce **rapid policy changes**, while budgetary stringency or *largesse* can lead to the imposition of sudden spending cuts or the equally sudden availability of funds for which there are no planned applications. In the second case, actually spending the money can be more important than what it is spent on, so that an **underspend** need not be reported.

These considerations make much business strategy theory irrelevant to this sector. However, Montanari and Bracker proposed a matrix for the analysis of services provided by public sector bodies. This might be applied at the level of local or national government, or an executive agency with a portfolio of services. The axes are an assessment of service efficiency and public attractiveness: naturally, political support for a service or organisation depends to a great degree on the extent to which the public need and appreciate it.

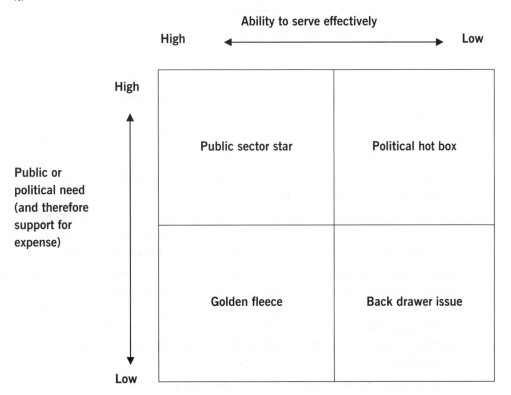

(a)   A **public sector star** is something that the system is doing well and should not change. It is essential to the viability of the system.

(b)   **Political hot boxes** are services that the public want, or which are mandated, but for which there are not adequate resources or competences.

(c)   **Golden fleeces** are services that are done well but for which there is low demand. They may, therefore, be perceived to be undesirable uses for limited resources. They are potential targets for cost cutting.

(d)   **Back drawer issues** are unappreciated and have low priority for funding. They are obvious candidates for cuts but, if managers perceive them as essential, they should attempt to increase support for them and move them into the **political hot box** category.

A similar concept, the Maslin Multidimensional matrix, has been proposed. This is also a two-axis, four-cell structure, with one axis dedicated to **client group needs** and wants and the other for any dimension that users might see as useful. This dimension might be, for example, the level of concern of the local community, of national government, the level of finance available, the level of staff expertise, or the level of activities currently undertaken.

The four cells are then defined by high and low levels of needs or wants and the extremes of the chosen second dimension.

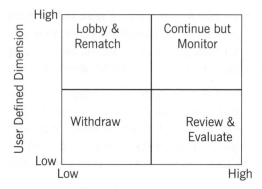

Needs (or wants) of the client growth

Public servants are under an obligation to deliver certain services in an effective and economical fashion. This implies that certain problems and choices are likely to appear repeatedly.

(a)   Plans must be made for the **delivery of services**. This may involve consideration of which **core competences** to maintain and develop, which services to carry on providing in-house and which to outsource.

(b)   Choices must also be made about procurement policy and the selection of suppliers to provide services required.

(c)   Budgets must be managed to provide mandated services. Choices must be made about **investment in physical and human resources** of all kinds.

(d)   Some **marketing** activity will be required, certainly in the form of **communication** with politicians, departmental staff, client groups and the wider public; and possibly in the form of **market research**, particularly in relation to the design and effectiveness of services.

(e)   Just as in business, there will be a requirement for continuing **innovation** in products and methods in the search for increased effectiveness and economy to deliver (for example) new services, or to find new ways of delivering services. These new ways of delivering services might include **public–private partnerships**, in which a public sector authority and one or more private sector companies combine to deliver a project. This will require the development of knowledge, assets and competences.

A public sector organisation's strategy will have three major elements.

- Marketing
- Service delivery
- Resource utilisation

As we have seen, co-operation between business organisations is now commonplace, both across and along the supply chain. Similar **cross-boundary links** are required in the public sector, both to meet client needs and to ensure that difficult problems do not disappear into the gaps between agencies.

9.2 Not for profit organisations

Even more than public sector organisations, charities need to operate both **economically** and **effectively**: they have an obligation both to those who depend on them and to those who finance them to do so. The techniques of business strategy are more applicable to charities than to the public sector, however, because their income is derived from **providing satisfaction to the donating public**, albeit in the form of providing a worthy cause to support. In addition, many charities do, in fact, operate mainstream businesses as a source of funds. They must therefore be particularly alive to **changing public concerns** when setting their objectives and be prepared to market their purpose as though it were a consumer product. Charities are, effectively, in competition with one another for donations.

The strategic management of charities is complicated by the element of **voluntary work** that exists within them. This is likely to be driven, at least in part, by very high ideals and may produce **ideological pressure** concerning the courses of action undertaken. Volunteers are likely to have their own ideas about how the organisation should be run, which is likely to constrain management ideas about control and reporting.

A major strategic concern will be to market the organisation's priorities and methods to its **internal stakeholders** as well as to the external donors who may be perceived to be its 'customers'. Both groups must be satisfied that the organisation is making proper use of the resources entrusted to it.

Strategic concern for charities

Haberberg and Rieple recognise three strategic concerns for charities.

- Organise and manage **internal structure** and systems so as to achieve the mission
- Develop and manage **fundraising** to provide consistent and predictable levels of income
- Demonstrate good **governance**

Section summary

Although **public sector** and **not for profit organisations** have different objectives to commercial organisations, they still need to develop strategies to deliver their objectives economically and effectively.

10   Evaluating strategic options

Introduction

Strategic choices are evaluated according to their suitability (to the organisation and its current situation), their feasibility (eg in terms of usefulness or competences) and their acceptability (eg to relevant stakeholder groups).

Once an organisation has identified its current strategic position, and the different potential strategic options available to it, it then has to choose which of these options it wants to pursue.

According to the rational model, individual strategies have to be evaluated against a number of criteria before a strategy or a mix of strategies is chosen. Johnson, Scholes and Whittington narrow these criteria down to three: **suitability**, **acceptability** and **feasibility**.

Suitability differs from feasibility and acceptability in that little can be done with an unsuitable strategy. However, it may be possible to adjust the factors that suggest a strategy is not acceptable or not feasible. Therefore **suitability should always be assessed first**.

10.1 Suitability

Suitability relates to the **strategic logic** of the strategy. The strategy must be consistent with the company's current strategic position and its operational circumstances.

- **Exploit** company strengths and distinctive **competences**?

- Rectify company **weaknesses**?

- **Neutralise** or deflect environmental **threats**?

- Help the firm to seize **opportunities**?

- **Satisfy the goals** of the organisation? (More generally, does the strategy fit with the company's mission and objectives?)

- **Fill the gap** identified by gap analysis?

- Generate/maintain **competitive advantage**?

- Involve an acceptable level of **risk**?

- Suit the **politics** and corporate **culture**?

A company should also consider three overall important strategic issues when assessing the suitability of an option.

- Does it **fit with any existing strategies** which the company is already employing, and which it wants to continue to employ?

- How well does the option actually address the company's strategic issues and **priorities**?

- Will the option contribute to a **sustainable competitive advantage** for the company, in the light of the competitive environment?

A number of the models which we have looked at earlier in this chapter and in preceding chapters in this Study Text could be useful for assessing the suitability of a strategy.

- Porter's generic strategies – For example, if an organisation is currently employing a cost leadership strategy and the basis of a proposed strategy is differentiation, this might not be suitable.

- Value chain – Similar issues could be identified in relation to the activities in the organisation's value chain: will the activities required for the proposed strategy 'fit' with the nature of the activities in the organisation's current value chain?

- BCG matrix – How will any new products or business units fit with the existing ones in an organisation's portfolio? Will they improve the balance of the portfolio?

- Ansoff's matrix – Is the choice of product–market strategy suitable? For example, in order for a market development strategy to be suitable there needs to be unsaturated markets available which the organisation could move into, and there must be distribution channels available so that the firm can gain access to the market. In addition, the firm's product or service has to be more attractive to customers than any existing competitor offerings so that the customers in the new market will want to switch to the organisation's product. Furthermore, the firm needs sufficient spare production capacity to be able to satisfy demand in the new market.

10.2 Acceptability (to stakeholders)

The acceptability of a strategy relates to whether it is acceptable to an organisation's stakeholders. As we identified in Chapter 2, the **key stakeholders** will be those with **high power** and **high interest** in an organisation or a strategy. It is particularly important that any potential strategy is acceptable to these key stakeholders.

The level of risk and return associated with the strategy are likely to be critical in determining how acceptable it is.

(a)   **Financial considerations**. Strategies will be evaluated by considering how far they contribute to meeting the dominant objective of increasing **shareholder wealth**.

   (i)   Return on investment
   (ii)   Profits
   (iii)   Growth
   (iv)   EPS
   (v)   Cash flow
   (vi)   Price/Earnings
   (vii)   Market capitalisation

(b)   **Customers**. Will the strategy give customers something they want? How will customers react to the strategy? Customers may object to a strategy if it means reducing service or raising price but, on the other hand, they may have no choice but to accept the changes.

(c)   **Management** have to implement the strategy via their staff.

(d)   **Staff** have to be committed to the strategy for it to be successful. If staff are unhappy with the strategy – or with any organisational changes which result from it – they could either resist the strategy, or else leave the organisation completely.

(e)   **Suppliers** have to be willing and able to meet the input requirements of the strategy.

(f)   **Banks** are interested in the implications for cash resources, debt levels etc.

(g)   **Government**. A strategy involving a takeover may be prohibited under legislation designed to prevent anti-competitive behaviour (eg the creation of a monopoly). Similarly, the environmental impact may cause key stakeholders to withhold consent.

(h)   **The public**. The environmental impact may cause key local stakeholders to protest. Will there be any pressure groups who oppose the strategy?

(i)   **Risk**. Different shareholders have different attitudes to risk. A strategy which changes the risk/return profile, for whatever reason, may not be acceptable.

10.3 Feasibility

Feasibility asks whether the strategy can in fact be implemented.

- Is there enough **money**?
- Is there the **ability** to deliver the goods/services specified in the strategy?
- Can we deal with the likely **responses that competitors** will make?
- Do we have access to **technology, materials and resources**?
- Do we have enough **time** to implement the strategy?

The 'Ms' model (which we considered in connection with the **resource audit**) could be useful for assessing feasibility. Does the organisation have the resources and competences it needs to implement the strategy successfully?

Strategies which do not make use of the existing competences, and which therefore call for new competences to be acquired, might not be feasible.

- Gaining competences via organic growth takes time.
- Acquiring new competences can be costly.

In Chapter 1 of this Study Text, we considered the management accountant's role in the strategy development process. A strategic management accountant could have an important role to play in providing information relating to the financial acceptability of a strategic option – for example, net present value and future cash flows – and its feasibility – for example, funding requirements and an organisation's ability to raise the finance needed.

10.4 Sustainability

Some organisations may feel it is appropriate to consider the longer-term prospects for a strategy under a separate heading of sustainability. This indicates that a firm should aim to adopt strategies which will deliver a long-term competitive advantage.

Section summary

Strategies should be assessed to ensure they are **suitable**, **acceptable** and **feasible**. Suitability should be assessed first as little can be done with an unsuitable strategy, whereas it may be possible to adjust the factors to make a strategy more acceptable or feasible.

11   Risk and cost behaviour

Introduction

Among the problems associated with strategic decision making is the lack of certainty associated with the forecasting techniques used. Whether or not probabilities can be assigned to outcomes, techniques exist for minimising the impact of this uncertainty, including CVP analysis.

Strategies deal with future events: the future cannot be predicted.

We can make a distinction between risk and uncertainty, but often the terms are used interchangeably.

(a)   **Risk** is sometimes used to describe situations where outcomes are not known, but their probabilities can be estimated.

(b)   **Uncertainty** is present when the outcome cannot be predicted or assigned probabilities.

Note. You will look at the strategic and operational risks an organisation faces in much more detail in Paper P3 – *Risk Management*.

The material we are looking at here does not attempt to replicate the material from P3, but it is a brief illustration of the way organisations need to take account of a wide range of potential risks when evaluating their strategic options.

11.1 Types of risk

KEY TERM

RISK is taken to mean both general unquantifiable uncertainty (eg political risk) and volatility, often measured by standard deviation.

Risk	Comment
Physical risk	Earthquakes, fire, flooding, and equipment breakdown. In the long term, climatic changes: global warming, drought (relevant to agriculture and water firms).
Economic risk	Assumptions about the economic environment might turn out to be wrong. Not even the government forecasts are perfect.
Financial risk	This term has a specific technical meaning: the risk to shareholders caused by debt finance. The risk exists because the debt finance might prevent capital growth or the payment of dividends, particularly when trading is difficult. The converse is that when business is buoyant, interest payments are easily covered and shareholders receive the benefit of the remaining profits.
Business risk	Lowering of entry barriers (eg new technology); changes in customer/supplier industries leading to changed relative power; changes to the firm's internal structure (eg its culture or technical systems); management misunderstanding of core competences; volatile cash flows; uncertain returns; changed investor perceptions increasing the required rate of return.
Political risk	Nationalisation, sanction, civil war and political instability can all have an impact on the business.
Exchange risk	This is the risk that changes in exchange rates affect the value of a transaction in a currency, or how it is reported.
Competitor risk	The risks to cash flows arising from the actions of competitors: for example, if a competitor introduces a new product, or reduces the price of its existing products.

11.2 Who suffers risk?

Risk and return are related. An investor will want a higher return to compensate for the increased risk of a project.

For example, investors in a company in a low-risk business might be satisfied with a return of, say, 15%, whereas in a comparable high-risk business the required return might be a minimum of 25%.

There may be a **minimum return** that shareholders will accept, allowing for the risk of the investment.

Different stakeholders in a company or a decision have different attitudes to risk.

(a)   **Shareholders** are able to **diversify their portfolios**, so they can have shares in a number of firms, some offering high return for high risk, others offering a low return for a low risk.

(b)   Key decision makers are **managers**, and their perceptions of risk are likely to be quite different.

11.3 The management accountant and risk

11.3.1 Targets for risk

If the primary financial target can be converted into a target rate of return for individual capital projects, how can risk be expressed in practical terms for decision makers?

(a)   A **premium** for risk can be added to the target DCF rate of return.

(b)   To protect cash flows, it might be made a condition of all new capital projects that the project should **pay back** within a certain period of time, say three to four years.

When assessing future cash flows and net present values of projects it may also be useful to consider the value of leaving different options open. This is the essence of real options theory, which we discussed in Chapter 3.

11.3.2 Risk appraisal in strategy evaluation

One of the problems arising when evaluating alternative strategies is the reliability of the data used.

(a) Business planners use operational research techniques to measure levels of uncertainty.

(b) Basic **probability theory** can be used to express the likelihood of a forecast result occurring. This would evaluate the data given by informing the decision maker that there is, for example, a 50% probability that an acceptable result will be achieved, a 25% chance that the worst result will occur and a 25% chance that the best possible result will occur. This evaluation of risk might help the executive to decide between alternative strategies, each with its own risk profile.

When evaluating a strategy, management should consider:

(a) Whether an individual strategy involves **an unacceptable amount** of risk. If it does, it should be eliminated from further consideration in the planning process.

(b) However, the risk of an individual strategy should also be considered in the context of the **overall portfolio** of investment strategies adopted by the company.

11.3.3 Risk and cost behaviour: operational gearing

CVP analysis (breakeven analysis) can be useful in strategic planning to assess the share of the market needed to break even or to achieve a target return with a particular strategy. For example, if a company is planning to make a new product for a particular market, and estimates of capital investment costs and fixed and variable running costs were fairly reliable, the company could assess the following for a number of different sales prices.

(a) How many sales would be required to break even each year, and so what market share would be needed.

(b) How many sales would be needed over a given period (of, say, three years) assuming a gradual increase in annual sales, in order to break even in DCF terms (ie achieve an NPV = 0). The required market share per year for each year of the project could then be assessed.

KEY TERM

COST-VOLUME-PROFIT ANALYSIS (CVP). 'Study of the effects on future profit of changes in fixed cost, variable cost, sales price, quantity and mix.' *(CIMA Official Terminology)*

A related risk is the **cost structure** of the business.

(a) A **high level of fixed costs** means that large losses are made if sales are less than breakeven, but that once breakeven is achieved, larger profits follow.

(b) A **high proportion of variable product costs** means that the total costs are always sensitive to actual production volumes. Losses are lower, but so are profits.

In other words, the business's **operational gearing** (the ratio of fixed to variable costs) is an important indicator of risk. Where there is a high proportion of fixed costs, a strategy might be more risky, although it promises a higher return. A high proportion of genuinely variable costs can mean more flexibility.

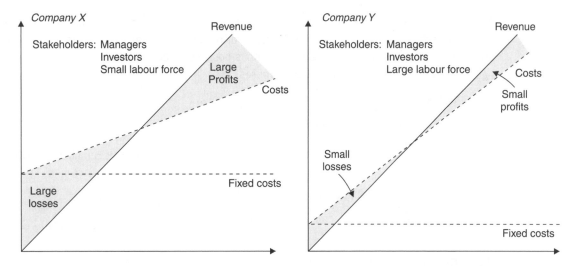

The two graphs have the same breakeven point, but X is much more sensitive to lower sales. It is more volatile. X promises higher profits, but risks higher losses than Y.

With any strategy there is a **stakeholder response risk**, an environmental factor which can intrude on the management accountant's cost behaviour diagrams. Bankers, employees and the Government are all interested in a business. If a business pursues a particular strategy, this might antagonise the Government of the country in which it is operating.

11.3.4 Probabilities and risk

Higher risks tend to be associated with higher returns. This is the principle underlying the Capital Asset Pricing Model, and we have already seen that the target DCF rate of return for capital expenditure projects may be varied according to the project's risk.

Some risks can be measured by probabilities.

(a)   An average expected profit or NPV can be measured as an expected value (EV) of the different probabilities.

(b)   Risk can be quantified as a standard deviation of expected profit or NPV.

 The Capital Asset Pricing Model is discussed in more detail in Paper F3 – *Financial Strategy*.

11.4 Example: uncertainty about sales demand, costs and profits

A company is trying to make a strategic decision about whether to introduce a new production process. The process would reduce unit variable costs of production significantly but would increase fixed costs of production substantially. Forecast sales demand is uncertain, for a range of different selling prices. Non-production costs are also uncertain. The key information in the question could be reduced to the following.

(a)   **Option 1**. Keep existing system

    (i)   Sales price could be anywhere in the range £9–£10.5 per unit
    (ii)   Sales quantity could be anywhere in the range 8.5 million to 11 million units
    (iii)   Profits in £ would be $(PQ)0.8 - 0.2Q - 100{,}000$ where:

    P = price
    Q = quantity sold

(b)   **Option 2**. Introduce new production system

    (i)   Sales price has to be £9 per unit or less
    (ii)   Sales quantity could be anywhere above 11 million units at the chosen price
    (iii)   Profit would be $(PQ)0.8 - 0.15Q - 400{,}000$

A suitable approach to tackling this problem would be to consider the profits that would be earned at a number of different price/quantity combinations, for both Options 1 and 2. A 'worst possible' and 'best possible' estimate could be made, and the various possible outcomes analysed and discussed. Some figures are shown below, for illustration purposes.

(a) **Option 1**

    (i)   Worse possible price   £9

              Quantity   8.5 million

              Profit = $(9 \times 8.5 \text{ million})0.8 - 0.2\,(8.5 \text{ million}) - 100{,}000$

                       =   £59.4m

    (ii)   Best possible price   £10.5

              Quantity   11 million

              Profit = $(10.5 \times 11 \text{ million})0.8 - 0.2\,(11 \text{ million}) - 100{,}000$

                       =   £90.1m

(b) **Option 2**

     Best possible price   £9

     Worst possible volume   11 million units

     Profit = $(9 \times 11 \text{ million})0.8 - 0.15\,(11 \text{ million}) - £400{,}000$

                 =   £77.15m

These could be used in a number of ways.

(a) If the probabilities of different outcomes were known they could be plotted on a decision tree.

(b) The outcomes might be used in a decision matrix, if they could be related to different sets of circumstances.

(c) An assessment of risk might be carried out.

Section summary

Strategies deal with future events, and the future cannot be predicted with any certainty. Techniques such as CVP analysis can be used to reduce this risk of uncertainty.

---

12   Decision techniques

Introduction

Decision-making processes can be supported by rational techniques, including decision trees, cost/benefit analysis, ranking and scoring, scenario building, decision matrices and sensitivity analysis.

This section describes a number of techniques to enable a systematic approach to be taken to certain strategic decisions.

12.1 Decision trees

KEY TERM

DECISION TREE. 'Pictorial method of showing a sequence of interrelated decisions and their expected outcomes. Decision trees can incorporate both the probabilities of, and values of, expected outcomes, and are used in decision making.'   (*CIMA Official Terminology*)

Decision trees are a useful tool for helping managers choose between different courses of action. The tree structure allows them to lay out options and investigate the possible outcomes of choosing these options.

There are **two stages in preparing a decision tree**.

(a)   **Drawing the tree itself**, to show all the choices and outcomes.

(b)   **Putting in the numbers**: the probabilities, outcome values and EVs. (EV is calculated as **probability** × **outcome**.) For example, if you have a 1% chance of winning £100, the EV of the winning is £1.

The role of decision trees in strategic planning is to assess which choices are **mutually exclusive**, and to try to give them some quantitative value. As such, they are useful in:

- Clarifying strategic decisions when they are complex
- Using risk (in probability terms) as an **input** to quantifying the decision options
- Ranking the relative costs and benefits of the options

12.2 Cost/benefit analysis

Cost/benefit analysis is a strategy evaluation technique often used in the public sector, where many of the costs and benefits of a project are intangible.

KEY TERM

COST/BENEFIT ANALYSIS involves a comparison between the cost of the resources used, plus any other costs imposed by an activity (eg pollution, environmental damage) and the value of the financial and non-financial benefits derived.

In many public sector decisions, a cost/benefit analysis is conducted on the following basis.

(a)   The project and its overall objectives are defined.

(b)   The benefits, including social benefits, are analysed in detail. It is not always easy to put a value on social costs.

(c)   The net benefits for the project are estimated, if possible. A road might reduce journey times, and so save money.

It can help businesses negotiate with public sector officials. For example, most large building projects have to get planning permission from the local authority. Local government officials will sometimes insist on certain social benefits to be included in a project.

12.3 Ranking and scoring

Ranking and scoring methods are less precise than decision trees. Some goals may be hard to quantify, and strategic decisions generally take more matters into account than can be dealt with by uncertain estimates of probability.

This is best illustrated by means of a simple example. The objectives are weighted in relative importance (so that minimising competitive threats is the most important).

	Objectives				
Strategic option	Growth in profit by over 10%	Reduce dependence on suppliers	Minimise competitive threats	Score	Rank
Do nothing	X	X	X	–	
Cut costs by subcontracting	✓	X	X	4	3rd
Expand product range	✓	X	✓	9	1st
Offer discounts to customers for fixed term contract	X	X	✓	5	2nd
Objective weighting	4	3	5		

In the example, expanding the product range would be chosen as the firm believes this will enhance profits and minimise competitive threats. Note that this is a deliberately simple example. In many cases, the strategies may not be mutually exclusive.

12.4 Scenarios

Scenario building is the process of identifying alternative futures. A strategy can be evaluated in terms of the various models of the future a company has.

Scenario planning and forecasting were discussed in more detail in Chapter 3 of this Study Text.

12.5 Decision matrices

A **decision matrix** is a way of comparing outcomes with a variety of circumstances. Outcomes can be selected on a number of bases, and the decision matrix clarifies the choice.

When a decision has to be made, there will be a range of possible actions. Each action will have certain consequences, or **payoffs**. The payoff from any given action will depend on the circumstances (for example, high demand or low demand).

For a decision with these elements, a **payoff table** can be prepared. This is simply a table with rows for circumstances and columns for actions (or *vice versa*) and the payoffs in the cells of the table. Here is an example.

Payoff table for decision on level of advertising expenditure: payoffs in $'000 of profit after advertising expenditure

| | | Actions: expenditure | | |
		High	Medium	Low
Circumstances	I	+50	+30	+15
of the economy	II	+20	+25	+5
	III	−15	−10	−5

Having worked out the consequences of different actions under different circumstances, we need to select a criterion for making our decision. Two basic decision rules cater for optimists and pessimists respectively.

(a) **Hope for the best**: the maximax rule can be applied in two equivalent ways:

   (i)   Maximise the maximum profit
   (ii) Minimise the minimum costs or losses

   Using this rule, we would decide on high expenditure as this offers the best of the favourable outcomes. Note that in this case, we are looking at economy condition 1, since this offers the highest profit: minimising cost or loss does not apply.

(b) **Expect the worst**: the minimax rule also has two equivalent versions:

   (i)   Maximise the minimum profit
   (ii) Minimise the maximum costs or losses

   Using this rule we examine economy condition 3 since this causes the greatest losses. Here we would choose low expenditure.

To consider only one payoff of each action may be thought unrealistic. The Hurwicz criterion seeks to remedy this by taking a **weighted average** of the best and worst payoffs of each action:

Weighted payoff = α × worst payoff × $(1 - \alpha)$ × best payoff

α is a number between 0 and 1, sometimes called the **pessimism-optimism index**. The value chosen reflects one's attitude to the risk of poor payoffs and the chance of good payoffs. The action with the highest weighted payoff is selected.

Another possible approach is to consider the extent to which we might come to regret an action we had chosen. This is the **minimax regret** rule.

Regret for any combination of action and circumstances	=	Payoff for best action in those circumstances	−	Payoff of the action actually taken in those circumstances

To apply this rule it is necessary to calculate the regret for each cell for each course of action.

Another technique which organisations could use to help consider the possible outcomes from a course of action is game theory, which we discussed in Chapter 3 of this Study Text.

12.6 Sensitivity analysis

KEY TERM

SENSITIVITY ANALYSIS can be defined as a 'modelling and risk assessment procedure in which changes are made to significant variables in order to determine the effect of these changes on the planned outcome. Particular attention is thereafter paid to variables identified as being of special significance.'

(*CIMA Official Terminology*)

Sensitivity analysis involves asking 'what if?' questions. By changing the value of different variables in a decision model, a number of **different outcomes** will be produced. For example, wage increases can be altered to 10% from 5%; demand for a product can be reduced from 100,000 to 80,000; the introduction of new processing equipment can be deferred by six months, on the revised assumption that there will be delays; and so on.

A particularly powerful decision-related technique is to establish the percentage change in each assumption that would lead to a different decision. This can give a good indication of overall risk and also show which variables need the closest monitoring.

12.7 Complications of strategic decisions

Remember that strategic decisions often involve a long timescale, and are based on data which may be unreliable. (For example, projected sales forecasts for a new product may be little more than educated guesses.)

The level of uncertainty involved means that strategic investment appraisal and analysis cannot ensure that an organisation makes the 'correct' investment decision. However, just as the rational model provides a framework for strategic planning overall, strategic investment analysis can give organisations a framework in which to make logical investment decisions.

Section summary

Rational techniques such as decision trees, cost/benefit analysis, ranking and scoring, scenario building, decision matrices and sensitivity analysis could all be useful in supporting the decision-making process.

Chapter Summary

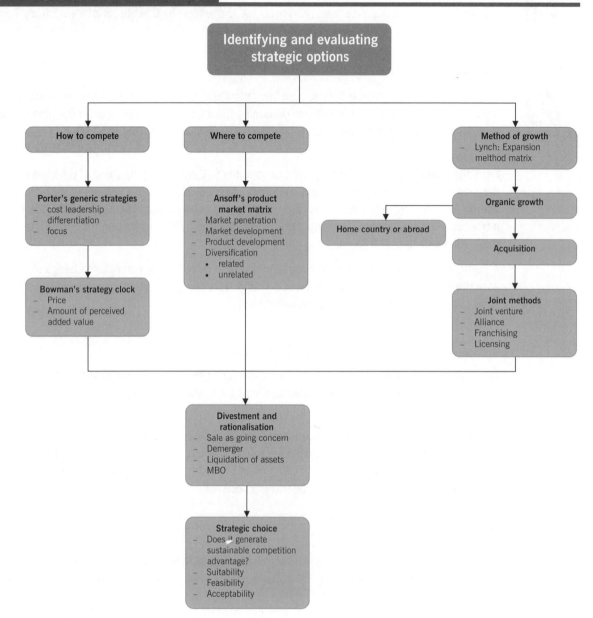

Quick Quiz

1   **Fill in the blanks**.

In the context of Porter's three generic strategies:

(1) ....*cost leadership*...... and (2) ....*differentiation*..... are industry wide strategies

(3) ..*focus*..... involves segmentation

2   According to Bowman's Strategy Clock, a hybrid strategy is one in which a firm:

(a)   Combines low price with low perceived product or service benefits
(b)   Pursues a low price strategy but offers better value than its competitors
(c)   Pursues a strategy which seeks both differentiation and a lower price than its competitors
(d)   Enhances margins by offering better products or services at a higher price than its competitors

3   What are two overall limitations of Porter's generic strategy approach?

4   The car manufacturer, Morgan, makes all its cars by hand and only serves a very small part of the market – car enthusiasts who like cars with a traditional design but performance resembling that of a sports car. Because the cars are hand made, they are expensive to buy.

What kind of generic strategy is Morgan pursuing?   *focus differentiation*

5   Fill in the product-market strategies identified by Ansoff's matrix.

Product

		Present	New
Market	Present	*Market penetration*	*Product development*
	New	*Market development*	*Diversification*

6   Why is innovation important in an organic growth strategy?

7   **Fill in the blanks** in the statement below, using the words in the box.

(1) ..*Acquisitions*..provide a means of entering a (2) ..*market*.. or building up (3) ..*market share*.. more (4) ..*quickly*..than would be the case if the company tried to develop its own (5) ..*resources*.. Corporate planners must however consider the level of (6) ....*risk*..... involved.

• risk	• quickly	• market
• market share	• resources	• acquisitions

8   Define a joint venture. What is the chief disadvantage of joint ventures?
  - *profit sharing*
  - *conflict of interest*
  - *confidential info*

9   What are the methods of divestment?
  - *Demerger*
  - *MBO*
  - *Sale of assets*
  - *Sale of going concern*

Answers to Quick Quiz

1   (1)   cost leadership
    (2)   differentiation
    (3)   focus

2   C   A firm pursuing a hybrid strategy seeks both differentiation and a lower price than its competitors.

        Option A describes a 'no frills' strategy; B describes a low price strategy; and Option D is a differentiation strategy.

3   •   Problems in defining the 'industry'.
    •   Problems in deciding whether strategies should be pursued at corporate level or SBU level.

4   Differentiation – focus. Morgan makes luxury cars for a narrowly defined sector of the market.

5

		Product	
		Present	*New*
Market	*Present*	Market penetration (for growth) or consolidation (to maintain position) or withdrawal	Product development
	New	Market development	Diversification

6   Innovation provides the organisation with a distinctive competence, and with the ability to maintain such a competence. Also it maintains the organisation's competitive advantage and market share.

7   (1) Acquisitions (2) market (3) market share (4) quickly (5) resources (6) risk

8   A joint venture is an arrangement where two firms (or more) join forces for manufacturing, financial and marketing purposes and each has a share in both the equity and the management of the business. The major disadvantage of joint ventures is that there can be conflicts of interest.

9   Sale as a going concern
    Sale of assets
    Demerger
    Management buyout/buy in

Answers to Questions

5.1 Hermes

(a)   Arguably, Hermes initially pursued a cost-focus strategy, by targeting the business segment.

(b)   It seems to be moving into a cost leadership strategy over the whole market although its competitive offer, in terms of lower costs for local calls, is incomplete.

(c)   The barriers to entry to the market have been lowered by the new technology. Gerbil phone might pick up a significant amount of business.

5.2 Road transport

The first step in a suggested solution is to think of how a company operating nationwide in general road haulage might diversify, while benefiting from synergies between its new business and its existing business. Perhaps you thought of the following.

(a)   To move from nationwide to international haulage, the company might be able to use its existing contacts with customers to develop an international trade. Existing administration and depot facilities in the UK could be used. Drivers should be available who are willing to work abroad, and the scope for making reasonable profits should exist. However, international road haulage might involve the company in the purchase of new vehicles (eg road haulage in Europe often involves the carriage of containerised products on large purpose-built vehicles). Since international haulage takes longer, vehicles will be tied up in jobs for several days, and a substantial investment might be required to develop the business. In addition, in the event of breakdowns, a network of overseas garage service arrangements will have to be created. It might take some time before business builds up sufficiently to become profitable.

(b)   Moving from general haulage to 'speciality' types of haulage, perhaps haulage of large items of plant and machinery, or computer equipment. The same broad considerations apply to speciality types of haulage. Existing depot facilities could be used and existing customer contacts might be developed. However, expertise in specialist work will have to be 'brought in' as well as developed within the company and special vehicles might need to be bought. Business might take some time to build up and if the initial investment is high, there could be substantial early losses.

Now try these questions from the Practice Question Bank	**Number**	**Level**	**Marks**	**Time**
	5.1–5.7	Intermediate	n/a	10 mins
	5.8	Examination	10	18 mins
	5.9	Examination	15	27 mins
	5.10	Examination	25	45 mins

INFORMATION SYSTEMS AND STRATEGY

 In Chapters 6 and 7 we examine the way that information and information systems can support business strategy.

In this chapter we look at the importance of the **systems** and the **technology**, and then in Chapter 7 we look at the strategic importance of **information** itself.

Information systems play an increasingly important role in contemporary organisations. For some, IS and IT are a source of competitive advantage in their own right, but, for many, IT's main role is to support the overall business strategy. Therefore it is important that the

organisation's IS/IT strategies are properly aligned with its business strategy.

Equally (as we see in Section 3 of this chapter) organisations need to ensure that their day to day operations are contributing effectively to the achievement of their overall corporate goals. This highlights the need for information about operational-level performance as well as strategic level performance.

Topic list	Learning outcomes	Syllabus references	Ability required
1 Strategic information systems	E1(b); E2(a)	E1(a) (i)	Evaluate
2 Information strategy	E1(a), E1(b), E2(a), E2(b)	E1(a) (i), E1(b) (ii), E2(a) (i), E2(b) (ii)	Evaluate
3 Strategic and operational information	E1(a)	E1(a) (i)	Evaluate

Chapter Overview

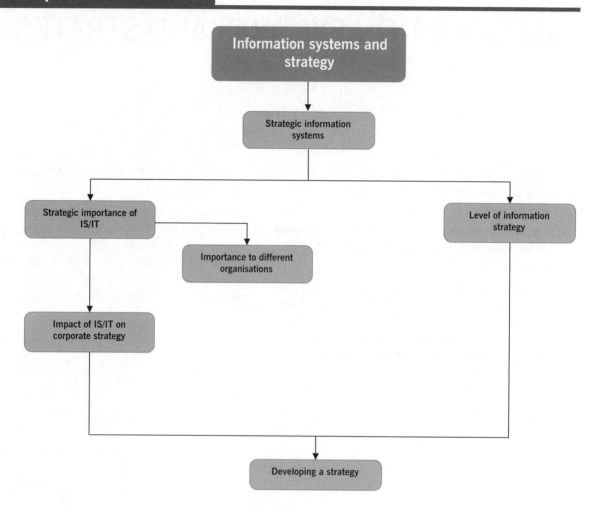

Introduction and overview

In order to manage the performance of their organisations effectively, managers need relevant and reliable performance information. In this chapter, we look at some of types of information system which could provide that information.

However, while information **systems** themselves are important to an organisation, the **information** which they provide is perhaps even more important. Ultimately, managers need information for decision making and control, and the role of the systems is to provide that information.

An underlying consideration for information strategy is that an organisation's information systems should provide the appropriate type and amount of information which management need to select, implement and control its chosen business strategy. However, this also means that an organisation's information strategy needs to be aligned to the business strategy, in terms of the type of information available. (For example, if an organisation is pursuing a differentiation strategy based on the high quality of its product then information about aspects of product quality will be required in order to measure and manage performance.)

Make sure you do not underestimate the importance of IT/IS to strategy. Very often an organisation's ability to deliver a strategy may depend on having sufficient IT capabilities to do so. Equally, an organisation's IT capabilities may be instrumental in shaping its strategy. For example, does it have sufficient IT infrastructure to support an e-commerce strategy?

Remember, in Chapter 4 we noted how an organisation's resources and capabilities contribute to its competitive advantage – and these resources could include its information systems and IT systems.

In this context, it is worth noting that the way an organisation manages and uses information could, in itself, become a source of competitive advantage – for example, if the organisation is able to respond to market trends or opportunities more quickly than its rivals on the basis of the information it gathered about those opportunities. Equally, gathering data and information about customers and customer requirements could also be useful in the context of customer relationship management (which we discuss further in Chapter 8 of this Study Text).

1   Strategic information systems

Introduction

Strategic information is used to **plan** the **objectives** of the organisation, and to **assess** whether the objectives are being met in practice. Therefore it is important that organisations have an information systems strategy so that they can meet their information requirements.

Organisations often have to consider three different strategies in relation to information: information systems (IS) strategy, information technology (IT) strategy and information management (IM) strategy. We will look at these in more detail throughout this chapter, but it is important you are aware of the different aspects of information strategy overall as you are reading through the chapter.

1.1 Strategic information

In Chapter 1, we highlighted the idea of a hierarchy of performance in organisations: covering strategic, tactical and operational levels of performance.

This idea of a hierarchy is also important in relation to the data and performance information required for decision making and control in organisations. We examine information systems, and the different levels of information they provide, later in this chapter.

Strategic planning, management control and operational control may be seen as a hierarchy of planning and control decisions (the Anthony hierarchy).

As well as highlighting the three levels in the hierarchy, it is also important to note the different characteristics of the information produced (and required) at different levels in the hierarchy:

Strategic information	Management (tactical) information	Operational information
• Derived from both internal and external sources	• Primarily generated internally (but may have a limited external component)	• Derived from internal sources; often includes 'transaction data' from transaction processing systems
• Summarised at a high level	• Summarised at a lower level	
• Relevant to the long term	• Relevant to the short and medium term	• Detailed, being the processing of raw data
• Concerned with the whole organisation	• Concerned with activities or departments, and with the efficiency/effectiveness of resource usage	• Relevant to the immediate term
• Often prepared on an *ad hoc* basis		• Task-specific
• Both quantitative and qualitative	• Prepared routinely and regularly	• Prepared very frequently
• Focus on planning; future orientation	• Based on quantitative measures (eg budgets, benchmarks)	• Largely quantitative, but often expressed in operational measures (eg units produced, transactions processed) rather than monetary terms
• Uncertain, as the future cannot be accurately predicted	• Some focus on planning, but greater focus on control	• Focus on control (rather than planning)

CASE STUDY

Case example: An evening newspaper

- **Operational information** will include supplies to and returns from vendors to support invoicing, costs of production, controls over inventories of paper, ink etc, hours worked by staff to support payroll, health and safety compliance.

- **Managerial (or tactical) information** will include levels of sales to plan production runs of each edition (up to seven a day in some cities), the quality of stories and likely interest in them to plan production runs, advertising sales and success of special editions, supplements etc, the weather on the day and its effects on sales. Clearly, the main information that will be used at this level will be the articles and stories themselves and the editorial team will decide inclusion and position of each.

- **Strategic information** includes the plans of rival newspaper owners, the policies of the press watchdogs, potential sources of new advertising revenues, new printing technologies, the costs and efficiency of the various printing plants operated by the firm, potential new markets for newspapers (eg free morning papers).

1.2 Strategic information systems

In order for managers or accountants to be able to measure the performance of their organisations, the relevant performance information needs to be available to them. This highlights the importance of information systems. Moreover, the reference to Anthony's hierarchy (above) highlights the importance of having different types of information systems which provide performance information at different levels (strategic, tactical and operational).

Strategic IT systems include Executive Information Systems **(EIS)**, Management Information Systems **(MIS)** and Decision Support Systems **(DSS)**. **Value added networks** facilitate the strategic use of information in order to add value.

1.2.1 Executive information systems (EIS)

KEY TERM

An EXECUTIVE INFORMATION SYSTEM (EIS) pools data from internal and external sources and makes information available to senior managers in an easy to use form. EIS help senior managers make strategic, unstructured decisions.

An EIS should provide senior managers with easy access to key **internal and external** information. The system summarises and tracks strategically critical information, possibly drawn from internal MIS and DSS, but also including data from external sources, eg competitors, legislation and external databases such as Reuters.

An EIS is likely to have the following **features**:

- Flexibility
- Quick response time
- Sophisticated data analysis and modelling tools

A model of a typical EIS is shown below.

An EIS

EIS
workstation

- Menus
- Graphics
- Communications
- Local processing

EIS
workstation

- Menus
- Graphics
- Communications
- Local processing

Internal data

MIS data
Financial data
Office systems
Modelling/analysis

External data

Share prices
Market research
Legislation
Competitors

EIS
workstation

- Menus
- Graphics
- Communications
- Local processing

1.2.2 Management information systems (MIS)

KEY TERM

MANAGEMENT INFORMATION SYSTEMS (MIS) convert data from mainly internal sources into information (eg summary reports, exception reports). This information enables managers to make timely and effective decisions for planning, directing and controlling the activities for which they are responsible.

An MIS provides regular reports and (usually) online access to the organisation's current and historical performance.

MIS usually transform data from underlying transaction processing systems into summarised files that are used as the basis for management reports.

MIS have the following characteristics:

- Support **structured** decisions at operational and management control levels
- Designed to report on **existing** operations
- Have little analytical capability
- Relatively **inflexible**
- Have an **internal** focus

1.2.3 Decision support systems (DSS)

KEY TERM

DECISION SUPPORT SYSTEMS (DSS) combine data and analytical models or data analysis tools to support semi-structured and unstructured decision making.

DSS are used by management to assist in making decisions on issues which are subject to high levels of uncertainty about the problem, the various **responses** which management could undertake or the likely **impact** of those actions.

DSS are intended to provide a wide range of alternative information gathering and analytical tools with a major emphasis upon **flexibility** and **user friendliness**.

DSS have more analytical power than other systems enabling them to analyse and condense large volumes of data into a form that helps managers make decisions. The objective is to allow the manager to consider a number of **alternatives** and evaluate them under a variety of potential conditions.

Executives at small and medium-sized companies are making critical business decisions every day based on the information available to them. This information can come from a variety of sources: opinions from peers and colleagues; a personal sense of intuition or business judgement; or data derived internally or externally to the organisation. This is worrying, however, given the lack of confidence in the data available to decision makers.

A 2007 report conducted by the Economist Intelligence Unit (EIU) found that nine out of ten corporate executives admitted to making important decisions on the basis of inadequate information.

This suggests that there are problems in the quality, amount and timeliness of information which is available as the basis for decision making. However, it also suggests there is a danger executives will be making sub-optimal decisions, because they simply do not have the relevant information to make the best decision in a timely manner.

1.2.4 Value added networks

Value added networks (VANs) are networks that facilitate the adding of value to products and (particularly) to services by the strategic use of information. Typically, VANs will link separate organisations together through electronic data interchanges (EDIs), contributing to the development of **business networks**.

Also, they are often business ventures in their own right, with companies subscribing to the services available. Good examples are the SABRE, Amadeus and Galileo airline flight booking systems. A simpler example is the EDI systems between manufacturers and their suppliers that facilitate the operation of just-in-time (JIT) logistics.

VANs give mutual competitive advantage to all their subscribers, but only so long as some competitors are left outside of the system. As soon as membership of the VAN (or a competing VAN) becomes a standard feature of the industry, the original competitive advantage is lost. Competitive advantage based on VAN membership can then only exist if there is more than one VAN and each VAN in the industry offers a different degree of benefit in terms of cost reduction or differentiation.

Section summary

Strategic information is used to **plan** the **objectives** of the organisation, and to **assess** whether the objectives are being met in practice. Strategic information (such as that provided by EIS and MIS) helps managers make strategic decisions.

2 Information strategy

Introduction

Information strategy can be divided into **information systems strategy**, **information technology strategy** and **information management strategy**. The strategic significance of information requires that information itself be managed strategically so that the systems, the technology and the information itself support the overall strategic policy.

As with so many other aspects of business strategy, the terminology used in the world of information strategy is not clearly defined. Terms such as 'information management' are used in slightly different ways by different groups of professionals. In this section we provide you with information that will help you to gain a fuller understanding of the ways in which various terms are used and of some of the range of meanings and connotations they possess.

2.1 Information and information systems

To begin with, let us consider the difference between **information** itself and the **means by which it is collected**, **processed**, **moved around and stored**. Information is intangible and in its most basic form exists in people's minds. However, there is a limit to the amount of information any one person can remember and make effective use of; as a result, **physical records** of information have been with us for thousands of years.

So, right from the beginning, we have a **distinction between information itself and the means by which it is handled**. Inscribed clay tablets that survive from ancient civilisations are an example of information technology; we can hold them in our hands, but the information they store is lost to us unless we can decipher the symbols used by the person who inscribed them.

Nowadays, we have a huge array of means in which we can store and manipulate information; many of these are electronic, but paper records are still fundamental to many aspects of information handling. We would not necessarily think of a handwritten memo as an example of information technology, such is its simplicity, but, in principle, it is.

Generally, today, information technology means **computers**: electronically based processing and storage systems and all the **peripherals**, **communication links** and **software** that go with them. The extreme complexity of these systems leads to the creation of large amounts of information relating specifically to their design, maintenance and operation, but this information is not their purpose: it is part of the technology itself.

The **information technology systems** we use in business exist to help us to make use of **information that is external to the overall system itself**, information that we need to carry on our business operations.

The immense potential of computer-based systems provides an increasingly wide range of ways in which we can exploit information in business. We need to decide how we are going to use the information we have, how we are going to obtain more information and how we are going to exploit the information technology that we use to handle it. The decisions we make about these problems constitute our **information strategy**.

2.2 Information strategy

KEY TERMS

The INFORMATION SYSTEMS (IS) STRATEGY is the long-term plan for systems to exploit information in order to support business strategies or create new strategic options.

The INFORMATION TECHNOLOGY (IT) STRATEGY is concerned with selecting, operating and managing the technological element of the IS strategy.

The INFORMATION MANAGEMENT (IM) STRATEGY deals with the roles of the people involved in the use of IT assets, the relationships between them and design of the management processes needed to exploit IT.

STRATEGIC INFORMATION SYSTEMS are systems at any level of an organisation that change goals, processes, products, services or environmental relationships with the aim of gaining competitive advantage.

Michael Earl's analysis of information strategy into three elements (IS, IT and IM) is useful. The first distinction he made was between the strategies for **information systems** and **information technology**.

2.2.1 Levels of information strategy

Information systems (IS) strategy

An IS strategy is concerned with specifying the systems (in the widest meaning of the word) that will best **enable the use of information to support the overall business strategy** and to deliver tangible benefits to the business (for example, through increased productivity, or enhanced profits). In this context, a 'system' will include all the **activities**, **procedures**, **records** and **people** involved in a particular aspect of the organisation's work, as well as the **technology** used.

The IS strategy is focused on **business requirements**, the demands they make for information of all kinds and the nature of the benefits that information systems are expected to provide.

This strategy is very much **demand-led** and **business-driven**: each SBU in a large organisation is likely to have its own IS strategy.

Information technology (IT) strategy

The IT strategy, by contrast, is technology focused and looks at the resources, technical solutions and systems architecture required to enable an organisation to implement its IS strategy.

IT strategies are likely to look at the **hardware and software** used by the organisation to produce and process information. They may also include aspects of data capture and data storage, as well as the transmission and presentation of information.

Information management (IM) strategy

Earl subsequently also highlighted the need for an IM strategy. The emphasis here is on management: managing the role and structure of IT activities within an organisation, and managing the relationships between IT specialists and the users of information. In this respect, a key feature of IM strategy is its focus on **roles and relationships**.

IM strategy also plays an important part in ensuring that information can be accessed by all the people who need it but, at the same time, access is restricted to only those people who need it.

We might sum up the three levels of information strategy in very simple terms by saying that: IS strategy defines **what** is to be achieved; IT strategy determines **how** hardware, software and telecommunications can achieve it; and the IM strategy describes **who** controls and uses the technology provided.

This model of information strategy has the advantage of being **internally consistent** and quite **simple** to understand. Unfortunately, the picture is spoiled by a different use of the term information management. You may come across a rather narrow use of this term to mean 'the approach taken to storing and accessing data'. Since this is really just an aspect of the IT strategy as defined above, we do not recommend the use of the term in this way.

Exam skills

Although you are not expected to have a detailed knowledge of IT systems, IS and IT are core elements of modern businesses, and they are likely to become increasingly important to business strategies.

Historically, however, examiners have noted that many students display a poor knowledge of the IS and IT aspects of the syllabus. Make sure you do not overlook these areas.

Very often an organisation's ability to implement a strategy successfully may depend on it having sufficient IT capabilities to do so. Equally, an organisation's IT capabilities may be instrumental in shaping its strategy. For example, does the organisation have sufficient competences to support an e-commerce strategy?

Also remember that an organisation needs to be able to collect data and turn it into useful information, for example either for management information or marketing information. Managers need this information as a basis for planning, decision making and control.

2.3 The need for a strategic approach

Earl argues that information systems and information strategy are too important to leave in the hands of technology professionals alone. He suggests the following characteristics of IT/IS strategy support this view:

- Involves **high costs**
- Is **critical to the success** of many organisations
- Is now used as part of the commercial strategy in the battle for **competitive advantage**
- Has an impact on **customer service**
- Potentially affects **all levels of management and staff** in an organisation
- May **lead to structural changes** within an organisation which require HR planning
- Affects the way **management information** is created and presented
- **Requires effective management** to obtain the maximum benefit
- Involves many **stakeholders** inside and outside the organisation, therefore stakeholder analysis is required

2.3.1 IS/IT is a high cost activity

Many organisations invest large amounts of money in IS, but not always wisely. The unmanaged proliferation of IT is likely to lead to expensive mistakes. Two key benefits of IT, the ability to **share** information and the **avoidance of duplication**, are likely to be lost. All IT expenditure should therefore require approval to ensure that it enhances rather than detracts from the overall information strategy. There is also the possibility that the failure of a very large IT investment might have a negative strategic impact on the organisation concerned, possibly even leading to business failure.

2.3.2 IS/IT is critical to the success of many organisations

When developing an IS/IT strategy a firm should assess **how important IT is** in the provision of products and services. The role that IT fills in an organisation will vary depending on the type of organisations. IS/IT could be:

- A **support** activity
- A **key** operational activity
- **Potentially** very important
- A **strategic** activity (without IT the firm could not function at all; eg Amazon, eBay)
- A source of **competitive advantage**

An organisation's information systems may not only support business strategy; they may also help determine corporate/business strategy. In particular:

(a) IS/IT/IM may provide a possible source of competitive advantage. This could involve new technology not yet available to others or simply using existing technology in a different way.

(b) Information systems may help in formulating business strategy by providing information from internal and external sources.

(c) Developments in IT may provide new channels for distributing and collecting information and/or for conducting transactions. The most fundamental illustration of this has been the way the internet has opened up opportunities for e-business and e-commerce.

   E-business is the use of electronic technologies (including the internet) to support and transform business processes, while **e-commerce** is the use of electronic technologies (including the internet) to buy and sell products and services.

Exam skills

When considering IS/IT in a strategic context it could be useful to consider how they contribute to an organisation's current strategic position. One way of doing this could be through a SWOT analysis.

For example:

Strength: A business might have a sophisticated customer database which enables it to send out targeted marketing messages to customers. Or a retailer might have an inventory management system which automatically reorders inventory lines according to sales being recorded on the shop tills, thereby allowing it to minimise the levels of inventory it needs to hold.

Weakness: A business's ordering system (either online or manual) is unreliable, and so customers cannot be confident that the goods they order will be delivered correctly or within an acceptable timescale.

Opportunity: If a business does not currently have a website which allows customers to purchase items online, the opportunity to develop such a website could provide a significant boost to its sales.

Threat: Conversely, if a competitor has recently upgraded their IT systems with the result that they can now offer a greater range of services to their customers and provide them with improved levels of service, this could pose a threat to an organisation, because customers may switch to using the competitor instead.

2.3.3 Information and competitive advantage

It is now recognised that information can be used as a source of competitive advantage. Many organisations have recognised the importance of information and developed an **information strategy**, covering both IS and IT.

Information systems should be tied in some way to **business objectives**.

(a)   The **corporate strategy** is used to plan functional **business plans** which provide guidelines for information-based activities.

(b)   On a year by year basis, the **annual plan** would try to tie in business plans with information systems projects for particular applications, perhaps through the functioning of a steering committee.

 We look at information and knowledge as potential sources of competitive advantage in the next chapter of this Study Text, particularly in the context of knowledge management and learning organisations.

2.3.4 IT can impact significantly on the business context

IT is an **enabling** technology, and can produce dramatic changes in individual businesses and whole industries. For example, the deregulation of the airline industry encouraged the growth of computerised seat-reservation systems. IT can be both a **cause** of major changes in doing business and a **response** to them.

2.3.5 IT affects all levels of management

IT has become a routine feature of office life, **a facility for everyone to use**. IT is no longer used solely by specialist staff.

2.3.6 IT and its effect on management information

The use of IT has permitted the design of a range of information systems. EIS, MIS, DSS, Knowledge Work Systems (KWS) and Office Automation Systems (OAS) can be used to improve the quality of management information.

IT has also had an effect on **production processes**. For example, Computer Integrated Manufacturing (CIM) changed the methods and cost profiles of many manufacturing processes. The techniques used to **measure and record costs** have also adapted to the use of IT.

2.3.7 IT and stakeholders

Parties interested in an organisation's use of IT are:

(a)   **Other business users** – for example to facilitate EDI.

(b)   **Consumers** – for example as reassurance that product quality is high; consumers may also be interested if information is provided via the internet.

(c)   **Employees** – as IT affects work practices.

(d)   **Governments** – eg telecommunications regulation, regulation of electronic commerce.

(e)   **IT manufacturers** looking for new markets and product development. User-groups may be able to influence software producers.

2.3.8 Other aspects

In addition to these arguments, we can identify the reasons below.

(a)   IS are by their nature open to external influences, particularly improvements and updates. A strategic view should be taken in order to obtain optimum benefit from these influences and prevent the proliferation of incompatible developments.

(b)   Environmental dynamism means that the need for information is constantly recreated in new ways.

(c)   Information is fundamental to strategic planning and so it should be managed strategically.

2.3.9 Advantages of a strategic approach

(a)   Competitive advantage is more easily attained.

(b)   There is **congruence** between the goal structure of the IS strategy and the overall corporate strategy.

(c)   Technical developments can be monitored and assessed with a view to introduction at a suitable time, rather than being ignored or introduced before they are properly developed.

(d)   Expenditure can be controlled strategically.

Question 6.1	Babbage and Newman

Learning outcome E1(a)

Babbage and Newman plc is a company with an established base of IT applications. The finance department has a fully computerised accounting system. The marketing department has developed a primitive customer modelling package. The production department 'does not need IT'.

The Finance Director is in charge of IT at Babbage and Newman. He proposes in the annual corporate budget a 10% increase in IT expenditure based on last year, for the relevant departments. This will enable system upgrades.

Comment briefly on the information strategy at Babbage and Newman.

2.4 Developing an IT strategy

When formulating an overall IT strategy, the following aspects should be taken into consideration:

(a)   What are the key business areas which could benefit most from an investment in information technology? What form should the investment take, and how could such strategically important units be encouraged to use such technology effectively?

(b)   How much would the system cost in terms of software; hardware; management commitment and time; education and training; conversion; documentation; operational manning; and maintenance and support? The importance of lifetime application costs must be stressed – the costs and benefits after implementation may be more significant than the more obvious initial costs of installing an IT function.

(c)   What criteria for performance should be set for IT systems? Two areas can be considered: the technical standard the information system achieves and the degree to which it meets the perceived and often changing needs of the user.

(d)   What are the implications for the existing workforce – have they the requisite skills to use the new systems, can they be trained to use the systems, and will there be any redundancies?

2.5 How IT is changing corporate strategy

It should be obvious that information systems and information technology should **support** corporate strategy, but there are also a number of ways IS/IT can **influence** corporate strategy.

In 1985, the *Harvard Business Review* published an article by Michael Porter and Victor Millar aimed at general managers facing the changes resulting from the rapid and extensive development of information technology. Although it was written a number of years ago, the article still has great relevance to the **strategic employment of information** systems and the use of information technology. It dealt with three main interlinked topics:

*   The ways in which IT had become **strategically significant**
*   How the **nature of competition** had changed
*   **How to compete** in the new, IT influenced environment

2.5.1 The strategic significance of IT

IT transforms the **value chain**. The value chain model (which Michael Porter devised) illustrates the way that businesses **add value** for the customers, through nine different activities: five primary, and four support.

We looked at the value chain in Chapter 4 of this Study Text.

Think also of the way the value chain links to Porter's generic strategies of cost leadership or differentiation (covered in Chapter 5).

Porter and Millar's article remarks that each of the value chain activities has both **physical** and **information** aspects and points out that, while until quite recently, technical advances were concentrated in the physical aspects, **current improvements tend to be IT-driven**.

Simple improvements are made by faster and more accurate processing of existing forms of data; more dramatic ones by creating new flows of previously unavailable information. This has a particular effect on the linkages between the various activities and extends the company's **competitive scope**, which is the range of activities it can efficiently undertake.

Porter and Millar provide a diagram of the value chain in which they give examples of the ways in which IT was influencing the various activities at the time the article was written (1985). Although the technologies themselves have developed since then, the ideas in the model are still very relevant.

Support activities	Firm infrastructure	Enterprise Resource Planning (ERPS)		Intranets	Extranets	
	Human resource management	Automated personnel scheduling				
	Technology development	Computer aided design e-business		Intranets	Extranets e-commerce capabilities	
	Procurement	Online procurement of parts (e-procurement)			Extranets	
		Automated warehouse – RFID and tagging systems

Electronic data interchange (EDI)

Inventory control | Flexible manufacturing

Computer aided manufacturing | Automated order processing

Vehicle tracking | Electronic marketing

CRM

EPOS

Customer databases | Remote servicing of equipment

Online scheduling of service and repairs

FAQs on website |
| | | Inbound logistics | Operations | Outbound logistics | Marketing and sales | Service |
| | | **Primary activities** | | | | **Margin** |

IT transforms the **product**. It is possible to view products as having physical and informational content, with the mix varying from product to product. **Diesel fuel**, for example, is an almost **entirely physical** product, though it is necessary to be aware that it will not work with petrol-engined vehicles. This Study Text, on the other hand, consists almost entirely of information, though, obviously, it has a physical aspect. An intermediate case would be an aircraft, which has a very obvious physical existence, but which cannot be used without a great deal of information on servicing, handling characteristics and the operation of its systems.

Porter and Millar make the point that there is an unmistakeable trend towards **supplying increasing amounts of information with products** as, for instance, in the case of freight and courier services that provide online tracking of consignments.

Slack *et al* in their text, *Operations Management*, also highlight that e-business has an impact in many areas of operations management:

- **Purchasing**: orders (EDI), funds transfer (EFT) and supplier selection. (More specifically, IT has also enabled e-procurement, which we discussed in Chapter 4 earlier in this Study Text.)

- **Production**: production planning and control, scheduling, inventory management, quality control

- **Marketing/sales and customer servicing**: opening new sales channels, internet sales, third-party logistics, customer services, CRM

- **Warehousing**: inventory management, forecasting (and real time updating)

IT and remote working

Developments in technology have been crucial in facilitating the growth of remote working (and home working). For example, remote workers need a laptop or personal computer, with reliable internet access, and secure remote access to a company's internal networks and internal messaging systems (eg sharepoints) in order to work from home effectively.

Video-conferencing (for example, through Skype or Google Video Chat) can also be valuable for contacting remote employees, particularly in relation to important matters which it may not be appropriate to discuss by email.

In general, technology has been essential for the development of remote working, because it provides opportunities for exchanges of information between employees working remotely and their colleagues or managers in a different location.

Exam skills

As well as thinking specifically how IT can affect the value chain, you should also be prepared to think how IT and e-business have affected business more generally.

For example:

The use of computer-aided design can lead to the faster production of new products and designs. Organisations could either use this speed as a basis for making designs cheaper (cost leadership) or, for example, in the clothing and fashion industry, as a means of getting the latest fashions to market more quickly than their rivals (differentiation).

Websites and email have changed the nature of communications between organisations and customers.

The internet has also changed the nature of the supply chain and channel structure; for example, by allowing customers to book flights and hotel rooms for their holidays directly from the airline company and the hotel, online, rather than having to use travel agents.

2.5.2 How IT changes the nature of competition

IT changes the **structure of industry** through its effect on the **five competitive forces**.

Porter's five forces model (which we discussed in Chapter 3 of this Study Text) can be used as a framework for assessing the strength of the competitive forces which affect the level of profit which can be sustained in an industry.

The relevance of it here is to consider how IT can change the nature of these five forces and therefore change the level of profits which can be sustained – for better or for worse.

Competitive rivalry – Developments in IT have been fundamental in the growth of online companies, which has meant that there is now increased competition, in many industries, between online and offline companies.

Threat of new entrants – IT could help create barriers to entry. For example, it could increase economies of scale through computer-controlled production methods, thereby meaning that potential new entrants would have to have similar technology to be able to compete effectively. Equally, improved levels of service based on expensive IT systems could also act as a potential barrier to new entrants.

Conversely, IT could also break down barriers to entry. For example, the development of telephone banking and online banking means that banks can be established without the need for an extensive network of high street branches (which would otherwise require large amounts of capital to establish).

Bargaining power of customers – One of the ways of reducing the bargaining power of customers is through 'locking them in' to a particular product or brand. A number of supermarkets and retailers have adopted this idea in their 'loyalty card' programmes. However, loyalty card programmes (such as Tesco's Clubcard) are also linked to data warehouses which then provide the retailer with information for targeted marketing campaigns. If supermarkets have detailed information about individual customers' spending habits and patterns, they can then send personalised marketing messages to customers with offers relating to products which they have bought previously or may be likely to buy in the future.

Threat of substitutes – In some cases, IS/IT can itself be the substitute product; for example in the way that videoconferencing could be seen as a substitute for business travel, or possibly in the way that e-books could be seen as a substitute for traditional printed copies of books.

Conversely, however, computer-aided design and manufacturing systems could be used to introduce new and reconfigured versions of existing products more rapidly to help fend off the threat from substitutes.

IT and competitive strategy

IT **enhances competitive advantage** in two principal ways:

- **Reducing costs**
- Making it easier to **differentiate products**

Perhaps the most obvious examples of IT-driven cost reductions have occurred in the automation of much clerical work that has been apparent since the introduction of mainframe computers in the middle of the 20th century.

However, although IT can be used to reduce costs, it is perhaps debatable whether this generates a long-term competitive advantage. For example, businesses increasingly use virtual conferencing as a means of cutting costs and imposing operational efficiency due to the ease with which data can be shared. However, if all the firms in an industry start using virtual conferencing, will this actually generate any competitive advantage for any individual firms in that industry?

Differentiation. One way an organisation might seek to differentiate itself from its competitors is by meeting customers' needs and requirements more closely than its competitors. The greeting card company 'Moonpig.com' has adopted such an approach by allowing customers to design their own cards online.

IT could also enhance competitive advantage by forming the basis of complete **new businesses.** It makes new businesses technically feasible; it creates derived demand for new products; and it creates new businesses inside old ones. The impact of Apple's iPod gives examples of all three effects. The device itself is based on the MP3 file format; a large **iPod ecosystem** of accessories has been created; and the product itself represents a departure from Apple's previous hardware and software strategies.

2.6 E-business strategies and benefits of e-business

More generally, we can identify three broad types of e-business strategy which a company can employ to help it gain a competitive advantage.

Cost and efficiency improvements: focus on improving efficiency and lowering costs by using the internet and other digital technologies as a fast, low-cost way to communicate and interact with customers, suppliers and business partners (eg use of email to communicate with customers; or EDI to communicate with suppliers).

Performance improvement in business effectiveness: make major improvements in business effectiveness – for example, the use of intranets can substantially improve information sharing, collaboration and knowledge management within a business or with its trading partners. Similarly, the provision of extranets can enhance customer service – for example, by enabling a customer to track the progress of a delivery.

Electronic technologies have enabled greater flexibility in organisation structures – for example, through the increase in home working and the development of virtual networks.

Product and service transformation: developing new internet-based products and services, or supporting entry into new markets (including e-commerce which enables access to a global marketplace).

In Chapter 8 of this Study Text we will look at **e-marketing**, which is an important way organisations can apply e-business and electronic technologies – for example, through the use of electronic communications to support customer relationship management.

Similarly, organisations can use e-business to help with **customer service**; for example, by providing the answers to frequently asked questions on their websites, and by providing information about the opening times of shops or offices.

2.6.1 Virtual arrangements

Network technologies are used by organisations to integrate workers across sites and working at home. Developments in broadband, particularly improved capacity and better data security, have improved the ability to communicate across sites and from **home**. Broadband telecommunications systems allow 'remote' computer users to communicate with each other, and to send and receive information.

A virtual organisation can be seen as an extension of the idea of network organisations. We will look at virtual organisations in Chapter 7 of this Study Text.

2.7 IT as a competitive necessity

Throughout this section, we have alluded to the potential which IT has as a source of competitive advantage for companies. However, it is important to note that companies only achieve competitive advantage by doing something different from their competitors, and they only achieve sustainable competitive advantage by doing something which their competitors cannot replicate over time.

For example, the first airline company to introduce self-service check-in kiosks gained a competitive advantage (or source of differentiation) by doing so. However, all the major airlines now have self-service check-in kiosks so they are no longer a source of competitive advantage. By contrast, not having them would place a company at a competitive disadvantage.

Equally, when the first logistics and shipping company allowed customers to track their packages via the web, this innovation was seen as a source of competitive advantage. Now, however, we expect to be able to track orders with all logistics and shipping companies.

Both of the examples above illustrate the importance of IT to modern business strategy. However, they also highlight that the majority of innovations which confer competitive advantage on the companies which adopt them first are subsequently shared and become routine.

In this respect, we can divide IT investments into two broad categories: those which provide an organisation with a competitive advantage over their rivals, and those which are necessary for the organisation to continue in business.

In effect, this distinction illustrates the difference between **threshold** competences resources and **core** competences, which we discussed in Chapter 1 of this Study Text. IT as a **competitive necessity** is essential for an organisation to continue in business, but it is not, by itself, a source of competitive **advantage**.

2.7.1 Customised applications and application platforms

In the same way that we can distinguish between IT as a source of competitive advantage and IT as a competitive necessity, we also need to distinguish between customised applications and generic software.

Although packaged software is vital to many businesses, gaining any competitive advantage or differentiation from a generic package is very difficult (because competitors can also use the package). Therefore, strategic IT investments are most often based on custom applications.

Crucially, a company needs its application platform to support current technologies. Therefore, a company's choice of application platform (such as the Microsoft application platform) can be a key part of creating competitive advantage.

2.7.2 The importance of managing technology

The success of an organisation's use of technology depends largely on how technology is selected, implemented and **managed**. For example, **information systems** may **fail to deliver the benefits expected** for any of the following reasons.

(a) They are used to tackle the **wrong problem** (ie the use of IT has not been thought through in the context of the wider organisation).

(b) Senior management are not interested.

(c) Users are ignored in design and development.

(d) No attention is given to behavioural factors in design and operation.

If an organisation develops and follows a realistic information strategy and information systems plan for information systems and technology then there is less chance that these problems will arise.

Organisations have typically gone through a process of evolution in the development and management of their IS strategy. Nolan identified six stages based on the level of expenditure involved.

Initiation: computers are introduced, usually by financial staff, in order to make cost savings.

Contagion: computers are introduced into other areas in an uncontrolled fashion, with varying degrees of success.

Control: senior managers, concerned about expenditure, create a central IT staff and concentrate control in its hands.

Integration: a need for innovative joint development by users and specialists is accepted and controls are loosened.

Data administration: the value of information is recognised and drives development; databases are set up.

Maturity: a strategic view is taken and IS strategy is incorporated into overall organisational strategy.

Obviously, factors other than the progression outlined in this model will affect expenditure, including the rapid fall in the cost of IT and the development of completely new technologies, such as video conferencing. The value of Nolan's model is the guidance it gives on how the **management of IT resources** might reasonably proceed and evolve.

Organisations typically go through a process of evolution in their IT strategy, moving from **simple automation of processes** such as bookkeeping to fully fledged **information-based business strategy**. Along the way they may pass through stages of expansion, centralised control of IT and wider dispersion of IT development. Different management techniques tend to be used as the process continues.

Exam skills

You should look out for scenarios in the integrated case study in which the management of IS and IT strategies appears to be deficient, and be prepared to offer sensible advice. The aim of IS and IT strategies should be to achieve strategic objectives while controlling costs: this will require the input of

user needs and practical experience to be combined with the IT specialist's knowledge of the available technology and how to make the best use of it.

However, note that it is important to distinguish between IS strategy (the business's requirements from the systems) and IT strategy (focusing on the hardware and software necessary to deliver the business requirements).

2.8 Developing an IT strategy

Just as business strategy should be subject to continuing review and development, it would be inappropriate to consider an information strategy as fixed and immutable. Developments both within the organisation and in the environment will inevitably require that the **information strategy be developed and subject to change**. Obvious potential influences include technical developments in hardware and software and changes in the business strategy itself. A simple guide to the continuing development of an information strategy might include the features outlined below.

(a)   There should be **constant reference to the overall business strategy**. This will shape the demand for information and thence the IS, IT and IM strategies. There may be companies in which the overall strategy is driven by the appearance of new technology, but it is important to be aware that, generally, this will not be the case and it will be **inappropriate to seek to adopt new technology for its own sake**.

(b)   **Compatibility of technologies** should be carefully considered.

(c)   Similarly, the **wider implications** of proposed developments must be thoroughly considered. Each part of the organisation should be able to make appropriate inputs into plans for change.

(d)   Where significant change is envisaged, it must be **properly planned**, possibly using a methodology such as Structured Systems Analysis and Design Methodology (SSADM). Hardware and software choices must be made, decisions must be taken about the extent to which work should be outsourced, if at all, and costs and benefits should be considered.

A successfully developed strategy will contribute to the success of the organisation. Its success may also be judged by the extent to which it performs three specific functions:

(a)   Prediction and definition of major areas of strategic choice

(b)   Indication of the degree of common ground between business and information managers on such matters as strategic assumptions, objectives and policies

(c)   Timely identification of the information resources required to implement the business strategy

2.8.1 Information needs

The identification of organisational **information needs** and the information systems framework to satisfy them is at the heart of a strategy for information systems and information technology.

The IS and IT strategies should complement the overall strategy for the organisation. It follows, therefore, that the IS/IT strategy should be considered whenever the organisation prepares other long-term strategies such as marketing and production.

2.8.2 Earl's three leg analysis

The writer Michael Earl observed that, in practice, there are three ways in which IS strategies develop. He identified these as the three 'legs' of IS strategy development:

● Business led (top down emphasis, focuses on business plans and goals)
● Infrastructure led (bottom up emphasis, focuses on current systems)
● Mixed (inside out emphasis, focuses on IT/IS opportunities)

A diagrammatic representation of the three legs follows.

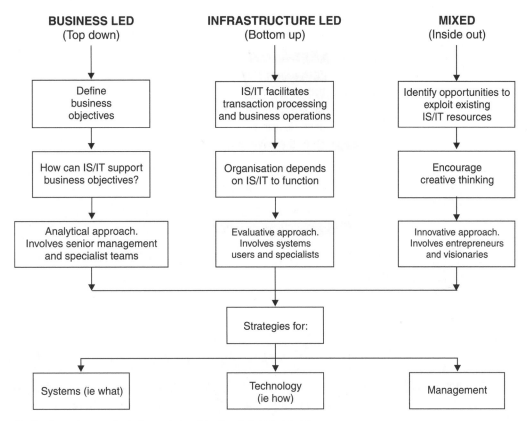

Earl's three leg analysis is explained in the following table.

Leg or approach	Comment
Business led (top down)	The **overall objectives** of an organisation are identified and then IS/IT systems are implemented to enable these objectives to be met. This approach relies on the ability to break down the organisation and its objectives to a series of business objectives and processes and to be able to identify the information needs of these. This is an analytical approach. The people usually involved are senior management and specialist teams.
Infrastructure led (bottom up)	Computer-based **transaction systems** are critical to business operations. The organisation focuses on systems that facilitate transactions and other basic operations. This is an evaluative approach. The people usually involved are system users and specialists.
Mixed (inside out)	The organisation encourages ideas that will **exploit existing IT and IS resources**. Innovations may come from entrepreneurial managers or individuals outside the formal planning process. This is an innovative/creative approach. The people involved are entrepreneurs and/or visionaries.

2.8.3 Enterprise analysis

KEY TERM

ENTERPRISE ANALYSIS involves examining the entire organisation in terms of structure, processes, functions and data elements to identify the key elements and attributes of organisational data and information.

Enterprise analysis is sometimes referred to as **business systems planning**. This approach involves the following steps.

 Ask a large sample of managers about:

- How they use information
- Where they get information
- What their objectives are
- What their data requirements are
- How they make decisions
- The influence of the environment

 Aggregate the findings from Step 1 into sub-units, functions, processes and data matrices. Compile a process/data class matrix to show:

- What data classes are required to support particular organisational processes
- Which processes are the creators and users of data

 Use the matrix to identify areas that information systems should focus on, eg on processes that create data

Enterprise analysis approach – strength	Comment
Comprehensive	The enterprise analysis approach gives a comprehensive view of the organisation and its use of data and systems.

Enterprise analysis approach – weaknesses	Comment
Unwieldy	The enterprise analysis approach results in a mountain of data that is expensive to collect and difficult to analyse.
Focused on existing information	Survey questions tend to focus on how systems and information are currently used, rather than on how information that is needed could be provided. The analysis has tended to result in existing systems being automated rather than looking at the wider picture.

 ## Section summary

Information strategy can be divided into **information systems strategy**, **information technology strategy** and **information management strategy**. The strategic significance of information requires that information itself be managed strategically so that the systems, the technology and the information support the business's overall strategic policy.

IT has the potential to **transform competition** in three ways: its effect on the **five competitive forces**, its potential for implementing **generic strategies**, and its contribution to the **emergence of completely new businesses**. However, IT strategy needs to support the overall business strategy.

3   Strategic and operational information

Introduction

Organisations need to have information systems in place to capture information about how well they are performing. **Critical success factors** (CSFs) can be used to determine an organisation's information requirements.

One of the key challenges that organisations face is linking their (long-term) strategy to their day to day operations. For example, a strategic plan might set revenue growth targets for an organisation over the next five years, but the operational plan will need to consider what practical steps will be taken to generate these revenue increases, in effect creating a road map that defines the detail of how the overall strategies are going to be put into action.

3.1 Information and performance

Management accounting models such as the balanced scorecard and the performance pyramid (which we discuss in more detail in Chapter 11 of this Study Text) align operational objectives and initiatives with an organisation's overall strategy and mission.

As with any other strategic project, if an organisation is going to implement a balanced scorecard successfully, it will need to think carefully about the steps involved:

Identify key outcomes – identify the key outcomes critical to the success of the organisation (this is similar to identifying the organisation's critical success factors)

Key processes – identify the processes that lead to those outcomes

KPIs – develop key performance indicators for those processes

Data capture – develop systems for capturing the data necessary to measure those key performance indicators

Reporting – develop a mechanism for communicating or reporting the indicators to staff (such as through charts, graphs or on a dashboard)

Performance improvement – develop improvement programmes to ensure that performance improves as necessary

3.2 Capturing performance information

Importantly, these 'steps' highlight that an organisation needs to have information systems in place to be able to capture the information it needs to assess how well it is performing.

As the context of strategic management accounting highlights, this performance information is likely to include non-financial performance, and could also include external elements (such as competitor performance or market growth) as well as information about the organisation's own financial performance.

3.2.1 Critical success factors (CSFs) and information requirements

The use of critical success factors (CSFs) can help to determine the information requirements of an organisation.

CSFs are a small number of key **operational goals** vital to the success of an organisation. If these operational goals are achieved, the organisation should be successful. CSFs are **measured** by **key performance indicators** (KPIs).

The CSF approach is sometimes referred to as the **strategic analysis** approach. The philosophy behind this approach is that managers should focus on a small number of objectives, and information systems should be focused on providing information to enable managers to monitor these objectives.

Two separate types of CSFs can be identified:

(a) **Monitoring** CSFs are important for **maintaining** business. A **monitoring** CSF is used to keep abreast of existing activities and operations.

(b) **Building** CSFs are important for **expanding** business. A **building** CSF helps to measure the progress of new initiatives and is more likely to be relevant at senior executive level.

One approach to **determining the factors** which are critical to success in performing a function or making a decision is:

* List the organisation's corporate objectives and goals
* Determine which factors are critical for accomplishing the objectives
* Determine a small number of KPIs for each factor

Note that most KPIs will be quantitative, and it is quite possible that CSFs will be quantitative as well.

One of the **objectives** of an organisation might be to maintain a high level of service direct from inventory without holding uneconomic inventory levels. This is first quantified in the form of a **goal**, which might be to ensure that 95% of orders for goods can be satisfied directly from inventory, while minimising total inventory holding costs and inventory levels.

The following **CSFs** might then be identified:

* **Supplier performance** in terms of quality and lead times
* Reliability of **inventory records**
* **Forecasting** of demand variations

The determination of **KPIs** for each of these CSFs is not necessarily straightforward. Some measures might use **factual**, objectively verifiable data, while others might make use of **'softer' concepts** such as opinions, perceptions and hunches.

For example, the reliability of inventory records can be measured by means of physical inventory counts, either at discrete intervals or on a rolling basis. Forecasting of demand variations will be much harder to measure.

Where measures use quantitative data, performance can be measured in a number of ways:

* In **physical quantities**, for example units produced or units sold
* In **money terms**, for example profit, revenues, costs or variances
* In **ratios** and **percentages**

Sequence	Explanation	Example (1) Public sector hospital service	Example (2) Mobile phone operator
Organisational goal	Overall strategy	Improve healthcare	Increase sales by entering new markets
Critical success factors (CSFs)	Operational goal: must be achieved for the overall strategy to be on track	Measurable reduction in time between booking an operation and receiving it	Establish network coverage in two countries in a year's time
Key performance indicators (KPIs)	Data sharing performance on CSF	For example % of patients seen after waiting: less than one month less than three months less than six months more than six months	% of country covered and date, reported monthly
Critical information requirements	Information requirements to generate KPI	Booking and operations data to enable accurate KPI to be compiled	Information about masts installed

3.2.2 Data sources for CSFs

In broad terms, we can identify four **general sources** of CSFs (based on Rockart's work in this area in the 1970s and 1980s).

(a)   The **industry** that the business is in. For example, in the supermarket industry, having the right product mix available in each store, and having products actually available on the shelves for customers to buy, will be prerequisites for an organisation's success, regardless of the detailed strategy it is pursuing.

(b)   The **company** itself and its situation within the industry (eg market leader or small company; competitive strategic, geographical location).

(c)   The **external environment**, for example consumer trends, the economy, and political factors of the country in which the company operates (PEST factors).

(d)   Temporal organisational factors, which are **areas of corporate activity** that are currently **unacceptable** and represent a cause of concern, such as high inventory levels. New laws or regulations could also be seen as temporary factors: eg if a regulator has recently fined a financial services company for mis-selling its products, then a possible CSF for the company would be: to ensure that similar mis-selling does not occur again in the near future.

More specifically, possible internal and external data sources for CSFs include:

(a)   **The existing system**. The existing system can be used to generate reports showing **failures to meet CSFs**.

(b)   **Customer service department**. This department will maintain details of **complaints** received, **refunds** handled, **customer enquiries** etc. These should be reviewed to ensure all failure types have been identified.

(c)   **Customers**. A survey of customers, provided that it is properly designed and introduced, would reveal (or confirm) those areas where **satisfaction** is high or low.

(d)   **Competitors**. Competitors' operations, pricing structures and publicity should be closely monitored.

(e)   **Accounting system**. The **profitability** of various aspects of the operation is probably a key factor in any review of CSFs.

(f)   **Consultants**. A specialist consultancy might be able to perform a detailed review of the system in order to identify ways of satisfying CSFs.

3.2.3 CSF approach: strengths and weaknesses

CSF approach – strengths	Comment
Takes into account environmental changes	The CSF approach requires managers to examine the environment and consider how it influences their information requirements.
Focuses on information	The approach doesn't just aim to establish organisational objectives. It also looks at the information and information systems required to establish and monitor progress towards these objectives.
Facilitates top management participation in system development	The clear link between information requirements and individual and organisational objectives encourages top management involvement in system (DSS, ESS) design.

CSF approach – weaknesses	Comment
Aggregation of individual CSFs	Wide-ranging individual CSFs need to be aggregated into a clear organisational plan. This process relies heavily on judgement. Managers who feel their input has been neglected may be alienated.
Bias towards top management	When gathering information to establish CSFs it is usually top management who are interviewed. These managers may lack knowledge of operational activities.
CSFs change often	The business environment, managers and information systems technology are subject to constant change. CSFs and systems must be updated to account for change.

3.3 Information audit

KEY TERM

An INFORMATION AUDIT aims to establish the information needs of users **and** how these needs could be met.

The audit has three stages.

Information needs assessment

This stage involves **gathering information**, usually through interviews and questionnaires.

Information users are asked what information they require, why they require it, when they require it and the preferred format.

People should be encouraged to think laterally about what information would help them do their job, rather than simply listing the information they currently receive.

To encourage wide-ranging thought, users should be asked to state the information they would like in an 'ideal world'. Unrealistic and uneconomic needs can be rejected (tactfully) at a later stage.

Information analysis

This stage **examines the information** provided by the existing information system. Both the quantity and the quality of the information are analysed. For example, the timing of information may reduce the quality of otherwise excellent information as it is provided too late to influence decision making. Slightly less accurate information, provided earlier, may be more desirable.

Gap analysis

This stage **compares** the information needs identified in Stage 1 with the information identified as being provided in Stage 2. Gaps between what is required and what is currently provided are identified.

'Information gaps' are analysed to evaluate the costs and benefits of closing the gap.

An information system **resource analysis** involves a review of **all** information systems and information technology used within an organisation. The review includes all aspects of hardware, software, communications devices, network topologies, systems development methodologies, maintenance procedures, contingency plans and IS/IT personnel. The review looks at all of these aspects in the context of the organisation's overall strategy and the IS/IT strategy.

Resource analysis is sometimes called **Current Situation Analysis (CSA)**. The analysis establishes the current status of IS/IT within the organisation. The CSA has similar problems to that of a cost-benefit analysis in that it relies on the **subjective judgements** of information users. A group of people using the same system for the same purpose may come up with different ratings for system efficiency and user friendliness.

Two techniques that could be useful when conducting a CSA are **Earl's grid** and the **applications portfolio**.

3.3.1 Earl's grid

Michael Earl suggests a grid to analyse an organisation's current use of information systems. Current systems are plotted on the following grid.

(a)   A system of poor quality and little value should be **disposed of** (divest).

(b)   A system of high business value and low technical quality should be **renewed** (invested in). An important system of low quality carries a high business risk.

(c)   A system of high quality but low business value should be **reassessed**. Is the system meeting an information need? Why is it under-utilised?

(d)   High-quality systems with a high business value should be **maintained** to preserve the high quality, and if possible **enhanced** in the quest for competitive advantage.

Establishing where to place systems on the grid is the difficult part. Consultation with system users and those for formulating and implementing information system strategy would be undertaken to form an opinion of each system. Again, judgements are subjective.

3.3.2 The strategic grid

The importance of IS/IT to an organisation was studied by McFarlan and McKenney in 1983.

They devised a matrix designed to show how important IS/IT currently is to an organisation, and how important it is expected to become in the future.

Strategic importance of **planned** information systems		Turnaround	Strategic
	High	Turnaround	Strategic
	Low	Support	Factory
		Low	High

Strategic importance of **current**
information systems

(a)   **Strategic** – Organisations in the strategic grid are ones for which IS/IT is crucial to their current and future success; for example, an online business cannot operate without its information systems. Similarly, information systems are likely to be strategically important in most financial service businesses.

(b)   **Turnaround** – Information systems currently have little strategic importance for organisations in the turnaround sector, but are expected to become more important in the future.

Indications that IS/IT is becoming strategically more important to an organisation might be: the appointment of an IT director for the first time; increasing IT budgets; or the board and senior management taking more interest in IT projects.

(c) **Support** – For organisations in the support quadrant, information systems currently have little strategic value, and their strategic importance is not expected to increase in the future. For example, organisations in this quadrant are likely to use IS/IT primarily for administrative systems to improve internal efficiency, but not for any key value-generating activities.

As a result, the level of investment in IS/IT is low, and there is little senior management involvement in it.

(d) **Factory** – Organisations in the factory quadrant see IS/IT as being strategically significant at the moment, but predict this will not be the case in the future. They do not feel that IS/IT will be crucial to their strategic development, nor that future IT applications will be a critical factor in future business success.

Nonetheless, the IT budget is likely to be significant in factory organisations, because IT is important in sustaining their existing business.

CASE STUDY

Case example: Supermarket industry

The supermarket industry provides an interesting context for analysing the strategic importance of IT to organisations.

Electronic point of sale (EPOS) tills in supermarkets compute customers' bills and update inventory records, and may also connect to suppliers' records so that they are aware when stock levels are running low and reorders are necessary. Supermarkets can also use the data collected from loyalty cards at the point of sale for marketing purposes. Therefore a supermarket's IT systems are a key part of its operations.

However, if all the major supermarket chains already use EPOS technology, then it could be argued that the technology doesn't currently provide any major source of competitive advantage, and as such EPOS technologies could be categorised in a 'factory' role (in terms of McFarlan and McKenney's grid).

However, although EPOS technology might be in a factory role, the retail industry is undergoing significant changes in relation to how customers do their shopping – through the development of e-commerce and online ordering, home deliveries, and 'click and collect' services for example. The industry is moving increasingly to a multi-channel environment, in which supermarkets' relationships with consumers will be online as well as in physical stores.

As such, IT is likely to have an increasingly important role to play in the business model in the future, meaning that supermarkets should be classified in the turnaround quadrant of the matrix.

3.3.3 Applications portfolio

The focus of McFarlan and McKenney's grid is on the importance of information systems to an organisation as a whole. However, Peppard developed the grid further to look at the importance of **individual applications** to organisations (rather than looking at the importance of information systems as a whole). As such, Peppard's **applications portfolio** is intended to offer more detailed analysis about the strategic impact of individual applications.

Strategic importance of individual applications in the predicted **future** competitive environment		High potential	Strategic
	High	High potential	Strategic
	Low	Support	Key operational
		Low	High

Strategic importance of individual applications
in the **current** competitive environment

(a)   **Support applications** are not critical to business success, but are designed to improve the productivity and efficiency of the internal activities of an organisation. Examples include an accounting system, or a payroll package.

(b)   **Key operational applications** support established core business activities. A production planning system is a good example; inventory control is another. These are critical for a business to maintain its performance relative to its competitors.

(c)   **Strategic applications** are vital to the organisation's future success. They seek to gain competitive advantage through innovation in support of business strategies. Finance/service companies are becoming increasingly dependent on information systems and technology.

(d)   **High potential applications** are applications likely to have a significant impact in the future environment. They are often innovative. However, a business must be careful not to invest too much too quickly in these systems in case there is no market acceptance.

Section summary

Critical success factors can help determine the information requirements of an organisation. If the information provided by an organisation's information systems does not currently satisfy the needs of its users, an information gap exists. Management will have to analyse the costs and benefits of closing that gap.

Chapter Summary

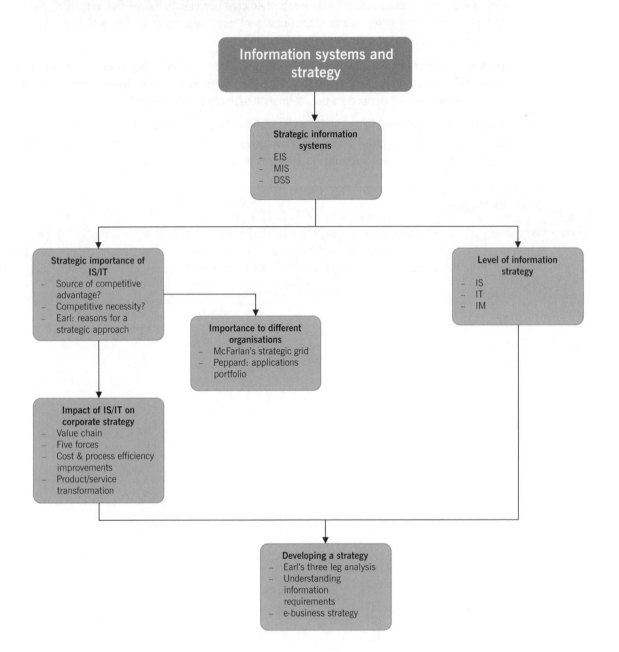

Information systems and strategy

Strategic information systems
- EIS
- MIS
- DSS

Strategic importance of IS/IT
- Source of competitive advantage?
- Competitive necessity?
- Earl: reasons for a strategic approach

Importance to different organisations
- McFarlan's strategic grid
- Peppard: applications portfolio

Level of information strategy
- IS
- IT
- IM

Impact of IS/IT on corporate strategy
- Value chain
- Five forces
- Cost & process efficiency improvements
- Product/service transformation

Developing a strategy
- Earl's three leg analysis
- Understanding information requirements
- e-business strategy

Quick Quiz

1   Which of the following are characteristics of operational (rather than strategic) information:

(i)   Derived from internal sources
(ii)   Focus on planning rather than control
(iii)   Prepared frequently

A   (i) and (ii)
B   (i) and (iii)
C   (ii) and (iii)
D   (i), (ii) and (iii)

2   Fill in the gap, for the type of system being described below.

..Management information systems.. convert data from mainly internal sources into information. This information enables managers to make timely and effective decisions for planning, directing and controlling the activities for which they are responsible.

3   Michael Earl identified nine reasons why a strategic approach was required for information systems, rather than allowing them to remain in the hands of the technology professionals.

List **three** of those reasons.

4   What are the three 'legs' of IS strategy development which Earl identified?   mixed, business, infrastructure

5   Organisations which see little or no strategic value in IS/IT and feel that IS and IT have little relevance to their current or future strategic success are in the ....B......... quadrant of McFarlan and McKenney's strategic grid.

A   Divest
B   Support
C   Turnaround
D   Factory

1. High cost of IT
2. Stakeholder mapping required
3. effects management information
4. critical to success
5. requires effective management
6 competitive advantage
7 affects all levels management & staff.
8 impacts customer service
9. May lead to structural changes.

Answers to Quick Quiz

1   B   (i) and (iii)

Operational information is derived primarily from internal sources – often from transaction processing systems. Operational information is prepared frequently and relates to the immediate term, whereas strategic information is often prepared on an *ad hoc* basis and relates to the longer term. However, the focus of operational information is primarily on control rather than planning – so option (ii) is incorrect.

2   **Management Information Systems (MIS)** convert data from mainly internal sources into information (eg summary reports, exception reports). This information enables managers to make timely and effective decisions for planning, directing and controlling the activities for which they are responsible.

3   Any three of the following:

- Involves **high costs**

- Is **critical to the success** of many organisations

- Is now used as part of the commercial strategy in the battle for **competitive advantage**

- Has an impact on **customer service**

- Potentially affects **all levels of management and staff** in an organisation

- May **lead to structural changes** within an organisation which require HR planning

- Affects the way **management information** is created and presented

- **Requires effective management** to obtain the maximum benefit

- Involves many **stakeholders** inside and outside the organisation, therefore stakeholder analysis is required

4   Business led; infrastructure led; mixed

5   B   Support

Organisations in the support quadrant see little or no strategic value in IS/IT and feel that it has little relevance to their current or future strategic success.

Answer to Question

6.1 Babbage and Newman

There is no strategy at all. The Finance Director regards IT as a cost. Moreover, the IT 'strategy' is directed to enhancing its existing base (eg in the accounts department) rather than areas where it might prove competitively valuable (eg in marketing).

Now try these questions from the Practice Question Bank	Number	Level	Marks	Time
	6.1–6.5	Intermediate	n/a	10 mins
	6.6	Examination	15	27 mins

BUSINESS APPLICATIONS OF INFORMATION AND INFORMATION TECHNOLOGY

 In the previous chapter we looked at the strategic importance of IS and IT. Now we will look at the strategic importance of **information** itself.

Organisations need to use information about both the external environment and internal performance to help determine strategy. Information is also important for allowing management to control an organisation and its performance (Section 1).

However, information can also be used to create knowledge; and knowledge management and organisational learning can both be important strategic capabilities in their own rights (Section 3).

The increasing amounts of data and information which organisations have to manage mean that it is important data is organised efficiently and can be accessed easily (Section 4).

This becomes even more of an issue in the context of Big Data (Section 5) due to the volume and variety of the data and the rate at which it becomes available to organisations.

Information systems – as well as information – play an increasingly dynamic role in contemporary organisations, and the internet has had a major impact on the structure of many organisations and how they do business. A significant aspect of this is the way the internet has opened up new business models through e-business and e-commerce activities (Section 6).

The internet also allows new marketing opportunities and ways of interacting with potential customers through the application of Web 2.0 technologies and social media (Section 7).

Topic list	Learning outcomes	Syllabus references	Ability required
1 Information for decision making and control	E1 (a)	E1(a)(i)	Evaluate
2 Information sources and management	–	–	–
3 Knowledge management	E1 (a), E1 (b)	E1(a)(ii); E1(a) (iii); E1(b)(i)	Advise
4 Databases and models	E1 (b), E2 (b)	E1(b)(i): E2(b)(ii)	Evaluate
5 Big Data	E2 (b)	E2(b)(iii); E2(b) (iv)	Evaluate
6 E-business and e-commerce	E2 (b)	E2(b)(iii)	Evaluate
7 Web 2.0 technologies and business strategy	E2 (b)	E2(b)(iii)	Evaluate
8 The IT department	–	–	–

Chapter Overview

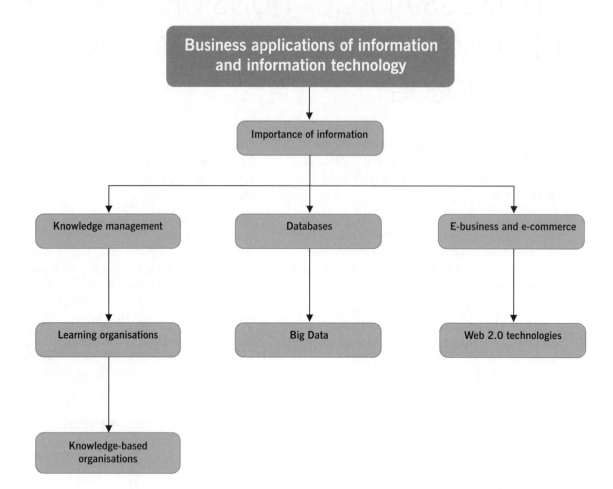

1 Information for decision making and control

Introduction

In order for it to be useful, management information must aid the decision-making process.

1.1 The need for information

In the last chapter, we looked primarily at the importance of information systems (IS) and information technology (IT) for organisations, their competitive position, and their strategies.

In this chapter, we will assess the importance of information itself.

Managers need information for three main reasons:

- To make effective **decisions**
- To **control** the activities of the organisation
- To **co-ordinate** the activities of the organisation

1.1.1 Information and decisions

Decision making is a key element of management. For example, a marketing manager must decide what price to charge for a product, what distribution channels to use, and how to promote the product. Equally, a production manager must decide how much of a product to make, while a purchasing manager must decide how much inventory to hold and whom to buy inputs from.

At a more strategic level, senior managers must decide how to allocate scarce financial resources among competing projects, how the organisation should be structured, or what business-level strategy an organisation should be pursuing.

In order to make effective decisions, managers need information from both inside and outside the organisation. For example, when deciding how to price a product, marketing managers need information about the way consumer demand will vary in relation to different prices, the cost of producing the product and the organisation's overall competitive strategy (since its pricing strategy will need to be consistent with this overall strategy).

1.1.2 Information and control

The management control process can be summarised in four key steps:

- Establish measurable standards of performance or goals
- Measure actual performance
- Compare actual performance against established goals
- Evaluate the results and take corrective action where necessary

In their text, *Contemporary Management*, Jones and George refer to the example of the package delivery company DHL. They note that DHL has a goal to deliver 95% of the packages it picks up by noon the next day. DHL has thousands of branch offices across the US which are responsible for the physical pick-up and delivery of packages, and DHL managers monitor the delivery performance of these offices on a regular basis. If the 95% target is not being achieved, the managers analyse why this is and then take corrective action as necessary.

In order to control operational activity in this way, the managers have to have information about deliveries and performance. In particular, the managers need to know what percentage of packages each branch office delivers by noon, and this information is provided through DHL's IT systems.

All packages to be shipped are scanned with handheld scanners by the DHL drivers, and details of the packages are sent wirelessly to a central computer at DHL's headquarters. The packages are scanned again when they are delivered, with the related delivery time being sent wirelessly back to the central computer. Therefore, managers can identify the percentage of packages which are delivered by noon the day after they were picked up, and can also break down this information to analyse delivery performance on a branch by branch basis.

1.1.3 Information and co-ordination

Another key element of management is co-ordinating the activities of individuals, departments or divisions in order to achieve organisational goals.

One area where this is particularly important is in relation to managing global supply chains. Organisations are using increasingly sophisticated IT systems to co-ordinate the flow of materials, work-in-progress, and finished products throughout the world.

Jones and George consider the example of Bose, the manufacturers of high-quality music systems and speakers. Almost all of the components which Bose uses in its speakers are purchased from external suppliers, and about 50% of its purchases are from foreign suppliers, many in the Middle East.

The challenge for Bose is to co-ordinate its globally dispersed supply chain in a way that minimises inventory and transportation costs. Bose employs a just-in-time production system, so it needs to ensure that component parts arrive at the relevant assembly plants just-in-time to enter the production process, and not before.

Equally, however, Bose has to be responsive to customer demands. This means that Bose and its supplier need to be able to respond quickly to changes in demand for different kinds of speakers, increasing or decreasing production as necessary.

In order to co-ordinate its supply chain, Bose uses a logistics IT system which provides it with real-time information about parts as they move through the global supply chain. When a shipment of parts leaves a supplier it is logged onto the system, and from that point Bose can track the supplies as they move around the globe to the assembly plant.

On one occasion, a significant customer unexpectedly doubled its order for Bose speakers, which meant that Bose had to increase its manufacturing output rapidly. Many of its components were stretched out across the supply chain. However, by using its logistics system Bose was able to locate the parts it needed, and accelerate them out of the normal delivery chain by moving them on air freight. In this way, Bose was able to get the parts it needed at the assembly plant in time to fulfil the customer's order.

1.2 Management accounting information

Management accounting information is used by managers for a variety of purposes.

(a) **To measure performance**. Management accounting information can be used to analyse the performance of the business as a whole, and of the individual divisions, departments or products within the business. Performance reports provide **feedback**, most frequently in the form of comparison between actual performance and budget.

(b) **To control the business**. Performance reports are a crucial element in controlling a business. In order to be able to control their business, managers need to know the following:

(i) What they want the business to achieve (targets or standards; **budgets**)
(ii) What the business is actually achieving (**actual performance**)

By comparing the actual achievements with targeted performance, and identifying **variances**, management can decide whether corrective action is needed, and then take the necessary action when required.

Much control information is of an accounting nature because costs, revenues, profits and asset values are major factors in how well or how badly a business performs.

(c) **To plan for the future**. Managers have to plan, and they need information to do this. Much of the information they use is management accounting information.

(d) **To make decisions**. Managers are faced with several types of decision.

    (i) **Strategic decisions** (which relate to the longer-term objectives of a business) require information which tends to relate to the organisation as a whole, is in summary form and is derived from both internal and external sources.

        In addition, strategic decision making:

- Is medium to **long term**
- Involves high levels of **uncertainty** and risk (the future is unpredictable)
- Involves situations that **may not recur**
- Deals with **complex** issues

    (ii) **Tactical and operational decisions** (which relate to the short or medium term and to a department, product or division rather than the organisation as a whole) require information which is more detailed and more restricted in its sources.

1.3 The decision-making process

The stages in making a decision are:

 Problem recognition

 Problem definition and structuring

 Identifying alternative courses of action

 Making and communicating the decision

 Implementation of the decision

 Monitoring the effects of the decision

Information and decision making

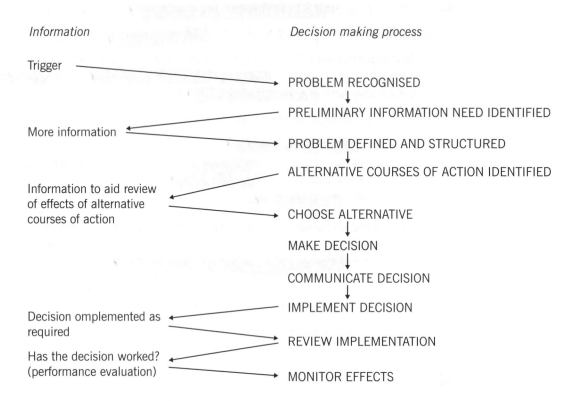

1.3.1 Problem recognition

Decisions are not made without **information**. The decision maker needs to be informed of a problem in the first place. This is sometimes referred to as the **decision trigger**.

1.3.2 Problem definition and structuring

Normally **further information** is then required. This further information is **analysed** so that the problem can be **defined** precisely.

Consider, for example, a company with falling sales. The fall in sales would be the **trigger**. **Further information** would be needed to identify where the deficiencies were occurring. The company might discover that sales of product X in area Y are falling, and the problem can be **defined** as:

'Decline of sales of product X in area Y due to new competitor: how can the decline be reversed?'

One of the purposes of **defining** the problem is to identify the **relationships** between the **various factors** in it, especially if the **problem is complex**.

1.3.3 Identifying alternative courses of action

Where alternative courses of action are identified, **information** is needed about the likely effect of each, so they can be **assessed**.

As a simple example, if our company wishes to review the price of product X in area Y, information will be needed as to the effect of particular price levels on demand for the product. Such information can include external information such as market research (demand at a particular price) and the cost of the product, which can be provided internally.

1.3.4 Making and communicating the decision

The decision is **made** after review of the information relating to alternatives. However, the decision is useless if it is not **communicated**. So, in our example, if the **marketing director** decides to lower the price

of product X and institute an intensive **advertising** campaign, nothing will happen unless the advertising department is informed, and also the **manufacturing** department, which will have to prepare new packaging showing the lower price.

1.3.5 Implementation of the decision

The decision is then **implemented**. For large-scale decisions (for example to relocate a factory 100 miles away from its current site), implementation may need substantial **planning**, detailed information and very clear communication.

1.3.6 Monitoring the effects of the decision

Once a decision has been implemented, information is needed so that its effects can be **reviewed**. For example, if a manufacturing organisation has installed new equipment in anticipation of savings in costs, then information will need to be obtained as to whether these are achieved in practice.

Exam skills

You could use this six-stage process as a means of analysing an exam question scenario and as a structure for your answer. What is the problem? What are the alternatives? How will your solution be implemented? And so on.

1.4 Risk and uncertainty in decision making

Decision making involves **making decisions now about what will happen in the future**. Obviously, decisions can turn out badly, or actual results can prove to be very different from the estimates on which the original decision was made because the necessary **information is not available** when the decision is made.

KEY TERMS

RISK involves situations or events which may or may not occur, but whose probability of occurrence can be calculated statistically and the frequency of their occurrence predicted from past records.

UNCERTAINTY involves situations or events whose outcome cannot be predicted with statistical confidence.

The management accountant, who must present relevant cost and revenue data to assist a manager who is about to make a decision, should consider two things.

(a)   If the figures are **only slightly in doubt** or the amounts themselves are not material, a **best estimate** with a note that the figures are not certain may be good enough.

(b)   If the amount or the **degree of uncertainty was large**, to present just one set of forecast figures would be unwise. For example, if a forecast of sales demand is 'anywhere between 1,000 and 10,000 units', it would be naive and unhelpful to prepare a **single point estimate** of sales – just one forecast figure – of, say, 5,000 units.

If the uncertainty in a situation does warrant special attention in the figures, the next problem is **how the uncertainty** in the figures should be presented.

There are various methods of bringing uncertainty and risk analysis into the evaluation of decisions. They include:

(a)   **Conservative estimates**: estimating outcomes in a conservative manner in order to provide a built-in safety factor.

(b)   Looking at the **worst possible** and **best possible** outcomes, as well as the most likely outcome, and reaching a decision which takes these into account.

(c)   **Sensitivity analysis**: any technique that tests decision options for their vulnerability to changes in a 'variable' such as expected sales volume.

(d)   Assessing **probabilities** and calculating, for each decision alternative, either the **expected value** of costs or benefits with, possibly, the standard deviation of the possible outcomes, or a probability distribution of the possible outcomes. **Decision trees** might be used to illustrate in a 'pictorial' or 'graphical' form the alternatives facing the decision maker.

1.5 Perfect information

Obtaining more information first about what is likely to happen can sometimes reduce the uncertainty about the future outcome from taking a decision. We can categorise information depending upon **how reliable** it is likely to be for predicting what will happen in the future and hence for helping managers to make better decisions.

KEY TERMS

PERFECT INFORMATION is information that predicts the future with perfect accuracy.

IMPERFECT INFORMATION is information which cannot be guaranteed to be completely accurate. Almost all information is, therefore, imperfect – but may still be very useful.

1.6 Factors that make information a valuable commodity

Information is now recognised as a valuable resource and a **key tool in the quest for a competitive advantage**.

Easy **access** to information, the **quality** of that information, and **speedy methods of exchanging** the information have become essential elements of business success.

Organisations that make **good use of information** in decision making and which use new technologies to access, process and exchange information are likely to be **best placed to survive** in increasingly competitive world markets.

In Chapter 4, we looked at resources and capabilities, and we discussed the concept of dynamic capabilities – and an organisation's ability to adapt to changes in markets or the environment more quickly or astutely than its competitors. The quality of information available to an organisation, and the way the organisation's management use that information, are likely to be crucial to the organisation's ability to respond effectively to changes in its environment.

We pick up on this point further shortly, when we look at knowledge management.

Section summary

In order to be useful, management information must aid the decision-making process. However, information is often imperfect, because it is impossible to predict the future with perfect accuracy.

2   Information sources and management

Introduction

Data and information come from sources both **inside** and **outside** an organisation. An organisation's information systems should be designed so as to obtain – or **capture** – all the relevant data and information required.

2.1 Internal information

Capturing data and information from **inside** the organisation involves designing a system for collecting or measuring data and information which sets out procedures for:

- What data and information is collected
- How frequently
- How data and information is processed, filed and communicated
- By whom
- By what methods

The accounting records

The accounting ledgers provide an excellent source of information regarding what has happened in the past. This information may be used as a basis for predicting future events.

2.2 External information

Formal collection of data from outside sources includes:

(a) A company's **tax specialists** will be expected to gather information about changes in tax law and how this will affect the company.

(b) Obtaining information about any new legislation on health and safety at work, or employment regulations, must be the responsibility of a particular person – for example, the company's **legal expert** or **company secretary** – who must then pass on the information to other managers affected by it.

(c) Research and development (R&D) work often relies on information about other R&D work being undertaken by another company or by government institutions. An **R&D official** might be made responsible for finding out about R&D work in other organisations.

(d) **Marketing managers** need to know about the opinions and buying attitudes of potential customers. To obtain this information, they might carry out market research exercises.

Informal gathering of information from the environment occurs naturally, consciously or unconsciously, as people learn what is going on in the world around them – perhaps from newspapers, television reports, meetings with business associates or the trade press.

Organisations hold external information such as invoices, letters and advertisements **received from customers and suppliers**. But there are many occasions when an active search outside the organisation is necessary.

KEY TERM

The phrase ENVIRONMENTAL SCANNING is often used to describe the process of gathering external information, which is available from a wide range of sources.

Sources of external information include:

(a) The Government

(b) Annual reports and press statements of competitors or other firms

(c) Advice or information bureaux

(d) Consultants

(e) Newspaper and magazine publishers

(f) Market research and other reports, for example from Mintel or the Economist Intelligence Unit

(g) Libraries and information services

(h) Increasingly, businesses can use each other's systems as sources of information, for instance via extranets or electronic data interchange (EDI)

(i)   **Electronic sources** of information are becoming more and more important:

    (i)   For some time there have been 'viewdata' services such as **Prestel** offering a very large bank of information gathered from organisations such as the Office for National Statistics, newspapers and the British Library. **Topic** offers information on the stock market. Companies like **Reuters** operate primarily in the field of information provision.

    (ii)   The **internet** is a vast source of information. A number of journals and articles are now published online, and many organisations also display information about themselves on their home pages.

Section summary

An information system should be designed to obtain information from **all relevant sources** – both internal and external – so that managers have the information they need to make properly informed strategic decisions.

---

3 Knowledge management

Introduction

The aim of **knowledge management** is to capture, organise and make widely available all the knowledge the organisation possesses, whether in recorded form or in people's heads.

Earlier in the chapter, we highlighted the potential strategic importance of information. The concept of knowledge management builds upon this, and reinforces the idea that information and knowledge could potentially be sources of competitive advantage for an organisation in their own right.

KEY TERMS

KNOWLEDGE MANAGEMENT is the systematic process of finding, selecting, organising, distilling and presenting information so as to improve comprehension of a specific area of interest. Specific activities help focus the organisation on acquiring, storing and utilising knowledge for such things as problem solving, dynamic learning, strategic planning and decision making.   *(CIMA Official Terminology)*

ORGANISATIONAL KNOWLEDGE is the collective and shared experience accumulated through systems, routines and activities of sharing across the organisation.   *(Johnson, Scholes and Whittington)*

Knowledge management is a relatively new concept in business theory. It is connected with the theory of the **learning organisation** and founded on the idea that knowledge is a major source of competitive advantage in business.

'Knowledge management refers to the set of business processes developed in an organisation to create, store, transfer and apply knowledge. Knowledge management increases the ability of the organisation to learn from its environment and to incorporate knowledge into its business processes.'   *(Laudon and Laudon, Management Information Systems)*

Studies have indicated that 20 to 30% of company resources are wasted because organisations are not aware of what knowledge they already possess. Lew Platt, Ex-Chief Executive of Hewlett Packard, has articulated this, saying 'If only HP knew what HP knows, we would be three times as profitable'.

Knowledge is thus seen as an important **resource** and may, in itself, constitute a **competence**: it can certainly **underpin** many competences, and knowledge management should be seen as a strategy to achieve competitive advantage; for example, through the sharing of cost reduction ideas across divisions, or through the diffusion of innovation.

In a knowledge management system, an organisation will appoint **knowledge managers** who are responsible for collecting and categorising knowledge, and encouraging other people in the organisation to use the available knowledge. The knowledge managers also monitor the use of knowledge in their organisation.

Some companies are now taking the idea of knowledge sharing one stage further and are adopting the practice of **knowledge brokering**. In knowledge brokering, companies look externally to find ways of improving internal business processes. In effect, knowledge brokering resembles benchmarking by allowing companies to find world-class solutions to problems, rather than having to invent their own solutions.

For example, a bank faced frequent complaints from customers about the length of the queues in its local branches. The bank staff responsible for reducing queuing times identified three potential sources of brokers: amusement parks, supermarkets and department stores. In each of these, it is important to keep queuing times under control. In time, the bank worked with an amusement park and a supermarket to redesign the layout of the windows in its branches, and the way it deployed staff between back office and customer-facing windows at busy times.

3.1 Organisational learning

Organisational learning is particularly important in the increasing number of task environments that are both complex and dynamic. It becomes necessary for strategic managers to promote and foster a **culture that values intuition, argument from conflicting views, and experimentation**. A willingness to back ideas that are not guaranteed to succeed is another aspect of this culture: there must be freedom to make mistakes.

3.2 Classifications of knowledge

The aim of **knowledge management** is to exploit existing knowledge and to create new knowledge so that it may be exploited in turn. This is not easy. All organisations possess a great deal of data, but it tends to be unorganised and inaccessible. It is often locked up inside the memories of people who do not realise the value of what they know. This is what Nonaka calls **tacit knowledge**.

KEY TERMS

TACIT KNOWLEDGE is personal, specific to context and hard to articulate.

EXPLICIT KNOWLEDGE is codified and easy to transmit in formal terms.

Even when knowledge is made **explicit** (available to the organisation) by being recorded in some way, it may be difficult and time consuming to access, as is the case with most paper archives. This is where knowledge management technology (such as groupware or intranets) can be useful.

Individual and organisational knowledge

In a similar way to how we can identify a distinction between tacit and explicit knowledge, we can highlight a distinction between **individual knowledge** and **organisational knowledge**.

Individual knowledge is held by an individual, but organisational knowledge is the collective co-ordination of a variety of pieces of knowledge or skill within an organisation.

An important element of organisational knowledge is that it is available to the organisation as a whole. Therefore, the organisation is not dependent on a single person or a small group of people as the sources of knowledge. The dangers of an organisation relying too much on individual knowledge would quickly become clear if the people holding that knowledge leave the organisation.

From 'tacit' to 'explicit' knowledge

Nonaka and Takeuchi describe four ways in which knowledge moves within and between the tacit and explicit categories.

(a) **Socialisation** is the informal process by which individuals share and transmit their tacit knowledge (for example, through the discussions between participants in a seminar or workshop).

(b) **Externalisation** converts tacit knowledge into explicit knowledge, thereby presenting it in a form that can be readily communicated. For example, writing up notes from a meeting and sharing them with colleagues who were unable to attend that meeting.

(c) **Internalisation** is the learning process by which individuals acquire explicit knowledge and turn it into their own tacit knowledge (ie 'learning by doing'). For example, applying some of the knowledge you gain from attending a BPP course, and applying it in your own job.

(d) **Combination** brings together separate elements of explicit knowledge and restructures them. For example, you could create your own revision notes based on the material in this Study Text, and any other study materials you have used.

Nonaka and Takeuchi's four generic strategies for transferring knowledge can be shown in the following matrix:

	To	
	Tacit Knowledge	Explicit Knowledge
From Tacit Knowledge	Socialisation	Externalisation
Explicit Knowledge	Internalisation	Combination

3.2.1 Information, knowledge and competitive advantage

Information and communications technologies have reduced the **cost** of storing and transmitting information, but they have also increased organisations' **capacity** for storing, processing and communicating information.

As access to information becomes easier and less expensive, skills and competences relating to the selection and efficient use of information become increasingly important to organisations. This reinforces the idea that information and information management could become a core competence and a source of competitive advantage for an organisation.

The resource-based approach to strategy – discussed in Chapter 1 – highlights that a successful organisation acquires and develops resources and competences over time, and exploits them to create competitive advantage.

The ability to capture and harness corporate knowledge has become critical for organisations as they seek to adapt to changes in the business environment, particularly those businesses providing financial and professional services. Therefore, as we have already mentioned, knowledge becomes a strategic asset. And organisation-specific knowledge, which has been built up over time, is a core competence that cannot easily be imitated.

Therefore, knowledge management can help promote competitive advantage through:

- The fast and efficient exchange of information
- Effective channelling of the information to:
    - Improve processes, productivity and performance
    - Identify opportunities to meet customer needs better than competitors
    - Promote creativity and innovation

However, the importance of meeting customer needs better than competitors means that organisations need to capture and analyse information about customers and potential customers rather than simply looking at internal processes.

We consider some further illustrations of this when we discuss databases, 'Big Data' and analytics later in this chapter and the next chapter —about strategic marketing.

CASE STUDY

Case example: Customer and supplier engagement

Like other high-end hotels, the Mandarin Oriental in Manhattan uses information systems and technologies to develop detailed knowledge of its customers. The hotel uses computers which keep track of guests' preferences, such as room temperature, check-in time, and television programmes, and store these in a large data repository.

Individual rooms in the hotels are networked to a central network server computer so that they can be remotely monitored or controlled. When a customer arrives at one of the hotels, the system automatically changes the room conditions, such as dimming the lights, setting the room temperature or selecting appropriate music based on the customer's digital profile. The hotels also analyse their customer data to identify their best customers, and to develop individualised marketing campaigns based on customers' preferences.

3.3 Learning organisations

Peter Senge (who is one of the main proponents of the learning organisation concept) argues that learning organisations are:

'Organisations where people continually expand their capacity to create the result they truly desire, where new and expansive patterns of thinking are nurtured, where collective aspiration is set free, and where people are continually learning to see the whole together.'   *(Peter Senge)*

Johnson, Scholes and Whittington also highlight the importance of knowledge in learning organisations:

KEY TERM

A **LEARNING ORGANISATION** is capable of continual regeneration from the variety of knowledge, experience and skills of individuals within a culture that encourages mutual questioning and challenge around a shared purpose or vision.   *(Johnson, Scholes and Whittington)*

The basic rationale for learning organisations is that in situations of rapid change, only those organisations which are flexible, adaptive and productive will be able to excel; and to achieve this flexibility and adaptability organisations need to harness people's commitment and capacity to learn at all levels.

While all people have the capacity to learn, if they are not given the tools and capacity to make sense of the situations they face, they will not be able to learn from them.

A learning organisation emphasises the **sharing of information and knowledge** both up and down the normal communication channels and horizontally through **social networks** and **interest groups**. It challenges notions of hierarchy and managers are facilitators rather than controllers. Such an organisation is inherently capable of change, because behaviours are adapted to reflect new knowledge (either about the external environment or about internal processes and performance). One of the main features of learning organisations is that they are continuously aware of, and interact with, their environments.

The concept of the learning organisation has much in common with that of **logical incrementalism**. The challenge is to combine the advantages of rational planning with the resilience and adaptability provided by the learning approach.

3.3.1 Characteristics of learning organisations

The basic idea behind the concept of the learning organisation is that learning should be treated as a core competence and a source of competitive advantage and, therefore, a learning organisation should be an environment where principles of learning can apply naturally.

As a result, a learning organisation should exhibit features such as:

(a)   People are not blamed for taking calculated risks that do not work out (ie to encourage people to experiment with new approaches; creative tension is embraced as a source of energy and renewal).

(b)   People's workloads are managed so that they have time to try out new ideas and/or to reflect on their experiences (ie to learn from their experiences, and from best practices of others).

(c)   Knowledge is transferred quickly and efficiently throughout the organisation.

(d)   Learning and development isn't seen as the preserve of a single organisational function (such as the HR department) but is regarded as a cross-departmental responsibility.

(e)   Individuals are provided with continuous learning opportunities (ie self-development is encouraged and training for this is provided).

(f)   There is an internal fit between learning activities and other aspects of performance management – such as the appraisal and reward structure – and the general culture of the organisation.

(g)   Individual performance is linked with organisational performance.

3.3.2 Team learning

Peter Senge argues that one of the important characteristics of learning organisations is team learning: 'the process of aligning and developing the capacities of a team to create the results its members truly desire'.

Central to team learning is the notion of dialogue and a genuine 'thinking together' between the team members.

 We look at the idea of team building and collaboration again in Chapter 10, in relation to building and managing effective teams in the context of organisational change. The focus in Chapter 10 is primarily on the role of leadership in building and managing teams, but the idea of team learning and 'thinking together' could also be useful in that context – for a leader to encourage dialogue with their team, rather than simply imposing new ideas on them.

3.4 Data, information and knowledge

There is an important conceptual hierarchy underpinning knowledge management. This distinguishes between **data, information** and **knowledge**. The distinctions are not clear-cut and, to some extent, are differences of degree rather than kind. An understanding of the terms is best approached by considering the relationships between them.

3.4.1 Data

We start with **data**. Data typically consists of individual facts, but in a business context may include more complex items such as opinions, reactions and beliefs. It is important to realise that a quantity of data, no matter how large, does not constitute **information**.

3.4.2 Information

Information is data that is **organised** in some useful way. For instance, an individual credit sale will produce a single invoice identifying the goods, the price, the customer, the date of the sale and so on. These things are data: their usefulness does not extend beyond the purpose of the invoice, which is to collect the sum due. Even if we possess a copy of every invoice raised during a financial year, we still only have data.

However, if we **process** that data we start to create information. For instance, a simple combination of analysis and arithmetic enables us to state total sales for the year, to break that down into sales for each product and to each customer, to identify major customers and so on. These are pieces of information: they are useful for the **management** of the business, rather than just inputs into its administrative systems.

3.4.3 Knowledge

Nevertheless, we still have not really produced any knowledge. Information may be said to consist of the relationships **between items of data**, as when we combine turnover with customer details to discover which accounts are currently important and which are not. We need to go beyond this in order to create knowledge.

The conceptual difference between data and information is fairly easy to grasp: it lies chiefly in the **processes** that produce the one from the other. The difference between information and knowledge is more complex and varies from setting to setting. This is not surprising, since knowledge itself is more complex than the information it derives from.

3.4.4 Differences between data, information and knowledge

A good starting point for understanding the difference is an appreciation of the importance of pattern: knowledge tends to originate in the **discovery of trends or patterns in information**. To return to our invoicing example, suppose we found that certain combinations of goods purchased were typical of certain customers. We could then build up some interesting customer profiles that would enhance our market segmentation and this in turn might influence our overall strategy, since we could identify likely prospects for cross-selling effort.

Another important aspect of the differences between data, information and knowledge is the relevance of **context.** Our sales invoice is meaningless outside its context; if you, as a marketing person, found an invoice in the office corridor, it would be little more than waste paper to you, though no doubt the accounts people would like it back. However, if you found a list of customers in order of annual turnover, that would be rather more interesting from a marketing point of view. The information is **useful outside of its original context** of the accounts office.

This idea also applies to the difference between information and knowledge. If you were a visitor to a company and found a copy of the turnover listing, it would really only be useful to you if you were trying to sell the same sort of thing to the same customers. Its value outside its context would be small. However, if you found a marketing report that suggested, based on evidence, that customers were becoming more interested in quality and less interested in price, that would be applicable to a wide range of businesses, and possibly of strategic importance. This highlights another characteristic of knowledge: that it is a key **source of comparative advantage**.

Here is a table that summarises the progression from data to knowledge.

	Data	Information	Knowledge
Nature	Facts	Relationships between processed facts	Patterns discerned in information
Importance of context	Total	Some	Context independent
Importance to business	Mundane	Probably useful for management	May be strategically useful: source of comparative advantage

There is one final important point to note here and that is that the **progression** from data to knowledge is not the same in all circumstances. The scale is moveable and depends on the general complexity of the setting. Something may be **information** within its own context. Something similar may be **knowledge** in a different context. The difference will often be associated with the scale of operations. Take the example of a customer going into insolvent liquidation with $200,000 outstanding on its account. For a small supplier with an annual turnover of, say, $10 million, a bad debt of this size would be of strategic importance and might constitute a threat to its continued existence. Advance notice of the possibility would be valuable **knowledge**. However, for a company operating on a global scale, the bad debt write-off would be annoying but still only one item on a list of bad debts – **data**, in other words.

3.5 Other ideas about knowledge

Individuals acquire knowledge in a variety of ways, including those listed below.

- Education and training
- Experience of work
- Observation of others
- Informal exchanges such as coaching and brain storming

Davenport and Prusak echo our earlier description of the relationship between data, information and knowledge and suggest that people **create knowledge from information by four processes**.

- **Comparison** with earlier experience
- **Consequences**: the implication of information
- **Connections**: relationships between items
- **Conversation**: discussion with others

3.6 Knowledge management (KM) systems

As we have noted, knowledge management (KM) is a key factor in realising and sustaining an organisation's success through improving its understanding of its environment and its processes.

Knowledge is increasingly being recognised as a critical organisational resource for competitive advantage in the contemporary economy. And one of the key objectives of KM is to capture, organise and store knowledge for use by an organisation and its staff or managers.

An important practical issue for organisations, however, is **how** to capture and exploit useful knowledge at different levels across the organisation and in different contexts.

Recognition of the value of knowledge, and understanding of the need to organise data and make it accessible, have provoked the development of sophisticated IT systems. Such systems deal, by definition, with **explicit knowledge**: that is, knowledge that is widely distributed.

Office automation systems are IT applications that improve productivity in an office. These include word processing and voice messaging systems.

Groupware is 'a collection of tools to assist collaborative work in an organisation'.

(CIMA Official Terminology)

Groupware products are designed to assist communication between members of a group, and capture information that the group is working with.

In a sales context, for instance, it would provide a facility for recording and retrieving all the information relevant to individual customers, including notes of visits, notes of telephone calls and basic data such as address, credit terms and contact name. These items could be updated by anyone who had contact with a customer and would then be available to all salespeople.

Groupware also provides such facilities as discussion databases and message boards, appointment scheduling, to-do lists, and jotters. Lotus Notes is a good example of a groupware product.

Workflow systems

KEY TERM

'A **WORKFLOW** is a series of tasks, which must be performed in order to achieve a specific result or outcome in an organisation.'
(CIMA Official Terminology)

For example, in order to purchase a new piece of equipment, a department may need to get some quotes from suppliers, prepare a business case, raise a purchase order (once the business case is approved) and match the purchase order to supplier invoice before approving the invoice for payment.

In a manual system, there is a chance that documents can get lost or out of order. Automated workflow systems avoid such problems by enabling documents to be moved over a network or maintained in a single database, which the appropriate users have access to at the required time. An automated workflow system can also include reminders which alert staff (or managers) when actions become due.

Intranet

An intranet is an internal network used to share information using internet technology and protocols. The **firewall** surrounding an intranet fends off unauthorised access from outside the organisation. Each employee has a browser, used to access a server computer that holds corporate information on a wide variety of topics, and in some cases also offers access to the internet. Applications include company newspapers, induction material, procedure and policy manuals and internal databases.

(a)   Savings accrue from the **elimination of storage**, **printing** and **distribution of documents** that can be made available to employees online.

(b)   Documents online are often **more widely used** than those that are kept filed away, especially if the document is bulky (eg manuals) and needs to be searched. This means that there are improvements in productivity and efficiency.

(c)   It is much easier to **update information in electronic form**.

Extranet

An extranet is a collaborative network which uses internet technology to join organisations, for example to link businesses with their suppliers. Extranets may be divided into **intronets** and **supranets**.

Intronet

When access to an intranet is extended to trusted external agencies, such as suppliers and customers, it becomes an **intronet**. The intronet's system content and functionality are under the control of the organisation that provides it. Intronets allow suppliers and customers to gain privileged access to data held by the host. This may form the basis of a long-term relationship if the external user becomes dependent on the system's information content.

Supranet

A **supranet** differs from an intronet in that it is set up in a co-operative fashion and control is not exercised by a single host. The aim is to ensure the overall efficiency of the consortium of entities concerned.

Security is a major issue for extranets and may require firewalls, server management, encryption and the issue of digital certificates.

Expert system

An **expert system** is a computer program that captures **human expertise** in a limited domain of knowledge. Such software uses a knowledge base that consists of facts, concepts and the relationships between them and uses pattern-matching techniques to solve problems. For example, many financial institutions now use expert systems to process straightforward loan applications. The user enters certain key facts into the system such as the loan applicant's name and most recent addresses, their income and monthly outgoings, and details of other loans. The system will then:

(a)   Check the facts given against its **database** to see whether the applicant has a good previous credit record

(b)   Perform **calculations** to see whether the applicant can afford to repay the loan

(c)   Make a **judgement** as to what extent the loan applicant fits the lender's profile of a good risk (based on the lender's previous experience)

(d)   **A decision is then suggested,** based on the results of this processing

IT systems can be used to store vast amounts of data in accessible form. A **data warehouse** receives data from operational systems, such as a sales order processing system, and stores it in its most fundamental form, without any summarisation of transactions. Analytical and query software is provided so that reports can be produced at any level of summarisation and incorporating any comparisons or relationships desired.

The value of a data warehouse is enhanced when **data mining** software is used. True data mining software **discovers previously unknown relationships** and provides insights that cannot be obtained through ordinary summary reports. These hidden patterns and relationships constitute **knowledge**, as defined above, and can be used to guide decision making and to predict future behaviour. Data mining is thus a contribution to organisational learning. (We look at data warehouses and data mining in more detail in the next chapter, in relation to strategic marketing.)

The US retailer Wal-Mart discovered an unexpected relationship between the sale of nappies and beer! Wal-Mart found that both tended to sell at the same time, just after working hours, and concluded that men with small children stopped off to buy nappies on their way home, and bought beer at the same time. Logically, therefore, if the two items were put in the same shopping aisle, sales of both should increase. Wal-Mart tried this and it worked.

The following table is an amended version of our earlier table distinguishing data, information and knowledge. This one includes the relevant IT systems.

	Data	Information	Knowledge
Nature	Facts	Relationships between processed facts	Patterns discerned in information
Importance of context	Total	Some	Context independent
Importance to business	Mundane	Probably useful for management	May be strategically useful
Relevant IT systems	Office automation Data warehouse	Groupware Expert systems Report writing software Intranet	Data mining Intranet Expert systems

However, note that KM is not just about IT systems. A successful KM implementation must also involve people and processes; for example, changing the corporate culture to encourage knowledge sharing.

3.7 A strategy for KM

An organisation that wishes to exploit its knowledge resource strategically should take a strategic approach.

A **top-down** strategy uses the **overall strategic plan** to identify the areas in which knowledge can be best exploited.

A **bottom-up** strategy is based on **research into existing key business processes** in order to determine important needs and issues.

However, in terms of actually developing and implementing a KM strategy, there are five main steps to consider.

(a) **Support from senior management**. Senior management support will be needed, not only to provide the necessary **resources** and to lead the development of a knowledge-based culture, but also because if senior managers are not seen to be supporting the strategy then other staff will not do so either.

(b) **Installing the IT infrastructure**. IT hardware and software will need to be acquired to ensure that the organisation has the capabilities to **capture, store and communicate knowledge**.

(c) **Developing the databases**. Advanced databases and database management systems may need to be developed, with the details of their design and structure being tailored to the type of knowledge the organisation is looking to capture.

(d) **Develop a sharing culture**. Knowledge is widely known to represent **power**, and staff are likely to want to hoard the knowledge they have already accumulated, rather than to share it. A **culture** of **knowledge sharing** must be developed.

(e) **Capturing and using the knowledge**. Existing knowledge needs to be captured and recorded in the databases. Staff then need to be trained how to use the databases and encouraged to do so.

Importantly, however, although there is an IT element to KM systems and their infrastructure, a KM strategy need not be IT-driven. **IT should support rather than dominate the strategy**. The **cultural aspects** of a KM strategy, and patterns of behaviour in an organisation, are likely to be just as critical to its success as the IT elements. IT cannot sustain KM by itself. For example, in order for knowledge to be shared between teams, members from the different teams must be prepared to share it.

In their text, *Management Information Systems*, Laudon and Laudon highlight that one apt observation about KM is 'Effective knowledge management is 80% managerial and organisational, and 20% technology'.

3.8 The benefits of KM

By definition, KM means that the knowledge and information possessed by individuals within an organisation is shared and can therefore be used by other people within the organisation.

However, as well as increasing an organisation's ability to compete and add value by virtue of its **greater knowledge base**, KM may also improve productivity through higher workforce **motivation**.

Also, if staff are encouraged to use knowledge this can help **improve efficiency**, and possibly lead to greater **innovation**. After all, the staff who work on a process are best placed to see whether that process could be improved, rather than management always telling them what to do. Similarly, the effective sharing of knowledge within an organisation could also improve **decision making** (because managers will consider factors which they might otherwise have overlooked).

3.8.1 Potential issues in implementing a KM system

Structure and culture – The current structure and culture of an organisation may not be conducive to sharing knowledge; for example, if there is little communication between departments in an organisation, or if staff are reluctant to share knowledge for fear that it will reduce their power within the organisation. These inherent barriers will have to be overcome in order for the system to be successful.

Technological infrastructure – If an organisation does not have a suitable network which allows information to be stored and accessed, one will have to be installed before knowledge can be shared across the organisation. There may be significant costs associated with installing such a network.

Incompatible systems and sources of information – Problems could arise if some divisions or departments record data or information in systems which are incompatible with those used by other divisions or departments. Such a situation will mean that data or information will have to be transferred into a new common format before they can be shared; but there is a risk that errors or omissions could result from the resulting conversion process.

Equally, it is possible that some information is not stored in a digital form at all, and so the organisation will have to decide how this material can be indexed and archived so that it can be accessed if it is needed in the future.

Resistance to change – Staff in different areas of an organisation may already have their own preferred ways of organising data. However, this may not be compatible with the common format in which data is being held on the network. Staff may be reluctant to change their current practices, particularly if they are not given adequate training in any new systems they are required to use, and if they are not given sufficient time to adapt to them.

Exam skills

The term knowledge-sharing systems is also sometimes used instead of knowledge management systems. For example, a question in your objective test exam could refer to the benefits of a knowledge sharing system or the problems of implementing one (rather than the benefits or problems of a knowledge management system). The benefits and problems remain the same, though, whichever terminology is used.

Section summary

There is a hierarchy between **data, information** and **knowledge**, and knowledge is the most useful as a source of competitive advantage.

Knowledge management aims to exploit existing knowledge and create new knowledge which, in turn, can be exploited.

All organisations possess a great deal of data, but much of it is disorganised and inaccessible. Knowledge management technology helps structure data in a way that makes it easily accessible so that it can be used to support knowledge.

4 Databases and models

Introduction

A database is a collection of data organised to service many applications. The database provides convenient access to data for a wide variety of users and user needs.

The way in which data is held on a system affects the ease by which the data is able to be accessed and manipulated. Many modern software packages are built around a database. A database provides a comprehensive set of data for a number of different users.

KEY TERMS

A DATABASE is a collection of data organised to service many applications. The database provides convenient access to data for a wide variety of users and user needs.

A DATABASE MANAGEMENT SYSTEM (DBMS) is the software that centralises data and manages access to the database. It is a system which allows numerous applications to extract the data they need without the need for separate files.

4.1 The characteristics of a database system

(a)   **Shared**. Different users are able to access the same data for their own processing applications. This removes the need for duplicating data on different files.

(b)   **Controls** to preserve the **integrity** of the database. Users should not be able to alter the data on file so as to **spoil** the database records for other users. However, users must be able to make **valid** alterations to the data.

(c)   **Flexibility**. The database system should provide for the **needs of different users**, who each have their own processing requirements and data access methods. The database should be capable of **evolving** to meet **future** needs.

4.2 Advantages and disadvantages

The **advantages** of a database system are:

(a)   Avoidance of unnecessary duplication of data

It recognises that data can be used for many purposes but only needs to be input and stored once.

(b)   **Multi-purpose data**

From (a), it follows that although data is input once, it can be used for several purposes.

(c)   **Data for the organisation as a whole, not just for individual departments**

The database concept encourages management to regard data as a resource that must be properly managed just as any other resource. Database systems encourage management to analyse data, relationships between data items, and how data is used in different applications.

(d)   **Consistency**

Because data is only held once, it is easier to ensure that it is up to date and consistent across departments.

(e)   **New uses for data**

Data is held independently of the programs that access the data. This allows greater flexibility in the ways that data can be used. New programs can be easily introduced to make use of existing data in a different way.

(f)   **New applications**

Developing new application programs with a database system is easier as a central pool of data is already available to be drawn upon.

(g)   **Flexibility**

Relational systems are extremely flexible, allowing information from several different sources to be combined and providing answers to *ad hoc* queries.

The **disadvantages** of a database system relate mainly to security and control.

(a)   There are potential problems of **data security** and **data privacy**. Administrative procedures for data security should supplement software controls.

(b)   Since there is only one set of data, it is essential that the data should be **accurate** and free from corruption. A back-up routine is essential.

(c)   Initial **development costs** may be high.

(d)   For hierarchical and network structures, the access paths through the data must be **specified in advance**.

(e)   Both hierarchical and network systems require intensive **programming** and are **inflexible**.

4.3 Using databases for planning

Planning will always involve an element of risk – as it deals with the **future**. Databases can at least ensure that information we have about the present and the past is available to aid planning. Organised data retrieval techniques make the data available in an effective way. In a world in which decisions must be ever more rapid, it is crucial to be able to access diverse, complex, multiple data sources and to analyse them to rapidly and correctly extract the knowledge they contain.

Databases can be used in conjunction with a variety of tools and techniques, eg decision support systems, Executive Information Systems, data warehousing, and data mining.

Financial and business planning is one of the most important activities an organisation undertakes. Often organisations use spreadsheets as the basis for their financial planning. However, spreadsheets were never designed for planning, although they have inherited the tasks. There may often be a benefit from using dedicated software to support planning decisions, rather than relying on spreadsheets to do the job.

CASE STUDY

Continental Airlines

Forecasting is critical to the airline industry. Managers at major airlines track many indicators and statistics – fluctuations in travel demand, oil prices, and changing currency rates – to make educated business decisions. All these data have significant impact on the costs of doing business and the profitability of a company.

The environment is very dynamic, so senior management need up to date information and forecasts, reflecting the rapid changes in the business and economic environments.

The US airline Continental Airlines traditionally recorded key performance indicators such as load factors, fuel efficiency, and on-time rates in Excel spreadsheets. This necessitated the time-consuming manual creation of thousands of monthly reports to get business decision makers the information they needed.

There was a huge price for such inefficiency. Because they spent so much time preparing reports and information, the financial planning and analysis team at Continental spent less than 20% of its time actually on analysis. This was much less than desired.

Moreover, the dependence on spreadsheets meant that much of the business logic used to prepare the numbers remained in individual employees' heads and on their desktop computers.

The head of Financial Planning and Analysis at Continental pointed out: 'Excel is a great tool – I don't think anyone can do without it. But Excel is just a spreadsheet. It shouldn't be a database tool, it shouldn't be a reporting tool, and it shouldn't be a communication tool.'

In 2008, although travel demand fell and oil prices skyrocketed, Continental executives saw an opportunity to change systems and processes to navigate the challenging times and emerge more efficient than ever.

They moved away from relying exclusively on Excel and implemented a suite of Hyperion EPM applications.

Within weeks of going live, Continental saw significant new efficiencies in analysing industry trends and performing strategic analysis. Additionally, Continental achieved the goal of generating an 18-month rolling forecast every month, updating executive insight and enabling better decision making. The financial planning and analysis team increased time spent on analysis by 80%. Uploading data for reports on

actuals was slashed from four hours to a matter of minutes. And moving critical data off of both people's laptops and network storage represented a huge improvement in data security.

However, potentially the most important benefit was the information and insights which became available for senior management. The goal for the financial planning team at Continental is simple: to give senior management the quickest, most complete picture of business conditions possible.

The head of Financial Planning and Analysis sums this up as follows: 'Our CFO needs to be able to come in every day, sign on to his dashboard, click on the button and see, "What's my outlook as of yesterday? What's changed since the prior day?"'

In the fast-changing airline industry, having that insight could be crucial for the success of the business.

4.4 Databases and marketing

The growth of the internet and e-commerce are allowing customers to build up information about online customers in databases. Emailing useful and relevant information to customers helps build stronger relationships with customers and may encourage them to make additional purchases.

We look at database marketing in more detail in Chapter 8.

Section summary

Databases provide convenient access to data for a wide variety of uses and users' needs. Databases can be used in strategic planning, and play an important role in database marketing.

5 Big Data

Introduction

The amount of data available to organisations is increasing ever more rapidly, and Big Data – with its characteristics of volume, velocity and variety – encapsulates the opportunities and challenges which the new sources of data present to organisations.

The ability to analyse these large, and unstructured, data sets and to uncover previously hidden patterns of information could be a key element of an organisation's competitive advantage.

In a number of places in this chapter we have been looking at the way organisations collect and use information to support their strategic and tactical decision making. Equally, we highlighted the way organisations can use data mining to uncover hidden relationships and patterns in data. We look at data mining again in the next chapter in the context of strategic marketing and discovering trends in customers' buying behaviours.

Organisations today have more transactional data than they have ever had before – about their customers, their suppliers and their operations.

More generally, the growth of the internet, multimedia, wireless networks, smartphones, social media, sensors and other digital technology are all helping to fuel a data revolution. In the so-called 'internet of things' sensors embedded in physical objects such as mobile phones, motor vehicles, smart energy meters, RFID tags, tracking devices and traffic flow monitors all create and communicate data which is shared across wired and wireless networks that function in a similar way to the internet. The timing and location of cash withdrawals from ATM machines could also be a potential source of data.

And consumers using social media, smartphones, laptops and tablets to browse the internet, to search for items, to make purchases and to share information with other users all create trails of data. Similarly, internet search indexes (such as Google Trends) can be a source of data for 'Big Data analytics'.

5.1 What is Big Data?

In a June 2011 report, *'Big data: The next frontier for innovation, competition and productivity'* McKinsey Global Institute defined Big Data as *'datasets whose size is beyond the ability of typical database software to capture, store, manage and analyse.'*

However, the most widely cited definition of Big Data is that given by the technology research firm, Gartner:

KEY TERM

BIG DATA is 'high-volume, high velocity and high-variety information assets that demand cost-effective, innovative forms of information processes for enhanced insight and decision making.' (*Gartner*)

5.1.1 Characteristics of Big Data (3 Vs)

Volume – Perhaps the main benefit of Big Data analytics comes from the ability to process very large amounts of information. The bigger the data, the more potential insights it can give in terms of identifying trends and patterns, and in terms of getting a deeper understanding of customer requirements. For example, as most customers use the internet, smartphones and social media in their everyday lives, these can now also be sources of data for organisations alongside any data they may capture internally – for example, from customer loyalty cards or the transactions recorded in EPOS tills.

However, the 'volume' aspect of Big Data also presents the most obvious challenges to conventional IT structures, due to volume of storage space required for the data.

Velocity – Refers to the increasing speed with which data flows into an organisation, and with which it is processed within the organisation.

Online retailers are able to compile records of each click and interaction a customer makes while visiting a website, rather than simply recording the final sale at the end of a customer transaction. Moreover, retailers who are able to utilise information about customer clicks and interactions quickly – for example, by recommending additional purchases – can use this speed to generate competitive advantage.

It is important to recognise that the competitive advantage an organisation can gain from 'velocity' relates to the speed with which data is processed and the velocity of a system's outputs, as well as the speed with which data initially flows into it.

Variety (or variability) – A common theme in relation to Big Data is the diversity of source data, with a lot of the data being unstructured (ie not in a database). For example, keywords from conversations people have on Facebook or Twitter and content they share through media files (tagged photographs, or online video postings) could be sources of unstructured data.

This variety presents a challenge to organisations as they need to find ways of capturing, storing and processing the data. If data is too big, moves too fast, or doesn't fit with the structures of an organisation's existing information systems, then in order to gain value from it an organisation needs to find an alternative way to process that data.

In this respect, 'Big Data analytics' is likely to be crucial to making use of the potential value of Big Data.

Big Data analytics – Refers to the ability to analyse and reveal insights in data which had previously been too difficult or costly to analyse – due to the volume and variability of the data involved.

The aim of Big Data analytics is to extract insights from unstructured data or from large volumes of data.

Being able to extract insights from the data available is crucial for organisations to benefit from the availability of Big Data – for example, to help them understand the complexity of the environment in which they are operating, and to respond swiftly to the opportunities and threats presented by it; or to develop new insights and understanding into what customers need or want.

However, the value of any insights which can be gained from Big Data also depends on the accuracy of the underlying data. This highlights another 'V' characteristic of Big Data: Veracity.

Veracity (truthfulness) – Although Big Data increases the volume of data available to organisations, for that data to be useful for decision making it needs to be reliable and truthful. If the data is not truthful (for example, due to bias or inconsistencies within it) this could reduce the value of any decisions which are informed by it. Moreover, hidden biases in the data could present significant risks to an organisation – if those biases lead to the organisation making 'incorrect' decisions.

5.2 Making use of Big Data

Historically, only the largest corporations have had sufficient resources to be able to process Big Data. Now, however, it is becoming possible for all organisations to access and process the volumes of Big Data potentially available to them, due to cost-effective approaches such as cloud-based architectures and open source software.

McKinsey's *Big Data* report suggests that 'Big data has now reached every sector in the global economy. Like other essential factors of production such as [physical] assets and human capital, much of modern economic activity simply couldn't take place without it.'

This suggests that the ability to capture and analyse Big Data, and the information gained by doing so, have become important strategic resources for organisations. Making effective use of Big Data could confer competitive advantage for an organisation. Alternatively, in time, competitors who fail to develop their capabilities to use Big Data and information as strategic resources could be left behind by those who do.

While these might initially seem to be quite bold claims, Big Data can certainly create value for organisations through its ability to drive innovation and by helping organisations gain greater and faster insights into their customers.

Similarly, analysing data from as many sources as possible when making decisions can also increase the amount of useful information available to managers when they are making decisions.

CASE STUDY

Case Study – Morrisons

The UK supermarket chain Morrisons uses weather forecasts to predict customers' purchasing patterns.

Morrisons has analysed five years of sales data and have identified how sales patterns change in line with increases or decreases in temperature. Although people make purchasing decisions as individuals, overall trends in their purchases show that we act as a 'human swarm'.

When temperatures fall during the winter, purchases of 'warming' food such as soup and porridge, as well as purchases of ready meals, increase. Therefore, when the weather forecast shows a fall in temperature, Morrisons increases the amount of these 'warming' foods it ships from its central distribution centre to its stores.

Similarly, Morrisons has identified that when weather forecasts in summer predict three or more consecutive days of hot, dry weather, demand for barbecue-related foods increases significantly. By reacting to the weather forecast, Morrisons can not only control the quantities of different products it ships from its warehouses to its stores, but can also ask its suppliers to change the volume of different products they supply. For example, if hot weather is forecast, Morrisons asks its supplier of minced beef to switch from producing ready meals (such as cottage pie) to producing beef burgers (which will be used for barbecues).

CASE STUDY

Case Study – Bravissimo

The lingerie and clothing retailer also uses local weather reports to change its online adverts in different parts of the UK as the weather changes. Bravissimo uses a software solution (called weatherFIT) to enable it to tailor online adverts in real time to respond to local weather data.

In the three months from March to May 2013, Bravissimo reported a 600% growth in revenue from its online adverts compared to the same period the previous year.

Bravissimo's senior marketing manager commented: 'Using [weatherFIT] to fine-tune our ... advertising and promotions by taking into account local weather conditions really boosted sales in the crucial run-up to the holiday season.'

5.3 The value of Big Data

McKinsey's *Big Data* report suggests there are five broad ways in which Big Data can create value for organisations:

Creating transparency – Making data more easily accessible to relevant stakeholders, in a timely manner, can create value in its own right – for example, by revealing insights from data which had previously been too costly or complex to process. This transparency could relate to data within an organisation as well as external data – through better integration and analysis of data produced by different parts of an organisation. For example, within a manufacturing company, integrating data from R&D, engineering and manufacturing units to enable concurrent engineering could significantly reduce time to market as well as improving quality.

However, in many cases the increased transparency resulting from Big Data is likely to relate to external data. For example, analysing shoppers' transactions, alongside social and geographical data, can reveal peer influence among customers – ie the extent to which shoppers' choices are shaped by their friends and neighbours as well as by the marketing efforts of the company itself.

Performance improvement – The increasing amount of transactional data they store in digital form provides organisations with an increasing amount of accurate and detailed performance data – in real or almost real time. By analysing variability in performance – and the causes of that variability – organisations then manage performance to higher levels. For example, if they can identify why certain products line are selling more slowly than expected, managers can either take action to improve sales of those lines, or else divert resources into more popular product lines.

Market segmentation and customisation – The volume and variety within Big Data enables organisations to create highly specific segments within its markets and to tailor its products and services precisely to meet those needs.

The idea of market segmentation (which we discuss in more detail in the next chapter) is already a key concept within strategic marketing. However, Big Data could facilitate the real-time micro-segmentation of customers for targeted promotions and advertising.

McKinsey also highlights that Big Data could also be valuable in segmenting public sector markets. Traditionally, public sector markets have not segmented citizens (service users) in the same way that private sector companies have segmented customers and potential customers. However, Big Data could enable public sector organisations to also tailor products and services more effectively.

Decision making – The sophisticated analytics tools which are used to uncover previously hidden patterns and trends in data could also be used to improve decision making. For example, trends identified in in-store and online sales for a retailer – in real time – could be used to manage inventories and pricing. In some cases, decisions will be made by managers in store (based on analytics from the datasets) but in other cases the decisions themselves could even become automated. So for example, a retailer could use algorithms to optimise decisions about inventory levels and pricing in response to current and predicted sales data.

New products and services – Companies can use data about social trends and consumer behaviours to create new products and services to meet customers' needs, or to enhance existing products and services so that they meet customers' needs more exactly. For example, the emergence of real-time location data, from traffic light sensors and satellite navigation systems, could enable insurance companies to refine the pricing of their insurance policies according to where, and how, people drive their cars.

More generally, Big Data could also provide new business opportunities in its own right. For example, Facebook's advertising business incorporates analysis of a user's actions as well as their friends' actions. Equally, Amazon could be seen as an example of a company which has built its business – and serves its customers – using data and analytics; for example, through the way it makes recommendations for customers linked to the purchases made by other customers with similar interests.

5.4 Data and customers

So far in this section we have looked at the way organisations can use Big Data to understand more about what their customers want. However, Web 2.0 technologies (which we will discuss later in this chapter) mean that data is increasingly available to customers as well as organisations.

For example, online customer reviews are now commonplace, and smartphone applications now enable customers to evaluate and compare product prices in real time. This increased availability of data creates a new market transparency which can give customers a greater insight into what they are buying and who they are buying from.

In this respect, the data helps customers to base purchasing decisions not only on price, but also on a company's social reputation – for example, in terms of customers' feedback in relation to the quality of service they have received.

5.5 Potential limitations of Big Data

Some critics have argued that Big Data is simply a buzzword, a vague term which has turned into an obsession in large organisations and the media. However, the critics argue that very few instances exist where analysing vast amounts of data has resulted in significant new discoveries of performance improvements for an organisation.

Correlation, not causation – The primary focus within Big Data is on finding correlations between data sets, rather than focusing on the cause of any trends and patterns. It can often be easier to identify correlations between different variables than to determine what – if anything – is causing that correlation. Correlation does not necessarily imply causality.

Similarly, if an organisation does not understand the factors which give rise to a correlation, it will equally not know what factors may cause the correlation to break down.

CASE STUDY

Case Study – Google Flu Trends

Google Flu Trends was presented as a means of tracking and predicting the spread of influenza across the US.

The program used algorithms which identified correlations between the symptoms people searched for online and flu symptoms.

However, after providing a swift and accurate account of flu outbreaks for several winters, in the 2012–3 season, Flu Trends overstated the spread of flu-like illnesses across the US by almost a factor of two.

The cause of this problem was that ultimately Google did not know what linked the search terms with the spread of flu, and Google's algorithms weren't designed to identify what caused what. They were simply finding statistical patterns in the data; and as such they focused on correlation rather than causation.

One explanation of the Flu Trends failure in 2012–3 was that there were a number of news stories in December about the dangers of flu, and these provoked internet searches by people who were healthy.

Sample population – While the data sets available through Big Data are often very large, they are still not necessarily representative of the entire data population as a whole. For example, if an organisation uses 'tweets' from the social networking site Twitter to provide insight into public opinion on a certain issue, there is no guarantee the 'tweets' will accurately represent the view of society as a whole. (For example, according to the Pew Research Internet Project, in 2013, US-based Twitter users were disproportionately young, urban or suburban, and black.)

5.6 Big Data and digitalisation in knowledge-based organisations

Earlier in this chapter, we discussed KM and learning organisations, and these discussions of Big Data remind us how knowledge – and the use of technology to support knowledge creation – are becoming increasingly important components of organisations' potential competitive advantage.

The increasing competitiveness of the global economy means that productivity gains or product improvements made by one company are often rapidly eliminated by their competitors' response.

In this respect, a company's process of **innovation** – and its ability to derive value from the information it has about products and markets – is likely to be critical to maintaining its competitive advantage in the face of a constantly changing market and economic environment. (This also echoes the idea of dynamic capabilities we discussed in Chapter 4.)

Equally, in the 'information society' which exists today, information is one of the most valuable assets which organisations have, and information management and KM are also likely to be essential parts of an organisation's competitive success, because they play a key role in value creation and productivity.

5.6.1 Knowledge-based organisations

Many organisations focus primarily on the routine tangible and observable activities that they carry out on a daily basis.

However, knowledge-based organisations also focus on two related processes which underlie these primary processes: the effective **application of existing knowledge**, and the **creation of new knowledge** to produce economic benefits. The success of knowledge-based organisations relies on their intangible assets – such as research, design, development, creativity, learning, and human capital.

Knowledge-based organisations have four goals in relation to knowledge management.

(a)   To ensure that knowledge from one part of an organisation is applied to activities in other parts of the organisation

(b)   To ensure that knowledge is shared over time so that the organisation benefits from past experience

(c)   To facilitate people from different parts of the organisation collaborating to create new knowledge

(d)   To provide opportunities and incentives for experimentation and learning

As we would expect, knowledge creation and knowledge sharing are key features of a knowledge-based organisation. And while it is important that knowledge is shared within an organisation – for example, between different departments – organisations are also realising that knowledge can often also be gathered and shared as a result of interactions with customers, suppliers, and possibly even competitors.

In this respect, initiatives such as **co-creativity** and **crowdsourcing** have been important for the creation and sharing of knowledge. (Procter & Gamble's 'Connect + Develop' programme, which we discussed in Chapter 4 of this Study Text, illustrates this point.)

However, while technological developments such as data warehousing and data mining have already helped to promote KM in organisations, and the advent of Web 2.0 technologies has helped organisations gather more information about customers, the volume and variety of Big Data means it has the potential to act as a source of even more knowledge to be created and shared.

In this context, however, Big Data presents two key challenges to organisations:

Information strategy – Organisations need to harness the power of information. Big Data is providing new ways to leverage information, but organisations need to be able to take advantage of them if they are going to be able to use the information to generate growth. How will they harness Big Data to improve strategic decision making – for example in evaluating potential new investments?

Organisations also have to have the infrastructural capacity to manage the **volume, variety and velocity** of the data available – and to process it – in order to maximise its value as a source of information and knowledge.

Data analytics – Organisations need to be able to draw insights from large and complex datasets, in order to understand and predict customer behaviours, and to improve customer satisfaction or to drive innovation.

5.6.2 Digitisation and business value

When considering the potential impact of digitisation on business, it is also important to acknowledge the point highlighted in McKinsey's report: *Finding your digital sweet spot*. The report argues that 'while online sales, social networking and mobile applications have received most of the buzz when it comes to digital', the greatest bottom-line impact may come from cost savings and changes beyond the interface between company and customer. If organisations focus too narrowly on the impact of digitisation on distribution channels only and the end-user customer interface, they will only gain a small proportion of the value that digitisation could provide.

As such, McKinsey's report suggests that technology (and digital transformation) can drive business value in four different ways:

- Enhanced connectivity
- Automation of manual tasks
- Improved decision making
- Product or service innovation

Tools such as Big Data analytics, apps, workflow systems and cloud platforms – all of which can enable business value – are too often applied selectively to certain parts of the organisation only, often around sales and marketing. However, they could also be used, equally beneficially, across a much wider range of activities.

Connectivity with customers, colleagues and suppliers

- Customer experience – Seamless, multi-channel experience; 'Whenever, wherever' service proposition
- Product and service innovation – New digital products and services; co-creation of new products

Decision making – based on Big Data and advanced analytics

- Enhanced corporate control – improved real-time management information systems, supporting improved decision making

Innovation of product, business models and operating models

- Distribution – digital augmentation of traditional distribution channels
- Marketing and sales – digital marketing; improved targeting with greater customer insights
- Fulfilment – digital fulfilment; virtual servicing and administration

In effect, McKinsey's report could be seen as reinforcing and updating Porter and Millar's ideas – which we considered in the previous chapter – about the impact IT can have on an organisation's value chain.

5.6.3 The value of digitisation to businesses

In our discussion of Big Data earlier, we mentioned how insights from Big Data could be used to adjust pricing in real time (in response to patterns of demand and inventory levels) but equally they could be used to forecast and manage operational capacity.

Similarly, while 'app' technology is typically focused on improving customer interactions, it could also be applied to a range of internal interactions – for example, procurement requests with suppliers.

Smarter and more complete application of digital investments can unlock 'trapped' value within an organisation, by improving information flows and reducing waste across it.

McKinsey's report *Finding your digital sweet spot* offers the following illustration of how 'digital' can benefit an organisation in different ways at an operational level.

A bank found that upgrading its digital channel led to a significant improvement in the richness and quality of its customer data which, in turn, increased the bank's marketing effectiveness. However, the improved customer data also drove better lending decisions by reducing risk, and digitisation also enabled customers to apply for a number of products online whereas previously the fulfilment process had been labour intensive.

5.6.4 Digitisation and 'the internet of things'

More generally, there are a number of ways which organisations can make use of digitisation and the information being created through the 'internet of things'.

Information and analytics

Monitoring behaviour – When products are embedded with sensors, companies can track the movements of the products and business models can be fine-tuned to take advantage of this detail. For example, insurance companies offer to install location sensors in customers' cars. These capture data on how well a car is driven, as well as where it travels. As a result, prices can be customised to the actual risk associated with operating the car, rather than being based on proxies such as a driver's age, gender or place of residence.

Similarly, **radio-frequency identification (RFID) tags** on products moving through the supply chain can be used to improve inventory management and to reduce working capital and logistics costs.

Situational awareness – Logistics managers for freight companies can use information about traffic patterns, weather conditions and vehicle locations to make adjustments to their vehicles' routes in order to reduce the risk of delays.

Decision analytics – Retail companies can monitor data from thousands of shoppers as they move through stores. Sensor readings and videos note how long shoppers spend at individual displays, while the stores also have information about what customers ultimately buy. Simulations based on the sensor readings, coupled with purchase records, can be used to increase revenues by optimising store layouts.

In relation to healthcare, sensors can be fitted to patients with heart problems and can monitor key indicators such as heart rate, rhythm, and blood pressure which could give medics early warning of conditions which could otherwise lead to unplanned hospitalisation and emergency treatment costs.

Automation and control

Process optimisation – Sensors on production lines provide data about temperature, pressure or ingredient mixtures (for example) to computers which analyse the data and then send signals back to the production line to adjust the process – for example, to reduce the temperature if it has become too high. Similarly, sensors can be used to adjust the position of an object as it moves down an assembly line to prevent the damage to the object, or the process jamming.

Resource consumption – 'Smart meters' can provide energy customers with visual displays showing their energy usage and the real-time costs of providing it. (Although customers may pay a fixed price per unit for their energy, the cost of producing energy varies substantially during a day.) Based on pricing and usage information, customers could then delay running energy-intensive processes from high-priced periods of peak energy demand to low-priced off-peak hours.

Section summary

Increases in the volume (amount), velocity and variety of data available to organisations present both opportunities and challenges. Data is only valuable to organisations if they can store and analyse it. However, provided they can do this, then Big Data can provide new insights which organisations can use to enhance their decision making.

6 E-business and e-commerce

Introduction

Very few businesses can afford to ignore the potential of the internet for driving forward strategy and activity at all levels. Internet usage can range from use of email at one extreme to the almost entirely virtual business model represented by audio and video downloads at the other.

E-commerce challenges traditional business models, makes global markets available to small businesses, transforms transparency of pricing, and offers new opportunities for market segmentation.

KEY TERM

E-COMMERCE is the use of electronic techniques, including the internet, to buy and sell products and services.

E-BUSINESS is the use of electronic techniques, including the internet, to transform key business processes.

The detail of this definition is important, because it highlights the distinction between e-commerce and e-business more generally. E-business includes not only online marketing and sales, but also the wider transformation of supply chain and channel management; manufacturing and inventory control; financial operations; and human resource management across an organisation in support of its business activities. As such, **e-business** could transform key business **processes** across value chains and supply chains. E-marketing could also be seen as an aspect of e-business, as could the development of new systems architectures (such as cloud-based storage). Crucially, though, **e-commerce** involves **transactions** – the sale of products and services to customers on the internet.

Exam skills

It is important to understand the distinction between 'e-business' and 'e-commerce', although the two terms are often confused. If an organisation is making use of electronic processes and internet technologies to support its operations, this is e-business. An electronic process only becomes **e-commerce** if there is a **financial transaction** involved.

6.1 Developing e-business capabilities

In order to implement a successful e-commerce strategy, organisations may need to reorganise their processes to make best use of the technology which is supporting the e-commerce system.

However, more generally, when looking at an organisation's capabilities in relation to e-business and e-commerce, we can identify four stages which organisations typically go through when introducing e-business:

- **Web presence** – The organisation has a website but, in effect, this just acts as a brochure on the internet. The organisation's web pages provide information about the organisation and its products or services, or might provide answers to frequently asked questions (FAQs).

- **Basic e-commerce** – The organisation makes purchases from its suppliers online and allows its customers to place orders and pay for them online. This enables the organisation to deal directly with suppliers and end-user consumers (and so could remove intermediaries from the supply chain) but there are no significant changes to the organisation's business model or its processes.

- **Integrated e-commerce** – The organisation uses electronic technology to develop closer relationships with its customers and suppliers (for example through real time processing and supply chain integration). The organisation uses the information it gathers about customers and their buying habits to target its marketing activities more precisely, and to improve customer relationship management.

- **E-business** – The organisation's operating systems are fully integrated, and require little human interaction. Electronic technology is fundamental to the organisation's business strategy.

Analysing its current position in terms of these four stages could help an organisation identify the areas it needs to develop in order to implement a successful e-business strategy.

Equally, analysing its current business activities could help it identify ways in which it could use electronic technologies and IT to change the way it carries out key activities in its value chain. Again, this could be seen as another application of Porter and Millar's ideas about IT and the value chain which we considered in the previous chapter.

6.2 The internet, e-business and the challenge to traditional business models

There are several features of e-business and the internet which make it radically different from traditional 'offline' business models.

(a)   It **challenges traditional business models** – because, for example, it enables product/service suppliers to interact directly with their customers, instead of using intermediaries (like high street retail shops, travel agents, insurance brokers, and conventional banks).

(b)   Although the internet is global in its operation, its benefits are not confined to large (or global) organisations. **Small companies** can move instantly into a global marketplace, either on their own initiative or as part of what is known as a 'consumer portal'.

(c)   It offers a **new economics of information** – because, with the internet, much information is free. People with internet access can view many of the world's major newspapers and periodicals without charge.

(d)   It supplies an almost incredible **level of speed** of communication, giving virtually instant access to organisations, plus the capacity to complete purchasing transactions within seconds.

(e)   **24-hour access**. Customers have access to a website 24 hours a day, 7 days a week. So an online 'shop' is never closed.

(f)   It has created **new and cheaper networks of communication** – between organisations and their customers (either individually or collectively), between customers themselves (through mutual support groups), and between organisations and their suppliers.

(g)   It stimulates the appearance of **new intermediaries** and the disappearance of some existing ones. Businesses are finding that they can cut out the middle man, with electronic banking, insurance, publishing and printing as primary examples.

CASE STUDY

A university can put its reading list on a website and students wishing to purchase any given book can click directly through to an online bookseller such as Amazon.com. The university gets a commission; the online bookseller gets increased business; the student gets a discount. Everyone benefits except the traditional bookshop.

(h)   It has led to **new business partnerships** through which small enterprises can gain access to customers on a scale which would have been viewed as impossible a few years ago.

(i)   Work is becoming **independent of location**. Clerical, administrative and knowledge work can be done at any location. This can reduce establishment and travelling costs, especially if people work from home, but the loss of personal interaction can affect **motivation** and **job satisfaction**.

(j)   The **nature of work** is changing since increased quantities of available data and more powerful methods of accessing and analysing it mean that greater attention can be paid to customising product offerings to more precisely defined target segments.

(k)   It promotes **transparent pricing** – because potential customers can readily compare prices not only from suppliers within any given country, but also from suppliers across the world.

(l)   It facilitates **personalised attention** – even if such attention is actually administered through impersonal, yet highly sophisticated IT systems and customer database manipulation.

(m)   It provides sophisticated **market segmentation** opportunities. Approaching such segments may be one of the few ways in which e-commerce entrepreneurs can create **competitive advantage**.

(n)   The web can either be a **separate** channel or a **complementary** channel to an existing 'offline' business.

(o)   A new phenomenon is emerging called **dynamic pricing**. Companies can rapidly change their prices to reflect the current state of demand and supply.

These new trends are creating **pressure** for companies. The main threat facing companies is that **prices will be driven down by consumers' ability to shop around**.

A key difference between e-commerce and 'traditional' commerce can also be seen from the 'role' of the consumer in marketing activity. In traditional marketing media, such as advertising and direct mail, the marketing message is initiated by the **supplier sending out a message** to potential customers. However, there is limited interaction with the customer. In electronic media, the **customer plays a much more active role**, for example visiting a website to find out information about a product or a supplier. There is a much greater degree of **interaction** between customer and supplier.

6.3 Varieties of e-commerce

E-commerce can be divided into four main categories.

B2B (business-to-business) – involves companies doing business with each other, for example when manufacturers sell to distributors and wholesalers sell to retailers. Pricing is based on quantity of order and is often negotiable.

B2C (business-to-consumer) – involves businesses selling to the general public, typically through catalogues with **shopping cart software**.

C2B (consumer-to-business) – a consumer posts their project with a set budget online and within hours companies review the consumer's requirements and bid on the project. The consumer reviews the bids and selects the company that will complete the project.

C2C (consumer-to-consumer) – an excellent example of this is found at eBay, where consumers sell their goods and services to other consumers. Another technology that has emerged to support C2C activities is that of the payment intermediary PayPal. Instead of purchasing items directly from an unknown, untrusted seller, the buyer can instead send the money to PayPal, which forwards it to the vendor's account.

The transaction alternatives between businesses and consumers are shown in the matrix below.

		Delivery by	
		Business	Consumer
Exchange initiated by	Business	B2B business models eg BusyTrade.com	B2C business models eg Amazon.com
	Consumer	C2B business models eg Priceline.com	C2C business models eg eBay.com

6.4 Marketplace channel structures

Channel structures are the means by which a manufacturer or selling organisation delivers products and services to its customers. The simplest channel structure is **direct**: the business deals directly with the customer without the assistance of any **intermediaries**. The more complex the channel structure, the more intermediaries (wholesalers and/or retailers) are used in the supply chain. Intermediaries offer a wide range of services and facilities: they include agents, traders, brokers, dealers, wholesalers/ distributors and providers of specialised information.

The main changes to channel structures facilitated through the internet include **disintermediation** (direct selling) and **reintermediation** (the creation of new intermediaries).

6.4.1 Disintermediation

Disintermediation is the removal of intermediaries in a supply chain that formerly linked a company to its customers. Instead of going through traditional distribution channels, with intermediaries such as a distributor, wholesaler, broker or agent, companies may now deal with every customer directly via the internet.

For example, in the hospitality industry, hotels have taken distribution back into their own hands by allowing guests to make bookings online – directly through the hotels' websites – rather than having to book through travel agents.

6.4.2 Reintermediation

Reintermediation is the establishment of new intermediary roles for traditional intermediaries that were disintermediated. In some cases, a new element of a supply chain simply replaces a single displaced element, such as Amazon.com replacing retailers. In other cases, a reintermediating entity replaces multiple supply chain elements. These new intermediaries do one of two things.

(a) Provide customers with **new**, **important value-added services** not provided in the new direct customer-supplier relationship. An example is Kelkoo which is a shopping/price comparison search engine.

Price comparison sites also increase **price transparency**, by allowing customers to compare the price of products or services offered by a range of providers.

For example, in the field of financial services, new intermediaries enable prospective customers to compare the interest rates and prices charged by different organisations for pensions, mortgages and other financial products. This means that the delivering companies are **losing control of the marketing** of their services, and there is a **downward pressure on prices**, especially for services which can legitimately be seen as mere commodities (eg house and contents insurance).

(b) Provide customers with **more efficient means** of transacting business.

The ever-increasing number of 'hubs', 'portals', 'aggregators', 'clearing houses' and 'exchanges' shows that entirely new ways of doing business are being created.

6.4.3 New types of intermediary

Search engines and directories – search engines, such as Google, provide search facilities based on data generated by software engines, that search the web. Directories such as Yahoo provide a general index of a large variety of different sites.

Search agents (Search bots) gather material from other sites. For example Shopbot searches across online shops to find the cheapest deals for customers.

Portals provide a gateway to the web and may also offer **signposting**, selected **links** and other services to attract users. Examples of web portals include Google, MSN and Yahoo.

'E-tailers' or consumer shopping sites such as Amazon. Since starting as simply a bookshop on the web, it has added a variety of products and types of services. By contrast, Tesco is an offline retailer which is offering web-based order and delivery services.

Virtual resellers are intermediaries that exist to sell to consumers. They are able to obtain products directly from manufacturers, which may hesitate to go directly to consumers for fear of **alienating retailers** upon which they still largely depend.

Forums, **fan clubs**, and **user groups** can play a large role in facilitating customer-producer feedback and supporting market research.

Financial intermediaries (eg PayPal). Any form of e-commerce will require some means of making or authorising payments from buyer to seller, and firms such as PayPal facilitate that payment.

6.5 Disadvantages of e-commerce

E-commerce presents a range of **new management and organisational issues** compared with 'traditional' business.

E-commerce involves an unusual mix of people – security, web technology, designers, marketing people – and this can be very difficult to manage. The e-business needs supervision by expensive specialists.

In spite of phenomenal growth the market is still fuzzy and undefined. Many e-businesses have only recently reported making any **profit**, the best-known example being **Amazon.com**, the internet bookseller.

Unless the e-business is one started completely from scratch, any new technology installed will **need to link up with existing business systems**, which could potentially take years of programming. Underestimating the time and effort involved is a common obstacle.

BPP
LEARNING MEDIA

The international availability of a website means that the **laws of all countries** that transactions may be conducted from have to be considered. The legal issues surrounding e-commerce are complex and still developing.

6.6 The internet in context

Commentators highlight so-called 'megatrends' which, coupled with the internet, are changing the face of businesses.

(a)   New **distribution channels**, revolutionising sales and brand management. In this respect, we can suggest that e-commerce may be increasing the **rivalry** between competitors in an industry.

(b)   The continued **shift of power** towards the consumer. For example, the ability to compare prices directly between different online retailers increases the **bargaining power of customers**.

(c)   **Growing competition** locally, nationally, internationally and globally. The internet removes some of the **barriers to entry** to an industry. For example, a 'shop' no longer has to incur overheads such as rent and rates because it can be set up online.

(d)   An acceleration in the **pace of business**, and linked to this an increased automation of business transactions and workflows.

(e)   The **transformation of companies** into 'extended enterprises' involving 'virtual teams of business, customer and supplier' working in collaborative partnerships.

(f)   **Reduced importance of location**. The availability of internet connections is making the physical location where people work less important.

(g)   A re-evaluation of how companies, their partners and competitors **add value** not only to themselves but in the wider environmental and social setting.

(h)   Recognition of '**knowledge**' as a strategic asset.

6.6.1 E-commerce strategy

Most observers and experts agree that a successful strategy for e-commerce cannot simply be bolted onto existing processes, systems, delivery routes and business models. Instead, management groups have, in effect, to start again, by asking themselves such fundamental questions as:

- What do customers want to buy from us?
- What business should we be in?
- What kind of partners might we need?
- What categories of customer do we want to attract and retain?

In turn, organisations can visualise the necessary changes at three interconnected levels.

Level 1   The simple **introduction of new technology** to connect electronically with employees, customers and suppliers (eg through an intranet, extranet or website).

Level 2   **Reorganisation** of the workforce, processes, systems and strategy – in order to make best use of the new technology.

Level 3   **Repositioning** of the organisation to fit it into the emerging e-economy.

So far, very few companies have gone beyond levels (1) and (2). Instead, pure internet businesses such as Amazon.com and eBay have emerged from these new rules: unburdened by physical assets, their competitive advantage lies in **knowledge management** and **customer relationships**.

Conventional thinking says that a company should pay no more to bring in a customer than the net present value of the stream of profits that the customer will subsequently generate. Yet in the e-commerce

context, investors have often rewarded companies for customer acquisition without asking any questions about how quickly those customers may disappear. The evidence suggests that many 'dot.com' enterprises remain unable to achieve sustained profitability or, indeed, any profitability at all.

6.7 Virtual arrangements

Network technologies are used by organisations to integrate workers across sites and working at home. And developments in broadband, particularly improved capacity and better data security, have improved the ability to communicate. Broadband telecommunications systems allow 'remote' computer users to communicate with each other, and to send and receive information.

6.7.1 Virtual organisations

KEY TERM

A VIRTUAL ORGANISATION is a temporary or permanent collection of geographically dispersed individuals, groups, organisational units (which may or may not belong to the same organisation) or entire organisations that depend on electronic linking in order to complete the production process.

The idea of a **virtual organisation** has attracted considerable attention as the usefulness of IT for communication and control has been exploited. The essence of the virtual organisation is the electronic linking of spatially dispersed components.

While there is some disagreement among academics as to a precise definition of the virtual organisation, a consensus exists with regard to **geographical dispersion** and the centrality of **information technology** to the production process. Many also agree that the virtual organisation has a temporary character. Other characteristics are a **flexible structure** and a **collaborative culture**.

Virtual organisations use networks to link people, assets and ideas, enabling a virtual organisation to ally with other organisations to create and distribute products and services without being limited by traditional organisational boundaries or physical locations. In a virtual network, one organisation can use the capabilities of another without being physically tied to that organisation.

The virtual organisation model is useful when a company finds it is cheaper to acquire products, services or capabilities from an external vendor, or when it needs to move quickly to exploit new market opportunities but lacks the time and/or resources to respond to the opportunities on its own.

However, an organisation is not 'virtual' simply because it uses IT extensively and has multiple locations but, nonetheless, the ability to share information between members of a virtual organisation is likely to be critical to its operation.

CASE STUDY

Case Study: Li & Fung

A number of fashion companies use the Hong Kong based company Li & Fung to manage the production and shipment of their garments. Li & Fung handles product development, raw material sourcing, production planning, quality assurance and shipping. However, Li & Fung does not own any fabric, factories, or machines, and it outsources all of its work to a network of more than 7,500 suppliers in over 30 countries around the world.

Customers place orders to Li & Fung over its private extranet. Li & Fung then sends instructions to appropriate raw material suppliers and factories where the clothing is produced.

Li & Fung's extranet tracks the entire production process for each order.

Working as a virtual company allows Li & Fung to remain flexible and adaptable so that it can design and produce the products ordered by its customers at short notice to keep pace with rapidly changing fashion trends.

CASE STUDY

Case Study: Amazon

Amazon.com is another example which is often cited as a virtual organisation.

Customers come to the Amazon website via Internet Service Providers (ISPs), often from links on other (affiliate) websites. Although Amazon processes the customers' orders, it does not hold much inventory itself. If a customer orders a book through Amazon it is likely the book will be despatched from the publisher's warehouse, and the delivery will be handled by a logistics or mail company. Nonetheless, the customer feels they are dealing with one organisation (Amazon) and not many different companies.

However, for this relationship to work, Amazon needs information from its partners – for example, it needs to know inventory availability and an estimate of delivery times so that it can provide this information for the customer when they make their order. Equally, Amazon needs to be confident that its partners will deliver the service they have agreed to provide (for example, if a partner says inventory will be available in 48 hours, then it needs to be available in 48 hours).

6.8 Building an 'e-commerce strategy'

A **strategy for e-commerce**, while not necessarily constituting the organisation's overall strategy, is likely to have wide implications and to involve and affect more than one function or department within the organisation. It should, therefore, be considered at the highest level of management and it should conform to the standard criteria for strategic choice: **suitability, acceptability** and **feasibility**.

6.8.1 Suitability

There are a few large organisations, such as Amazon, whose overall strategy is based on e-commerce. However, for most companies, e-commerce will be a **supplement to more traditional operations**, with the website forming a supplementary medium for communication and sales. It is important that the e-commerce strategy supports the overall strategy. One way of approaching this would be to consider the **extended marketing mix** and the need for **balance, consistency** and **mutual support** between the elements.

A very simple example would be to consider the question of whether to confine the website to an essentially communications role, or to incorporate a fully featured online shopping facility. A specialist chain store dealing in, say, camping and outdoor equipment would expect to expand its market if it developed online shopping. On the other hand, a manufacturer of specialist luxury goods, such as the most expensive fountain pens, would probably have a policy of distributing through carefully selected retailers. It is unlikely that online shopping would appeal to the target market segment: they would probably enjoy the shopping experience and would want to try the products before they bought them.

6.8.2 Acceptability

The e-commerce strategy must be **acceptable to important stakeholders**. Distributors are particularly important here. Pursuing our luxury goods example we would expect that retailers chosen for their attractive premises, skilled and attentive staff and air of luxury would be unhappy to find their position usurped by a website.

6.8.3 Feasibility

Feasibility is a matter of **resources**. The fundamental resource is cash, but the availability of the **skilled labour** needed to establish and administer a website will be crucial to the e-commerce strategy. It may be appropriate to employ **specialist consultants** for these purposes.

Under this heading, we might identify the following points for consideration.

(a)   The first thing to do is to try to establish precise **objectives** for the new strategy element. It may not be possible to do this conclusively, and consideration of objectives may have to proceed alongside the processes outlined below, all passing through several iterations.

(b)   An estimate and analysis of **costs** and **benefits** should be undertaken. This should cover all the possible options, such as what services are to be offered, whether a full catalogue is to be put online, whether internet selling is envisaged, whether a search function is required and so on.

(c)   A detailed **budget** should be prepared, probably using estimates from the cost and benefit analysis. Where internet selling is to be offered, pricing policy must be established: there is a theory that customers expect goods and services to be discounted when sold online, since they are aware that administrative costs are likely to be lower than in more traditional forms of distribution.

(d)   **Specific technical requirements**

- Web hosting software
- Server computers (more than one system to provide redundancy)

6.8.4 Launch

It may be appropriate to launch the website to a restricted number of potential customers in order to ensure that its functionality is satisfactory. This might be done on a regional basis, with promotion through appropriate press and TV channels. When a national launch is approved, it will be necessary to promote the website nationally and to ensure that the web address is included in all corporate stationery and display material.

6.8.5 E-commerce and e-marketing

We look at marketing and e-marketing (digital marketing) in more detail in the next chapter, but it is important to be aware of the links between e-commerce and e-marketing.

Just as a marketing strategy needs to support the business strategy for a 'traditional' business model, so an organisation's marketing strategy needs to support its e-commerce strategy.

However, the interactive nature of e-commerce means that e-marketing has a number of characteristics which differentiate it from traditional marketing.

These can be summarised as **6 I's**:

- **Independence of location** – global communications potentially allow access to markets that couldn't be reached before

- **Industry structure** – redesigning business processes; redrawing market segments

- **Integration** – sharing customer feedback and customer requirements throughout the whole business

- **Interactive** – customers can seek information and initiate dialogue rather than receiving marketing information

- **Individualisation** – communications can be tailored to specific customers, rather than sending one standard message to everyone

- **Intelligence** – information gathered about customer perceptions of products and services can be used to help shape marketing strategy

Exam skills

Although an organisation can gain a number of benefits from having a website, not all websites have the same levels of functionality, or user friendliness.

For example, is a website which simply allows customers to look at a range of products likely to have as much business benefit as one which also allows customers to make orders online?

If you are asked to advise how an organisation could benefit from having a website, or how it could benefit from improving its website, try to think of practical issues about the functionality of the website. However, also consider any issues it would need to address in making the improvements; for example, the potential security issues involved in taking online transactions.

Also, the design of the website itself could affect its effectiveness. Is it easy for users to navigate or search? Does it make it easy for users to contact the organisation (eg by email or phone)? What information does the website provide users (eg Frequently Asked Questions)? Does the website have any animations which bring its products and services to life? Do all users get the same information, or is there a 'members' section which can only be accessed via a username and password? Are viewers invited to provide an email address and then receive e-newsletters from the organisation? Can the website be viewed in different languages or is it restricted to one language?

Section summary

The **internet and e-commerce** allow organisations to challenge traditional business models, and have changed the relationship between vendors and customers. However, a business's e-commerce strategy needs to be consistent with its overall business strategy.

7 Web 2.0 technologies and business strategy

Introduction

Technologies known collectively as Web 2.0 have spread rapidly among consumers in recent years. As the popularity of Web 2.0 has grown, companies have noted the way consumers have engaged with the technologies, and have realised this could have important business implications – particularly in relation to marketing and new product development strategies.

Web 2.0 technologies can provide firms with opportunities in a range of activities – from market research, marketing, collaboration, innovation and design.

The phrase 'Web 2.0' has become synonymous with a new generation of web technologies and softwares and, possibly more importantly, their impact on how web users interact with content, applications and each other. Web 2.0 allows people across the world to connect with each other 24 hours a day, 365 days a year.

7.1 User experience and participation

Web 2.0 allows internet users (and potential customers for businesses) to no longer simply be recipients of information, but to participate in the creation, sharing and evaluation of content. In other words, users can actively take part in 'many to many' communications. A crucial aspect of Web 2.0 is that it focuses on **user experience** and **participation**.

Again this is important for businesses; Web 2.0 allows firms of all sizes to engage with customers, staff and suppliers in new ways. In particular, it allows firms to have a more customer-focused approach to new product development – because customers can actually be involved in the design of the new products.

Web 2.0 has highlighted the significance of **dynamic social interactions** in the environment, rather than considering business, and business transactions, as a set of static processes.

We have already identified the **importance of knowledge** to businesses, and Web 2.0 plays an important role in this 'knowledge economy' through supporting creativity, **collaboration**, **knowledge sharing**, and ultimately innovation.

The idea of **collaboration** is also very important when considering how Web 2.0 technologies could affect business strategies. The potential impact could be huge if organisations find it becomes as efficient to do business through collaborating **outside** the organisation's structure, rather than doing business within the organisation's own structure.

In effect, collaboration is an extension of the idea of **outsourcing**. Outsourcing provides for specific processes to be outsourced **to** specific companies, whereas in collaboration anybody can contribute to the discussion in progress. (The collaborative online encyclopaedia – Wikipedia – is probably the best known illustration of this.)

We will now consider some of the key aspects of Web 2.0.

Web-based communities

Probably the most popular aspect of Web 2.0 has been social networking sites, such as Facebook, which now has more than 500 million unique visitors.

Web-based communities are enhanced by:

- **Social networking** – Social networks (such as Facebook and MySpace) allow users to make contact with other users. As well as mass-market social networks, a number of smaller, more focused **niche social networks** have also begun to emerge. The value of these sites is that they allow users to connect with others with whom they share a common interest. For example, LinkedIn is a network for businesspeople looking to build business contacts, and also to advertise their skills and experience to potential employers or clients.

- **Blogs** – Blogs provide an easy way for users to publish their own content, and are usually text based. Users can publish audio and visual content as podcasts, and the growth of sites such as YouTube illustrates how popular podcasts have become.

  The microblogging site Twitter provides a platform for people who want to publish very short blogs – of up to 140 characters each.

- **Wikis** – Wikis allow user groups to collaborate in contributing and editing content. Wikipedia, the collaborative online encyclopaedia, is the best-known example of this.

- **Instant messaging** – This allows real-time conversations between two or more participants using pop-up dialogue boxes (eg instant messaging is now available in Skype).

These web-based communities mean that web **users are now participants in the web experience** rather than simply being observers. Moreover, these communities allow people to get to know each other and to interact, regardless of their physical, geographical location.

A key aspect behind Web 2.0 is **open source software**. Open source software such as Linux (the software which Google runs on) is free to use. Because open source services are free, they can reach a far greater number of people than services which users have to pay for.

7.2 Socialisation of knowledge sharing

Web 2.0 technologies encourage the socialisation of knowledge sharing through:

- **Tagging of information** – A tag is a keyword assigned by a user to describe a piece of information (such as a file, an image, or an internet bookmark). Tagging is a key feature of many Web 2.0

applications and is commonly used on file storing and file sharing sites. Once a file has been tagged, the tag allows it to be found again when a relevant search enquiry is made.

Tags are examples of **metadata**, which is 'data about other data'. The title, author and publication date of a book are examples of metadata about a book, and this data could help a user find the book they are looking for.

Tagging also highlights an important point which businesses need to consider. The new technologies mean that the amount of information on the internet is rising constantly. However, information is no use if it can't be found. Search engine optimisation is therefore increasingly important for businesses – making sure the information on the business's website is 'findable' and relevant.

- **Mashups** – A mashup is a web publication that combines data from more than one source into a singe web page. For example, a restaurant review website could take the location details of all the local restaurants in an area and map them onto a single Google map page.

- **Feedback** on sources of information.

- **Promoting collective intelligence** – Collective intelligence refers to both structured and unstructured group collaboration. It describes the way people's opinions or behaviours can be aggregated so that others can learn from their collective decision making.

    The online auction site eBay uses collective intelligence to let potential buyers see how efficient and trustworthy vendors are. Equally, Amazon and a number of online sites include product reviews allowing people who have purchased an item to comment on the item and rate its performance.

    Amazon also uses collective intelligence to make product recommendations based on purchasing patterns. When a user selects an item to buy, they are presented with a list of other items purchased by people who have already bought the current selection, which may encourage the user to make follow-up purchases.

User-generated content (UGC): Websites can now have sections of content created by their readers. One of the main ideas behind Web 2.0 technologies is that users can generate the content of sites themselves, and the technologies allow users to create, capture and share information across the web. The video streaming website YouTube and the image and video hosting website Flickr are popular examples of content sharing sites.

Consumer-generated content (CGC): Websites can now contain shared feedback from consumers; for example, product reviews. This has important implications for businesses, because it means customers can communicate with other (potential) customers very easily. If a customer receives poor customer service, they can now tell everyone else about it, which could damage the business's reputation, and lead to a decline in sales.

The most widely known example of CGC is the user reviews developed by Amazon noted above. Many customers read users' product reviews when considering prospective purchases.

In this respect, an important feature of Web 2.0 technologies is that they use **open standards** to enable connectivity between applications.

(Open standards mean that the rights normally reserved for copyright holders are provided in the public domain. Open standards are publicly available, and are developed, approved and maintained via a collaborative and consumer-driven process. Consequently users can share technologies with each other.)

Collaboration, based on shared knowledge, can be assisted by:

- Virtual team management.

- File sharing.

- Collaborative working – both internally and with partners, suppliers and customers. This improves the ability to customise and integrate applications.

7.2.1 Enterprise 2.0

Enterprise 2.0 technology enables businesses to work across the web, regardless of location. This increases the use of virtual teams (involving people inside and outside a business) to identify and exploit new business opportunities.

Enterprise resource planning (ERP) software was an important development in business technologies, allowing business systems to be integrated and automated, but a potential danger with ERP software is that it can understate the role that people still have to play in business. Even when systems are automated, people are still required to identify new opportunities for growth, or to intervene when the systems flag up problems.

In an increasingly knowledge-based society, people are critical to the development, evolution, and overall success of a business. Enterprise 2.0 acknowledges this, and recognises that **businesses need people**, **processes** and **technology** all working together to make them successful.

7.3 Evolution of web services

Although it would be wrong to think of Web 2.0 as simply being a software upgrade from some kind of 'Web 1.0', it is useful to look at the evolution of Web 2.0 web functionalities and services compared with the first generation equivalents.

Web 2.0	Web 1.0 (predecessor)
Wikipedia (collaborative encyclopaedia)	Britannica Online (online version of published encyclopaedia)
Content published through wikis (participative)	Content managed through content management systems (published)
Participation (many to many knowledge sharing)	Publishing (one to many knowledge dissemination)
Syndication (sharing content across sites)	Stickiness (keeping people on your site)
Cost per click advertising (revenues charged on the basis of content being actively accessed)	Page views (advertising revenues being charged on the basis of content displayed)
Web services (real connectivity between applications)	Screen scraping (accessing data being displayed by another IT application)
Tagging	Directories
Napster (peer to peer file sharing)	Mp3.com (online music store)
Flickr (photo sharing site)	Ofoto (photo repository site)
Blogging/Twitter	Personal websites

7.4 Applications of Web 2.0 for business

In recent years, we have seen the emergence of a number of new online companies. Most are probably run by young entrepreneurs for whom technology will play a key role in their business strategy.

(a)   The business can find partners, collaborators, customers and suppliers through social networks and blogs.

(b)   It can use blogs, and social networks for publicity and to market itself, and it can encourage customers to leave feedback on its site (customer generate content).

(c)   It can manage the development, creation and delivery of its products through virtual workspaces and wikis that support collaboration, innovation and the management of workflow. The collaborative nature of Web 2.0 enables external third parties to participate in product development.

(d)   It can get market intelligence through blogs and online reference sites. It can also get feedback on how customers perceive its own products or services.

Staff – Importantly also, if the businesses want to attract and retain young, dynamic employees they will need to provide them with tools they are familiar with, and offer a work environment that fits with their lifestyle.

Marketing – Web 2.0 can also have significant implications for marketing approaches. Teenagers and young adults can be an important demographic for many businesses, and sites such as Facebook and Twitter play an important part in their lives. In this way, running campaigns through popular social networking sites can offer businesses a way of engaging with these users, allowing them to access a demographic which has traditionally been difficult to reach. Marketers can also use pre-existing social networks as a mechanism for promoting **viral marketing** campaigns. In these, a company will generate an initial marketing message, but people then pass it along to their friends and contacts through their social networks.

However, if companies do engage in social networking or publish blogs they need to monitor how these are perceived by the online communities. **Brand management** remains very important – perhaps even more so because of the way users can publish negative feedback on poorly designed or presented content.

Conversely, though, favourable customer review comments on products or services can be very useful PR material for an organisation.

 We will examine the value of the internet in a marketing context – in particular, social media marketing – in more detail in the next chapter.

Ethical and legal implications of Web 2.0

While Web 2.0 technologies could offer businesses a number of advantages, it is important that they are managed responsibly.

Security considerations – The increased use of web-based interfaces makes businesses vulnerable to malicious attacks on their internet applications. There have been a number of 'phishing' scams where hackers have tried to obtain financial information about customers and users.

Consequently, businesses need to ensure they have real-time sufficient security systems in place to detect any suspicious activities, and thereby to protect their customers.

Data protection – When handling personal data, businesses must ensure data is only used for the purpose it was provided. Data must be fairly and lawfully processed, and data requests must be relevant and not excessive. If companies hold data, they are responsible for ensuring it is accurate, and kept up to date. Data must not be kept for longer than is necessary, and it must be kept secure.

Copyright – Web 2.0 technologies make it much easier for staff to publish material on the internet. However, businesses need to ensure that they do not publish material if they do not have permission to do so, and if they do not credit the copyright holder. This applies to videos, images, pictures and music as well as text.

Employment policies – Businesses will need to ensure their HR policies are up to date and deal with flexible working arrangements, email use, privacy, use of social networking sites during office hours etc.

Staff also need to recognise that they are in a **position of trust**. For example, staff dealing with personal details have a duty to keep them confidential. Equally, they must not post any libellous or inappropriate content on their company's website. To this end, anonymous postings should be prohibited.

However, it appears that a number of businesses are aware of the legal and HR issues relevant to Web 2.0 technologies. In interviews with a number of business executives, McKinsey & Company found that 'participatory initiatives' had been stalled by legal and HR concerns. These risks differ markedly from previous technology adoptions, where the chief downsides were perceived as high costs and poor execution.

7.5 Web 2.0 and emergent strategies

The nature of Web 2.0 technologies means that they encourage participation and a bottom-up approach. In the context of business strategy, this is very different to the prescriptive, top-down approach suggested by the rational model.

By allowing web users to provide feedback and share ideas, Web 2.0 is encouraging a model in which people outside an organisation can have an impact on that organisation's strategy.

Moreover, the internet becomes, in effect, a research tool, where companies can find out customers' opinions about products and services. Web 2.0 allows businesses to aggregate opinions from many different individuals to guide idea generation and strategic decision making.

In this way, customer networks and social interaction have become much more important in marketing.

Section summary

Web 2.0 technologies allow businesses new ways of interacting with customers, suppliers and staff. What distinguishes Web 2.0 technologies from previous technologies is the degree of participation they require to be effective. Web 2.0 technologies are truly interactive and rely on users to participate in the creation and sharing of ideas, rather than simply being recipients of information.

Our references to e-commerce and Web 2.0 technologies have highlighted how important technologies are to contemporary businesses. In this context, therefore, we need to acknowledge the role that IT departments play in maintaining businesses' IT infrastructures, but we also need to consider the issue of how the IT departments themselves are structured.

8 The IT department

Introduction

The main choice about organising the IT specialists is whether they should be centralised or decentralised. There is a tension between **control** and **relevance to local conditions**. An **information centre** is an important aspect of the IT department, providing rapid support to users together with an element of supervision.

KEY TERMS

A CENTRALISED IS/IT department involves all IS/IT staff and functions being based at a single central location, such as head office.

A DECENTRALISED IS/IT department involves IS/IT staff and functions being spread out throughout the organisation.

There is no single 'best' structure for an IS/IT department – an organisation should consider its IS/IT requirements and the merits of each structure.

8.1 Centralisation

Advantages of a centralised IS/IT department:

(a) Assuming centralised processing is used, there is only one set of files so everyone uses the same data and information.

(b) It gives better security/control over data and files so it is easier to enforce standards.

(c) Head office is in a better position to know what is going on.

(d) There may be economies of scale available in purchasing computer equipment and supplies.

(e) Computer staff are in a single location, more expert staff are likely to be employed and career paths may be more clearly defined.

Disadvantages of a centralised IS/IT department:

(a) Local offices might have to wait for IS/IT services and assistance.
(b) Reliance on head office, so local offices are less self-sufficient.
(c) A system fault at head office will impact across the organisation.

Centralisation is appropriate in a coherent integrated organisation where all locations or departments are doing much the same thing and there is no equivalent for specialised systems. A chain of supermarkets would be a good example. This is sometimes called the 'star organisations' approach.

A degree of decentralisation or **partial distribution** may be appropriate where departments or sites are doing similar things but with different data: there can be commonality of systems but local processing may be appropriate. An example would be a manufacturer operating on several sites and using the same production control system at each installation: different products, manufacturing processes and inventory levels might make distributed systems appropriate.

8.2 Decentralisation

Advantages of a decentralised IS/IT department:

(a) Each office can introduce an information system specially **tailored** for its individual needs so local changes in business requirements can be taken into account.

(b) Each office is more self-sufficient.

(c) Offices are likely to have quicker access to IS/IT support/advice.

(d) A decentralised structure is more likely to facilitate accurate IS/IT cost/overhead allocations.

Disadvantages of a decentralised IS/IT department:

(a) Control may be more difficult – different and uncoordinated information systems may be introduced.

(b) Self-sufficiency may encourage a lack of co-ordination between departments.

(c) Increased risk of data duplication, with different offices holding the same data on their own separate files.

Full decentralisation may be seen in a network organisation, especially where there are incompatible legacy systems. There is unlikely to be any central IT management function, though there will probably be co-ordination by agreement. Information sharing and integration will be a priority, but may be difficult to achieve.

8.3 The information centre

KEY TERM

An INFORMATION CENTRE (IC) is a small unit of staff with a good technical awareness of computer systems, whose task is to provide a support function to computer users within the organisation.

ICs, sometimes referred to as **support centres**, are particularly useful in organisations which use distributed systems and so are likely to have hardware, data and software scattered throughout the organisation.

8.3.1 Help

An IC usually offers a **help desk** to solve IT problems. Help may be via the telephone, email, through a searchable knowledge base or in person. **Remote diagnostic software** may be used which enables staff in the IC to take control of a computer and sort out the problem without leaving their desk. The help desk needs sufficient staff and technical expertise to respond quickly and effectively to requests for help. IC staff should also maintain good relationships with hardware and software suppliers to ensure their maintenance staff are quickly on site when needed.

8.3.2 Problem solving

The IC will maintain a **record of problems** and identify those that occur most often. If the problem is that users do not know how to use the system, training is provided. Training applications often contain analysis software, drawing attention to trainee progress and common problems. This information enables the IC to identify and address specific training needs more closely. If the problem is with the system itself, a solution is found, either by modifying the system or by investment in new hardware or software.

8.3.3 Improvements

The IC may also be required to consider the viability of suggestions for improving the system, and to bring these improvements into effect.

8.3.4 Standards

The IC is also likely to be responsible for setting, and encouraging users to conform to, common **standards**.

(a)   Hardware standards ensure that all of the equipment used in the organisation is compatible and can be put into use in different departments as needed.

(b)   Software standards ensure that information generated by one department can easily be shared with and worked upon by other departments.

(c)   Programming standards ensure that applications developed by individual end-users (for example complex spreadsheet macros) follow best practice and are easy to modify.

(d)   Data processing standards ensure that certain conventions such as the format of file names are followed throughout the organisation. This facilitates sharing, storage and retrieval of information.

8.3.5 Security

The IC may help to preserve the security of data in various ways.

(a)   It may develop utility programs and procedures to ensure that back-ups are made at regular intervals.

(b)   The IC may help to preserve the company's systems from attack by computer viruses, for instance by ensuring that the latest versions of anti-virus software are available to all users, by reminding users regularly about the dangers of viruses, and by setting up and maintaining 'firewalls', which deny access to sensitive parts of the company's systems.

8.3.6 End-user applications development

An IC can help applications development by providing technical guidance to end-user developers and to encourage comprehensible and well-documented programs. Understandable programs can be maintained or modified more easily. Documentation provides a means of teaching others how the programs work. These efforts can greatly extend the usefulness and life of the programs that are developed.

8.4 Outsourcing IT/IS services

KEY TERM

OUTSOURCING is the contracting out of specified operations or services to an external vendor.

The arrangement varies according to the circumstances of both organisations.

Outsourcing arrangement			
Feature	Timeshare	Service	Facilities Management (FM)
What is it?	Access to an external processing system on a time-used basis	Focus on specific function, eg payroll	An outside agency manages the organisation's IS/IT facilities. The client retains equipment but all services provided by FM company
Management responsibility	Mostly retained	Some retained	Very little retained
Focus	Operational	A function	Strategic
Timescale	Short term	Medium term	Long term
Justification	Cost savings	More efficient	Access to expertise; better service; management can focus on core business activities

Managing such arrangements involves deciding **what** will be outsourced, choosing a supplier and the supplier **relationship**.

8.4.1 How to determine what will be outsourced

(a)   What is the system's **strategic importance**? A third-party IT specialist cannot be expected to possess specific business knowledge.

(b)   Functions with only **limited interfaces** are most easily outsourced, eg payroll.

(c)   Do we know enough about the system to manage the arrangement?

(d)   Are our requirements likely to **change**?

The arrangement is incorporated in a contract sometimes referred to as the **Service Level Contract** (SLC) or **Service Level Agreement** (SLA).

Element	Comment
Service level	Minimum levels of service with penalties, for example: • Response time to requests for assistance/information • System 'uptime' percentage • Deadlines for performing relevant tasks
Exit route	Arrangements for an exit route, transfer to another supplier or move back in-house.
Timescale	When does the contract expire? Is the timescale suitable for the organisation's needs or should it be renegotiated?

Element	Comment
Software ownership	This covers software licensing, security and copyright (if new software is to be developed).
Dependencies	If related services are outsourced, the level of service quality agreed should group these services together.
Employment issues	If the organisation's IT staff move to the third party, employer responsibilities must be specified clearly.

8.4.2 Advantages of outsourcing arrangements

(a) Outsourcing can remove uncertainty about **cost**, as there is often a long-term contract where services are specified in advance for a **fixed price**.

(b) Long-term contracts (maybe up to ten years) encourage **planning** for the future.

(c) Outsourcing can bring the benefits of **economies of scale**. For example, an IT company's research into new software may benefit several of its clients.

(d) A specialist organisation is able to **retain skills and knowledge**. Many organisations' IT departments are too small to develop good people.

(e) New skills and knowledge become available. A specialist company can **share** staff with **specific expertise** between several clients.

(f) **Flexibility**. Resources may be scaled up or down depending upon demand.

8.4.3 Disadvantages of outsourcing arrangements

(a) Information and its provision is **an inherent part of business and management**. If the information system is outsourced, the organisation will have less control over the system. If controls are subsequently relaxed, or the quality of information falls, this could damage the organisation's competitive position.

(b) Information strategy can be used to gain **competitive advantage**. Opportunities may be missed if a third party is handling IS services.

(c) The organisation will lose the **knowledge of key staff**, which again may weaken its competitive position.

(d) An organisation may have highly **confidential information** and to let outsiders handle it could be seen as **risky** in commercial and/or legal terms.

(e) The organisation is vulnerable if the outsourced company stops trading. For example, if an organisation outsources some of its software systems, and then the software provider goes bankrupt, the organisation could lose important information (such as software codes and updates).

(f) An organisation may find itself **locked in** to an unsatisfactory contract.

Section summary

The growth of e-commerce highlights the importance of businesses' IT systems being well maintained. However, businesses face a number of questions about how their IT departments should be structured: in particular, whether they should be centralised or decentralised, and whether IT services should be retained in-house or outsourced.

Chapter Summary

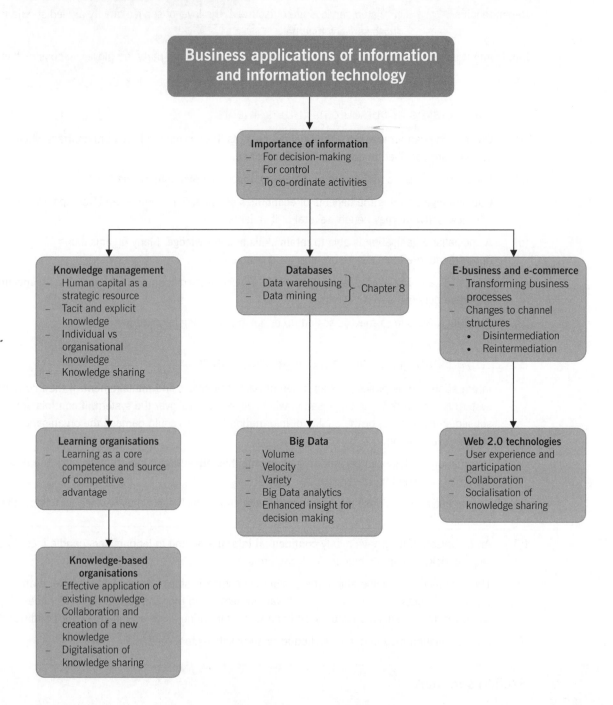

Business applications of information and information technology

Importance of information
- For decision-making
- For control
- To co-ordinate activities

Knowledge management
- Human capital as a strategic resource
- Tacit and explicit knowledge
- Individual vs organisational knowledge
- Knowledge sharing

Databases
- Data warehousing
- Data mining
} Chapter 8

E-business and e-commerce
- Transforming business processes
- Changes to channel structures
  - Disintermediation
  - Reintermediation

Learning organisations
- Learning as a core competence and source of competitive advantage

Big Data
- Volume
- Velocity
- Variety
- Big Data analytics
- Enhanced insight for decision making

Web 2.0 technologies
- User experience and participation
- Collaboration
- Socialisation of knowledge sharing

Knowledge-based organisations
- Effective application of existing knowledge
- Collaboration and creation of a new knowledge
- Digitalisation of knowledge sharing

Quick Quiz

1   What is the difference between data and information?

2   The process by which individuals share and transmit knowledge (represented as moving **from** tacit **to** tacit in Nonaka and Takeuchi's matrix) is known as:

   A   Combination
   B   Externalisation
   C   Internalisation
   Ⓓ   Socialisation

3   Which of the following should be characteristics of a learning organisation?

   (i)   Knowledge is transferred quickly and efficiently throughout the organisation.

   (ii)   People are encouraged to experiment with new approaches, even if they prove to be unsuccessful.

   (iii)   Learning and development is regarded as a cross-departmental responsibility.

   A   (i) and (ii)
   B   (i) and (iii)
   C   (ii) and (iii)
   Ⓓ   (i), (ii) and (iii)

4   What are the 'V' characteristics which are often used to define Big Data? *volume, variety, velocity*

5   Which one of the following is not associated with Web 2.0 technologies?

   A   Wikipedia
   B   Tagging
   Ⓒ   Screen scraping
   D   Blogging

Answers to Quick Quiz

1   Information is data that is organised in some useful way.

2   D   Socialisation

Socialisation is the informal process by which individuals share and transmit their tacit knowledge.

3   D   (i), (ii) and (iii) should all be characteristics of a learning organisation.

4   Volume, Velocity and Variety (Variability) are the three most commonly cited 'V' characteristics. However, a fourth characteristic – 'Veracity' (truthfulness) – is sometimes also added to these.

Remember Gartner's definition (in Section 5.1): Big Data is 'high-volume, high-velocity and high-variety information assets that demand cost-effective, innovative forms of information processes for enhanced insight and decision making'.

5   C   Screen scraping involves accessing data being displayed by another IT application. This is the predecessor technology to web services which allow real connectivity between applications.

Now try these questions from the Practice Question Bank	Number	Level	Marks	Time
	7.1–7.5	Intermediate	n/a	10 mins
	7.6	Examination	25	45 mins

CUSTOMERS AND MARKETING

 Marketing plays a key part in a business's strategy, and can help a business fulfil its mission and maximise long-term owner value.

Products and customers are the two key aspects of marketing (Sections 1 and 2), because they are the sources of revenue for an organisation.

The product view of marketing looks at issues such as direct product profitability and branding.

Customers' demands will dictate decisions for investment in new products, development of existing ones and setting up of new outlets. They will also affect the standards adopted for quality control, and the extent to which they can be enticed away by competitors' products will affect the planned advertising spend.

In this chapter we have included an overview of some key marketing issues, considering both the importance of attracting new customers and also retaining existing (profitable) customers (Section 3).

We have also highlighted the increasing importance of information in strategic marketing, and the role of databases, data warehouses and data mining in enabling organisations to store data about their customers (Section 5).

We finish the chapter by looking at the way the internet has allowed organisations to develop new, digital marketing activities (digital marketing; Section 6).

Topic list	Learning outcomes	Syllabus references	Ability required
1 Marketing	A1(d)	A1(d) (iii)	Recommend
2 Marketing: products, customers and segmentation	A1(d)	A1(d) (iii)	Recommend
3 Relationship marketing and customer loyalty	A1(d)	A1(d) (iii)	Recommend
4 Reviewing the customer portfolio	A1(d)	A1(d) (iii)	Recommend
5 Databases and marketing	E2(b)	E2(b) (i)	Evaluate
6 Digital marketing	E2(b)	E2(b) (ii)	Evaluate

Chapter Overview

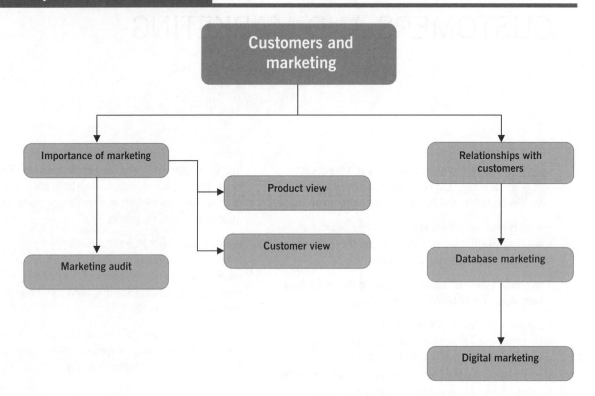

1   Marketing

Introduction

Marketing as a concept of the way business should be done must be distinguished from marketing as a business function. Operational marketing is the best-developed form of the latter.

1.1 The nature of marketing

'Strategic management' and 'marketing' share a number of ideas and models but they are not the same thing. 'Marketing' contributes to strategic management and is ultimately subordinate to it.

What is marketing?

> **Marketing** is the management process responsible for identifying, anticipating and satisfying customer requirements profitably.   *(Chartered Institute of Marketing)*

While useful in its way, the CIM definition is not the only one we might consider; in fact there are many. Dibb, Simkin, Pride and Ferrel suggest the following:

> 'Marketing consists of individual and organisational activities that facilitate and expedite satisfying exchange relationships in a dynamic environment through the creation, distribution, promotion and pricing of goods, services and ideas.'

This is a more detailed definition and has the advantage of being very specific about the activities it includes under the umbrella term 'marketing'.

Finally, let us consider what Philip Kotler says:

> 'The marketing concept holds that the key to achieving organisational goals lies in determining the needs and wants of target markets and delivering the desired satisfactions more efficiently and effectively than the competition.'

Kotler's statement is very important because it identifies four key concepts in marketing:

(a)   Identifying **target markets**
(b)   Determining the **needs and wants** of those markets
(c)   Delivering a **product offering** which meets the needs and wants of those markets
(d)   Meeting the needs of the market **profitability**

David Jobber (in *Principles and Practice of Marketing*) reinforces these points by highlighting that marketing-oriented companies strive for competitive advantage by serving customers better than the competition.

In relation to this, Jobber highlights the differences between businesses that are **marketing-oriented**, or market-driven, and those that are **internally** oriented, or **production-oriented** (ie businesses which focus on production and cost efficiency rather than customer satisfaction).

Market-oriented organisations	Internally (production) oriented organisations
Organisation's activities are focused on providing customer satisfaction	Convenience in production is considered to be most important
Understand the criteria which customers use to make purchasing decisions and match these with the marketing mix	Assume that price and product performance are key to most sales
Segment the market according to customer differences, and tailor marketing strategies accordingly	Segment the market by product

Market-oriented organisations	Internally (production) oriented organisations
View market research as an investment which can yield rewards through improved understanding of customer wants or needs	Rely on anecdotes and received wisdom
Welcome change, appreciating that change is inevitable to maintain a strategic fit between an organisation, its strategies, and its environment	Prefer the *status quo*, and tend to resist change
Try to understand competitors' objectives and strategies, in order to try to anticipate competitive actions	Ignore competition
Treat marketing expenditure as an investment which yields future benefits	Treat marketing expenditure as a luxury which rarely (if ever) produces benefits
Reward employees who take risks and are innovative	Avoid risk or innovation, and continue with the *status quo*
Seek latent needs for products or services, or previously untapped markets	Stick with existing products and markets
Seek to respond quickly to product and market opportunities	Ask 'Why rush?' and end up missing windows of opportunity
Strive for competitive advantage	Are happy to copy existing offerings already available in the market
Seek to be efficient and effective (doing the right things, as well as doing them in the right way)	Focus solely on efficiency (doing things in the right way, in order to reduce costs)

[Table based on: Jobber, D. *Principles and Practice of Marketing*. (6th edition)]

It is important to recognise that successfully implementing the marketing concept requires the whole organisation to be responsible for meeting customer needs. A focus on 'satisfying customer needs' has to underpin everything that the organisation does; it is not solely the responsibility of the marketing department.

 In Chapter 2 of this Study Text, we discussed stakeholders and stakeholder management, and in this chapter we examine how an organisation develops and manages relationships with one of the main groups of stakeholders – customers.

1.2 Marketing and strategic management

In the context of this Study Text, rather than just looking at 'marketing' in its own right, it is more important to think about the relationship between marketing and strategic management. The two are closely linked since there can be no corporate plan which does not involve products/services and customers.

Corporate strategic plans guide the overall development of an organisation. Marketing planning is subordinate to corporate planning but makes a significant contribution to it and is concerned with many of the same issues. The marketing department can also be an important source of information for the development of corporate strategy. The corporate audit of product/market strengths and weaknesses, and much of its external environmental analysis, is likely to be directly informed by the **marketing audit**.

Specific marketing strategies will be determined within the overall corporate strategy. To be effective, these plans will be interdependent with those for other functions of the organisation.

(a)   The **strategic** component of marketing planning focuses on the direction which an organisation will take in relation to a specific market, or set of markets, in order to achieve a specified set of objectives.

(b)   Marketing planning also requires an **operational** component that defines tasks and activities to be undertaken in order to achieve the desired strategy. The **marketing plan** is concerned uniquely with **products** and **markets**.

Marketing management aims to ensure the company is pursuing effective policies to promote its products, markets and distribution channels. This involves exercising strategic control of marketing, and the means to apply strategic control is known as the **marketing audit**. Not only is the marketing audit an important aspect of **marketing control**, but it can be used to provide much information and analysis for the **corporate planning process**.

1.3 Marketing audit

KEY TERM

In *Principles and Practice of Marketing*, Jobber defines a MARKETING AUDIT as 'a systematic examination of a business's marketing environment, objectives, strategies, and activities, with a view to identifying key strategic issues, problem areas and opportunities'.

The marketing audit provides the basis upon which a plan of action to improve marketing performance can be built. It also provides answers to the following questions in relation to a firm's marketing strategy:

- Where are we now?
- How did we get here?
- Where are we heading?

The answers to these questions depend on an analysis of the **internal** and **external** environment of a business, invoking models such as PEST and SWOT (which we reviewed earlier in this Study Text).

In effect, the marketing audit is the marketing equivalent of the corporate **strategic analysis** which is carried out in the strategic analysis stage of the rational model.

The **internal marketing audit** focuses on those areas which are under the control of marketing management, whereas the **external marketing audit** looks at those forces over which marketing has no control (eg GDP growth).

The results of the marketing audit are a key determinant of the future direction of the business, and may even give rise to a redefined mission statement for the business as a whole.

Jobber identifies five aspects of a marketing audit:

(a) **Market analysis**. This looks at:

    (i) Market **size**, market **growth** and trends

    (ii) **Customer analysis** and buyer behaviour

    (iii) **Competitor analysis** – competitors' objectives and strategies; market shares and profitabilities; competitors' strengths and weaknesses; barriers to entry

    (iv) Analysis of different **distribution channels** and their relative strengths and weaknesses

    (v) **Supplier analysis** – trends in the supply chain; power of suppliers; strengths and weaknesses of key suppliers

(b) **Strategic issues analysis**. This involves considering the suitability of the organisation's **marketing objectives** in relation to the marketplace and any changes in the market. Points to consider are likely to include: market segmentation; basis of competitive advantage; core competences; positioning; and product portfolio.

(c) **Review of marketing mix effectiveness** – including an analysis of product, price, promotion and distribution.

(d) **Marketing structure** – including marketing **organisation** (does the organisation of the marketing department fit with the strategy and the market); marketing **training**; and intra- and inter-departmental **communication** (for example, how well does the marketing department communicate with production departments).

(e) **Marketing systems**. Three different types of system are considered:

    (i) Marketing information systems: What information do they provide about current performance? Is this information sufficient?

(ii)   Marketing planning systems

(iii)   Marketing control systems: Can the systems provide an evaluation of marketing campaigns (accurately and on a timely basis)? Do the systems evaluate the key variables affecting company performance?

We can expand on some elements of the market analysis section of the marketing audit.

Market size: Refers to both actual and potential (forecast) size. A company cannot know whether its market share objectives are feasible unless it knows the market's overall size and the position of competitors. Forecasting areas of growth and decline is also important (eg what stage is a product at in its life cycle? How durable is the market?).

Customers: The analysis needs to identify who a company's (or a brand's) customers are, what they need, and characteristics of their buying behaviour (where, when and how they purchase products or services. For example, are there significant geographical variations in customer requirements or product usage?). This kind of customer analysis could help to point out opportunities for a company – for example, to expand further into areas where product usage is currently low.

Companies need to monitor changing customer tastes, lifestyles, behaviours, needs and expectations so that they can continue to meet existing customer needs effectively, as well as seeking out new customer needs which have not yet been met.

Competitor analysis: We have already discussed competitor analysis in Chapter 3 of this Study Text, but competitor analysis is important in the specific context of the marketing audit as well as in an organisation's environmental analysis more generally.

Competitor analysis helps an organisation understand its competitive advantages/disadvantages compared with its competitors. It can also provide valuable insights into competitors' strategies, which in turn could help an organisation develop its own strategies to achieve (or sustain) an advantage over its competitors.

An analysis of individual competitors will cover: Who are the competitors? What are their strategies and objectives? What are their strengths and weaknesses? How are they likely to respond to the organisation's own strategies? (ie what is the competitor's response profile?)

Distribution channels: The company will need to evaluate its current arrangements for delivering goods or services to the customer. Changes in distribution channels can open up new fields of opportunity (most notably in the growth of e-commerce facilitated by the internet).

1.3.1 Market sensing

In order to maximise the benefit an organisation can get from market analysis and external appraisal, its managers need to be skilled in market sensing.

KEY TERM

MARKET SENSING: How the people within an entity understand and react to the external marketplace, and the way it is changing.

Market sensing does not relate primarily to the gathering and processing of information about the market (market research) but, instead, how this information is **interpreted** and **understood** by decision makers in a company, so that that company can fulfil customers' requirements more successfully than its competitors.

For example, some market signals may be hard to pick up, even though they may be of long-term significance. However, companies that are able to identify those signals should be in a better position to respond to them than companies which have failed to pick up the signals.

1.4 Marketing and the management accountant

The role of the management accountant in marketing is to provide the company with the information it requires in order to be able to market itself successfully. However, in order to do this, the accountant must first understand the nature of the information they will be asked to provide, and whether it is product- or customer-led.

Products or customers?

The aim of most commercial organisations is to maximise the wealth of their shareholders via the twin aims of increasing revenues and minimising costs. In order that an organisation can analyse its revenues (and thereby work out how to increase them) it is important that the management accountant can produce information on **where revenues come from**.

However, there is a debate over whether these revenues ultimately come from products or customers.

The **product view** follows the idea that the products a company sells are the source of its earnings and so the more products a company sells, the greater its revenues will be.

The **customer view** believes that customers are the source of revenue and, as such, customer relationships and loyalty are the drivers of success.

The distinction between these two views of marketing – and which one a firm decides to follow – can have important implications for how the firm decides its strategy.

1.5 The product view

Direct product profitability analysis (DPP)

If an organisation adopts the product view and decides that products are its source of revenue, then issues such as its **product portfolio** and the **product life cycle** (which we discussed earlier in this Study Text) will be crucial considerations in developing its strategy.

It will also be important that an organisation can accurately assess the profitability of its products in order to maximise the returns it can make.

In this respect, direct product profitability can also play a key part in helping an organisation develop its strategy.

 We introduced the idea of direct product profitability in Chapter 4 earlier in this Study Text.

DPP was originally introduced and developed by consumer goods manufacturers to help them assess the profits that retailers generated by stocking their products. The manufacturers could then use that information when negotiating terms and conditions with the retailers.

However, today DPP is primarily used by retailers in order to determine which products to put on their shelves. For example, supermarkets can analyse the relative profitability of every branded and non-branded product they sell, and thus maximise the contribution to profit being generated by the limited retailing space they have available.

1.6 Brand strategies

If organisations are adopting a product view of marketing, then brands and brand strategy are also likely to be an important aspect of their marketing approach. For example, should the organisation brand its products or not; and if it does, what should its branding strategy be?

1.6.1 Why brand?

According to Kotler a **brand** is 'a name, term, sign, symbol or design or combination of them, intended to identify the goods or services of one seller or group of sellers and to differentiate them from those of competitors'.

Another way of considering this issue is the concept of **brand equity**. Brand equity is the asset that the marketer builds to ensure continuity of satisfaction for the customer and profit for the supplier. The 'asset' consists of consumer attitudes, distribution channels and other relationships.

The reasons for branding are:

(a)   It is a form of **product differentiation** that can make it possible to change premium prices. (Think, for example, of designer clothes labels. The kudos attached to the brand means that the clothes can be sold for significantly higher prices than non-branded equivalents.)

(b)   The more a product is similar to competing goods, the more branding is necessary to create a separate **product identity**.

(c)   It leads to a more ready **acceptance** of a manufacturer's goods by wholesalers/retailers. The power of the retailer is reduced and it is easier for the manufacturer to enter new markets.

(d)   It facilitates **self-selection** of goods in self-service stores and also makes it easier for a manufacturer to obtain the optimum **display space** in shops and stores.

(e)   It reduces the importance of **price differentials** between goods.

(f)   **Brand loyalty** in customers gives a manufacturer more control over marketing strategy and choice of channels of distribution.

(g)   Strong brands form **barriers to entry**.

(h)   Brands can have much **longer life cycles** than products, especially when the technology is developing rapidly.

(i)   A strong brand name may allow a firm to **enter unfamiliar markets** or **introduce new products** or marketplaces more quickly and with less risk than a firm without a strong brand would be able to.

1.7 Brand strategy and marketing strategy

Brand positioning is a crucial part of marketing strategy because, in order to develop an effective marketing strategy, a firm also has to decide how to position its product or service in the marketplace.

KEY TERM

POSITIONING: The 'act of designing the company's offer and image so that it occupies a distinct and valued place in the target customers' mind'.   (Kotler and Keller, *Marketing Management*)

As its name implies, positioning involves finding an appropriate position for a product or service in the marketplace so that consumers think about that product or service in the 'right' way. Equally, brand positioning involves identifying the optimal location of a brand in the minds of consumers, and in relation to its competitors, to maximise the potential benefit of the brand to the company which owns it.

If we consider the general functions of a brand (as listed below), we can see how closely they are also linked to the logic of positioning:

*   To distinguish a company's offering, and to differentiate one particular product from competitor products

*   To deliver an expected level of quality and satisfaction

*   To help with promotion of the product and to develop awareness of it

Brand positioning should help to guide marketing strategy by clarifying: what a brand is; how it is unique or how it is different from competing brands; and why consumers should purchase and use the brand.

Once a brand's positioning strategy has been determined, the brand's marketers can then develop and implement their marketing strategy to create, strengthen or maintain brand associations. In this respect, obtaining an appropriate combination of the 'marketing mix' elements (4 Ps, or 7 Ps) will be very important when designing the marketing campaigns to support the brand.

Product – The product (or service) is central to brand equity because it is the primary influence on consumers' experience with a brand, as well as on what they hear about a brand from others, and about what a company can tell consumers about the brand in any marketing communications.

Products must be designed, manufactured, marketed, sold, delivered and serviced in a way which creates a positive brand image with customers. If a company does not have a product or service which satisfies customer needs (particularly in relation to perceived quality and value), that company will not be able to develop a successful brand, or engender any customer loyalty to that brand.

The importance of acquiring and retaining loyal customers has led to relationship marketing becoming a priority for branding. The marketers who are most successful at building customer-based brand equity will be those who ensure they understand their customers, and understand how to deliver value to their customers before, during and after purchase.

Price – The price element of the marketing mix pricing policy for a brand is very important because it can play a key role in shaping consumers' perceptions of a product (eg as being high, medium, or low priced). However, price often also has an association with quality; and consumers often infer the quality of a product or service on the basis of its price.

In some cases, consumers are willing to pay a premium for certain brands because of what they represent. But in terms of preparing a marketing strategy to develop a brand, it is important to ensure that the price is consistent with the perceived quality or value of a product to the customer. The benefits delivered by a product, and its competitive advantages compared with rival products, can often have a significant impact on what consumers believe to be a fair price.

In this context, the concept of **value pricing** could be very useful. The objective to value pricing is to identify the right blend of product quality, product costs and product prices to satisfy both the needs and wants of consumers and also the profit targets of the company.

Place – The manner in which a product is sold or distributed can have a profound impact on the sales success of a brand. In this respect, channel strategy (the way firms distribute their products to consumers) is important for building and maintaining a brand.

Channel strategy involves deciding whether to sell directly to customers or to sell through third-party intermediaries (eg wholesalers, or retailers). In either case, however, it is important to ensure that the shop's image is aligned to the brand's image – for example, it would not seem appropriate to use a discount retailer for selling a brand which seeks to emphasise high quality and luxury as differentiating factors.

Another important decision in relation to channel strategy is whether to sell online, offline, or through a combination of both.

For many companies, the best channel strategies will be ones which develop an integrated shopping experience, combining physical stores and internet. For example, Nike sells its products through a range of department and clothes shops as well as through some of its own 'Nike Town' shops. Alongside this, Nike's own e-commerce website (store.nike.com) allows customers to buy directly from it online, while a number of the other shops which stock Nike products also have their own e-commerce websites.

Promotion – It should be obvious that the aim of promotion and marketing communications is to increase consumers' knowledge of a brand and to entice them to buy that brand.

Companies have a wide range of potential communication options they could use for a marketing campaign: for example, broadcast media, print media, direct response (eg phone calls), online advertising; consumer and trade promotions; or event marketing and sponsorship. Crucially, however, when deciding on its promotion strategy, a company must evaluate the effectiveness and efficiency with which that strategy affects brand awareness, and how it creates or strengthens favourable brand associations.

1.7.1 Branding strategies

Kotler has identified the following five strategies a company can use once it has established its brand(s).

(a)   **Line extension** – an existing name is applied to new variants of existing products, for example Coca-Cola launching Coke Zero, or Coca-Cola with Lime.

(b)   **Brand extensions** – using an existing brand to launch a product in a new category, for example Virgin Group extending its brand from airlines, to railways, mobile phone services, banking and fitness centres.

(c)   **Multibranding** – launching several brands in the same category, for example Kellogg's offers breakfast cereals with their own brands – such as All Bran, Cornflakes, Coco Pops, Rice Krispies.

(d) **New brands** – an organisation may launch a new brand into the market. The new brand can be used to compete with existing rivals, but can be marketed as something new and fresh. Equally, if the new brand fails, its failure should be less likely to damage the existing brand.

(e) **Co-branding** – two brands are combined in an offer, for example Sony PlayStations were offered in a package with Tomb Raider game.

The decision as to whether a brand name should be given to a range of products or whether products should be branded individually depends on quality factors.

(a) If the brand name is associated with quality, all goods in the range must be of that standard.

(b) If a company produces different quality (and price) goods for different market segments, it would be unwise to give the same brand name to the higher and the lower quality goods because this could deter buyers in the high quality/price market segment.

Section summary

Marketing plays an important role in strategic management since an organisation cannot have a strategic plan which does not involve products/services and customers. The marketing audit is an important aspect of marketing control, but can also provide information and analysis for the corporate planning process.

Another important factor in shaping an organisation's marketing strategy will be whether it views revenue as coming ultimately from products or customers.

2 Marketing: products, customers and segmentation

Introduction

The strategy of a business is often oriented towards its customers. Marketing seeks to identify customers and their needs, and to encourage them to buy. Segments are groups of customers with similar needs that can be **targeted** with a distinctly **positioned** marketing **mix**.

2.1 Products and customers

KEY TERM

A PRODUCT (goods or services) is anything that satisfies a need or want. It is not a 'thing' with 'features' but a package of benefits. For example, a compact disc and hi-fi system provide recorded music, and other benefits. From most customers' point of view, the electronics inside are not important as long as they are reliable and deliver a certain quality of sound.

The immediate task of a marketing manager with respect to the **products** of the organisation may be any of the following:

- To create demand (where none exists)
- To develop a latent demand
- To revitalise a sagging demand
- To attempt to smooth out (synchronise) uneven demand
- To sustain a buoyant demand (maintenance marketing)
- To reduce excess demand

Many products might satisfy the same customer need. On what basis might a customer choose?

(a) **Customer value** is the customer's estimate of how far a product or service goes towards satisfying their need(s).

(b) Every product has a cost, so the customer must trade off between expenditure and value.

(c)   According to Kotler, customers must feel they get a better deal from buying an item than by the alternatives.

Companies must make a distinction between the **customer** and the **consumer**.

(a)   The **customer** is the person or organisation buying the product or service. For example, a cat's owner will buy food for the cat.

(b)   The **consumer** is the person who uses the product or receives the benefit of the service. In the case of cat food, the cat is the consumer, not the purchaser.

Marketing has a role in the organisation's **value chain**. The end result of a value chain is a product or service which has both a price in line with **customer perceptions of value** and a cost that allows the producer to make a **margin or profit**.

2.2 The importance of developing a market orientation in strategic planning

An organisation commits itself to supplying what customers need. As needs change, so must the goods or services produced. **Marketing orientation enables a firm to adapt to the environment**.

(a)   By applying the marketing concept to product design the company might hope to make more attractive products, hence to achieve sustained sales growth and make higher profits.

(b)   Profits come from not only individual transactions with customers, but also the customer's propensity to deal with the firm rather than its competitors.

Strategic planning involves making decisions about the choice of **product-market strategies** – developing new products and new markets that will fill the '**profit gap**'. A marketing orientation should help planners to identify more successfully what products or markets would earn good profits for the organisation.

Having decided on a competitive strategy a firm must then decide on:

*   Which target markets should be developed
*   How the firm should offer its product or service in comparison with competitors
*   How to establish a **marketing system** and organisation for the firm
*   How to develop a **marketing plan** and then implement and control it

2.3 Buyer behaviour

The decision to make a purchase can be very simple, very complex or somewhere between the two.

Nonetheless, it is important that organisations try to understand **why** buyers purchase their goods or services.

It might be tempting to think that consumers make purchasing decisions wholly on the basis of the value for money they obtain from buying a particular product or service. However, consumer behaviour is also shaped by a range of different needs and requirements, which Maslow identified as a 'hierarchy of needs':

*   Physiological needs
*   Safety needs
*   Social needs
*   Status/ego needs
*   Self-fulfilment needs

The type of need which a product or service addresses could, in turn, help shape the strategy which a firm uses for marketing and selling that product or service. For example, the purchasing decisions involved in buying a luxury sports car (fulfilling a status/ego need) are likely to be very different to those involved in buying everyday groceries such as bread and milk (to meet physiological needs). Equally, the marketing and sales strategies a sports car company uses to sell sports cars are likely to be very different to the approach a supermarket takes in relation to selling bread and milk.

It is also important to remember that buyers do not always proceed rationally. In this respect, the distinction between individual consumers and industrial buyers can be significant, because the purchasing decisions and motivations of industrial buyers tend to be more logical than those of individual consumers.

In marketing, a market is defined in terms of its **buyers** or **potential buyers**:

- **Consumer markets** (eg for soap powder, washing machines, TV sets, clothes)
- **Industrial markets** (eg for machine tools, construction equipment)
- **Government markets** (eg for armaments and, in the UK, medical equipment)
- **Reseller markets**
- **Export markets**

2.3.1 Consumer goods

Consumer goods are ready to be used by the consumer without the need for any further commercial processing. Consumer goods are further classified according to the method by which they are purchased.

	Features	Examples
Convenience goods	Purchased regularly in small amounts of low unit value. Has close substitutes. Everyday purchases and likely to be produced by several manufacturers. Promoting a unique image for the product, for example by **branding**, is important.	Toothpaste Bread Coffee Chocolate
Shopping goods	Goods for which customers are more discriminating. Usually have a higher unit value and are bought less frequently, usually from a specialist outlet with a wide range on offer.	Cars Furniture Hi-fi equipment Household appliances, such as washing machines and cookers
Speciality goods	The manufacturer, either by product design or advertising, has become associated in the public mind with a particular product. The customer will ask for it by name and seek out a dealer who sells it.	Rolls-Royce cars Wedgwood pottery

2.3.2 Industrial or business-to-business markets

In industrial markets, the customer is another firm. The industrial market, more than the consumer market, is influenced by the general state of the economy and the Government's economic policy.

Derived demand. The demand for industrial goods and services is derived from the demand for the product or service to which they contribute. For example, the demand for aluminium is, in part, derived from the demand for cans, which might itself be derived from demand for beer or soft drinks.

Industrial buyers are more **rationally motivated** than consumers in deciding which goods to buy. Sales policy decisions by a supplier are therefore more important than sales promotion activities in an industrial market. Special attention should be given in selling to quality, price, credit, delivery dates, after-sales service, etc. The size of order which can be supplied may also be an important factor; whether or not the supplier has the capacity to meet the buyer's demands.

These rational motivations make it difficult for an untried newcomer to break into an industrial goods market.

2.3.3 Organisational buying behaviour

The organisational buying behaviour process has some similarities with consumer buyer behaviour, but is supposedly more rational.

- How are needs recognised in a company?
- What is the type of buying situation?
- How is a supplier selected?
- How will performance be reviewed after purchase?

2.3.4 Factors in the motivation mix of business or government buyers

Business or government buyers are motivated as follows:

(a) **Quality** and reliability.

(b) **Price**. Where profit margins in the final market are under pressure, the buyer of industrial goods will probably make price the main purchasing motivation (particularly if the buyer's own competitive strategy is focused on cost minimisation and cost leadership).

(c) **Budgetary control** may encourage the buying department to look further afield for potential suppliers to obtain a better price or quality of goods.

(d) **Fear of breakdown**. Where a customer has a highly organised and costly production system, they will want to avoid a breakdown in the system due to a faulty machine or running out of inventory.

(e) **Credit**. The importance of credit could vary with the financial size of the buyer.

(f) **Delivery**. Generally, buyers want delivery without delay; even for orders which can sometimes be on a much larger scale than those made by individual consumers.

(g) **Purchasing procedures**. The availability of written quotations, legal contracts, or service level agreements could be important for business buyers. Again, the buyers are also likely to be interested in the credit terms (and/or bulk discounts) available.

2.4 Market segmentation

Both consumer and industrial markets can usefully be segmented, and several bases exist for the process. The aim is to identify a coherent segment that is both valid and attractive.

Much marketing planning is based on the concepts of **segmentation and product positioning**. Segmentation identifies target markets in which the firm can take a position. A market is not a mass, homogeneous group of customers, each wanting an identical product. Market segmentation recognises that every market consists of potential buyers with different needs, and different buying behaviour. It is relevant to a **focus strategy**.

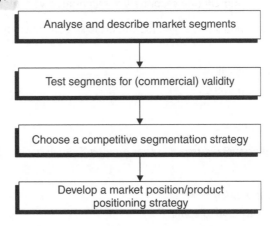

KEY TERM

MARKET SEGMENTATION is 'the subdividing of a market into distinct and increasingly homogeneous subgroups of customers, where any subgroup can conceivably be selected as a target market to be met with a distinct marketing mix'.

(Kotler)

There are two important elements in this definition of market segmentation:

(a) Although the total market consists of widely different groups of consumers, each group consists of people (or organisations) with **common needs and preferences**, who perhaps react to 'market stimuli' in much the same way.

(b) Each market segment can become a **target market for a firm**, and would require a unique marketing mix if the firm is to exploit it successfully.

Reasons for segmenting markets

Reason	Comment
Better satisfaction of customer needs	One solution will not satisfy all customers
Growth in profits	Some customers will pay more for certain benefits
Revenue growth	More customers may be attracted by what is on offer, in preference to competing products
Customer retention	By targeting customers, a number of different products can be offered to them
Targeted communications	Segmentation enables clear communications as people in the target audience share common needs
Innovation	By identifying unmet needs, companies can innovate to satisfy them
Segment share	Segmentation enables a firm to implement a focus strategy successfully

2.5 Identifying segments

An important initial marketing task is the **identification of segments** within the market. Segmentation applies more obviously to the consumer market, but it can also be applied to an **industrial market**. An important basis for segmentation is the nature of the customer's business.

(a) One basis will not be appropriate in every market, and sometimes two or more bases might be valid at the same time.

(b) One basis or 'segmentation variable' might be 'superior' to another in a hierarchy of variables. These are **primary and secondary segmentation variables**.

CASE STUDY

An airport cafe conducted a segmentation exercise of its customers. It identified a number of possible segments:

- Business travellers
- Airport employees
- Groups
- Single tourists

However, further analysis revealed that running through each of these categories was the same key distinction:

- Those 'in a hurry'
- Those with time to spare

For marketing purposes, this latter segmentation exercise was more useful, and the firm was able to develop an 'express menu' for those in a hurry.

Customers could be classified into customer segments using a variety of other **segmentation** bases such as:

(a)   Geography – location of the customers

(b)   Socioeconomic group, or social class

(c)   Stage in the family life cycle

(d)   Level of education

(e)   Personal wealth

(f)   Lifestyle

(g)   Behaviour – based on their attitudes to and use of the product, and the benefits they expect to receive

2.6 Segmentation of the industrial market

Industrial markets can be segmented with many of the bases used in consumer markets such as geography, usage rate and benefits sought. Additional, more traditional bases include customer type, product/technology, customer size and purchasing procedures.

(a)   **Geographical location**. Some industries and related industries are clustered in particular areas. Firms selling services to the banking sector might be interested in the City of London.

(b)   **Type of business** (eg service, manufacturing)

   (i)   **Nature of the customers' business**. Accountants or lawyers, for example, might choose to specialise in serving customers in a particular type of business. An accountant may choose to specialise in the accounts of retail businesses, and a firm of solicitors may specialise in conveyancing work for property development companies.

   (ii)   **Components manufacturers specialise in the industries of the firms to which they supply components.**

(c)   **Use of the product**. In the UK, many new cars are sold to businesses, as company cars. Although this practice is changing with the viability of a 'cash alternative' to a company car, the varying levels of specification are developed with the business buyer in mind (eg junior salesperson gets a Ford Fiesta; regional manager gets a Ford Mondeo).

(d)   **Type of organisation**. Organisations in an industry as a whole may have certain needs in common. Employment agencies offering business services to publishers, say, must offer their clients personnel with experience in particular desktop publishing packages. Suitable temporary staff offered to legal firms can be more effective if used to legal jargon. Each different type of firm can be offered a tailored product or service.

(e)   **Size of organisation**. Large organisations may have elaborate purchasing procedures, and may do many things in-house. Small organisations may be more likely to subcontract certain specialist services.

2.7 Segment validity

A market segment will only **be valid if it is worth designing and developing a unique** marketing mix for that specific segment. The following questions are commonly asked to decide whether or not the segment can be used for developing marketing plans.

Criteria	Comment
Can the segment be measured?	A market segment might be easy to define but hard to measure. For example, if 'people with a conservative outlook to life' is a segment, how would this be measured?
Is the segment big enough?	There has to be a large enough potential market to be profitable.
Can the segment be reached?	There has to be a way of getting to the potential customers via the organisation's promotion and distribution channels.
Do segments respond differently?	If two or more segments respond in the same way to a marketing mix, the segments are effectively the same. There is no point in distinguishing them from each other.
Can the segment be reached profitably?	Do the identified customer needs cost less to satisfy than the revenue they earn?

2.8 Segment attractiveness

A segment might be valid and potentially profitable, but is it potentially attractive?

(a)   A segment which has **high barriers to entry** might cost more to enter but will be less **vulnerable to competitors**.

(b)   For firms involved in **relationship marketing**, the segment should be one in which a **viable relationship** between the firm and the customer can be established.

The most attractive segments are those whose needs can be met by building on the company's strengths and where forecasts for **demand**, **sales profitability** and **growth** are favourable.

Target markets

Because of limited resources, competition and large markets, organisations are not usually able to sell with equal efficiency and success to the entire market; that is, to every market segment. It is necessary to select **target markets**. The marketing management of a company may choose one of the following policy options.

KEY TERMS

UNDIFFERENTIATED MARKETING: produce a single product and hope to get as many customers as possible to buy it; that is, ignore segmentation entirely.

CONCENTRATED MARKETING: the company attempts to produce the ideal product for a single segment of the market (eg Rolls-Royce cars for the wealthy).

DIFFERENTIATED MARKETING: the company attempts to introduce several product versions, each aimed at a different market segment. For example, manufacturers of soap powder make a number of different brands, marketed to different segments.

It is important to assess company strengths when evaluating attractiveness and targeting a market. This can help determine the appropriate strategy, because once the attractiveness of each identified segment has been assessed it can be considered along with relative strengths to determine the potential advantages the organisation would have. In this way preferred segments can be targeted.

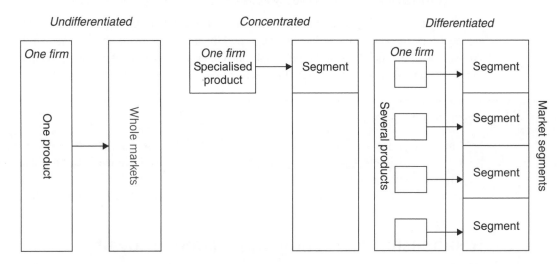

The major **disadvantage of differentiated marketing** is the additional costs of marketing and production (more product design and development costs, the loss of economies of scale in production and storage, additional promotion costs and administrative costs etc). When the **costs of further differentiation of the market exceed the benefits** from further segmentation and **target marketing**, a firm is **over-differentiated**.

The major **disadvantage of concentrated marketing** is the business risk of relying on a single segment of a single market. On the other hand, specialisation in a particular market segment can give a firm a profitable, although perhaps temporary, competitive edge over rival firms.

The choice between undifferentiated, differentiated or concentrated marketing as a marketing strategy will depend on the following factors.

(a)   The extent to which the product and/or market is **homogeneous**. **Mass marketing** may be 'sufficient' if the market is largely homogeneous (for example, for safety matches).

(b)   The **company's resources** must not be overextended by differentiated marketing. Small firms may succeed better by concentrating on one segment only.

(c)   The product must be sufficiently **advanced in its life cycle** to have attracted a substantial total market, otherwise segmentation and target marketing is unlikely to be profitable, because each segment would be too small in size.

Remember, the ideal mix for a convenience good (requiring a heavy emphasis on distribution and sales promotion) will be different from that for an industrial good (where price, design, quality and after-sales service are more important).

2.8.1 Micromarketing

Segmentation, as part of target marketing, looks likely to play an increasingly important role in the marketing strategies of consumer organisations in the years ahead. The move from traditional mass marketing to **micromarketing** is rapidly gaining ground as marketers explore more cost-effective ways to recruit new customers. This has been brought about by a number of trends:

(a) The ability to create large numbers of product variants without the need for corresponding increases in resources is causing markets to become overcrowded.

(b) The growth in minority lifestyles is creating opportunities for niche brands aimed at consumers with very distinct purchasing habits.

(c) The fragmentation of the media to service ever more specialist and local audiences is denying mass media the ability to assure market dominance for major brand advertisers.

(d) The advance in information technology is enabling information about individual customers to be organised in ways that enable highly selective and personal communications.

In our discussions of Big Data in the previous chapter, we noted that Big Data could help organisations segment their markets in more detailed ways, and the last bullet point above relates to this same issue. We will revisit this point about the potential 'individualisation' of marketing messages in more detail later in this chapter when we look at digital marketing (e-marketing) and its characteristics.

Section summary

Segments are groups of customers with similar needs that can be targeted with a distinct marketing mix. Both consumer and industrial markets can be segmented, and the aim is to identify coherent segments that are both valid and attractive.

---

3 Relationship marketing and customer loyalty

Introduction

Customer relationship marketing means using marketing resources to retain, rather than simply attract, customers. It focuses on establishing **loyalty** among the existing customers.

We mentioned earlier in this chapter that organisations can adopt either a product view or a customer view of marketing. We now examine customer-based aspects of marketing, in particular relationship management, customer retention and customer profitability analysis.

Relationship marketing

In *Principles and Practice of Marketing*, David Jobber notes that many companies find that 80% of their sales come from 20% of their customers. This highlights how important it is for companies to retain their existing high-volume and highly profitable customers, as well as those with strong potential to become high-volume, high-profit customers in the future.

This emphasis on **customer retention** has led to an increasing focus on customer relationship management. Sales and marketing staff should no longer be looking solely to make a one-off sale, but to create a long-term relationship, which is mutually beneficial for the company and the customer.

This is the logic behind relationship marketing and customer relationship management.

Relationship marketing is the use of marketing resources to maintain and exploit a firm's **existing customers**, rather than using marketing resources solely to attract new customers.

Firms can implement their relationship marketing strategy through effective **customer relationship management**.

KEY TERM

CUSTOMER RELATIONSHIP MANAGEMENT is the establishment, development, maintenance and optimisation of long-term, mutually valuable, relationships between consumers and organisations.

What customer relationship management involves	Company benefits realised as a result
• Organisations must become 'customer centric' • Organisations must be prepared to adapt so that they take customer needs into account and then deliver them • Market research must be used to assess customer needs and satisfaction	• Improved customer retention • Improved cross-selling • Improved profitability (per customer and in general)

3.1 The need for customer relationship management (CRM)

There are several reasons why customer relationship management (CRM) is an important consideration.

(a) Customers are inherently more willing to switch suppliers and less likely to be loyal to a specific company or brand than they have been in the past. (The internet has also had an impact on customer loyalty. For example, price comparison websites may reduce customer loyalty if customers see that an alternative supplier offers a product or service more cheaply than their current provider. However, by developing a relationship with its customers, an organisation will move away from competition based on price alone.)

(b) It is cheaper to focus on retaining existing customers than to have to attract new ones. Attracting new customers is expensive due to low initial prices or promotion expenses for instance.

(c) In mature markets, existing customers provide the most likely source of future earnings.

(d) Strategy to widen the range of products available would make no sense if existing customers could not be retained.

CASE STUDY

Mobile phone services

The mobile telecommunications industry traditionally suffers from high customer attrition ('churn') rates. In a message to staff at the beginning of 2012, the CEO of T-mobile (before it became part of EE) highlighted that 'it is critical we fix churn... For every customer who renews their contract with T-mobile, we lose one. That is a dead end, not a growth path. We have established a plan ... that will improve the customer experience and enrich how we interact with our customers.'

A key part of T-mobile's plan was improving customer relationship management; emphasising the importance of customer renewals before looking to acquire new customers.

However, one of the most common complaints received across the mobile phone industry is that loyal (existing) customers don't get the same deals as new customers. If this remains the case, though, the industry's business model appears to be geared more towards acquisition rather than retention.

Dave Chaffey outlines three phases of CRM (particularly in relation to e-business and e-commerce management):

- Customer **acquisition**
- Customer **retention**
- Customer **extension**

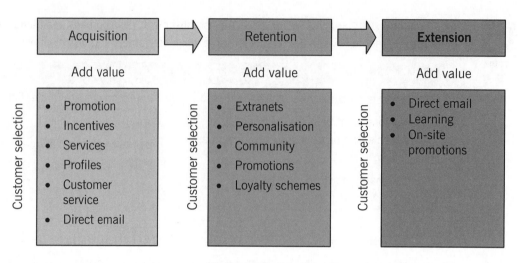

Chaffey's three phases of customer relationship management

Customer acquisition is the process of attracting customers for their first purchases.

Customer retention ensures that customers return and buy for a second time. The organisation keeps them as customers. This is most likely to be the purchase of a similar product or service, or the next level of product or service.

Customer extension introduces products and services to loyal customers that may not wholly relate to their original purchases. These are additional, supplementary purchases.

In recent times emphasis has increased on building and **maintaining good long-term relationships** with customers. This is because such relationships are more profitable than constantly searching for new customers.

At a tactical level, relationship marketing also needs to be supported by the effective use of data and databases to gather and analyse information about customers and potential customers.

Data mining (which we look at in more detail later in this chapter) can therefore be very important in supporting relationship marketing, and the volume of data available for organisations to analyse could be increased significantly through the expansion of **Big Data** (which we discussed in the previous chapter).

3.1.1 Customer retention in service businesses

An important element in a service business's ability to retain customers will be the degree to which it continues to meet the needs of its customers.

However, in order to be able to do this, the business will need to research the needs of its customers, so that it can then measure how well it is performing in relation to its customers' needs. These needs are likely to vary according to the nature of the business: for example, reliability is important in a bank; comfort is more likely to be important in a hotel.

One framework which a business can use for assessing the quality of service it provides its customers is the **SERVQUAL methodology** (developed by Zeithanl, Parasurman and Berry). This covers five dimensions of service quality, and customer feedback is sought in relation to the five dimensions.

(a) **Tangibles**: for example, appearance of facilities; is equipment up to date; are staff well dressed?

(b) **Reliability**: for example, are bookings processed accurately; if services are promised by a certain time, are they delivered by that time?

(c) **Responsiveness**: do staff react to queries promptly, and courteously?

(d) **Assurance**: do staff inspire confidence; if customers have problems, are staff sympathetic and reassuring?

(e) **Empathy**: are customers treated as individuals; do staff have the customers' best interests at heart?

The SERVQUAL methodology then allows businesses to improve their performance by gauging the gap between how well they think they are performing and customers' expectations of how well they should be performing. Staff and managers may believe they are delivering a good-quality service; customers may not agree, though.

3.2 Differences between transactional and relationship marketing

Transactional	Relationship
Importance of single sale	Importance of customer relations
Importance of product features	Importance of customer benefits
Short timescale	Longer timescale
Less emphasis on service	High customer service
Quality is concern of production	Quality is concern of all
Competitive commitment	High customer commitment
Persuasive communication	Regular communication

(From: Adcock, Bradfield, Halborg and Ross, *Marketing: Principles and Practice*)

3.3 Relationship marketing strategies

A number of strategies can be implemented in relation to customer relationship marketing and to develop loyalty towards an organisation.

Strategy	CRM implications	Examples
Develop appropriate staff incentive schemes	Encourages staff to work harder to retain existing customers	Reward staff based on customer satisfaction and feedback, rather than number of new customers attracted
Provide consistent standards	Customers more likely to return if they receive consistently good service Familiarity with good staff encourages loyalty	Implement measures to reduce staff turnover
Obtain senior management buy-in	If senior management prioritise staff retention, staff will too	Build customer retention into the organisational strategy Develop a customer-focused approach at all levels
Monitor customer relationships and act appropriately	By understanding the behaviour of customers, improvements to secure their loyalty can be made	Establish regular contact with customers Assess customer satisfaction and loyalty Determine reasons for loss of a customer Address reasons to prevent future loss of custom

Strategy	CRM implications	Examples
Obtain detailed customer information	Allows the firm to: • Identify customer needs • Develop improved ways of meeting those needs • Specifically target customers and bring relevant new products or services to their attention	Customer loyalty/reward cards can provide invaluable information about the buying habits and patterns of customers
Develop specific loyalty focused strategies	Directly encourages the customer to return	Introduce loyalty cards Appoint dedicated account managers for key customers
Implement procedures to monitor and influence all aspects of the customer relationship	Provides the customers with a good experience of the company encouraging them to be loyal Monitors the success of the relationship allowing weak areas to be identified and improved	Total quality management (TQM)
Implement systems that can support customer relationship management	Provides high level of information to the firm, allowing better understanding of the relationship; this in turns helps understand how it can be improved	Analytical customer databases Automated sales management systems Systems to track customer spending and profitability

3.4 Wider relationship marketing

Adrian Payne and his colleagues at the Cranfield School of Management have suggested that relationship management extends beyond the customer. They developed the **'Six Markets' model** which recommends building relationships in six markets as shown in the following table.

Market	Who makes up the market	CRM implications
Customer markets	Customers are the final buyers of the product or service	Superior customer value can only be delivered if appropriate relationships exist in each of the markets
Referral markets	People/institutions that introduce new customers, for instance banks, agencies or existing customers	Build strong relationships in this market to ensure new customers are introduced
Supplier markets	All suppliers to the company	By working closer with suppliers the firm can better meet the needs of the final consumer
Recruitment markets	Potential staff, as well as key stakeholders in the recruitment market such as agencies and careers advisers	Good staff are crucial to provide good service to customers. To attract good staff the firm must: • Develop an appealing corporate image • Build relationships with the key stakeholders in this market

Market	Who makes up the market	CRM implications
Influence markets	Any person, group or company that can influence customer purchases, such as analysts, pressure groups, brokers or consumer groups	The firm needs a good Personal Relations (PR) department to ensure the firm is presented favourably in this market
Internal markets	Everyone internal to the organisation; each department is a customer and a supplier to other departments	Develop strategies that: • Ingrain a client service mentality • Discourage departmental rivalry • Encourage each department to view its work in relation to serving the customers

Section summary

Customer relationship marketing focuses on establishing **loyalty** in the existing customer base. Payne suggested that relationship marketing extends beyond the customer and developed the 'Six Markets' model to demonstrate where relationships should be built.

4   Reviewing the customer portfolio

Introduction

The **customer base** is an asset to be invested in, as future benefits will come from existing customers, but not all customers are as important as others. It will help you in evaluating the customer portfolio if you consider the customer base as an asset worth investing in.

CASE STUDY

(a)   In September 2009, the online jewellery retailer Bidz.com acquired the intellectual property and trademark registration of Whitehall Jewelers (also incorporating Lundstrom Jewelers, Mark Bros. Jewelers, and White Star Private Label). However, as well as acquiring a well-known brand (Whitehall Jewelers) with its associated history and goodwill, Bidz.com acquired the customer mailing list with over 800,000 names and addresses.

(b)   Supermarket loyalty cards reward customers with bonus points, saving them money, or allowing them to redeem points for products according to how much they spend.

(c)   Many banks lose money on student accounts, in the hope that they will earn it back later in the customer's life cycle.

As we noted earlier in this chapter, a **marketing audit** involves a review of an organisation's products and markets, the marketing environment, and its marketing system and operations. The profitability of each product and each market should be assessed, and the costs of different marketing activities established.

Information obtained about markets:

(a)   **Size of the customer base**. Does the organisation sell to a large number of small customers or a small number of big customers?

(b)   **Size of individual orders**. The organisation might sell its products in many small orders, or it might have large individual orders. Delivery costs can be compared with order sizes.

(c)   **Sales revenue and profitability**. The performance of individual products can be compared, perhaps as follows:

Product group	Sales revenue		Contribution to profits	
	£'000	% of total	£'000	% of total
B	7,500	35.7	2,500	55.6
E	2,000	9.5	1,200	26.7
C	4,500	21.4	450	10.0
A	5,000	23.8	250	5.6
D	2,000	9.5	100	2.2
	21,000	100.0	4,500	100.0

An imbalance between sales and profits over various product ranges can be potentially dangerous. In the figures above, product group 'A' accounts for 23.8% of turnover but only 5.6% of total contribution, and product group 'D' accounts for 9.5% of turnover but only 2.2% of total contribution.

(d)   **Segments**. An analysis of sales and profitability into export markets and domestic markets.

(e)   **Market share**. Estimated share of the market obtained by each product group.

(f)   **Growth**. Sales growth and contribution growth over the previous four years or so, for each product group.

(g)   Whether the **demand** for certain products is **growing, stable or likely to decline**.

(h)   Whether **demand is price sensitive** or not.

(i)   Whether there is a growing tendency for the market to become **fragmented**, with more specialist and 'custom-made' products.

Information about current marketing activities

- Comparative pricing
- Advertising effectiveness
- Effectiveness of distribution network
- Attitudes to the product, in comparison with competitors

4.1 Customers

Key customer analysis investigates six main areas of customers, in order to identify which customers offer most profit.

Many firms – especially in business-to-business markets – sell to a relatively small number of customers. **Not all customers are as important as others**. The checklist below can help identify the most important.

Strategic importance evaluation guide		High	Medium	Low	N/A
1	Fit between customer's needs and our capabilities, at present and potentially.				
2	Ability to serve customer compared with our major competitors, at present and potentially.				
3	'Health' of customer's industry, current and forecast.				
4	'Health' of the customer, current and forecast.				
5	Customer's growth prospects, current and forecast.				
6	What can we learn from this customer?				
7	Can the customer help us attract others?				
8	Relative **significance**: how important is the customer compared **with other** customers?				
9	What is the **profitability** of serving the customer?				

4.2 Customer analysis

Key customer analysis considers six main areas of customer analysis. A firm might wish to identify which customers offer most profit. Small businesses are especially prone to overtrading.

Area	Detail
Key customer identity	• Name of each key customer • Location • Status in market • Products they make and sell • Size of firm (capital employed, turnover, number of employees)
Customer history	• First purchase date • Who makes the buying decision in the customer's organisation? • What is the average order size, by product? • What is the regularity/periodicity of the order, by product? • What is the trend in size of orders? • What is the motive in purchasing? • What does the customer know about the firm's and competitors' products? • On what basis does the customer reorder? • How is the useful life of the product judged? • Were there any lost or cancelled orders? For what reason?
Relationship of customer to product	• What does the customer use the product for? • Do the products form part of the customer's own service/product?
Relationship of customer to potential market	• What is the size of the customer in relation to the total end-market? • Is the customer likely to expand, or not? Diversify? Integrate?
Customer attitudes and behaviour	• What interpersonal factors exist which could affect sales by the firm and by competitors? • Does the customer also buy competitors' products? • To what extent may purchases be postponed?
The financial performance of the customer	How successful is the customer?

4.3 Customer profitability analysis (customer account profitability)

Although we have highlighted the importance of customer retention in the context of customer relationship management, it is ultimately only beneficial for entities to develop and nurture relationships with customers who are profitable for them. Therefore, organisations can benefit from undertaking customer profitability analysis in conjunction with customer relationship management, so that they focus their efforts on retaining profitable customers.

Customer profitability analysis is an analysis of the total sales revenue generated from a customer or customer group, less all the costs that are incurred in servicing that customer group.

KEY TERM

CUSTOMER PROFITABILITY ANALYSIS (CPA). 'Analysis of the revenue streams and service costs associated with specific customers or customer groups.'   *(CIMA Official Terminology)*

The total costs of servicing customers can vary depending on how they are serviced.

(a)   **Volume discounts.** A customer who places one large order is given a discount, presumably because it benefits the supplier to do so (eg savings on administrative overheads in processing the orders – as identified by an ABC system).

(b) **Different rates** charged by power companies to domestic as opposed to business users. This in part reflects the administrative overheads of dealing with individual customers. In practice, many domestic consumers benefit from cross-subsidy.

Customer profitability is the 'total sales revenue generated from a customer or customer group, less all the costs that are incurred in servicing that customer or customer group.'

It is possible to analyse customer profitability over a single period but more useful to look at a longer timescale. Such a multi-period approach fits in with the idea of **relationship marketing** discussed earlier in this chapter, with its emphasis on customer retention for the longer term.

Question 8.1	Profitable customers

Learning outcomes A1(d)

Seth Ltd supplies shoes to Narayan Ltd and Kipling Ltd. Each pair of shoes has a list price of £50 each; as Kipling buys in bulk, Kipling receives a 10% trade discount for every order over 100 shoes. It costs £1,000 to deliver each order. In the year so far, Kipling has made 5 orders of 100 shoes each. Narayan Ltd receives a 15% discount irrespective of order size, because Narayan Ltd collects the shoes, thereby saving Seth Ltd any distribution costs. The cost of administering each order is £50. Narayan makes 10 orders in the year, totalling 420 pairs of shoes. Which relationship is the most profitable for Seth?

Customer profitability analysis (CPA) focuses on profits generated by customers, and suggests that **profit does not automatically increase with sales revenue**. CPA can benefit a company in the following ways.

(a) It allows a company to **identify and retain the most profitable customers**.

(b) It enables a company to **focus resources** on the most profitable areas.

(c) It identifies unexpected **differences in profitability** between customers.

(d) It enables a company to **stop supplying to unprofitable customers**, or to **work out a way of increasing the profitability of those customers**; for example, imposing a minimum order size, or varying delivery charges depending on the size of an order.

(e) An appreciation of the costs of servicing clients assists in **negotiations** with customers.

(f) It helps quantify the **financial impact** of proposed changes.

(g) It helps highlight the **cost** of obtaining **new** customers and the **benefit** of retaining existing customers.

(h) It helps to highlight whether **product** development or **market** development is preferable.

4.3.1 Limitations of CPA

However, there are also some limitations of CPA.

(a) Practical **calculations can be very difficult** – in particular assigning indirect costs to different activities or customers. If costs are wrongly apportioned then customer profitability will be distorted.

(b) CPA tends to be used on single products but, in practice, **customers may buy a range of products**. Although a customer may not be profitable on the single product being assessed, they may be across the range of products they buy. CPA could overlook this, leading to **flawed decision making**.

(c) CPA may also lead to flawed decision making if it only looks at **current revenues and costs**, and **overlooks the life cycle value** of the customer. Although a customer may not currently be very profitable, their profitability may increase as they move through their life cycle. For example, university students may not be very profitable customers for banks during their student days, but if they become business executives in the future they could then become very profitable.

4.4 Identifying profitable customers/segments

To analyse customer profitability successfully, it may be necessary to structure **accounting information systems** to take account of the many factors by which customers can be analysed.

An important area in marketing strategy is **retaining** customers, so as to generate new business from them. But how do you identify which customers, or customer groups, generate the most profit?

(a)   First, divide the customer base into segments (for example, by purchase value, by frequency of purchases, by geographical region, by method of ordering (in store, by phone, or online), by number of different products bought, or by payment method).

(b)   Then, calculate the annual revenues earned (net of direct production costs) from each of the segments.

(c)   Finally, calculate the annual costs of serving each of the segments (for example, delivery costs, promotional costs, cost of processing orders, sales returns or warranty costs, and any special costs due to last-minute orders. This will involve the adoption of activity based costing (ABC) techniques).

(d)   By comparing revenues with costs it is possible to identify which segments are the most profitable.

Remember, this consideration must be brought into the design of management information and administration systems. The firm's existing customer groupings, as reported in management accounts, may reflect administrative measures rather than their strategic value.

Question 8.2	Choosing data

Learning outcomes A1(d)

Busqueros Ltd has 1,000 business customers spread fairly evenly over the UK. The sales force is organised into 10 regions, each with 100 customers to be serviced. There are sales force offices at the heart of each region. Information is collected on a regional basis. The marketing director has recently carried out an analysis of the major customers by sales revenue. There are five significant customers, who between them account for 20% of the sales revenue of the firm. They do not get special treatment. What does this say about customer profitability analysis in Busqueros Ltd?

4.4.1 Accounting systems

To analyse customer profitability successfully it may be necessary to structure accounting information systems to take account of the many factors by which customers can be analysed. A **relational database**, whereby information can be structured in many different ways, offers a useful approach.

How do you apportion costs to customer segments? Assume you have a customer base of 15,000 people. You have just spent £20,000 on an advertising campaign and 5,000 new customers have been found. How do you allocate the cost of the campaign? You do not know whether each new customer was attracted by the campaign, or by word of mouth.

Different customer costs can arise out of the following:

- Order size
- Sales mix
- Order processing
- Transport costs (eg if JIT requires frequent deliveries)
- Management time
- Cash flow problems (eg increased overdraft interest) caused by slow payers
- Order complexity (eg if the order has to be sent out in several stages)
- Inventory holding costs can relate to specific customers
- The customer's negotiating strength

4.4.2 Product attributes

The nature of the product (its **attributes**) may be a mix of the varying requirements of different customers. Hence some customers will be offered greater value than they need at a price they are unwilling to pay. The sales volume to this market segment and resulting profit will be less than it might be with a simpler product. This must be set against the potential extra cost and complication of offering a special product.

4.4.3 Example

Here is a possible layout for a **customer profitability analysis**.

	£'000
Gross sales	1,072
Less discounts	(45)
Net sales	1,027
Production	
Less production costs	(510)
	517
Marketing	
Less: Specific marketing costs:	
Sales calls	(10)
In-store promotions	(5)
Customer bonuses	(5)
Less: Share of other marketing costs:	
Sales force management	(10)
Customer service	(10)
	477
Distribution	
Less: Specific distribution costs:	
Transportation	(5)
Packaging	(17)
Refusals	(2)
Outstanding debts	(30)
	423
Less: Shares of distribution costs:	
Order processing	(4)
Inventory holding	(24)
Warehousing	(20)
Collecting debts	(10)
Customer contribution	365

Such a report can highlight the variations in the cost of servicing different individuals or firms which can then be applied as follows:

(a) **Directing effort to cutting customer specific costs.** Installing an electronic data interchange (EDI) system can save the costs of paperwork and data input.

(b) **Identifying those customers who are expensive to service**, thereby suggesting action to increase profitability.

(c) **Using CPA as part of a comparison with competitors' costs.** A firm which services a customer more cheaply than a competitor can use this cost advantage to offer extra benefits to the customer.

(d) Indicating cases where **profitability might be endangered**, for example by servicing customers for whom the firm's core competence is not especially relevant.

CPA might provide answers to the following questions. (Obviously a firm undertaking work for one major customer will find it easier to answer these questions than one which works for many customers.)

(a) What **profit/contribution** is the organisation making on sales to the customer, after discounts and selling and delivery costs?

(b) What would be the **financial consequences** of losing the customer?

(c)   Is the customer buying in order sizes that are **unprofitable** to supply?

(d)   What is the level of **inventory** required specifically to supply these customers?

(e)   Are there any other **specific costs** involved in supplying this customer, eg technical and test facilities, R&D facilities, special design staff?

(f)   What is the ratio of net contribution per customer to total investment?

4.5 Customer life cycle value

Customer life cycle value (CLV) is the present value of the future cash flows attributed to the life cycle of an organisation's relationship with a customer.

In theory, CLV shows how much each customer is worth to an organisation; and therefore shows that organisation how much it should be prepared to spend on acquiring and retaining that customer. For example, it is not worth an organisation offering promotions and incentives whose value is greater than the customer's life cycle value to that organisation.

The concept of the **customer life cycle** is less developed than the product and industry life cycle models. However, it could still usefully be used in conjunction with customer account profitability by considering the following:

(a)   **Promotional expense** relating to a single customer is likely to be heavily **front-loaded**: it is much cheaper to retain a customer than to attract one.

(b)   It is likely that **sales** to a customer will start at a low level and increase to a higher level as the customer gains confidence, though this is not certain and will vary from industry to industry.

(c)   A customer who purchases a basic or commodity product initially may move on to **more differentiated products** later.

(d)   In consumer markets, career progression is likely to provide the individual with steadily increasing amounts of disposable income, while the **family life cycle** will indicate the ranging nature of likely purchases as time passes.

In practice, firms have to make some assumptions in order to calculate CLV. Two key assumptions are:

(a)   **Churn rate**. The percentage of customers that end their relationship with the organisation in any given period. Organisations tend to assume that churn rate remains constant but if, for example, churn rate turns out to be lower than this assumed level, CLV should be higher than anticipated.

(b)   **Retention cost**. The amount of time and money the company has to spend in order to retain an existing customer, for example through customer service, or special offers and other promotional incentives.

In addition, any attempt to estimate life cycle costs and revenues should also consider existing and potential environmental impacts including, in particular, the likely actions of competitors and the potential for product and process innovation.

However, these external factors increase the degree of uncertainty in any customer value calculations over the longer term. For example, what is the probability of retaining customers in the future if competitors introduce new products? Or what is the probability that customers will buy additional products in the future if the company develops new products?

Section summary

Key customer analysis investigates six main customer characteristics in order to identify which customers offer most profit.

Customer profitability analysis is an analysis of total sales revenue generated from a customer or customer group, less all the costs incurred in servicing that customer or group.

5 Databases and marketing

Introduction

Information and knowledge about customers can help organisations manage their marketing campaigns more effectively. **Database marketing** illustrates how organisations can use databases to assist with the direct marketing of products.

However, a consequence of the increasing importance of data is that businesses are having to hold and manage ever-increasing amounts of data (about sales, revenues, customers, competitors etc). Two techniques designed to utilise the ever-increasing amounts of data held by organisations are **data warehousing** and **data mining**.

KEY TERM

DATABASE MARKETING is the analysis and use of customer databases in supporting communication and other relationship-building contacts with customers. Customer data held in computerised databases can be interrogated and manipulated in various ways through the process of data mining.

Database marketing techniques can be used for a range of relationship marketing projects, including:

(a)   Identifying the most profitable customers, using RFM analysis (**R**ecency of the latest purchase, **F**requency of purchases and **M**onetary value of all purchases).

(b)   Developing new customers (for example, by collecting data on prospects, leads and referrals).

(c)   Tailoring messages and offerings, based on customers' purchase profiles. (Actual customer buying preferences and patterns are a much more reliable guide to their future behaviour than market research, which gathers their 'stated' preferences.)

(d)   Personalising customer service, by providing service staff with relevant customer details.

(e)   Eliminating conflicting or confusing communications: presenting a coherent image over time to individual customers. In this respect, it is important to differentiate the message to different customer groups. (For example, companies must avoid sending 'Dear first-time customer' messages to long-standing customers!)

However, an organisation must be careful that it does not distribute spam (unsolicited or unwanted emails) via the internet.

5.1 Databases and new customers

An organisation's customer database and potential customer database represents a major source of trade. The company can use it to generate repeat business, or to stimulate new business.

When advertising, companies don't only target new customers, but also the existing ones they already have listed in their databases. **Keeping contact with existing customers** is a good way to generate repeat business, but also to be able to promote new products to the right people – the people who would be most interested in buying them.

Obtaining **names of potential new customers** is now quite easy, because there are companies who specialise in selling the information of individuals who wish to be contacted by relevant businesses.

However, there is a cost involved in this method, which is why it is also important for organisations to keep records of all the potential customers they come into contact with so that they can build up their own database.

Ultimately, the **aim of marketing databases is to generate revenues**, so the more information organisations can hold about customers and potential customers the better. The more the organisation knows about potential customers, the better chance it should have of targeting the right people in a marketing campaign.

In an effort to **target potential customers more effectively**, organisations can use database marketing to build models of their target demographic group. These models then allow them to focus their advertising budgets on these target groups, in the hope that this will result in an improved return on investment (ROI) on their advertising spend.

Information gathering is therefore an important process, and organisations need to attract potential customers who are willing to divulge information about themselves. Offering prizes and/or promotional campaigns through newsletters or 'ezines' can help achieve this.

If **records are stored and organised effectively**, an organisation should be able to implement new marketing strategies and (targeted) campaigns more quickly and easily. For example, by grouping individuals together according to shared characteristics (age, income, gender etc) organisations can generate targeted mailing lists of potential customers who share a set of desired characteristics.

Moreover, having a comprehensive database can also **help with forecasting**. Future trends for sales and marketing can be modelled based on the results of previous projects. By studying the past purchases of consumers, analytical software allows data analysts to predict broad trends in purchasing habits which can give an insight into customers' future purchasing behaviour.

However, it is important that organisations keep their database **up to date, and well organised**. Having outdated or invalid entries could cause confusion and waste time. For example, there is no point in trying to contact business customers who have gone out of business.

There is also an **ethical/legal dimension** to consider when managing databases. Often unsolicited calls do not generate any business and can be annoying for the recipient. But, more importantly, companies need to ensure their databases comply with the law. In the UK, data must be kept up to date, be relevant, and must only be used for the purpose the customer intended or can reasonably expect it to be used for.

5.2 Data warehousing

KEY TERM

A DATA WAREHOUSE consists of a database, containing data from various operational systems, and reporting and query tools.

Data warehouse – A data warehouse is a large-scale data collection and storage area, containing data from various operational systems, plus **reporting** and **query tools** which allow the data to be analysed. The key feature of a data warehouse is that it provides a single point for **storing a coherent set of information** which can then be used across an organisation for **management analysis** and decision making.

The data warehouse is not an operational system, so the data in it remains static until it is next updated. For example, if a supermarket introduces a customer credit card, the history of customers' transactions on their cards could be stored in a data warehouse, so that management could analyse spending patterns.

However, although the reporting and query tools within the warehouse should facilitate management reporting and analysis, data warehouses are primarily used for **storing** data rather than analysing data.

A data warehouse contains data from a range of **internal** (eg sales order processing system, nominal ledger) and **external sources**. One reason for including individual transaction data in a data warehouse is that if necessary the user can drill down to access transaction level detail. Data is increasingly obtained from newer channels such as customer care systems, outside agencies or websites.

Maintenance of a data warehouse is an iterative process that continually refines its content. Data is copied to the data warehouse as often as required – usually either daily, weekly or monthly. The process of making any required changes to the format of data and copying it to the warehouse is usually automated.

The result should be a coherent set of information available to be used across the organisation for management analysis and decision making. The reporting and query tools available within the warehouse should facilitate management reporting and analysis and should be flexible enough to allow multidimensional data analysis, also known as **online analytical processing** (OLAP). Each aspect of information (eg product, region, price, budgeted sales, actual sales, time period etc) represents a different dimension. OLAP enables data to be viewed from each dimension, allowing each aspect to be analysed in relation to the others.

5.2.1 Features of data warehouses

A data warehouse is subject-oriented, integrated, time-variant, and non-volatile.

(a) **Subject-oriented**

A data warehouse is focused on data groups, not application boundaries. Whereas the operational world is designed around applications and functions such as sales and purchases, a data warehouse world is organised around major **subjects** such as customers, supplier, product and activity.

(b) **Integrated**

Data within the data warehouse must be consistent in format and codes used – this is referred to as **integrated** in the context of data warehouses.

For example, one operational application feeding the warehouse may represent **sex** as an 'M' and an 'F' while another represents **sex** as '1' and '0'.

While it does not matter how **sex** is represented in the data warehouse (let us say that 'M' and 'F' is chosen), it **must** arrive in the data warehouse in a **consistent integrated** state. The data import routine should cleanse any inconsistencies.

(c) **Time-variant**

Data is organised by time and stored in time-slices.

Data warehouse data may cover **a long time horizon**, perhaps from five to ten years. Data warehouse data tends to deal with **trends** rather than single points in time. As a result, each data element in the data warehouse environment must carry with it the time for which it applies.

(d) **Non-volatile**

Data **cannot be changed** within the warehouse. Only load and retrieval operations are made.

Organisations may build a single central data warehouse to serve the entire organisation or may create a series of smaller **data marts**. A data mart holds a selection of the organisation's data for a specific purpose.

A data mart can be constructed more quickly and cheaply than a data warehouse. However, if too many individual data marts are built, organisations may find it is more efficient to have a single data warehouse serving all areas.

The components of a data warehouse are shown in the following diagram.

Components of a data warehouse

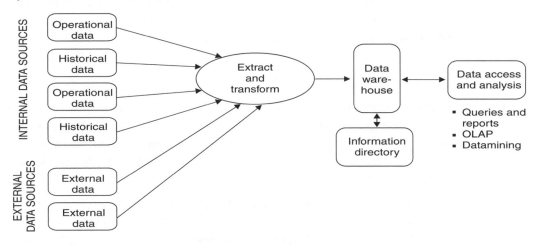

5.2.2 Advantages of data warehouses

Advantages of setting up a data warehouse system include:

(a)   **Support for strategic decision making**. The warehouse provides a single source of authoritative data which can be analysed using data mining techniques to support strategic decision making.

(b)   Decision makers can access data without affecting the use of operational systems.

(c)   **Data quality**. Having a single source of data available will reduce the risk of inconsistent data being used by different people during the decision-making process.

(d)   Having a wide range of data available to be queried easily encourages the taking of a wide perspective on organisational activities.

(e)   **Speed**. Data warehousing can enable faster responses to business queries, not only by storing data in an easily accessible central repository, but also by using OLAP technologies.

(f)   Data warehouses have proved successful in some businesses for:

    (i)   Quantifying the effect of marketing initiatives

    (ii)   Improving knowledge of customers

    (iii)   Identifying and understanding an enterprise's most profitable revenues streams

In this way, data warehouses (and data mining) allow organisations to use the data they hold to help improve their competitiveness, and could help them gain a competitive advantage over their rivals.

5.2.3 Limitations of data warehouses

Some organisations have found they have invested considerable resources implementing a data warehouse for little return. To benefit from the information a data warehouse can provide, organisations need to be flexible and prepared to act on what they find. If a warehouse system is implemented simply to follow current practice it will be of little value.

Other limitations exist, particularly if a data warehouse is intended to be used as an operational system rather than as an analytical tool. For example:

(a)   The data held may be outdated.

(b)   An efficient regular routine must be established to transfer data into the warehouse.

(c)   A warehouse may be implemented and then, as it is not required on a day to day basis, be ignored.

There is also an issue of **security**. The management aim of making data available widely and in an easily understood form can be at variance with the need to maintain confidentiality of, for example, payroll data.

This conflict can be managed by **encrypting** data at the point of capture and **restricting access** by a system of authorisations entitling different users to different levels of access. For this to work, the data held must be classified according to the degree of protection it requires: users can then be given access limited to a given class or classes of data. Encryption at the point of capture also exerts control over the **unauthorised uploading** of data to the data warehouse.

5.3 Metadata

Metadata is data about data. In the same way that a nutritional standards label gives you information about the contents of a tin of food, so metadata gives you information about the data in a data warehouse. For example, metadata might include the time data is loaded into the warehouse, the source of the data, or when an entry into the warehouse was last updated. A software information model can create metadata for a data warehouse.

Metadata also describes the way the data is structured, and assists users in finding and accessing data in the warehouse. It can also help users understand what that data means. However, metadata also plays an important role in ensuring the quality of data held in a warehouse. Metadata specifies what is supposed to be in the data warehouse, and documents what is actually there. Good metadata allows data to be loaded into a database more quickly, and equally allows users to fulfil subsequent information requests more quickly.

5.4 Data mining

While a data warehouse is effectively a large database which collates information from a wide variety of sources, data mining is concerned with the discovery of meaningful relationships in the underlying data.

KEY TERM

DATA MINING software looks for hidden patterns and relationships in large pools of data.

Data mining is primarily concerned with **analysing data**. It uses statistical analysis tools to look for **hidden patterns and relationships** (such as trends and correlations) in large pools of data. The value of data mining lies in its ability to highlight previously unknown relationships.

In this respect, data mining can give organisations a **better insight into customer behaviours**, and can lead to **increased sales through predicting future behaviour**.

A classic example of this is Wal-Mart's findings in the 1990s, that young fathers, sent by their partners to buy nappies on the way home from a hard working week, would often add some bottles of beer to their checkout basket. By putting beer next to nappies in the shopping aisles, Wal-Mart saw Friday evening beer sales across the US increase significantly.

Similarly, a number of supermarkets now have customer loyalty cards (for example, Tesco's Clubcard). When a customer pays for their shopping using a loyalty card, the supermarket can also create a record of the items the customer has bought. The purchasing behaviour of customers can be used to create a profile of what kind of people the cardholders are.

Data mining techniques could be applied to customers' purchasing information to identify patterns in the items which were purchased together, or what types of item were omitted from shopping baskets, and how the make-up of customers' baskets varied by different types of customer. The supermarket could then target its promotions to take advantage of these purchasing patterns.

In this way, by identifying patterns and relationships, data mining can **guide decision making**.

True data mining software discovers **previously unknown relationships**. The hidden patterns and relationships the software identifies can be used to guide decision making and to **predict future behaviour**.

Data mining uses statistical analysis tools as well as neural networks, fuzzy logic and other **intelligent techniques**.

5.4.1 Patterns uncovered through data mining

The types of relationships or patterns that data mining may uncover may be classified as follows.

Relationship/ Discovery	Comment
Classification or clustering	These terms refer to the identification of previously unrecognised patterns within the database, which can be used to organise the data into groups with common characteristics or profiles. For example, data mining may find that unmarried males aged between 20 and 30, who have an income above $75,000, are more likely to purchase a high performance sports car than people from other demographic groups. This group could then be targeted when marketing material is produced/distributed.
Associations	One event can be linked or correlated to another event – as in the Wal-Mart beer and nappies example.
Sequences	One event leads to another event. For example; buying a new car will be followed by taking out insurance on that car. By identifying purchasing sequences in this way, organisations can target their marketing activities based on customers' recent purchases.
Forecasting	Trends are identified within the data that can be extrapolated into the future, and can therefore lead to predictions about the future (for example, due to seasonal variations in purchasing patterns).

5.4.2 The potential impact of Big Data

In the previous section, we mentioned the example of how Tesco uses Clubcard data to analyse customer purchasing behaviour.

However, the expansion of Big Data can provide organisations with a far greater volume and variety of data which could be used in predicting customer behaviours and building relationship marketing campaigns.

Section summary

Data warehouses and data mining are important techniques for using the data held by an organisation.

A **data warehouse** consists of a database, containing data from various operational systems, and reporting and query tools, and is used to collate a coherent set of information which can be used in decision making. **Data mining** involves discovering new patterns and relationships in the underlying data.

6 Digital marketing

Introduction

Digital marketing is the application of IS and internet techniques to achieve marketing objectives. Most marketing activities can be enhanced by the use of such techniques, including branding, customer service and sales.

Exam skills

Although we have called this section 'Digital marketing', you could equally see references in exam questions to electronic marketing or e-marketing. Both terms refer to the way electronic communication technologies can be used to accomplish marketing objectives, and so could be used interchangeably as the key terms at the start of the next section illustrate.

6.1 Digital technologies and their impact on marketing

KEY TERMS

DIGITAL MARKETING involves the application of the technologies which form online channels – such as the internet, email, smartphones, tablets, digital television and games consoles – to achieve marketing objectives.

E-MARKETING can be described as the application of the electronic communication technologies – such as the internet, smartphones, tablets and digital televisions – to achieve marketing objectives.

Kotler et al in *Principles of Marketing* provide a useful summary of how changes in communication technology have given rise to the growth of digital marketing:

> '*Advances in communications technology are causing remarkable changes in the ways in which companies and customers communicate with each other. The digital age has spawned a host of new information and communication tools – from smartphones and iPods to satellite and cable television systems to the many faces of the internet (e-mail, social networks, blogs, brand websites and so on). These ... new digital media have given birth to a new marketing communications model.*
>
> *Although television, magazines, newspapers and other mass media remain very important, their dominance is declining. In their place, advertisers are now adding a broad selection of more-specialised and highly targeted media to reach smaller customer segments with more personalised, interactive messages. The new media range from speciality cable television channels and made-for-the-Web videos to internet catalogues, e-mail, blogs, mobile phone content and online social networks. In all, companies are doing less broadcasting and more narrowcasting.*'

Marketing objectives include identifying, anticipating and satisfying customer requirements profitably.

- **Identifying** – using the internet to find out customers' needs and wants

- **Anticipating** – the demand for digital services

- **Satisfying** – achieving customer satisfaction raises issues over whether the site is easy to use, whether it performs adequately and how the physical products are dispatched

Essentially, digital marketing means using digital technologies to help sell goods or services. The basics of marketing remain the same – creating a strategy to deliver the right messages to the right people. What has changed is the number of options available. These include pay per click advertising, banner ads, email marketing and affiliate marketing, interactive advertising, search engine marketing (including search engine optimisation) and blog marketing.

Though businesses will continue to make use of traditional marketing methods, such as press and television advertising, direct mail and PR, digital marketing adds a whole new element to the marketing mix and is a valuable complement, as the extract from Kotler *et al* illustrates. Digital marketing gives businesses of any size access to the mass market at an affordable price and, unlike TV or print advertising, it allows truly **personalised marketing.**

6.1.1 Push vs pull marketing

Another consequence of the emergence of digital technologies has been an increase in 'pull' marketing strategies compared to traditional 'push' marketing strategies.

Push strategies – An organisation transmits messages about its products or services to prospective customers, to try to ensure those customers are aware of the product. However, as such, the customer is only a **recipient of the information** – for example, when they see a banner advert on a website.

Pull strategies – By contrast, pull marketing seeks to draw potential customers towards a company, and to encourage the customer to find out more about that company. In pull marketing, the customer has an active role to play in **seeking out information**. For example, a blog posting by a company could encourage potential customers to search for more information about it and its products. Similarly, a number of companies now have Facebook pages, which aim to enhance customers' experiences of interacting with their brands.

6.1.2 Key marketing functions the internet can perform

(a) **Creating company and product awareness** – communicating essential information about the company and its brands. Such information may have a financial orientation to help attract potential investors, or it may focus on the unique features and benefits of its product lines.

(b) **Branding** – is a marketing communications activity. The intent is to have the public perceive a brand in a positive manner. With the amount of advertising being devoted to the internet increasing each year, the frequency of visits to a site will also increase. Consequently, a company's website will play a more prominent role in building its brand image. Online communications should therefore be similar in appearance and style to communications in the traditional media so as to present a consistent brand image.

(c) **Offering incentives** – many sites offer discounts for purchasing online. Electronic coupons, bonus offers, and contests are now quite common. Such offers are intended to stimulate immediate purchase before a visitor leaves a website, and also to encourage repeat visits.

(d) **Lead generation** – the internet is an interactive medium. Visitors to a site leave useful information behind when they fill in boxes requesting more information (eg name, address, telephone number, and email address). A site may also ask for demographic information that can be added to the company's database. This information is retained for future mailings about similar offers, or can be turned over to a sales force for follow-up if it is a business-to-business marketing situation.

(e) **Customer service** – in any form of marketing, customer service is important. Satisfied customers hold positive attitudes about a company and are therefore more likely to return to buy more goods. Right now, customer service is perceived as a weak link in internet marketing. Customers are concerned about who they should call for technical assistance or what process to follow should goods need to be returned.

Some customer service tactics commonly used include frequently asked questions (FAQs) and return email systems. It is apparent that organisations will have to spend more time and money developing effective customer service systems.

(f) **Email databases** – organisations retain visitor information in a database. Emailing useful and relevant information to prospects and customers helps build stronger relationships. An organisation must be careful that it does not distribute spam (unsolicited/unwanted email) on the internet.

(g) **Online transactions** – organisations are capable of selling online if the website is user friendly. The ability to sell online could potentially be the most important benefit the internet provides for a company. However, if a company website is hard to navigate, and it proves difficult for customers to make a purchase online, this will reduce the company's ability to generate online sales.

Websites and online ordering also enable organisations in the supply chain to link together to achieve efficiencies in business-to-business transactions. The ability to track and monitor orders via an extranet can also be valuable (particularly for B2B customers), so websites which provide this facility could play a part in customer retention.

Technology and website designs

Developments in technology mean that companies have to continuously monitor the media through which they interact with potential customers.

'User experience' is very important for customers. Since potential customers no longer only access websites from PCs, but also from tablet computers or smartphones, they are likely to expect a user experience built around these different devices. Therefore, a well-designed 'app' or a web page designed for the screen size of the device it is being accessed from could help enhance a mobile user's impression of a company.

Earlier in the chapter we discussed the concept of customer relationship management, and its three elements of customer acquisition, retention and extension.

The internet and online techniques can play an important role in these, perhaps most extensively in relation to customer acquisition.

The internet offers a number of methods for **acquiring customers**.

Search engines – Search engines (such as Google) mean that when users search for relevant key words or phrases links to the company's website will appear in their search results. In turn, **search engine optimisation** can be used as a technique for improving the company's position in the search engine listings.

Pay per click (or cost per click) advertising – Companies can pay other websites to display a banner on their website, with the hope that potential customers will click on the banner which then links through to the company's own website.

Affiliate marketing – A company rewards affiliates for each visitor or customer who comes to the company's website through the affiliate's own marketing efforts. Amazon is probably the best-known example of an affiliate network, with an extensive range of sites directing customers to Amazon to buy books or music tracks that the affiliates have mentioned on their web pages.

Business blogs – Companies can use blogs to showcase the knowledge and expertise of their employees, and thereby hopefully attract new customers.

Comparison sites – Comparison sites (such as moneysupermarket.com) allow potential customers to compare the price and features of different products, and if a product compares favourably to competitor products this should encourage potential customers to buy it.

Viral marketing – Social networks are used to increase brand awareness, for example through video clips or images being passed from one user to another.

Retention

The internet can also be useful for helping to **retain customers**, for example through the use of **personalised reminder emails**, possibly with discount codes or other incentives, to customers who have not purchased anything recently.

Online communities – The creation of online communities and forums could also help retain customers' interest in a product or service. However, these forums can also have an additional benefit from companies. By reading customers' feedback and comments, businesses can improve their understanding of customer needs, and can take steps to improve their products or services to address any issues which are currently attracting criticism on the forums.

Extension

Recommendations – Probably the best-known examples of customer extension are the 'recommendations' which customers are given on Amazon. Amazon's data modelling software allows it to monitor products which customers often buy together. Therefore, when existing customers log back in to Amazon they are given recommendations of other products they might like to buy, based on their previous purchases.

However, recommendations are not only made when customers log on; they also occur at the point a customer makes a purchase. For example, if a customer purchases a television, they might then be asked at the checkout if they also want to buy a television stand to go with their television.

6.1.3 Specific benefits of digital marketing

(a) **Global reach** – a website can reach anyone in the world who has internet access. This allows you to find new markets and compete globally for only a small investment.

(b)   **Lower cost** – a properly planned and effectively targeted digital marketing campaign can reach the right customers at a much lower cost than traditional marketing methods.

(c)   **The ability to track and measure results** – marketing by email or banner advertising makes it easier to establish how effective your campaign has been. You can obtain detailed information about customers' responses to your advertising.

(d)   **24-hour marketing** – with a website your customers can find out about your products even if your office is closed.

(e)   **Personalisation** – if your customer database is linked to your website, then whenever someone visits the site, you can greet them with targeted offers. The more they buy from you, the more you can refine your customer profile and market effectively to them.

(f)   **One-to-one marketing** – digital marketing lets you reach people who want to know about your products and services instantly. For example, many people take their smartphone or tablet with them wherever they go. Combine this with the personalised aspect of digital marketing, and you can create very powerful, targeted campaigns.

(g)   **More interesting campaigns** – digital marketing lets you create interactive campaigns using music, graphics and videos. You could send your customers a game or a quiz – whatever you think will interest them.

(h)   **Better conversion rate** – if you have a website, then your customers are only ever a few clicks away from completing a purchase. Unlike other media which require people to get up and make a phone call, post a letter or go to a shop, digital marketing is seamless.

Together, all of these aspects of digital marketing have the potential to add up to more sales.

As a component of e-commerce, it can include information management, public relations, customer service and sales.

6.2 Web 2.0 and social media marketing

In the previous chapter, we mentioned briefly how Web 2.0 technologies could be used to facilitate **viral marketing**, and also to monitor consumers' feedback and comments on a product or brand.

KEY TERM

SOCIAL MEDIA MARKETING refers to the process of acquiring customers and attracting the attention of potential customers through social media sites.

Web 2.0 technologies have changed the way companies interact with customers, and have also changed the way customers (or potential customers) interact with content and each other. As we noted in Chapter 7, Web 2.0 technologies – and specifically social media sites – allow users to provide information about themselves and this information can be valuable to marketers.

For example, marketers could analyse the people who 'like' their brands or products on Facebook, and identify those who fit their target demographic. By observing the chatter among those fans on social media, marketers could identify not only sentiments about their own brands, and competitor brands, but the more wider interests of its target demographic – for example, celebrities and TV shows talked about; events that are frequently discussed; topics (articles, video clips or photos) which are commonly shared; and websites which are commonly visited.

In turn, marketers can use this information to help shape their own marketing activity – for example, buying banner adverts on websites which are frequently mentioned; buying advertising space in a TV show being discussed; getting a named celebrity to endorse their product or brand; and developing partnerships with other brands in other industries (where those brands are popular with the target demographic).

Social media and targeted marketing

More generally, social media marketing enables organisations to target relevant marketing messages to narrowly defined market segments, based on the data they have gathered and analysed about their customers and potential customers. This kind of data-powered, targeted marketing is likely to be not only more effective, but also more cost efficient than traditional forms of mass (eg television or newspaper) advertising.

CASE STUDY

Shake Shack

Although the US fast food company, Shake Shack, is much smaller than competitors like McDonald's and Burger King, it has used its social media presence to increase its sales very successfully.

While the industry giants like McDonald's and Burger King frequently advertise on traditional media (such as television or billboards), Shake Shack has instead focused on building an audience through social media platforms like Instagram and Vine – which have a disproportionately high usage among the country's youth population.

And Shake Shack's approach appears to be paying off because not only has its brand won the goodwill of the US's younger fast food eaters, it has also generated a cult-like following online.

A report by Goldman Sachs related to the company's IPO in January 2015 highlighted that Shake Shack 'does essentially no traditional marketing, but has a strong presence on social media, which speaks to its relevance among Millennials' (people born around the turn of the Millennium). 'Using both Vine and Instagram as examples, its followers are much larger than what its system sales would suggest.'

Goldman Sachs' report pointed out that although McDonald's sold more than 300 times as much fast food as Shake Shack – which has fewer than 40 restaurants in the US – McDonald's Instagram following was only approximately 3 times as large (500,000 compared to 155,000 followers).

Moreover, Shake Shack's use of social media means that its marketing activities have a minimal cost, whilst at the same time enabling it to reach the demographic group (Millennials) who are about to become the largest segment of the population.

Based on an article by Roberto Ferdman in The Washington Post: *Where Shake Shack has McDonald's – and most other fast food chains – beat*, February 25, 2015, www.washingtonpost.com

CASE STUDY

Social media and promotions

Discounts are a very important marketing tool for attracting new customers or clients to a company, and a number of companies now distribute special offers and promotional codes via Facebook. In effect, the companies are offering discounts to users who 'like' their Facebook page. Importantly, the promotional codes are offered exclusively to people who 'like' a company or brand's page on Facebook.

By using promotional codes in this way, a company could hope to encourage loyalty among its Facebook fans, but it can also gather information about them (for example, email address; age) if users have to provide these details in order to validate their code.

Similarly, companies are encouraging customers to 'follow' them on Twitter, to receive voucher codes as well as updates on other special offers.

However, the value of social media comes from allowing companies to engage with customers and build relationships with them, not simply from selling to them.

For example, Starbucks communicates with fans on Facebook on an ongoing basis, with a stream of offers and benefits, only some of which are revenue generating. Starbucks' Facebook page combines its offers with stories about the brand, the history of its coffees, and the history of Starbucks' stores. Moreover, Starbucks' Facebook page also incentivises people to 'share' the page with friends. In turn, this sharing adds to the number of customers (and potential customers) Starbucks can build a relationship with.

By September 2013, Starbucks was liked by over 35 million people on Facebook, and had more than 4.3 million Twitter followers.

6.2.1 Potential limitations of social media

In recent years, there has been considerable hype about the growth of social media. However, some commentators still urge caution about the impact that social media actually has on purchasing decisions. In particular, questions are raised about the sort of information which people exchange on social networking sites.

People use social media mainly to socialise, not to buy goods or services. As a result, much of the information that is exchanged is non-commercial in nature, and so may be of limited value to businesses.

Clearly, there is some overlap between the conversations people have about their social lives and conversations about products, services and brands. In this respect, social networking platforms may be a good way for companies to 'listen' to what customers are saying about their brands.

Similarly, social media can be very useful for networking, building relationships and engaging with customers and prospects. However, the actual expenditure generated through social media has, so far, been relatively low, and other marketing channels may remain more relevant and powerful for influencing customers' purchasing decisions.

For example, many brands boast very large numbers of Facebook fans or 'likes'. But marketing directors could be justified in asking what benefits these 'likes' actually bring a brand. Simply 'liking' a brand on Facebook doesn't mean that someone is going to purchase that brand.

Potential threat to companies/brands – Social media also gives customers the power to transmit/share messages which may not be the messages the companies actually want to be transmitted (for example, if a guest has had an unsatisfactory meal in a restaurant, or stay in a hotel, they can publicise this on review sites such as TripAdvisor).

Equally, conversations between social networkers may not be in the best interests of a company. For example, many Facebook groups are set up to complain about organisations.

In this way, the internet and social media are not simply increasing the role of the consumer in the marketing process; they could also be seen to be increasing consumers' power over the marketing process – and disrupting an organisation's ability to control that process.

CASE STUDY

Potential risks from social media

In September 2013, accounting firm Grant Thornton published a report titled 'Social media risks and rewards'. The report explored the increasing use of social media by large companies and the new types of risk that such communication brings. The growing importance of social media among big business is evident from the report's findings:

- More than half (55%) of the executives who responded to the survey feel that social media will be an important component of corporate marketing efforts going forward.

- Two-thirds (66%) of respondents expected their company's use of social media to increase slightly or significantly over the next 12 months.

Social media risks

The report identifies four main risks from using social media:

(1) Damage to brand reputation
(2) Disclosure of proprietary and/or confidential information
(3) Corporate identity theft
(4) Legal, regulatory and compliance violations

'Nearly three quarters (71%) of executives surveyed were concerned about the potential risks involved in the use of social media, but believe the risks can be mitigated or avoided'.

The report highlights some examples of companies which have failed to manage their social media communications effectively, including the following by Gap and Netflix:

Gap – In 2012, Hurricane Sandy struck parts of the US causing severe devastation; retailer Gap posted a tweet via Twitter which advised customers to 'stay safe, and perhaps shop at Gap.com'. Gap apologised shortly afterwards and removed the message.

Netflix – The US Securities and Exchange Commission (SEC) investigated Netflix in 2012 after the company's CEO, Reed Hastings, posted information on Facebook which boosted its share price.

Reed Hastings' postings raised an interesting issue about social media communications and associated risks. As social media starts to play an increasing role in how businesses communicate, careful consideration needs to be given to ensuring that private messages expressing personal opinions are not perceived as official corporate communications.

Source: Grant Thornton, *Social media risks and rewards,* www.grantthornton.com

6.3 Developing an effective digital marketing plan

Planning for digital marketing does not mean starting from scratch. Any online or digital communication must be **consistent with the overall marketing goals** and **current marketing efforts** of the organisation.

The key strategic decisions for digital marketing are common with strategic decisions for traditional marketing. They involve selecting target customer groups and specifying how to deliver value to these groups. Segmentation, targeting, differentiation and positioning all contribute to effective digital marketing.

The **SOSTAC® planning framework** developed by Paul Smith provides a structured and effective approach to marketing strategy. It can be used by managers in the private, public and non-profit sectors.

S = Situation analysis	Where are we now? What is the external environment in which we are operating? What are our own strengths and weaknesses?
O = Objectives	Where do we want to get to? What is our goal?
S = Strategies	How do we get there? What do we need to do to be successful?
T = Tactics	What are the individual steps we need to take to achieve our objective?
A = Actions	What are the things we need to do? What is our 'to-do' list? Who will do what?
C = Control	What will we measure to know we are succeeding? How will we know when we have arrived?

The planning framework is expanded in the diagram below to show the techniques/actions that make up each stage:

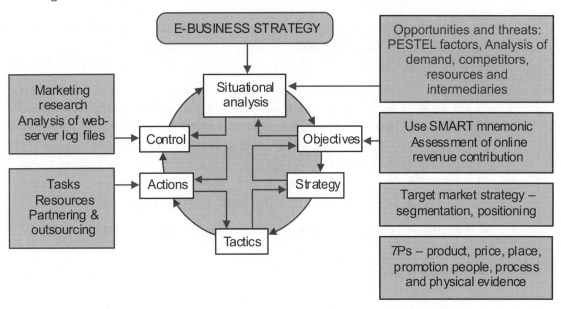

SOSTAC® Framework for digital marketing planning

The process of developing an effective digital marketing plan will include the following.

Competitor analysis	Scanning competitor internet sites
	Competitor benchmarking to compare e-commerce services within a market
	Competitive intelligence systems give a structured approach to monitoring and disseminating information on competitor activities
Intermediary analysis	Identify and compare intermediaries for a marketplace
	Search portals and look for new approaches for traffic building
	Research whether competitors are using disintermediation or reintermediation
Internal marketing audit	Focus on e-market measurement:

<table>
<tr><td>Channel promotion</td><td>Channel behaviour</td><td>Channel satisfaction</td><td>Channel outcomes</td><td>Channel profitability</td></tr>
<tr><td>Acquisition costs Referrers</td><td>Who? How?</td><td>Opinions? Attitudes? Brand impact?</td><td>Leads? Sales?</td><td>ROI? Profitability?</td></tr>
</table>

	Applying web analytics tools to measure the contribution of leads, sales and brand involvement currently delivered by online communications such as search engine marketing, online advertising and email marketing in conjunction with the website
	Create online CRM capabilities to understand customers' characteristics, needs and behaviours and to deliver targeted, personalised value
Objective setting	Online revenue contribution
Strategy	Identify target market by assessing size, segments, needs and competitive action
	Online value proposition (OVP)

Tactics	Use internet to vary the extended product
	Look at new channel structures
	Research people replacements: autoresponders, email notification, call-back facility, FAQs, on-site search engines and virtual assistants
	Branding
	Managing the continuous online marketing communications such as search engine marketing, partnerships, sponsorships and affiliate arrangements and campaign-based digital marketing communications such as online advertising, email marketing and microsites to encourage usage of the online service and to support customer acquisition and retention campaigns

6.4 Characteristics of the media of digital marketing

The employment of digital marketing may be analysed and planned using the six I's.

- Independence of location
- Industry structure
- Integration
- Interactivity
- Individualisation
- Intelligence

The six I's of marketing, developed at Cranfield by McDonald and Wilson in 1999, summarise the ways in which the internet can add customer value and hence improve the organisation's marketing effectiveness.

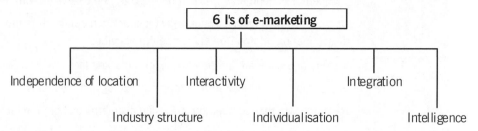

By considering and questioning each of these aspects of the new media, marketing managers can develop plans to accommodate the characteristics of the new media.

Independence of location	Do you exploit any opportunities to deliver information-based products and services electronically?
	Electronic media gives the possibility of communicating globally – giving opportunities of selling into markets that may not have been previously accessible.
Industry structure	Industry restructuring includes the following:
	Redesigning business processes
	Redrawing the market map in form of new market segments or increasing the marketing boundaries
	Adopting IT enabled services (ITeS)
Integration	Do you have detailed knowledge of individual customers, influencers or consumers?
	Do you share this knowledge across all customer-facing parts of the business?
	Advertising products/services on the web is easy. It is more difficult, but absolutely crucial, to gather vital customer information, obtain customer feedback, use existing knowledge about the customer and exploit the web's interactive nature to add value through product configuration, online pricing and so on.

Interactivity	Do you use interactive media to allow your customers to communicate with you?
	Do you listen to what they say and respond appropriately in a continuing dialogue?
	Traditional media are mainly '**push**' media – the marketing message is broadcast from company to customer – with limited interaction. On the internet it is usually a customer who seeks information on a web – it is a '**pull**' mechanism.
	The growing use of carefully targeted direct mail as a means of communicating with individual customers has led some to call this 'the age of addressability'.
Individualisation	Do you use your customer knowledge to tailor products and services to the needs of particular individuals or segments?
	Do you tailor all your communications to the characteristics of the recipients?
	Communications can be tailored to the individual unlike traditional media where the same message is broadcast to everyone.
Intelligence	Do you inform your marketing strategy with intelligence gleaned from your operational systems at the customer interface eg through analysis of customer needs, segmentation, prioritising segments according to customer lifetime value etc?
	The internet can be used as a low cost method of collecting marketing information about customer perceptions of products and services. The website also records information every time a user clicks on a link. Log file analysers will identify the type of promotions or products customers are responding to and how patterns vary over time.

Example

The best-known example of electronic commerce, bookselling, exemplifies how the internet can be used for an interactive dialogue with a known customer.

Websites such as Amazon.com exploit the web's interactive nature to allow the customer to search for books on particular topics, track the status of an order placed earlier, ask for recommendations of books similar to their favourites, read reviews placed by other customers, and so on. The website builds knowledge of the customer which allows it, for example, to notify them by email if a new book appears on a topic of particular interest.

6.5 Digital marketing and the 7 Ps

More specific concepts for the development of digital marketing may be based on the 7 Ps of the service marketing mix.

- The augmented **product** can be extended through web information and interactivity.

- **Pricing** can be made transparent; dynamic pricing may be used.

- The global reach of the internet has significant implications for **place**, with the creation of new marketplaces and channel structures.

- **Promotion** can be previously targeted via customer databases.

- **People** can be replaced by software to a varying extent.

- **Processes** may be automated.

- **Physical evidence** consists of the customer's experience of using the organisation's digital marketing tools in general and of its website in particular.

Marketing on the internet brings many new opportunities not readily available or affordable using conventional marketing methods.

The marketing mix is the combination of marketing activities that an organisation engages in so as to best meet the needs of its targeted market. Because of changes in the market and the behaviour of the customers, future marketing should focus more on delivering value to the customer and become better at placing the customer – and not the product – in the centre. In some texts, the 4 Ps have been renamed the 4 Cs.

- Product becomes **customer value**
- Place becomes **customer convenience**
- Promotion becomes **customer communication**
- Price becomes **customer cost**

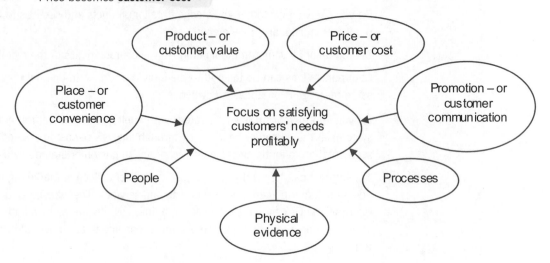

We will now show how the internet and e-commerce provides the opportunities for the marketer to vary the seven elements of the marketing mix.

Exam skills

We have mentioned above how the traditional 4 Ps of the marketing mix have been extended to 7 Ps for the service marketing mix. If you are faced with a question about marketing issues for a service company, make sure you think about the characteristics of services which distinguish them from products: they are **intangible** so customers cannot physically see the features of the item they are buying; they cannot be stored for later use, because the customer is an essential part of the transaction. This customer involvement means there is a very large degree of **variability** in the customers' experiences of service transactions.

6.5.1 Product (or customer value)

What does buying products online offer which purchasing offline does not?

(a)   The ability to deliver interactivity and more detailed information through the internet is the key to enhancing the augmented or extended product offering online.

(b)   The buyer knows immediately about product features, the facts, not a salesperson's interpretations.

(c)   The buying process is customised for returning visitors, making repeat purchases easier. Organisations can also offer immediately ancillary products along with the main purchase. EasyJet, for example, can readily bundle its flights, hotels and car hire through suitable design of its website.

(d)   The product can also be customised to consumers' needs, eg nike.com offers customised trainers to users online. Users can design and see their trainers online before they order.

6.5.2 Price (or customer cost)

The internet has made **pricing very competitive**. Many costs such as store cost and staff cost have disappeared for completely online stores, placing price pressures on traditional retailers.

(a)   The internet increases customer knowledge through **increased price transparency** since it becomes much quicker to shop around and compare quoted prices by visiting supplier websites. Even more significant is the use of price comparison sites by consumers. Sites such as Kelkoo.com (or Kelkoo.co.uk in the UK) give a single location that empowers the consumer to quickly find out the best price from a range of suppliers for a range of products from books and CDs to white goods. Such easy access to information helps to maintain prices within the online world.

(b)   **Dynamic pricing** gives the ability to test prices or to offer differential pricing for different segments or in response to variations in demand. For some product areas such as ticketing it may be possible to dynamically alter prices in line with demand. Tickets.com adjusts concert ticket prices according to demand and has been able to achieve 45% more revenue per event as a result. Dynamic pricing is used widely in airline and hotel industries, but it is also increasingly used in restaurants; for example, by offering people a discount to eat at quieter times of the day, rather than at peak lunch time or evening services.

(c)   Different types of pricing may be possible on the internet, particularly for digital, downloadable products. Software and music have traditionally been sold for a continuous right to use. The internet offers new options such as payment per use, rental at a fixed cost per month or a lease arrangement. Bundling options may also be more possible.

(d)   The growth of **online auctions** also helps consumers to dictate price. The online auction company eBay has grown in popularity with thousands of buyers and sellers bidding daily.

(e)   E-pricing can also easily reward loyal customers. Technology allows repeat visitors to be tracked, easily allowing loyalty incentives to be targeted towards them.

(f)   Payment is also easy; PayPal or online credit cards allow for easy payments. However, the downside to this is internet fraud, which is growing rapidly around the world.

6.5.3 Place (or customer convenience)

Allen and Fjermestad argue that the internet has the greatest implications for **place** in the marketing mix since it has a global reach.

E-commerce models

Types of marketplaces	Set up by	Main aim
Controlled by sellers	Single vendor seeking many buyers	To retain value and power in any transaction
Controlled by buyers	One or more buyers	To shift value and power in marketplace onto the buyer's side Buyer intermediaries can also be there to act as agents
Neutral marketplaces	Third-party intermediaries to match many buyers to many sellers	To match buyers to sellers at an auction Commission based

Choosing a marketplace depends on four factors:

- Are there transactions or benefits to be realised?
- Is the electronic market for the product developing quickly?
- Does company have substantial market share or buying power?
- Would a neutral intermediary be beneficial?

Types of e-commerce marketplace

- B2C and B2B (can be combined or separate eg Dell)
- C2C (eBay)
- Auctions (eBay)
- Consumer reviews (Bizrate)
- Customer bids (priceline)

The emergence of new **channel structures** – disintermediation, reintermediation and countermediation (which we consider in connection with e-commerce in Chapter 9) – also affects the 'place' where online transactions occur.

Navigation – there are three aspects of navigation that are key to achieving competitive advantage online.

(a) **Reach** – this is the potential audience of the e-commerce site. Reach can be increased by moving from a single site to representation with a large number of different intermediaries.

(b) **Richness** – this is the depth or detail of information which is both collected about the customer and provided to the customer. This is related to the product element of the mix.

(c) **Affiliation** – this refers to whose interest the selling organisation represents – consumers or suppliers. This particularly applies to retailers. It suggests that customers will favour retailers who provide them with the richest information on comparing competitive products.

Localisation – providing a local site, usually a language-specific version, is referred to as localisation. A site may need to support customers from a range of countries; they may have different product needs, language differences and cultural differences.

6.5.4 Promotion (or customer communication)

Marketing communications are used to inform customers and other stakeholders about an organisation and its products.

(a) There are new ways of applying each of the elements of the **communications mix** (advertising, sales promotions, PR and direct marketing), using new media such as the web and email. Most organisations today have some form of web page used in most, if not all, advertisements. Placing banner advertisements on other web pages is a common form of e-promotion. Web public relations (WPR) is another approach to promoting online. Newsworthy stories based on product or service launches can be placed on the company's web page, or WPR articles sent to review sites for consumers to read.

(b) The internet can be used at different stages of the **buying process**. For instance, the main role of the web is often in providing further information rather than completing the sale. Think of a new car purchase. Many consumers will now review models online, but most still buy in the real world.

(c) Promotional tools may be used to assist in different stages of **CRM** from customer acquisition to retention. In a web context this includes gaining initial visitors to the site and gaining repeat visits using, for example, direct email reminders of site proposition and new offers.

(d) The internet can be integrated into **campaigns**. For example, we are currently seeing many direct response print and TV ad campaigns where the web is used to manage entry into a prize draw and to profile the entrant for future communications.

These general technological trends have an impact across the promotional mix.

Promotion activity	Impact/opportunity	Examples of supporting technology
Advertising	Reach more customers worldwide	Websites and ads
	Target audiences more specifically	Specialist TV channels
	Increase response via interactivity	Direct response TV, SMS text messaging
Sales promotion	Target segment/individual interests and preferences	Customer databases, EPOS data
	Facilitate/motivate response	Online entry/coupons
	Online discounts (lower admin costs)	Online transaction
Direct marketing	Personalised, one-to-one messages	Database
	Permission-based database/contacts to enhance response rate	Email, website, SMS requests for info
	Speed and interactivity of response	Email and website links
	Direct response/transaction	E-commerce sites
PR and publicity	Speed of information dissemination and response to crisis/issues	Email media releases and online information
Marketing/sales support	Publicising sponsorships	Website
	Publicising exhibition attendance	Website/email clients
	Up to date information for sales force and call centre staff	Access to product/inventory and customer database
Internal marketing	Staff access to information relevant to their jobs	Intranet newsletters, bulletins, policy information
	Co-ordination/identification of dispersed offices and off-site staff	Email, tele- and video-conferencing
Network marketing	Supplier/client access to information relevant to business relationship	Extranet: access to selected information

6.5.5 People

The **people** element of the marketing mix is the way an organisation's staff interact with customers and other stakeholders during sales and pre- and post-sales. Smith and Chaffey suggest that online, part of the consideration for the people element of the mix is the consideration of the tactics by which people can be replaced or automated.

(a)   **Autoresponders** automatically generate a response when a company emails an organisation, or submits an online form.

(b)   **Email notification** may be automatically generated by a company's systems to update customers on the progress of their orders. Such notifications might show, for example, three stages: order received; item now in stock; order dispatched.

(c)   **Call-back facility** requires that customers fill in their phone number on a form and specify a convenient time to be contacted. Dialling from a representative in the call centre occurs automatically at the appointed time and the company pays.

(d)   **Frequently Asked Questions (FAQ)** can pre-empt enquiries. The art lies in compiling and categorising the questions so customers can easily find both the question and a helpful answer.

(e)　**On-site search engines** help customers find what they are looking for quickly. Site maps are a related feature.

(f)　**Virtual assistants** come in varying degrees of sophistication and usually help to guide the customer through a maze of choices.

6.5.6 Process

The **process** element of the marketing mix is the internal methods and procedures companies use to achieve all marketing functions such as new product development, promotion, sales and customer service. The restructuring of the organisation and channel structures described for product, price, place and promotion all require new **processes**.

6.5.7 Physical evidence

The physical evidence element of the marketing mix is the tangible expression of a product and how it is purchased and used. In an online context, physical evidence is **customers' experience of the company through the website** and associated support. It includes issues such as ease of use, navigation, availability and performance. Responsiveness to email enquiries is a key aspect of performance. The process must be right to enable an acceptable response within the notified service standards such as 24 hours.

Benefits of digital marketing
It promotes **transparent pricing** – because potential customers can readily compare prices not only from suppliers within any given country, but also from suppliers across the world.
It facilitates **personalised attention** – even if such attention is actually administered through impersonal, yet highly sophisticated IT systems and customer database manipulation.
It provides sophisticated **market segmentation** opportunities. Approaching such segments may be one of the few ways in which e-commerce entrepreneurs can create **competitive advantage**.
The web can either be a **separate** or a **complementary** channel.
A new phenomenon is emerging called **dynamic pricing**. Companies can rapidly change their prices to reflect the current state of demand and supply.

These new trends are creating **pressure** for companies. The main threat facing companies is that **prices will be driven down by consumers' ability to shop around**.

Section summary

Digital marketing (or **e-marketing**) involves the use of digital technologies to achieve marketing objectives and enhance marketing activities. **Social media** marketing can also be used to acquire customers, or to attract the attention of potential customers, through social media sites.

The characteristics of digital marketing can be summarised as 6 I's:

- Independence of location
- Industry structure
- Integration
- Interactivity
- Individualism
- Intelligence analysed

Chapter Summary

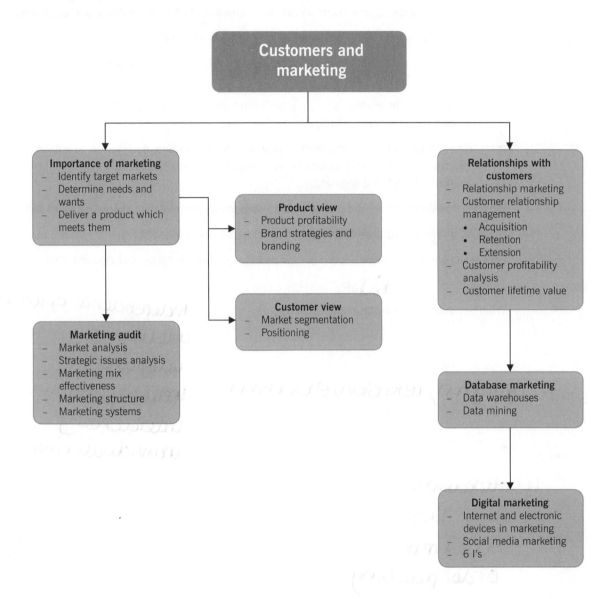

Customers and marketing

Importance of marketing
- Identify target markets
- Determine needs and wants
- Deliver a product which meets them

Product view
- Product profitability
- Brand strategies and branding

Customer view
- Market segmentation
- Positioning

Marketing audit
- Market analysis
- Strategic issues analysis
- Marketing mix effectiveness
- Marketing structure
- Marketing systems

Relationships with customers
- Relationship marketing
- Customer relationship management
  - Acquisition
  - Retention
  - Extension
- Customer profitability analysis
- Customer lifetime value

Database marketing
- Data warehouses
- Data mining

Digital marketing
- Internet and electronic devices in marketing
- Social media marketing
- 6 I's

Quick Quiz

1 Give an example showing why there should be a correlation between employee and customer loyalty.

2 Which of the statements below describes differentiated marketing?

(a) The company attempts to produce the ideal product for a single segment of the market (eg Rolls-Royce cars for the wealthy).

(b) This policy is to produce a single product and hope to get as many customers as possible to buy it, ignoring segmentation entirely.

(c) The company attempts to introduce several product versions, each aimed at a different market segment. For example, manufacturers of soap powder make a number of different brands, marketed to different segments.

3 What are the three phases of customer relationship management which Dave Chaffey identifies?

4 How can different costs arise with different customers? Give five examples.

5 Data warehousing involves discovering new patterns and relationships in underlying data.

True or false? *false*

6 What are the six I's of digital marketing?

Independence of location
intelligence
integration
industry structure
interactivity
individualisation

3 acquisition, retension, extension

4. discounts
order size
sales mix
order processing
Transport costs

Answers to Quick Quiz

1   Reduced staff turnover in service firms can result in more repeat business because of improved service quality due to more knowledgeable staff.

2   (c)

3   Customer acquisition; retention; extension

4   Five from:

- Order size
- Sales mix
- Order processing
- Transport costs (eg if JIT requires frequent deliveries)
- Management time
- Cash flow problems (eg increased overdraft interest) caused by slow payers
- Order complexity (eg if the order has to be sent out in several stages)
- Inventory holding costs can relate to specific customers
- The customer's negotiating strength

5   False. Data mining involves discovering new patterns and relationships in underlying data.

6   Independence of location, industry structure, interactivity, individualisation, integration and intelligence

Answers to Questions

8.1 Profitable customers

You can see below that the profit earned by Seth in servicing Narayan is greater, despite the increased discount.

	Kipling	Narayan
Number of shoes	500	420
	£	£
Revenue (after discount)	22,500	17,850
Transport	(5,000)	–
Administration	(250)	(500)
Net profit	17,250	17,350

8.2 Choosing data

The information reflects sales force administration and convenience. However, it might obscure an analysis of customer profitability, in which case presenting information by customer size might be more important than geography.

Now try these questions from the Practice Question Bank	Number	Level	Marks	Time
	8.1– 8.5	Intermediate	n/a	10 mins
	8.6	Examination	17	30 mins

LEADING CHANGE

Part C

UNDERSTANDING ORGANISATIONAL CHANGE

 Change management is one of the most frequently discussed topics in business strategy. Such discussions may reflect why it is important for an organisation to change, the impact that changes will have on the organisation, or an organisation to change successfully.

In Chapter 3 of this Study Text, we identified how opportunities and threats in the external environment could act as triggers for organisational change. By contrast, the focus in this chapter will be more on the impact of organisational change on an organisation itself.

We begin by analysing the causes of strategic change, before moving on to look at the speed with which changes need to be implemented and how extensive their impact will be across an organisation (Section 2). Next we highlight the importance of understanding the context of the change, particularly with respect to the culture or an organisation (Sections 3 and 4).

Some models view change as a rational linear process, while others see it in less structured terms, but, however it is perceived, in order for a change to be successful, it has to be effectively managed (Sections 5 and 6).

There will be some stakeholders who support a change while others are likely to resist it. Force field analysis (Section 7) provides a way of assessing the driving and resisting forces for any change event. However, in order to implement change successfully, an organisation will have to overcome any resistance to it (Section 8).

Topic list	Learning outcomes	Syllabus references	Ability required
1 Introduction to change management	C1(a)	–	Evaluate
2 Types of change	C2(a)	C2(a) (i)	Evaluate
3 The context of change	C2(a)	C2(a) (i)	Evaluate
4 Culture and change	C1(a)	C2(a) (i)	Evaluate
5 Stage models of change	C2(a)	C2(a) (ii)	Evaluate
6 Other models of managing change	C2(a)	C2(a) (ii)	Evaluate
7 Force field analysis	C2(a)	C2(a) (ii)	Evaluate
8 Managing resistance to change	C2(a), C3(b)	C2(a) (iii), C3(b)(i)	Evaluate
Appendix			
9 Organisational structure	–	–	–

Chapter Overview

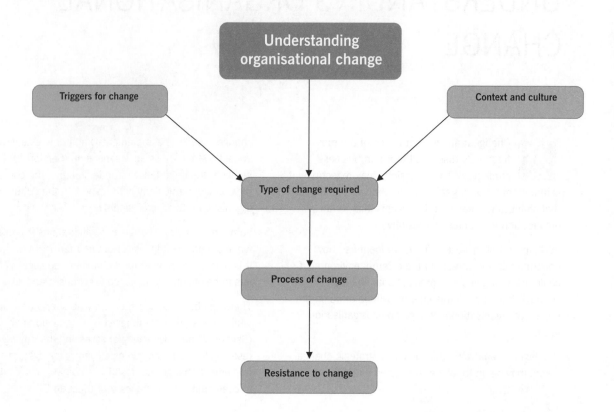

1   Introduction to change management

Introduction

It is very hard to ignore the impact of change on contemporary businesses. However, the visibility of change in this way also highlights the importance of understanding and managing the impact of change on businesses and the people who work for them. Implementing and managing change is often an integral part of strategy implementation.

However, before we start to look at any change management theories and models, we will consider some of the practical issues involved in organisational change by using a case study.

CASE STUDY

McDonald's fast food restaurants

Society's attitudes to fast food have been changing in recent years, and in order to remain successful the fast food industry will need to recognise those changing customer needs and respond to them.

Concerns about rising obesity levels and advances in healthcare have highlighted the importance of a healthy diet. Increased access to mass communications (television, internet) have meant that consumers are becoming more informed about issues and are demanding better choices in convenience foods.

Meeting stakeholder needs

Changing **customer needs and requirements** illustrate the more general issue that the business environment is not static, but evolves over time, reflecting changes in the broader social environment.

However, customers are not the only important stakeholder whose interests McDonald's need to consider.

Other stakeholders include:

Business partners – including franchisees and suppliers (McDonald's restaurants are run by franchisees).

Employees – when taken together, the McDonald's corporation and its franchisees employ approximately 1.5 million people, with more than 35,000 restaurants spread across about 120 countries.

Opinion leaders – including governments, the media, health professionals and environmental groups. McDonald's is very conscious of its corporate social responsibility, and constantly looks to adapt its operations to increase the positive impact it can have on society.

Responding to customers' needs

McDonald's conducts market research and listens to what its customers want to see on its menu, and also to understand customer opinions about brand image, quality, service, cleanliness and value.

One of the messages which emerged from this research in recent years was that customers wanted more choice, with healthier and lighter food options. Customers also wanted greater visibility in food labelling and more information about what they were eating: for example, how much fat and how much salt their meals contained.

Creating menu changes

McDonald's took a twofold approach to converting these customer findings into menu changes. On the one hand, they improved existing products, on the other, they created new ones.

Improving existing products – changes included introducing new cooking oil blends which were low in saturated fat, and reducing the amount of salt used when preparing the meals.

New products – these include new salad and deli choice ranges, which contain lower levels of fat. Also, McDonald's has introduced wraps (which are seen as healthier than a burger and fries), which it hopes will appeal to calorie-conscious consumers.

McDonald's also provides customers with extensive nutritional labelling, both in-store and on the company website. Packaging includes recommended daily intakes (for example of fats or carbohydrates) so that customers can see how their food choices relate to their overall daily requirements.

However, despite the product changes, the menu options are still consistent with McDonald's brand. The packaging, presentation and service are still recognisably McDonald's.

McDonald's experience

The 'customer experience' is another important aspect of the McDonald's brand, and the company is looking to enhance service and technology so that the convenience of a McDonald's experience is aligned to customers' needs.

In 2013, McDonald's announced a new ordering system which was designed to improve customer experience in the ordering process. Under the new system, once customers have placed their order at a register they then move away from the register while that order is being fulfilled. This means that the cashiers can continue to serve other customers while food is being cooked, rather than having to hold customers in a queue waiting for food to come out of the kitchen.

Customers are given order numbers on receipts, and an overhead screen displays the order numbers that are ready. Staff then bring the completed orders to the collection points, which are at the opposite end of the counter to the cash registers.

McDonald's is also looking to its digital strategy to help improve customer experience – for example, by introducing tablet computers at the counter to allow consumers to select different ingredients for their meals, and by introducing new payment options such as Apple Pay.

Communicating the changes

Although making the changes to products and processes is important, it is equally important to communicate the changes to the consumer – particularly in relation to new products. To this end, McDonald's developed advertising campaigns which were designed to highlight the new healthier food options, countering public perceptions of McDonald's as only selling unhealthy meals.

McDonald's has made use of a variety of advertising media – print, billboards, television and the internet – and it targets its audience for each media type carefully. For example, website and social media advertising is designed to be appealing to teenagers and young adults, so is both interactive and informative, making use of the latest design and technology.

The McDonald's example illustrates how change occurs in a social context. This is an important point to recognise, because change management does not simply involve a choice between technological, organisational or people-oriented solutions. Rather, it involves finding solutions which combine these factors to provide integrated strategies which help improve performance and results.

Change management is a crucial part of any project which leads or enables people to accept new processes, technologies, systems, structures and values. Change management consists of the set of activities which help people move from their present way of working to a new, and hopefully improved, way of working.

KEY TERM

We can define CHANGE MANAGEMENT as 'the continuous process of aligning an organisation with its marketplace and doing it more responsively and effectively than competitors'.

(Berger)

It is also important to identify the importance of adopting a **contingency approach** to change management. There isn't a single correct way to manage change. Selecting a way to manage a change depends on the **nature** and the **context** of the change, and the **organisation** undergoing the change.

Kanter points out that effective organisations are adept at handling the triggers of change, even when the triggers may appear to be threats.

For example, an unwanted takeover bid may require immediate and dramatic responses. But by managing the situation to **create the environment of a crisis**, the organisation may induce a willingness among all

stakeholders to act as one in the defence of the organisation. Therefore the crisis can actually act as a galvanising event, and lead to rapidly agreed responses, without incurring any resistance. (As we see later in this chapter, resistance to change is often a problem in change management processes.)

1.1 The need for change

Any organisation that ignores change does so at its own peril, because its inactivity is likely to weaken its ability to manage future scenarios.

The management guru, Peter Drucker, argues that a 'winning strategy' will require information about events and conditions outside the organisation, because only once an organisation has that information can it prepare for the new changes and challenges which arise from shifts in the external environment.

This does not, however, mean that implementing a strategic change will necessarily improve an organisation's performance.

CASE STUDY

Marks & Spencer

In 1993, the UK was experiencing a recession, and all the major retailers were suffering as consumers looked to cut back on their spending.

Marks & Spencer's (M&S) chief executive at the time, Richard Greenbury, decided to concentrate on the company's traditional core businesses of clothing and food to steer it through this difficult time.

The strategy appeared to be successful, and M&S's profits rose steadily over the next few years and Greenbury planned to double the number of European stores by the year 2000.

However, the face of high street retail was changing, and a number of new companies such as Monsoon and Gap were emerging. They segmented the market, and offered customers cheaper, more socially aware designs than M&S.

Additionally, Tesco, Sainsbury's and Waitrose challenged M&S for some of its core business in the food sector. These companies eroded M&S's competitive advantage by offering products of similar quality at better value, thereby making M&S's product lines look expensive.

M&S's results in 1998 showed that falling sales had caused profits to halve from the previous year.

Luc Vandevelde became CEO in 2000, and he introduced new designers and new product ranges (eg Per Una) and switched to cheaper overseas suppliers to face the increased competition in the clothing market. (M&S had historically only used UK suppliers and had built up strong relationships with them, using the quality of its produce as a strong source of competitive advantage.)

As profits continued to fall, M&S sold off its European operations, and decided to concentrate on its core UK businesses, opening a number of homeware and food only stores.

Celebrity endorsements, such as David Beckham's 'DB07' children's clothing range, were also introduced.

Profits began to rise again in mid-2002 as a result of these activities, and then the top board posts were separated as Mr Vandevelde remained as chairman but handed over the CEO role to Roger Holmes.

By 2004 sales had slowed again, and M&S had to fight to stave off a takeover bid from the retail tycoon, Sir Philip Green. The policy of sourcing products directly from overseas continued, with the Far East and Eastern Europe being the key locations. However, M&S continued to lose market share in its core business areas to competitors such as Asda and Next.

In 2005 M&S reacted to slowing sales by cutting prices to try to put pressure on its rivals.

It also introduced a new promotional brand – Your M&S – which has become the main focus for its advertising and in-store merchandising. The 'Your M&S' brand was designed to portray a more modern and youthful image for M&S. To support this newer image, M&S has also been rolling out a new store format across all its stores – making them brighter and more spacious.

The new look, combined with successful advertising campaigns in 2005–6 (for example the clothing campaign featuring Twiggy, and the food adverts with the slogan 'This is not just food, this is M&S food'), led to a resurgence in performance in 2006–7.

However, the economic downturn in 2008–9 meant that shoppers once again became more conservative in their spending. Price once more became a key issue, and M&S responded to this in their food stores with their '2 Dine for £10' offers – offering customers a 'restaurant experience' for less. Rather than competing on price with other food retailers, M&S effectively started competing with restaurants: offering customers a main meal, vegetables, and dessert for two, with a bottle of wine, for just £10. In other words, customers could get a restaurant-standard meal for £10, although they had to eat it in their own homes rather than a restaurant.

When Marc Bolland became CEO of M&S in 2010, he pledged to turn the company into an international, multichannel retailer. In the period 2010 to 2013 the company made significant investments in revamping its website and modernising its IT systems, as well as opening stores abroad.

However, the £2.3bn spent on projects over the three years, has failed to yield an increase in M&S's profits. The quarter to June 2014 was the 12th consecutive quarter in which M&S reported a decline in non-food sales. Like for like sales in non-food merchandise in the quarter fell by 1.5%, due in part to a £150m overhaul of the company's website, which resulted in shoppers having to re-register to use the website as well as having to take time to work out how to use the new site.

Perhaps even more importantly, M&S appeared to be making little progress towards becoming a truly multi-channel retailer. The company's Head of Development, Digital Stores admitted that many of M&S's customers don't consider it all when they are thinking about multichannel, and they don't even think to look at M&S's website when they are shopping online.

In 2014, multichannel sales (online, including mobile and personal devices) only accounted for around one tenth of M&S's total sales.

1.2 The process of change

In the same way that choosing a business strategy encourages an organisation to assess its current **position**, evaluate its strategic **choices**, and then decide upon a course of action to **implement**, we can also view change management as a sequence of stages.

For an organisation to respond to the need for change, it needs a way of **planning for** and **implementing changes**.

Organisations may need to make strategic changes for lots of different reasons. For example:

- Dealing with changes in the global economy and global markets

- Allowing an organisation to grow, either organically or through mergers or acquisition

- Responding to customer pressures (for example, car manufacturers moving towards producing more environmentally friendly cars in response to consumer concerns about carbon emissions and pollution)

- Restructuring or reorganising the business

- Implementing new technologies and business processes

Although each change situation should be considered individually, we can still identify some general steps which could be followed during a major change initiative.

Change processes usually begin with a change '**trigger**' which can either be **external** to the organisation or **internal** (ie from within the organisation).

Triggers include:

External events

- Changes in the economic cycle (for example, an economic downturn)

- New laws or regulations affecting the industry

- Stiffer competition from rivals or from new entrants

- Arrival of new technology (for example, the impact of faster communications and digital downloads on music and film entertainment)

Internal events

- Arrival of new senior management with different strategies, priorities and styles

- A new organisation structure which prompts changes to job responsibilities

- Implementation of new technologies or working practices

- The acquisition of new knowledge or skills, creating both the pressure to change and the ability to do so

- Changes in the activities of the organisation which require adaptation and learning (for example, with the development of a new product line)

- Relocation of the business to different city or country

Poor performance can also be an internal trigger for change, although the wish to improve performance could also be triggered by external pressures to become more competitive.

A change trigger will initiate change in an organisation. However, a key question for management is how to manage the change to get the best outcome.

In response to the trigger, some tentative plans about possible changes are prepared. Wherever possible, an organisation should consider a range of alternatives, and consider the advantages and disadvantages of each. **Stakeholders'** probable reactions to the changes should also be considered.

A preferred solution should then be chosen from the range of alternative options, and a **timetable** for implementing the changes should be established. The **speed** at which change is implemented is likely to depend on the nature of the change and people's anticipated reactions to it.

The plan for change then needs to be **communicated** to everyone who will be involved in implementing it, before the actual implementation stage gets underway.

Balogun and Hope Hailey summarise the process of change in a change flow chart, outlined below.

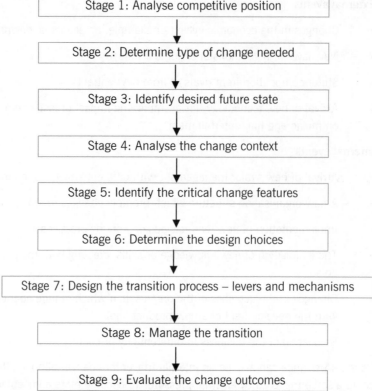

Stage 1: Analyse competitive position

Stage 2: Determine type of change needed

Stage 3: Identify desired future state

Stage 4: Analyse the change context

Stage 5: Identify the critical change features

Stage 6: Determine the design choices

Stage 7: Design the transition process – levers and mechanisms

Stage 8: Manage the transition

Stage 9: Evaluate the change outcomes

Stages 1 and 2 of the flow chart can be summarised as the '**why and what**' of change, while Stages 3 to 9 can be summarised as the '**how**' of change.

Managing strategic change is a key part of implementing corporate strategy.

Note that both strategic management and change management involve an analysis of current position, an evaluation of possible choices and a decision about the appropriate course of action to take. Therefore the ideas of suitability, acceptability, and feasibility which we considered in Chapter 5 are also relevant to decisions about strategic change.

We discussed a number of the environmental factors which could act as external triggers for change in Chapter 3 of this Study Text. PEST analysis can often be a useful way of identifying environmental factors (opportunities or threats) which could act as indirect external triggers for change. Similarly, Porter's five forces can help to identify direct external triggers for change.

1.3 Mergers and acquisitions

Acquisitions, mergers and other business combinations may require substantial changes in the organisation structure in order to benefit from new synergies, value chain linkages or core competences. They may also lead to changes in the culture of an organisation.

We looked at mergers and acquisitions as strategic options earlier in this Study Text, and we identified the respective advantages and disadvantages of them as methods of growth. However, in the context of change management it is worth pointing out that there are a number of different reasons why organisations may join together through a merger or an acquisition.

This is important because it means there are a number of different (potential) change management issues depending on the context of the merger or acquisition.

Let us consider some of the different issues which arise from a range of possible reasons for a merger or acquisition.

Reason for acquisition	Possible issues to consider
Growth	• Senior management team required to deliver a significant change in performance • Likely to be new arrivals in the senior management team • Importance of aligning cultures • Administrative efficiencies; integration in some areas if beneficial to results
Synergy	• Senior management teams need to work closely together on key areas of strategy • Other areas of business left intact
Diversification	• Loosely coupled management teams • Some administrative efficiencies, but businesses retain separate identities and branding
Integration	• Integrated senior management team • Merged administrative systems; core process tightly coupled • Pooled resources, better services for customers • Single corporate identity. Overcoming cultural problems is key. (Complex 'dual' structures can sometimes result if merger partners retain their own systems and structure after the merger is completed.)
Defensive measures	• Response to mergers/acquisitions by rivals: may be unexpected by staff • Crisis management techniques may be required • Low performance from staff if they are confused about the process

If the motive behind the deal is simply that there is **pressure on senior management to do a deal**, then potentially many of the issues above may apply.

1.3.1 Post-acquisition issues

After an acquisition, the incoming management will want to integrate the firm they have acquired into the parent company's structure and systems. This will involve visible changes to names and signage, but also deeper changes to organisational structures, culture, job roles, staff numbers and management systems.

However, statistically, around 70% of acquisitions fail, meaning that they do not create any wealth for the shareholders of the acquiring company.

Key reasons for these failures (and therefore key areas of change which need to be managed) are:

(a) **Poor communication**   In particular, poor communication to staff, resulting in a failure to establish trust and a commitment to a joint future.

(b) **Poor structure**   The structure of the new company does not follow the logic of the acquisition.

(c) **Cultural differences**   Issues of cultural incompatibility are often cited as problem areas when implementing mergers and acquisitions. Therefore organisations need to consider the compatibility of the respective cultures when considering the suitability of the merger or acquisition.

However, the amount of **cultural integration** required actually depends on the reason for the merger.

If core processes are going to be combined for economies of scale, then integration is important and needs to be given management time and attention. If a company is acquiring a portfolio of diverse businesses, cultural integration may only be necessary at senior management level.

CASE STUDY

Daimler/Chrysler

In 1998, Daimler Benz, the German car manufacturer best known for its Mercedes premium brand, merged with the US company, Chrysler, a volume car manufacturer. The merged company, Daimler Chrysler, became the world's largest car manufacturer.

However, although the deal was originally billed as a merger of equals, in practice it was a takeover by Daimler. Interestingly, by March 2001 the share price had fallen to just over 60% of what it had been in November 1998.

A number of reasons were identified for the poor performance of the new Group:

* US and German **business cultures were different**. Possibly because of cultural problems in the new Group, many key Chrysler managers left after the merger.

* Mercedes was a premium brand which had been extended to making smaller cars. Chrysler depended on high volumes, not a premium product. Therefore the distinction between 'premium' and 'volume' businesses got blurred.

* The new Group did not properly exploit economies of scale, such as sharing components. There was a degree of technology sharing among the engineers, and this did result in some success stories, such as the Chrysler 300 model. However, many critics argued that the merger **could not deliver the synergies** which had been expected because the businesses were never successfully integrated. In effect, they seemed to be running two independent product lines: Daimler and Chrysler.

* **Productivity and efficiency** at Chrysler was far lower than industry norms. (In 2000, each vehicle took Chrysler around 40 hours to make, compared with approximately 20 for the US factories of competitors such as Honda and Toyota.) In addition, its purchasing was inefficient, and fixed costs were too high for the size of the company. Overall, Chrysler's performance was much weaker than Daimler had realised going into the deal.

Ultimately, the Daimler Chrysler merger failed to produce the trans-Atlantic automotive powerhouse that had been hoped for, and in 2007 Chrysler was sold to a private equity firm that specialises in restructuring troubled companies. In December 2008, Chrysler received a $4bn loan from the US Government to stave off bankruptcy. Nonetheless, Chrysler eventually filed for bankruptcy in April 2009.

While it was by no means the only reason why it failed, the failure to implement change effectively and to integrate the companies after the merger was a major contributing factor to the failure of the merger.

Fiat Chrysler

Despite filing for bankruptcy, Chrysler remained in business, and over the period 2009 – 2014 Fiat acquired an increasingly large stake in the company. By January 2014, it had acquired all the shares, and Chrysler Group became a subsidiary of Fiat.

In May 2014, a new group – Fiat Chrysler Automobiles (FCA) – was established, with two main operating subsidiaries: FCA Italy (previously Fiat Group Automobiles) and FCA US (previously Chrysler Group).

However, the question now is whether Fiat Chrysler will be any more successful than Daimler Chrysler was.

Impact on the customer

It is very easy for managers to become so focused on a deal that **customers get forgotten**. However, if managers take their eye off the ball, they are in danger of forgetting the main reason for their existence.

Competitors will be looking out for opportunities to exploit any weaknesses arising from a merger or acquisition, and this could be a serious threat if the merged organisations' product offering or customer service standards slip.

1.4 Internally generated change

Internally generated change is likely to be managed more proactively, creatively and effectively than externally generated change.

This is because there is clear ownership of the change, but also because the organisation has a prior knowledge and understanding of the change. Because the trigger for change is internal to the organisation, the organisation can control the nature and timing of the change in a way it cannot do when it has to react to external triggers.

A survey by the Chartered Institute of Personnel and Development (CIPD) in the UK found that during the 1990s the top 50 UK companies moved from having, on average, one major reorganisation every five years to having one every three years.

Although external market conditions can lead to restructuring through downsizing or cost-cutting, there may also be internal change triggers which force organisations to review their size and structure.

Reorganisation and restructuring can occur as a result of internal triggers aimed at internal improvement:

- Efficiency or effectiveness
- Centralisation or decentralisation
- Flattening of organisational hierarchy

In more general terms, managing strategic change is a key part of implementing corporate strategy, and reorganisation can often come about as part of an organisation's strategy implementation.

- Expansion into new markets
- Introduction of a new product or service
- Change in organisational culture

 When considering the implementation of strategic plans, businesses need to make sure that organisation structures match with business strategy. You should be familiar with different organisational structures from your previous studies at E1 level, but we have included a summary of different organisational structures as an appendix to this chapter.

The relationship between structure and strategy has important implications for change management: if business strategy or organisational structure, or both, are being changed, the new strategy and structure need to fit together for any change to be implemented successfully.

1.5 Internal growth

We mentioned earlier that firms may grow through mergers and acquisitions, but firms may also grow internally through organic growth.

Greiner looked at the way organisations grow, and identified a series of phases through which growing companies tend to pass. Importantly, in the context of change management, Greiner also postulated that this growth was made up of prolonged periods of **evolution** – in which organisational practices remained

relatively constant – and periods of **revolution** in which there was substantial turmoil and change in the organisation's life.

In this way, Greiner presented organisational growth as a series of five phases, each of which results in a revolutionary crisis that takes it on to the next phase:

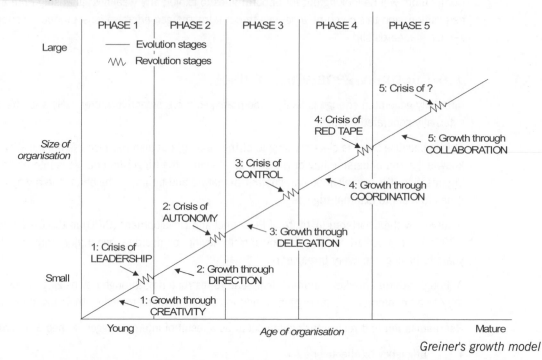

Greiner's growth model

Greiner's model suggests that an organisation cannot expect growth and development to be a smooth, evolutionary process. As an organisation grows it reaches critical points at which the existing ways of doing things are no longer efficient or effective. These critical points are the revolutionary periods at which managers need to **find a new set of organisational practices** which can then form the basis for the next period of evolutionary growth.

1.5.1 Creativity and the crisis of leadership

In the birth stage of an organisation, the emphasis is on creating a product or a market. The culture of the organisation will be essentially entrepreneurial, and communication among staff will be informal. As the organisation starts to grow, however, the entrepreneur and the organisation will need more sophisticated competencies to cope with increasing volumes of production and a larger workforce. Increased numbers of employees cannot be managed exclusively through informal communication. Investment is likely to be required to continue expansion, which will require further financial control. Therefore, the founding entrepreneurs find themselves burdened with management responsibilities – the crisis of leadership. A solution to this crisis would be to install a strong business manager who can implement a more formal control mechanism and pull the organisation together.

1.5.2 Direction and the crisis of autonomy

However, the control mechanisms and the organisation structure which are put in place as the result of the first crisis become inadequate as the firm continues to grow. Staff are frustrated at bureaucracy, centralised control, and narrowly defined job assignments. They find themselves restricted by a cumbersome and centralised hierarchy and this leads to the crisis of autonomy.

This crisis of autonomy makes it necessary for the firm to start to **delegate** and allow the managers and staff some discretion over decision making. This delegation accompanies the application of a more decentralised organisational structure. Local managers are given responsibility for running their own plants and markets.

1.5.3 Delegation and the crisis of control

A consequence of the delegation and discretion allowed to local managers is that senior management at the top of the firm begin to feel a loss of control – a crisis of control. Co-ordination across the firm suffers, and those at the top now seek to reassert their control over the firm as a whole.

1.5.4 Co-ordination and the crisis of red tape

Co-ordination and control may be necessary in ensuring the efficient allocation of scarce resources. Managers still have local and delegated authority, but have to justify their actions to the centre, which Greiner describes as a 'watchdog audience at headquarters'. Formal planning procedures and control programmes are established and reviewed rigorously. However, in turn, the staff begin to resent what they see as unnecessary bureaucracy and rigid procedures, implemented by managers who are not familiar with local conditions, and this leads to a crisis of red tape. Procedures take precedence over problem solving, and innovation is suppressed.

1.5.5 Collaboration – and the crisis of '?'

A successful escape from the crisis of red tape results in a growth of 'interpersonal collaboration'. This is difficult to achieve, requiring some fundamental changes in culture to allow problem solving through teams and more flexible structures. Innovation and experiments in new practice are encouraged throughout the organisation. The importance of the corporate centre is reduced, with a concomitant reduction in the number of headquarters staff.

The final crisis is named by Greiner as 'The ? crisis', one that he could not fully identify back in 1972 (when he published his model). With some foresight, however, he speculated that this crisis would result from increasing stress in the workplace, the 'psychological saturation of employees who grow emotionally and physically exhausted by the intensity of teamwork and the heavy pressure for innovative solutions'.

1.5.6 General points about Greiner's model

Overall, Greiner's model provides some useful insights into the process of organisational growth, although Greiner himself highlights some of the challenges it presents to managers of growing organisations.

Knowing which stage of development an organisation is at – Management has to recognise when an organisation reaches a 'crisis' point, and to know which crisis point it is at, otherwise they may impose the wrong solution.

Solutions breed new problems – Managers often fail to realise that the solution to one problem eventually becomes the cause of a future problem. For example, the decision to delegate in time causes the crisis of control. This is not to say that the solutions themselves were not appropriate when they were implemented, but it is a reminder that a solution will not remain valid forever. In essence, this suggests that management need to try to predict when the next revolution (or crisis) is imminent so that they can work on a solution to deal with that crisis.

In addition, a general observation about Greiner's model is that it seems to imply that growth is the normal state of affairs for all organisations. However, this is not always the case; and, for example, Greiner's model provides no insight into how to deal with organisational decline.

1.6 Managing decline

So far, we have focused largely on change management in the context of organisational growth, but changes may also be required to help an organisation overcome a decline in performance.

There are a number of factors which may contribute to organisational decline, but some of the more common ones are:

- Decline in demand for products or services, leading to a decline in revenues

- High cost structures, leading to a decline in competitiveness compared with rivals

- Poor financial control, exemplified either by spending not being kept under control, or by management not having suitable information to assess the performance of the business

- Overtrading, leading to excess pressure on the organisation's cash flow

- Too much diversification, causing a business to move away from, and neglect, its core business

In many cases, managers' strategic priorities for reversing the decline will centre on:

- Increasing competitiveness (for example through new product development, or product differentiation) in order to increase revenue

- Reducing costs in order to improve efficiency

However, when looking at ways of reducing costs, it is important that an organisation considers all of its processes and structures, and does not only look for a quick fix solution, such as reducing labour costs through redundancies.

While reducing staff numbers can help cut costs, a business needs to think through the implications of making dramatic staff cuts. If, for example, these lead to a reduction in the quality of the products or services offered to customers, they may inflict long-term damage to the business's reputation and its future prospects. Equally, if employee morale is damaged too severely this could have further detrimental consequences for the business, particularly among unionised workforces which may vote for strike action.

Nonetheless, in some cases, the decline in a business's performance means that managers have to take drastic action and make significant changes to its strategy:

Retrenchment – Retrenchment looks at the ways a business can drastically reduce its expenditure. This could involve redundancies, closing offices or branches, reducing the quality of materials used in a product, or moving the business's premises to locations where operating costs are cheaper.

However, retrenchment could also involve selective downsizing. For example, if one market is declining, or the company is proving unprofitable in one market (for example, due to technological changes) it could downsize in that market (or withdraw from it completely) and focus instead on another market which is more profitable. In this way, the company is able to focus its resources on the areas which are most profitable for it.

Turnaround – If a business appears to be in terminal decline, and is facing closure or takeover, there is a need for rapid and extensive change in order to achieve **cost reduction** and **revenue generation**.

However, cost cutting by itself is unlikely to be sufficient to turn around a business. The wider causes of its decline must be identified and addressed.

Divestment – Divestment involves the sale of part of an organisation's activities or one (or more) of its business units. For example, having tried unsuccessfully to expand into the US grocery market, Tesco decided to pull out of that market and sold its 'Fresh n Easy' stores in 2013.

Liquidation – A business unit is closed and its assets are sold. Liquidation should normally be viewed as a last resort, because it is an admission of failure by the organisation's management and is likely to damage the reputation of the remaining parts of the business.

1.7 Operational change

Although we have considered change management at a general strategic level, organisations also have to manage changes at a more tactical or operational level. A number of the issues we considered in the previous chapter may be relevant here. For example, business processes may need to be improved

through **business process re-engineering** (BPR); or a firm may have a culture of **continuous improvement** and **total quality management** (TQM).

In this context, it is also worth mentioning the Japanese idea of **kaizen** – the continuous improvement of a process or product.

Continuous improvement, by its very nature, involves constant adaptation and change, because it encourages workers to always be looking for better ways of doing things and for innovating processes.

You should be familiar with the concepts of lean systems, continuous improvement and business process re-engineering from your previous studies (in Paper E1).

The context of organisational culture could also be important here. For example, if an organisation wants to encourage continuous improvement, does its culture encourage staff to innovate and try to find new ways of doing things – or does it penalise them if they try new things which prove not to be successful? We will look at aspects of organisational culture in more detail later in this chapter.

1.8 Links between triggers

Although we have mentioned a number of possible change triggers, it is important to appreciate that triggers do not exist in isolation.

Once a trigger has been 'pulled', it is likely to set off a chain reaction of interrelated events.

Leavitt's organisational system model expressed this neatly, by considering organisational change as the result of the interaction between four components: task, structure, people and technology.

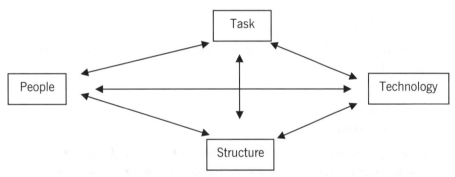

Components of change (Leavitt)

Whatever the trigger for change, change managers must always consider the impact the change will have on these four interrelated variables, and therefore their organisation as a whole.

Burke and Litwin subsequently expanded this idea to create a model of organisational performance and change in which they suggest 12 variables need to be used to analyse the factors of organisational change.

They are:

- Mission and strategy
- Structure
- Task requirements and individual skills/abilities
- External environment
- Leadership
- Management practices
- Working environment
- Motivation
- Individual and organisational performance
- Organisational culture

- Systems (policies and procedures)
- Individual needs and values

1.9 Problem identification as a precursor to change

The first two boxes in Balogun and Hope Hailey's change flow chart (which we showed earlier in this chapter) illustrate that an organisation needs to analyse its competitive position before determining the type of change required.

We look in more detail later at the different types of change an organisation can face, but at this point it is important to note that, regardless of the type of change, it is necessary to **clearly identify the problem or the reason for the change before undertaking** a change programme.

A review of strategy can often highlight the need to address a specific issue relating to the internal or external business environment. So problem identification can act as a trigger for change.

Perhaps more importantly, if there are no problems in the way the business is currently working, it will be difficult to persuade staff of the need to change. Problems with the current strategy, or the results it is delivering, provide one of the forces needed to drive change.

Problem identification can also be used to encourage participation at all levels in an organisation. Although the focus is at an operational level rather than a strategic level, the Japanese approach of kaizen involves all workers in problem identification and the quest for continuous improvement.

Note, however, that the trigger for change might not always be a problem which has happened or already exists. Organisations can try to foresee the need for change by being proactive. For example, if an organisation can anticipate changes in the marketplace and identify the impact they might have on its business then it could plan how to deal with those external changes in advance rather than having to react to them.

1.10 Levels of change

At this point, it is also worth pointing out that change can occur at the different levels within an organisation:

- Individuals
- Structures and systems
- Organisational climate

Changing individuals involves changing their skills, values, attitudes and behaviours. Any such individual changes have to support the overall organisational changes required. However, ultimately organisational changes can only be achieved if the individual people working for an organisation change as necessary.

Changing structures and systems involves changing the formal and informal organisational structures in place: for example, changing business processes, or changing roles, responsibilities and relationships.

Changing the organisational climate involves changing the way people relate to each other in an organisation; the management style; and the overall culture of the organisation. For example, this might involve creating a culture of high interpersonal trust and openness between staff.

The presence of these three levels means that a change manager needs to ensure they use appropriate methods in order that the desired change is achieved at each level.

Section summary

Change can be triggered by a wide range of factors, some of which are external to an organisation, and some of which stem from within it.

Organisations need to change and adapt to deal with changes in their environment and to improve their performance and results. The detail of any change management programme will depend on its context, but in general terms change management is likely to require an organisation to assess its current position, evaluate the choices it has for how to change, and then decide upon a course of change action to implement.

Change management can be defined as 'the continuous process of aligning an organisation with its marketplace and doing it more responsively and effectively than competitors'.

2 Types of change

Introduction

There are a wide range of triggers which could lead an organisation's managers to recognise the need for strategic change. Consideration of the broader contexts of the **environment** and the organisation's **strategic capability** could both show that large-scale developments are necessary. The need to put strategy into action may call for more detailed but no less far-reaching adjustment of processes, relationships, technologies and so on. In any event, the management of change starts with an understanding of **two main considerations**:

(a) The **type** of change required
(b) The **wider context** of the change

Importantly, these considerations mean that the particular management challenges involved in initiating and implementing change can vary considerably according to the change scenario in question.

2.1 Speed and scale of change required

When faced with any potential change situation, an organisation has to analyse the **nature of the change**, in order to identify the most appropriate way of managing the change.

Change can be classified in relation to the **extent** of the change required and the **speed** with which that change needs to be achieved.

Speed – Change can range from an all at once, 'big bang' change to a series of step by step, incremental changes.

Extent – The extent of change can range from an overall **transformation** of an organisation's central assumptions, culture and beliefs to a **realignment** of its existing assumptions. Although a realignment may affect the way an organisation operates at a practical level, it will not lead to an underlying change in the organisation's culture.

In their book *Exploring Strategic Change*, Balogun and Hope Hailey illustrate that there are four main types of change, based on differences in the speed and extent of change required. They present these types of change in a matrix, with the two axes being the **nature** of the change required (speed) and the **scope** of the change required (extent).

The measure of the scope of change is whether or not the methods and assumptions of the existing **paradigm** must be replaced. (The paradigm is the set of assumptions and beliefs which are taken for granted in an organisation and define that organisation and its culture. We look at the concept of the paradigm in more detail later in this chapter when we discuss culture and change.)

The **nature** of change may be incremental and built on existing methods and approaches, or it may require a 'big bang' approach if rapid response is required, as in times of crisis.

Scope of change

Nature of change		Realignment	Transformation
	Incremental	Adaptation	Evolution
	'Big bang'	Reconstruction	Revolution

(a)   **Adaptation** is the most common type of change. An adaptive change realigns the way an organisation operates, but does not require the development of a new paradigm. It proceeds step by step.

(b)   **Reconstruction** can also be undertaken within an existing paradigm but requires rapid and extensive action. It is a common response to a long-term decline in performance, or to a changing competitive context.

(c)   **Evolution** is an incremental process that leads to a new paradigm. It may arise from careful analysis and planning or may be the result of **learning processes**. Evolutionary change is often undertaken in anticipation of the need for future change. Its transformational nature may not be obvious while it is taking place.

(d)   **Revolution** is a rapid and wide-ranging response to extreme pressures for change, and can often be triggered by changes in the competitive conditions an organisation is facing. Because revolution is both wide ranging and fast paced, it is likely to involve a number of simultaneous initiatives, dealing with different aspects of a business. Revolution will be very obvious and is likely to affect most aspects of both what the organisation does and how it does them.

You may notice the overlap between Balogun and Hope Hailey's ideas and Greiner's growth model which we discussed in the last chapter. Greiner also talked of evolution and revolution, suggesting that an important aspect of successful change management is understanding the **nature of the change required**.

While Balogun and Hope Hailey talk about realignment and transformation, Johnson, Scholes and Whittington categorise types of strategic change as being either **incremental** or **transformational**.

Again, however, a matrix can be used; change is either **incremental** or **transformational**, and the approach to managing change is described as being either **reactive** or **proactive**.

Incremental change is characterised by a series of small steps, and does not challenge existing organisational assumptions or culture. It is a gradual process, and can be seen as an extension of the past. Management will feel that they are in control of the change process. There is also a feeling that incremental change is reversible. If the change does not work out as planned, the organisation can revert to its old ways of doing things.

Transformational change is characterised by major, significant change being introduced relatively quickly. The existing organisational structures and the organisational culture are changed. Transformational change is likely to be a top-down process, initiated, and possibly imposed, by senior management. However, unlike incremental change it requires new ways of thinking and behaving, and leads to discontinuities with the past. Consequently it is likely to be irreversible.

Transformational change may come about because:

- The organisation is faced with **major external events** that demand large-scale changes in response

- The organisation **anticipates major changes** in the environment and initiates action to make shifts in its own strategy to cope with them

- Strategic drift has led to deteriorating performance and so leaves the organisation now requiring **significant changes to improve performance**

Johnson, Scholes and Whittington's change matrix reflects these different change categories, but also highlights how management's response differs according to the different change categories.

Nature of change

Management role		Incremental	Transformation
	Proactive	Tuning	Planned
	Reactive	Adaptation	Forced

The importance of **proactive management** is that it implies that organisational change may be undertaken **before** it is imposed by events. It may, in fact, result from the process of forecasting and be a response to expected developments.

Forced change (for example, where an organisation has to make significant and rapid change due to changes in the external environment) is likely to be both painful and risky for an organisation.

Although these change matrices are a useful summary of types of change, we also need to recognise that the degree of change varies so, in practice, there is a **continuum** between **adaptive** changes and **transformation**.

Also, the **severity** of the change depends on **where** it is experienced, or by whom. Redundancies may be an **adaptive** response to changed product market conditions for an organisation, and will preserve the future of the organisation. However, for the people experiencing them, they are likely to be **transformational changes**.

 The scale and nature of organisational change required can also influence the way in which the change process needs to be managed in order for it to be successful. We look at different approaches and styles of change management later in this chapter and in the next chapter of this Study Text.

2.2 Hard or soft change

The relative physical and organisational impacts of a change should also affect the way it is implemented. In this respect, change can be classified as either **hard** (mechanistic) or **soft** (people based). Is the change a purely technical, systems-oriented one, or will it also affect people?

The aspect of the business undergoing change should influence the way change is implemented. If the change is relatively routine and technical in nature (for example, the machines in a factory are being upgraded) then existing knowledge can be applied in a mechanistic manner to implement the change.

A 'hard' model of change is similar to the 'rational' model of decision making. In short, there is a **description** of the current situation, **options** for change are evaluated, and the change is **implemented**. The process is logically in a sequence and is linear. Feedback comes at the end of the process.

Hard models of change can be looked at as following three sequential phases:

- **Define**: clarify objectives; perform systems diagnostics and systems analysis
- **Design**: determine options; evaluate solutions
- **Implement**: implement solution; appraise and monitor performance

However, purely 'mechanistic' changes are uncommon, and most changes have a degree of impact of people orientation. Consequently, approaches to change implementation need to take account of **personal interrelationships** and **emotional responses**. Also, they have to reflect the volatile and dynamic nature of the change environment.

Paton and McCalman in their book *Change Management* contrast the characteristics of hard and soft change situations, which can be summarised as follows:

Hard	Soft
Objectives, constraints and performance indicators are predominantly quantifiable	Objectives are likely to be subjective, interrelated and hard to quantify
Environmental forces are relatively static	The environment is likely to be volatile and complex
Timescales known with reasonable certainty	Timescales will be uncertain
The change environment is clearly defined and has minimal interaction with external forces	The change environment is unbounded, and characterised by having many internal and external interactions
The problem being addressed by the change can be clearly and concisely defined	It is difficult to define problem characteristics
May be defined in systems/technological terms	The problem is likely to be defined in interpersonal and social terms
The resources required to achieve a solution are reasonably well known	Resource requirements are likely to be uncertain
The number of viable potential solutions is limited, and the organisation has knowledge of them	There will be a wide range of solutions, all of which may appear relevant and interconnected
Structured approaches will produce good results	No clear solution methodology is visible
Consensus about the best way forward can be reached easily	There is a lack of consensus about the way forward, arising from a lack of common perception of the problem

2.2.1 Illustration of hard versus soft changes

Senior illustrates the differences between the hard and soft models of change by looking at how they could be applied to improving performance in a call centre.

Hard changes

Stages	Tasks	Example
1 *Situation analysis*	Formally identify need for change, and obtain agreement that change is needed.	'Response times at our call centre are too slow'.
2 *Identify objectives and constraints*	An objective is a desired outcome; a constraint is something that inhibits the outcome being achieved.	Objective – response times must be better than a competitor's response times. Constraint – there are not enough people and/or recruiting more is too expensive.
3 *Identify performance measures*	This will show if the change has been successful once it is implemented.	90% of calls to be answered within three rings.

Stages	Tasks	Example
4 *Generate options*	There could be many possible ways of reaching objectives, all of which can be considered.	For example: • Change processes to reduce the length of each call, thereby freeing up time to answer more. • Relocate call centre to a lower-cost environment such as India. • Abandon the call centre and go for internet-only ordering – but this is outside the scope of the problem definition.
5 *Develop promising options*	Some ideas may be more promising than others. However, for the promising options, a review of who is involved and how it will work is essential. This could involve detailed plans and budgets, computer simulations and so on.	The practicalities of each option are looked at (eg how easy is it to develop a call centre in India?).
6 *Evaluate options against performance measures*	Each option is evaluated in terms of the performance criteria in Stage 3. Will it deliver the desired result? It is important that any model used does represent the system accurately.	It is important to consider risk here.
7 *Develop implementation strategies*	The preferred option is selected.	This may involve informing staff, training them, reassuring them, pilot or dual running and so on. It could involve redundancy, if the relocation option is chosen.
8 *Carry out the change*	The changes are put in place from a certain date.	For example, new procedures become live – or the new call centre operational.

The **hard system** model is most suitable where 'difficulties' can be easily identified. However, it is less suitable in situations where it is harder to define the problem, obtain information or come to conclusions. Senior classifies these situations as 'messes' and suggests that soft models of change should be applied to '**messes**' while hard models should be applied to '**difficulties**'.

In this respect, soft models of change could be seen more like **emergent strategies**, and hard models of change more like rational, **prescriptive strategies**.

2.2.2 Soft models of change

Three different approaches can be taken to dealing with change situations.

Resolve the problem	A satisfactory solution can be employed based on what worked in the past in a similar situation – this is referred to as **satisficing**. It lacks analytical rigour. In our call centre example above, a knee-jerk reaction might be to increase the number of staff, if that has improved service standards in the past: but note that other options have not been considered.

Solve the problem	This is like the hard systems model. Problem solvers try to quantify messes and, so to speak, turn them into quantifiable 'difficulties'.
	However, a mess is a series of interlocking problems, and attempts to quantify and break it down may destroy the holistic nature of the problem.
	Poor call centre service standards may be the result of poor training. However, high staff turnover may mean that call operators are not experienced, and the training department cannot cope. High staff turnover may be caused by boredom in the job, lack of good pay, an inappropriate management style and so on.
Dissolve the problem	This is to change the nature of the problem. In the call centre example above, one 'option' to deal with the problem was to abolish the call centre completely and change over to internet-only ordering: here the problem has been redefined as a customer access problem.
	However, a problem cannot be simply defined away. Changes to the organisation structure and the wider system may be needed to deal with the problem finally.
	Most 'messes' require systems to be redefined at many levels. For example, co-ordination problems can be solved by formal mechanisms such as changing people's jobs.

Section summary

When considering a strategic change, managers need to analyse the speed and extent of the change required. They also need to assess whether management's role is proactive or reactive, and whether the change is hard (systems based) or soft (people based). All of these factors will affect the way the change is implemented.

3 The context of change

Introduction

Many organisations have a poor track record of bringing about strategic change.

This is often because they fail to grasp that it is the **implementation** of the change, rather than the **formulation** of it, that is the hard part of the process. For strategic change to become reality, it is necessary to change the way in which the individuals within an organisation behave.

This means that there is a personal and cultural dimension to change management, and it is not simply an exercise in mechanical restructuring or the introduction of new systems.

The context of change is provided by the **organisational setting**; this has many aspects and can, therefore, be very complex. A change agent faces a wide range of choices about how change should be implemented in the specific context of their organisation.

We can look at the context of change by reference to what Balogun and Hope Hailey call the **change kaleidoscope**.

The kaleidoscope was created to help managers design a **change management approach which is appropriate** to their organisation, and it offers eight headings for the **context** in which change occurs (**contextual features**).

One of the eight contextual features is **scope** which we have discussed in relation to the type of change. The rest of the contextual features are discussed below.

In relation to scope, a change manager also needs to consider how much of an organisation is going to be affected by the change: a single division or department, or the whole organisation?

The headings represent a wide range of influences and the specific considerations affecting the impact of each may vary from organisation to organisation. For example, the first on the list, **time available**, may be largely determined by stakeholder sentiment in one organisation and by anticipated political change in another, with different aspects of the market situation influencing both.

3.1 Contextual features of change

(a)   The **time available** may vary dramatically, but can often be quite limited when responding to competitive or regulatory pressure. Organisations in crisis have little time, but those looking at longer-term strategic development normally have more time to change.

(b)   The **preservation** of some organisational characteristics and resources may be required. Do certain ways of working need to be maintained? Do particular groups of staff need to be retained? Do specific organisational competences need to be preserved?

(c)   **Diversity** of general experience, opinion and practice is likely to ease the change process: homogeneity in these factors is unlikely to do so.

(d)   The **capability** to manage and implement change is obviously important. To a great extent, this depends on past experience of change projects, both among managers and among lower-level staff.

Capability can be analysed at three levels:

(i)   **Individual**: are individuals able to cope with the transition they will have to undertake?

(ii)   **Managerial**: do managers have the ability to help their staff through the transition process?

(iii)   **Organisational**: does the organisation as a whole have sufficient resources with the knowledge and ability required to manage the types of change required?

(e)   **Capacity** to undertake change depends on the availability of resources, particularly **finance**, **IS/IT**, and management time and skill. We have looked at the importance of IS/IT to strategy earlier in this Study Text, but it is important to note that unrealisable or outdated systems could become a blockage in the change process.

(f)   The degree of workforce **readiness** for change will affect its success. Are staff aware of the need for change, and are they committed to making the personal changes required of them?

Readiness may be contrasted with **resistance** to change, which can exist at varying levels of intensity and may be widespread or confined to pockets.

(g)   The **power** to effect change may not be sufficient to overcome determined resistance among important **stakeholder groups**. This can apply even at the strategic apex where, for example, major shareholders, trustees or government ministers may constrain managers' freedom of action.

Stakeholder analysis is very important because stakeholders can affect an organisation's capacity to change, so an organisation needs to ensure that its proposed changes are acceptable to key stakeholder groups.

An examination of context leads to four questions:

(a)   Is the organisation able to **achieve** the change required?

(b)   Does the context affect the **means** by which change should be achieved?

(c)   Should the context itself be **restructured** as a preliminary to strategic change?

(d)   Will constraints present in the context make it necessary to proceed in **stages** rather than implementing the changes all at once?

3.2 Design choices

As well as the eight contextual features, the change kaleidoscope identifies six design choices which affect change implementation itself.

Once a change agent has considered the context of the change process, they can then select a change approach from the menu of design choices.

Change path – The change path refers to the type of change (the nature and scope of change) that needs to be undertaken for the required outcome to be achieved.

Change start point – The change start point is the point where change is initiated and developed. For example, is the change **top-down** or **bottom-up**? Will the change initially be applied to a **pilot site** and then extended to the whole organisation, or will it immediately be rolled out across the whole organisation?

Change style – The change style is the management style of the implementation. We look at change management styles later, but it is important to realise there is a range of possible styles for managing change – ranging from highly **collaborative**, to **directive** and then **coercive**. However, there is no single 'correct' style of management. Style needs to be appropriate to the change context.

Change target – Deciding which organisational level to intervene at is an important design choice. For example, does a change process try to change employees' values, or focus on behavioural change, or does it instead try to change the performance objectives and outputs of employees?

Change interventions – The change interventions are the levers and mechanisms which need to be deployed to implement the change. They include:

- Technical interventions (structures and systems)
- Political interventions
- Cultural interventions (changing the culture in the organisations)
- Interpersonal interventions (education, communication, training, personal development)

Change roles – This determines who is responsible for leading and implementing the changes. These roles may include:

- Leadership (for example, the individual responsibility which lies with a senior manager such as the MD or the CEO)

- External consultants who facilitate the process

- Change action team

3.2.1 Comments on the kaleidoscope

Balogun and Hope Hailey stress that the kaleidoscope is not intended to prescribe formulaic design choices for particular contexts.

In the same way as a real kaleidoscope continuously rearranges the same small pieces of coloured glass to produce different images, the eight contextual features in the model are constantly reconfigured to produce different scenarios for each change situation.

As a result, the change designs also vary according to individual situations.

Also, the importance of the eight contextual features on the design choices does not come from the impact of isolated, individual features, but from the impact of all of them together.

3.3 Top-down or bottom-up change

Balogun and Hope Hailey's kaleidoscope highlights the importance of context in change management, and their change matrix highlights the potential variety in the scope and nature of the change which an organisation could face.

However, we also need to recognise that the starting point for change (top-down or bottom-up) can in itself affect the change.

3.3.1 Top-down change

In a top-down change, the direction, control and initiation of the change come from the **strategic apex** of the organisation.

Top-down change usually involves a programme of change **determined** and implemented by the **senior management** or their representatives.

Top-down change may need to be **imposed** on an organisation. In a crisis or turnaround situation, there may be no alternative but to impose change on the organisation.

3.3.2 Bottom-up change

The logic behind emergent, or bottom-up, change is that the responsibility for change should not rest solely with senior management.

While top-down change offers the benefits of speed and clarity, it is unlikely to **encourage ownership or commitment** to the required changes.

By contrast, bottom-up change involves consultation with staff so that employees contribute to the themes and ideas in the changes.

This collaborative approach to change gives the employees a sense of ownership of the change process.

However, there are some limitations to a bottom-up approach:

(a)   Because it involves consultation and emerges from the organisation, it can be **slower to implement** than a top-down approach.

(b)   Bottom-up change can produce much more **unpredictable consequences** than top-down change because it is subject to interpretation and negotiation by the staff who put the change in place.

(c)   Senior management have less control over the change process, because it has to be participative and collaborative.

(d)   A top-down, or directive, approach to change (as would be necessary for a reconstruction or a revolution) leads to a cultural web developed by one person (usually the CEO) or a small group of people (senior management). By contrast, a bottom-up, collaborative approach leads to a wider range of employees being involved in the process of vision and cultural web development.

3.4 Adaptation and continuous change

The change matrices illustrating the nature and scope of change have highlighted that while some changes can be rapid, one-off events (revolutions or reconstructions), other changes take place much more gradually.

Although 'adaptation' is less dramatic than a 'revolution', it can be equally important for an organisation. In essence, adaptive change is about making organisations more efficient, or better, at what they already do.

Adaptive change occurs when an organisation's environment changes slowly, and is altered in little stages. One of the advantages of this is that it **minimises the resistance faced** at any time.

Also, although many models and approaches to change present a 'change event' as a one-off occurrence, this is not always the case.

We have already mentioned that many organisations view change as a means of reaching a visionary future state. However, this ignores the fact that for some organisations change management is most realistically about what Buchanan and McCalman call a **'perpetual transition management'**.

In this case, a key aspect of successful change management is managers' ability to deal with **constant change**.

For Buchanan and McCalman change is not simply a stage process. Instead, they suggest that **four interlocking management processes** or layers need to be in place to implement and sustain major organisational changes.

(a) **Trigger layer**: Identification of needs and opportunities for major change.

(b) **Vision layer**: Establishing the future development of the organisation by articulating a vision of the future and communicating this effectively.

(c) **Conversion layer**: Mobilise support in the organisation for the new vision as being the most appropriate way of dealing with the triggers of change.

　　　This has important implications for management: everyone involved in making change work has to feel part of the change, and has to accept the logic behind it. If they are not involved, they are liable to the 'you've introduced this without consulting us' syndrome, which could lead to them resisting the changes, and therefore reducing their effectiveness.

(d) **Maintenance and renewal layer**: Identifying ways in the changes are sustained and enhanced through alterations in attitudes, values and behaviours, thereby avoiding regression back to 'old' ways of doing things.

Many change initiatives fail to achieve the results which had been hoped for. And the reason for this is often that there are inherent tendencies in an organisation to preserve the *status quo*.

Therefore, approaches to change management which focus on planning and vision (at the start of the change process) are in danger of overlooking the vital importance of **sustaining and renewing organisational change**: that is, recognising that change is an ongoing process.

3.5 Change adept organisations

The increasing dynamism and complexity of their external environments means that change has increasingly become a way of life within organisations. For example, in order to remain competitive in the global economy, organisations need to manage complex information flows (about opportunities and threats), grasp new ideas quickly, and spread those ideas throughout their enterprise.

An organisation's ability to maintain its competitive position is likely to depend not only on its resources and competences but also on its ability to respond to opportunity and threats.

The number and variety of change triggers an organisation faces (both internal and external) means that change is created almost constantly and at many levels in an organisation. Although there may occasionally be revolutionary strategic changes (often triggered by external forces), changes also occur almost every day through the actions of people engaged in their work.

Therefore, rather than viewing it as a departure from the past, organisations need to view change as a way of life, and as a means of improving their ability to thrive in competitive markets in the future. Rosabeth Moss **Kanter** describes organisations which embrace change in this way, and manage it successfully, as change adept organisations.

Kanter argues that change adept organisations have three key attributes, each of which also has implications for the role of leaders within an organisation.

(a) **The imagination to innovate**

　　　The need for improvement and innovation never ceases – products and processes which are a source of competitive advantage today simply become the industry standard in future. (For example, when they were first introduced, self-service check-in facilities at airports were a source of differentiation for the airlines which had them; now they are used by all the airlines.)

To encourage innovation, effective leaders help to develop new concepts, models and applications of technology that set an organisation apart from its competitors.

Crucially, though, the source of these innovations and improvements should not be confined to research and development; employees across the organisation should be seen as a source of new ideas and improvements.

(b) **The professionalism to perform**

Leaders provide personal and organisational competence, supported by workforce training and development, which enables staff to use their skills to a very high operational standard and to deliver value to (increasingly demanding) customers.

A key issue here is not simply that the employees within an organisation have the underlying skills and capacity to be able to perform well, but that the routines and infrastructure within an organisation support their ability to do so.

(c) **The openness to collaborate**

Leaders develop relationships with partners who can extend the organisation's reach, enhance its product or service offerings, or energise its practices.

In this respect, supply chain management, as well as more strategic alliances and collaboration (eg joint ventures) can all be crucial in maintaining an organisation's competitive advantage.

These three attributes are sometimes also referred to as the 'three Cs':

- **Concepts** – knowledge and ideas

- **Competence** – the skill to operate anywhere at a high standard

- **Connections** – the ability to form successful relationships, and to gain access to external resources and competences around the world

3.5.1 Leadership in change adept organisations

Kanter also observed that in order to make their organisations more responsive to change – and to manage change effectively within them – leaders need to demonstrate seven key skills:

(a) **Tune into the environment** – Leaders need to create a network of 'listening posts' to listen and learn from what is happening in the environment; for example, by understanding what key stakeholders such as customers and suppliers want (or need) from an organisation. Equally 'listening posts' within an organisation (for example, team leaders or supervisors) could prove valuable for understanding the needs of employees.

(b) **Challenge the prevailing organisational wisdom** – The current ways of working may not always be the best ones for an organisation, so leaders need to challenge assumptions and look at issues from different perspectives, rather than simply accepting the *status quo*.

(c) **Communicate a compelling aspiration** – Leaders need to have a clear vision of what they want to achieve, and to communicate this with conviction to other people. There are likely to be many sources of resistance to overcome, so if a leader is not able to 'sell' the proposed changes effectively, they will not be able to overcome this resistance.

(d) **Build coalitions** – According to Kanter, while it may seem obvious that gaining the support of key individuals is vital to successfully implementing a change, this is often one of the most neglected steps in the change process. Leaders need the support and involvement of people who have the resources, knowledge and influence ('political clout') to make change happen.

(e) **Transfer ownership to a working team** – Leaders cannot introduce changes by themselves. One of the key reasons for building a coalition which supports the change is that the members of the

coalition (as resource owners and influencers) can then enlist other people to implement the change. The implementation team can then build its own identity and concentrate on the task.

(f)   **Learn to persevere** – It is virtually inevitable that something will go wrong – or critics will emerge – during the course of a change programme. However, leaders need to persevere with the changes through the difficult times in order to reap the results in the end. The beginning of a change programme will be exciting, and the end will be satisfying, but it is the hard work in the middle which requires the leaders' perseverance – for example, to maintain the momentum, and to address unexpected issues which arise.

(g)   **Make everyone a hero** – It is very important that leaders remember to recognise and reward achievements. The extent to which people's efforts are recognised and rewarded is likely to be crucial in determining their motivation and enthusiasm for any future change programmes.

3.6 Continuous and discontinuous change

The 'scope of change' axis on Balogun and Hope Hailey's change matrix illustrates that change can either take place within the existing organisational paradigm or else can lead to the creation of a new paradigm.

Continuous change comprises small-scale incremental changes, which do not alter the organisational paradigm. Tushman calls this type of change '**convergent**' reflecting the fact that changes do not alter the underlying strategy of the organisation.

Discontinuous change results in a radical change in the firm's environment or operations. This change can be a sudden one-off change, or can be the result of a series of incremental changes. Discontinuous change is sometimes also described as '**frame-breaking**'.

The existence of discontinuous change is very significant in the unfreeze process.

Characteristics of discontinuous change

(a)   **Magnitude of change**: Discontinuous change means doing things in fundamentally different ways from the way they were previously done. The whole nature of the business is reshaped.

(b)   **Organisational fit**: Because the new strategic imperatives are inconsistent with the old ways of doing business, the old organisational structure is unlikely to fit with the new business model. This can lead to new organisational structures.

(c)   **Strategic vision**: Discontinuous change is nearly always linked to a reshaping of the overall corporate strategy.

(d)   **Multiple changes**: The magnitude of the change means that discontinuous change often affects several aspects of an organisation simultaneously – for example, strategy, structure, staffing and systems.

(e)   **Unclear future state**: At the outset, it is impossible to know precisely where discontinuous change will lead. Because discontinuous change involves the movement to a **new paradigm**, it is impossible to predict the detail of that paradigm in advance.

(f)   **Leadership**: The leadership of discontinuous change cannot be delegated: because of the magnitude of the change, the CEO and other top executives must be involved with the change.

(g)   **Speed of change**: Discontinuous change often involves rapid implementation, particularly if the change is a response to an external crisis.

The environment where frame-breaking change is necessary can be highly volatile, suggesting that unless an organisation changes quickly to meet the changed circumstances it may go out of business. In such a situation, there is a risk attached to any delay in the change process.

3.6.1 Dangers of simplistic classification

Before we leave this section, it is again worth considering that there is a danger of simply categorising change into two distinct categories – essentially either some kind of low-level, operational change or a kind of corporate earthquake.

This distinction is too simplistic, and we need to acknowledge a middle ground between convergent change and frame-breaking change. We could see this middle ground as 'frame-stretching' rather than 'frame-breaking'.

Frame-stretching change might involve the following features:

(a)   Parts of the corporate mission may be revised but the whole is not replaced.

(b)   Some elements of the power structure at the top of an organisation may change but not the whole management team.

(c)   Some modifications may be needed around the whole business, though they do not require wholesale redesign of every major process.

(d)   Some aspects of the organisational structure might be changed but the basic elements and the overall balance of size and shape will remain largely the same.

3.7 Uncertainty and change

In Chapter 1 of this Study Text, we suggested that the rational model of strategic planning underplays the level of uncertainty and complexity in strategy development. In that context, we introduced Stacey's ideas of chaos and complexity.

These ideas of chaos and complexity also have important implications for organisational change.

The interaction between a system and its environment has the potential for significant disruption. And if a system (in this case, an organisation) is operating in a chaotic and complex environment, the potential for disruption is increased still further.

Stacey argues that the complexity and instability of the business environment mean that organisations are operating in **unpredictable circumstances**. Consequently, there is no value in setting a prescriptive strategy. The reality is so complex that the **linear assumptions** between **cause** and **effect** cannot be justified.

Instead strategy should be allowed to emerge and adapt to the changes in the environment.

The importance of this for business strategists is that because organisations are operating in an unpredictable environment, **strategy becomes virtually impossible to model** because the future cannot be known with any certainty.

For example, could strategists looking at three- or five-year plans in 2006 have predicted the global economic downturn and crisis in the financial markets in 2008–9?

One other characteristic of chaotic systems is that they oscillate between **steady states** and **states of flux**; and at the end of a period of turbulence a new order will emerge. Strebel makes an important point here when he refers to the way **changes in technology** lead to 'breakpoints' in the development of an organisation. For example, look at how the development of the internet has triggered changes through new e-commerce opportunities. Could these have been anticipated 20 or more years ago?

Another important consequence of these ideas about chaos is that it **challenges the way organisations manage change**.

The traditional rational model would suggest that change is somehow internally generated and an organisation can, to some extent, control the change. However, the chaos theory approach suggests that organisations **cannot ultimately predict or control the change** in the longer term, however well they have planned for the future.

Instead, change management becomes a means of **responding to**, and **coping with**, the uncertainties created by an unpredictable environment.

3.7.1 Thriving on chaos

The management guru Tom Peters has argued that in this age of rapidly changing information technology, 'chaos' and constant change are now integral parts of companies' success. Peters argues that constant change is something that companies should pursue, rather than discourage.

In his book *Thriving on Chaos*, Peters argues that companies have to adapt by creating open information societies and knowledge sharing, encouraging employees to be responsible and adaptable, and by flattening hierarchical organisational structures.

Peters suggests that successful companies will embrace a policy of **constant innovation**, and will understand the value of **speed in responding to the opportunities** created by the volatility and dynamism in the external environment. (Developments in information technologies are one of the key drivers of this.) Conversely, companies need to rid themselves of 'the evils of bureaucracy', which Peters suggests will prevent them from being able to introduce change quickly and successfully.

Section summary

When facing a strategic change, an organisation needs to consider the **context of the change**, and the change kaleidoscope illustrates the contextual features it should consider. It is also important to note that change could be **continuous**, rather than simply a one-off, **discontinuous** event.

Equally, the organisation needs to consider whether change needs to be **imposed** by senior management or whether it can **emerge** from within the organisation.

4 Culture and change

Introduction

In the same way that we can look at the way individuals 'feel' and 'behave' we can also look at the way organisations do. Also, like individuals, organisations can adapt to their surroundings – changing their appearance, beliefs and behaviours.

Nevertheless, organisational culture has a very important impact on the management of change. Every organisation will have its own cultural blueprint which dictates how it interacts with its environment and manages its people.

Understanding the relationships between an organisation's culture and its (changing) environment greatly assist the organisation in managing change.

In their text, *Exploring Corporate Strategy*, Johnson, Scholes and Whittington argue that 'Strategic developments can only be successful if they recognise and address the cultural aspects of the change at hand'.

In other words, change cannot be isolated from the organisation overall, and needs to be linked to the culture of the organisation.

Two important characteristics of successful strategic change initiatives highlight this:

Alignment – ensuring that all the components of the change plan form an integrated whole. This means they are consistent within themselves, but are also linked into the whole organisational system.

Attunement – mirroring the preferred organisation culture, and ensuring that all aspects of the change are carried out in line with organisational values, and with sufficient attention to the human side of change.

If you think about the change kaleidoscope and the elements of context outlined above, you can see that they are all affected to some extent by **cultural considerations**. For example, even the adequacy or otherwise of the time available may be affected by culturally influenced attitudes to speed of action, caution and risk.

Johnson, Scholes and Whittington bring these ideas of culture and change together to create what they call the **cultural web**. The web helps an organisation analyse its current culture and identify which aspects of this culture need to be changed in order for the organisation to be able to achieve its strategic goals.

4.1 The cultural web

The cultural aspects which need to be considered when managing change can be illustrated in the cultural web.

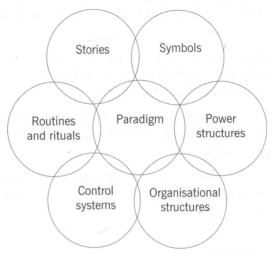

The cultural web (Johnson, Scholes and Whittington)

The web comprises six physical manifestations of culture:

(a)   **Stories** – The past events and people talked about inside and outside the company. Who and what are talked about most in these stories can illustrate the behaviour an organisation encourages, and the sorts of things it values.

(b)   **Rituals and routines** – The daily behaviour and actions of people that signal what is considered acceptable. This determines what is expected to happen in given situations, and what is valued by management.

(c)   **Symbols** – The visual representations of an organisation including logos, premises and dress can illustrate the nature of that organisation. Also, verbal representations such as language and titles can also act as symbols of the nature of an organisation.

(d)   **Organisational structures** – This includes both the formal structure defined by the organisation chart, and the unwritten lines of power and influence that indicate whose contributions are most valued. Structure is likely to reflect power.

(e)   **Control systems** – The ways that the organisation is controlled. These include financial systems, quality systems, and rewards (including the way they are measured and distributed within the organisation). Looking at the areas which are controlled most closely can indicate what is seen as most important to an organisation, and where most attention is focused.

(f)   **Power structures** – The pockets of real power in the company. This may involve one or two key senior executives, a whole group of executives, or even a department. The key is that these people have the greatest amount of influence on decisions, operations, and strategic direction.

These cultural elements all combine to underpin **the paradigm**. The paradigm signifies the **basic assumptions and beliefs** that an organisation's decision makers **hold in common** and **take for granted**.

Note that the paradigm is a slightly different concept from **culture**. The paradigm represents **collective experience** and is used to make sense of a given situation. It is thus essentially conservative and inhibiting to innovation, while an innovative **culture** is entirely feasible.

4.1.1 Challenging the paradigm

The entrenched assumptions and habits of mind which represent the **paradigm** constitute an important obstacle to strategic change. Therefore, if change is to be achieved, the existing organisational paradigm has to be challenged. A key part of the 'unfreeze' aspect of change management may need to be changing organisational behaviours and the paradigm.

Changing routines

Routines are the **habitual behaviours** that members of the organisation display both internally and externally. They are not procedures or processes but the **wider ways of doing things** that are typical of the organisation.

The problem of routines is that they can subvert change efforts. For example, it is unlikely that simply explaining required new processes and procedures will lead to their effective adoption: existing routines will mould the way they are put into operation.

When a **top-down change programme** requires the introduction of new methods, the detail of implementation can be driven by the careful identification of **critical success factors** and the **competences** they demand.

When change is to be introduced in a **less directed** way, change agents may focus on routines, **extending** existing ways of doing things towards what is required and then '**bending** the rules of the game' when sufficient stakeholder support has been created.

Symbolic processes

The importance of symbolic processes in the context of change is that they can often be used as levers of change. However, it is important to understand that the significance of a given symbol may vary from person to person; this makes their use as a tool of management difficult.

(a)   New **rituals** can be introduced and old ones abolished in order to communicate and implement change. For example, the replacement of a strictly hierarchical approach to management with a culture of coaching and empowerment can be signalled and reinforced by the introduction of social occasions such as office parties that will allow staff to meet relatively informally.

(b)   Formal **systems and processes** can have symbolic aspects, typically when they signal status and power relationships, but also when they direct attention to new concerns, such as customer service.

(c)   Changes to **physical aspects** of the workplace can have strong symbolic effect as, for instance, when open-plan offices or hot desking are introduced.

(d)   The **behaviour** of leaders and change agents has a very powerful symbolic effect and must reflect intended change if the intention is not to be undermined: staff will respond far better to example than to edict.

(e)   **Language** can have symbolic significance beyond the bald meaning of the words used. Well-chosen words can inspire and motivate change; similarly, the use of badly chosen words can undermine their inherent meaning.

(f)   **Stories** have an important symbolic role, but are not easy to exploit since much corporate communication is automatically dismissed as mere marketing puff.

Power and politics

Politics is about the exercise of **power** and the use of **influence**. Managers and other important individual stakeholders establish and exploit **power structures** and **networks of influence** that are intertwined with both formal hierarchies and the informal aspects of the organisation's life. The implementation of strategy is inevitably influenced by the operation of these structures and networks. Change management is also, therefore, subject to political influence and change managers should take due account of political processes.

Change managers can use political activity to achieve the following goals:

- Building the **power base**
- Overcoming **resistance**
- Achieving **compliance**

4.1.2 Example of the cultural web

The example below shows some of the questions which the cultural web asks about an organisation. It also illustrates some of the expressions of culture that could be generated by the web, based on an example of a car repair workshop.

Cultural web	Examples (based on a car repair workshop)
Stories	
What stories do people tell about the organisation? What do these stories say about the values of the organisation?	They're always the cheapest on the market; they do things the cheapest way they can.
What reputation is communicated among customers and other stakeholders?	They are known for having high numbers of customer complaints, and for doing shoddy work.
What do employees talk about when they think of the history of the organisation?	The founder started the company with a $10,000 loan from a friend.
Rituals and routines	
What do employees expect when they come to work?	Employees have their time sheets examined by the boss.
What do customers expect when they walk in?	Customers expect to hear the radio playing and to be given a mug of coffee while they wait for their cars.
What would be immediately obvious if it changed?	Workshop repainted and new machinery installed.
What behaviour do the routines encourage?	Lots of talk about money, and especially how to cut costs.
Symbols	
What language and jargon is used? Is it well known and usable by all?	Mechanics use jargon which customers don't understand to describe parts and problems.
What aspects of strategy are highlighted in publicity?	Adverts and leaflets say they won't be beaten on price.
Are there any status symbols?	No, the boss wears an overall, like the staff.

Cultural web	Examples (based on a car repair workshop)
Organisational structure	
Is the structure formal or informal? Flat or hierarchical?	Flat structure: Owner, Mechanics, Receptionist.
What are the formal lines of authority?	Mechanics report to the owner (who is also a mechanic).
Are there any informal lines of authority?	The receptionist is the owner's wife so she discusses customer complaints directly with him.
Do structures encourage co-operation and collaboration?	Each mechanic looks after himself. There is no sharing of tools or jobs.
Control systems	
What process has the strongest controls?	Costs are tightly controlled. Customers are billed for all parts used.
What process has the weakest controls?	Quality is not seen as important. Getting work done as cheaply as possible is emphasised ahead of quality.
Is emphasis on rewarding good work or penalising poor work?	Employees' pay is deducted if actual costs on a job exceed quotes by more than 10%.
Power structures	
Who has the real power in the organisation?	The owner.
How strongly held are the beliefs of the people with power?	The owner believes strongly in a low cost model, and is prepared to lose repeat customers in order to keep costs down.
How is power used or abused?	The threat of having their pay docked keeps mechanics working to this low cost model.
What are the main blockages to change?	The owner insists that his low cost model is the best way to run the business and won't invest in any new equipment if it will cost lots of money.

4.1.3 The cultural web, business strategy and change

The importance of the cultural web for business strategy is that it provides a means of looking at cultural assumptions and practices, to make sure that **organisational elements are aligned with one another**, and **with an organisation's strategy**.

If an organisation is not delivering the results its management wants, management can use the web to help diagnose whether the organisation's **culture is contributing to the underperformance**.

The cultural web may be used as a tool to establish specific implications of the desired overall strategic change by facilitating comparison between the current position and the desired future outcome.

For example, consideration of power structures may make it clear that there should be a move away from some aspects of uncontrolled devolution of power and towards a clearer definition of responsibility.

Similarly, it might be decided that dress is a powerful symbol and that providing all customer-facing staff with a corporate uniform will give them a greater sense of pride and identity in their work.

4.2 McKinsey 7 'S' model

Like the cultural web, the **McKinsey 7 'S' model** is a useful way of looking at organisations facing organisational change. The model represents the organisation as a set of interconnected and interdependent sub-systems, some of which are seen as 'hard' (quantifiable or easily defined) and some of which are 'soft' (more subjective and less easily defined).

Although the model was designed to show how the various aspects of a business relate to one another, it can also illustrate how change will affect both the organisation as a whole, and individual people and functions within it.

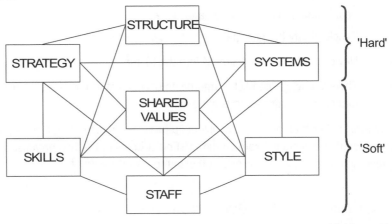

McKinsey 7 'S' model

The organisation's **structure** determines the division of tasks in the organisation and the hierarchy of authority from the most senior to junior.

Strategy is the way in which the organisation plans to outperform its competitors, or how it intends to achieve its objectives. **Systems** include the technical systems of accounting, personnel, management information and so forth.

These 'hard' elements are easily quantified or defined, and deal with facts and rules. However, certain 'soft' elements are equally important.

Staff are the people in the organisation (who have their own complex concerns and priorities) and **skills** are those things that the organisation does well. **Shared values** are the guiding beliefs of people in the organisation about why it exists, while **style** includes the shared assumptions, ways of working and attitudes of management (especially senior management).

Shared values thus approximate closely to the 'paradigm', underpinning management beliefs.

4.3 Culture and mergers/acquisitions

Issues of cultural incompatibility have often been cited as problem areas when implementing a merger or acquisition, and are often considered to be an important reason why mergers fail. The case study example of Daimler/Chrysler earlier in this chapter illustrates that one of the factors which contributed to the failure of the merger was the difference in culture of the two organisations.

If we apply the McKinsey 7 'S' model back to the reasons which we identified for the poor performance of the merger Daimler/Chrysler group we can see that:

(a)   US and German business cultures were different (so the **styles** of the two companies were different).

(b)   Many key Chrysler managers left after the merger (so there were problems with **staff** in the merged organisation).

(c)   Mercedes was a premium brand which had been extended to making smaller cars. Chrysler depended on high volumes, not a premium product (so the **strategies** of the two companies were different).

(d)   The new Group did not properly exploit economies of scale, such as sharing components. The merger did not deliver the synergies which had been expected because the businesses were never successfully integrated and, in effect, seemed to carry on running two independent product lines. (So, the merger didn't integrate the **systems** of the two companies.)

In more general terms, signs of a culture clash following a merger or acquisition might be:

*   People talk in terms of 'them' and 'us'

*   People glorify the past, talking of the 'good old days'

*   Newcomers are not integrated into the team

*   There is obvious conflict – arguments between staff members, refusal to share information, formation of cliques and coalitions

However, rather than running the risk of cultural issues disrupting a merger or acquisition, it would be sensible for managers to examine the existing cultures of the two organisations at the start of the integration process, while looking at the suitability of the deal.

4.4 Change and national cultures

As well as considering change in the context of organisational culture, we need to consider how different **national cultures** can affect the way organisations change.

Differences between national cultures can be stronger than between different organisations.

(a)   **Organisational culture** is something we learn afresh each time we join a different workforce, and is therefore easy to pick up and put down as appropriate.

(b)   **National culture** is something we are born into, and therefore is generally non-negotiable; it is something inherent to all of us.

This last point is often used to explain why management approaches developed in Japan that have been successful there, such as TQM and kaizen, may not work in Western companies because the national cultures are so different. Of course, it might be added that Japanese approaches may not work even in other Asian countries, such as South Korea, because their cultures are sufficiently different from Japan's. However, the underlying point is clear: business practices cannot be divorced from their social context.

This has important implications for managing change, particularly major transformational change, because it suggests change managers need to pay attention to **national cultural characteristics**.

Section summary

Many aspects of change will be affected to some extent by cultural considerations. Therefore it is important to establish the impact of a strategic change by comparing the current cultural position with that of the desired future position.

5 Stage models of change

Introduction

We have identified a number of situations which might act as triggers for change in an organisation. However, it is also important that organisations realise that change is an ongoing process and needs to be addressed all the time.

In the modern market economy, change is inherent in society. Not only do technologies change, so too do social norms, tastes and trends, demographic profiles and people's expectations of employment. In fact, almost every aspect of collective human life is subject to constant change.

The context of change – within a complex and dynamic environment – means it is wrong to think a visionary 'future state' can always be reached through some highly programmed way.

Moreover, successful change management requires more than simply recognising a change trigger and acting on it. Successful exploitation of a change situation requires:

- Knowledge of the circumstances surrounding a situation

- Understanding of the interactions in that situation

- Awareness of the potential impact of the variables associated with the situation (as in Leavitt's model highlighting the interaction between task, structure, people and technology)

Nevertheless, many organisations do view change as a highly programmed process which follows a 'formula' and it is useful for us to consider a framework for change:

Recognition – Identify the problem that needs to be rectified

Diagnosis – Break down the problem into component parts

Solution – Analyse possible alternatives
Select preferred solution
Apply preferred solution

5.1 Lewin's three-stage model (the 'ice cube' model)

Although the essence of change is that it enables a person, department or organisation to move from a current state to a future state, Lewin suggested that organisational changes actually have **three steps** (stages): '**unfreeze**', '**change**' (or '**move**') and '**freeze**' or '**refreeze**'. (In this Study Text we refer to the third stage as 'refreeze' because we think it describes the process more clearly. However, in his original model, Lewin actually referred to the stage simply as 'freeze'.)

It is important to note that change involves 're-learning': not merely learning something new, but trying to unlearn what is already known and practised in an organisation. This is a key part of the 'unfreeze' stage.

| Unfreeze | → | Change | → | Refreeze |

Lewin: Unfreeze-change-refreeze model

5.1.1 Unfreeze

This first step involves unfreezing the current state of affairs, and creating the motivation to change. This means defining the current state of an organisation, highlighting the forces driving change and those resisting it and picturing a desired end state.

Crucially, the unfreeze stage involves making people within an organisation ready to change: making them aware of the **need (trigger) for change**, and creating a **readiness to change** among the workforce.

A key part of this stage is **weakening the restraining forces** that are resisting change, and **strengthening the driving forces** that are promoting change.

Approaches to the unfreeze stage include:

(a)   Physically **removing** individuals from their accustomed routines, sources of information and social relationships, so that old behaviours and attitudes are less likely to be reinforced by familiarity and social influence.

(b)   **Consulting** team members about proposed changes. This will help them to feel less powerless and insecure about the process. It may also involve them in evaluation and problem solving for more effective change measures – which will create a measure of ownership of the solutions. This, in turn, may shift resistant attitudes.

(c)   **Confronting** team members' perceptions and emotions about change. Failure to recognise and deal with emotions only leads to later problems. Negative emotions may be submerged, but will affect performance by undermining commitment.

(d)   Positively **reinforcing** demonstrated willingness to change: validating efforts and suggestions with praise, recognition and perhaps added responsibility in the change process.

If the need for change can be 'sold' to the team as immediate, and its benefits highlighted – for example, by securing individuals' jobs for the future – the unfreeze stage can be greatly accelerated.

Either way, effective **communication**, explaining the need for change, is essential for the unfreeze process to work successfully.

(**Note**. We have touched on the idea of 'resistance to change' here. We look in more detail at ways for dealing with resistance to change later in this chapter.)

'Unfreezing' an organisation may sound simple enough in theory but, in practice, it can be very difficult because it involves making people ready to change.

Rational argument will not necessarily be sufficient to convince individuals of the need to change, particularly if they stand to lose out from the change, or will have to make significant personal changes as a result of the change.

Sometimes the need for change may be obvious to all employees – for example, the arrival of a new competitor in the market leading to a dramatic reduction in market share.

However, if the need for change is less obvious, then the 'unfreezing' process may need to be 'managed' in some way, to make staff appreciate the need for change.

For example:

*   Encourage debate about the appropriateness or effectiveness of the current way of operating (including current management styles)

*   Publish information showing how the organisation compares with its competitors in key performance areas

 In Chapter 11 of this Study Text, we discuss performance management, and one of the ways organisations can analyse their performance is by benchmarking against competitors' performance. Benchmarking could therefore be useful as part of the unfreeze stage of a change process.

5.1.2 Change (or 'move')

The change (or 'move') stage involves learning new concepts and new meanings for existing concepts. This is the **transition stage**, by which an organisation moves from its current state to its future state.

It is important that an organisation encourages the **participation** and **involvement** of its staff in this phase so that they do not feel alienated by the change process.

This phase is mainly concerned with identifying the new, desirable behaviours or norms; communicating them clearly and positively; and encouraging individuals and groups to '**buy into**' or '**own**' the new values and behaviours.

Change is facilitated by:

(a)   **Identification**: encouraging individuals to identify with role models from whom they can learn new behaviour patterns. For example, the team leader should adopt the values and behaviours they expect the team to follow. Team members who have relevant skills, experience and/or enthusiasm may be encouraged to coach others.

(b)   **Internalisation**: placing individuals in a situation in which new behaviours are required for success, so that they **have** to develop coping behaviours. Pilot schemes or presentation of the changes to others may help in this process.

5.1.3 Refreeze (freeze)

The refreeze stage involves internalising new concepts and meanings. It focuses on **stabilising (refreezing) the new state of affairs**, by setting policies to embed new behaviours, and establishing new standards.

It is crucial that the **changes are embedded** throughout an organisation to ensure that staff do not lapse back into old patterns of behaviour.

Once new behaviours have been adopted, the refreeze stage is required to consolidate and reinforce them, so that they become integrated into the individual's habits, attitudes and relationship patterns.

(a)   **Habituation effects** (getting accustomed to the new situation) may be achieved over time, through practice, application and repetition.

(b)   **Positive reinforcement** can be used to reward and validate successful change. For example, an element of a staff bonus scheme could be dependent on staff members adopting the new methodology.

5.2 Gemini 4Rs framework for planned strategic change

Although Lewin's three-stage model of strategic change is probably the best-known stage model of change, it is not the only one.

Management consultants Gouillart and Kelly describe the process of business transformation (major change) in four stages, in a framework known as the **Gemini 4Rs framework**.

For Gouillart and Kelly, a transformation process must create a new corporate vision, create new opportunities for an organisation, and introduce new ways of doing things.

According to Gouillart and Kelly, such a process needs the four 'Rs' to be present if it is to be successful.

5.2.1 Reframing

Reframing is the process of setting a corporate vision.

It involves asking fundamental questions about what the organisation is and what it is for.

The reframing element of a change process should:

- **Achieve mobilisation**: create the will and desire to change
- **Create the vision** of where the organisation is going
- **Build a measurement system** that will set and measure progress against those targets

5.2.2 Restructuring

Restructuring is the process of removing elements of an organisation which do not add value. Although it primarily involves looking at the organisation's structure, it may also involve cultural changes.

Restructuring activity should include:

- **Constructing an economic model** to show in detail how **value is created** and where resources should be deployed
- **Aligning the physical infrastructure** with the overall plan
- Redesigning the work architecture so that **processes interact to create value**

 The ideas of value creation here link back to Porter's idea of the value chain (see Chapter 4), and they also highlight the importance of having a good 'fit' between organisational structure and strategy.

5.2.3 Revitalising

Revitalising is the process of finding **new products and markets**, and ensuring a good fit with the competitive environment.

Revitalising activities include:

- **Achieving market focus** and identifying new market opportunities
- **Inventing** new businesses or products
- **Changing the rules of competition** by exploiting technology

5.2.4 Renewal

Renewal is the process of developing individuals, to ensure that their skills are aligned to organisational requirements.

Renewal ensures that the people in the organisation support the change process, and acquire the necessary skills to contribute to it.

Renewal activities should include:

- **Creating a reward system** in order to motivate
- **Supporting individual learning** to develop learning as a competence within the organisation

5.3 Evaluation of stage models and Lewin's ideas

Although the three-stage model provides a useful outline of the change process, it is not a planning tool for the process.

There is a danger that some managers may view 'unfreeze' as a planning session, before using 'move' as implementation and 'refreeze' as a post-implementation review.

Unfortunately, such an approach ignores the fundamental issue that **people will only change if they feel and appreciate the need to do so**. If this need is not properly communicated, the change process will not harness the energy of key players effectively, and will not tackle any potential resistance within an organisation.

Moreover, some critics argue that Lewin's model is based on the simplistic assumption that organisations are stable and static, so change only results from concentrated effort, and even then, the change that results is one-directional. However, the counter argument is that **change is multidirectional and ubiquitous,** and is often a **continuous process**, not the structured process Lewin's model would suggest.

5.3.1 'Biological' models

We should also note that both Lewin's three-stage model and the 4 Rs model imply a structured, planned approach to change in the same way that the rational model views strategic planning as a logical, structured process.

However, in the same way that we can look at emergent processes of strategy development as an alternative approach to the rational model, so we can also suggest **less prescriptive approaches to change management**.

In particular, Gareth Morgan presents an alternative approach which considers the organisation as a biological organism which is continually changing. Such an approach seems appropriate given the complexity of modern society and its constant changes.

Morgan suggests that in the same way a living organism continually interacts with its environment, changing it and responding to changes in it, and interacting with other creatures in it, so too does any organisation. Regardless of its industry or sector, an organisation affects its environment (eg by fulfilling the needs of its clients, or by using scarce resources). Equally, an organisation comes into contact with potential collaborators or competitors, and has to respond to changes that occur in the external environment.

In this context, change can be seen as a **dynamic capability** – an organisation understanding how and when to change.

We need to recognise, however, that change involves two complementary factors, and each is essential for an organisation to derive the fullest benefit from change.

One of these factors is clearly the **readiness** and **ability to change** different aspects of the organisation without wrecking the rest of the entity.

The other factor is the ability to maintain a **sense of continuity** in order for change to be recognisable as a change from one thing to another, rather than just the disappearance of one thing and its replacement. If an organisation changes, then for it to remain that organisation (albeit in a changed form) then some aspect of it has to stay the same.

What this also implies, then, is that the **management of stability** is as important as the **management of difference**, when managing change.

Section summary

Stage models of change suggest a structured process of moving from a current state to a future state. Lewin's three-stage model (unfreeze, change, refreeze) illustrates this process, although it is important not to overlook the human aspect of change. People will only change their behaviour if they appreciate the need for change.

---

6 Other models of managing change

Introduction

Although Lewin's stage model of change provides a clear overview of the change process, it doesn't offer any insights into how managers can manage change through the process. Other models draw on project management ideas to suggest how the change process can be managed.

6.1 Bullock and Batten, planned change

A number of approaches to managing the change process draw on the discipline of **project management**. One example of this is Bullock and Batten's model.

Bullock and Batten identify four 'steps' to changing an organisation:

Exploration – Verifying the need for change, and acquiring any resources for the change to go ahead (for example, human expertise; IT systems).

Planning – The planning step involves key decision makers and technical experts. A diagnosis of the current position is completed, and actions are arranged into a change plan. This plan is then approved by management, before moving on to the action phase.

Action – Actions are completed according to the plan, with feedback mechanisms which allow some replanning if activities go off track or get behind schedule.

Integration – The integration phase starts once the action stage has been completed. Integration involves aligning the changes which have been made with other areas of an organisation and formalising the changes; for example, through company policies and reward systems.

However, while Bullock and Batten's model provides a clear sequence of stages, it (like other models derived from project management ideas) assumes that change can be defined and moved towards in a planned way.

The project management approach simplifies the change process by isolating one part of the organisation to make the necessary changes.

Such an approach implies that organisational change is a technical problem which can be solved by using a definable technical solution. This would work well for isolated issues, but less well when organisations face more complex changes – for example, to 'go global'.

6.2 Kotter – eight step model

John Kotter analysed a number of organisations going through change, and highlighted eight key lessons which could be learned from this analysis. In 1995, Professor Kotter published an article in the *Harvard Business Review* in which he converted these eight lessons into an eight step model for managing change.

(1)   **Establish a sense of urgency** – Discuss the current competitive position and look at potential future scenarios. Increase the 'felt need for change' (in other words, promote the driving forces for change).

(2)   **Form a powerful guiding coalition** – Assemble a powerful group of people who can work well together to promote the change.

(3)   **Create a vision** – Build a vision to guide the change effort, together with strategies for achieving it.

(4)   **Communicate the vision** – The vision, and accompanying strategies and new behaviours, need to be communicated. Kotter stresses that effective communication is crucial in change management.

(5)   **Empower others to act on the vision** – This includes getting rid of obstacles to change such as unhelpful structures or systems. People need to be allowed to experiment.

(6)   **Plan for and create short-term wins** – Look for and advertise short-term visible improvements because these will help sustain the driving forces for change. Kotter suggests that these short-term wins should be planned into the change programme, and people should be publicly rewarded for making improvements.

(7)   **Consolidate improvements and produce still more change** – Promote and reward those who are able to further advance and work towards the vision. Maintain the energy behind the change process by introducing new projects, resource and change agents.

(8)   **Institutionalise new approaches** – Ensure that everyone understands that the new behaviours and systems will lead to corporate success.

Kotter's eight step model is popular with managers, and highlights two key issues – the importance of having a 'felt need' for change in an organisation, and importance of communication throughout the change process.

However, there is a danger that Kotter's approach will create an early burst of energy at the start of a change programme followed by a sequence of routine processes. Steps 6, 7 and 8 – 'plan', 'consolidate', 'institutionalise' – seem to suggest a straightforward process which can be embedded into an organisation. But, in practice, the challenges and excitement of the early stages of a change management project need to be maintained throughout.

6.3 Beer and Nohria – Theory E and Theory O

Beer and Nohria (writing in the *Harvard Business Review* in 2000) suggest that although each organisation's change is unique, each change is ultimately a variant of two underlying approaches. Beer and Nohria call these underlying approaches 'Theory E' and 'Theory O'.

Theory E starts from the premise that the purpose of change is to **increase economic value**, often expressed as shareholder value. The focus of change is on formal structure and systems, and change is seen as a top-down process, often with extensive help from external consultants. Theory E changes are planned and programmatic, and usually involve the use of economic incentives, drastic layoffs, downsizing and restructuring.

Theory O is concerned with developing an organisation's **human capability** to implement strategy, and to develop corporate culture through **organisational learning**. The focus of change is on culture and cultural adjustment, rather than structure and systems, and the process is participative (rather than being top-down). Consequently, change is emergent rather than planned and programmatic, with an emphasis on feedback and reflection.

However, both approaches have drawbacks. Theory E approaches ignore the feelings and attitudes of employees, and may lead to a fall in motivation and commitment, and the loss of the creativity needed to sustain competitive advantage. Conversely, by trying to maintain positive relationships with staff, Theory O approaches may mean that organisations avoid taking difficult decisions; for example, decisions about how to reverse a decline in customer numbers or market share.

Moreover, Beer and Nohria argue that, in practice, organisations cannot use only one of these theories alone. Instead, a company should implement both Theory E and Theory O at the same time. However, this then leaves managers with the problem of how to combine the relevant elements from both approaches, and to resolve the tension between Theories E and O in a way that obtains the benefits of each while minimising the negative consequences.

Yet at the same time, Beer and Nohria argue that this 'problem' should also be the objective of managers leading change. Their objective should be to integrate E and O in a way that resolves the tension between the two, allowing organisations to satisfy their shareholders and yet also have the capacity and capabilities to adapt and survive as viable institutions in the long run.

For example, an organisation should look to make changes to the corporate structure and systems at the same time as making changes to the dynamic of the corporate workplace and its culture. In other words, it needs to combine elements of 'hard' change and 'soft' change (which we look at in more detail in the next chapter). Equally, consultants should be used to get managers and staff to think about, and not just act blindly on, a set of procedures. Often the presence of consultants can make managers abdicate any sense of leadership; however, managers should be encouraged to use consultants as a tool to help them make better decisions and become better leaders, not to replace them as leaders.

The contrast between Theory E and Theory O mirrors the contrast between a prescriptive, rational model approach to strategy and emergent approaches to strategy, which we looked at in Chapter 1 of this Study Text.

Section summary

One of the criticisms of Lewin's stage model is that it doesn't give any insights into how change should be managed. Change managers can draw on project management ideas to help them here. Communication is also crucial throughout the change process.

7 Force field analysis

Introduction

In the 'unfreeze' stage of the three-stage model, we highlighted the interaction of driving forces promoting change, and resisting forces preventing it. Lewin recognised the importance of this interaction and so, alongside the three-stage model, he also introduced the idea of force field analysis.

Force field analysis assists change management by examining and evaluating – in a summary form – the forces 'for' and 'against' the change.

Force field analysis consists of identifying the factors that promote or hinder change. In order for change to be successfully implemented, promoting forces need to be exploited and the effect of hindering forces need to be reduced, so that the driving forces for change outweigh those forces resisting change.

It is traditional to represent these forces by **arrows** whose individual dimensions correspond to their perceived strengths. Promoting and hindering forces are then shown pointing from opposite sides to a vertical line. This representation is useful for purposes such as brainstorming and staff briefings, but two lists in order of magnitude are just as useful for purposes of analysis.

The example below concerns a public sector organisation that is introducing performance review.

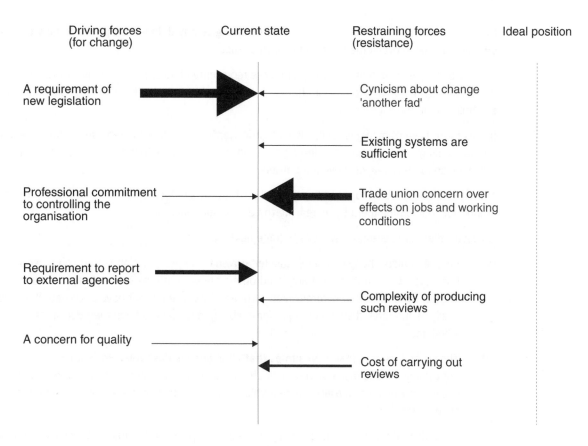

Example of force field analysis

Senior (drawing on the advice of Carnall and Huczyuski and Buchanan) suggests a practical route to applying the force field analysis idea.

(a) Define the problem in terms of the current situation and the desired future state.

(b) List the forces supporting and opposing the desired change and assess both the strength and the importance of each one.

(c) Draw the force field diagram.

(d) Decide how to strengthen or weaken the more important forces as appropriate and agree with those concerned. Weakening might be achieved by persuasion, participation, coercion or bargaining, while strengthening might be achieved by a marketing or education campaign, including the use of personal advocacy.

(e) Identify the resources needed.

(f) Make an action plan including event timing, milestones and responsibilities.

Elements of the culture of an organisation may also emerge as important forces promoting or hindering changes. So the **cultural web** can also be used alongside force field analysis as a diagnostic tool in looking at the forces driving and resisting change.

Exam alert

Note the possible link between force field analysis and stakeholder analysis. In a case study scenario, you may need to identify who the key stakeholders are, and then identify whether they will be driving forces for change or whether they will resist change.

You may also need to recommend ways in which various stakeholders could be managed to overcome their resistance to change.

Note, however, that force field analysis itself **doesn't give any detailed insights into how to manage change**, or how to overcome the resistance to change.

Lewin's basic idea was that the change process represented two opposing fields of force, one encompassing the driving forces for change, the other encompassing the resisting forces (as in the example on the previous page).

In this form, Lewin's model is relatively straightforward: the central line represents the current situation, and in a change scenario we can identify both those sets of forces that are trying to effect change and those which are resisting or providing barriers.

Management action therefore needs to be directed towards reducing the resisting forces, turning them around, or overcoming them by increasing the drivers for change.

However, there are several drawbacks to force field analysis.

(a)   First, it depicts change as being **'insider' driven** – the presumption is that some people in the business are committed to change and others are not, and the task is to tilt the balance in favour of those who have that commitment. Although Lewin would not have approved of it, this can easily be interpreted as a technique for enabling managers to force their decisions on an unwilling workforce.

(b)   The second issue is that it **presumes that all change is desirable**. Presentations of this model do not usually include discussion of how change should be resisted, yet there are probably as many occasions when a proposal is undesirable or unworkable as there are ones where it is to be encouraged.

(c)   Force field analysis, as it is generally presented, depicts all the driving forces as operating in the same direction, and all the resisting forces as running in the opposite direction. In practice, the key influences in a situation – usually the more powerful stakeholders – are pointing in varying directions, as in the illustration below.

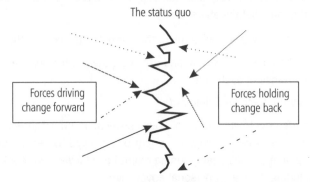

Force field: The 'real' context of Lewin's model

The point of this second illustration is that it reflects the complexity of the force fields in a change scenario more accurately than the simple illustration we showed earlier. For example, people may resist change for different reasons and so different solutions will be needed to manage their resistance to change.

The second illustration also highlights not only the different strengths of the forces either driving or resisting change, but also how far they are opposed. A resisting force that is almost vertical is easier to turn around to support the change than a resistance which is horizontally opposed to the change.

Resisting forces are central to Lewin's approach to change management. It is therefore important both to identify these resisting forces and then also to think of ways to deal with them. (Before doing this, though, bear in mind a point made earlier, that not all change is desirable.)

Sources of resistance are generally linked to human interests – hygiene factors mostly, to use Herzberg's concept. Senior has set out the following as the main sources of individual resistance:

- Fear of the unknown
- Dislike of uncertainty
- Potential loss of power
- Potential loss of rewards
- Potential lack of or loss of skills

These sources of resistance spring from direct human concerns. Interestingly, Senior also identifies a number of organisational resistances, such as resource constraints, or inertias resulting from the interlocked nature of the different features and processes of the organisation. But for the most part organisational resistances feed back to human concerns. Where they do not, there is unlikely to be a strategic change problem, but perhaps a technical problem of issues such as co-ordination or process design.

Section summary

Force field analysis illustrates a summary of the forces promoting change and the forces resisting change.

---

8 Managing resistance to change

Introduction

Force field analysis has introduced the idea of resistance to change, and identified that organisations need to overcome this resistance in order for change to be implemented successfully.

We now look at ways of managing resistance to change in more detail.

While some people within an organisation may accept, co-operate with, or even support a change programme, it is likely that others will resist it.

In the simplest terms, when management is faced with resistance to change, they have two underlying choices for how to deal with that resistance.

(a)   **Overcoming resistance** through strengthening the driving forces for change, for example increasing management pressure, enhancing fears of dismissal and so forth.

(b)   **Reducing resistance** by weakening the forces that currently hold down output, for example through job redesign, or through the adoption of a more people-centred management style.

The essential characteristic of **overcoming resistance** as a strategy for change is that increasing any of the 'push' factors driving change will prompt an opposite reaction on the other side of the force field equilibrium. Management seemingly gets what it wants – for example, an increase in production – but at the cost of more tension, conflict, suspicion and hostility.

On the other hand, by **reducing resistance**, the same objective is accomplished – again, for example, production is increased – but there is a much lower level of resistance.

So, at the simplest level, force field analysis suggests that there are two ways of managing this resistance to change:

- Strengthening your own side
- Weakening the opposing forces

However, this still leaves a number of questions unanswered. In particular, how much coercion should be used to make people change, or how much should people be encouraged to participate in the change process and help identify solutions themselves.

How much **coercion** should be used?

(a) Some element of coercion may ultimately be necessary. However, it helps if, for example, a supposedly neutral consultant can be persuaded to suggest measures supported by the proponents of the innovation.

(b) Involving people in diagnosing problem situations (eg in quality circles) wins over 'hearts and minds'.

8.1 Resistance to change

Leaders and managers of change sometimes cannot understand why individuals or groups of individuals do not embrace the changes that are being introduced. This failure to embrace change is often labelled as resistance to change.

No matter how much an organisation overall welcomes change, it will still face a degree of resistance from employees, suppliers, customers, distributors or other stakeholders.

One of the key issues here is that people resist change because they feel comfortable with what they know, but they fear the unknown and the uncertainty which goes with it.

8.1.1 Reasons for resisting change

Kotter and Schlesinger identify four main reasons why people will resist organisational change:

(a) **Parochial self-interest** – People will resist change if they think they will lose something of value as a result of the change. In these cases, people focus on their own best interests rather than those of the organisation. For example, managers might resist a change in organisational structure if they fear it will reduce their authority within an organisation.

(b) **Misunderstanding and lack of trust** – People will resist change when they do not understand the implications of the change and perceive that the disadvantages arising from it will outweigh the advantages. Such situations can often arise due to poor communication; for example, where poor communication leads to the spreading of rumours among employees. Equally, this type of resistance can often occur when trust is lacking between the person initiating the change and the employees.

(c) **Different assessment of the situation** – Managers may believe a change is beneficial, but if staff assess the situation differently and believe that the costs of the change will outweigh its benefits (either for themselves, or for the organisation as a whole) they will resist the change.

In some cases, this resistance may be beneficial for the organisation. For example, employees may identify practical problems with a proposed change that managers had not foreseen, so their resistance means the organisation can avoid the problems which would otherwise have arisen if the change had been implemented.

(d) **Low tolerance of change** – Some people will resist change because they fear they will not be able to develop the new skills and behaviour that will be required of them. In addition, some people value security and stability in their work, and will resist change because it will mean they have to move outside their 'comfort zone'.

Change is often a difficult process for the individuals involved, and so resistance to a change programme should always be expected.

Potential areas of resistance need to be identified. Then appropriate tactics need to be agreed to overcome the resistance anticipated among different stakeholders.

Schein adopts a similar approach to force field analysis when looking at resistance to change. He argues that there are two forces acting on every individual undergoing change.

Learning anxiety: The anxiety associated with learning something new. Will I be able to deal with the new situation? Will I fail? Will gaps in my knowledge or skills be exposed?

Survival anxiety: This concerns the pressure to change. What if I don't change? Will I be left behind?

Used in conjunction with force field analysis, we can see survival anxiety as a driving force for change, and learning anxiety as a restraining force.

Schein suggests that there are two principles to enable change to work:

- First, survival anxiety must be greater than learning anxiety.
- Second, learning anxiety needs to be reduced, rather than survival anxiety being increased.

Schein advises that increasing people's **sense of psychological safety** is crucial in reducing learning anxiety, and therefore in managing change.

He recommends a number of ways this can be done:

- Presenting a compelling vision of the future
- Training
- Involving the learner in discussions about the change
- Establishing support groups (for example, mentors or counsellors)
- Using consistent systems and structures across the change

8.2 Kotter and Schlesinger's approaches to resistance

Kotter and Schlesinger also highlighted that overcoming resistance to change is a critical aspect of managing the change process.

They identified six approaches to dealing with resistance to change, with a key underlying theme being that **communication is critical** in overcoming resistance to change.

Approach	Comment
Education and communication	This approach assumes that resistance is caused by ignorance. Communicating the reasons for the change and the outcomes will undermine resistance to the change. Communicating the 'vision' for change, and the potential benefits of the change may also help overcome negative perceptions.
	In effect, this approach involves 'selling' the change to those people who are currently resisting it.
Participation and involvement	Get people involved in the change process. If staff are involved in the change process and feel they have contributed to the design of the changes they are less likely to resist them.
	Getting people involved may also help reduce concerns about the impact of change and their ability to cope.
	Those potentially affected can help to:
	• Identify problem situations
	• Define the problem and its causes
	• Define solutions
	• Develop strategies for implementation
Facilitation and support	There are a number of ways to facilitate and support people facing change.
	These could include counselling services for those experiencing difficulties or stress, or else simply the availability of a line manager for staff to talk to about their concerns.
	Support could also include training for those staff who need new technical or business skills to deal with changes to their jobs.
	If the change involves making people redundant, they should also be supported, and this support can include outplacement counselling and/or generous redundancy packages.

Approach	Comment
Negotiation and agreement	Negotiation is often necessary where there are strong unions, so changes to working practices may be considered in exchange for extra pay.
	Negotiation involves discussion with employees to resolve areas of dispute about the changes – for example, remuneration, hours of work, or changes to terms and conditions.
	The negotiations may involve offering incentives to workers to encourage them to accept changes – for example, offering them additional payments to take on more demanding duties.
Manipulation and co-optation	In this case, resistance is undermined in a more covert manner, perhaps by the way information is presented or by a political process. For example, the company can manipulate the debate (eg by invoking public opinion).
	However, if individuals feel they are being manipulated this could increase the resistance to change.
	It is also important to consider whether there are any ethical issues at stake here. Given the ethical principle of integrity, how ethical is it to manipulate (or even deceive) people into accepting change?
Coercion, implicit and explicit	Where management have power, this appears the easiest way – sometimes it is the only way.
	Individuals are forced to accept change, for example by being threatened with redundancy if they do not.
	This sort of tactic can often be successful if rapid change is required.
	However, such aggressive tactics are not always desirable because people resent them, even if their resistance is overcome.

Each approach will be suited to different circumstances, based on the respective power of each party, and the type of change being experienced.

Kotter and Schlesinger's approaches to change management illustrate there are a variety of ways of managing change and resistance to change, so it is important that change leaders select an appropriate method for managing change.

The appropriateness of different methods will depend, in part, on the degree of collaboration or conflict which is expected from staff.

Kotter and Schlesinger's scale of change management approaches

Kotter and Schlesinger's work is important because, as well as identifying ways of managing resistance, they make the link between triggers of resistance and ways of managing change.

We looked earlier at Kotter's eight step model, and a number of the steps in this model of change management could also be seen as ways of overcoming resistance to change.

Section summary

Organisations need to **overcome resistance to change** in order for change to be successfully implemented. The methods used to deal with resistance will vary according to the change context, and the degree of collaboration or conflict which may be expected from staff. Kotter and Schlesinger identified six approaches for dealing with resistance to change.

Chapter Summary

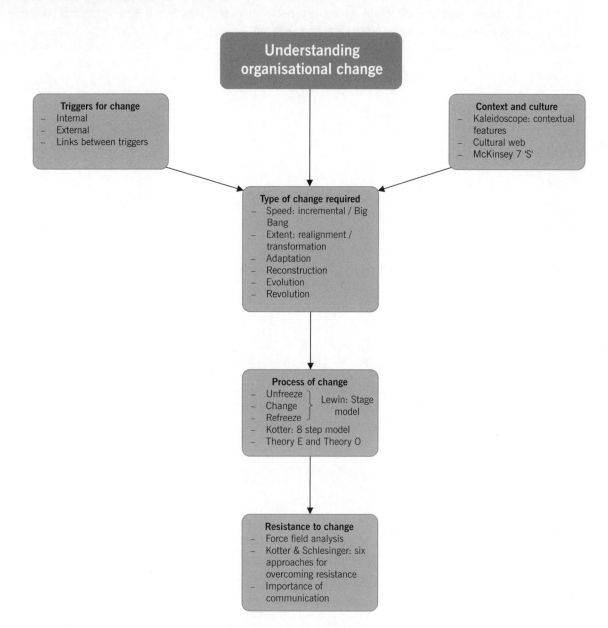

Understanding organisational change

Triggers for change
- Internal
- External
- Links between triggers

Context and culture
- Kaleidoscope: contextual features
- Cultural web
- McKinsey 7 'S'

Type of change required
- Speed: incremental / Big Bang
- Extent: realignment / transformation
- Adaptation
- Reconstruction
- Evolution
- Revolution

Process of change
- Unfreeze ⎫
- Change ⎬ Lewin: Stage model
- Refreeze ⎭
- Kotter: 8 step model
- Theory E and Theory O

Resistance to change
- Force field analysis
- Kotter & Schlesinger: six approaches for overcoming resistance
- Importance of communication

Quick Quiz

1   A new CEO has just joined a business from a competitor organisation, and he wants to change the organisation structure in his new company to make it more streamlined. Is the trigger for this change internal or external?   *internal*

2   Leavitt considered organisational change as the result of interaction between four components. What are they?

3   According to Lewin's three-stage model, which one of the following activities is part of the 'unfreezing' stage?

    A   Publicising success stories of divisions which have embraced a change
    B   Creating new performance management and reward schemes
    C   Explaining the need for change
    D   Training staff in new ways of working

4   Depending on the speed and extent of the change required, organisational change can be classified as adaptation, reconstruction, evolution or revolution.

    Which of the following describes an organisational change which can be introduced incrementally, and which realigns – rather than transforms – an organisation's existing processes and culture?

    A   Evolution
    B   Adaptation
    C   Reconstruction
    D   Revolution

5   Who suggested the model of an organisation as a biological organism which is constantly changing?

    A   Schein
    B   Morgan
    C   Carnall
    D   Kotter

6   Reducing resistance to change involves strengthening the driving forces for change. True or false?   F

7   What are Kotter and Schlesinger's six approaches for dealing with resistance to change?

Answers to Quick Quiz

1   Internal. Although the CEO has only recently joined from outside the organisation, he is promoting the changes in his role of CEO.

2   Task, structure, people, technology

3   C

Explaining the need for change is part of the unfreezing stage.

Retraining staff is part of the 'change' stage, while publicising success stories and creating new reward schemes are part of the 'refreezing' stage.

4   B   Adaptation

By definition, a change whose nature is incremental (as opposed to 'Big Bang') and whose extent (scope) is realignment is an adaptation in Balogun and Hope Hailey's classification.

5   Gareth Morgan considers an organisation as a biological organism which is constantly changing.

6   False. Reducing resistance to change involves weakening the forces that are resisting change. Overcoming resistance involves strengthening the driving forces for change.

7   (i)   Education and communication
     (ii)   Participation and involvement
     (iii)   Facilitation and support
     (iv)   Negotiation and agreement
     (v)   Manipulation and co-optation
     (vi)   Coercion

Now try these questions from the Practice Question Bank

Number	Level	Marks	Time
9.1 – 9.5	Intermediate	n/a	10 mins
9.6	Intermediate	15	27 mins

APPENDIX

9 Organisational structure

9.1 Types of organisational structure

The syllabus for Paper E1 includes discussion of different types of organisational structure, so you are assumed to already be aware of these by the time you come to study E3.

It is important that you know the different structures an organisation could take, and the characteristics of different structures, so that you could assess whether they are appropriate for an organisation or a proposed strategy being described in a question scenario in E3.

The table below summarises seven basic organisational structures.

Structure	Advantages	Disadvantages
Functional (also called **Unitary (U) organisational form**) • Departments defined by their function, ie what they do • Traditional, common-sense approach used by many organisations • Centralised authority (so suited to centralised organisations)	• Based on work specialisation, therefore logical • Pooling of expertise, by grouping specialised tasks and staff together • Firm can benefit from economies of scale • Relatively simple lines of control • Senior managers close to the operation of their function • Controlled by strategic leaders/CEO • Offers career structure	• Doesn't reflect business processes by which value is created • Hard to identify where profits/losses are made on individual products • People do not have an understanding of how the whole business works • Problems in co-ordinating the work of different specialisms • Communication problems between functions • Unlikely to be entrepreneurial • Managers focus on short-term routine activities rather than longer-term strategic developments

Structure	Advantages	Disadvantages
Multi-divisional (also called **M-form**) • Business divided into autonomous regions or product businesses, each with its own revenues, expenditures and profits • Appropriate if organisation produces a number of different products or services, so relevant divisional/business splits exist • Communication between the divisions and head office is restricted • Corporate centre focuses on higher level strategic controls, aimed at ensuring divisions play their part in ensuring corporation as a whole achieves its goals • Divisions focus on managerial and operational controls	• Focuses attention of subordinate management on business performance and results • Enables contribution of various activities to be evaluated • Management by objectives is the natural control default • Corporate centre focuses on corporate strategy • Gives authority to junior managers therefore prepares them for future senior positions • Increases motivation among divisional managers	• Division is partly insulated by holding company from shareholders and capital markets, which ultimately reward performance • Different product divisions may function better as independent companies • Divisions more bureaucratic than they would be as independent companies • Can be hard to identify completely independent products/markets • Divisionalisation only possible at a high level • Conflict between divisions for resources • Divisions may think short term and concentrate on profits rather than shareholder value • Can be difficult to evaluate relative performance of different divisions
Holding company • An extreme form of multi-divisional structure in which the divisions are separate legal entities		
Matrix • Attempts to ensure co-ordination across functional lines via **dual authority** in the organisation structure • Management control between different functions, while at the same time maintaining functional departmentalisation • Can be a mixture of functional, product and territorial organisation	• Offers flexibility • Improves communication • Dual authority gives the organisation multiple orientation so that functional specialists do not get wrapped up in their own concerns • Provides a structure for allocating responsibility to managers for end results • Provides for inter-disciplinary co-operation and a mixing of skills and expertise	• Difficult to implement • Dual authority threatens a conflict between managers; managers may also feel their authority is threatened • One individual with two or more bosses is more likely to suffer role stress at work • Can be more costly – eg project managers are additional jobs that would not be required in a more simple structure • The consensus and agreement required may slow down decision making

Structure	Advantages	Disadvantages
Transnational • Attempts to reconcile global scope and scale with local representatives • Similar to matrix, but responds specifically to globalisation challenges • National units are independent operating entities, but also provide capabilities, such as R&D, that are used by the rest of the organisation	• Shared capabilities allow national units to achieve global, or at least regional, economies of scale • Responsiveness to local conditions	• Makes great demands on managers both in their immediate responsibilities and in the complexity of their relationships with the organisation • Complexity of the organisation can lead to difficulties of control and the complications introduced by internal political activity
Team-based • Extends matrix structure by utilising cross-functional teams • Business processes used as the basis of the organisation, with each team being responsible for the processes relating to an aspect of the business		
Project-based • Similar to team-based except that projects have finite life and so, therefore, do the project teams dealing with them		

9.2 Centralisation vs decentralisation

Another important aspect of an organisation's structure is the level at which decisions are taken, and here there is a contrast between centralised organisations (in which the authority for most decisions remains with the upper levels of the organisation's hierarchy) and decentralised organisations (in which the authority to make specific decisions is delegated to people at lower levels in the organisation's hierarchy). Consequently, decentralisation allows local managers to respond flexibly to local market conditions without constantly having to refer back to head office.

Advantages of centralisation

(a)   Decisions can be **co-ordinated** more easily, and management have better control over decisions.

(b)   **Goal congruence**. Decisions taken centrally should be based on overall objectives, whereas decentralised decisions may be influenced by short-term or local objectives of the people making the decisions.

(c)   **Standardisation**. For example, in any country McDonald's customers expect to find standard menus and pricing. If local managers were allowed to take decisions about changing menus or prices, this could undermine the business model.

(d)   **Resource allocation**. Centralised decision making should allow resource usage to be co-ordinated effectively between different functions and divisions, based on overall corporate objectives.

(e)   **Economies of scale**. For example, companies might be able to get bulk discounts if they co-ordinate all their purchasing requirements and make a single order. Similarly, the corporate centre may be able to obtain cheaper bank loans and finance than local divisions (which have less assets to secure a loan against).

(f)   **Speed of decision making**. For example, when a quick decision is required in response to a crisis, it may not be practical to involve local managers.

Disadvantages of centralisation

(a)   **Reduced morale and job satisfaction**. Local managers and divisional staff may be frustrated at their inability to take decisions, and this could reduce their job satisfaction and motivation.

Equally, the fact that senior managers are having to take all the decisions and aren't delegating any could also increase the pressure and stress the senior managers feel they are under.

(b)   **Limited opportunities**. If junior managers are not given any opportunities for decision making this could hinder their career development, by preventing them gaining experience which could be useful in more senior management positions (ie experience of decision making).

(c)   **Imperfect information**. Local managers may have greater knowledge about operational activities or local market conditions than senior management or head office staff. Therefore, senior management may have to delegate some decisions, or else risk damaging the quality of decisions taken due to their imperfect information.

(d)   **Communication time**. Although centralisation can be useful for making rapid decisions (eg in a crisis) it may take longer for decisions taken centrally to be communicated to different divisions and functions than if the decisions had been taken locally.

The nature of these advantages and disadvantages means that an organisation might find that an effective approach to decision making will be to centralise corporate-level strategic decisions, and decentralise tactical or operating decisions.

9.3 The changing business environment

Major environmental changes have affected many aspects of the way businesses and other organisations operate, including the way in which they are structured. Here are some examples.

(a)   Changes in products and process methods have come from new and innovative firms, particularly in Asia.

(b)   There is mounting pressure for increased corporate social responsibility and for more attention to be paid to stakeholders other than owners.

(c)   The rapid development of IS and IT has revolutionised the way information (both external and internal) can be used for competitive advantage.

These changes mean that the classical model of the organisation is no longer necessarily the most appropriate.

9.4 Developments in organisation theory

A number of writers on organisations and management have made similar recommendations about the need for **innovation**, **flexibility**, **communication**, **empowerment**, **leveraging of knowledge** and a **network approach to organising resources** both within the organisation and outside its boundaries.

Remember also the comments we made about **collaboration** in the context of Web 2.0 technologies in Chapter 7. Collaboration is another illustration of the way organisations can use resources from outside their boundaries, rather than controlling all the resources within their boundaries.

9.4.1 Contingency theory

The contingency approach suggests that many aspects of the management of organisations, including the way they are structured, arise as a result of the varying influences to which they are subjected. Here are some possible influences on organisation structure.

Influence	Comment
Age	• The older the organisation, the more formalised its behaviour. Work is repeated, so is more easily formalised and standardised. • Organisation structure reflects the age of the **industry's** foundation.
Size, growth and degree of centralisation	The larger the organisation, the **more elaborate** its structure will be, the larger the average size of the units within it, the more formalised its behaviour (for consistency).
Co-ordination and leadership	Mutual adjustment, direct supervision and standardisation all have consequences for organisation structure.
Skills of managers and workers	Can people be left alone to do the job, or do they require close supervision?
Geographical dispersion	An organisation with several sites will have a different organisation structure from one located in a single place.
Fashion and culture	Bureaucracies, for example, are deeply unfashionable, but they are often the best at doing certain kinds of work. Indeed, **Burns and Stalker**, who developed the concept of organic and mechanistic organisations, held that neither type of organisation had any intrinsic merits, as the key variables were **product-markets** and **technology**.
Control and environment	The more an organisation is subject to **external control or influence** (eg by government, holding company) the more centralised and formalised its structure. The power needs of organisational members (to control others, or at least to control their own working conditions) can lead to centralisation.

9.4.2 Kanter

In her book *The Change Masters*, Rosabeth Moss Kanter identified two contrasting organisational responses to the problems produced by change and innovation.

(a) The **segmentalist** approach is unable to create an integrated response to new problems because of its strongly compartmentalised, mechanistic structure and methods. Managers produce solutions to the aspects of the problem that concern their own responsibilities and no one takes an overview.

Firms which have a segmentalist approach find it hard to innovate.

(b) The **integrative** approach looks at the whole problem. Divisions work together rather than focusing solely on their own problems, and the organisation is prepared to innovate to solve problems, even to the extent of changing its structure and the way it does things. Innovation flourishes under this approach.

The integrative approach requires management to deploy three important sets of skills:

(a) **Power skills** are needed in order to persuade others to take risks.
(b) **Problem management** skills focus on employee participation and working in teams.
(c) **Change design and construction skills**.

Kanter makes recommendations for the managers of segmentalist organisations that wish to move to a more integrative style:

(a) Encourage a **culture of pride** in the firm's achievements.

(b) Improve **lateral communication** – encouraging teams and departments to work together and share ideas.

(c) Widen the **distribution of information** about company plans, so that people throughout the organisation can influence change and make suggestions.

(d) Devolve and decentralise power as low down the hierarchy as possible, **delayering** where possible to reduce unnecessary layers of hierarchy.

(e) Increase **opportunities for innovation** – allow teams more time to research and develop ideas.

9.4.3 The third wave

It is now commonplace to see the influence of advances in IS as creating a 'third wave' of economic development comparable to the development of agriculture and the industrial revolution. Whether or not a change of such magnitude is taking place, there is no doubt that there have been a number of very important IS-based developments in the nature of work and the way it is organised.

(a) **Mass customisation** of products via one-to-one marketing, web-based trading, the accumulation of customer information and the development of large **relationship marketing** databases.

(b) **Disintermediation** is taking place both within organisations, as a result of delayering made possible by IS, and in the marketplace. Customers can deal direct with producers via their websites, or with a new kind of distributor typified by Amazon. **Network organisations** represent a mosaic of productive relationships that transcend older models based on the ownership of resources.

(c) **Network economies** arising from the number of devices in use are becoming more important than economies of scale, which depend on the number of items produced. As the take-up of any device incorporating an aspect of communications increases, so the usefulness and hence the value of an individual device grows as well.

(d) The importance of the **service sector** and the **knowledge worker** is accelerating and the **leveraging of knowledge** itself is rising in importance as a business resource.

Hope and Hope identified 'the ten key issues of the management information wave':

(a) **Strategy** should be innovative (thinking 'outside the box'), based on core competences and organised using networks and alliances (for example, with suppliers and customers).

(b) **Customer value** should be based on product leadership, operational excellence or customer knowledge.

(c) **Knowledge management**: leverage human capital, market data and internal IS, to create competitive advantage.

(d) **Business organisation**: base on networks rather than hierarchies.

(e) **Market focus** should be on the best (most profitable) customers, not on volume of sales. (Customer account profitability could be a useful measure here.)

(f) **Management accounting** should be relevant and empowering. It should look to manage the business (for example, processes and business drivers), not just the numbers. So rather than simply reporting costs, management accountants should also look for ways to reduce costs, for example through value chain analysis, benchmarking, or business process re-engineering.

(g) **Measurement and control** measures should not constrain innovation. There needs to be a balance between control and empowerment.

(h)   **Shareholder value** depends on human capital, not physical assets. Human capital plays a crucial role in delivering future returns to shareholders.

(i)   **Productivity** is about people's ability to create value, not simply utilising non-current assets.

(j)   **Transformation**: abandon the classical approach and Scientific Management; embrace the third wave.

Ezzamel *et al* suggest the following characteristics of 'new wave management':

●   Flexible supervision and employee self-discipline, rather than rules and regulation with discipline imposed by management

●   Development of people, rather than hierarchical control

●   Participative problem solving, rather than having solutions directed by management

●   Multifunctional teams, instead of 'silos' of single-function specialists

●   Continuously evolving responsibilities and tasks, instead of narrowly defined jobs and responsibilities

When looking at different forms of management, it may also be useful to consider Stacey's concepts of ordinary and extraordinary management (which we introduced in Chapter 1 of this Study Text).

Ordinary management is based on hierarchy and bureaucracy, with an emphasis on team building and consensus. It essentially follows a rational model approach to strategy, with changes being introduced progressively and incrementally. Control is mainly exerted through 'negative feedback control': any deviations from expected results or patterns of behaviour are investigated and controlled.

Extraordinary management is much more informal. It involves a system of self-organisation, through informal creative networks and contacts, rather than formal structures. These creative networks build on 'tacit' knowledge and encourage organisational learning and innovation.

Interestingly, however, Stacey does not suggest that an organisation should adopt one type of management or the other. Rather, he suggests that operational matters and operational staff should be managed using ordinary management, while strategic management and organisational development may actually be better suited to an extraordinary management context.

9.5 New structural models

New approaches to the structure of organisations (such as flexible firms or virtual organisations) form part of the syllabus for Paper E1. On this basis, they can be seen as assumed knowledge for Paper E3.

Flexibility may be important in a strategic context for a number of reasons:

(a)   **Speed of change.** Firms have to respond quickly to the need for change in turbulent and dynamic business conditions.

        This may also include being able to respond quickly to new competitors who enter a market.

(b)   **Impact of technology.** New technologies lead to changes in the products produced by suppliers and demanded by consumers. Shortening product life cycles means firms need to be able to respond to changes in product specification more quickly.

        Technology has also led to changes in the **nature of the competition** firms face, with new online companies entering the market alongside established competitors.

        In addition, technology has changed the ways people can work, with the growth of the internet leading to an increase in levels of **remote- or home-working**, meaning workers no longer need to be based at a firm's own offices.

(c) **Flexibility and staffing**

Multi-skilling: One element of flexibility is in the multi-skilling of staff; which gives firms the ability to redeploy staff in different roles as required.

Flexible remuneration: A second element of flexibility could be the flexibility of remuneration packages offered to employees. This could include not only profit-sharing and performance-related pay, but also the offer of 'cafeteria' approaches where employees are allowed to customise their own reward packages to a degree (for example, through healthcare, gym memberships, or buying additional leave). Such an approach allows employees to design a remuneration package which best suits their needs, and in doing so, it could also help boost employee morale and staff retention.

Flexible hours: A third element of flexibility relates to the hours which staff work: for example, the use of **flexible working hours**, **shift working**, or **job sharing schemes**. The increasing use of **home-working** could also be seen as an extension of the idea of greater flexibility around working hours – giving staff the flexibility to work from remote locations rather than having to come into a central office. The attraction of being able to work at home some days should be obvious for employees, but it can also be an advantage to a business: for example, by using systems such as 'hot desking', a firm can reduce the amount of office space and office furniture it needs.

Flexible numbers of staff: A fourth element of flexibility – and the one which could potentially have the greatest impact on the structure of firms – is flexibility in relation to the **numbers of staff** employed.

If a firm employs staff on a temporary contract basis, rather than on a full-time basis, the number of staff it uses can be increased or decreased according to changes in demand for its services or the products those staff help to make.

This idea of using contract staff to perform non-core work was taken up by Charles Handy in his concept of the '**shamrock**' organisation.

New organisational structures include **virtual**, **network**, and **shamrock** organisations. Typically, these modern approaches feature loose, delayered, organic relationships, exploitation of IS by empowered knowledge workers, and a flexible approach to mission and strategy. However, the shamrock organisation in particular, with its emphasis on **core staff** and **peripheral workers** (with activities either outsourced or performed by self-employed contract staff) is indicative of a new casualisation of labour, with implications for security and benefits at all levels.

Boundaryless organisations

Jack Welch (the long-time CEO of General Electric) introduced the idea of 'The Boundaryless Organisation'.

Welch's view was that cultural, geographical and organisational boundaries which separated employees hindered efficiency, and so companies should look to make these boundaries more permeable; for example, by encouraging the exchange of information and ideas between different departments, and by developing cross-functional teams.

This idea of breaking down boundaries can also be extended to organisations' relationships with their customers and suppliers. For example, if organisations develop closer relationships with their suppliers this could help supply chain management. Equally, developing relationships with customers could help organisations gain a better understanding of what their customers want.

However, interdependency and trust are crucial in the boundaryless organisation. Staff will have to trust their co-workers, and recognise that they are all mutually accountable for the organisation's successes (or mistakes).

Nonetheless, despite (or perhaps because of) the proliferation of new models of organisational structure, it is crucial that management adopt the most appropriate structure for the organisation they are running. Although there may now be more variables to choose from, the underlying concept of aligning structure and strategy remains a key aspect of strategy implementation.

BPP LEARNING MEDIA

9.6 The new organisation and the management accountant

The new approaches will involve **management accountants in providing more information** to more people than previously, for decision making, for control and for reward and motivation. This may also lead to the management accountant having to deliver more detailed measures of performance.

The looser, more innovative ways of working mentioned above will be of particular significance to the management accountant. Here are some examples.

(a)   All **traditional routines** such as invoice processing will be challenged by, for instance, empowerment and network approaches.

(b)   **Cost management**. Challenging traditional routines will lead to challenging all cost areas to identify whether they add value or not. This means the accountant's role is no longer confined to **cost control**, but also extends to identifying opportunities for **cost reduction**.

(c)   **Activity-based management** of costs may come to prominence within an organisation, with cross-functional responsibility centres predominating. This is likely to require a **revision of budgetary control systems**.

(d)   Functions, including some aspects of finance work, may be **outsourced** and **network structures** may be used both inside and outside the organisation: the accountant will have to provide and use control information in new ways.

(e)   **Decisions** may be made lower down the organisation, but they must still be made on sound grounds. Management accounting information will be more widely distributed, especially to **self-managing teams**, and there may be a requirement for control systems that will facilitate dispersed decision making but prevent its abuse.

(f)   **Flexible patterns of employment** may lead to increased staff turnover with consequent loss of experience and cultural control. This may increase the need for closer rather than looser control of the work of temporary staff and teleworkers.

(g)   **Performance measurement**. Similarly, there may be a greater need for performance measurement for knowledge and contract workers. At the same time, normal cost accounting for labour will become more complicated as pay rates and the split into direct and indirect labour become more problematic.

The way labour costs are budgeted will also need to be revised, to reflect any changes in the mix between contract staff and permanent employees.

(h)   The overall system of control will depend on whether the organisation is one that depends on the knowledge and skills of its workforce, invests in and trusts them, or whether it uses flexible approaches to **exploit** them more effectively. A balance must be struck between empowerment and control.

(i)   The problem of motivating and rewarding the creative individual will be complicated by the move to **team working**.

LEADING AND MANAGING CHANGE

 The dynamics of the external environment mean that organisations' strategies will inevitably change and evolve.

Change management is therefore an integral and important part of strategic management (Section 8).

However, we begin this chapter by looking at the importance of **communication** in the change process (Section 1). It is important that the way change is communicated, and the style in which it is managed, is appropriate to the context of the change episode in question.

Leaders have a crucial role in communicating change but, more generally, they also have to create a context in which changes can be implemented successfully (Section 2).

Leadership is a key factor in a change programme. Organisations need their leaders to have the vision to identify changes, and then deliver them (Section 4).

However, leaders not only have to manage change at a strategic level; they also need to build and manage effective teams which can implement a strategy effectively (Section 5).

In any change scenario, it is important that the changes which are recommended are ethical and any staff who might be affected by them are treated fairly (Section 6).

Topic list	Learning outcomes	Syllabus references	Ability required
1 Change and communication	C2(a), C3(a)	C2(a)(iii), C3(a)(ii)	Evaluate
2 Why change succeeds or fails	C3(a), C3(b)	C3(a)(i), C3(b)(ii)	Evaluate
3 Change and the individual	–	–	–
4 Leading change	C3(a)	C3(a)(ii)	Evaluate
5 Building and managing effective teams	C1(b)	C1(b)(i)	Evaluate
6 Business ethics in change management and the implementation of strategic plans	C3(a)	C3(a)(i)	Evaluate
7 Change in practice	C3(a)	C3(a)(i)	Evaluate
8 Change management and strategy implementation	C1(a)	C1(a)(i)	Evaluate
Appendix			
9 Project management and implementing projects	–	–	–

Chapter Overview

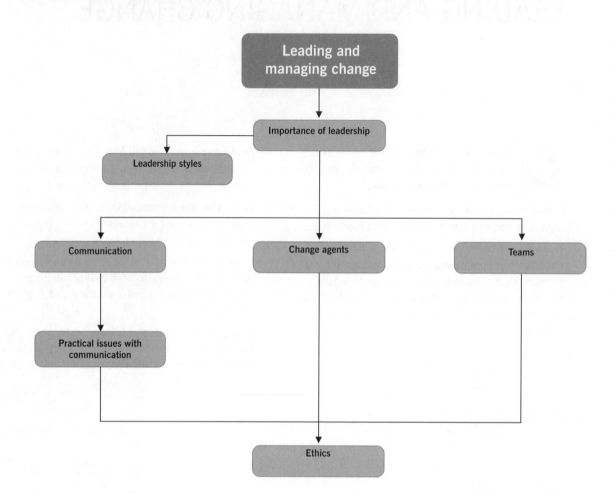

1   Change and communication

Introduction

In the previous chapter, we saw that there are three basic stages to a change implementation process (unfreeze, move, refreeze) and we highlighted the role of change 'triggers' in initiating the process of change.

However, in order to implement a change, a change manager needs to use a number of levers to actually unfreeze and move an organisation, and then sustain the changes that have been put in place. Communication plays a key role in this change process, but the management style used when implementing change can also affect the effectiveness of that change.

1.1 The importance of communication in managing change

Although there is often a presumption that staff and other stakeholders will oppose change – hence the section in the previous chapter about managing resistance to change, and Kotter and Schlesinger's styles for overcoming resistance to change – in many cases staff will **accept change** when they can see it could be **beneficial to them**, or that it is **necessary for the organisation**. Nonetheless, **resistance to change** can often be caused where the reasons why change is required have not been properly communicated.

This again highlights the importance of **communication as a change lever**, and reinforces Kotter's point (in relation to his eight step model) that effective communication is crucial in change management.

However, effective communication doesn't just happen by itself, and managers across an organisation are responsible for the communication process. (Communication is not solely the responsibility of the HR or marketing departments.) Not surprisingly, communication skills are increasingly regarded as a critical skill set for leaders in organisations, and accordingly communication skills training is becoming an increasingly important component of leadership development programmes.

Whetten and Cameron suggest that leading change is the most common activity that requires, and demonstrates, leadership. Leading change can, in effect, be seen as the essence of leadership, because it requires a whole range of leadership capabilities:

*   Communicating and inspiring people to future visions
*   Motivating and empowering people
*   Influencing and handling conflict

Moreover, leaders may have to display these capabilities in a context which recognises individual and cultural differences.

1.1.1 Leaders' roles in communication

Careful planning and management, along with clarity and consistency, are key factors in effective communication. Unfortunately, many communications focus solely on the **delivery of the message** itself, and neglect the **planning** and **management of the communications process**. For example, the speed offered by email means it is often seen as an effective means of communication when the context of the message means it is not.

When planning communications about organisational changes, a leader must consider a number of issues:

*   The way in which people are used to receiving communications
*   The impact that the changes will have on different stakeholders
*   Developing a clear, consistent message that is meaningful to the stakeholders
*   Select and use appropriate communication channels
*   Develop measurable objectives for the communications
*   Measure the effectiveness of the communication effort, and adjust the communication strategy as necessary (ie if it is proving not to be effective)

Once the communication strategy has been devised, then the message delivery itself becomes important. A leader may use a range of different communication skills – for example, presentation skills – to help deliver a message, but it is critical to remember that effective communication involves **listening** as well as **informing**.

The leader must know and understand their audience, and what their information needs are. Listening to stakeholders (audiences) not only helps to identify what their information needs are, but involving them in communications can provide valuable input and feedback.

The following questions could be asked to help assess the effectiveness of a leader's – or an organisation's – communications:

- Do they know exactly what they want their audience (eg employees, customers) to understand, think and do in response to their communication?

- Is the message consistently aligned with the organisation's vision, goals and objectives? (And, in the case of an organisation: is the leadership team delivering a consistent message?)

- Is the communication a two-way process?

- Do they measure the effectiveness of their communication?

- Do they use the results of previous programmes (and feedback from them) to adjust future communication initiatives to improve effectiveness?

- Do they know how stakeholders prefer to receive communications (eg face to face, email)?

More generally, the idea of communication being a two-way process could also be viewed in the context of Ashridge Management College's four management styles – tells, sells, consults and joins – which were discussed in the E2 syllabus.

Where leaders adopt a 'tells' style, communications are one-way, and neglect feedback or input from the audience; communications are also still largely one-way when a leader adopts a 'sells' style. However, in 'consults' or 'joins' styles, leaders and managers involve team members in discussions. This can encourage greater motivation and commitment among team members, but means the decision-making process is likely to be longer than under a 'tells' or 'sells' style.

Two of the obstacles to organisational change can often be employee resistance and staff turnover. If leaders ask for their employees' feedback, and respond to their concerns honestly and openly, this can help reduce employees' resistance – although it will not necessarily overcome it entirely. Similarly, engaging with employees, and involving them in the change process, may make them more inclined to stay with the organisation.

Staff turnover could be reduced further by using the change process as a means of enriching employees' roles – although this is likely to be effective if managers understand which employees want their roles to be enriched, and how they want them to be enriched.

1.1.2 Relating strategic change to an operational level

Bridges and Mitchell – in their article *Leading transition: A new model for change* – highlight that leaders and managers must be aware of the stress related to a period of change, and should be encouraged to use clear, consistent communication and focus on connections with, and concern for, the people being affected by change.

Bridges and Mitchell's model characterises three stages of transition (which, in a way, could be seen as similar to the three stages of Lewin's ice cube model):

(a)   Saying goodbye to the existing, familiar way of doing things

(b)   Shifting into neutral

(c)   Moving forward with the new way of doing things

However, Bridges and Mitchell also focus on the importance of leaders assisting people through the change process by communicating the 4 Ps of transition:

(a)   **Purpose** – why change is necessary

(b)   **Picture** – where the change will lead, and what the future position will look and feel like when it is reached

(c)   **Plan** – steps to be taken to reach the future goal; how the organisation can get there

(d)   **Part** – what each person needs to do to contribute to achieving the future goal

The 'part' aspect of Bridges and Mitchell's 4 Ps highlights that, although strong leadership is crucial to business success, an entity can ultimately only succeed when employees and managers at every level understand where the entity is going and how their actions help it achieve its goals.

This also has important implications for the communications required in support of an organisational change. Although the change itself might be at a strategic level, it is important that staff understand how it will affect them, and what the benefits of it will be for them. As such, most employees are likely to be more interested in the operational features of the change, rather than the high-level strategic aspects. Equally, though, if communications programmes fail to tell the employees what they want to know – or need to know – then those communications will ultimately be unsuccessful.

Exam skills

Although communications in relation to change may often be directed towards employees, effective communication could equally improve relationships with other key stakeholder groups – for example customers and suppliers. How will the changes affect them? What benefits will the changes bring them?

However, communication can be a double-edged sword. Poor communication can damage a change process just as much as effective communication can help it.

For example, employees will resent hearing about changes which affect them from sources other than management, for example the press. If staff members feel that managers are not being open and honest with them, resistance to change will be increased.

Honesty – even if it means admitting that all the details have not yet been finalised – is better than cover-ups.

The table below summarises the role of communication in the context of Lewin's change process:

Change phase	Communication purpose
Unfreeze	Creating readiness for change; spread understanding of the need for change
Move	Provide individuals with the explanation about the changes; reduce uncertainty about the impact of the changes
	Enable staff to make any changes required of them
Refreeze	Keep staff informed of the progress of the change process

1.2 Communication channels

There are a wide variety of communication channels available:

- Conferences, or videoconferences
- Seminars and workshops
- Briefings and departmental meetings
- One-to-one meetings with managers
- Memos
- Manuals and information packs
- Newsletters (electronic or in hard copy)
- Announcements on notice boards (on intranet as well as hard copy)
- Email
- Websites

This variety of possible channels available means it is important to select a channel which is appropriate to the message being delivered and the audience.

In general, complex, non-routine change situations are best delivered through rich forms of communication – usually face to face interactions. Face to face communication – especially in small groups – allows people the opportunity to ask questions and raise concerns they may have.

Less rich forms of communication – such as written and electronic means – are usually better suited to routine, less complex changes.

1.2.1 Dangers of communication by email

Email is a useful mechanism for distributing a standard message to a large number of people at one time. However, email can be impersonal and 'soulless' so it is usually not appropriate for delivering messages of an emotional nature, particularly ones which convey bad news (eg redundancy).

Communication efforts should include clear and plentiful opportunities and routes for **feedback**, so that omissions, poorly constructed messages, misunderstandings and anxiety can be dealt with.

Care must be taken with **emotional aspects** of communication so that appropriate media, language and symbols are used.

1.2.2 Timing of communications

The time at which actions are taken can be selected for tactical effectiveness.

(a)   A **crisis** can be used to justify extensive change, so monitoring a mounting crisis and delaying action until it is ripe may enhance acceptance.

(b)   **Windows of opportunity** may occur as, for example, when a takeover occurs.

(c)   **Messages** about timing must be coherent so that, for example, rapid action is not undermined by the retention of procedures that enforce long time frames.

(d)   Fear and anxiety about change may be reduced if unpleasant consequences can be **decoupled in time** from the main change programme. An example would be a programme of redundancy that does not commence until other change objectives, such as the outcomes of product and market reviews, have been implemented.

More generally, the timing of communications can be critical, and Balogun and Hope Hailey suggest that the following key factors need to be considered in relation to the timing of communications:

(a)   **Control announcements carefully**: employees will resent hearing about changes from other sources.

(b)   **Manage rumours**: try to minimise the opportunity for rumour by communicating information as quickly as possible.

(c)   **Communication too late**: this can mean staff have insufficient time to come to terms with, and adjust to, changes; but this needs to be balanced against leaving people in a position of uncertainty for too long.

(d) **Announcements should be honest and accurate**: if this doesn't happen, management will soon lose their credibility and distrust will build up among staff. Even if not all information is available, staff can be given a clear timetable of when further details will be provided.

Balogun and Hope Hailey identify three main phases of communication:

(i) **Readiness**: in the early phases of the change process, communication is about creating a readiness for change, with the key goals being promoting understanding and building commitment.

(ii) **Explanation**: as change starts to get underway, staff need information, but also need to know about the support available to them. Staff are likely to be experiencing uncertainty, so communication will also be crucial in reducing ambiguity as far as possible.

(iii) **Update**: as changes start to become embedded, there needs to be continual updates of progress, as different stages are reached.

1.2.3 Job losses

The threat of job losses associated with change is likely to be bad for morale and to provoke resistance. Redundancy programmes must be managed with care.

(a) A single, rapid and extensive round of cuts is preferable to a long drawn out programme of smaller reductions: the former can be stressful but the latter creates **long-term uncertainty and anxiety**.

(b) Where **delayering** is required, it may be possible to concentrate the job losses among managers identified as being opposed to change: these are likely to be more senior figures.

(c) Those who lose their jobs should be dealt with as **sympathetically and compassionately** as possible; the provision of services such as outplacement, counselling and retraining may help.

1.2.4 Quick success

Momentum for change can be created by putting simple but highly visible improvements into successful operation. Even where the overall position is difficult and requires a complex solution, such **quick wins** are often available: it is common for them to emerge in the form of suggestions from the lower echelons of the organisation.

Even where there are no obvious easy options, it may be possible to create some by **concentrating the available resources** on specific problems rather than spreading them too thinly.

1.3 Stakeholders and communication channels

Stakeholder	Their needs	What they want to know	How to communicate
Shareholders	Reassurance	That there is well thought through strategy; how the strategy will benefit them	The press Financial statements AGM Website
Suppliers	Information	How the changes will affect their working relationship	Face to face meetings with major suppliers Letters/email to small suppliers
Customers	Motivation	That they will still be able to buy the products they want That the service they receive will continue uninterrupted	The press Advertisements

Stakeholder	Their needs	What they want to know	How to communicate
Senior managers	Acknowledgement and involvement	How they will be involved and opportunities in the new structure Reassurance over employment positions	One-to-one meetings
Staff	Reassurance Help to adapt	Training and support Job security	Briefings One-to-one with line manager
Line managers	Reassurance Involvement	Opportunities to be involved and opportunities to learn Job security	Briefings One-to-one with senior manager/HR
The press	A good story	What is happening, the rationale, and whether the changes are under control	Briefings

Although this table illustrates that change will need to be communicated to a range of external as well as internal stakeholders, we focus here on the internal stakeholders, and how change is managed within an organisation.

Balogun and Hope Hailey's change kaleidoscope shows that one of the design choices in a change project is choosing which change intervention to use.

Successful change implementation ultimately requires an organisation to deploy a range of levers to change all the relevant organisational subsystems shown in the cultural web.

Levers will need to be designed to remove the barriers to change in the existing web, and to create new structures, systems, routines and so on, as defined by the new cultural web.

The number of levers required is likely to depend on the scope of the project. The greater the extent of the change, the more change initiatives that are likely to be required.

Communication, **education**, **training** and **personal development** initiatives (including possibly coaching and counselling) are all likely to be required to help individuals undertake the changes required of them.

However, managers will also need to ensure that changes across an organisation are **mutually supportive**.

For example, if there is a focus on improved teamwork, then the rewards system needs to reflect this and not simply reward individual performance. If the rewards system recognises individual performance, then the behaviour it encourages could undermine the rhetoric of the change.

1.4 Five styles for managing change

We have already mentioned the importance of communicating appropriately and effectively in managing change. However, it is also important that the overall style in which the change is managed is appropriate to the context. (You may notice some similarities between these styles for managing change and Kotter and Schlesinger's styles for overcoming resistance to change, which we looked at earlier.)

Johnson, Scholes and Whittington identify five styles of change management:

- Education and communication
- Collaboration/participation
- Intervention
- Direction
- Coercion/edict

1.4.1 Education and communication

Education and communication is an approach based on persuasion: the reasons for change and the means by which it will be achieved are explained in detail to those affected by it. This style is appropriate when change is **incremental**.

This style is **time consuming**, but can be useful if there has been misinformation in the past. However, it is a top-down approach and depends on a **willingness to accept management's plans** as appropriate. This may not, in fact, be present.

If the willingness to change is initially missing, managers may also need to have a **negotiation strategy**.

In other words, they may need to negotiate with staff to resolve any issues, overcome any resistance and avoid any future conflicts. However, the negotiation process is likely to be a lengthy, time-consuming one.

1.4.2 Collaboration/participation

Collaboration, or **participation**, brings those affected by strategic change into the change management process. For example, this may include drawing them into issue identification, prioritisation and the creation of new routines to implement newly established strategy. This approach may improve decision quality by bringing wider experience and knowledge to bear.

However, it may be time consuming and it will be **subject to the influence of the existing culture** and **paradigm**, which may limit its potential effectiveness. This approach is both **ethical**, in basic deontological terms, and advantageous in practice, since it can nurture a positive attitude, thus building both **readiness** and **capability** for change. It is suited to incremental change.

1.4.3 Intervention

Intervention is undertaken by a **change agent** who delegates some aspects of the change process to teams or individuals, while providing guidance and retaining overall control. Delegated aspects can include both design and implementation activities. Final responsibility for achieving the necessary change remains with the change agent, but this kind of participation can build **commitment** and a **sense of ownership**. This style is appropriate for incremental change.

1.4.4 Direction

Direction is a top-down style in which **managerial authority** is used to establish and implement a change programme based on a clear future strategy. It is thus suited to **transformational change**.

It has the potential advantages of speed and clarity, but may lead to **resistance**. Its success depends in part on the **adequacy of the proposed strategy**: if this is inappropriate, the best managed of change programmes will still not result in wider strategic success.

1.4.5 Coercion

Coercion is an **extreme form of direction**, being based on the use of power to impose change. It is likely to provoke opposition due to the lack of participation or consultation, but it may be the best approach in **times of confusion or crisis**. At such times there may simply not be time to consult, because decisions need to be taken quickly.

1.5 Using change management styles

Although we have looked at five change management styles in isolation, there may be advantages to making use of more than one of the change management styles at any one time.

1.5.1 Context

Specific aspects of the organisational context will influence the use that can be made of the five styles. Clear and appropriate **direction** can be a strong motivating force and may enhance **readiness** to change, while **collaboration/participation** and **intervention** may help to build **capability** to change.

1.5.2 Scope and nature

Using Balogun and Hope Hailey's change matrix (scope and nature of change) we might suggest that progression down the list of change management styles corresponds reasonably well with progression from top left to bottom right of the matrix.

In **adaptation**, where time is not critical and the extent of the change required is small, styles from the collaborative-communicative end of the spectrum may be appropriate.

Revolution, on the other hand, will require a great element of **direction** and even of **coercion**.

The intermediate cases are likely to require a combination of **participation** and **direction**, with the emphasis on the former in **evolution** and on the latter in **reconstruction**.

As with all change processes, the likely success of different change management strategies is context-specific: what works in one context will not necessarily work in another.

Again, the change kaleidoscope could be a useful tool here. Key **contextual features** will affect the decision about which styles of management might be appropriate.

For example, an organisation with little time to deliver change, and a low readiness for change may need to use dramatic and directive means of unfreezing their current position. But an organisation with more time to deliver change could afford more communication and discussion with staff.

1.5.3 Power structures

In many cases, it will be appropriate to **echo an organisation's normal power structure** when managing change. Direction or intervention are likely to be more suitable in a firmly hierarchical organisation than they would be in a network or learning organisation, except in time of crisis, for example.

1.5.4 Personality type

Management style is a tool. Good managers will be capable of using a **style appropriate to the conditions** they have to work in. However, many managers' personality types will incline them to the **style with which they are most comfortable**. But this style may not be appropriate to the context of the change.

1.5.5 Combining styles

It will often be appropriate to use a combination of styles in a change programme, **taking different approaches with different stakeholders**. Providers of capital are likely to respond better to **education and communication** than to **direction**, for example, while something approaching **coercion** may be necessary in some internal areas simply because of the pressure of time.

Most of the time, a **mixed approach between coercive change and adaptive change** is suitable. Adaptive change may be too slow, whereas coercive change is often resented and may not be 'refrozen' into the organisation's future state.

1.6 Context-sensitive change

The strategic change needed to implement a new corporate strategy often involves a need to change an organisation's skills, style and operating culture.

Pettigrew and Whipp's research identified that there are five interrelated factors which need to be considered in order to manage strategic change successfully:

(a) **Environmental assessment**. Strategy constantly emerges from a review of the environment and competitors' actions.

(b) **Leadership style**. Leaders are constrained by the actual situation of their organisation.

(c) **Linking strategic and operational change**. The strategy will allow for evolution over time, as issues become apparent in its implementation.

(d) **Manage human resources**. It is important to manage the knowledge, skills and attitudes of the organisation as a whole. Long-term learning and development are crucial for an organisation to develop its full potential.

(e) **Coherence**. This is the most complex of the five factors. It attempts to combine the other four into a consistent whole, which is reinforced by a set of complimentary support mechanisms:

- Consistency – the goals of the organisation must not conflict with each other.
- Consonance – the whole process must respond well to its environment.
- Competitive advantage – the change must deliver competitive advantage to the organisation.
- Feasibility – the strategy must be feasible given the resources the organisation has available to it.

The organisation needs to develop a balanced approach to change that is internally efficient while also adapting successfully to external changes.

Potentially, organisations may wish to pursue emergent strategic change in favour of prescriptive change because it is less disruptive.

However, emergent models of change take a long-term approach and so may have limited usefulness when the organisation faces a short-term strategic crisis.

Consequently, there may be occasions when strategic circumstances force prescriptive change.

Ultimately, the choice of which strategy to use to manage change – and therefore also to manage corporate strategy – depends on the situation facing the organisation at the time.

1.7 Reardon and Rowe – leadership style inventory

Rowe, Reardon and Bennis in their paper, *The leadership style inventory,* reinforce the importance of adopting a leadership style which is appropriate to the context in which it is being used. Rowe *et al* highlight that while leaders and managers often address the technical dimensions required in a change, they fail to consider what it takes to actually implement the change at different stages of the change process.

Rowe *et al* argue that there are only a few 'Strategic leaders' who recognise that leading change requires the integration of diverse interests and skills, and also that multiple styles of leadership are likely to be needed to effectively implement organisational change. Effective leadership involves selecting a leadership style which matches the needs of the group being led. Leaders also need to adapt their style to the urgency of the task to be accomplished.

1.7.1 Leadership styles

However, although they highlight that leaders need to adapt their styles for different circumstances, Rowe *et al* have still identified four basic styles to which leaders are pre-disposed. These styles are based around two key characteristics:

- How adaptive are leaders when dealing with the issues they face?
- How do leaders communicate with, persuade and motivate staff during the process of change?

Rowe *et al*'s resulting leadership style inventory identifies four basic leadership styles: commanding, logical, inspirational, and supportive.

Commanding leadership style

- Focuses on performance
- Short-term goal orientation
- 'Commanders' are highly productive and results oriented
- They learn better through their own success and failure than through input from others

Logical leadership style

- Insistence on covering all alternatives
- Long-term goal orientation
- Use of analysis and questioning
- Leaders learn by reasoning things through
- The 'logical' style is particularly effective when the goal is strategy development

Inspirational leadership style

- Focuses on developing meaningful visions for the future, through focusing on radically new ideas
- Leaders learn by experimentation
- Leaders show a high level of concern for assuring cohesiveness of the members of the organisation
- Encourage others to follow the vision
- Leaders are inquisitive and curious, and satisfy their curiosity by finding radically new solutions

Supportive leadership style

- Tries to create consensus
- Emphasis on openness and transparency
- Leaders operate more as facilitators than directors
- Leaders learn by observing outcomes and how others react to their decisions

As such, the four leadership styles can be summarised in the following table:

	Focuses on	Persuades by	Makes changes	Learns by
Commanding	Results	Directing	Rapidly	Doing
Logical	Innovation	Explaining	Carefully	Studying
Inspirational	Opportunities	Creating trust	Radically	Questioning
Supportive	Facilitating work	Involvement	Slowly	Listening

(Source: Rowe, A., Reardon, K. and Bennis, W., *The leadership style inventory*)

Section summary

Effective communication is critical for the successful implementation of organisational change. However, it is also important to use an appropriate management style for the type of change being managed. Management styles and types of change form a spectrum: the education and communication style works best for an adaptive change, while direction or coercion works best for revolutionary change.

2   Why change succeeds or fails

Introduction

We have highlighted the importance of context in change management and the different management styles which can be used in the change process. We will now look at some of the specific factors which can contribute to the success of a change management programme.

2.1 What makes change go well?

Studies carried out by Prosci Research (www.prosci.com) have identified that there are a number of common factors which contribute to the success of change management projects:

(a)   **Effective support from senior management**: active, visible, ongoing support throughout the life of the initiative, acting as role models and ambassadors for change

(b)   **Buy-in from front-line managers and employees** which gets the change moving and maintains momentum through the project

(c)   **Continuous and targeted communication** throughout the project, tailored for different interested parties

(d)   **An experienced and credible change management team** who maintain good internal working relationships

(e)   **A well-planned and well-organised approach** which is suited to the type of change being managed

However, one very interesting conclusion this research highlighted is that in order to buy into the change, employees need to **hear about change from two people**:

(a)   The most senior person involved in the change
(b)   Their line manager

The senior official – possibly even the CEO – should communicate the general business message around the change to the organisation as a whole, while the line manager should communicate more personal messages, such as the impact the change might have on an individual's roles and responsibilities.

2.2 Why does change fail?

By contrast to the research looking at the ways that make change management successful, Professor John **Kotter**, one of the leading authors on change, picked out **eight key aspects of the change process** which could cause a change initiative to fail if they were not managed correctly.

In turn, Kotter suggests possible antidotes which could be used to overcome the reasons for failure. In effect, the antidotes can be seen as a framework for successful change leadership. (You may recognise this 'framework' as Kotter's eight step model for managing change, which we looked at in the previous chapter.)

Reason for failure	Possible antidotes
Not enough sense of urgency	**Establish a sense of urgency by:** • Examining market or competitive pressures • Identifying potential crises or major opportunities • Ensuring that levels of dissatisfaction with current position or perception of future threat are sufficient to kick-start the change and maintain momentum

Reason for failure	Possible antidotes
Failure to create a powerful support base	**Form a powerful guiding coalition by**: • Assembling a group with enough power to **lead the change effort** (without an effective change management team, any change management project is likely to fail) • Encouraging the group to work together as a team • Ensuring that key stakeholders are engaged
Vision not clearly developed	**Create a vision by**: • Having a clear understanding of what the change needs to achieve • Developing clear strategies for achieving the vision
Vision poorly communicated	**Communicate the vision by**: • Using a variety of media to communicate the new vision and strategies. Within this, it will also be important to **highlight the benefits** of the changes • Teaching new behaviours by the example of the guiding coalition senior management • Ensuring people have a shared understanding and commitment to the direction of the change
Obstacles block the vision	**Empower people to act on the vision**: • Senior management demonstrably tackling obstacles to change • Ensuring that all the people who are needed to make the change happen have the necessary resources and authority to achieve their goals
Failing to create short-term wins	**Plan for and create short-term wins by**: • Planning for visible performance improvements • Identifying smaller goals along the way to the ultimate target so that success can be demonstrated. Being able to demonstrate success will maintain momentum • Recognising and rewarding employees involved in improvements
Systems, policies and skills not aligned	**Consolidate improvements and produce more change by**: • Changing systems, structures and policies that don't fit the vision • Hiring, promoting and developing employees who can implement the vision • Building on improvements in the organisation as and when they occur to continue to move the change forward
Failing to anchor changes in the corporate culture (not refreezing)	**Institutionalise new behaviours by**: • Explaining how the new behaviours will deliver corporate success • Developing the means to ensure leadership development and succession • Ensuring knowledge about the new approaches is captured and shared

Adapted from Cameron and Green, *Making sense of change management* and based originally on an article by Kotter in the *Harvard Business Review*

One additional factor which could jeopardise the success of a change management project is a **lack of change management/implementation expertise** and skills within an organisation's senior management team. Change does not just happen on its own; management need to define the change programme, ensure the necessary resources are allocated to it, and drive it forward. However, for example, if the senior management team do not have any previous experience of change programmes, and do not allocate sufficient resources to it, its success could be jeopardised.

2.2.1 IT in change management

Although Kotter doesn't specifically mention it, we should also consider the role of IT in the potential success or failure of any change programme.

Businesses have become increasingly dependent on effective IT systems, and this often creates tensions between the IT and operational departments in organisations.

Despite the best of intentions, IT and operational departments end up clashing and blaming each other for problems which emerge during projects.

However, effective change relies on an integrated shift of people, systems and processes – supported by IT. For example, if a business wants to introduce a new e-commerce strategy, for that strategy to be successful it will need an IT infrastructure which can support online transactions etc.

Therefore a lack of confidence and trust between the IT and operational teams, which are critical to the success of change, is unlikely to lead to a successful project.

2.3 The importance of mentoring and coaching

We noted above that one of the factors which threatens the success of a change management project is a lack of expertise and experience of leading change among an organisation's senior management team.

As we note later in this chapter, one way an organisation can overcome this weakness is by using an external change agent to help it manage change.

However, the dynamism of the global environment in which contemporary organisations exist; the need to respond to opportunities and threats more quickly and effectively than competitors; and the need to control cost and increase efficiency are likely to mean that the ability to implement organisational changes effectively could, in itself, become an important capability for an organisation.

As such, an organisation may look to develop its own change management capabilities rather than having to rely on external change agents to lead change programmes for it.

In their 2011 research on sustainable organisational performance ('Sustainable organisational performance: What really makes a difference?') the Chartered Institute of Personnel and Development (CIPD) identified capability building as one of the key themes in achieving sustainable performance. This capability building relates to equipping people with the requisite knowledge and skills, not just for their current job, but also for future challenges.

Ineffective management and leadership can affect an organisation's profit and performance, just as other organisational weaknesses can; therefore it is in organisations' best interests to develop their management and leadership teams through training and development, and mentoring and coaching.

Leaders and senior managers often find themselves dealing with complex, multifaceted problems, and this is particularly likely to be the case in relation to organisational changes. However, at the same time, leaders are often faced with diaries packed with meetings and other commitments which mean they have little quality time to reflect and consider the decisions they need to make. This context means that leaders can gain considerable value from working with an external coach or mentor who can act as a sounding board for their ideas and help them clarify their thinking process.

2.3.1 Coaching

Coaching is one of the key developmental tools for encouraging workplace learning and growth (ie where the focus is on acquiring new skills and competences rather than just attending formal training events).

Lloyd and Rosinski (in *Coaching, culture and leadership*) suggest that coaching is about unleashing people's potential to meet meaningful goals, and is essentially a developmental process through which the coach helps the learner find their own solutions, discover new opportunities and implement actions.

Similarly, Starr (in *The Coaching Manual*) emphasises that coaching is a way of encouraging learning, rather than telling or instructing someone. Through a conversation or series of conversations the coach provides support and helps the coachee develop insights and come to their own solutions.

Although there are many different views of coaching, and many definitions in the past have equated coaching with instructing – where someone more skilled shows someone less skilled how to do something – much of the current thinking on coaching sees it as an approach whereby the coach is not essentially passing on knowledge but instead **drawing out knowledge and learning** from the individual.

2.3.2 Mentoring

The terms coaching and mentoring are often used interchangeably. However, many authors would argue that they are not the same. Parsloe and Wray (in *Coaching and Mentoring: Practical Methods to Improve Learning*) suggests that a mentor is a broader role than a coach and is more concerned with the **longer-term** acquisition of skills for career development. A mentor tends to have the role of adviser or counsellor, and helps the mentee develop insight and understanding, through intrinsic observation of the mentor.

2.3.3 The coaching process and the GROW model

There are many different models of coaching, but one which is widely used is the GROW model, developed by Sir John Whitmore, which suggests a coach should follow four key steps in a coaching session.

(a) **Goals**: identify the goals for the coaching session and for the learner in the short and longer term. The purpose of this stage is to be very clear on the behaviours the learner is seeking to develop or change. Without a clear focus on goals, it is difficult to determine what might be appropriate ways of meeting the needs.

(b) **Reality**: the coach then explores the current situation or the 'reality' now. Why does the learner feel they have this need? How does this link to their current job? Here the coach is trying to encourage the learner to identify the 'gap' between where they are now and where they want to be. From this part of the coaching process the learner should be identifying the nature and size of the development gap. At this point, the coach may get the learner to rethink their goals as it may become apparent that the goals first identified are not the real problem or issue.

(c) **Options**: having identified the goals and the development gap, the coach then encourages the learner to identify possible development options. It is important at this stage that the coach tries to elicit ideas from the learner rather than giving them suggestions since the point of coaching is to encourage ownership and self-reliance.

(d) **What**: once options have been explored the final stage is to agree what exactly the learner will do and when they will do it. This stage of 'action planning' is crucial since both parties agree what has been settled and when this will happen. The coach needs to agree the type of support they will provide and how progress will be monitored.

2.3.4 Applying the GROW model

The primary role of the coach in the coaching session is to ask questions to draw out the development plan from the learner. Some of the key questions for each stage of the coaching process are shown below.

Although these questions are generic, think how they could be applied in the context of leading change, or overcoming resistance to change in the course of change management.

(a) **Goals**

- What do you want to achieve from this session?
- What would be your ideal outcome in the short or long term (in terms of behaviours and goals)?
- Why is this important to you?

(b)   **Reality**

- What is happening now?
- Why is it happening?
- How often is it happening?
- When does this happen?
- Who is involved?
- What are the consequences of this?

(c)   **Options**

- What could you do to achieve your objectives?
- What else could you do?
- What would be the benefits/limitations of that course of action?

Note. The coach can input options but these should be posed as suggestions only after the learner has come up with their ideas, if the coach thinks other ideas would be of benefit.

(d)   **What**

- What are you going to do?
- When are you going to do it?
- What obstacles might you encounter?
- Who needs to know?
- What support do you need?
- How and when will you require that help and support?

2.3.5 Potential benefits of coaching and mentoring

In addition to the fact that time spent with a coach or mentor gives the leader space to think ideas through, such sessions could have a number of benefits for someone leading a change programme.

(a)   The process of explaining their ideas and issues to the coach or mentor helps the leader clarify their own thinking.

(b)   Having their thinking challenged in a safe environment gives the leader the chance to develop their ideas further; or, if necessary, change their ideas and plans with no loss of face, and with no adverse consequences.

(c)   A coach or mentor, as an outsider to the leader's organisation, can ask apparently daft questions which are actually highly challenging – such as 'Why would you want to do that?' or 'What would happen if you didn't do that?' which will encourage the leader to think critically about the change programme as a whole.

(d)   An external coach or mentor should not be affected by politics or power struggles within the organisation.

(e)   An external coach who has previously worked with other leaders in relation to leading change may also be able to bring in new ideas from outside the organisation.

Section summary

There are a number of factors which contribute to the success of change management projects, but having a clear vision for a project, and communicating effectively, are particularly important.

3 Change and the individual

Introduction

So far we have looked at change as something which affects organisations. However, it is also important to appreciate that change affects individual people as well, and their reactions and response to change have to be appreciated.

One of the more common themes in modern business management is that 'people are a firm's best asset' and, in the context of change management, this may be particularly true.

All changes are ultimately made by people, and the success of a change project is achieved by people, even if their role is in planning or designing systems and processes.

Yet the critical role of people in the change process also highlights a crucial risk in change management. A **key part of change management is about dealing with people**, and unfortunately people are not always rational or logical.

Therefore, as well as possibly being a firm's best asset, people can potentially be its biggest liability.

If organisations do not understand their people, and their reactions to potential changes, the risk of change programmes failing increases.

Therefore, although our main focus is on organisational change, we also need to recognise that, in order for an organisation to change, the individuals within it are also likely to have to change to some degree.

Therefore when managing change, a change agent will have to consider how to change individuals' behaviours to support the change programme.

3.1 Approaches to managing change

There are a number of approaches to managing individual change.

3.1.1 Behavioural approach to change

This approach focuses on how one individual can change another's individual behaviour through reward and punishment in order to achieve intended results.

The implications for business are an organisation needs to get its **reward strategies** right, and reward people for following change.

3.1.2 Cognitive approach to change

This approach is founded on the idea that people's emotions and problems are a result of the way they think. Individuals react in the way they do because of the way they appraise the situation in which they find themselves. In the context of change, individuals need to look at the way they limit themselves through sticking to old ways of thinking, and replace that with new ways of being.

However, there are some drawbacks to this approach.

In particular, there may be a lack of recognition of the inner emotional world of the individual, and the positive and negative impact that this can have when attempting to manage change. Some obstacles to change need to be worked through, and cannot simply be made all right by reframing or positive talk.

3.1.3 Psychodynamic approach to change

The word 'psychodynamic' is based on the idea that, when facing change in their external world, an individual can experience a variety of **internal psychological states**. Although this approach has now been applied to the workplace, the original research by Elizabeth Kübler-Ross involved observing the way terminally ill patients come to terms with being informed about their conditions.

Kübler-Ross realised that patients go through five stages as they come to terms with their diagnosis.

Denial – The initial reaction is one of disbelief; trying not to accept the news, pretending that it did not happen.

Anger – Once people acknowledge what is happening, disbelief gives way to anger. For example, people want to know 'Why me?' or 'How could such a thing happen to me?'.

Bargaining – Instead of continuing to be angry, the patient now desperately tries to find a way of remedying the situation.

Depression – When it becomes apparent that bargaining is not going to provide any escape from the situation, the scale and impact of the situation becomes realised, and patients recognise that they will be losing their life as they knew it. They experience a sense of grief and depression for that loss.

Acceptance – The patients have now come to terms with the reality and inevitability of their situation. While they are not necessarily happy about it, they are nonetheless prepared for it.

Adam, Hayes and Hopson developed Kübler-Ross's ideas to apply them to business, and added the concepts of 'experimentation', 'discovery' and 'integration' after the acceptance stage in the original model.

Experimentation – Staff begin to think that some of the changes 'out there' might be worth thinking about.

Discovery – As staff enter the 'new world' that has changed they may actually discover that things are not as bad as they had imagined. Perhaps the organisation was telling the truth after all, when it said the changes would provide new opportunities and a better way of working. In which case, they then begin to **integrate** this 'new world' into their own.

The complexity of this psychodynamic approach has important implications for business. When introducing change, businesses to need to **treat people as individuals** and understand their emotional states when responding to change. Change cannot simply be forced through.

3.1.4 Humanistic psychology approach to change

For many years, we have been led to believe that organisations are ruled by the **rational mind**. However, humanistic psychology moves away from this rational approach and argues that managers need to have an emotional apathy with a situation and to be present emotionally in the situation in order to be fully effective.

This approach also emphasises the importance of development and growth, and maximising the potential of staff.

Section summary

In any change programme it is vital to consider the impact change will have on an organisation's staff as individuals. People respond to change in different ways, and develop their own ways of coping with change. In this way, change cannot simply be considered a mechanical process.

4 Leading change

Introduction

Effective leadership is crucial in times of change. A leader will have to not only identify the vision for change but also communicate that to the organisation. The challenge leaders face in any change situation will depend on the scale, time frame and possible implications of the change.

Change management is a comprehensive effort to lead an organisation through transformation. However, to be successful the transformation effort must be actively led and managed, with a clear set of objectives and an agreed plan for achieving these objectives.

A crucial problem organisations have to address is how they can **manage change** in the fast-moving environment of contemporary business, while also **maintaining control** and their **core competences**.

Designing, evaluating and implementing successful change strategies depends to a significant extent on the quality of the senior management team and, in particular, that team's ability to design an organisation in a way to facilitate the change process.

Knowledge brought forward

Although we are focusing here on change management, a number of the skills needed to manage change successfully are similar to those required in project management. You should already be familiar with the concepts and techniques of project management from your studies at E2, but we have provided a very brief recap of some of the issues in implementing and managing projects as an appendix at the end of this chapter.

4.1 Who leads change?

Although a CEO plays an important role in leading change, it is not only the responsibility of the CEO.

Whetten and Cameron pointed out:

> '... the most important leadership demonstrated in organisations usually occurs in departments, divisions, and with teams and with individuals who take it upon themselves to enter a temporary state of leadership ...'

Inevitably, though, leading change will also require competences in influencing and conflict handling, because people may need to be persuaded of the value and benefits of change.

Change may create conflict between individuals and their environment – and, often, within individuals themselves.

We have already noted that change can make people uncomfortable, which is why so many people resist it. Organisational change also creates potential conflict between management (who may be identified as the causes or agents of change) and employees (who often feel like the 'victims' of it).

Managing change is, in essence, a process of facilitating internal and external **conflict resolution**. So, change leaders have to play a dual role of not only leading a business forward, but also resolving any conflicts which are created during the course of the change process.

Whetten and Cameron suggest five key steps as to how a leader can encourage those involved with change to be positive about that change. (Note the similarities between this list and the points we identified earlier in this chapter as to why change succeeds or fails. This reiterates the importance of leadership to the change process.)

(a)   **Establishing a climate of positivity**: This is about focusing on the positive, rather than dwelling on negative aspects of the change. To do this requires identifying 'positive energisers', people who are optimistic and enthusiastic about the change and then enable them to have opportunities to

interact with others and influence them. Leaders also need to display compassion in dealing with people experiencing change – supporting staff, providing positive feedback and recognising that mistakes may occur if staff are faced with new challenges. Another part of establishing a positive climate is to focus on people's strengths and successes.

(b)   **Create 'readiness' for change**: This is about helping people understand the reasons for change and its importance and urgency. One suggestion made by Whetten and Cameron is to use benchmarking to show areas for achieving higher levels of performance, showing that higher standards are achievable by looking at relevant comparators. They link this to the idea of 'unfreezing', getting people to let go of the past and identify a better future.

(c)   **Articulating a vision**: Developing and communicating a vision of the future, which illustrates the benefits of the change. Whetten and Cameron comment:

'Positive change seldom occurs without a leader articulating a vision of abundance ... by abundance we mean a vision of a positive future, a flourishing condition, and a legacy about which people care passionately.'

(d)   **Generating commitment to the vision**: Once the vision has been articulated, the next step is to get people to sign up to and adopt the vision.

(e)   **Institutionalising the change**: This final change is about making the new change part of everyday working life. This involves continually reinforcing the new ways and finding ways to communicate, celebrate and reward achievement.

4.2 Change roles

We can identify a number of key players in the change process.

Change leader: The success of the change programme is based on a key, pivotal figure. This leader may be the CEO, the MD, or another senior manager acting as an internal change agent.

Change advocate: Who proposes the change.

Change sponsor: Who legitimises the change, and has overall authority over the change progamme and the individuals who will implement it. The change sponsor approves the high-level direction of the programme and any subsequent changes in scope of it.

Change agent: Who implements the change. Change agents seek to initiate and manage a planned change process.

Change targets/recipients: Although they do not lead the change, it is important in any change programme to remember the change targets – these are the people who undergo the change.

Other changes roles to consider are:

External facilitators: External consultants may be appointed to help co-ordinate the change process.

Change action team: A team of people within the organisation may be appointed to lead the changes. This team may take the form of a steering committee. If the team does not include any influential senior managers it will need the backing of more powerful individuals to support any major change efforts.

Functional delegation: The responsibility for managing change may be assigned to a particular function – often the HR department. This approach is probably most suitable when the skills needed to manage the change reside within a particular department. However, unless the department head is a powerful authority figure, they will need the backing of a more powerful figure to spearhead significant changes.

4.3 Change agents

For change to be effective, it needs to be effectively implemented. Many organisations seek to use change agents to facilitate change.

KEY TERM

A CHANGE AGENT is an individual or group that helps to bring about strategic change in an organisation.

Although a change agent might be a single person (sometimes called a **champion of change**, or a **change master**), change agency could equally be spread among the members of a group, such as a project team or the management team more generally. Outsiders, such as consultants, may share in change agency and have the responsibility for driving and 'selling' the change.

The role of the change agent varies depending on the brief they are given. It may include:

- Defining the problem
- Examining what causes the problem and considering how this can be overcome
- Suggesting possible solutions
- Selecting an appropriate solution
- Implementing the change
- Communicating information about the change throughout the organisation

The change agent must possess the skills to manage the transition process, but must also have the determination to see the change through.

Rosabeth Moss Kanter identified seven '**power skills**' which change agents need in order to help them overcome resistance to change in organisations.

- An ability to collaborate effectively

- An ability to develop relationships based on trust and high ethical standards

- An ability to work independently, and without relying on senior management to provide visible support

- An ability to work across different business functions and business units

- Self-confidence, tempered with humility

- A willingness to stake personal rewards on results being achieved, and to take satisfaction from achieving them

- Respecting the process of change, as well as the substance of the change

The following additional skills and attributes could also be important for a change agent more generally:

(a)   **Communication skills** – and the ability to communicate effectively with people at all levels within an organisation.

(b)   **Networking skills** to establish and maintain contacts, both within and outside an organisation.

(c)   **Negotiation and 'selling' skills** – negotiating with stakeholders in the business to obtain resources for a project, or to resolve conflict; selling the vision of change to key stakeholders to increase support for a change programme. Alongside this, a change agent also needs to have **influencing skills**, to be able to convince potential sceptics about the benefits of a change programme, and thereby to overcome their resistance to it.

(d)   An awareness of organisational 'politics', and an ability to manipulate and exploit triggers for change.

(e)   **Sensitivity** to the impact which changes could have on different stakeholders, and tact and diplomacy in dealing with the different stakeholders.

(f)   An understanding of the relevant processes, coupled with a willingness to question current processes and practices and to challenge existing assumptions and beliefs.

(g)   **Creativity** – an ability to think creatively, and to avoid becoming bogged down in the detail of how to do every individual task.

(h)   Financial analysis skills: to assess the financial impacts of proposed changes, or to be able to look at how changes to operations and systems can deliver a desired financial goal.

(i)   **Flexibility** to be able to respond to shifts in project goals or objectives; or to adapt in response to internal or external factors which affect the change process.

(j)   Change agents also need the flexibility to see the strategic picture as well as being able to identify operational and process issues.

An important point that Kanter highlights is that a change agent needs to be able to adapt to cope with the complexities of modern organisations.

In particular, a change agent needs to:

(a)   Be able to work across a range of business units and functions and across a network of different stakeholders

(b)   Be an effective collaborator, able to work in ways that enhance collaboration across different functions and divisions

Importantly, though, a change agent should not be selected just because they have good general project management skills. The change agent must be **directly involved in the change process**, and must see clear linkages between their future success in an organisation and the effective implementation of the change.

4.3.1 The champion of change model

The **champion of change model** recognises the importance of change being led by a **change agent**.

Senior management are the change strategists, and decide in broad terms what is to be done. There is a need for powerful advocacy for change at the strategic apex. This will only occur if senior management are themselves agreed on the need for change. This is a role requiring a clear vision of what the change is to achieve.

Senior management appoint a change agent to drive change through. Senior management has three roles:

- Supporting the change agent, if the change provokes conflict between the agent and interest groups in the organisation

- Reviewing and monitoring the progress of the change

- Endorsing and approving the changes, and ensuring that they are publicised

The change agent has to win the support of functional and operational managers, who have to introduce and enforce the changes in their own departments. The champion of change has to provide advice and information, as well as evidence that the old ways are no longer acceptable.

The change agent galvanises managers into action and gives them any necessary support. The managers ensure that the changes are implemented operationally, in the field. Where changes involve, say, a new approach to customer care, it is the workers who are responsible for ensuring the effectiveness of the change process.

It is important to realise that **successful change is not something exclusively imposed from above**. There is a sense in which middle and junior managers are **change recipients** in that they are required to implement new approaches and methods. However, they are themselves also **change agents** within their own spheres of responsibility. They must be committed parts of the change process if it is to succeed.

4.3.2 External change agents

Although a change agent can be selected from within the organisation which is experiencing change, many organisations choose to use external consultants as change agents.

The advantages of using an external change agent include:

Expertise – An external agent may need to be brought in because the organisation doesn't have the capabilities or skills required internally.

Best practice – Additionally, an external agent can recommend '**best practice**' approaches, drawing on their experience from working with other organisations.

Collaboration – An external agent who has expertise and experience in managing change can collaborate with people from the organisation, and together they can make sense of the change situation and what needs to be done. The external agent can work with members of the organisation to facilitate the change process, and in doing so the organisation's leaders and managers can gather expertise from the agent.

Resources – An external agent may be required simply because an organisation doesn't have the capacity to dedicate an existing member of their internal staff to the role. In particular, an external change agent may be able to devote themselves to the change process on a full-time basis; something which internal members of staff may not be able to do.

Fresh perspective – Even if an organisation has the skills and resources necessary to manage change internally, it can still be useful to bring in someone with a fresh perspective, who can take an **independent view** of the change required. This fresh perspective may enable them to see things that people familiar with the organisation had stopped noticing, or had chosen to stop noticing due to internal politics within the organisation.

Section summary

A **change agent** is an individual or group that helps to bring about strategic change in an organisation.

For change to be effective, it needs to be effectively implemented. For this reason, many organisations seek to use change agents to facilitate change.

5 Building and managing effective teams

Introduction

In most organisations, staff do not work in isolation from their colleagues. Instead, they work as part of a team, or a group.

Therefore, when considering change management, we need to assess not only how individuals react to change, but also how groups do. Perhaps more importantly, though, leaders need to consider how they can develop effective teams which enable the changes to be implemented successfully.

One of the key issues in successfully implementing change is obtaining a shared perception among those affected, of the issues and implication associated with the change.

5.1 How groups respond to organisational change

In an organisation, the employees and management are used to working in a particular way. They develop or establish a set of relationships with the work environment.

A change process inevitably leads to some kind of **shift in the work environment**, the routine or the composition of the group.

The members of a group in an organisation may respond in different ways to the change. In other words, some may support the change, while others may oppose it.

If those people who oppose the change are very influential in the group, they can sway the responses of the other people in the group, so that the change will not be successfully implemented.

Equally, if the dominant members of the group support the change, they can influence the other members of the group to help ensure the change is successfully implemented.

In both situations, there are likely to be some people who are neutral, and will accept whatever decision is finally taken by the employees and management.

In a way, the group dynamic could be seen as similar to a force field: some members of the group will be driving forces for change, while others will resist change.

For the change to be successfully implemented, the driving forces need to be stronger than the resisting forces.

Group resistance to change is often manifest through strike action. For example, if management propose changes which workers don't like, in extreme cases, the workers respond by taking strike action. In particular, this may be the case with **unionised workforces**, where trade unions will support their members in a dispute with management. The strike action can only be resolved by the workers accepting management's proposal, or by management backing down and heeding to the workers' grievances about the changes.

5.2 Stakeholder analysis and change

When considering a change exercise, a stakeholder analysis could be a useful starting point because it can help analyse what each of the **interested parties will stand to gain or lose from the change process**. In this way, it could highlight the potential benefits of the process which management can use to help rally support.

It could also instruct management that they need to find ways to compensate or compromise those who feel that they stand to lose more than they gain from the change. If such people are influential members of a group they might otherwise persuade other members of the group to resist the change.

5.3 The role of groups in change

Peter Senge in his analysis of the learning organisation argues that **teams**, not single individuals, are the key to successful organisations in the future, and individuals have to 'learn how to learn' in the context of the team.

In this respect, teams and groups can also be useful to the process of change.

Often they can be used as a **source of support** during the change process; members can support and counsel each other during the changes.

Sensitivity training, undertaken in groups or established teams, can help people involved in change talk openly about issues that they find difficult to discuss any other way. Often groups of this nature will have a facilitator, but the facilitator is not a leader and so leaves the group to discuss a topic by themselves.

During periods of change and uncertainty, these discussions will often concentrate on group members' fears and concerns about the change. However, by discussing their concerns with their peers, group members can often gain reassurance that they are not alone in facing the change and this can help them feel more positive.

We have discussed the concept of learning organisations in Chapter 7 earlier in this Study Text. However, learning organisations are also interesting to consider in the context of change management. Learning organisations learn from their external environments and adapt to them. Change, for learning organisations, becomes natural and ongoing, and not something which only occurs in times of crisis or pressure.

5.4 Building teams after change

Change programmes often lead to changes in the composition of work teams. Therefore, the new teams which are created after a change programme need to re-establish themselves to ensure they operate as effectively as possible.

5.4.1 Aspects of teams

KEY TERM

A **TEAM** is a 'small number of people with complementary skills who are committed to a common purpose, performance goals and approach for which they hold themselves mutually accountable'.

(Katzenbach and Smith, 1994)

(a) **Work organisation**. Teams combine the skills of different individuals and avoid complex communication between different business functions.

(b) **Control**. Fear of letting down the team can be a powerful motivator, hence teams can be used to control the performance and behaviour of individuals. Teams can also be used to resolve **conflict**.

(c) **Knowledge generation**. Teams can generate ideas.

(d) **Decision making**. Teams can be set up to investigate new developments and decisions can be evaluated from more than one viewpoint.

(e) **Communication**. Teamwork can enhance the flow of information.

(f) **Social needs**. People generally have a need for company and social interaction.

Woodcock identified the following building blocks which help to build effective teams.

Issue	Contribution to building an effective team
Leadership	Adopting a leadership style that fits the task, team and situation
Membership	Ensuring a suitable mix of competences and member roles
Climate/culture	Striving to create a co-operative atmosphere and style based on trust
Objectives	Clarifying and articulating specific, meaningful and achievable goals which can be shared by the whole team
Achievement	Creating opportunities to learn; celebrating learning and improvement
Work methods	Developing workable procedures for task and group functioning
Creativity	Facilitating generation of new ideas (eg through brainstorming); respecting and reinforcing ideas and risk taking
Review and control	Regularly evaluating and feeding back on team performance and improvement needs
Communication	Facilitating openness and honesty, information sharing, ideas generation and constructive feedback
Interpersonal relations	Helping members to get to know one another; controlling conflict; facilitating trust and co-operation
Individuals	Giving team members opportunities to grow and develop within and through the team (eg by multiskilling)

5.4.2 Multidisciplinary teams

In many cases, particularly in relation to projects, teams will be deliberately structured as multidisciplinary teams. Multidisciplinary teams bring together individuals with different skills and specialisms, so that their skills, experience and knowledge can be pooled or exchanged. Team working of this kind encourages freer and faster communication between disciplines in the organisation.

(a)   Team working increases workers' **awareness of their overall objectives** and targets.

(b)   Team working **helps to generate solutions to problems**, and suggestions for improvements, since a multidisciplinary team has access to more 'pieces of the jigsaw'.

(c)   Team working **aids co-ordination across functional boundaries**, by increasing the flow of communication, informal relationships and co-operation.

(d)   Team working also increases the flexibility and speed of response to customers.

 Here too, aspects of knowledge management and learning organisations which we discussed in Chapter 7 could also be relevant. We have noted that knowledge management promotes the fast and efficient exchange of information, and can help to promote creativity and innovation through effective channelling of information. In this respect, bringing people from different parts of an organisation together into multidisciplinary teams could help to promote information and knowledge sharing.

However, despite the potential benefits of multifunctional teams, they can also create difficulties due to the matrix structures which they can create – with employees feeling responsible both to a team and their functional department. Moreover, the members of the team may have a range of different backgrounds, work cultures, and terminologies – all of which increase the challenge facing the team leader in creating a sense of team identity, role clarity and co-operative working.

5.4.3 Development of the team

The **performance** and **effectiveness** of teams is influenced by a range of factors:

(a)   **Size** is important: larger groups can do more work, but individual productivity tends to fall. This is called the **Ringelmann effect**. This effect is held to be the product of **social loafing**, which arises when group members believe they will not receive a fair share of reward if they make a great effort, nor appropriate blame if they make an inadequate one.

(b)   **Cohesion** enhances output. Cohesion is reduced by membership turnover and if members have divided loyalties. Similarity of status enhances cohesion.

(c)   **Group roles**. Groups often develop roles that are played by individuals spontaneously. More formal roles are acknowledged by mechanisms such as election. Personal predisposition and talent are important in the emergence of such figures as leaders and nurturers in groups. We return to this concept later when we discuss the work of Belbin on team roles.

5.4.4 Tuckman's stages of team development

Tuckman identified four stages in team development, and leaders and managers should be prepared to manage and exploit these different stages when creating teams:

 Forming

The team is just coming together, and may still be seen as a collection of individuals. Each member wishes to impress their personality on the group. The individuals will be trying to find out about each other, and about the aims and norms of the team. There will at this stage probably be a wariness about introducing new ideas. The objectives being pursued may as yet be unclear and a leader may not yet have emerged. This period is essential, but may be time wasting: the team as a unit will not be used to being autonomous, and will probably not be an efficient agent in the planning of its activities or the activities of others.

Storming

This frequently involves more or less open conflict between team members. There may be changes agreed in the original objectives, procedures and norms established for the group. If the team is developing successfully this may be a fruitful phase as **more realistic targets** are set and **trust** between the group members **increases**.

Norming

A period of settling down: there will be agreements about work sharing, individual requirements and expectations of output. **Norms and procedures** may evolve which enable methodical working to be introduced and maintained.

Performing

The team sets to work to execute its task. The difficulties of growth and development no longer hinder the group's objectives.

5.4.5 Characteristics of effective teams

(a) Each individual gets the support of the team and a sense of identity and belonging that encourages loyalty and hard work on the group's behalf.

(b) There is high level of commitment to the achievement of the group's **targets and goals**. Goals are aligned with a well-defined vision or sense of purpose, and are clearly communicated.

(c) Skills, information and ideas are shared, so that the team's capabilities are greater than those of the individuals. **Synergy** is achieved through the pooling of skills.

(d) New ideas can be tested, reactions taken into account and persuasive skills brought into play in group discussion for **decision making** and **problem solving**. The team provides a focus for **creativity** and **innovation**, especially in multidisciplinary teams. Good ideas are followed up, and people are rewarded for innovation and **appropriate risk taking**.

(e) Each individual is encouraged to participate and contribute and thus becomes personally involved in and committed to the team's activities. Equally, control and discipline are enhanced by commitment to the team's expectations.

(f) Goodwill, trust and respect can be built up between individuals, so that communication is encouraged and potential problems more easily overcome. This can contribute to **empowerment** when responsibility and authority are delegated to self-managing teams.

    (i) Feedback is freely asked for and constructively given as a way of evaluating and developing individual and team performance. Team members are willing to examine errors and limitations without making personal attacks, so that the group can learn from its mistakes.

    (ii) Conflict is not suppressed. The group openly confronts and investigates problems, with commitment to finding mutually satisfactory solutions.

(g) There is clear understanding of the team's role in the organisation's activity, particularly in terms of key values such as customer care and quality.

    (i) Team members have a positive attitude towards change, and are willing to accept and facilitate changes which are in line with the team's purpose and goals.

    (ii) Team member resources are identified, acknowledged, utilised and developed. Opportunities are sought to meet individuals' higher-level needs for challenge, responsibility and development in the work.

5.4.6 Benefits of using teams to implement change

The characteristics of effective teams highlight that teams have a number of potential benefits for organisations in general.

Equally, when looking to implement change in an organisation, a change leader should consider the potential advantages of using a team to do this, rather than trying to do it alone.

(a)   **Identifying potential solutions** – If the team is made up of people from different parts of the organisation they will bring with them **different skills and experience**. As such, they may be able to identify a wider range of insights and potential solutions to a problem than a change leader working alone might be able to identify. The team can then develop a change programme which benefits from the insights and ideas of all its members.

(b)   **Evaluating solutions** – Similarly, the knowledge that team members have of different parts of the organisation can be used to evaluate whether a proposed change is appropriate for different departments or divisions. And the range of skills and knowledge among the team members means the team may be able to identify problems with a proposed solution which an individual change leader may not spot.

(c)   **Stakeholder involvement and communication** – If departments or divisions know they have been represented in the process of designing the changes, they may be more willing to accept the changes. For example, members of the finance department may be more likely to accept changes if they know the financial controller or the financial director have been part of the change team.

Similarly, staff may be more amenable to a change if it is communicated to them by a member of their department.

5.4.7 Problems with teams

Unfortunately, team working in organisations as a whole, or in the context of implementing change, is rarely such an undiluted success as the previous sections might suggest. There are certain constraints involved in working with others which can reduce the effectiveness of teams.

(a)   Awareness of **group norms** and the desire to be acceptable to the group may **restrict individual effort**.

(b)   **Too much discord**. Where an individual is a member of more than one group, conflicting roles and relationships can cause difficulties in communicating effectively.

(c)   **Personality problems** will arise if one member dislikes or distrusts another; is too dominant or so timid that the value of their ideas is lost; or is so negative in attitude that constructive communication is rendered impossible.

(d)   **Rigid leadership** and procedures may stifle initiative and creativity in individuals. Team working requires that managers share power with the team. Some managers find this difficult to do. Also, a coaching style of management is most appropriate for teams and this must be learned.

(e)   **Differences of opinion** and political conflicts of interest are always likely.

(f)   **Too much harmony**. Teams work best when there is room for disagreement. They can become dangerously blinkered to what is going on around them, and may confidently forge ahead in a completely **wrong** direction. Janis describes this as '**groupthink**'. The cosy consensus of the group prevents consideration of alternatives, constructive criticism or conflict. Alternatively, efforts to paper over differences may lead to bland recommendations without meaning.

(g)   **Corporate culture and reward systems**. Teams will fail if the company promotes and **rewards the individual at the expense of the group**. Similarly, when team rather than individual output is measured, it is easier for unmotivated individuals to get by with minimal effort.

This point could have important implications when setting performance objectives and targets. For example, members of a sales team are eligible for performance-related bonuses according to the number of sales they make individually; this is likely to encourage the sales staff to keep potential leads to themselves rather than sharing them with colleagues in the team.

We look at performance measurement and performance management in Chapters 11 and 12 of this Study Text, but the general point to note here is the way that the performance measures chosen can affect behaviours within a team or an organisation.

(h)   **Too many meetings**. Teams should not try to do everything together. Not only does this waste time in meetings, but team members are exposed to less diversity of thought. Decision making by teams can be excessively time consuming and may not offer any advantage over the normal process of decision making by individual managers after consultation.

(i)   **Powerlessness**. People will not bother to work in a team or on a task force if its recommendations are ignored.

(j)   **Risky shift**. Group processes are such that individual characteristics can be reinforced and become exaggerated (for example, people who are natural risk takers will be prepared to accept even greater risks as part of a group). The 'risky shift' occurs when a group collectively, after discussion, makes decisions about risk differently than if the members of the group had been acting individually. One of the main problems with this for organisations is that groups are often likely to accept riskier decisions than the members of the group would have been prepared to accept if they had had individual responsibility for the decisions.

5.4.8 Problems of using teams to implement change

Although we have noted (in Section 5.4.6 above) that it can be beneficial to use teams to implement change in an organisation, there could nevertheless be problems from doing so:

Speed of decision making – As a team will need to discuss any proposals before reaching a decision about what to do, this is likely to mean that the decision-making process is slower than if a change leader took decisions by themselves. The process will be slowed further if there are significant differences of opinion within the team which need to be resolved before a decision can be taken. The time taken to reach a decision could be a particular issue in times of crisis, when a rapid ('Big Bang') change is required.

The problems of '**groupthink**' and **risky shift** could also be problematic here:

(a)   Members of the team may accept the consensus of the group and support decisions affecting the change programme which are not beneficial to the organisation as a whole (group think).

(b)   The team may support riskier courses of action and decisions than its members would have been prepared to accept individually (risky shift).

5.4.9 Teams and accountability

In team-based organisations, accountability is focused at the team level, rather than on individuals. As such, members of the team feel mutually accountable to each other, and therefore the team as a whole is accountable for its performance and results, rather than specific individuals.

In practice, the paradigm of individual accountability is so strong in many organisational cultures that holding a team accountable for its collective output, rather than evaluating the contributions of individuals, can be very difficult. However, from a customer's perspective, they are not concerned with who individually was responsible for a substandard product, or even who will fix it – just as long as the problem is resolved. The team (as a whole) is responsible for producing the product, and equally they are collectively accountable for fixing things when they go wrong.

There is an important caveat here, though, which links directly to the idea of accountability and control in a performance measurement context: teams should only be held accountable for those aspects of performance which they can control. For example, if an organisation has a centralised procurement policy which means a team cannot purchase an additional machine it needs to cope with increased demand, the team should not be held accountable for failing to satisfy that demand.

Equally, however, teams can only be jointly accountable for their combined results if the people within the team can influence each other's behaviour. So, for example, a performance appraisal system should include feedback from team mates, and this should be seen as equally important as a manager's feedback.

Encouraging **mutual accountability** for **shared objectives** may involve the following:

(a)   Involving team members in formulating a 'team charter': an agreement that clearly states what the team wants to accomplish, why its goals are important, and how the team will work together to achieve results.

(b)   Clear articulation and periodic reminders of the team's task objectives and their place in the organisation's activity as a whole. This is particularly important in the case of geographically dispersed teams (such as on the road sales teams, project teams whose members are based at different sites, and 'virtual' teams of people working from home connected by computer and/or telephone). The team leader needs to maintain a constant overview of the team's activity and progress, through monitoring and feedback.

(c)   Involving the team in setting specific targets and standards, and agreeing methods of organising work and team processes (frequency and purpose of communications, meetings and so on). Again, this is particularly important if team members work apart for some or all of the time.

(d)   Raising awareness of team roles and the complementary value of different member contributions: this will help to avoid any misunderstandings about roles and responsibilities and help all members to feel valued. (We look at Belbin's team roles shortly, but this point is especially relevant to team members with less 'visible' or glamorous roles, such as Implementers, Completer-Finishers and Team Workers.)

(e)   Giving regular feedback on performance, improvements, progress and results, so all members are aware of where they are in relation to targets and standards and can learn and adjust performance accordingly. This supports commitment to continuous improvement and skill development.

(f)   Inviting feedback and suggestions from team members, and responding positively to them, so they feel they can genuinely influence work methods and drive improvements.

(g)   Positively reinforcing behaviour that demonstrates commitment to the team (collaboration) as well as commitment to the task (performance): through rewards; public recognition, thanks and praise; the awarding of greater responsibility. People's efforts should be focused on team performance rather than individual 'star' performance.

(h)   Exploiting formal and informal communication channels and media to ensure that team members continually share information and ideas, and generally maintain contact (particularly in dispersed, virtual or independent-working teams).

5.5 Team roles

Belbin's classic study of team roles identified the most effective character mix in a team. Belbin's findings identified eight necessary roles that should be played by team members:

Member	Role
Co-ordinator	Presides and co-ordinates: balanced, disciplined, good at working through others
Shaper	Highly strung, dominant, extrovert, passionate about the task itself, a spur to action
Plant	Introverted, but intellectually dominant and imaginative; source of ideas and proposals but with disadvantage of introversion
Monitor-evaluator	Analytically (rather than creatively) intelligent; dissects ideas, spots flaws; possibly aloof, tactless – but necessary
Resource-investigator	Popular, sociable, extrovert, relaxed; source of new contacts, but not an originator; needs to be made use of
Implementer	Practical organiser, turning ideas into tasks; scheduling, planning and so on; trustworthy and efficient, but not excited; not a leader, but an administrator
Team worker	Most concerned with team maintenance – supportive, understanding, diplomatic; popular but uncompetitive – contribution noticed only in absence
Finisher	Pushes the team to meet deadlines, attends to details; promotes urgency and follow-through; not always popular

The **specialist** joins the group to offer expert advice when needed. Notice that one team member may play two or more roles.

5.6 The role(s) of the team leader

Adair's model of **action-centred leadership** provides a framework for the leadership and management of any team or organisation. Adair's model identifies three core management responsibilities:

- Achieving the task
- Managing the team
- Managing individuals

Although Adair's model was developed to describe the complexity of the leadership context in general, it is particularly relevant here – since it identifies the challenge for a leader in addressing the needs of team members as individuals, as well as the needs of the team as a whole. However, the nature of the model – comprising three interrelated variables – means the needs of the team and its members cannot be detached from the requirement to perform (ie to achieve the task at hand).

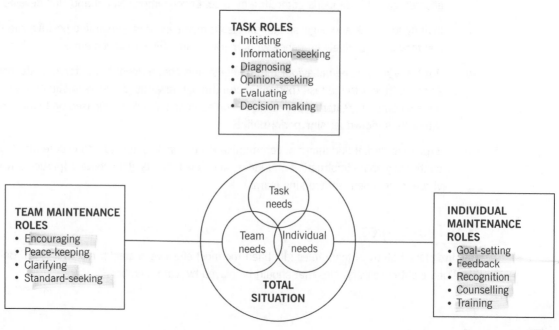

Section summary

In many organisations, staff do not work in isolation from their colleagues, but as part of groups or teams. A change programme within an organisation may require leaders or managers to build and develop effective teams which can implement the change – and subsequently perform – successfully.

6 Business ethics in change management and the implementation of strategic plans

Introduction

The process of change often raises serious questions of ethics and value: for example where people are encouraged or even forced to take on new roles, or even more acutely when structural changes in an organisation may lead to people being made redundant.

We have mentioned many times in this Study Text already that all organisational changes affect people, and so it is therefore important that the potential ethical implications of any change programme are assessed before that programme is undertaken.

For example, organisational change can often lead to:

- Loss of individual roles and jobs
- New individual roles and jobs
- New organisational or departmental strategy

It is important that any people affected by these changes are treated fairly and are not unnecessarily disadvantaged by them.

6.1 Consultation processes

In this respect, we should highlight the importance of having a consultation process in advance of any planned change programme.

The consultation process should be taken in such areas as:

- Establishing whether change is necessary and if so to what extent
- Identifying options for change
- Evaluating options for change
- Taking the strategic decision as to what kind of change to implement
- Designing and then putting into practice the implementation plan

The question of consultation is important because:

(a) It is often seen as ethically worthwhile in its own right, empowering and enabling people who otherwise might see their individual rights overridden

(b) It can be argued that many of the areas where conflicts of value and ethics occur come about due to inadequate consultation processes

A well-known model of consultation is provided by Tannenbaum and Schmidt who depict it in relation to the power that is implicitly available to parties to the consultation process.

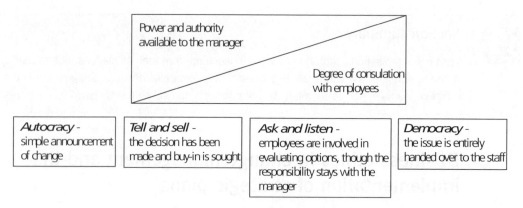

The Tannenbaum-Schmidt model of consultation and power

The idea behind the model is that the degree of consultation that a manager engages in amounts to a passing across of their power and authority. The more that a manager (genuinely) consults with employees (and we could add here other stakeholders as well) the more they are giving some of the responsibility for the change to those who are consulted.

(a) At one extreme, a manager retains all power by identifying and analysing a change autonomously, generating options and deciding between them, formulating how to put the change into practice and then right at the end just telling others what will happen.

(b) At the other, a manager decides that the issue would be best resolved by giving it to the staff to deal with, and they are allowed full authority to do what they believe is best. And in between there are progressive stages moving partially from one extreme to the other.

Certain assumptions are built into this model, of which an important one is whether or not the consultation process is genuine. Many managers, for a variety of reasons, may misrepresent what they are doing when they engage in a dialogue with staff. A few examples of how this may happen are given below.

Type of misrepresentation	Example
Unintentional misrepresentation	A manager may be carrying on an activity that they see as 'tell and sell' where they have already made up their mind about the change but want to lead the staff through their thought processes in order to achieve the degree of commitment they require. So they ask the employees to consider how to solve a certain problem. The employees, on the other hand, may feel that they are being given the opportunity to contribute to the formulation of the solution.
Deliberate misrepresentation	A manager may feel that if the choice they have already made is publicised then there will be a concerted attempt by the workforce to resist or subvert it. So rather than act with overt secretiveness they pretend that they are consulting more openly than is actually the case.
Self-deception	Nowadays, consultation is often regarded as good management practice. Most managers will want to think of themselves as good managers. As a result they may fail to realise that they have a distinct bottom line, and go ahead with a consultative process even though subconsciously they have no intention of following it through.
Weakness of position	Often a manager may feel unable to contest a strongly held opinion concerning change – perhaps a forceful major investor has a strong view about what kind of change is appropriate. So they conceal this from the workforce as it would erode their authority.

The reason to detail these examples is that a radical change to the organisation represents a major event in its cultural development. The good or harm to employee-employer relationships that results from the quality of the change management process can have a lasting effect on the capacity of the business to meet future changes appropriately. For example, if staff feel a change process has been managed poorly, this is likely to adversely affect their morale and their productivity.

6.2 Consultation and stakeholders

In the process of **consultation**, the most important parties that need to be consulted are:

- Those who have **sufficient power and influence** to drive forward or hold up the change process
- Those who are **most vulnerable** to any potential changes

In practice, the same group is usually the main target of consultation – namely the workforce, as they have a great deal of potential power to prevent a change happening (or at least to make a quite different kind of change emerge from the process) and they are often the people at most risk, for example because of the possibility of losing their jobs.

Depending on the scale of the change, it may be that other parties are also consulted: for something that might affect the capital structure of the company then the majority shareholders will be asked for their views; while for a change that might result in relocation of premises, local residents might be consulted.

When considering any change process, it is important to remember the differences in power which different people in the process have. Senior management have the power to shape the process whereas workers may feel vulnerable to change.

In this context, there could be ethical questions as to whether management are introducing changes in the best interests of their organisation as a whole, or to benefit their self-interest.

Johnson, Scholes and Whittington suggest a useful matrix that helps us understand the position of stakeholders in a change scenario.

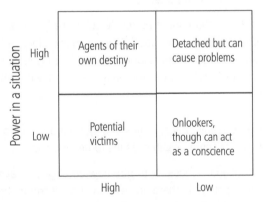

The position of stakeholders in change contexts

The most ethically important quadrant is probably the low power–high vulnerability one. People in this quadrant have to rely on others for their protection. For example, a retired person living close to the factory cannot directly influence what happens but has to hope that others will not subject him or her to unnecessary risks of toxic pollution.

In contrast the 'high power–high vulnerability' quadrant (usually employees and managers) is often the one which is most directly affected by change. People in this quadrant are vulnerable to what happens but have a chance to act on the situation with some reasonable degree of impact.

6.3 Potential ethical issues arising from change situations

Exam skills

In the integrated case study exam you should always be alert to any ethical issues which may be implied in the case study scenario. Equally you should ensure that any courses of action you recommend to an organisation uphold ethical practices in line with the CIMA Code of Ethics for Professional Accountants.

The indicative syllabus content associated with Learning outcome A2(a) indicates that you need to be able to apply the CIMA Code of Ethics for Professional Accountants (Parts A and B) in the context of the implementation of strategic plans. Make sure you are familiar with the contents of the Code before you sit your exam, so that you can identify any ethical issues which may arise in change management scenarios, and can make appropriate recommendations in your answers about how to deal with those issues.

As you read through the scenarios in the case study, think whether they raise any issues in relation to the five fundamental principles of the CIMA Code of Ethics, or whether they pose any potential threats to complying with them.

The five fundamental principles are:

- Integrity
- Objectivity
- Professional competence and due care
- Confidentiality
- Professional behaviour

The Code of Ethics makes clear that the professional accountant must react and respond if they uncover a threat to compliance with the fundamental principles. You should be prepared to advise on the alternative courses of action an accountant should take if they discover any such potential threat. An appropriate response may be to discuss the matter with a line manager and then subsequently with the internal audit department or the audit committee.

Alternatively, if the matter cannot be resolved internally, the accountant should consider taking advice from CIMA's ethics helpline, and possibly even seeking legal advice. If the accountant still cannot resolve the dilemma between their responsibility to their employee and their obligations to the ethical code they may ultimately have to resign from the organisation they currently work for.

The precise nature of any ethical issues arising from a scenario will be determined by the nature of the scenario but here are some possible issues to be aware of.

(a)   If an organisation is looking to hire new employees, have they followed a fair and equitable recruitment policy? Is there any evidence of discrimination?

(b)   If an organisation is looking to reduce its head count, has it imposed any compulsory redundancies on its staff or has it tried to manage the process through natural wastage and by consulting with its staff? Could the organisation be guilty to a charge of unfair dismissal? Equally, has the organisation treated all its employees fairly, or is there any evidence of discrimination (eg by age, gender, or race)?

(c)   Has an organisation intimidated its staff to support a particular course of action? For example, by threatening them with redundancy if they do not support proposed changes?

(d)   Are staff being manipulated to support change?

(e)   Are the accounting staff being pressurised to produce reports which materially misrepresent the facts of a case?

(f)   If an organisation is negotiating new contracts does it have any vested interests in the contract being awarded to a particular company?

(g)   Are staff misinformed about the nature/extent of change being considered?

(h)   Are schemes designed to increase profit/reduce costs putting profit before (customer) safety?

(i)   Do any proposed schemes contravene regulations, technical or professional standards?

(j)   Is process automation putting jobs at risk?

(k)   Skills obsolescence – The value of workers' skills may decrease due to changes in production technology or the production process. Job-specific skills obsolescence can occur when job requirements change, because workers' existing skills do not fully equip them to do their new job. In this context, does an organisation provide its workers with training to do their new job? Does it allow them flexibility to move into different roles within the organisation? Or does it simply make them redundant?

(l)   Age discrimination – If businesses are looking to expand or recruit new staff, they cannot discriminate against applicants on grounds of age. Researchers have found that many businesses inherently prefer to take on younger workers ahead of older ones, but if a candidate is rejected on the grounds of age alone this is not only unethical, but also illegal in many countries.

However, in any scenarios, we need to remember that an organisation has a duty of responsibility to its owners as well as its employees. There may be times when it is necessary to reduce staff costs in order to safeguard the future of the business. In such a situation, we cannot simply say it is unethical to make people redundant.

The list above is by no means exhaustive, and hopefully you can think of other examples, but it should give you some pointers as to the sorts of things you should be looking out for in case studies about change.

Section summary

Strategic changes may often raise ethical issues, and change managers need to consider the ethical implications when assessing the suitability and acceptability of a proposed change.

7 Change in practice

Introduction

We now bring together a number of the change management issues we have considered to look at an example where organisational change is required.

For this, we look at the case of a **turnaround**, where a business is in severe decline and faces either closure or takeover.

Although change management is often linked to expansion and growth, this is not always the case. Change management skills could equally be needed if an organisation needs to change its business strategy in response to falling revenues or profits.

Such a situation could possibly lead to the **divestment** of a business unit or part of an organisation, or its **liquidation**. Alternatively, the organisation could try to address its decline by means of a **turnaround**.

7.1 Turnaround

When a business is in terminal decline and faces closure or takeover, there is a need for rapid and extensive change in order to achieve cost reduction and revenue generation. This is a **turnaround strategy**. We can identify **seven elements of such a strategy**.

7.1.1 Crisis stabilisation

The emphasis is on reducing costs and increasing revenues. An emphasis on reducing direct costs and improving productivity is more likely to be effective than efforts to reduce overheads.

(a)   **Measures to increase revenue**

- Tailor marketing mix to key market segments
- Review pricing policies to maximise revenue
- Focus activities on target market segments
- Exploit revenue opportunities if related to target segments
- Invest in growth areas

(b)   **Measures to reduce costs**

- Cut costs of labour and senior management
- Improve productivity
- Ensure clear marketing focus on target market segments
- Financial controls
- Strict cash management controls
- Reduce inventory
- Cut unprofitable products and services

Severe cost cutting is a common response to crisis but it is unlikely to be enough by itself. The **wider causes of decline** must be addressed.

7.1.2 Management changes

It is likely that new managers will be required, especially at the strategic apex. There are four reasons for this:

(a)   The old management allowed the situation to deteriorate and **may be held responsible by key stakeholders**.

(b)   **Experience of turnaround management** may be required.

(c)   Managers brought in from outside will not be **prisoners of the old paradigm**.

(d)   A **directive approach** to change management will probably be required.

7.1.3 Communication with stakeholders

The support of key stakeholder groups – groups with both a high level of power and a high degree of interest in an organisation, such as the workforce and providers of finance – is likely to be very important in a turnaround; it is equally likely that stakeholders did not receive full information during the period of deterioration. A **stakeholder analysis** (discussed earlier in this Study Text) should be carried out so that the various stakeholder groups can be informed and managed appropriately.

7.1.4 Attention to target markets

A **clear focus on appropriate target market segments** is essential. Indeed, a lack of such focus is a common cause of decline. The organisation must become customer-oriented and ensure that it has good flows of marketing information.

7.1.5 Concentration of effort

Resources should be concentrated on the best opportunities to create value. It will almost certainly be appropriate to **review products and the market segments** currently served and eliminate any distractions and poor performers. A similar review of internal activities would also be likely to show up several candidates for **outsourcing**.

7.1.6 Financial restructuring

Some form of **financial restructuring** is likely to be required. In the worst case, this may involve trading out of insolvency. Even where the business is more or less solvent, capital restructuring may be required, both to provide cash for investment and to reduce cash outflows in the shorter term.

7.1.7 Prioritisation

The eventual success of a turnaround strategy depends in part on management's ability to **prioritise necessary activities**, such as those noted above.

8 Change management and strategy implementation

Introduction

We end our review of change management by revisiting its role in business strategy, to highlight why change management is so important in implementing business strategy.

The key role of change management in strategy implementation can be illustrated by looking at the key elements of strategic management. The diagram below illustrates these:

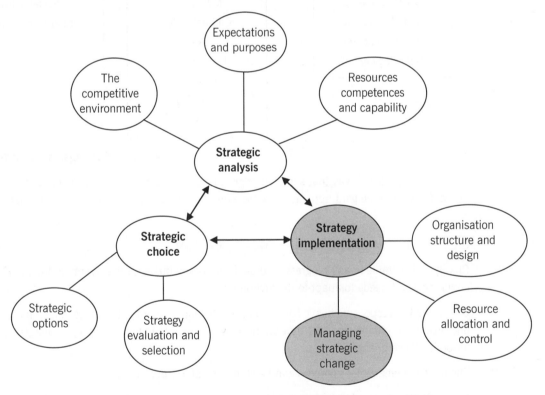

Summary of the elements of strategic management
(*Diagram adapted from* Johnson, Scholes and Whittington, *Exploring Corporate Strategy*)

KEY TERM

STRATEGIC CHANGE is 'the proactive management of change in organisations to achieve clearly defined strategic objectives or to allow the organisation to experiment in areas where it is not possible to define strategic objectives precisely'.   (Lynch, *Strategic Management*)

This definition – particularly the first half of it – clearly identifies the central role which change management plays in strategic implementation. Managing strategic change is one of the key components of strategy implementation.

We can also illustrate how change can affect all the aspects of an organisation but also, in turn, how a strategy implementation could require changes in all the aspects of an organisation.

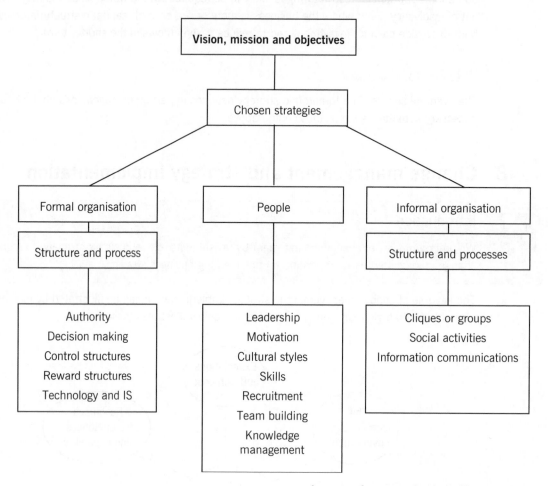

Aspects of an organisation affected by change

However, in the same way that some strategists favour a prescriptive view of corporate strategy and others favour an emergent approach, so there are diverse viewpoints on how best to manage change.

8.1 Strategy and change management

Change is inevitable in any progressive organisation. Any business that wants to thrive in an ever-changing world needs to adapt to its environment.

One of the key responsibilities for an organisation's management is to detect trends inside and outside the organisation to identify changes that are needed and then to initiate a change management process to introduce those change.

The change management process can be summarised in three steps:

(a) **Strategic planning and design**: form a change management team, define the vision and strategy, design a programme from which to manage the change and determine the tools needed for implementation

(b) **Strategy implementation**: communicate the vision and implementation to staff, manage staff responses and lead them through the change; maintain momentum

(c) **Evaluation and readjustment**: look at the results, track performance against targets, modify structure if necessary, plan for the future but continue to monitor performance

However, in the same way that corporate strategy can be either **prescriptive** or **emergent**, so can strategic change and change management.

Some researchers view the management of change as clear and largely predictable (the prescriptive approach) while others argue that change has a momentum of its own and the consequences are less predictable (the emergent approach).

Under the **prescriptive approach**, change is seen as the **implementation actions** that result from the deliberate decision to pursue a chosen strategy, and where the way to move from one state to another can be clearly identified.

In **emergent theories**, change can sometimes mean the whole process of developing the strategy, as well as the actions that result after it has been developed. Therefore change may involve **experimentation**, **consultation** and **learning** for those involved.

Prescriptive models tend to treat people simply as 'objects' and do not involve them in the change process.

Such approaches assume that change can be imposed upon the employees concerned. Imposing change may be necessary in some circumstances – for example, closing a factory – but in situations where the organisation needs the ongoing support and co-operation of its employees such a prescriptive approach may be inappropriate.

Also, prescriptive approaches to change assume that it is possible to move clearly from one state to another. However, this may not be possible if the environment itself is turbulent, and therefore the desired 'future state' is unclear.

Section summary

It will be unusual for an organisation's strategy to remain unchanged for any length of time as environmental developments mean that strategies will change and evolve. The management of change is therefore an integral and important part of strategic management.

Further reading

Although this Study Text is designed to provide you with all the coverage you need for your E3 exam, if you wish to do any further reading around change management issues the following texts offer some very useful material:

Balogun, J. and Hope Hailey, V. (2008) *Exploring Strategic Change.* (3rd edition). Harlow, Essex: Pearson Education.

Cameron, E. and Green, M. (2012) *Making Sense of Change Management.* (3rd edition). London: Kogan Page.

Whetten, D. and Cameron, K. (2011) *Developing Management Skills.* (8th edition). Harlow, Essex: Pearson Education.

Chapter Summary

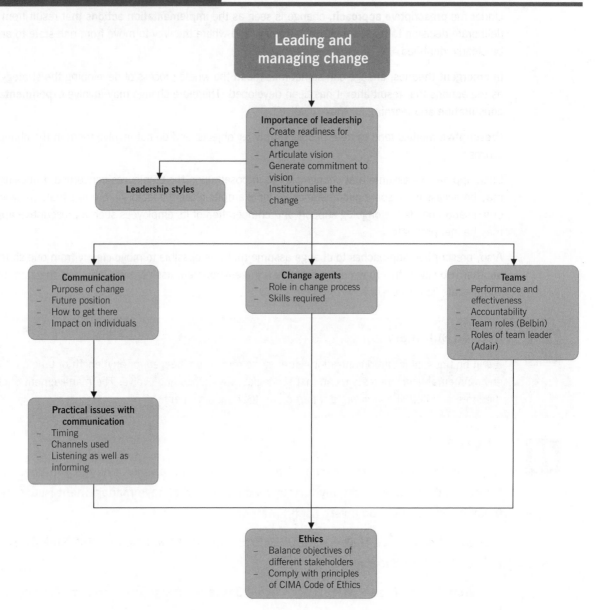

Leading and managing change

Importance of leadership
- Create readiness for change
- Articulate vision
- Generate commitment to vision
- Institutionalise the change

Leadership styles

Communication
- Purpose of change
- Future position
- How to get there
- Impact on individuals

Change agents
- Role in change process
- Skills required

Teams
- Performance and effectiveness
- Accountability
- Team roles (Belbin)
- Roles of team leader (Adair)

Practical issues with communication
- Timing
- Channels used
- Listening as well as informing

Ethics
- Balance objectives of different stakeholders
- Comply with principles of CIMA Code of Ethics

Quick Quiz

1 List three issues a leader must consider when planning a communication about organisation changes.

2 Which styles of management are required to effect revolution?

3 In a message to staff, a leader has communicated: where a change will lead the organisation and what the future position will look like once it is reached; the steps which need to be taken to reach the future goal; and what each person needs to do to help achieve that goal.

 According to Bridges and Mitchell's model – 4 Ps of transition – which 'P' has the leader failed to communicate?

 A Part
 B Picture
 C Plan
 D Purpose

4 Identify three potential benefits of coaching or mentoring for someone who is about to lead a change programme.

5 What is a change agent?

6 Which of the following is not one of the three core management responsibilities in Adair's model of action-centred leadership?

 A Managing the process
 B Achieving the task
 C Managing individuals
 D Managing the team

Answers to Quick Quiz

1   Any three from:

- How are people used to receiving communications
- What impact will the changes being communicated have on different stakeholders
- Is the message being communicated clear and consistent, and meaningful to the stakeholders
- What communication channels will be used
- What are the objectives for the communications
- How can the effectiveness of the communication be measured, and how can the communication strategy be adjusted if it proves not to be effective

2   Direction and, possibly, coercion

3   D   Purpose

The leader has failed to communicate why the change is necessary.

4   Three from:

(a)   The process of explaining their ideas and issues to the coach or mentor helps the leader clarify their own thinking.

(b)   Having their thinking challenged in a safe environment gives the leader the chance to develop their ideas further; or, if necessary, change their ideas and plans with no loss of face, and with no adverse consequences.

(c)   A coach or mentor, as an outsider to the leader's organisation, can ask challenging questions which encourage the leader to think critically about the change programme as a whole.

(d)   A coach who has previously worked with other leaders in relation to leading change may also be able to bring in new ideas from outside the organisation.

5   A change agent is an individual or group that helps to bring about strategic change in an organisation.

6   A   Managing the process

Adair's model identifies the three core management responsibilities as being: achieving the task; managing the team; and managing individuals.

Now try these questions from the Practice Question Bank	Number	Level	Marks	Time
	10.1 – 10.5	Intermediate	n/a	10 mins
	10.6	Examination	20	36 mins
	10.7	Examination	12	22 mins

APPENDIX

9   Project management and implementing projects

You should already be familiar with project management techniques from studying the E2 syllabus, and they are not included specifically in the E3 syllabus. Nonetheless, implementing organisational change can often also involve project management, so we have included a brief recap of some key project management issues here.

The objective of project management is to deliver a successful project. A project will be deemed successful if it is completed at the **specified level of quality**, **on time** and **within budget**.

Constraint	Comment
Quality	The end result should conform to the project specification. In other words, the result should achieve what the project was supposed to do.
Budget	The project should be completed without exceeding authorised expenditure.
Timescale	The progress of the project must follow the planned process, so that the 'result' is ready for use at the agreed date. As time is money, proper time management can help contain costs.

Quality, **cost** and **time** are traditionally regarded as the yardsticks against which project success is measured, although it is increasingly common to add a fourth constraint, **scope**, and even to use it to **replace quality** as a fundamental constraint and target. The **scope** of a project defines all the work that is to be done and all the deliverables that constitute project success. Under this analysis, the quality constraint is restricted to a narrower meaning and the difference between scope and quality becomes the difference between doing a job and doing it well – or badly.

The process involved in project management can be summarised in the figure below.

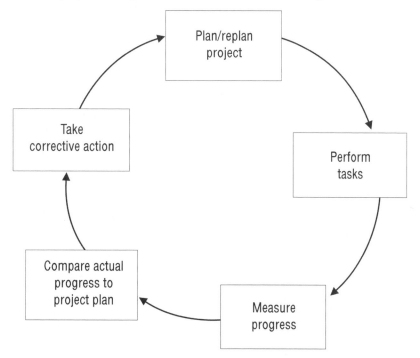

Management challenges presented by projects

Challenge	Comment
Team building	The work is carried out by a team of people often from varied work and social backgrounds. The team must 'gel' quickly and be able to communicate effectively with each other.
Expected problems	Expected problems should be avoided by careful design and planning prior to commencement of work.
Unexpected problems	There should be mechanisms within the project to enable these problems to be resolved quickly and efficiently.
Delayed benefit	There is normally no benefit until the work is finished. The 'lead in' time to this can cause a strain on the eventual recipient who is also faced with increasing expenditure for no immediate benefit.
Specialists	Contributions made by specialists are of differing importance at each stage.
Potential for conflict	Projects often involve several parties with different interests. This may lead to conflict.

IMPLEMENTING STRATEGY

Part D

STRATEGIC PERFORMANCE MANAGEMENT

However well designed they are, the ultimate test of strategies is their impact on organisational performance. Therefore, it is very important that managers measure performance effectively, to assess how well an organisation is performing against its objectives.

Historically, organisations have relied purely on financial measures, but this created some problems, particularly in relating the short term to the long term.

Performance measurement is all about **communicating the objectives** of an organisation and concentrating efforts towards them. **Strategic control** (Section 2) indicates the need for a review of strategic performance over **critical success factors** not solely in relation to financial performance – although many organisations

still use the traditional budgetary control process as the main basis for measuring performance.

Modern performance measurement systems should include indicators of **non-financial performance** as well as financial performance. The **balanced scorecard** (Section 4) is one way by which both **financial and non-financial** (strategic) performance can be measured. Other multidimensional models of performance – the **performance pyramid**, and the **building blocks** model – are described in Sections 6 and 7 respectively.

The building blocks model also highlights some of the key characteristics which effective targets should demonstrate. The effective use of targets and rewards (Section 9) can motivate employees and thereby also improve performance.

Topic list	Learning outcomes	Syllabus references	Ability required
1 Performance management and control	–	–	Recommend
2 Strategic control and critical success factors (CSFs)	D1(b)	D1(b)(ii)	Recommend
3 Performance measures: financial and non-financial	D1(a), D1(b)	D1(b)(i)	Recommend
4 The balanced scorecard	D1(a), D1(b)	D1(a)(ii)	Evaluate
5 Developing a performance measurement system	D1(b)	D1(b)(i)	Recommend
6 Performance pyramid (Lynch and Cross)	D1(a), D1(b)	D1(a)(ii)	Evaluate
7 Building block model (Fitzgerald and Moon)	D1(a), D1(b)	D1(a)(ii)	Evaluate
8 Measuring performance in manufacturing businesses	–	–	Recommend
9 Targets and rewards	D1(b)	D1(b)(iv)	Recommend

Chapter Overview

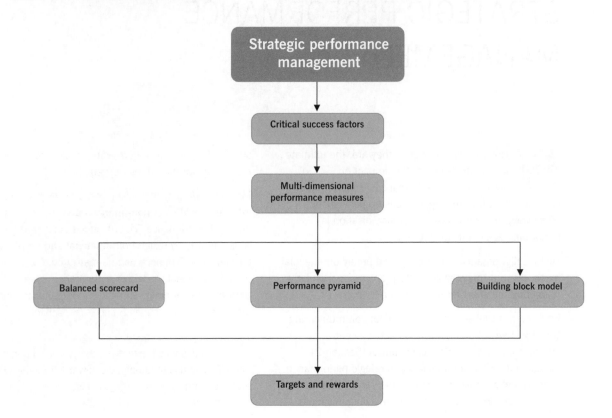

1 Performance management and control

1.1 Performance management and control

In Chapter 1 of this Study Text, we noted that the structure of the book broadly follows the sequence of the rational model – understanding strategic position, evaluating strategic choices and implementing strategy. However, it is important not to overlook the **feedback loop** in the model – representing review and control – which links strategy implementation back to strategic position.

Now that the organisation has implemented a strategy, what impact has this had on its performance and its competitive position? What can be done to improve the organisation's performance further?

In order to answer these questions an organisation has to measure and analyse its performance, and use this analysis to inform subsequent strategic decisions. These activities are at the heart of performance management. Performance management aims to improve an organisation's performance and ensure that its goals are being met.

Performance management systems are plans, with set guidelines and targets, to help organisations measure how efficiently their goals and objectives are being met, and to identify areas where performance can be improved. Performance management systems can also be linked to reward programmes, so that employees are rewarded for helping an organisation to reach its goals (for example, through profit-related pay schemes).

Historically, performance management tended to focus on either people management (eg performance appraisals) or performance monitoring (eg reporting on key performance indicators). However, the concept of performance management is now much wider and includes: strategic planning, performance measurement and monitoring, business intelligence, analytics, people management, financial planning and budgeting, data warehousing, risk management, business process re-engineering, knowledge management, performance scorecards, and key performance indicators (KPIs).

The reference to KPIs indicates how performance management plays a crucial role in checking an organisation's progress towards its objectives. **KPIs** should monitor how well a business is performing against its **critical success factors** (CSFs). In turn, the CSFs are the aspects of an organisation's activity which are central to its future success.

A performance management system should be derived from the company's strategic **objectives** so that it supports those objectives. It should also change over time as the strategies of the organisation change and should be flexible enough to remain coherent with the objectives of the organisation.

A performance management system should have clear links between performance measures at the **different hierarchical levels of the organisation** so that all departments and areas strive towards the same goals. Examples of models of measurement that seek to capture this alignment include the **balanced scorecard** and the **performance pyramid**. These models are considered in more detail later in this chapter.

By definition, however, in order for an organisation to be able to manage its performance – and to ensure its goals are being met – it must first have established its goals and objectives. In this respect, strategic planning (establishing an organisation's mission, objectives and goals) is a prerequisite before any performance management can take place. Once an organisation's goals have been set, and its operational performance targets have been set, then it can begin to measure whether these goals and targets are being achieved.

In this way, performance **measurement** is an important control in the organisation. However, performance also needs to be **managed** via judicious target setting that reinforces strategic goals and objectives.

1.2 Control systems

Introduction

All systems of control can be analysed using the **cybernetic model**. The essence of this model is the **feedback** of control action to the controlled process: the control action itself being generated from the comparison of actual results with what was planned.

1.2.1 Cybernetic control

To some extent, planning and controlling are two sides of a single coin, since a plan is of little value if it is not put into action, while a system of control can only be effective if the people running it know what it is they are trying to achieve.

In the cybernetic system, an objective is established: for the organisation, this might be the current year's budget. Actual achievement is measured, perhaps by means of monthly reports, and a process of comparison takes place. In the organisation, managers fulfil this role by comparing budget and actual figures. They then take control action to make up for any failure to achieve the plan. This control action feeds back into the activity of the organisation and its effects should become apparent in the next monthly report. This **feedback loop** is the essence of any control system, though sometimes it may be difficult to discern its existence and operation.

KEY TERMS

FEEDBACK occurs when the results (outputs) of a system are used to control it, by adjusting the input or behaviour of the system. Businesses use feedback information to control their performance.

SINGLE LOOP FEEDBACK results in the system's behaviour being altered to meet the plan.

DOUBLE LOOP FEEDBACK can result in changes to the plan itself.

Emmanuel *et al* describe **four necessary conditions that must be satisfied before any process can be said to be controlled**. These will help us to put control into a wider context still.

(a) **Objectives** for the process being controlled must exist, for without an aim or purpose control has no meaning.

(b) The **output of** the process must be **measurable** in terms of the dimensions defined by the objectives.

(c) A **predictive model** of the process being controlled is required so that causes for the non-attainment of objectives can be determined and proposed corrective actions evaluated.

(d) There must be a **capability of taking action** so that deviations of attainment from objectives can be reduced.

It is important to understand that this concept of control involves more than just measuring results and taking corrective action. Control in the broad sense embraces the formulation of objectives – deciding what the things that need to be done are – as well as monitoring their attainment by way of feedback. Management accountants working in senior management will be major contributors to the objective-setting process for two reasons.

(a) As Drucker pointed out, the most crucial aspect of performance management in business is economic success; therefore **financial targets remain vital ones**.

(b) Targets are only useful if **performance can be measured**: performance measurement is a major aspect of management accountancy.

1.3 Performance measurement

Performance measurement aims to assess how well something or somebody is doing in relation to previous or expected activity, or in comparison with other processes or people.

KEY TERM

PERFORMANCE MEASUREMENT is the 'process of assessing the proficiency with which a reporting entity succeeds, by the economic acquisition of resources and their efficient and effective development, in achieving its objectives. Performance measures may be based on non-financial as well as on financial information'.

(CIMA Official Terminology)

1.3.1 The purpose of performance measurement

Performance measurement has become such an accepted part of business life that sometimes we lose sight of its purpose.

(a)   Performance measurement is part of the overall cybernetic (or feedback) control system, providing the essential **feedback** spur to any necessary control action.

(b)   It is a major input into communications to **stakeholder groups**, including the widening field of corporate reporting.

(c)   It is intimately linked to **incentives** and **performance management** systems, providing evidence of results against agreed objectives.

(d)   Motivation may be enhanced since managers will seek to achieve satisfactory performance in areas that are measured.

Neely summarised the purpose of performance measurement in his '**Four CPs of Performance Measurement**':

(a)   **Check Position** – how well are we doing? (This should look at both financial and non-financial factors.)

(b)   **Communicate Position** – to stakeholders so that they know how the business is performing.

(c)   **Confirm Priorities** – setting targets for business and developing action plans to help achieve them.

(d)   **Compel Progress** – measuring performance is a strong driver for change, especially if it is linked to reward.

1.3.2 Approaches to performance measurement

An important aspect of the management accountant's role is to help implement and control strategies through performance measurement.

There are a number of key areas to consider when determining the approach to adopt towards performance evaluation in a given set of circumstances.

Area to consider	Comments
What is evaluated?	Some approaches concentrate on the performance of the organisation as a whole, while others look at strategic business units, divisions, functions or the individual.
Who wants the evaluation?	Some approaches are based on the viewpoint of a single interest group such as investors. Others take in the views of various interest groups (for example employees).
What are the objectives of the organisation?	Is there a single goal or many goals? Are the goals short or long term?
Are quantitative measures or qualitative measures appropriate?	Quantitative measures (eg ROI or number of rejects) may not seem relevant but qualitative measures (eg customer satisfaction) are sometimes perceived to be too subjective.

Area to consider	Comments
What targets are used to assess performance?	Measures are meaningless unless they are compared against something. Common sources of comparison are historic figures, standards/budgets, similar external activities, similar internal activities, indices and trends over time.

Question 11.1	Product leadership

Learning outcome D1(b)

How could product leadership be measured, besides considering market share?

1.4 Budgets as a control mechanism

KEY TERM

BUDGETARY CONTROL is the process whereby the 'master budget, devolved to responsibility centres, allows continuous monitoring of actual results versus budget, either to secure by individual action the budget objectives or to provide a basis for budget revision'. *(CIMA Official Terminology)*

Budgets are a vital control mechanism in organisations, and offer an important way of **linking strategy to operations**. Budgets provide a quantitative expression of how strategic plans will be implemented over a period of time, and as such they play a key role in **communicating ideas** and **performance targets** across different departments and business units.

We can summarise the purposes of budgets through the mnemonic 'PRIME':

Purpose	Comment
Planning	Budget holders are forced to plan how to achieve targets that should ensure the organisation's overall strategic plan is achieved (eg for sales, margins, quality levels).
	The budgeted planning process should also help to co-ordinate aims and activities across different departments.
Responsibility	Budgets help allocate responsibility, and specify which managers control which costs.
	(However, the ideas of accountability and control are important here. Managers' performance should only be assessed in relation to the costs and resources which they control.)
Integration	The process of preparing budgets should help ensure that the planned activities of one area of an organisation do not conflict with another. (For example, if the production department forecasts an increase in production, but the sales department forecast a decrease in sales.)
Motivation	If managers and employees are involved in setting the budget targets, this will increase their motivation in trying to achieve the targets.
	However, it is important that budget targets are felt to be achievable, otherwise they will serve to be demotivating.
Evaluation	Budgets allow trends in performance to be identified and investigated. For example, if actual performance is falling below budget, the reasons for the variance can be investigated, and action taken to correct the shortfall as necessary.
	In this respect, budgets act as a key strategic control, and they can be used for both financial control (eg sales, profits) and non-financial control (eg error rates, customer satisfaction levels).

Budgets can be used for both planning and control by management, and are widely recognised as management tools which can facilitate the management task of leading a business towards its goals.

In effect, planning and control are two sides of the same coin. The budget reflects an organisation's objectives and targets (plans) – for example, its expected sales for the coming year, and the resources it anticipates it will need to achieve those sales. However, during the year, the organisation's management will compare actual performance with budget, and should take any corrective actions it deems necessary if actual performance is worse than budget.

However, budgets can sometimes also have negative effects. These include:

(a) There is no incentive to try to achieve budgeted figures if the budget is unrealistic.

(b) A manager may build slack into their budget targets to ensure the budget can be met.

(c) A manager may simply aim to 'achieve' the target but do no more than that.

(d) A manager may go on a 'spending spree' if budgeted funds remain unspent.

(e) The budget may focus on short-term results rather than longer-term consequences (eg cutting marketing expenditure in order to meet budgeted operating profit in one year, but potentially sacrificing future growth as a result).

Some of these negative effects also illustrate the distinction between strategic and operational levels of a business. For example, the managers who set the budgets are often not responsible for attaining them, and therefore targets which managers think are realistic at a strategic level may be considered unrealistic once they are translated into an operation level.

Similarly, an operational manager may seek to reduce spending in the short term (on marketing, in the illustration above) whereas that spending may have generated greater than proportional benefits in the future, and so would have benefited the whole organisation in the longer term.

This again highlights the importance of **goal congruence** within organisations, but the 'integration' aspect of budgeting should also help to encourage **communication** and **co-ordination** between the different parts of an organisation, which will be necessary to achieve goal congruence.

Section summary

Controls are vital for an organisation to assess how well it is performing against its strategic plans. However, plans and controls need to be reviewed together. A plan is of little use if it is not put into action, while a system of control can only be effective if the people overseeing it know what they are trying to achieve.

2 Strategic control and critical success factors (CSFs)

Introduction

In Chapter 2 earlier in this Study Text, we looked at strategic planning, and we identified the way organisations need to translate their mission into strategic objectives and goals.

In turn, if an organisation is going to achieve its goals, it will have to ensure it performs well in key areas. These key areas can be identified as **critical success factors**.

KEY TERM

A CRITICAL SUCCESS FACTOR (CSF) is 'An element of the organisational activity which is central to its future success. CSFs may change over time, and may include items such as product, quality, employee attitudes, manufacturing flexibility and brand awareness'.

(CIMA Official Terminology)

CSFs are those components of strategy which are particularly valued by customers, and therefore at which the organisation must excel to outperform its competitors. As such, CSFs are underpinned by the core competences which will lead to an organisation's success.

2.1 Objectives, CSFs and key performance indicators (KPIs)

It is important to understand how objectives, CSFs and KPIs relate to each other.

Once an organisation has established its objectives, it needs to identify the key factors and processes that will **enable it to achieve those objectives**. These key factors are the CSFs – in effect, the building blocks which will enable an organisation to implement its mission and thereby achieve future success.

In an effective organisation, the factors that are crucial to success will influence all aspects of its operations, especially those relating to people. For example, if a company identifies excellent customer service as a CSF, then its recruitment process, training, appraisal and reward systems should all be geared towards promoting customer-service skills in its staff.

However, once an organisation has identified its CSFs, it also needs to know whether it is delivering on them. This is done by using KPIs, which **measure how well the organisation** is performing against its CSFs. KPIs are the hard data which tell the organisation how well it is performing. KPIs must be measurable.

Remember, in Chapter 2 we introduced the idea of a hierarchy in which CSFs and KPIs support an organisation's ability to achieve its mission and objectives.

An organisation's mission expresses its fundamental objectives. CSFs are the building blocks which will enable it to implement its mission and achieve future success. KPIs are the measures which indicate whether or not the CSFs are being achieved. In this context, when thinking about KPIs, it could also be useful to consider whether they are 'SMART'.

2.1.1 Example of CSFs and KPIs

We can illustrate the relationship between objectives, CSFs and KPIs by looking at an example of a supermarket.

Let us assume it has defined **two of its objectives** as follows:

*   To ensure the loyalty of its customers ('to generate lifetime loyalty')
*   To ensure its prices are at least 2% cheaper than the average of rival supermarkets' ('to create value for customers')

The supermarket then needs to identify the **CSFs** which will help it achieve those objectives. Possible CSFs could be:

*   Stocking the goods that customers most want to buy
*   Making the shopping experience as pleasant as possible
*   Refining internal processes to operate the business on a cost-effective basis
*   Using economies of scale to source appropriate goods as cheaply as possible

Then in order to **measure how well it is performing** against these CSFs, the supermarket needs to set **KPIs**. Example KPIs could be:

*   The proportion of goods taking more than a week to sell
*   Results of customer feedback surveys
*   Percentage of customers who are repeat customers
*   Market share
*   Cost measures and progress against savings targets
*   Cost savings in procurement; results of benchmarking prices or costs against rivals

2.1.2 CSFs and information systems

In Chapter 7 we highlighted that managers need information for decision making and control. By virtue of being the areas in which an organisation needs to outperform its competitors if it is to be successful, CSFs can also be used to help determine the information requirements for an organisation's executive information systems (ie because they identify the areas of performance about which managers need most information).

It will be difficult and expensive to capture, store and analyse all of the various types of information which could be available for decision making and control – particularly with the advent of 'Big Data'. Therefore managers need to determine, in advance, what is most relevant to them, so that information systems can be tailored to focus on those areas, and provide managers with the information which is most relevant to them.

In this respect, CSFs could also act as a trigger for change in relation to an organisation's information systems. If an organisation's current information systems cannot provide managers with the information they need to monitor performance in key business areas, then the systems will need to be changed to ensure that they can provide that information in future. For example, if an organisation's information systems focus primarily on reporting financial performance, but the organisation has identified quality as being a CSF, then it will need to ensure that it captures and analyses information about the quality of its products or services.

2.1.3 CSFs and behaviour

It is also important to consider the potential impact of CSFs and KPIs on behaviour. Once certain areas of performance are highlighted as 'key' – and staff know that performance in those areas is being measured – staff are likely to focus on those areas, possibly at the expense of other areas.

In this respect, it is vital that the range of indicators selected is balanced across the organisation as a whole. This is one of the reasons which could encourage an organisation to use multidimensional performance measures – such as the balanced scorecard.

In order to be successful, organisations have to perform well across a range of key processes. Therefore CSFs and KPIs should focus on key operational processes, and **should not focus only on financial performance**.

 Thinking about an organisation's stakeholders could also be instructive here. A company's shareholders (as its owners) will have a keen interest in its performance, primarily its financial performance.

However, shareholders are not the only stakeholders, and performance measures will also be required to reflect the interests of other key stakeholders – in particular customers.

Also, remember that not-for-profit organisations, charities or government bodies are likely to have a different range of performance measures to those of commercial organisations.

Michael Goold and John Quinn write: 'Most companies take pride in fostering a performance-driven culture that emphasises profitability as the key goal for business management ... [but] ... too much emphasis on budgetary control and short-term profit can disguise strategic problems'.

2.2 Gaps and false alarms

Many firms have spent time measuring the wrong things – the trick is to remove 'false alarms' from performance measures and replace them with measures that fill gaps in coverage. **Gaps** (important areas which are neglected) include:

- New product introduction
- Customer satisfaction
- Employee involvement

However, a number of problems could emerge if firms concentrate on measuring gaps, and then look for ways of filling them.

- Short-term measures predominate over long-term measures

- Financial proxies (eg EPS) predominate over reality

- Efficiency takes precedence over effectiveness

- Economy takes precedence over efficiency

- Individual department performance measures take precedence over how departments are linked together to satisfy the customers

2.3 The product life cycle and control systems

In Chapter 4 earlier in this Study Text, we discussed the concept of the product life cycle and the importance of organisations trying to develop a balanced portfolio of products, at different stages in their life cycles.

However, the product life cycle can also be relevant when deciding upon CSFs and performance measures, and the information required in relation to them. The table below illustrates some possible factors which could be considered at each stage of the life cycle.

	Introduction	Growth	Maturity	Decline
Information needed	The environment Potential market size and buyer value	Market growth Market share Marketing effectiveness Competitor information and effectiveness of marketing	Competitors' costs Limiting factors	Rate of decline When to exit Realisable asset values
Critical success factors	Time to develop and launch	Growth in share Sustainable competitive advantage	Contribution per unit of limiting factor Customer retention rates	None
Performance measures	Evaluate using DCF of life cycle cash flows Lead indicators of market success, eg advertising effectiveness, distributor acceptance	DCF evaluation of marketing costs Specific marketing objectives Market share	ROI Profit margin Operating cash flow Market share	Free cash flow compared with opportunity costs of assets used

Section summary

Strategic control is bound up with measurement of performance, which often tends to be based on financial criteria. Techniques for strategic control suggest that companies develop strategic milestones (eg for market share) to monitor the achievement of strategic objectives, as a counterweight to purely financial issues.

Critical success factors are the few key areas where things must go right for the organisation to flourish.

3 Performance measures: financial and non-financial

Introduction

Performance measures must be relevant both to a clear objective and to operational methods, and their production must be cost effective.

Although measuring financial performance is important, if an organisation focuses solely on financial performance measures, other critical aspects of performance could get overlooked.

3.1 Deciding what measures to use

It should be obvious that different measures will be required, and appropriate, for different businesses. Determining which measures are used in a particular case will require **preliminary investigations** along the following lines.

(a)   The **objectives/mission** of the organisation must be **clearly formulated** so that when the factors critical to the success of the mission have been identified they can be translated into performance indicators.

(b)   **Measures** must be **relevant** to the way the organisation operates. Managers themselves must believe the indicators are useful.

(c)   **The costs and benefits of providing resources** (people, equipment and time to collect and analyse information) to produce a performance indicator must be carefully **weighed up.**

3.2 Financial modelling and performance measurement

Financial modelling might assist in performance evaluation in the following ways:

(a)   **Identifying the variables** involved in performing tasks and the relationships between them. This is necessary so that the model can be built in the first place. Model building therefore shows what should be measured, helps to explain how a particular level of performance can be achieved, and identifies factors in performance that the organisation cannot expect to control.

(b)   **Setting targets for future performance.** The most obvious example of this is the budgetary control system described above.

(c)   **Monitoring actual performance.** A flexible budget is a good example of a financial model that is used in this way.

(d)   **Co-ordinating long-term strategic plans with short-term operational actions.** Modelling can reflect the dynamic nature of the real world and evaluate how likely it is that short-term actions will achieve the longer-term plan, given new conditions.

3.3 Profitability, activity and productivity

In general, there are three possible **points of reference for measurement**:

(a) **Profitability**

Profit has two components: **cost and income**. All parts of an organisation and all activities within it incur costs, and so their success needs to be judged in relation to cost. Only some parts of an organisation receive income, and their success should be judged in terms of both cost and income.

(b) **Activity**

All parts of an organisation are also engaged in activities (activities cause costs). Activity measures could include:

(i) Number of orders received from customers, a measure of the effectiveness of marketing

(ii) Number of machine breakdowns attended to by the repairs and maintenance department

Each of these items could be measured in terms of **physical numbers**, **monetary value**, or **time spent**.

(c) **Productivity**

This is the quantity of the product or service produced in relation to the resources put in; for example, so many units produced per hour or per employee. It defines how efficiently resources are being used.

The **dividing line between productivity and activity is thin**, because every activity could be said to have some 'product', or if not can be measured in terms of lost units of product or service.

Question 11.2	Invoicing

Learning outcome D1(b)

An invoicing assistant works in a department with 3 colleagues. She is paid £16,000 per annum. The department typically handles 10,000 invoices per week.

One morning she spends half an hour on the phone to her grandfather, who lives in Australia, at the company's expense. The cost of the call proves to be £32.

Required

From this scenario identify as many different performance measures as possible, explaining what each is intended to measure. Make any further assumptions you wish.

3.4 Financial performance measures

Financial measures (or **monetary measures**) should be very familiar to you. Here are some examples, accompanied by comments from a single page of the *Financial Times*.

Measure	Comment
Profit	The commonest measure of all. Profit maximisation is usually cited as the main objective of most business organisations: 'ICI increased pre-tax profits to £233m'; 'General Motors... yesterday reported better-than-expected first-quarter net income of $513 (£333m) ...'
Revenue	'The UK businesses contributed £113.9m of total group turnover of £409m'.
Costs	'Sterling's fall benefited pre-tax profits by about £50m while savings from the cost-cutting programme were running at around £100m a quarter'; 'The group interest charge rose from £48m to £61m'.

Measure	Comment
Share price	'The group's shares rose 31p to 1278p despite the market's fall'.
Cash flow	'Cash flow was also continuing to improve, with cash and marketable securities totalling $8.4bn on March 31, up from $8bn at December 31'.

The important point to note here is that the monetary amounts stated **are only given meaning in relation to something else**. Profits are higher than last year's; cash flow has improved compared with last quarter's.

We can generalise the above and give a list of benchmarks against which financial results are usually placed so as to become measures.

- **Budgeted** sales, costs and profits
- **Standards** in a standard costing system
- The **trend** over time (last year/this year, say)
- The **results of other parts** of the business
- The **results of other businesses**
- The **economy** in general
- **Future potential** (eg a new business in terms of nearness to breaking even)

3.5 The profit measure

Profit has both advantages and disadvantages as a measure of performance.

Measure	Comment
Single criterion.	Easier to manage, as the sole concern is the effect on the bottom line.
Analysis has a clear objective: ie the effect on future profits.	Easier than cost/benefit analysis, for example.
A broad performance measure that incorporates all other measures.	'If it does not affect profit it can be ignored.'
Enables decentralisation.	Managers have the delegated powers to achieve divisional (and therefore Group) profit.
Profitability measures (eg ROI) can compare all profit-making operations even if they are not alike.	This ignores the balance between risk and return.
Encourages **short-termism** and focus on the annual cycle, at the expense of long-term performance.	Examples: cutting discretionary revenue investments, manipulating of accounting rules, building up inventories.
Profit differs from **economic income**.	
A firm has to satisfy **stakeholders** other than shareholders, such as the Government and the local community.	This may include environmental/ethical performance measures.
Liquidity is at least as important as profit.	Most business failures derive from liquidity crises.
Profit should be related to **risk**, not just capital employed.	Rarely done.
Profits can **fluctuate** in times of rapid change.	For example, as a result of exchange rate volatility.
Profit measures cannot easily be used to motivate **cost centre** managers.	They do not control profit.

Measure	Comment
Not useful for new businesses.	Most start-ups will be unprofitable for at least two years.
Easily manipulated.	Especially over a single period: think back to your cost accounting studies and the effect of stock changes on profit under absorption costing, for example.
Pure profit-based measures do not consider **capital spending**.	Growth in asset levels can be uncontrolled; alternatively, productive capacity may be allowed to decline.

3.5.1 Ratios

Ratios are a **useful** way of measuring performance for a number of reasons.

(a) It is easier to look at **changes over time** by comparing ratios in one time period with the corresponding ratios for periods in the past.

(b) Ratios are often **easier to understand** than absolute measures of physical quantities or money values. For example, it is easier to understand that 'productivity in March was 94%' than 'there was an adverse labour efficiency variance in March of $3,600'.

(c) Ratios relate one item to another, and so help to **put performance into context**. For example, the profit/sales ratio sets profit in the context of how much has been earned per $1 of sales, and so shows how wide or narrow profit margins are.

(d) Ratios can be **used as targets**. In particular, targets can be set for ROI, profit/sales, asset turnover, capacity fill and productivity. Managers will then take decisions which will enable them to achieve their targets.

(e) Ratios provide a way of **summarising an organisation's results**, and **comparing them with similar organisations**.

3.5.2 Percentages

A percentage expresses one number as a proportion of another and gives meaning to absolute numbers.

Measure	Comment
Market share	A company may aim to achieve a 25% share of the total market for its product, and measure both its marketing department and the quality of the product against this.
Capacity levels	These are usually measured in percentages. 'Factory A is working at 20% below full capacity' is an example which indicates relative inefficiency.
Wastage	This is sometimes expressed in percentage terms. 'Normal loss' may be 10%, a measure of inefficiency.
Staff turnover	This is often measured in this way. In the catering industry for example, staff turnover is typically greater than 100%, and so a hotel with a lower percentage could take this as an indicator both of the experience of its staff and of how well it is treating them.

3.6 Quantitative and qualitative performance measures

It is possible to distinguish between **quantitative information**, which is **capable of being expressed in numbers**, and **qualitative information**, which **can only be expressed in numerical terms with difficulty**.

An example of a **quantitative performance measure** is 'You have been late for work twice this week and it's only Tuesday!'. An example of a qualitative performance measure is 'My bed is very comfortable'.

The first measure is likely to find its way into a staff appraisal report. The second would feature in a bed manufacturer's customer satisfaction survey. Both are indicators of whether their subjects are doing as good a job as they are required to do.

Qualitative measures are by nature **subjective and judgemental** but this does not mean that they are not valuable. They are especially valuable when they are derived from several different sources because then they can be expressed in a mixture of quantitative and qualitative terms which is more meaningful overall: 'seven out of ten customers think our beds are very comfortable' is a quantitative measure of customer satisfaction as well as a **qualitative** measure of the perceived performance of the beds.

3.7 Non-financial performance measures

KEY TERM

NON-FINANCIAL PERFORMANCE MEASURES are 'measures of performance based on non-financial information which may originate in and be used by operating departments to monitor and control their activities without any accounting input. Non-financial performance measures may give a more timely indication of the levels of performance achieved than financial measures do, and may be less susceptible to distortion by factors such as uncontrollable variations in the effect of market forces on operations.'

(CIMA Official Terminology)

Here are some examples of non-financial performance measures.

Areas assessed	Performance measure
Service quality	Number of complaints Proportion of repeat bookings Customer waiting time On-time deliveries
Production performance	Set-up times Number of suppliers Days' inventory in hand Output per employee Material yield percentage Schedule adherence Proportion of output requiring rework Manufacturing lead times
Marketing effectiveness	Trend in market share Sales volume growth Customer visits per salesperson Client contact hours per salesperson Sales volume forecast versus actual Number of customers Customer survey response information
Personnel	Number of complaints received Staff turnover Days lost through absenteeism Days lost through accidents/sickness Training time per employee

Question 11.3

Hotel

Learning outcome D1(b)

The Taybridge Hotel is a luxury hotel, on the outskirts of a town in the south west of England. The local area is popular with tourists. Like all of the other hotels in the area, the Taybridge is privately owned, and is not part of a chain. Although the Taybridge has a restaurant and a gym, these are for residents' use only.

Required

Suggest some suitable performance criteria for the Taybridge Hotel.

3.7.1 The importance of measuring non-financial performance

An important element of performance management is developing appropriate performance metrics. As far as possible, performance measures should be linked to a company's strategy, value drivers and CSFs, as well as short-term and long-term goals. Crucially, CSFs and organisational goals are often non-financial, which means that the performance measures used to assess how well they are being achieved also need to be non-financial.

Therefore, while it is important for organisations to measure and monitor their financial performance, there are likely to be disadvantages to focusing solely on financial performance, as discussed below.

3.7.2 Concentration on too few variables

If performance measurement systems focus entirely on those items which can be expressed in monetary terms, there is a danger managers will **concentrate solely on those variables** and ignore other important variables that cannot be expressed in monetary terms.

For example, pressure from senior management to **cut costs and raise productivity** will produce **short-term benefits** in cost control but, in the **long term**, managerial performance and motivation is likely to be affected, labour turnover will increase and product quality will fall.

Reductions in cost can easily be measured and recorded in performance reports, employee morale cannot. Performance reports should therefore include not only costs and revenues but also other important variables, to give an indication of expected future results from present activity.

Moreover, in an increasingly competitive business environment, price is only one of the factors which may affect a consumer's purchasing decision. Companies (particularly those pursuing differentiation strategies) are also competing in terms of **product quality**, **delivery**, **reliability**, **after-sales service** and **customer satisfaction**. Research and development, **innovation** and intellectual property could also be important elements of an organisation's competitive advantage. And if these variables are important elements in a company achieving its strategy successfully, then it follows that the company should also measure its performance in respect of them.

In this context it could also be useful to think of a company's relationship with its customers.

Many companies are now looking to use **relationship marketing** techniques to help build longer-term relationships and loyalty among their customers. The quality of service given to customers (including after-sales service) and customer satisfaction are likely to be very important in maintaining these relationships with customers.

This again highlights the importance of measuring how well a company is performing in such areas.

3.7.3 Lack of information about quality

Traditional responsibility accounting systems also fail to provide **information on the quality or importance of operations**. Drury provides the following example:

> 'Consider a situation where a purchasing department regularly achieved the budget for all expense items. The responsibility performance reporting system therefore suggests that the department was well managed. However, the department provided a poor service to the production departments. Low-cost suppliers were selected who provided poor quality materials and frequently failed to meet delivery dates. This caused much wasted effort in chasing up orders and prejudiced the company's ability to deliver to its customers on time.'

3.7.4 Measuring success, not ensuring success

Financial performance indicators have been said to simply **measure success**. What organisations also require, however, are performance **indicators that ensure success**. Some of these indicators, which are **linked** to an organisation's **CSFs** such as quality and flexibility, will be **non-financial** in nature.

For example, consider a pizza delivery company. When a customer is choosing which pizza company to buy their pizza from, key factors in their decision will be the price of the pizza, the toppings available and the taste of the pizza. However, they could also be influenced by the time they will have to wait for their pizza to be delivered. If one company can deliver their pizza in 20 minutes, but another one says they will only be able to deliver the pizza in an hour, there is a good chance the customer will choose to place their order with the first company.

It is possible that the speed of delivery could even become a factor which one of the pizza delivery companies uses to differentiate itself from its rivals, in which case it will be very important for that company to measure how long it takes to deliver its pizzas to its customers, because 'delivery time' has effectively become one of its CSFs.

Equally, non-financial performance indicators can identify areas where an organisation's **performance is currently relatively weak**, and therefore needs to be improved in order to make the organisation more competitive. For instance, in the pizza delivery example, the second company might find it needs to reduce the time it takes to deliver its pizzas to make itself more competitive.

3.7.5 Leading and lagging indicators

The way in which non-financial indicators can allow an organisation to assess how well it is performing against its CSFs also means they can act as leading indicators whereas most traditional financial indicators tend to be lagging indicators, reporting on past performance and past events.

As such, lagging indicators do not necessarily help managers or directors to understand the future challenges an organisation will face. By contrast, leading indicators can point to future performance successes or problems. For example, declining customer satisfaction levels could point to future revenue issues and a longer-term erosion of the value of a company's brand.

3.7.6 Not linked to long-term organisational strategies

Another issue with financial performance measurement systems is that they generally focus on **annual or short-term performance** (against financial targets) and so may not be directly linked to longer-term organisation objectives. For example, financial performance measures will not assess how well an organisation is **meeting customer requirements**.

However, non-financial objectives (such as achieving customer loyalty, or new product development) may be vital in achieving – and sustaining – profitability, competitiveness and other longer-term strategic goals.

Once again, there is potentially a **trade-off between the short term and the long term** here. For example, new product development may be an important strategic goal, but the costs involved in research and development may hinder short-term accounting performance.

3.8 Interaction of financial and non-financial performance indicators

The reference to new product development in the previous section also highlights the **importance of the interaction between financial and non-financial performance indicators**. For example, measuring the number of new products developed in a period is a non-financial performance indicator, but developing new products is only valuable to an organisation if they help it increase revenue and profitability.

Financial and non-financial performance indicators interact with each other even though they measure separate activities or aspects of performance.

The table in Section 3.7 above lists a number of non-financial performance indicators. Performance indicators looking at production performance, for example, **measure activity but not cost**. However, activity and cost are linked. For instance, if there are problems with the **quality** of output from a production process, then the goods produced will have to be reworked and fixed before they can be shipped to customers. This reworking will add to **production costs**. Therefore, if the organisation improves quality standards in its processes, reworking costs will be reduced.

Equally, if the organisation is having to rework goods, this may delay production schedules. However, if the organisation also has a target for **on-time deliveries** it could face a dilemma. If the goods are delayed in production, then they may have to be delivered by express courier or some other out of hours delivery service to ensure they are delivered on time. However, this would increase delivery costs compared with a standard delivery service. So, if management want to focus on the cost of deliveries, they may have to accept a lower number of on-time deliveries. However, in turn, if customers do not receive their goods on time, they may not place any repeat orders with the company.

This illustrates the different aspects of both financial and non-financial performance that management need to consider, but also indicates that they may, on occasion, need to accept a trade-off between the two.

Another common example of this is the relationship between market share (non-financial) and profit margin (financial). If an organisation is trying to increase its **market share**, it may try to do this by **discounting** its products or offering some kind of **special offer** on them. While the discounts and offers may enable the organisation to gain market share (at least in the short term before competitors react), they may also lead to lower profit margins (for example as discounts reduce the revenue received per product sold).

We can also see the link between financial and non-financial performance in relation to **customer service**. For example, if customers receive good-quality service from an organisation, they are more likely to be loyal to that organisation and use it again than if they have received poor service. In this way, there can be a direct link between good-quality service, customer retention, and future sales revenue.

The balanced scorecard (discussed in Section 4) explicitly combines financial and non-financial performance indicators through its four perspectives of: financial; customer; internal business; and innovation and learning performance. By integrating these four perspectives, the scorecard highlights the importance of non-financial aspects of performance (eg customers, internal process efficiency) in delivering financial success for an organisation.

The performance pyramid (Section 5) and Fitzgerald and Moon's building block model (Section 6) also highlight how non-financial aspects of performance are crucial in shaping an organisation's financial performance.

However, while it can be beneficial to monitor performance in a range of areas, managers should avoid measuring too many aspects of performance. Instead they must concentrate on the metrics that are most important (ie **key** performance indicators), in order to avoid succumbing to information overload.

Nonetheless, when identifying which metrics to measure, it is important to balance traditional financial measures with non-financial ones.

In particular, measures should be selected to provide a balance of leading and lagging indicators. Most traditional, financial performance measures are lagging indicators, connected with past performance and past events. However, such indicators do not necessarily help managers or directors to understand the future challenges an organisation will face.

By contrast, leading indicators can point to future performance successes or problems. For example, declining customer satisfaction levels could point to future revenue issues and a longer-term erosion of the value of a company's brand.

 Remember also the distinction we highlighted in Chapter 1 between strategic management accounting and 'traditional' management accounting. One of the aspects which distinguishes strategic management accounting is the emphasis placed on non-financial factors (in addition to financial ones).

3.9 The performance measurement manifesto

Eccles argues that financial measures alone are inadequate for monitoring the progress of business strategies based on creating customer value, satisfaction and quality, partly because they are **historical** in nature and partly because they cannot measure current progress with such strategies directly. He also notes the impulse to **short-termism** given by such measures.

In the same way that we have already done in this section, Eccles argues there is a need for a performance measurement system that includes both financial and non-financial measures. The measures chosen must be **integrated**, so that the potential for discarding non-financial measures that conflict with the financial ones is limited. Eccles argues that too often firms prioritise financial measures above non-financial ones, and if the two clash the financial priorities take precedence. However, Eccles points out that **non-financial measures** such as quality, customer satisfaction and market are now equally important as purely financial measures.

For Eccles, the development of a good system of performance measurement requires activity in five areas.

(a)   The **information architecture** must be developed. This requires the identification of performance measures that relate to strategy and the gradual, iterative development of systems to capture the required data.

(b)   An appropriate **information technology strategy** must be established.

(c)   The company's **incentives system** must be aligned with its performance measures. Eccles proposes that qualitative factors should be addressed by the incentive system.

(d)   **External influences** must be acknowledged and used. For example, benchmarking against other organisations may be used, while providers of capital should be persuaded to accept the validity of non-financial measures.

(e)   **Manage the implementation** of the four areas above by appointing a person to be responsible overall as well as department agents.

3.10 Triple bottom line

On several occasions we have highlighted the potential danger that a focus on financial performance measures only will lead to a short-termist approach in organisations.

In this respect, the concept of 'triple bottom line' which we discussed in Chapter 2 could also be important, because it looks at **social responsibility** and the longer-term **sustainability** of an organisation's actions, rather than their short-term consequences.

By including metrics linked to the triple bottom line (social justice; environmental quality; economic prosperity) in its performance measurement system, an organisation should be encouraged to act in a more socially responsible manner.

However, there could be practical difficulties associated with incorporating a triple bottom line approach into an organisation's performance measurement system – in particular, relating to how the organisation measures (or quantifies) the level of waste or emissions it produces.

Equally, at a more general level, as we noted in our discussions of CSR in Chapter 2, there may be some critics who argue that a company's primary aim should be to maximise the wealth it generates for its shareholders, rather than focusing on the social and environmental consequences of its action. For example, proposals to improve working conditions in its factories or to reduce emissions would help a company's performance in relation to the triple bottom line, but if those proposals lead to a reduction in profits in the short term this could lead to them being opposed by shareholders who are more interested in the level of profits the company is generating.

3.11 Value for money audits

Value for money audits can be seen as being of particular relevance in not-for-profit organisations. Such an audit focuses on **economy**, **efficiency** and **effectiveness**. These measures may be in conflict with each other. To take the example of higher education, larger class sizes may be **economical** in their use of teaching resources, but are not necessarily **effective** in creating the best learning environment.

Section summary

Performance measures can be both financial and non-financial. A growing recognition of the limitations of relying solely on financial performance measures has led to non-financial measures being developed, based on operational performance.

Nonetheless, commercial organisations need to remember that maximising profit is likely to remain one of their key goals, so they cannot ignore the financial aspect of performance.

4 The balanced scorecard

Introduction

The balanced scorecard tries to integrate the different measures of performance by highlighting the linkages between operating and financial performance. This scorecard offers four perspectives on performance:

- Financial
- Customer
- Innovation and learning
- Internal business

A theme so far has been that financial measurements do not capture all the strategic realities of the business, but it is equally important that financial measurements are not overlooked. A failure to attend to the 'numbers' can rapidly lead to failure of the business.

Nonetheless, financial measurements do not capture all the strategic realities of a business so businesses need to look at both financial and non-financial measures. A technique which has been developed to integrate the various features (financial and non-financial) of corporate success and to make organisations more strategy focused is Kaplan and Norton's **balanced scorecard**.

Business failures

The global recession in 2007–8 meant that there were articles about business failures almost every day in the newspapers. These articles often mentioned the reason given for the failure, and the state of economy was often portrayed as the number one cause.

However, this tended to obscure a rather more painful truth. The reason for the business failure was often the business itself.

An article in a local newspaper in Tupelo, Mississippi, illustrated this point. The article looked at three food outlets in the town which had failed in 2009, and noted the owners' reasons for the failure. The reasons given were 'poor timing and the economy'.

However, customers who had been to the businesses noted that all three had three things in common: high prices, poor service and mediocre food.

One in particular – a sandwich shop – stood out. It had an ordering process that involved standing in line to order, and then moving to another station and standing in line to repeat your order and pay for it. The total wait for an expensive and really poor take-out sandwich was over 45 minutes. The shop was located in a mall, and four units away from a Mexican restaurant that was not only surviving but positively thriving. So it seems the economy was not the main reason for business failure after all!

The more pertinent point is that businesses – and particularly small businesses – are often launched and operated without the resources needed to succeed. To be successful, a business needs to supply a cost effective solution to customer needs.

If businesses don't understand their markets, their customers or their competition, and if they don't have a clear vision or direction which is executed by management, they are likely to fail.

(Adapted from article, 'Who's to blame for most business failures' on www.articlesbase.com, 19 January 2010)

The BALANCED SCORECARD approach is 'an approach to the provision of information to management to assist strategic policy formulation and achievement. It emphasises the need to provide the user with a set of information which addresses all relevant areas of performance in an objective and unbiased fashion. The information provided may include both financial and non-financial elements, and cover areas such as profitability, customer satisfaction, internal efficiency and innovation'. *(CIMA Official Terminology)*

The balanced scorecard seeks to translate **mission** and **strategy** into **objectives** and measures, and focuses on **four different perspectives**. For each of the four perspectives, the scorecard aims to articulate the **outcomes** an organisation desires, and the **drivers** of those outcomes.

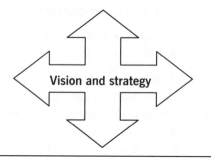

Financial perspective

How should we create value for our shareholders to succeed financially?

(covers traditional measures such as growth, profitability and shareholder value, with measures set through talking directly to the shareholders)

Internal business process

What business processes must we excel at to achieve financial and customer objectives?

Vision and strategy

Customer perspective

To achieve our vision, how should we appear to our customers?
What do new and existing customers value from us?
(cost, quality, reliability etc)

Innovation and learning perspective

How can we continue to create value and maintain the company's competitive position through improvement and change?
(acquisition of new skills; development of new products)

Performance targets are set once the key areas for improvement have been identified, and the balanced scorecard is the **main monthly report**.

The scorecard is **balanced** in the sense that managers are required to think in terms of all four perspectives, to **prevent improvements being made in one area at the expense of another**.

Broadbent and Cullen identify the following **important features** of this approach:

- It looks at both **internal and external matters** concerning the organisation.
- It is related to the key elements of a company's strategy.
- Financial and non-financial measures are linked together.

Kaplan and Norton have found that organisations are using the balanced scorecard to:

- Identify and align strategic initiatives
- Link budgets with strategy
- Align the organisation (structure and processes) with strategy
- Conduct periodic strategic performance reviews with the aim of learning more about, and improving, strategy

Kaplan and Norton suggest that using the balanced scorecard can also help an organisation improve its strategic performance:

(a) The process of identifying key outcomes and drivers should help individuals and divisions become more aware of how their work fits in with the organisation's strategy.

(b) Giving individuals and divisions regular reports on their performance against key measures will help them monitor their own performance, and identify areas for improvement.

(c)   The scorecard as a whole should provide senior management with regular information on how their organisation is performing against key measures, and therefore how well strategies are being implemented.

4.1 Problems with using the scorecard

As with all techniques, problems can arise when the balanced scorecard is applied.

Problem	Explanation
Conflicting measures	Some measures in the scorecard such as research funding and cost reduction may naturally conflict. It is often difficult to determine the balance which will achieve the best results.
Selecting measures	Not only do appropriate measures have to be devised but the number of measures used must be agreed. Care must be taken that the impact of the results is not lost in a sea of information.
	The innovation and learning perspective is, perhaps, the most difficult to measure directly, since much development of human capital will not feed directly into such crude measures as rate of new product launches or even training hours undertaken. It will, rather, improve economy and effectiveness and support the achievement of customer perspective measures.
	When selecting measures it is important to measure those which actually add value to an organisation, not just those that are easy to measure.
Expertise	Measurement is only useful if it initiates appropriate action. Non-financial managers may have difficulty with the usual profit measures. With more measures to consider this problem will be compounded.
	Measures need to be developed by someone who understands the business processes concerned.
Interpretation	Even a financially trained manager may have difficulty in putting the figures into an overall perspective.
Management commitment	The scorecard can only be effective if senior managers commit to it. If they revert to focusing solely on the financial measures they are used to, then the value of introducing additional measures will be reduced.
	In this context, do not overlook the **cost** of the BSC. There will be costs involved in data gathering and in measuring the performance of additional processes.

It may also be worth considering the following issues in relation to using the balanced scorecard.

(a)   It doesn't provide a single aggregate summary performance measure; for example, part of the popularity of ROI or ROCE comes from the fact they provide a convenient summary of how well a business is performing.

(b)   In comparison to measures like EVA (which we discuss in Chapter 12), there is no direct link between the scorecard and shareholder value.

(c)   Culture: Introducing the scorecard may require a shift in corporate culture; for example, in understanding an organisation as a set of processes rather than as departments.

(d)   Equally, implementing the scorecard will require an organisation to move away from looking solely at short-term financial measures, and focus on longer-term strategic measures instead.

The scorecard should be used **flexibly**. The process of deciding **what to measure** forces a business to clarify its strategy. For example, a manufacturing company may find that 50% to 60% of costs are represented by bought-in components, so measurements relating to suppliers could usefully be added to the scorecard. These could include payment terms, lead times, or quality considerations.

4.2 Linkages in the scorecard

Disappointing results might result from a **failure to view all the measures as a whole**. For example, increasing productivity means that fewer employees are needed for a given level of output. Excess capacity can be created by quality improvements. However, these improvements have to be exploited (eg by increasing sales). The **financial element** of the balanced scorecard 'reminds executives that improved quality, response time, productivity or new products, benefit the company only when they are translated into improved financial results', or if they enable the firm to obtain a sustainable competitive advantage.

4.3 Implementing the balanced scorecard

The introduction and practical use of the balanced scorecard is likely to be subject to all the problems associated with balancing long-term strategic progress against the management of short-term tactical imperatives. Kaplan and Norton recognise this and recommend an iterative, four-stage approach to the practical problems involved.

(a)   **Translating the vision**: the organisation's mission must be expressed in a way that has clear operational meaning for each employee.

(b)   **Communicating and linking**: the next stage is to link the vision or mission to departmental and individual objectives, including those that transcend traditional short-term financial goals. This stage highlights an important feature of the scorecard: that it translates strategy into day to day operations.

(c)   **Business planning**: the scorecard is used to prioritise objectives and allocate resources in order to make the best progress towards strategic goals.

(d)   **Feedback and learning**: the organisation learns to use feedback on performance to promote progress against all four perspectives.

4.3.1 Other implications of using the balanced scorecard

(a)   Like all performance measurement schemes, the balanced scorecard can influence behaviour among managers to conform to that required by the strategy. Because of its comprehensive nature, it can be used as a wide-ranging driver of organisational change.

(b)   The scorecard emphasises **processes** rather than **departments**. It can support a competence-based approach to strategy, but this can be confusing for managers and may make it difficult to gain their support.

4.3.2 A word of warning

Kaplan and Norton never intended the balanced scorecard to replace all other performance measurement systems a business may use. They acknowledge that financial measures and financial results remain important, but suggest businesses can use the scorecard to help deliver strategic goals.

Kaplan and Norton have also acknowledged that the scorecard needs to recognise the **linkages** between **strategic**, **tactical** (management) and **operational levels** in organisations. In this context, they recognise that indicators measured in the scorecard often focus on the strategic level, rather than looking at the practical, day to day operational levels.

Increasingly, organisations are looking to be able to identify the linkages between these levels, and to drill down and identify the sources and root causes behind the underperformance at a strategic level.

4.3.3 Strategy maps

As an extension to the balanced scorecard, Kaplan and Norton also developed the idea of strategy maps, which could be used to help implement the scorecard more successfully.

Strategy maps identify six stages:

(a)   Identify **objective**. Identify the key objectives of the organisation.

(b)   **Value creation**. In the light of the key objectives, determine the main ways the organisation creates value.

(c)   **Financial perspective**. Identify financial strategies to support the overall objective and strategy.

(d)   **Customer perspective**. Clarify customer-oriented strategies to support the overall strategy.

(e)   **Internal processes**. Identify how internal processes support the strategy and help to create value.

(f)   **Innovation and learning**. Identify the skills and competences needed to support the overall strategy and achieve the objectives.

The 'map' illustrates that the four perspectives in the scorecard are clearly linked but, perhaps more importantly, the **sequence of the stages** illustrates that there is a **hierarchy among the perspectives**. The financial perspective is the highest level perspective. The measures and goals an organisation seeks to achieve in relation to the other perspectives should, in turn, help that organisation achieve its financial goals.

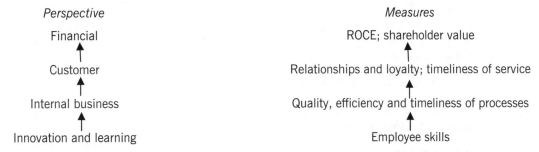

In this way, the strategy map highlights how the four perspectives of the scorecard help create value, with the overall aim of helping an organisation achieve its objectives. It can also help staff appreciate the way that different elements of performance management are linked to an organisation's overall strategy.

However, it is also important to recognise that the **balanced scorecard only measures performance. It does not indicate that the strategy an organisation is employing is the right one**. 'A failure to convert improved operational performance into improved financial performance should send executives back to their drawing boards to rethink the company's strategy or its implementation plans.'

Practical steps in developing a scorecard

As with any other projects or changes, if an organisation is going to implement a scorecard successfully, it will need to think carefully about the steps involved.

Identify key outcomes – Identify the key outcomes critical to the success of the organisation (this is similar to identifying the organisation's CSFs).

Key processes – Identify the processes that lead to those outcomes.

KPIs – Develop key performance indicators for those processes.

Data capture – Develop systems for capturing the data necessary to measure those key performance indicators.

Reporting – Develop a mechanism for communicating or reporting the indicators to staff (for example, through charts, graphs or on a dashboard).

Performance improvement – Develop improvement programmes to ensure that performance improves as necessary.

4.4 Examples of indicators

Exam skills

In the integrated case study exam you may be asked to recommend some indicators organisations can use to measure performance. If you are, do not just give generic measures, but tailor them specifically to the organisation and the situation described in the case study scenario.

The exact measures an organisation uses will depend on its context, but the indicators below suggest some possible measures for each scorecard category.

Financial perspective
Increase monthly turnover
Increase monthly operating profit (by division)
Improve asset utilisation
Increase market share
Increase ROI
Increase cash flow
Customer perspective
Increase market share
Number of new customers attracted
Extend product range
Customer satisfaction rating
Number of recommendations or referrals
Customer retention rates
Level of returns/refunds
On-time delivery
Percentage of sales from new products (introduced in the last two years)
Internal business processes
Reduce inventory levels
Reduce lead times
Minimise wastage/errors
Actual delivery dates of new products/services in line with plan
Reliability and usability (for websites in online business)
Security of transactions and credit card handling

Innovation and learning perspective (learning and growth)
Develop new products
Time to market (time taken for new product ideas to become 'live')
Percentage of sales from new products (introduced in the last two years)
Number of new products introduced (< two years) compared with competitors
Ideas from employees
Adaptability and flexibility of staff
Reward and recognition structure for staff

KEY POINT

The scorecard can be used by both profit and not-for-profit organisations because it acknowledges the fact that both financial and non-financial performance indicators are important in achieving strategic objectives.

4.5 The balanced scorecard and enterprise management solutions

Strategic Enterprise Management (SEM) refers to the methods of management, and the related tools, that businesses can use when making high-level strategic decisions.

SEM focuses primarily on strategic management rather than operational management, with a view to allowing organisations to improve their business processes and procedures, and their business decision making, in order to sustain a competitive advantage in a competitive business environment.

SEM can be seen as an extension of the BSC approach, because it encourages senior managers to combine financial and strategic measures when formulating business decisions.

SEM software provides organisations with the capability to support financial consolidation and to manage strategy and performance through a single piece of software (such as SAP Strategic Enterprise Management; SAP SEM).

SAP's SEM software supports:

(a) **Financial reporting** – it can generate financial and management account information to allow managers to monitor the financial performance of business units and divisions.

(b) **Planning, budgeting, and forecasting.**

(c) **Corporate performance management and scorecards** – the software allows managers to develop KPIs that support balanced scorecards and economic value added scorecard methodologies. The software allows managers to link both operational and strategic plans and to develop scorecards and performance measures based on both financial and non-financial data.

(d) **Risk management** – the software helps managers identify, quantify, and analyse business risks within their business units and thereby to identify risk-reducing activities.

4.6 Strategic scorecards vs balanced scorecards

Strategic scorecards are similar to balanced scorecards because they consist of summary reports of financial and non-financial information to provide a summary of the organisation's progress towards its strategic goals.

However, they are an advance on balanced scorecards because:

- They normally include information on external factors that could affect the strategy
- They explicitly consider risk factors
- They are not confined to quantitative metrics
- They are explicitly strategic whereas many balanced scorecards focus on operational performance

The CIMA Strategic Scorecard™

CIMA has worked with The International Federation of Accountants (IFC) to develop a strategic scorecard as the centrepiece of a framework of enterprise governance.

Strategic position List all key issues eg • Competitor activity • Legislative developments	**Strategic options** List all options eg • Divestment • Outsourcing • New products • New markets
Strategic implementation List all key initiatives underway eg • Progress of IT project • Recent launch	**Strategic risks** All major process issues and risks eg • Risk appetite • Risk management • Capabilities

Adapted from CIMA Strategic Scorecard – executive summary (2007)

(1)   **Strategic position**: information to allow assessment of current and likely future position

This should include **internal** data such as competences and resources and **external** data such as economic, market and competitive developments.

Tools that may be used for internal assessment may be mapping the firm's position against the CSFs for the industry, benchmarking against resources and competences of rivals. External assessment may include environmental analysis, scenario planning, SWOT analysis and stakeholder mapping. 'Headlights' information on long-term currents in the industry and market could also be included to stimulate discussion.

The scorecard may also record process issues under this heading such as how well this data is presently being collected, the quality of the data being included under this heading, and whether there have been any unexpected external events that the board had not been alerted to.

(2)   **Strategic options**: a list of current options under consideration or previously discussed but not yet active

This provides assurance to the board that management are identifying new options on a continuous basis rather than resting on the firm's laurels, and also provides a concise summary of options to enable the board to act as a strategic parent and to discuss at meetings.

Tools that can assist in categorising these are the Boston portfolio matrix, Ansoff's product/market growth vector diagram and evaluation models such as the suitability, acceptability and feasibility framework of Johnson, Scholes and Whittington.

The scorecard may also record process issues under this heading such as whether there are processes in the divisions to carry out innovation, the quality of information gathering on developments in the industry, and the availability of resources and incentives to innovate. Data on effectiveness, such as whether others have grasped opportunities that the firm missed, could be included.

(3)   **Strategic implementation**: key milestones for the board and to monitor implementation of the agreed strategy

All strategic initiatives that are undertaken should include attainable milestones and timelines as well as the CSFs that must be achieved if the strategy is to succeed. These should be summarised in this section and progress against them recorded.

Tools here could include attainment against the steps in recognised project management approaches (eg PRINCE 2 or PERT), quality and process improvement systems (eg Six Sigma) or the perspectives of the balanced scorecard.

The scorecard may also record process issues under this heading such as whether there are project and change management methodologies in use, whether the firm has an SEM solution configured to track strategic implementation, and whether there are weaknesses in these such as whether any strategic initiatives have gone off the rails.

(4) **Strategic risks** (or strategy for risks): major risks that affect the achievement of the firm's strategic goals and key issues such as its risk appetite

The Enterprise Risk Management (ERM) approach recognises that risk management needs to encompass all the firm's risks such as operational, financial, compliance, regulatory and strategic because these can impact on shareholder value significantly.

Strategic risk management requires that the board monitors three components:

Risk appetite: how willing it and its investors are to take risks.

Strategic risks facing the organisation as a consequence of external events as well as in consequence of the strategies and actions management have followed.

Risk treatment processes: how risks are identified and management within the organisation.

Section summary

The balanced scorecard is a performance measurement scheme which translates mission and strategy into objectives and measures. Balanced scorecards encourage key performance indicators to be measured across four interdependent perspectives, rather than focusing purely on financial performance.

The four perspectives (financial; customer; internal business process; and innovation and learning) help ensure that other factors of corporate success (eg customer service; employee satisfaction and training) are given appropriate attention by management alongside financial performance.

5   Developing a performance measurement system

Introduction

KPIs and the balanced scorecard highlight the importance of developing appropriate internal measures for monitoring the performance of a business or process.

However, it is important that an organisation selects what it is going to measure carefully so that it is controlling the outputs and processes which contribute to its CSFs.

As we have already discussed in Section 2 of this chapter, understanding, measuring and managing CSFs is increasingly important to ensuring the prosperity of organisations. CSFs, and the performance measures used to measure whether they are being achieved, need to link daily activities to the organisation's strategies.

In this respect the following factors are important in developing a performance measurement system.

- Identify the key outputs required from an activity

- Identify the key processes in providing the outputs

- Identify the interfaces of the activity with other parts of the firm, or with other processes in the value chain

- Develop KPIs for key processes

- Identify data sources for KPI information

  The data required will vary considerably depending on what is being measured. The table below illustrates some of the aspects that could be measured.

Aspect of performance	Data sources For KPIs
Physical efficiency	Time to output Staff – customer ratios Chargeable time vs slack time
Perceptions and attitudes	Customer satisfaction surveys Customer retention/client turnover Staff turnover Peer group rating
Compliance	Key deadlines met Accuracy of documentation Data security – number of security breaches
Competence	Quality and training of staff in key positions Ability of management in controlling the process
Comparators	Benchmarking: Historical (year on year) Compared to best practice

- Develop reporting system

  Note that the desire to measure these performance indicators may highlight to an organisation that its information systems cannot provide the information it wants from them.

  In this context, the desire to report on CSFs and performance indicators may prompt changes to an organisation's information systems.

Section summary

CSFs, and the performance measures used to assess whether they are being achieved, link daily activities to an organisation's strategies. If an organisation does not know its CSFs, performance measurement can become a random process creating a range of reports which do not measure an organisation's progress against its intended strategic direction.

---

6 Performance pyramid (Lynch and Cross)

Introduction

The **performance pyramid** derives from the idea that an organisation operates at different levels, each of which has different (but supporting) concerns.

6.1 Performance across a range of dimensions

There have been a number of ideas concerning the measurement of performance across a range of dimensions. For example, as long ago as 1952 General Electric undertook a measurements project which concluded that there were eight key results areas (or CSFs);

- Profitability
- Market position
- Productivity
- Product leadership
- Personnel development
- Employee attitudes
- Public responsibility
- Short- vs long-term balance

6.2 The performance pyramid

The **performance pyramid** (developed by Lynch and Cross) stems from an acknowledgement that traditional performance measures which focused on financial indicators such as profitability, cash flow and return on capital employed did not address the driving forces that guide an organisation's ability to achieve its strategic objectives.

Instead of focusing purely on financial objectives, the pyramid focuses on a range of **objectives** for both **external effectiveness** (related to customer satisfaction) and **internal efficiency** (related to flexibility and productivity), which Lynch and Cross propose are the driving forces upon which company objectives are based. The status of these driving forces can then be monitored and measured by the indicators at the lower levels in the pyramid – measures of quality, delivery, cycle time and waste.

However, a crucial point behind the presentation of the model as a pyramid is that, although the organisation operates at different levels, each of which has a different focus, it is vital that each different level supports each other. In this way, the pyramid explicitly makes the link between **corporate level strategy** and the **day to day operations** of an organisation.

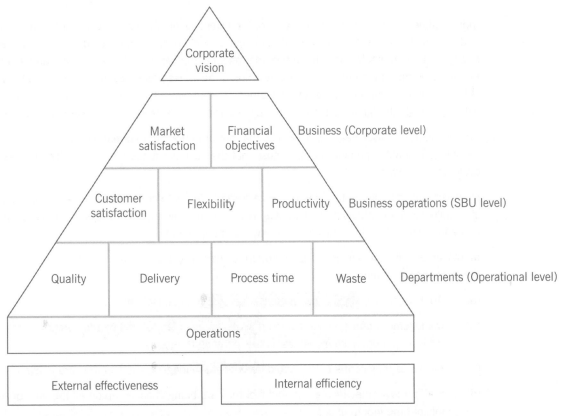

Note. When looking at any appraisal of costs it is crucial to understand the **processes driving** the costs rather than simply looking at them as figures in the management accounts.

(a)   At **corporate level** the vision is developed and **financial** and **market objectives** are set in accordance with it.

(b) At **strategic business unit** level, strategies are developed to achieve these financial and market objectives.

   (i)   **Customer satisfaction** is defined as meeting customer expectations.

   (ii) **Flexibility** indicates responsiveness of the business operating system as a whole.

   (iii) **Productivity** refers to the management of resources such as labour and time.

(c) These in turn are supported by more specific **operational** criteria.

   (i)   **Quality** of the product or service, consistency of product and fit for the purpose

   (ii) **Delivery** of the product or service, ie the method of distribution, its speed and ease of management

   (iii) **Process time** (or cycle time) of all processes from cash collection to order processing to recruitment

   (iv) **Waste** meaning the elimination of all non value added activities

The pyramid highlights the **links** running between the **vision for the company** and **functional objectives**. For example, a reduction in process time should lead to increased productivity and hence improved financial performance. The links within the pyramid help to ensure not only **goal congruence** but also a **consistency of performance** across all business areas, and a balanced approach.

6.3 Strengths and weaknesses of the performance pyramid

The performance pyramid clearly links the performance measures at the different hierarchical levels of the organisation (Anthony's hierarchy), and encourages operational performance measures to be linked to strategic goals.

Individual departments need to be aware of the extent to which they are contributing to strategic aims, and their performance measures should link operational goals to strategic goals. This, in itself, is a strength, but perhaps the key strength of the model is the fact that it links this **hierarchical view** of performance measurement with an appreciation of **business processes** and the need to focus all business activities on the **requirements of the customer**. (In this respect, the model contains echoes of Porter's value chain which highlights the importance of business processes creating **value** for the customer.)

The model also makes clear the measures that are of interest to **external** parties (such as customer satisfaction, quality and delivery) and those that the business focuses on **internally** (such as productivity, cycle time and waste).

However, critics argue that the performance pyramid tends to concentrate on two main groups of stakeholders: shareholders and customers. However, it could also be necessary to look at measures which relate to other stakeholders (such as employees or suppliers).

Moreover, as with the balanced scorecard, critics have pointed to some practical problems that apply to the performance pyramid.

(a) Applying it may significantly increase the **cost** of organisational control.

(b) **Management effort**, which could otherwise be devoted to running the business, could be used in devising performance measures and responding to reports.

(c) Measures may **conflict**. This could demotivate managers who feel they are in a 'no win' situation.

(d) Staff turnover may increase if staff feel they are being checked up on all the time or have to spend lots of time inputting data.

Section summary

The performance pyramid is an alternative performance measure to the balanced scorecard, and looks at how different performance measures will be required at different levels of an organisation.

7 Building block model (Fitzgerald and Moon)

7.1 Measuring performance in service businesses

Performance measurement in service businesses has often been perceived as difficult due to the nature of services compared with products.

There are **five major characteristics** of services that **distinguish services from manufacturing**.

(a) **Intangibility** refers to the lack of substance which is involved with service delivery. Unlike goods (physical products such as confectionery), there is no substantial material or physical aspects to a service: no taste, feel, visible presence and so on. For example, if you go to the theatre, you cannot 'take' the play with you.

(b) **Inseparability/simultaneity**. Many services are created at the same time as they are consumed. (Think of dental treatment, for example.) No service exists until it is actually being experienced/consumed by the person who has bought it.

(c) **Variability/heterogeneity**. Many services face the problem of maintaining **consistency in the standard of output**. It may be hard to attain precise standardisation of the service offered, but customers expect it (such as with fast food).

(d) **Perishability**. Services are innately perishable. The services of a beautician are purchased for a period of time.

(e) **No transfer of ownership**. Services do not result in the transfer of property. The purchase of a service only confers on the customer access to or a right to use a facility (for example, using a public transport system).

Fitzgerald and Moon developed the **building block model** as an attempt to overcome the perceived problems associated with performance measurement in service businesses.

The model identifies three so-called building blocks – **dimensions, standards and rewards** – which can be used as the basis for performance measurement in service businesses.

Dimensions	
Results	
• Competitiveness	
• Financial performance	
Determinants	
• Quality of service	
• Flexibility	
• Resource utilisation	
• Innovation	

Standards	**Rewards**
• Ownership	• Clarity
• Achievability	• Motivation
• Fairness	• Controllability

Dimensions are the areas of performance which yield the specific performance metric for a company. These dimensions are then split into **results** and **determinants** (the factors which shape the results). The logic behind this is that controlling and improving performance in relation to the determinant should then lead to improvements in the results.

(a) **Results**

    (i)   **Competitive performance**, focusing on factors such as sales growth and market share

    (ii)   **Financial performance**, concentrating on profitability, liquidity, capital structure and market ratios

(b) **Determinants** (of those results)

    (i)   **Quality of service** looks at matters like reliability, responsiveness, courtesy, competence and availability/accessibility. These can be measured by customer satisfaction surveys.

    (ii)   **Flexibility** refers to an organisation's ability to deliver at the right speed, to respond to precise customer specifications, and to cope with fluctuations in demand.

    (iii)   **Resource utilisation** considers how efficiently resources are being utilised. This can be problematic because of the complexity of the inputs to a service and the outputs from it and because some of the inputs are supplied by the customer.

    (iv)   **Innovation** is assessed in terms of both the innovation process and the success of individual innovations. Individual innovations should be measured in terms of whether they have led to improvements in the other five performance criteria (results and determinants).

(c) **Standards**

Standards are the **measures** used to monitor an organisation's performance in each of the dimensions chosen. (In effect, **determinants** in the building block model are **CSFs**, while **standards** are **KPIs**.)

In order for standards to be effective, employees must view them as **fair** and **achievable**, and must take **ownership** of them.

    (i)   To ensure that employees take **ownership** of standards, they need to **participate** in the budget and standard-setting processes. They are then more likely to **accept** the standards, feel more **motivated** as they perceive the standards to be achievable and **morale** is improved. The disadvantage to participation is that it offers the opportunity for the introduction of **budgetary slack**.

    (ii)   **Achievability** – Standards need to be set **high enough** to ensure that there is some **sense of achievement** in attaining them, but **not so high** that there is a **demotivating** effect because they are felt to be unachievable. It is management's task to find a **balance** between what the organisation perceives as achievable and what employees perceive as achievable.

    (iii)   **Fairness** – It is vital that equity is seen to occur when applying standards for performance measurement purposes. The performance of different business units should not be measured against the same standards if some units have an inherent advantage unconnected with their own efforts. For example, divisions operating in different countries should not be assessed against the same standards.

(d) **Rewards**

Rewards are the motivators which encourage employees to work towards the standards set.

Three issues need to be considered if the performance measurement system is to operate successfully: **clarity**, **motivation** and **controllability**.

    (i)   **Clarity**. The organisation's objectives need to be **clearly understood** by those whose performance is being appraised; that is, they need to know what goals they are working towards.

(ii)   Individuals should be **motivated** to work in pursuit of the organisation's strategic objectives. Goal clarity and participation have been shown to contribute to higher levels of motivation to achieve targets, providing managers accept those targets. Bonuses can be used to motivate.

(iii)   Managers should have a certain level of **controllability** for their areas of responsibility. For example, they should not be held responsible for costs over which they have no control.

Dimension	Type	Example measures
Competitive performance	Competitor focused	Market share Prices Product features
	Customer focused	Customer retention Customer numbers
Financial performance	Profitability	Profit Working capital cycle
	Liquidity	Bad debts
Quality of service	Reliability	Punctuality Dependability of service and staff
	Responsiveness	Response times Number of phone lines Delivery speed (for goods ordered online or by phone)
	Courtesy	Politeness Respect to customers
	Competence	Staff skill Expertise Knowledge Diligence
	Availability	Product availability Product range
	Accessibility	Ease of finding site
Flexibility	Delivery speed	Customer waiting time Time from customer enquiry to job completion
	Coping with demand	Spare capacity to deal with peak times Overtime worked
	Response to customer specification	Customer feedback surveys (degree to which advice or assistance is tailored to customer needs) Range of staff and skills
Resource utilisation	Productivity	Labour hours worked Skill levels of work performed by staff grade
	Premises	Percentage of area used for value-adding services, or customer-facing services
Innovation	Cost	Development cost per new service line
	Speed	Time taken from concept being devised to service being offered to customers

Section summary

The characteristics of services can potentially make it more difficult to measure the performance of service businesses than manufacturing ones. However, the building block model offers a useful range of performance measures for measuring service performance.

8 Measuring performance in manufacturing businesses

Introduction

A wide range of measures exists for measuring manufacturing performance. They range from simple cost/output efficiency measures to more complex ideas relating to quality and innovation.

A number of performance indicators can be used to assess operations. They are particularly relevant to the internal business and customer perspectives of the balanced scorecard.

- Quality
- Number of customer complaints and warranty claims
- Lead times
- Rework
- Delivery to time
- Non-productive hours
- System (machine) down time

These indicators can also be expressed in the form of ratios or percentages for comparative purposes. Like physical measures, they can be produced quickly and trends can be identified and acted upon rapidly. Examples of useful ratios might be as follows:

(a) **Machine downtime: total machine hours**. This ratio could be used to monitor machine availability and can provide a measure of machine usage and efficiency.

(b) **Component rejects: component purchases**. This ratio could be used to control the quality of components purchased from an external supplier. The measure can be used to monitor the performance of new suppliers.

(c) **Deliveries late: deliveries on schedule**. This ratio could be applied to sales made to customers as well as to receipts from suppliers.

(d) **Customer rejects/returns: total sales**. This ratio helps to monitor customer satisfaction, providing a check on the efficiency of quality control procedures.

(e) **Value added time: production cycle time**. Value added time is the direct production time during which the product is being made and value is therefore being added.

8.1 Advanced manufacturing technology

The advent of **advanced manufacturing technology (AMT)** has meant that many organisations will need to modify their performance measures so that the information they provide will be useful in controlling operations in the new manufacturing environment.

8.2 Performance measurement for manufacturing

Performance measurement in manufacturing is increasingly using non-financial measures. Malcolm Smith identifies four overarching measures for manufacturing environments.

- **Cost**: cost behaviour
- **Quality**: factors inhibiting performance
- **Time**: bottlenecks, inertia
- **Innovation**: new product flexibility

8.2.1 Cost

Possible non-financial or part-financial indicators are as follows:

Area	Measure
Quantity of raw material inputs	Actual vs target number
Equipment productivity	Actual vs standard units
Maintenance efforts	No. of production units lost through maintenance No. of production units lost through failure No. of failures prior to schedule
Overtime costs	Overtime hours/total hours
Product complexity	No. of component parts
Quantity of output	Actual vs target completion
Product obsolescence	% shrinkage
Employees	% staff turnover
Employee productivity	Direct labour hours per unit
Customer focus	% service calls; % claims

8.2.2 Quality

Integrating quality into a performance measurement system suggests attention to the following items:

Area	Measure
Quality of purchased components	Zero defects
Equipment failure	Downtime/total time
Maintenance effort	Breakdown maintenance/total maintenance
Waste	% defects; % scrap; % rework
Quality of output	% yield
Safety	Serious industrial injury rate
Reliability	% warranty claims
Quality commitment	% dependence on post-inspection % conformance to quality standards
Employee morale	% absenteeism
Leadership impact	% cancelled meetings
Customer awareness	% repeat orders; number of complaints

KEY TERM

TOTAL QUALITY MANAGEMENT (TQM) is an 'integrated and comprehensive system of planning and controlling all business functions so that products or services are produced which meet or exceed customer expectations. TQM is a philosophy of business behaviour, embracing principles such as employee involvement, continuous improvement at all levels and customer focus, as well as being a collection of related techniques aimed at improving quality such as full documentation of activities, clear goal-setting and performance measurement from the customer perspective'. *(CIMA Official Terminology)*

8.2.3 Time

A truly just-in-time system is an ideal to which many manufacturing firms are striving. Time-based competition is also important for new product development, deliveries etc. The management accounting focus might be on throughput, bottlenecks, customer feedback and distribution.

Area	Measure
Equipment failure	Time between failures
Maintenance effort	Time spent on repeat work
Throughput	Processing time/total time per unit
Production flexibility	Set-up time
Availability	% stock-outs
Labour effectiveness	Standard hours achieved/total hours worked
Customer impact	No. of overdue deliveries Mean delivery delay

8.2.4 Innovation

Performance indicators for innovation can support the 'innovation and learning' perspective on the balanced scorecard. Some possible suggestions are outlined below:

Area	Measure
The ability to introduce new products	% product obsolescence Number of new products launched Number of patents secured Time to launch new products
Flexibility to accommodate change	Number of new processes implemented Number of new process modifications
Reputation for innovation	Media recognition for leadership Expert assessment of competence Demonstrable competitive advantage

8.3 Activity-based measures of performance

Many writers have seen the potential of the activity-based approach to management accounting to provide new performance indicators. For example, if the number of purchase requisitions is a cost driver for a number of purchasing, receiving and accounting activities then it would be possible to compare the resources which ought to be employed to process a given number of requisitions with the resources actually employed.

8.4 Use of experience curves

Experience curves can also be used in strategic control of costs. Experience curves suggest that as output increases, the cost per unit of output falls. This fall in cost results from:

(a) **Economies of scale** – in other words an increased volume of production leads to lower unit costs, as the firm approaches full capacity.

(b) A genuine **'learning effect'** as the workforce becomes familiar with the job and learns to carry out their tasks more efficiently. As a process is repeated, it is likely that costs will reduce due to **efficiency, discounts** and **reduced waste**.

(c) **Technological improvements**.

8.5 Target costing

This brings us on to **target costing**, an approach used in Japan. This is based on the principle that a product must have a target price that will succeed in winning a target share of the market.

When a product is first manufactured, the **target cost** will usually be well below the current cost, which is determined by current technology and processes, and experience effects. Management then sets benchmarks for improvement towards the target costs, by improving technologies and processes.

Target costing is thus, in effect, a process of establishing what the cost of the product should be over the entire **product life cycle**.

(a)   In the short run, because of development costs and the learning time needed, costs are likely to exceed price.

(b)   In the longer term, costs should come down (eg because of the experience curve) to their target level.

Section summary

A range of financial and non-financial measures will also be useful for measuring manufacturing performance. These range from simple cost and output efficiency measures to more complex ideas relating to quality and innovation.

9 Targets and rewards

Introduction

Targets and rewards are tools that can be used to motivate employees to achieve corporate goals. It is important to strike a balance between setting targets which are too challenging – and therefore not achievable – and too easy, and therefore do not stimulate performance improvement.

9.1 Communicating performance targets

Kaplan and Norton's original intention of how the balanced scorecard should be used was as a means of **translating mission and strategy into objectives**, and measures into four different perspectives. They also saw it as a means of communicating mission and strategy, and using the **measures to inform employees about the key drivers of success**.

Interestingly, Kaplan and Norton intended the scorecard to be a **communication** and **information** system, **not a control system**.

By definition, performance targets and objectives have to be set before performance can be measured against them. Equally, the targets must be communicated across an organisation so that managers and staff know what they are trying to achieve.

Some extracts from the UK National Health Service (NHS) Institute for Innovation and Improvement website provides a useful summary of the importance of communicating strategy and objectives.

'Performance management enables organisations to articulate their business strategy, align their business to that strategy, identify their key performance indicators (KPIs) and track progress, delivering the information to decision-makers.

As an organisation, you need to define your strategy and communicate it effectively to staff, so there is a clear link between the strategic objectives and every work group within your hospital.

The balanced scorecard plays a key role within performance management, enabling you to clarify your organisation's vision and strategy, translating them into tangible objectives and measures. Balanced scorecards allow you to measure and monitor performance and assign Key Performance Indicators (KPIs), giving you the ability to track and optimise performance based on those indicators.

KPIs help you define and measure progress towards organisational goals. As the primary means of communicating performance across the organisation, KPIs should focus on a range of areas. Once an organisation has analysed its mission, identified all its stakeholders, and defined its goals, KPIs offer a way of measuring progress towards those goals.'

As these extracts highlight, KPIs provide one way of communicating performance targets. And, as we noted earlier in this chapter, **budgets** provide another way of communicating performance targets.

In both cases, however, in order for performance targets to be effective it is important that they encourage **goal congruence** across all levels of the performance hierarchy. The targets set for individual departments or business units must be properly aligned to an organisation's overall targets. And, in turn, the targets and objectives set for individual members of staff must support those set for their department or business unit. In theory, if staff objectives and targets are derived from departmental and organisational objectives, then if every individual achieves their objectives, then their department will achieve its objectives, and if every department achieves its objectives then the organisation as a whole will achieve its objectives.

However, for targets to be meaningful and effective in motivating employees, they need to link to larger organisational objectives. If employees are unable to see how their efforts – and the targets they are being set – contribute to the organisation's overall performance, they are less likely to be motivated to achieve those targets.

In practice, one way targets and objectives can be communicated to individual members of staff is through an annual appraisal process (which is discussed in Papers E1 and E2 and so is assumed knowledge for E3). Targets and objectives can be set at the start of the year, and then performance against those targets can be assessed at the end of the year.

9.2 The importance of targets

On several occasions in this Study Text, we have noted that human knowledge and skills are a strategic resource for an organisation, and that they can play a vital role in achieving sustainable competitive advantage.

As such, aspects of human resource management (such as setting **performance targets** and **reward management**) also play an important role in the performance management and control of the organisation. In this respect, human resource management (HRM) follows a similar control model as is used for the overall strategic and operational control of an organisation:

 Goals are set.

 Performance is measured and compared with target.

 Control measures are undertaken in order to correct any shortfall.

 Goals are adjusted in the light of experience.

However, it is crucial to recognise that these goals link to both strategic and operational success. Effective performance management requires that the strategic objectives of the organisation are broken down into layers of more and more detailed sub-objectives, so that **individual performance** can be judged against personal goals that support and link directly back to corporate strategy.

More generally, the HRM process within an organisation also needs to support the organisation's corporate strategy by ensuring that the right number of employees are in place, with the necessary skills and knowledge, and whose behaviour and approach to their work is consistent with the organisation's culture.

9.3 Target selection

In relation to appraisals and performance rating, performance management acts as a control system in measuring people's achievement against targets. However, in order for performance management to be beneficial, it is important to select the right measures or targets at the outset when setting performance goals. Staff are likely to pay most attention to those aspects of performance which are measured most closely; so if the 'wrong' performance measures or targets are set, this could lead to staff behaviour being different to that originally intended, and ultimately adversely affecting performance.

CASE STUDY

Bankers' bonuses

In the aftermath of the global financial crisis of 2008–9, a lot of media attention has focused on bankers' bonuses. A number of investment banks link employees' annual bonuses to the amount of money they earn in that year, a short-term approach which can influence employees' decision making.

Critics argue that the bonuses encourage short-term, risky behaviour that maximises profits in the short term but could potentially be loss-making in the longer term.

The sub-prime mortgage crisis in the US in 2007 was a good example of this. The mortgage bond market proved extremely profitable for the banks in the short term, but once mortgage holders started defaulting on their loans, the banks had to foreclose them, causing the loans to be written off.

During the bull market (before 2007) certain financial packages made a great deal of money for the banks in the short term, resulting in their staff receiving large bonuses. However, those same financial packages failed shortly afterwards, triggering the financial crisis.

The individual performance measures selected should be relevant to the overall objectives of the organisation. Individuals' objectives must reflect the overall strategic initiatives management are taking. For example, if management is focusing on quality, performance measures must reflect this by measuring employees on their contribution to achieving quality targets.

Some employees respond well to difficult targets and are motivated to attain them. Others may find the targets daunting and feel they are unachievable, and indeed there may be valid reasons why they believe this. For example, in an economic downturn, a number of businesses reduce the amount they spend on their IT budgets. Therefore, if a salesperson in an IT company was given a target of increasing sales 25% on the prior year they would appear to be justified in thinking this target is unachievable.

Equally, care must be taken when using certain measures, for instance numbers of sales, as the basis for rewarding employees. As an example, here are some possible negative consequences of using sales numbers as a primary performance measure.

(a)   The salesperson might offer potential customers large discounts in order to make the sale (but with the effect that the company makes a loss on the sale).

(b)   The salesperson is concerned solely with the immediate sale, which may lead to poor after-sales service, low customer satisfaction levels and poor customer retention.

(c)   The salesperson might use expensive promotions that actually generate less in sales value than they cost, but which allow the salesperson to register a number of sales.

(d)   Once a salesperson has reached their target figure for a period they might look to defer future sales into the next period.

It may be better to use a balanced mix of targets – for example, setting customer care and customer profitability targets as well as the number of sales made.

It is also important to make sure whatever goals are set that these are capable of being controlled by the individual, otherwise the individual is likely to become demotivated.

In addition, if processes are being redesigned, and job roles are changing, performance measures must be adapted to reflect the new jobs and responsibilities.

However, it is important that people are not given too many objectives and targets. There is a danger that people could become overwhelmed by the sheer number of goals they are expected to meet, but with the result that they do not know what their priorities are or what aspects of their work they should give most attention to.

Finally, it is useful to remember the acronym SMART when setting performance targets: are the targets specific, measurable, achievable, relevant and time-bounded?

9.4 Stretch targets

Although we have just identified the importance of targets being perceived as achievable, it is equally important that targets remain challenging and so cannot be achieved too easily. In this context, the notion of setting 'stretch targets' could be useful in helping to improve performance in organisations.

A stretch target is one that an organisation cannot achieve simply by working a little harder or a little smarter. To achieve a stretch target, people have to devise new strategies and new ways of achieving that target.

Jack Welch is credited with introducing the concept of stretch targets while he was president of GE. He noted that 'We have found that by reaching for what appears to be the impossble, we often actually do the impossible; and even when we don't quite make it, we inevitably wind up doing much better than we would have done.'

Welch's logic is that stretch targets energise people; they invigorate them in ways which ordinary targets do not. Employees tend to rise to the standard set for them when they are faced with a challenge. So the more that is expected of them, the more they will achieve.

The danger, however, with setting targets which appear to be unachievable is that people will treat them as such, and will therefore not bother trying to achieve them. If stretch targets seem overwhelming and unachievable, they will sap employees' intrinsic motivation to achieve them. As such, there is a fine line between good stretch targets, which can energise an organisation, and bad ones which crush morale and demotivate staff.

Equally, to promote and sustain high levels of performance, targets need to be linked to **reward**. If staff attain the targets which are set for them, but are not recognised and rewarded for doing so (not necessarily with financial rewards), then they may be less motivated to try to achieve similar targets set for them in future.

Likewise, staff (or departments more generally) need to be given sufficient resources to be able to fulfil the targets set.

Finally, if an individual's work performance is dependent on work done by other people (and many jobs involve co-operation and interdependence with other people) an individual reward scheme (eg an individual bonus scheme) may not always be effective, since individual performance can be affected by what other people have done.

9.5 Rewards and motivation

You should recall from your studies for Paper E2 that the relationship between rewards and motivation is complex and there is only a limited degree of correlation between pay levels and work performance and motivation. The ideas behind **Maslow's hierarchy of needs** and **Herzberg's 'motivation-hygiene' theory** could both be relevant here.

Maslow's hierarchy of needs suggests that monetary rewards are more likely to motivate low-paid staff (because the money they earn will enable them to meet their physiological and safety needs – for example, for food and housing). However, as employees become progressively better paid, money is less likely to be a motivating factor for them. Instead, a sense of respect and achievement ('esteem'), and a sense of fulfilment ('self-actualisation') are likely to be more important for such employees.

Similarly, Herzberg's theory suggests that, although employees will be dissatisfied if they feel they have a poor salary, monetary rewards alone do not generate satisfaction and motivation in the longer term. Instead, non-financial factors such as a sense of achievement, recognition, increased responsibility, opportunities for advancement and growth, plus the nature of the work itself are more likely to motivate employees.

Nonetheless, traditional pay systems have featured monetary incentives intended to improve performance.

9.6 Performance-related pay

In Section 9.4, we noted the importance of linking performance to reward, and one way this can be done is through performance-related pay (PRP) schemes, where remuneration is directly linked to an assessment of performance, usually measured against pre-agreed objectives. (These schemes are also sometimes known as merit pay.)

Performance-related pay can either be based on an individual's performance against their own objectives (individual PRP) or it can be based on a team's performance against its objectives (group PRP).

Individual PRP schemes have the benefit of controllability, since each employee has control over their own rewards rather than being dependent on the effort (or lack of effort) of other members of their team. However, a danger of individual PRP schemes is that they may lead to a lack of teamwork as each member of the team seeks to maximise their own performance.

Conversely, while group PRP schemes should encourage teamwork, they have the potential disadvantage that members of a team who work less hard benefit from the efforts of those members of the team who work harder.

More generally, there is a danger that PRP schemes will lead employees to focus on those aspects of their performance which they know are being measured, to the detriment of other parts of their role. In other words, 'What gets measured, gets done'.

Performance-related pay takes many forms. As well as merit pay, it can also include commissions, piecework, and knowledge- or skill-related pay.

Commissions are often used as a form of remuneration for sales staff. These staff are likely to receive a relatively low basic salary, supplemented by a commission based on the level of sales they make.

One advantage of commission schemes is that they should help to motivate sales staff to achieve higher sales, thereby aligning the interests of individual staff members with those of the organisation.

Another advantage (for an organisation) is that they mean that a proportion of staff costs become variable costs; so if a salesperson only makes a relatively low level of sales, the amount the organisation pays them is also relatively low.

However, a potential disadvantage of commission schemes is that they may lead to dysfunctional behaviour. For example, they could adversely affect teamwork as each individual tries to maximise their own commission. They could also encourage sales staff to 'put the sales target above the customer', and pressurise a customer to buy something before they have time to think about the purchase, or possibly even if they don't really want to make the purchase. This is likely to be disadvantageous to a company in

the long run, though, because a customer is unlikely to buy from them again, if they are unhappy with the way they have been treated.

Under a **piecework scheme**, an individual is paid a price for each unit of output, so the higher their output the more they receive. However, the inherent danger of such a scheme is that the payment is based on quantity, not quality, so some kind of quality control will also be necessary to ensure that an individual is not paid for substandard work.

Knowledge- or competence-related pay reflects a situation where an employee receives a pay increase, or a bonus, in return for increasing their competences or knowledge. Such a situation frequently occurs in the accountancy profession, where trainee accountants receive a higher salary once they have passed their exams.

9.6.1 Profit-related pay

Profit-related pay can also be seen as a type of group PRP scheme. In a profit-related pay scheme, part of an employee's remuneration is linked to the profitability of their organisation. So, for example, a profit target could be set at the beginning of each year; then, if the organisation's profit for the year exceeds that target figure, employees will become eligible for their bonuses.

The logic of profit-related pay schemes is that rewarding employees for the success of their organisations should help motivate them to increase their performance – in order to contribute to the success of the organisation overall. They may also encourage loyalty to an organisation, since in many cases employees lose their entitlement to a bonus when they leave the organisation.

However, a significant disadvantage of profit-related pay is that it could lead to a conflict between short-term and long-term performance, and hence between the directors or managers of a company and its shareholders.

If the managers of a company know that their bonuses depend on annual (short-term) profits, they may be motivated to take actions to boost the short-term profitability of the company. However, those actions may not generate value for the company in the longer term, and may end up damaging the longer-term profitability of the company. As such, the managers' actions will also be inconsistent with the primary objective of their companies – which is to maximise the wealth of their shareholders.

One alternative means of remuneration which could be used to help align the interests of managers and directors with those of shareholders is **share options** (or employee share option plans (ESOP)).

In particular, the time period (vesting period) which must pass before share options can be exercised means that they should encourage a company's management to focus on the longer-term success of the company, rather than simply focusing on short-term performance.

9.7 Target setting and performance-related pay

The logic of performance-related pay should be pretty clear: if an organisation can find a way of linking the personal objectives of its employees to its corporate objectives, then better goal congruence should result. If employees' performance is then linked to financial reward, for example in the form of bonuses, then there should be a mutual benefit for employees, employer and owners resulting from objectives being met.

However, a key factor in the success of PRP schemes will be the performance measures and targets actually set.

Remember the building block model we looked at earlier in the chapter. In this model, Fitzgerald and Moon suggest that effective targets (or performance standards) should have the following three characteristics:

(a)   **Fairness** (equity) – When targets are being set across an organisation (for various managers and staff over a range of departments or functions) care needs to be taken to ensure that the targets set are equally challenging, rather than being easier for some managers/staff to achieve than others.

(b)   **Ownership** – The targets should be accepted and agreed by the managers or staff they relate to. Where individuals participate in the setting of their targets they are more likely to accept them – and be motivated by them – rather than simply having the targets imposed on them.

(c)   **Achievability** – The most effective targets are ones which are challenging yet achievable. If employees feel that a target is too difficult and is therefore unachievable, their inability (either real or perceived) to reach the target is likely to demotivate them.

Exam skills

Although the building block model was developed as a framework for performance measurement specifically in service industries, the characteristics of 'standards' and 'rewards' which Fitzgerald and Moon identified can usefully be considered in relation to reward systems as a whole.

The effectiveness of standards (or targets) is affected by the principles of fairness, ownership and achievability.

The effectiveness of reward schemes is affected by the principles of clarity, ability to motivate, and controllability.

The issue of clarity also links back to the ideas of 'SMART' and performance objectives being 'specific' and 'measurable'. If an employee's performance objectives are not clearly defined, how can the employee be assessed on whether they have achieved their objectives or not?

Question 11.4	Performance standards

Learning outcome D1(a)

Morale among the managers in the residential lettings division of a nationwide estate agents firm has been falling in recent years, although morale in the house sales division has remained high.

The HR Director has been trying to find out why this is, and he has identified that one of the main reasons is that virtually all the managers in the house sales divisions achieve their annual performance targets and therefore receive a bonus, while less than 5% of the managers in the lettings division achieve their targets.

Which of the characteristics which Fitzgerald and Moon identify for effective performance standards does the estate agency need to improve?

A   Achievability
B   Fairness and Achievability
C   Ownership and Fairness
D   Fairness

9.8 Problems of using performance measures

Although using performance measures is a necessary and integral part of performance management and control, there are nevertheless problems associated with their use.

Berry, Broadbent and Ottley identify the following list of possible problems related to the use of performance measures:

(a)   **Tunnel vision** (undue focus on the aspects of performance being measured to the detriment of other aspects of performance). For example, if a performance measure for an accountancy firm is the staff utilisation ratio in terms of chargeable hours as a proportion of total hours, this may lead to an insufficient amount of time being spent on staff development or training.

(b) **Sub-optimisation** (focus on some objectives so that others – which could bring greater success – are not achieved). For example, if an audit partner focuses too much on winning new clients, this may lead to inadequate time being given to managing relationships with existing clients and supervising the work being done on the audits of those clients.

(c) **Myopia** (focusing on short-term success or goals at the expense of longer-term objectives and long-term success). For example, the audit firm might be focused on maximising client revenues rather than investing in the technology to provide automated audit software which will generate efficiency savings in the future.

(d) **Measure fixation** (a focus on measures and behaviour in order to achieve specific performance indicators which may not be effective. In effect, focusing more on the measures themselves, rather than underlying goals and objectives.). For example, if the audit firm knows that the cost of the audit is being measured this could mean it focuses on reducing the costs of its audits. However, this may lead it to use staff who are too junior for the complexity of the work involved for particular clients. This may also lead to client dissatisfaction (and loss of clients) or extra costs when a more senior member of staff has to re-do work which is unsatisfactory or incomplete.

(e) **Misrepresentation** ('creative' reporting or deliberate manipulation of data to make a result appear better than it actually is). For example, the audit firm may produce a report saying that 90% of its clients have expressed complete satisfaction with the service they have received. But if the firm only sent its client satisfaction survey to a carefully selected number of clients, rather than all of its clients, the satisfaction score is misleading.

(f) **Misinterpretation** (misunderstanding the performance data; for example, due to a failure to recognise the complexity of the environment in which an organisation operates and therefore the influences on performance). Within the accountancy firm, one partner might be focused on winning new business from large, national clients, another concerned with winning new business from small, local clients, while a third might be focused on selling additional services to existing clients. In this scenario, the motives of the different partners create a complex environment in which the objectives of the firm's key players may conflict. If the firm wins lots of business from large, national clients, how will this affect its capacity to take on extra business from small, local clients?

(g) **Gaming** (deliberate distortion of performance to secure some strategic advantage). This might include deliberate underperformance in the current period to avoid higher targets being set in future periods. For example, assume an audit manager spots an opportunity to sell some additional services to a client, but knows the audit firm is already on target to exceed budgeted profit for the current period. The manager may suggest that the consultancy work begins in the next period, with the hope that the additional services help create a favourable performance to budget in that period as well.

(h) **Ossification** (an overly rigid system, or an unwillingness to change the performance measure scheme once it has been set up). For example, the questions in the audit firm's questionnaire may be poorly designed and don't give clients the opportunity to comment on some aspects of the firm's offering. However, because the firm gets good responses from the questionnaire in its current form, it may be unwilling to change the questionnaire.

9.8.1 Tunnel vision and performance targets

Berry, Broadbent and Ottley's concept of tunnel vision also reiterates the point that 'What gets measured gets done'.

If particular performance targets or objectives are set, employees will know that their performance is likely to be appraised against those targets. Therefore, employees will concentrate on achieving the targets which are measured in preference to other possible aspects of their role. However, this could have negative side effects, as the following two short examples illustrate:

(a) The manager of a fast food restaurant was striving to achieve a bonus which was dependent on minimising the amount of chicken pieces and burgers which were wasted. The manager earned

the bonus, but did so by instructing staff to wait until the chicken pieces or burgers were ordered before cooking them. However, the long waiting times which resulted led to a huge loss of customers in the following weeks.

(b)   Sales staff at a company met their sales targets by offering discounts and extending payment terms. In some cases, they even made credit sales to customers they felt might never pay. As a result, the sales staff achieved their targets at the expense of the company's profitability. However, the sales staff were not concerned by profits, because they were motivated by a bonus scheme which was based solely on the level of sales they achieved.

More generally, the problems of performance measurement highlighted by Berry, Broadbent and Ottley also highlight the issue of **congruence between the goals of individuals and the goals of the organisation**.

Individual goals may be financially or non-financially oriented, and relate to remuneration, promotion prospects, job security, job satisfaction and self-esteem.

Each **individual** may face a **conflict** between taking action to ensure organisational goals and action to ensure personal goals.

9.8.2 Ways in which the problems may be reduced

(a)   **Involvement of staff** at all levels in the development and implementation of the scheme should help to reduce gaming and tunnel vision.

(b)   A **flexible use** of performance measures should help to reduce measure fixation and misrepresentation.

(c)   Keeping the performance measurement system under **constant review** should help to overcome the problems of ossification and gaming.

(d)   Give careful consideration to the **dimensions of performance**. Quantifying all objectives should help to overcome sub-optimisation, while a focus on measuring customer satisfaction should reduce tunnel vision and sub-optimisation.

(e)   Consideration should be given to the **audit of the system**. Expert interpretation of the performance measurement scheme should help to provide an idea of the incidence of the problems, while a careful audit of the data used should help to reduce the incidence and impact of measure fixation, misinterpretation and gaming.

(f)   **Recognition of the key features** necessary in any scheme (a long-term view/perspective amongst staff, a sensible number of measures, benchmarks which are independent of past activity) should help to overcome the range of problems listed above.

Section summary

Performance targets need to be established and communicated to staff in order that actual performance can be compared with the targets.

Rewards are used to motivate employees towards the achievement of corporate targets. If attainable targets are set, and attractive rewards are offered, this should increase employees' motivation to help an organisation to achieve its goals.

Chapter Summary

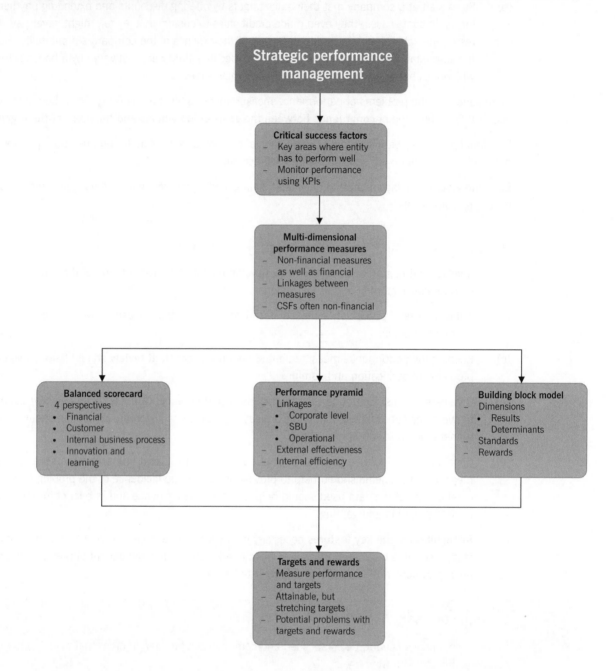

Strategic performance management

Critical success factors
- Key areas where entity has to perform well
- Monitor performance using KPIs

Multi-dimensional performance measures
- Non-financial measures as well as financial
- Linkages between measures
- CSFs often non-financial

Balanced scorecard
- 4 perspectives
  - Financial
  - Customer
  - Internal business process
  - Innovation and learning

Performance pyramid
- Linkages
  - Corporate level
  - SBU
  - Operational
- External effectiveness
- Internal efficiency

Building block model
- Dimensions
  - Results
  - Determinants
- Standards
- Rewards

Targets and rewards
- Measure performance and targets
- Attainable, but stretching targets
- Potential problems with targets and rewards

Quick Quiz

1   **Fill in the blanks** in the statements below, using the words in the box.

The aims of performance measurement are as follows:

- (1) .... the (2) .... of the company

- Concentrating (3) .... towards objectives

- Part of the (4) .... process where (5) .... is compared with the (6) ....

•	plan	•	objectives	•	control
•	feedback	•	efforts	•	communicating

2   List **four** examples of non-financial performance measures that can be applied to an assessment of marketing effectiveness.

3   What are the four perspectives of the balanced scorecard?

....

....

....

....

4   Which of the following is **not** one of the specific operational criteria contained in the performance pyramid?

A   Flexibility
B   Process time
C   Delivery
D   Quality

5   In the building blocks model, which of the following are classified as **determinants** of performance?

(i)   Innovation
(ii)   Quality of service
(iii) Motivation

A   (i) and (ii)
B   (i) and (iii)
C   (ii) and (iii)
D   (i), (ii) and (iii)

6   One of a professional service firm's KPIs is the number of new clients it attracts each year. This KPI has been in place for a number of years while the firm's market has been growing, and while the firm has also enjoyed considerable growth. However, overall market growth has slowed significantly in recent years, and recent industry research has shown that client retention is now more important to sustaining profitability than attracting new clients.

Which of the following problems of performance measurement does the firm appear to be suffering from?

A   Myopia
B   Measure fixation
C   Misinterpretation
D   Gaming

Answers to Quick Quiz

1   (1) Communicating (2) objectives (3) efforts (4) control (5) feedback (6) plan

2   Four from the following:

Trend in market share	Sales volume growth
Customer visits per salesperson	Client contact hours per salesperson
Sales volume forecast vs actual	Number of customers
Customer survey response information	

3   Financial
     Customer
     Internal business processes
     Innovation/learning

4   A   Flexibility

The four elements of the performance pyramid at operational level are: quality, delivery, process time, and waste.

5   A   (i) and (ii)

In the building block model, the four determinants of performance are: quality of service, flexibility, resource utilisation and innovation.

Motivation relates to the rewards which encourage employees to work towards the standards set.

6   B   Measure fixation

The firm remains committed to using a specific performance indicator (the number of **new** clients) even though that indicator may not be effective. As a result, the firm appears to be focusing more on the measure than the underlying goal – of sustaining its profitability.

Myopia involves prioritising short-term issues over longer-term ones; gaming relates to the deliberate distortion of performance to secure some strategic advantage; while misinterpretation arises when an organisation misunderstands the performance data it is analysing.

Answers to Questions

11.1 Product leadership

Qualitative measures ought to be available in the form of reviews by consumer magazines, newspapers, and trade press, awards, endorsement by public figures, and direct comment from customers.

11.2 Invoicing

Invoices per employee per week: $10,000/4 = 2,500$ (activity)
Staff cost per invoice: £0.12 (cost/profitability) $16,000/(2,500 \times 52)$
Invoices per hour: $2,500/(7 \times 5) = 71.4$ (productivity). (Assume employee works 5 days a week, 7 hours per day.)
Cost of idle time: £32 + £4.28 = £36.28 (cost/profitability). (Cost of phone call + ½ hour lost productivity $(½ \times £0.12 \times 71.4)$)

You may have thought of other measures and probably have slight rounding differences.

11.3 Hotel

Financial performance: Revenue growth; net profit margin; variance analysis (eg expenditure on wages, power, catering, bedrooms); revenue per available room; profit per available room

Competitive performance: market share (rooms occupied on a total percentage of rooms available locally); competitor occupancy; competitor prices; bookings; vacant rooms as a proportion.

Resource utilisation: Occupancy rate (rooms occupied/rooms available); energy and water usage per room

Quality of service: complaints, results of room checks; guest satisfaction scores (results of questionnaires; Scores/comments on review websites (eg Trip Advisor); level of repeat bookings (customer loyalty)

11.4 Performance standards

The correct answer is: B   Fairness and Achievability

Fairness – The disparity in the proportion of managers receiving a bonus suggests that it is easier for managers in the house sales division to achieve their targets than for their colleagues in the letting division. In order to be fair, the targets for both divisions should be equally challenging.

Achievability – The most effective targets are ones which are challenging yet achievable. If the targets are too difficult to achieve (as they seem to be in the house sales division) the managers' inability to achieve the target is likely to demotivate them, and they may stop trying to achieve the target.

Now try these questions from the Practice Question Bank	Number	Level	Marks	Time
	11.1–11.5	Intermediate	n/a	10 mins
	11.6	Examination	25	45 mins

PERFORMANCE MEASUREMENT

Although non-financial aspects of performance are becoming increasingly important, aspects of financial performance remain very important for organisations, and management accountants have a key role in generating and analysing financial performance information (Section 1).

In Sections 3–4, we discuss the appraisal of particular business units and divisions, using profit-based measures such as ROI and RI.

We then consider some more themes in controlling performance with the ultimate aim of increasing shareholder value (Section 7).

Many large firms are organised into strategic business units. Multinational firms, in particular, have specific management problems in relation to setting objectives and performance assessment (Section 8).

Transfer prices (Section 9) are a way of promoting divisional autonomy, but the transfer price needs to be fair, neutral and administratively simple. Otherwise, prices may be set in such a way as to improve the results of one subsidiary at the expense of another.

We finish by looking at some of the issues in measuring divisional performance, in particular controllability and short-termism.

Topic list	Learning outcomes	Syllabus references	Ability required
1 The role of the management accountant in strategic performance evaluation	D1(b)	D1(b)(v)	Recommend
2 Using contribution margin as a measure of performance	D1(a)	–	Evaluate
3 Divisional performance: return on investment (ROI)	D1(a)	D1(a)(ii)	Evaluate
4 Divisional performance: residual income (RI)	D1(a)	D1(a)(ii)	Evaluate
5 Comparing profit centre performance	D1(a)	D1(a)(i)	Evaluate
6 Interfirm comparisons and performance ratios	D1(a)	D1(a)(i)	Evaluate
7 Value based management	D1(a)	D1(a)(i)	Evaluate
8 International subsidiaries	D1(a)	D1(a)(i)	Evaluate
9 Transfer pricing	D1(a)	–	Evaluate
10 Divisional performance and control	D1(a)	–	Evaluate
11 Strategic management styles	–	–	–

Chapter Overview

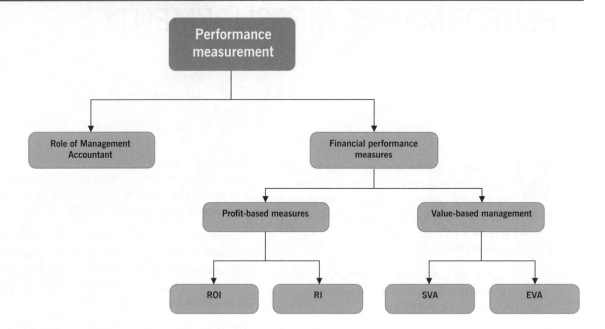

1 The role of the management accountant in strategic performance evaluation

Introduction

Although the management accountant's role is no longer limited to measuring financial performance, management accountants nevertheless have a crucial role to play in measuring, and evaluating, financial performance.

In the previous chapter, we highlighted the importance of non-financial aspects of an organisation's performance, particularly where those aspects of performance link directly to the organisation's CSFs.

Nonetheless, financial aspects of performance remain crucial to organisations, particularly to companies whose primary objective is to maximise the value they create for their shareholders. Here is a reminder of CIMA's definition of performance measurement.

KEY TERM

PERFORMANCE MEASUREMENT: 'The process of assessing the proficiency with which a reporting entity succeeds, by the economic acquisition of resources and their efficient and effective development, in achieving its objectives. Performance measures may be based on non-financial as well as on financial information.'

(CIMA Official Terminology)

Similarly, while the role of the management accountant has been changed in recent years – particularly in the context of strategic management accounting – measuring financial performance remains a key part of the management accountant's role. In this final chapter of the Study Text, we focus on the measurement of financial performance, and some of the techniques which can be used to evaluate an organisation's financial performance.

1.1 The role of the management accountant

In Chapter 1 of this Study Text, we looked at the role of the management accountant, primarily in relation to strategy development. However, a number of the elements of the accountant's role are central to performance measurement, and the 'review and control' aspects of the strategic management process.

The following points are taken from the *CIMA Official Terminology* defining the role of Chartered Management Accountants:

- Generation, communication and interpretation of financial and non-financial information for management and other stakeholders.

- Provision of specific information and analysis on which decisions are based.

- Monitoring of outcomes against plans and other benchmarks and the initiation of responsive action for performance improvement.

- Derivation of performance measures and benchmarks, financial and non-financial, quantitative and qualitative for monitoring and control.

CIMA also highlights that Chartered Management Accountants can bring the following two key skills to organisations:

- **Analysis** – Analysing the narrative behind the figures and using it to make business decisions.

- **Communication** – Knowing what information management needs and explaining the numbers to non-financial managers.

Exam skills

In this chapter, we will look at various techniques which can be used for measuring divisional performance. However, when assessing divisional performance it is very important that the measures a management accountant uses reflect the nature of the division. Divisions can be categorised into three different categories of **responsibility centre**:

Cost centres – A division incurs costs but has no sales revenue. Financial performance measures should focus on costs (eg total cost, cost per unit, cost variances), but cannot measure profit (because the division has no sales revenue).

Non-financial performance measures (for example, relating to productivity, or quality) could also be measured.

Profit centres – A division has both costs and revenues, and the divisional manager is responsible for these. However, the divisional manager is not responsible for the level of investment in the division.

Financial performance measures should focus on sales, profits and margins, but should not include ROI, RI or EVA (because these are affected by the asset base).

Customer-related non-financial measures (eg market share; customer satisfaction) could also be measured.

Investment centres – Divisional managers are responsible not only for revenues and costs, but also for working capital and capital investment decisions.

Financial performance measures could include ROI, RI or EVA as well as ones focusing on sales, profits and margins.

Section summary

The management accountant has a crucial role to play in performance measurement, which includes providing financial and non-financial information to managers.

Communication is an important part of a Chartered Management Accountant's role, including knowing what information managers need, and explaining financial performance to non-financial managers.

2 Using contribution margin as a measure of performance

Introduction

The basic concept of **contribution** can be used strategically if questions about strategic factors are examined in relation to the contribution to profit they generate. It could also be appropriate to measure the performance of SBUs in relation to the contribution to profit they generate.

KEY TERM

CONTRIBUTION MARGIN can be defined as 'the difference between sales volume and the variable cost of those sales, expressed either in absolute terms or as a contribution per unit'.

The contribution per unit is 'often related to a key or limiting factor to give a sum required to cover fixed overhead and profit, such as contribution per machine hour, per direct labour hour or per kilo of scarce raw material'.

(a)   A **contribution centre** is a profit centre where expenditure is calculated on a marginal cost basis.
(b)   **Contribution per unit of limiting factor** is a measurement for optimising the use of scarce resources.

Contribution margins are also used for measuring performance in terms of **breakeven analysis**.

2.1 Contribution and strategic decisions

2.1.1 Product market issues

Consider, for example, a situation where a car manufacturer wishes to launch a new model, the success of which is crucial to corporate survival. Fixed costs are the capital required to develop the vehicle and tool up, which will appear in the breakeven equation as depreciation, development costs and operational fixed costs. Variable costs will have been identified and reliable sales forecasts will have been obtained. From this data, two figures can be computed:

(a)   The number of vehicles required to **break even**

(b)   The number of vehicles required to generate **adequate returns** over the life of the model or the investment and, significantly, what this represents in terms of market penetration and market share

Johnson, Scholes and Whittington argue that breakeven analysis has a useful role in appraising and controlling strategy. Questions can be asked based on the breakeven model.

- What is the **probability** of achieving the desired levels of market penetration?

- Do the **conditions in the market** lend themselves to achieving that desired penetration?

- Will the **competitors** allow a profitable entry?

- Are the **cost and quality** assumptions feasible?

- Are the **funds available**, not just to complete the development but to establish the production capacity and skilled manpower to achieve the desired penetration?

2.1.2 Exit

Firms with high exit barriers may use contribution as the main tool for decision making. Ward cites the example of a coal mine, as to the type of decisions taken. High exit barriers result from:

- The actual costs of closure, redundancy and so on
- The cost of reopening the mine, if demand for coal and prices picks up
- Costs which will not be avoided by the closure

2.2 Applying contribution margin accounting to divisional performance measurement

A danger with contribution margin analysis is that firms in a competitive industry might be tempted to sell at prices which cover marginal costs, but fail to earn an adequate return on **sunk fixed costs**.

Applying the principle that managers should only be accountable for costs and revenues which they can control directly, it follows that short-term controls for profit centres should focus on contribution margins. This is because only revenues and variable costs are **controllable** in the short run.

However, some directly attributable fixed costs might also be controllable, or at least avoidable, in the short term if the scale of business operations was significantly reduced. Fixed costs can therefore be classified as follows:

(a)   Costs which are **directly attributable** to a particular activity, and which tend to rise or fall in steps as the scale of activities is increased or lowered.

(b)   **Unavoidable costs**. Many fixed costs are committed, or not directly attributable to any particular activity.

One way of measuring profit for an investment centre or a profit centre is as follows.

	£
Sales revenue	X
Less variable cost of sales	(X)
Equals contribution	X
Less directly attributable fixed costs (avoidable/controllable)	(X)
Equals gross profit	X
Less share of unavoidable (committed*/uncontrollable*) fixed costs	(X)
Equals net profit	X

(* In the short term. In the long term, all fixed cost items should be controllable and 'variable'.)

Section summary

Contribution margins can be used for measuring performance and as a tool for decision making.

3 Divisional performance: return on investment (ROI)

Introduction

Profit centre organisation reflects the structure of authority in the organisation, and managers are made accountable and rewarded on the basis of profit centre results.

Return on investment (ROI) is a convenient measure, which ties in easily with the firm's accounts. However, there are measurement and valuation problems, especially in relation to non-current assets. These can encourage managers to take decisions which are not in the firm's best long-term interest. ROI does not easily account for risk.

ROI is based on **organisation structure**, not business processes, and is only suitable to products at the mature phase of the life cycle.

Many large firms are organised into **strategic business units** (SBUs).

KEY TERM

A STRATEGIC BUSINESS UNIT (SBU) is a 'section, usually a division, within a larger business organisation, that has a significant degree of autonomy, typically being responsible for developing and marketing its own products or services'.   (*CIMA Official Terminology*)

A typical SBU is a division of the organisation 'where managers have control over their own resources, and discretion overt the deployment of resources within specified boundaries'.   (*Ward*)

The performance of these business units is complicated by the degree of autonomy their managers enjoy.

We have covered DCF and contribution margin accounting first for these reasons:

(a) Both techniques are, in theory, applicable to controlling and assessing strategies and can be applied to **divisional performance measurement**.

(b) DCF addresses the issue in terms of **cash flows**.

In practice, many firms use more 'traditional' accounting based measures, such as ROI. First some definitions.

RETURN ON CAPITAL EMPLOYED (ROCE)

$$\frac{\text{Profit before interest and tax} \times 100}{\text{Average capital employed}}$$

ROCE indicates the productivity of capital employed. The denominator is normally calculated as the average of the capital employed at the beginning and end of the year. Problems of seasonality, new capital introduced or other factors may necessitate taking the average of a number of periods within the year.

RETURN ON INVESTMENT (ROI)

$$\frac{\text{Profit before interest and tax} \times 100}{\text{Operations management capital employed}}$$

ROI is often used to assess managers' performance. Managers are responsible for all assets (normally defined as non-current assets plus net current assets).   (*CIMA Official Terminology*)

ROI is normally used to apply to investment centres or profit centres. These normally reflect the existing organisation structure of the business.

ROI shows how much profit in accounting terms has been made in relation to the amount of capital invested. For example, suppose that a company has two investment centres, A and B, which show results for the year as follows:

	A	B
Profit after depreciation, before tax and interest	£60,000	£30,000
Assets generating income	£400,000	£120,000
ROI	15%	25%

Investment centre A has made double the profits of investment centre B, and in terms of profits alone has therefore been more 'successful'. However, B has earned a much higher ROI. This suggests that B has been a more successful investment than A.

The main reasons for the widespread use of ROI as a performance indicator are:

(a)   **Financial reporting**. It ties in directly with the accounting process, and is identifiable from the income statement (profit and loss account) and the statement of financial position (balance sheet), the firm's most important communications media with investors. Therefore it is easy for investors to understand.

(b)   **Aggregation**. ROI is a very convenient method of measuring the performance for a division or company as an entire unit.

(c)   It can be used to **compare divisions**. Because ROI provides a percentage figure rather than an absolute amount, it can be used to compare performance in divisions of different sizes.

3.1 Measurement problems: non-current assets

The problems with ROI relate to accurate measurement.

3.1.1 Net assets

It is probably most common to use **return on net assets**. There are two main problems:

(a)   If an investment centre maintains the same annual profit, and keeps the same assets without a policy of regular non-current asset replacement, its ROI will increase year by year as the assets get older. This can give a false impression of improving 'real' performance over time.

The dangers of this are twofold:

(i) Managers will avoid buying new assets (even though they may be needed to improve performance).

(ii) Management might wrongly think the divisions with the newest assets are the worst performing, leading them to be shut down.

(b) It is not easy to **compare fairly** the performance of one investment centre with another. Non-current assets may be of different ages or may be depreciated in different ways.

3.1.2 Return on gross assets

(a) **Advantage**. Ignoring depreciation removes the problem of ROI increasing over time as non-current assets get older and get depreciated.

(b) **Disadvantages**

(i) Measuring ROI as return on gross assets ignores the **age factor**. Older non-current assets usually cost more to repair and maintain. An investment centre with old assets may therefore have its profitability reduced by repair costs.

(ii) **Inflation and technological change** alter the cost of non-current assets. If one investment centre has non-current assets bought ten years ago with a gross cost of £1 million, and another investment centre, in the same area of business operations, has non-current assets bought very recently for £1 million, the quantity and technological character of the non-current assets of the two investment centres are likely to be very different.

3.1.3 ROI: replacement cost

The view that ROI should be measured in terms of **replacement cost** (either net or gross) is connected to the arguments in favour of **current cost accounting**. In a period of price inflation, ROI based on historical costs is difficult to interpret because it will become higher as assets get older, as profits will be measured in current-year money.

3.1.4 Measurement problems: what are 'assets' anyway?

Prudence and other accounting principles require items such as R&D to only be carried forward as an investment in special circumstances.

Many 'costs' enhance the long-term revenue-earning capacity of the business; **brands**, for example. Many firms have capitalised brands for this reason. For decision-making and control purposes, brand expenditure might be better treated as an investment.

3.1.5 The target return for a group of companies

If a group of companies sets a target return for the Group as a whole, or if a company sets a target return for each SBU, it might be company policy that no investment project should go ahead in any subsidiary or investment centre unless the project promises to earn at least the target return. For example, it might be Group policy that:

(a) There should be no new investment by any subsidiary in the Group unless it is expected to earn at least a 15% return

(b) Similarly, no non-current asset should be disposed of if the asset is currently earning a return in excess of 15% of its disposal value

(c) Investments which promise a return of 15% or more ought to be undertaken

Problems with such a policy are:

(a)   Investments are appraised by DCF whereas actual performance will probably be measured on the basis of ROI.

(b)   The target return makes no allowance for the different risk of each investment centre.

(c)   In a conglomerate an identical target return may be unsuitable to many businesses in a group. The financial returns and investment costs of a division will vary according to its location, the type of business it engages in, and the stage it is at in its product life cycle. A company needs to remember this when assessing the performance of different divisions.

(d)   Managers **may reject profitable investment opportunities**, and thereby not act in the best interests of their shareholders. For example, assume a division currently earns an ROI of 12%, the estimated ROI on a new project is 10%, but the company's cost of capital is 8%.

The project's estimated ROI is greater than the cost of capital and so it should be accepted because it will increase shareholder wealth. However, a divisional manager whose performance is measured in terms of ROI will reject the project because its expected return (10%) is less than the 12% the division is currently generating.

3.2 Example: the problem with setting a target ROI

Suppose an investment in a non-current asset would cost £100,000 and make a profit of £11,000 pa after depreciation. The asset would be depreciated by £25,000 pa for 4 years. It is Group policy that investments must show a minimum return of 15%.

The DCF net present value of this investment would just about be positive, and so the investment ought to be approved if Group policy is adhered to.

Year	Cash flow (profit before dep'n) £	Discount factor 15%	Present value £
0	(100,000)	1.000	(100,000)
1	36,000	0.870	31,320
2	36,000	0.756	27,216
3	36,000	0.658	23,688
4	36,000	0.572	20,592
		NPV	2,816

However, if the investment is measured year by year according to the accounting ROI it has earned, we find that its return is less than 15% in year 1, but more than 15% in years 2, 3 and 4.

Year	Profit £	Net book value of equipment (mid-year value) £	ROCE
1	11,000	87,500	12.6%
2	11,000	62,500	17.6%
3	11,000	37,500	29.3%
4	11,000	12,500	88.0%

In view of the low accounting ROI in year 1, should the investment be undertaken or not?

(a)   Strictly speaking, investment decisions should be based on IRR, and should not be guided by short-term accounting ROI.

(b)   Even if accounting ROI is used as a guideline for investment decisions, ROI should be looked at over the full life of the investment, not just in the short term. In the short term (in the first year or so of a project's life) the accounting ROI is likely to be low because the net book value of the asset will still be high.

In our example, it is conceivable that the Group's management might disapprove of the project because of its low accounting ROI in year 1. This approach is short-termist, but it nevertheless can make some sense to a company or group of companies which has to show a satisfactory profit and ROI in its published accounts each year, to keep its shareholders satisfied with performance.

3.3 Possible behavioural implications of ROI: short-termism and lack of goal congruence

Managers are judged on the ROI earned by their centre each year. This motivates them into taking decisions that increase their centre's short-term ROI. An investment desirable to the Group might not be so appealing to the individual investment centre. This demonstrates a lack of **goal congruence**.

In the short term, a desire to increase ROI might lead to projects being taken on without due regard to their risk.

Any decisions which benefit the company in the long term but which reduce the ROI in the immediate short term would reflect badly on the manager's reported performance.

We have already suggested that using ROI as a performance measure may prevent managers buying new assets. This is an example of short-sighted decision making. The manager's decision is being based on the affect it will have on ROI in the short term, rather than the longer-term benefits to the business which may accrue from having the new assets.

However, we need to remember that ROI is a measure of historic performance – it describes performance in the past year. But this may not be an accurate guide as to what future earnings may be, and ultimately, shareholders will be interested in the future earnings which a company can deliver.

Question 12.1	Manipulation

Learning outcome D1(a)

Describe any methods you can think of (and their implications) which managers would use to manipulate the return on investment figures, if ROI was calculated as:

$$\text{Return on total assets} = \frac{\text{Profit before interest, tax, depreciation}}{\text{Gross non-current assets} + \text{total current assets}}$$

3.4 ROI, strategy and product-market issues

3.4.1 ROI reflects organisation structure, not business processes

ROI is based on the existing organisation structure of a business:

(a)   Business process re-engineering suggests that many organisation structures are badly designed in themselves.

(b)   The use of ROI in a responsibility accounting framework perpetuates the bad effects of the existing organisation structure.

(c)   All investment projects may involve the co-operation of many departments in a business, along the whole extent of the value chain.

3.4.2 Product life cycle: ROI is not suitable to all phases

Product-market issues are also relevant. ROI is suited to the **mature phase**, when the market is established. ROI is also best suited to cash cows on the BCG matrix.

3.4.3 ROI aggregates all products in a portfolio

We have seen that many firms have a **portfolio of products** in different stages of the life cycle – in fact this is necessary for the firm's long-term survival. ROI does not suggest the right strategic action to be taken with regard to new products or declining products (rising stars, question marks or dogs).

Section summary

Return on investment (ROI) is based on organisational structure, not business processes, and is best suited to products at the mature phase of the life cycle. The problems with ROI relate to accurate measurement.

4 Divisional performance: residual income (RI)

Introduction

Residual income (RI) gets around some of the problems of ROI, by deducting an imputed interest charge for the use of assets from profits.

An alternative way of measuring the performance of an investment centre, instead of using ROI, is residual income (RI).

KEY TERM

RESIDUAL INCOME is 'profit minus a charge for capital employed in the period'.

(CIMA Official Terminology)

RI is calculated as 'Earnings before interest and tax – (invested capital × imputed rate)'.

The imputed cost of capital might be the organisation's cost of borrowing or its weighted average cost of capital. Alternatively, the cost of capital can be adjusted to allow for the risk characteristics of each investment centre, with a higher imputed interest rate being applied to higher risk centres.

4.1 The advantages and disadvantages of RI compared to ROI

The advantages of using RI are:

(a)   RI will increase when:

   (i)   Investments earning above the cost of capital are undertaken
   (ii) Investments earning below the cost of capital are eliminated

(b)   RI is more flexible since a different cost of capital can be applied to investments with different risk characteristics.

(c)   The cost of financing a division or an investment is highlighted to division managers through the use of the cost of capital figure.

The weakness of RI is that it does not facilitate comparisons between investment and organisations of different sizes, because it uses an absolute figure rather than a percentage.

4.1.1 RI versus ROI: marginally profitable investments

RI increases if a new investment is undertaken which earns a profit in excess of the imputed interest charge on the value of the asset acquired. When a manager is judged by ROI, a marginally profitable investment would be less likely to be undertaken because it would reduce the average ROI earned by the centre as a whole.

RI does not always point to the right decision, because notional interest on accounting capital employed is not the same as IRR on cash investment. However, RI is more likely than ROI to improve when managers make correct investment/divestment decisions, and so is probably a 'safer' basis than ROI on which to measure performance.

4.2 Example: ROI versus RI

Suppose that Department H has the following profit, assets employed and an imputed interest charge of 12% on operating assets.

	Department H	
	£	£
Operating profit	30,000	
Operating assets		100,000
Imputed interest (12%)	12,000	
Return on investment		30%
Residual income	18,000	

Suppose now that an additional investment of £10,000 is proposed, which will increase operating income in Department H by £1,400. The effect of the investment would be:

	£	£
Total operating income	31,400	
Total operating assets		110,000
Imputed interest (12%)	13,200	
Return on investment		28.5%
Residual income	18,200	

If the Department H manager is made responsible for the department's performance, they would resist the new investment if they were to be judged on ROI, but would welcome the investment if they were judged according to RI, since there would be a marginal increase of £200 in RI from the investment, but a fall of 1.5% in ROI.

The marginal investment offers a return of 14% (£1,400 on an investment of £10,000) which is above the 'cut-off rate' of 12%. Since the original ROI was 30%, the marginal investment will reduce the overall divisional performance. Indeed, any marginal investment offering an accounting rate of return of less than 30% in the year would reduce the overall performance.

RI should not be used as a means of making asset purchasing decisions; nevertheless, it may be a useful alternative to ROI where there is a conflict between purchase decisions indicated by a positive NPV in discounted cash flow, and the resulting reduction in divisional ROI which 'reflects badly' on management performance.

4.3 General issues with RI

Some of the disadvantages we identified in relation to using ROI as a performance measure also apply to RI:

(a) It can lead to short-termist decision making by discouraging managers from replacing non-current assets which would increase the cost of their capital assets.

(b) The financial returns and investment costs of a division will vary according to its location, the type of business it engages in, and the stage it is at in the product life cycle. A company needs to remember this when assessing the performance of different divisions.

(c) RI (like ROI) is a measure of historic performance, but it does not give an indication of what future earnings may be, despite this being an important consideration for shareholders.

Section summary

An alternative to ROI for measuring the performance of an investment centre is **residual income** (RI). This avoids some of the problems with ROI by deducting from profit an interest charge for the use of assets. However, RI does not facilitate comparison between investment centres, nor does it relate the size of a centre's income to the size of the investment.

5 Comparing profit centre performance

Introduction

Profit centres are often compared. Problems arise when managers are judged on matters they cannot control. A variety of measures involving **contribution** are used to isolate controllable costs.

Problems in measuring **divisional performance** include allocation of head office costs, and different asset valuations.

When departments within an organisation are set up as profit centres, their performance will be judged on the profit they earn. This performance might be compared on the basis of profit/sales ratios, contribution earned per unit of scarce resource, or profit growth rates.

5.1 Dysfunctional decisions and goal congruence

A profit centre manager might take decisions that will improve their own centre's performance at the expense of other parts of the business.

- Profit centre managers tend to put their own profit performance above everything else.
- Profit centres are not isolated entities, but related divisions within a single organisation.

Question 12.2	Head office

Learning outcome D1(a)

What are the likely behavioural consequences of a head office continually imposing its own decisions on divisions?

5.2 Comparing profit centre performance

Shillinglaw suggested that four profit concepts could be used to measure and report divisional profit internally within a company. Each has its own purpose.

(a)   **Contribution**

(b)   **'Controllable profit'** – contribution minus all the division's fixed costs controllable by the manager.

(c)   **Controllable margin** – controllable profit minus all other costs directly traceable to the division.

(d)   **Net profit or net contribution**, less a share of service centre costs and general management overhead. However, 'net profit' is the least useful of the four, because the allocation of general overhead costs must inevitably be largely arbitrary.

5.2.1 Contribution

A principle of responsibility accounting is that profit centre managers should only be held accountable for those revenues and costs that they are in a position to control. Increases in production volume, within the relevant range of output, will raise profit by the amount of increase in contribution.

A divisional performance statement based on contribution might appear as follows.

	Division A £'000	Division B £'000	Total £'000
Sales	80	100	180
Less variable costs	60	50	110
Contribution	20	50	70
Less fixed costs			50
Profit			20

(a) Divisional performance can be improved by increasing the sales price, or volume of sales, or reducing the unit variable cost.

(b) The relative profitability of Divisions A and B could be compared by means of their C/S ratios (in this example, 25% and 50% respectively).

(c) If there is a production limiting factor, performance could also be measured in terms of contribution per unit of limiting factor. In our example, if there is a shortage of cash for working capital acting as a restriction on output, and if Divisions A and B use £2,500 and £8,000 in working capital respectively, the contribution per £1 of working capital employed would be £8 for Division A and £6.25 for Division B (so that a transfer of some production resources from B to A might be profitable under these circumstances).

5.2.2 Controllable profit

One drawback to using contribution alone as a measure of divisional performance is that although it indicates the short-term controllable results of the division, it gives no indication as to **longer-term underlying profitability**.

In the following example, closure of Division X might be justified, since there would be a net saving in annual running costs of £5,000.

	Division X £'000	Division Y £'000	Total £'000
Sales	70	120	190
Less variable costs	50	80	130
Contribution	20	40	60
Less directly attributable fixed costs	25	25	50
Profit of the division	(5)	15	10
Less fixed costs (general)			8
Company profit			2

5.2.3 Controllable margin

A further refinement of this approach to profit centre accounting is to make a distinction between fixed costs over which the centre manager has short-run discretionary control, for example advertising costs and sales promotion expenditures, and fixed costs over which the manager has no personal control, such as their own salary, or depreciation of assets.

		Division X £'000	Division Y £'000	Total £'000
	Sales	70	120	190
	Less variable costs	50	80	130
(1)	Contribution	20	40	60
	Less fixed costs directly attributable to manager's discretionary control	8	20	28
(2)	Profit attributable to the manager	12	20	32
	Less fixed costs directly attributable to the profit centre, outside the manager's control	17	5	22
(3)	Profit attributable to the profit centre	(5)	15	10
	Shared fixed costs			8
	Company profit			2

5.2.4 Net profit: after charging a proportion of shared fixed costs

An argument against measuring profit on the basis of contribution less directly attributable fixed costs is that no one is made responsible for earning a sufficiently large profit to ensure that shared fixed costs are covered, and that the organisation as a whole is profitable.

5.2.5 The problems of absorption costing

Absorption costing systems are perhaps the 'traditional' method of accounting for divisional performance, but they have some serious drawbacks:

(a) **They are not a method of responsibility accounting**, in that managers cannot control the general fixed costs charged to their division, and are not properly responsible for them.

(b) **The method of apportioning fixed costs can vary**, according to the basis chosen.

5.2.6 RI and interdepartmental comparisons.

With an RI method of reporting divisional profits, four different 'profit' figures can be identified, as follows. It is quite possible that divisions will do better or worse, in comparative terms, according to which measure is used.

		Division A £'000	£'000
	Sales: external		310
	internal transfers		210
			520
	Variable costs of goods sold internally and externally	220	
	Variable divisional expenses	20	
			240
(1)	**Controllable contribution**		280
	Controllable divisional overhead		90
(2)	**Controllable profit**		190
	Depreciation and other expenses on controllable fixed assets (eg lease costs)	50	
	Interest on controllable fixed assets	15	
			65
(3)	**Controllable residual income**		125
	Depreciation and other expenses on non-controllable fixed assets	20	
	Allocated central expenses	40	
	Interest on non-controllable fixed assets	10	
			70
(4)	**Net residual income**		55

5.3 Head office as a profit centre or investment centre: charging for services

One way of improving the responsibility accounting system might be to establish head office as a profit centre or investment centre in its own right.

5.4 Service departments

The same cost distinctions should be made for service department costs.

(a) The department might incur costs that are variable with the volume of activity. Variable costs should be identified, and control reporting should compare actual costs with a flexed budget.

(b) The department's directly attributable fixed costs should be identified, because these are the running costs that would be saved if the department were to be closed down.

5.5 Making non-current assets controllable

Non-current assets are 'controllable' by divisional managers if they have the authority to purchase or dispose of assets. A temporary surplus of non-current assets will reduce the division's short-term ROI or RI as the assets are 'controllable'. The manager could dispose of the assets to prevent this, but they may be needed in the future and so disposal might be inappropriate. A way around this is to establish a head office 'pool' of non-current assets from which non-current assets can be obtained when required, and returned to when they become surplus to requirements.

5.6 Added value

KEY TERM

Although added value can be measured in different ways, the broad concept is that ADDED VALUE equals sales minus the costs of materials and bought-in services.

Managers are then made responsible for the following:

(a) Total value added earned

(b) The way in which value added is divided between labour costs, non-current asset depreciation, profit

(c) Value added earned per unit of key resource (per machine hour, say, or direct labour hour)

Division B

	£'000	£'000
Sales		400
Materials	160	
Bought-in services	80	
		240
Value added		160
Direct labour	70	
Indirect labour	50	
Depreciation	30	
		150
Profit		10

Section summary

When comparing **profit centres**, managers should only be held accountable for those revenues and costs that they are in a position to control. Controllable costs can be isolated using a variety of methods involving **contribution**.

6 Interfirm comparisons and performance ratios

Introduction

As well as comparing profit centres within a Group, comparisons are made between **companies in an industry**. Problems include a lack of information and different accounting policies. As well as monitoring performance from the investor's point of view, such schemes can be used in **competitive analysis**. **Ratio analysis** might be useful in this context.

Interfirm comparisons are comparisons of the performance of different companies, subsidiaries or investment centres.

6.1 The purpose of interfirm comparisons

(a) One company can compare its performance against another, as part of **competitive analysis or benchmarking**.

(b) **Senior management** can compare the performance of different subsidiary companies within their Group.

(c) **Investors** can compare different firms in an industry.

(d) A company's **status** as a potential takeover target, or as a potential takeover threat, can be evaluated.

A financial comparison between rival public limited companies might cover:

- The best profits record (ROI, growth in profits and EPS)
- The best financial structure (financial gearing, debt ratio, interest cover)
- The 'best quality' profits or best growth prospects (P/E ratio comparison)
- The best cash flow position

6.2 Which firms should be compared with each other?

It is unrealistic to assume that all firms ought to be able to earn comparable ROI.

- Some industries are more profitable than others.
- Some companies need a big investment in non-current assets.

There are a number of basic requirements for an interfirm comparison to be successful:

(a) The companies compared must all belong to a **similar industry** to enable comparison.

(b) Reports might be given in the form of lists of **ratios**. If ratios are to be helpful for control purposes, comparisons should be limited to companies of roughly the same size.

(c) The results of each of the participants must be adjusted so that, as far as possible, the same **accounting policies** are used for each.

6.3 Performance ratios

Ratios are useful in that they provide a means of comparison of actual results:

- With a budget, or desired target
- With ratios of previous years' results, in order to detect trends
- With ratios of other companies or divisions
- With industry or governmental indices

6.3.1 Ratios from financial statements

You should be familiar with the statement of financial position (balance sheet) and income statement (profit and loss account) ratios.

(a) **Income statement ratios** include profit margin (profit/sales) which can be analysed as follows, in a hierarchy of subsidiary ratios.

(i) $\dfrac{\text{Production cost of sales}}{\text{Sales}}$ which can be broken down into:

(1) $\dfrac{\text{Material costs}}{\text{Sales value of production}}$ or $\dfrac{\text{Material costs}}{\text{Total costs of production}}$

(2) $\dfrac{\text{Works labour cost}}{\text{Sales value of production}}$ or $\dfrac{\text{Labour costs}}{\text{Total cost of production}}$

(3) $\dfrac{\text{Production overheads}}{\text{Sales value of production}}$ or $\dfrac{\text{Production overheads}}{\text{Total costs of production}}$

(ii) $\dfrac{\text{Distribution and marketing costs}}{\text{Sales}}$

(iii) $\dfrac{\text{Administrative costs}}{\text{Sales}}$

(b) **Statement of financial position ratios** include the following, broken down further:

(i) **Asset turnover** (sales/capital employed), which can be analysed by class of asset (eg sales/non-current assets)

(ii) **Working capital ratios** covering liquidity (eg current ratio, current assets/current liabilities) and turnover periods for receivables, payables and inventory (eg credit period taken by credit customers)

(iii) Gearing ratios covering borrowings

Question 12.3	Strategic significance

Learning outcome D1(a)

What might be the strategic significance of the following, when compared with the industry average?

(a) A high non-current asset turnover
(b) High gearing
(c) Far higher non-current assets but lower labour costs

Question 12.4	Subsidiaries

Learning outcome D1(a)

Calculate and compare the ROI, asset utilisation and profitability of the two subsidiaries whose results are shown below.

	A Ltd £	B Ltd £
Capital employed	300,000	800,000
Net profit	60,000	120,000
Sales	1,250,000	2,400,000

6.4 The calculation of ROI in interfirm comparisons

There are several issues to consider when deciding how to measure both the return and the capital employed.

6.4.1 Return

Definition of return. Return might be taken as profit after tax. However, when interfirm comparisons are being made, this would be unsuitable, for two reasons:

(a)   The **tax rate** applicable to one company's profits may be different from the tax rate applicable to another's.

(b)   One company might be financed largely by borrowing, receiving tax relief on interest payments. Another company might be entirely equity financed.

Measuring return (profit). When there is a comparison between the results of subsidiaries within the same Group or the results of investment centres within a single company, there may be a problem with **transfer prices**.

6.4.2 Capital employed/investment

Should assets be valued on the basis of historical cost, replacement cost, disposal value, current value or some other similar inflation-adjusted basis?

(a)   Historical cost has the severe drawback that in a period of inflation, the balance sheet value of older non-current assets can fall below their 'realistic' current value, and so the measurement of ROI will give a misleading (excessively high) percentage return.

(b)   Depreciation charges against non-current assets might also fail to reflect the loss of value from using the assets during the period, when historical cost accounting is used.

(c)   Replacement cost or current cost might be difficult to estimate whereas historical cost is a readily known value.

(d)   Disposal value is only useful when the non-current assets are readily marketable (eg property) but in such cases a target return on disposal value represents an opportunity cost of the investment.

6.4.3 The accounting policies of different companies

Typical differences in accounting policies and asset acquisition methods between one firm and another are:

*   The assumed life of non-current assets
*   The method of depreciation used
*   Accounting for intangible non-current assets, such as development costs and goodwill
*   Inventory valuation methods
*   Renting accommodation instead of buying the freehold or leasehold
*   Purchasing operating non-current assets or leasing/renting them

Section summary

Interfirm comparisons are comparisons of the performance of different companies, subsidiaries or investment centres. Ratios are useful in that they provide a means of comparison of actual results.

7 Value based management

Introduction

A management team is required by an **organisation's shareholders** to **maximise the value of their investment** in the organisation and a plethora of performance indicators is used to assess whether or not the management team is fulfilling this duty.

7.1 Shareholder value

Since the primary objective of commercial organisations is normally assumed to be maximising the wealth of their shareholders, it follows that performance measures should evaluate how well the organisations are acheving this.

However, most of the financial **performance measures** used by organisations are based on information from their published accounts. Not only do these indicators often give **conflicting messages**, but they can also be easily **manipulated** and often provide **misleading** information. Earnings per share, for example, is reduced by capital-building investments in research and development and in marketing. Perhaps more importantly, though, critics of profit-based performance measures (such as ROI and RI) argue that profits can be influenced by management through the accounting policies they choose. Similarly, as we noted earlier, ROI and RI are often criticised for discouraging asset replacement – and promoting short-termist decision making. (Choosing not to invest in new assets may preserve ROI or RI in the short term, but it could impede growth and innovation in the future.)

What is more, the **financial statements** themselves **do not provide a clear picture of whether or not shareholder value is being created**. The income statement (profit and loss account), for example, indicates the **quantity** but not the **quality** of earnings, and it does not distinguish between earnings derived from operating assets as opposed to non-operating assets. Moreover, **it ignores the cost of equity financing** and only takes into account the costs of debt financing, thereby penalising organisations which choose a mix of debt and equity finance.

The statement of cash flows (**cash flow statement**) also fails to provide appropriate information as large, positive cash flows are possible when organisations underspend on maintenance, or undertake little capital investment, to increase short-term profits at the expense of long-term success. On the other hand, an organisation can have large negative cash flows for several years and still be profitable.

A **shareholder value approach** to performance measurement involves moving the focus away from short-term profits to a **longer-term view of value creation**, the motivation being that it will help the business stay ahead in an increasingly competitive world.

Individual shareholders have varying definitions of shareholder value as different shareholders value different aspects of performance.

- Financial returns in the short term
- Short-term capital gains
- Long-term returns or capital gains
- Stability and security
- Achievements in products produced or services provided
- Ethical standards

(It is unlikely that the last two alone make a company valuable to an investor.)

These factors and others will all be reflected in a company's share price, but stock markets are notoriously fickle and tend to have a short-term outlook.

7.1.1 Shareholder value analysis

Wider share ownership and more knowledgeable investors are forcing companies to understand the techniques by which their companies are being judged. The terminology **shareholder value** is used widely to describe a range of shareholder-focused performance indicators developed by various consultancies.

One approach is **shareholder value analysis (SVA)**, devised by Alfred Rappaport (*Creating Shareholder Value,* 1986).

KEY TERM

SHAREHOLDER VALUE is the 'total return to the shareholders in terms of both dividends and share price growth, calculated as the present value of future free cash flows of the business discounted at the weighted average cost of the capital of the business less the market value of its debt'.

(CIMA Official Terminology)

Shareholder value = (corporate value – debt)

Where business value is calculated as the PV of free cash flows from operations plus the value of any marketable assets held.

The value of a corporation can be established by developing a future **cash flow forecast** and converting it into a present value, discounted at the cost of capital. The total value of the business is then found by taking away the value of any debt and adding any value from external investments.

Dividing the result by the number of shares gives the **shareholder value per share**.

This technique has been used extensively in acquisition situations and is often known as **cash flow return on investment (CFROI)**.

7.1.2 Drivers of shareholder value

Rappaport proposes that this **single figure value** for a business be calculated by **reference to seven 'value drivers'**, which drive the generation of **cash**.

(a) **Sales growth rate**: percentage increase in annual sales revenue. An increase in profitable sales should increase free cash flow.

(b) **Operating profit margin**: operating profit as a percentage of sales revenue. An organisation should try to maximise its profit margin. Margins can be increased either by increasing prices, or reducing costs.

   The return on capital generated by a business depends on the combination of profit margins relative to turnover (margin) and the ability to generate turnover from capital invested (efficiency). In order to improve return on capital, a business needs an improvement in the combination of margin and efficiency.

(c) **Cash taxation rate**: tax payable as a percentage of operating profit. The more tax incurred, the more of the shareholders' value the Government takes.

(d) **Fixed capital investment rate**: the amount invested in fixed (non-current) assets as a percentage of sales revenue. Cash invested in non-current assets reduces free cash flows even though it may lead to growth.

(e) **Working capital investment rate**: working capital (inventory, receivables) as a percentage of sales revenue. A similar principle applies for fixed capital investment rate: reducing the amount of cash tied up as working capital will increase free cash flows.

(f) **Life of the business (or project)**: number of years for which sales are forecast. The longer a firm can realistically expect to generate future sales, the greater the present value of those sales and hence the business value.

(g) **Cost of capital**: present value depends on the discount rate employed (WACC). The lower the cost of capital a company incurs (and therefore the discount rate it has to use), the higher the present value of future cash flows.

The first five drivers ((a)–(e)) can be used to prepare cash flow forecasts for a suitable period. The length of this period should be defined according to the likely period of a company's competitive advantage (driver (f)). Discounting these cash flows at the cost of capital (driver (g)) leads to the value of the business's operations.

Identifying the value drivers in a company is also important when deciding what performance measures are the most meaningful to measure. One way to ensure that a company uses meaningful performance metrics is to link those metrics to value drivers. For example, a metric of 'new product sales' could be useful to measure how well a company is achieving sales growth.

In this respect, the drivers should not all be treated equally. Different drivers will be more important than others in different businesses. For example, for a hotel business, with a high fixed cost base, the most important driver is sales, meaning that occupancy rates are a key performance measure for hotels. By contrast, for a bank lending to corporate customers, profits are driven by the margin between the rate at which the bank borrows and that at which it lends. That margin is usually slim, so for the bank, more value will be created by improving interest margins and reducing operating costs than by increasing the volume of business.

Value creation does not occur and costs do not arise evenly across an organisation, so managers should have a firm grasp of the key cost and value drivers affecting their operations. Some of these may be located outside the organisation, elsewhere in the value network, so the ability to influence suppliers and distributors may be crucial to success.

More generally, the choice of generic strategy interacts with cost and value: strict control of cost is obviously fundamental to cost leadership, while differentiation will inevitably have cost implications associated with such matters as brand communications, product quality and customer service.

Moreover, the structure of costs and value creation is likely to change over time as, for example, illustrated by the cost and profit aspects of the product life cycle.

According to Johnson, Scholes and Whittington, applying SVA requires a whole new mindset, termed **value based management**. Central to this way of thinking is the identification of the cash generators of the business, or **value drivers**, such as those identified by Rappaport. These will be both external and internal. For example, **competitive rivalry** is a major external value driver because of its direct impact on margins.

7.2 Value based management

KEY TERM

VALUE BASED MANAGEMENT is 'a managerial process which effectively links strategy, measurement and operational processes to the end of creating shareholder value'.   *(CIMA Official Terminology)*

Value based management (VBM) consists of three elements:

(a) **Strategy for value creation** – ways to increase or generate the maximum future value for an organisation

(b) **Metrics** – for measuring value

(c) **Management** – managing for value, encompassing governance, remuneration, organisation structure, culture and stakeholder relationships

VBM highlights that management decisions designed to lead to higher profits do not necessarily create value for shareholders. Often, management are under pressure to meet short-term profit targets, and they are prepared to sacrifice long-term value in order to achieve these short-term targets. For example, management might avoid initiating a project with a positive net present value if that project leads to their organisation falling short of expected profit targets in the current period.

Profit-based performance measures may therefore obscure the true state of a business. By contrast, VBM seeks to ensure that analytical techniques and management processes are all aligned to help an organisation maximise its value. VBM does this by focusing management decision making on the key drivers of value, and making management more accountable for growing an organisation's intrinsic value.

Therefore, whereas profit-based performance measures look at what has happened in the past, VBM seeks to maximise returns on new investments. What matters to the shareholders of a company is that they earn an acceptable return on their capital. They are not only interested in how a company has performed in the past, but also in how it is likely to perform in the future.

7.2.1 Creating shareholder value

Although it is easy to identify the logic that companies ought to be managed for shareholder value, it is much harder to specify how this can be achieved. For example, a strategy to increase market share may not actually increase shareholder value.

Good-quality information is essential in a VBM system, so that management can identify where value is being created – or destroyed – in a business. For example, continuing the previous example, there is no value in increasing market share in a market if that market is not profitable.

An organisation will need to identify its value drivers, and then put strategies in place for each of them. When identifying its value drivers, an organisation may also find that its organisational structure needs reorganising, to ensure that it is aligned with the processes which create value.

7.2.2 Measurement

VBM will lead to a change in the performance metrics used in a company. Instead of focusing solely on historical returns, companies also need to look at more forward-looking contributions to value: for example, growth and sustainability. The performance measures used in VBM are often non-financial.

7.2.3 Managing value

In today's companies, the intellectual capital provided by employees plays a key role in generating value. VBM attempts to align the interests of the employees who generate value and the shareholders they create value for. Otherwise VBM could drive a wedge between those who deliver economic performance (employees) and those who harvest its benefits (shareholders). In practice, this equates to remuneration structures which include some form of share-based payments.

Successfully implementing VBM will also involve cultural change in an organisation. The employees in the organisation will need to commit to creating shareholder value. Value is created throughout the company not just by senior management, so employees all need to appreciate how their roles add value.

Nonetheless, visible leadership and strong commitment from senior management will be essential for a shift to VBM to be successful.

However, as with any change programme, implementing VBM could be expensive and potentially disruptive, particularly if extensive restructuring is required.

7.2.4 Elements of VBM

A comprehensive VBM programme should consider:

(a) **Strategic planning** – strategies should be evaluated to establish whether they will maximise shareholder value

(b) **Capital allocation** – funds should be allocated to the strategies and divisions that will create most shareholder value

(c) **Operating budgets** – budgets should reflect the strategies the organisation is using to create value

(d) **Performance measurement** – the economic performance of the organisation needs to lead to increases in share prices, because these promote the creation of shareholder wealth

(e) **Management remuneration** – rewards should be linked to the value drivers, and how well value-based targets are achieved

(f) **Internal communication** – the background to the programme and how VBM will benefit the business need to be explained to staff

(g) **External communication** – management decisions, and how they are designed to achieve value, must be communicated to the market; the market's reaction to these decisions will help determine movements in the organisation's share price

All the consultants who have followed Rappaport's ideas work from the same principles.

(a) **Profit** has become discredited as a performance measure.

(b) The traditional cost of capital used in the income statement interest figure is inadequate. A composite measure taking into account the complex **capital structure** of a business is needed.

(c) What really needs to be measured is **how well the business is performing for the shareholders**.

7.3 How does business strategy promote increased shareholder value?

A diagram helps to show how strategy drives the business towards increased shareholder value, which for many businesses is the primary objective of strategy.

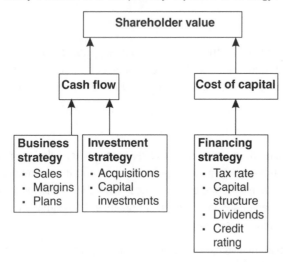

(Adapted from *CIMA Insider*, March 2001)

Adopting a value based approach to managing an enterprise has wide-ranging implications.

Culture: shareholder value must be accepted as the organisation's purpose. This may have greatest impact at the **strategic apex**, whose members may have had different ideas on this subject. However, the importance of creating shareholder value must be emphasised in all parts of the business.

Nevertheless, it is crucial that management do not overlook underlying business processes in the quest for value-based metrics. Core business processes (for example, quality management, innovation, and customer service) should still be monitored alongside value-based metrics.

Relations with the market: shareholder value should be reflected in share price. The company's senior managers must **communicate effectively with the market** so that their value-creating policies are incorporated into the share price. However, they must not be tempted to manipulate the market. This may be a difficult area to manage as executive rewards should reflect the share price. One way in which management can communicate performance to the market is through performance indicators. These metrics should then, in turn, form the basis of the performance targets for divisional managers to achieve.

Strategic choices: the maximisation of shareholder value must be the object of all strategic choices. This will affect such matters as **resource allocation** and HR policies and will have particular relevance to the evaluation of expensive projects such as acquisitions and major new product development.

Demergers and shareholder value

In March 2010, telecoms groups Cable & Wireless and Carphone Warehouse both underwent demerger deals. The management of both companies argued that splitting up their groups into two clearly defined businesses would help unlock shareholder value.

However, some investors are concerned that companies do not rush to demerge simply because demergers have become the flavour of the month in a sluggish market where bankers are looking for new sources of fees.

The sentiment among investors remains that a deal – whether it is a merger or a demerger – must only be done because it creates value for shareholders.

However, research carried out into demerged European companies suggests that demerger activity does usually create shareholder value. A report published by UBS in March 2010 showed that 75 European companies demerged since 2000 outperformed Europe's top 300 groups by 16% a year.

As if to reinforce this, when the newly demerged retail and telecoms arms of Carphone Warehouse made their stock market debut, the combined market capitalisations of the demerged companies was 10% higher than the old Carphone group.

The author of the UBS report anticipates there will be a 'flurry' of spin-offs in the near future. However, he points out that not all demergers do well. While the share price of AstraZeneca has soared since it was split from its parent, ICI, the demerger of Mondi from AngloAmerican has seen the parent outperform the spin-off.

Nevertheless, the spin-off part of the business often performs better than the larger parent, and one reason for this is the demerger throws light upon parts of the business that were hidden to investors beforehand.

The demerger of the former British Gas business illustrates how a successful demerger can unlock shareholder value, as the value of shares has risen almost ten-fold since the Group's demerger (in 1997) into Centrica, BG Group and National Grid. However, as one long-standing Centrica executive commented, management have to be mature to deliver value on the demerger. 'To give shareholder value, management have to make sure the right components go with the right business, and not be steered by various factions with the business.'

(Adapted from FT.com article 'Spin-offs show demergers are staging comeback' 29 March 2010)

7.4 Economic value added

Many organisations use profit-based measures as key measures of their financial performance. However, there are two significant problems with these types of measures, considering that performance measures in commercial organisations should evaluate how well those organisations are maximising the **wealth of their shareholders**.

(a)   **Profit ignores the cost of equity capital**. Companies only truly generate wealth when they generate a return in excess of the return required by providers of both equity and debt capital. In financial statements, however, although the calculation of profit takes into account the cost of debt finance (interest), it ignores the cost of equity finance.

(b)   Profits calculated in accordance with accounting standards **do not accurately reflect the wealth that has been created**.

Economic value added (EVA) tries to overcome the problems of accounting profit as the basis of performance measurement, by using **economic profit** instead. Economic profit is derived after adjusting traditional accounting profits for the write-offs that are made for **value building expenditures** such as research and development, training, and advertising.

KEY TERM

ECONOMIC VALUE ADDED (EVA)™: 'A measure which approximates a company's profit. Traditional financial statements are translated into EVA statements by reversing distortions in operating performance created by accounting rules and by charging operating profit for all of the capital employed. For example, written-off goodwill is capitalised, as are extraordinary losses and the present value of operating leases. Extraordinary gains reduce capital'.

(Stern Stewart)

EVA = Adjusted operating profits after tax* – (Adjusted invested capital × Imputed rate of interest)

* Stern Stewart calls this net operating profit after tax (NOPAT).

The principles of EVA are that:

- Investment leads to assets regardless of accounting treatments
- Assets once created cannot be diminished by accounting action

Such an approach creates some notable differences when compared with information based on traditional accounting concepts and conventions. The prudence concept, for example, requires revenue expenditure (such as maintenance expenditure on plant and machinery) to be written off to the income statement in the accounting period in which it is incurred. This is to reflect the fact that such expenditure may have no long-term benefits. It is, therefore, not very surprising that if management are assessed using performance measures calculated using traditional accounting policies, they are unwilling to invest in or spend money on activities which immediately reduce the current year's profit.

Although the logic behind EVA is similar to that of RI (in other words, subtracting an imputed interest charge from the profit earned by a company or division), the calculation of EVA is different to RI because the net assets used as the basis of the invested capital are usually valued at their **replacement cost** and are **increased by any costs that have been capitalised** (see below).

There are also **differences in the way that NOPAT is calculated**, compared with the profit figure that is used for RI. There are three main reasons for adjusting accounting profits to derive NOPAT:

(a) Costs which would normally be treated as expenses in the financial statements, but which are considered within an EVA calculation as **investments building for the future**, are added back to derive a figure for 'economic profit'. These costs are included instead as assets in the figure for net assets employed; in other words, they are deemed to be investments for the future. Costs treated in this way include items such as **research and development expenditure**, and **advertising costs**.

(b) **Cash accounting versus accruals**. Investors are primarily interested in cash flows, so accounting adjustments for non-cash items, such as allowances for doubtful debts, are eliminated.

(c) Investors, who are interested in maximising their wealth, will be interested in the continuing performance of the company. Therefore **one-off, unusual items** of profit or expenditure should be ignored.

7.4.1 Accounting adjustments in calculating EVA

In practice, there are a very large number of adjustments that have to be made when converting accounting profit to economic profit. However, the main adjustments can be summarised as follows:

Types of item	Comment
Value-building expenditure	Expenditure on **marketing and promotions**, **research and development**, and **staff training** – which will generate value for the business in future periods – should be capitalised. If any such expenditure has been charged as an expense in the income statement, it should be **added back to profit**, and also **added to capital employed** in the year in which the expenses were incurred.

Types of item	Comment
Depreciation	The charge for depreciation in the income statement should be **added back to profit**, and a **charge for economic depreciation** made instead. The value of non-current assets (and therefore capital employed) should also be adjusted to reflect the revised charge.
	Economic depreciation reflects the true change in value of assets during the period.
	[**Note**. If no detail is given about economic depreciation in a question scenario, then you should assume that accounting depreciation is a reasonable approximation for it, and therefore you do not need to make any change to the depreciation figure.]
Provisions	Provisions, allowances for doubtful debts, inventory write-downs, and deferred tax provisions are deemed to represent over-prudence on the part of the financial accountant, with the result that the 'true' value of capital employed is understated. Therefore they should all be **added back to capital employed**.
	Any movements in provisions recognised as income or expenses in the income statement also need to be **removed from NOPAT**.
Non-cash expenses	All non-cash items (eg goodwill) are treated with suspicion, on the basis that if the costs were 'real', cash would have been paid for them.
	Any non-cash expenses should be **added back to profits**, and to **capital employed**.
Operating leases	Operating leases should be **capitalised** and **added to capital employed**. Otherwise, the inconsistency in treatment between operating and finance leases means that firms can take advantage of operating leases to reduce the capital employed figure, and in doing so increase EVA. In effect, EVA treats all leases **as finance leases**.
	Any **operating lease charges** in the income statement should be added back and removed from NOPAT.
	In principle, **depreciation** should then be charged on the assets acquired under finance leases. However, remember that accounting depreciation is replaced with **economic depreciation** when calculating EVA.

However, note that **no additional adjustments are made to the tax charge** in relation to the tax on other adjustments made when calculating NOPAT (eg adding back value-building expenditure to profit).

7.4.2 Example: calculating EVA

A company has reported operating profits of $21 million. This was after charging $4 million for the development and launch costs of a new product that is expected to generate profits for 4 years. Taxation is paid at the rate of 25% of the operating profit.

The company has a risk-adjusted weighted average cost of capital of 12% per annum and is paying interest at 9% per annum on a substantial long-term loan.

The company's non-current asset value is $50 million and the net current assets have a value of $22 million. The replacement cost of the non-current assets is estimated to be $64 million.

Required

Calculate the company's EVA for the period.

Solution

Calculation of NOPAT

	$m
Operating profit	21
Add back development costs	4
Less one year's amortisation of development costs ($4 million/4)	(1)
	24
Taxation at 25% (of original operating profit)	(5.25)
NOPAT	18.75

Calculation of economic value of net assets

	$m
Replacement cost of net assets ($22 million + $64 million)	86
Add back investment in new product to benefit future	3
Economic value of net assets	89

Calculation of EVA

The capital charge is based on the **weighted average cost of capital**, which takes account of the cost of share capital as well as the cost of loan capital. Therefore the correct interest rate to use is 12%.

	$m
NOPAT	18.75
Capital charge (12% × $89 million)	(10.68)
EVA	8.07

Question 12.5	Calculating EVA

Learning outcome D1(a)

B division of Z Co has operating profits and assets as below:

	$'000
Gross profit	156
Less: Non-cash expenses	(8)
Amortisation of goodwill	(5)
Interest @ 10%	(15)
Profit before tax	128
Tax @ 30%	(38)
Net profit	90
Total equity	350
Long-term debt	150
	500

Z Co has a target capital structure of 25% debt/75% equity. The cost of equity is estimated at 15%. The capital employed at the start of the period amounted to $450,000. The division had non-capitalised leases of $20,000 throughout the period. Goodwill previously written off against reserves in acquisitions in previous years amounted to $40,000.

Required

Calculate EVA for B division.

7.4.3 Replacement costs or balance sheet costs?

In the earlier example in 7.4.2, the scenario identified that the replacement cost of the non-current assets was estimated to be $64 million, which meant we were able to use the replacement cost figure in the calculation.

However, **balance sheet costs** (assets' costs in the statement of financial position) **will often be used as an estimate of replacement costs**. The other adjustments (for example, adding back development costs) will still be made to calculate the economic value of net assets, as in the example in 7.4.2.

However, if balance sheet costs are used instead of replacement costs, EVA will be distorted because there is no attempt to adjust for inflation. The cash costs and revenues in the calculation will be measured in current prices, but the non-current asset costs and depreciation charges will be based on historical prices from the year when the assets were acquired. Consequently, the asset costs and depreciation charges are likely to be understated if they are not adjusted to reflect inflationary price movements. As a result, EVA is likely to be overstated.

7.4.4 Using EVA as a performance measure

EVA (like RI) gives an absolute measure, rather than a percentage value of performance, and if EVA is positive it indicates an organisation is generating a return greater than that required by the providers of finance. In other words, a positive EVA indicates that an organisation is creating wealth for the shareholders.

Consequently, directors should be encouraged to either:

(a)   Invest in divisions where the returns from those divisions exceed the cost of capital; or

(b)   Close down divisions, or harvest assets, where the return is less than the cost of capital. In turn, the proceeds from any sales can either be reinvested in other divisions, or returned to shareholders as dividends.

7.4.5 Evaluation of EVA

The **advantages** of EVA include the following:

(a)   **Real wealth for shareholders**. Maximisation of EVA will create real wealth for the shareholders. Maximising the present value of future cash flows will help **maximise shareholders' wealth**.

(b)   **Less distortion by accounting** policies. The adjustments within the calculation of EVA mean that the measure is based on figures that are **closer to cash flows than accounting profits**.

(c)   **Consistent with net present value (NPV)**. EVA is consistent with the idea of NPV, showing the return on projects in excess of the cost of financing them. Any projects which would generate a positive NPV will also increase EVA.

(d)   **An absolute value**. The EVA measure is an absolute value, which is easily understood by non-financial managers.

(e)   **Treatment of certain costs as investments thereby encouraging expenditure**. If management are assessed using performance measures based on traditional accounting policies they may be unwilling to invest in areas such as advertising and development for the future because **such costs will immediately reduce the current year's accounting profit**. EVA recognises such costs as investments for the future and thus they do not immediately reduce the EVA in the year of expenditure. This will **reduce the temptation** (which may occur under ROCE or ROI) **to short-termism**.

EVA does have some **drawbacks**, though:

(a) **Dependency on historical data**. EVA is based on historical accounts, which may be of **limited use as a guide to the future**. In practice, the influences of accounting policies on the starting profit figure may not be completely negated by the adjustments made to it in the EVA model.

(b) **Number of adjustments needed to measure EVA**. Making the necessary adjustments can be problematic as sometimes a **large number of adjustments** are required.

(c) **Comparison of like with like**. EVA is an absolute measure, so larger companies in size may have larger EVA figures than smaller companies, simply because they are bigger, not because they are performing better. **Allowance for relative size** must be made when comparing the relative performance of companies. In this respect, ROI (which shows a percentage measure) may be better for comparing performance between companies of different size.

(d) **Difficulty in estimating WACC**. Many organisations use models such as the CAPM for estimating WACC. However, this is not a universally accepted method of determining the cost of equity.

7.5 Example: EVA and strategic decisions

Recommend which plc, X or Y, to invest funds in. Justify your decision.

Profit and loss account for the previous year (£m)

	X	Y
	£	£
Sales	26.0	62.0
Cost of sales	18.0	47.0
Gross profit	8.0	15.0
Production overheads	1.2	2.4
Advertising	0.6	2.0
Depreciation	1.1	1.6
Training	0.1	1.8
R&D	0.6	2.0
Bad debt expense	0.2	0.3
PBIT	4.2	4.9
Investment base	26.5	40.3

Solution

Traditional ROI techniques would give X plc 15.8% and Y plc 12.1%, and therefore choose X plc for investment. However, this ignores the fact that Y is more heavily involved in developing the long-term future of its company by spending on training, advertising and R&D. These items, under EVA, would be added back to obtain a comparison using operational expenses.

Adjusted ROI	X	Y
Original profit	4.2	4.9
Training	0.1	1.8
Advertising	0.6	2.0
R&D	0.6	2.0
New profit	5.5	10.7
New ROI	20.8%	26.4%

There is still a lack of information here to make a final decision, although the original analysis and decision to invest in X plc has been considerably refined. Business risk, market dynamics, previous year's results, competitor comparisons, and investment portfolio issues will all affect the analysis.

7.6 EVA and strategy

As well as considering how EVA is calculated, it is worth thinking how the elements of EVA might affect a firm's strategy.

For example, possible ways of increasing net operating profit might be:

Increased revenues:

- Higher sales volumes: market penetration; product development; innovation (new products in early stages of product life cycle); build barriers to entry (eg patent protection)

- Higher prices: branding; product differentiation; quality of product/service

- Cross-selling and customer retention: customer relationship management

- Customer profitability

Reduced operating costs:

- Cost reduction programmes, and target costing of products

- Productivity and efficiency initiatives (eg review of staffing levels)

- Outsourcing of non-core areas

- Vertical integration (to gain access to materials and markets), and to generate greater economies of scale

- Relocation – to benefit from cheaper rents, labour costs etc (international relocation could also have the benefit of reducing tax)

7.7 Market value added (MVA)

Market value added (MVA) is the difference between the market value of a company and the economic book value of capital employed.

This might be thought of as being related to EVA, being the NPV created for shareholders over the life of the company. The difference is that EVA is essentially **historic**, while MVA is assumed (under the efficient market hypothesis) to be the market's assessment of the firm's ability to add value **in the future**. It is similar to Rappaport's idea of business value and his list of **value drivers** is relevant. The idea of market valuation, however, brings into play all the variables that affect market expectations, such as the firm's ability to win the trust of investors and investors' understanding of the business.

KEY TERM

MARKET VALUE ADDED is 'the difference between a company's market value (derived from share price) and its economic book value (the amount of capital that shareholders and debt holders have committed to the firm throughout its existence, including any retained earnings)'.   *(CIMA Official Terminology)*

Put another way, MVA is 'the difference between what investors put into the company as capital and what they could get out by selling at today's market price' (Al Ehrbar). In theory, **MVA is the present value of all future EVAs**. However, **market sentiment** will always affect the share price too.

The difficulty with this measure is that while capital employed (monies invested by shareholders in the company) represents investments made in the **past**, market value is the present value of **future** cash flows. So what does MVA (ie the difference between these two) really represent? In addition, shareholders are buying and selling shares all the time. There must be as many measures of MVA for a company as there are individual shareholders.

7.8 Total shareholder return (TSR)

Total shareholder return (TSR) is the total percentage return to shareholders over a given period.

TSR is defined as the **total percentage return to shareholders over a period** using the formula:

$$\frac{\text{Dividend per share} + \text{Movement in share price}}{\text{Share price at the start of the period}}$$

This measure is very simple to calculate, and can be used to compare performance of similar companies. As with MVA, however, it is not immune to market sentiment.

Section summary

Shareholders require managers to **maximise the value of their investment** in the organisation. Performance indicators assess how well this is carried out.

Economic value management hinges on the idea of an economic profit, which is derived after adjusting traditional accounting profits for the write-offs that are made for **value building expenditures** such as training and advertising. By adding such expenditures back to accounting profit, better comparison can be made between companies.

Market value added is the difference between the market value of a company and the economic book value of capital employed.

Total shareholder return is the total percentage return to shareholders over a given period.

8 International subsidiaries

Introduction

The task of setting objectives within a multinational is complex, and it is important that performance standards set for international subsidiaries are realistic.

Exam skills

In a case study scenario, you may be asked to consider the difficulties of performance measurement facing a Group with subsidiaries or operations in different parts of the world. Make sure you think about the specific difficulties which are relevant to the scenario: don't just discuss general issues.

The following factors could all affect performance in foreign subsidiaries or operations.

(a)   **Capital structure**. Where foreign subsidiaries are financed partly by loans, the differing rates of interest in each country might affect the relative profitability of subsidiaries.

(b)   **Cost structure**. Overseas subsidiaries may have a different operational gearing.

(c)   **Accounting policies**. In each country, the subsidiary may adopt a different rate of depreciation so that profits and asset values are not comparable. Profits can be transformed into losses by accounting policies.

(d)   **Government policy**. There will be differences in the levels of grants or concessions from the national government and in the rate of taxation and interest.

(e)   **Transfer prices** for goods and services between the subsidiaries may be set in such a way as to improve the results of one subsidiary (or head office) at the expense of another (eg if goods are transferred from a subsidiary to head office at cost, the subsidiary will get no profit and the head office will obtain the goods at a low price).

(f)   **Workforce**. A justification for expanding into developing countries is to take advantage of lower wages. However, an organisation also needs to recognise **cultural differences** between countries.

(g)   **Exchange rate fluctuations** may turn profits into losses and *vice versa*.

(h)   **Risk**. Some overseas operations may be a greater risk than others so that higher returns may be required from them.

(i)   **Life cycle**. The same product may be at different stages in its product life cycle in each country.

(j)   **Transport**. If a subsidiary in, say, the UK is performing much worse, and incurring higher unit costs of production than a comparable subsidiary in, say, Germany, it may still be uneconomic to switch production from the UK to Germany because the extra costs of transport to the UK may exceed the savings in the costs of production.

(k)   **Domestic competition**. The market of the overseas subsidiary may face a unique configuration of Porter's five forces.

(l)   **Different economic conditions**.

Increasing demands that larger companies adopt the principles of **corporate social responsibility** complicate the problem of controlling the activities of foreign subsidiaries. The corporate **mission statement** can be useful here, if it incorporates the aspirations and standards promoted by all stakeholder groups, not just those of shareholders. Such a mission statement can be incorporated into divisional performance measurement schemes that can also reflect the particular national and industrial circumstances of each division.

8.1 International comparisons

If the firms or subsidiaries being compared operate in different countries there will be certain problems for performance measurement.

(a)   **Realistic standards**. It may be difficult to establish realistic standards for each different country. Performance standards should take account of local conditions, considering local opportunities as well as any restrictions on the activities of an operating unit in a particular country.

(b)   **Controllable cash flows**. Care must be taken to determine which cash flows are controllable and to separate these from those outside the control of local management. In particular, the distortions caused by local taxation laws should be eliminated.

(c)   **Currency conversion**. Considerable friction and difficulty in measuring performance can be caused by the use of inappropriate currency conversion rates.

(d)   **Basis for comparison**. Following on from the problem of setting realistic standards of performance, central management must exercise care when attempting to compare performance between the different countries.

8.1.1 Reporting considerations for international subsidiaries

Normal procedures may have to be adjusted.

(a)   **Reports**

     (i)   **Standardised** to allow comparative analysis between subsidiaries
     (ii)   Use an agreed **common language** and currency
     (iii)   **Frequent** as necessary to allow proper management
     (iv)   Cover all the **information needs** of headquarters

(b)   **Meetings**

     Meetings between HQ executives and subsidiary management allow for more intensive information exchange and monitoring, and minimise misunderstandings. They do, however, take up time and resources, and are generally not as regular as reports.

(c)   **Information technology**

     The transmission speed of mail and internet communications makes close monitoring of marketing and financial performance much easier. Video conference meetings allow both financial and time savings to be made.

(d)   **Control of intermediaries**

The problem with controlling 'outsiders' is that there is no control by **ownership**. In the final analysis **negative controls** such as legal pressures or threats to discontinue relationships can be used, resulting perhaps in loss of business. The best control is through good selection and by making it clear to intermediaries that their interests and the company's coincide.

8.2 Exchange rates and transfer pricing

The most obvious problem is the exchange rate, but Ward argues that this may not be serious:

(a)   A firm which makes an investment in a factory intends to use the factory, not sell it. So while changes in exchange rates alter the value of the original investment, this does not matter so much in the long term, providing that the subsidiary is making a profit at the same rate, in local terms.

(b)   This might seem a rather dangerous assertion but it is sometimes asserted that long-term differences in rates of exchange result from inflation.

In practice, many companies have to budget for exchange rate changes which affect their plans. A firm can lock itself into a particular exchange rate by hedging or other financing. Jaguar used this when, as an independent British company, most of its sales were in the US. Hedging instruments were used to protect its profits from any fall. As well as operational issues, such as the acquisition of funds and hedging contracts, there is the obviously vexed problem of performance assessment.

It might be helpful to illustrate this with a question.

Question 12.6	Overcapacity

Learning outcome D1(ii)

Enharmonic Changes Ltd is a company with two European factories: at Sharp in the UK and at Pflatte in South Africa. The company is facing overcapacity at Sharp even though it is the most productive plant. The company makes Andantes. The relative performance of each factory at rates of £1 = 200 Yen and 14 Yen = 1 South Africa Rand (ZAR) is as follows.

	Sharp		Pflatte	
	£	Yen equiv (200Y: £1)	South African Rands	Yen equiv (14Y: 1 ZAR)
Selling price	100	20,000	2,000	28,000
Cost of production	75	15,000	1,600	22,400
Gross profit	25	5,000	400	5,600
Margin		25%		20%

In Japanese Yen terms, the UK factory has a higher margin, but the actual profits from making and selling Andantes in South Africa are higher than in the UK.

(a)   However, given the overcapacity in the UK, and given transportation cost at £10 per andante from the UK to South Africa, should the UK factory be used as a sole source for the South African plant? Assume that Pflatte pays Sharp in sterling for the Andantes. Assume that profits are remitted to Japan in ZAR. Assume the £: Yen and ZAR: Yen relationships are as above, but that £: ZAR rates are as follows:

(i)   £1 = 20 ZAR
(ii)   £1 = 15 ZAR

(b)   What would be the position if Andantes were shipped over directly, and Pflatte did **not** pay Sharp any money for the components?

There are particular problems in the management of overseas subsidiaries:

(a)   How much **control**? There is always a tension between autonomy and centralisation.

(b)   **Staffing**. Expatriate managers are often expensive. Housing costs, school fees etc often have to be paid. In addition, there are cultural problems in adjusting to the country and the way of doing business.

Section summary

Objective setting for multinationals is complex. Problems arise with performance management due to the difficulties of setting realistic standards for different countries, controllability of cash flows and currency conversion. Levels of control and staffing can also be problems when managing overseas subsidiaries.

9   Transfer pricing

Introduction

Transfer pricing is used to encourage optimal performance by keeping track of costs incurred throughout a business. Ideally, prices should be set by reference to the **external market**, but where this is not possible transfer prices will have to be **negotiated**, or head office might **impose** a transfer price.

KEY TERM

TRANSFER PRICE is the 'price at which goods or services are transferred between different units in the same company. May be set on a number of bases, such as marginal cost, full cost, market price or negotiation. For the transfer of goods between units in different countries, tax implications mean that the respective governments have to accept the method used. They are likely to insist on **arm's-length transfer prices**'.

(*CIMA Official Terminology*)

Where there are **transfers of goods or services between divisions**, the transfers could be made 'free' to the division receiving the benefit. For example, if a garage and car showroom has two divisions, one for car repairs and servicing and the other for sales, the servicing division will be required to service cars before they are sold. The servicing division could do its work for the car sales division without making any record of the work done. However, unless the cost or value of such work is recorded, management cannot keep a check on the amount of resources (such as labour time) being used up on new car servicing. It is necessary for control purposes that some record of the interdivisional services should be kept. Interdivisional work can be given a cost or charge: a **transfer price**.

Transfer prices are a way of promoting **divisional autonomy**, ideally without prejudicing the measurement of **divisional performance** or discouraging overall **corporate profit maximisation**. The management accountant must devise a method of transfer pricing which meets three criteria:

- **Equity** (provides a fair measure of divisional performance)
- **Neutrality** (avoids the distortion of business decision making)
- **Administrative simplicity**

The transfer price should provide an '**artificial**' **selling price** that enables the transferring division to earn a return for its efforts, and the receiving division to incur a cost for benefits received, and should be set at a level that enables profit centre performance to be measured 'commercially'. This means that the transfer price should be a **fair commercial price**.

9.1 Transfer pricing with constant unit variable costs and sales prices

An ideal transfer price should reflect **opportunity cost**. Where a **perfect external market price exists** and unit variable costs and sales prices are constant, the opportunity cost of transfer will be one or other of the following:

- External market price
- External market price less savings in selling costs

9.2 Example: transferring goods at market price

A company has two profit centres, A and B. Centre A sells half of its output on the open market and transfers the other half to B. Costs and external revenues in a period are as follows.

	A £	B £	Total £
External sales	8,000	24,000	32,000
Costs of production	12,000	10,000	22,000
Company profit			10,000

Required

What are the consequences of setting a transfer price at market price?

If the transfer price is at market price, A would be happy to sell the output to B for £8,000, which is what A would get by selling it externally.

	A £	A £	B £	B £	Total £
Market sales		8,000		24,000	32,000
Transfer sales		8,000		–	
		16,000		24,000	
Transfer costs			8,000		
Own costs	12,000		10,000		22,000
		12,000		18,000	
Profit		4,000		6,000	10,000

The consequences are as follows:

(a) **A earns the same profit** on transfers as on external sales. B must pay a commercial price for transferred goods.

(b) A will be indifferent about selling externally or transferring goods to B because the profit is the same on both types of transaction. B can therefore ask for and obtain as many units as it wants from A.

9.3 Adjusted market price

Internal transfers, in practice, are often cheaper than external sales, with savings in selling and administration costs, bad debt risks and possibly transport/delivery costs. It would seem reasonable for the buying division to expect a **discount** on the external market price.

If profit centres are established, however, and unit variable costs and sales prices are constant, there are two possibilities.

(a) Where the supplying division has spare capacity the ideal transfer price will simply be the **standard variable cost of production**.

(b) When there is a scarce production resource, the ideal transfer price will be the variable cost of production plus the contribution forgone by using the scarce resource instead of putting it to its most profitable alternative use.

9.4 Cost-based approaches to transfer pricing

Cost-based approaches to transfer pricing are often used in practice, where there is no external market for the product being transferred, or the external market is imperfect due to limited external demand.

9.4.1 Transfer prices based on full cost

Under this approach the full standard cost (including fixed overheads absorbed) incurred by the supplying division in making the product is charged to the receiving division. If a **full cost plus** approach is used, a profit margin is also included in this transfer price.

A company has two profit centres, A and B. Centre A can only sell half of its maximum output externally because of limited demand. It transfers the other half of its output to B which also faces limited demand. Costs and revenues in a period are as follows:

	A £	B £	Total £
External sales	8,000	24,000	32,000
Costs of production in the division	12,000	10,000	22,000
(Loss)/profit	(4,000)	14,000	10,000

If the transfer price is at full cost, A in our example would have 'sales' to B of £6,000 (ie half of its total costs of production). This would be a cost to B, as follows:

	A £	A £	B £	B £	Total £
Open market sales		8,000		24,000	32,000
Transfer sales		6,000		–	
Total sales, inc transfers		14,000		24,000	
Transfer costs			6,000		
Own costs	12,000		10,000		22,000
Total costs, inc transfers		12,000		16,000	
Profit		2,000		8,000	10,000

The transfer sales of A are self-cancelling with the transfer costs of B so that total profits are unaffected. The transfer price simply spreads the total profit of £10,000 between A and B. Division A makes no profit on its work and, using this method, would prefer to sell its output on the open market if it could.

9.4.2 Transfer prices based on full cost plus

If the transfers are at cost plus a margin of, say, 25%, A's sales to B would be £7,500.

	A £	A £	B £	B £	Total £
Open market sales		8,000		24,000	32,000
Transfer sales		7,500		–	
		15,500		24,000	
Transfer costs			7,500		
Own costs	12,000		10,000		22,000
		12,000		17,500	
Profit		3,500		6,500	10,000

Compared to a transfer price at cost, A gains some profit at the expense of B. However, A makes a bigger profit on external sales in this case because the profit mark-up of 25% is less than the profit mark-up on open market sales, which is (£8,000 – 6,000)/£6,000 = 33%. The transfer price does not give A a fair revenue or charge B a reasonable cost, and so their profit performance is distorted. It would seem to give A an incentive to sell more goods externally and transfer less to B. This may or may not be in the best interests of the company as a whole.

Division A's total costs of £12,000 will include an element of fixed costs. Half of Division A's total costs are transferred to Division B. However, from the point of view of Division B the cost is entirely variable.

Suppose that the cost per unit to A is £15 and that this includes a fixed element of £6, while Division B's own costs are £25 per unit, including a fixed element of £10. The total variable cost is really £9 + £15 = £24, but from Division B's point of view the variable cost is £15 + £15 = £30. This means that Division B will be unwilling to sell the final product for less than £30, whereas any price above £24 would make a contribution.

9.4.3 Transfer prices based on variable cost

A variable cost approach entails charging the variable cost that has been incurred by the supplying division to the receiving division. As above, we shall suppose that A's cost per unit is £15, of which £6 is fixed and £9 variable.

	A		B			Company as a whole
	£	£	£	£	£	£
Market sales		8,000		24,000		32,000
Transfer sales at variable cost		3,600		–		
($\frac{£9}{£15} \times 6,000$)						
		11,600		24,000		
Transfer costs			3,600			
Own variable costs	7,200		6,000		13,200	
Own fixed costs	4,800		4,000		8,000	
Total costs and transfers		12,000		13,600		22,000
(Loss)/Profit		(400)		10,400		10,000

The problem is that with a transfer price at variable cost the supplying division does not cover its fixed costs.

9.5 Transfer prices based on opportunity costs

It has been suggested that transfer prices can be set using the following rule.

Transfer price per unit = **standard variable cost** in the producing division plus the opportunity cost to the organisation of supplying the unit internally.

The opportunity cost will be one of the following:

(a)   The maximum **contribution forgone** by the supplying division in transferring internally rather than selling externally.

(b)   The **contribution forgone** by not using the same facilities in the producing division for their next best alternative use.

(c)   If there is no external market for the item being transferred, and no alternative uses for the division's facilities, the transfer price = standard variable cost of production.

(d)   If there is an external market for the item being transferred and no alternative use for the facilities, the transfer price = the market price.

9.6 Transfer pricing when unit variable costs and sales prices are not constant

When unit variable costs and/or unit selling prices are not constant there will be a profit-maximising level of output and the ideal transfer price will only be found by careful analysis and sensible negotiation.

(a)   The starting point should be to establish the output and sales quantities that will optimise the profits of the company or group as a whole.

(b)   The next step is to establish the transfer price at which both profit centres, the supply division and the buying division, would maximise their profits at this company-optimising output level.

(c)   There may be a range of prices within which both profit centres can agree on the output level that would maximise their individual profits and the profits of the company as a whole. Any price within the range would then be 'ideal'.

9.7 Problems in transfer pricing

(a)   If transfer prices are set at **full cost** the transferring division makes no profit.

(b)   If **full cost plus** is used the problem is how to set the margin at a level that all parties perceive as being fair.

(c)   If **variable cost** is used the transferring division does not cover its fixed costs but two-part prices (the variable cost transfer price plus a fixed annual fee) might be used to overcome this.

(d)   Transfer prices based on **standard cost** are fairer than transfer prices based on actual costs because if actual costs are used the transferring division has no incentive to control its costs: it can pass on its inefficiencies to the receiving division.

(e)   On the other hand, standards may become out of date so it is advisable to have an agreement to revise them periodically.

9.8 Negotiated transfer prices

When authority is decentralised to the extent that divisional managers negotiate transfer prices with each other, the agreed price may be finalised from a mixture of accounting arithmetic, politics and compromise.

Interdepartmental disputes about transfer prices are likely to arise and these may need the intervention of head office to settle the problem.

(a)   **Head office imposition**. Head office management may impose a price which maximises the profit of the company as a whole.

(b)   On the other hand, head office management might restrict its intervention to the task of **keeping negotiations in progress** until a transfer price is eventually settled.

Where **negotiation** is necessary there should be an understanding of the 'risk/return' profile. Tomkins suggests the following methodology, which head office can apply when mediating in disputes.

(a)   **Identify the outer bounds of the transfer price**. In other words, at what transfer price does the buying division end up earning the entire group profit, and at what transfer price does the selling division earn the entire group profit?

(b)   **Variability**. At each transfer price, compare each division's expected profits and the variability of the profits.

(c)   Incorporate **risk attitudes** in a fair transfer price, so that the profit-share between divisions takes the riskiness of the project into consideration.

9.9 International transfer prices

When firms transfer goods and services **internally**, but also **internationally**, the transfer price mechanism allows them to **move value from one country to another** without actually engaging in trade. Bearing in mind the difficulty discussed above of establishing the level at which a transfer price should be set, we may say that a 'low' price effectively moves value into the receiving country, while a 'high' one moves it into the transferring country.

9.9.1 Using transfer prices

This ability to decide in which country value (and particularly **profit**) is created is extremely useful.

(a)   It can be used to **manage taxation**.

    (i)   Profit can be minimised in states with high taxes on profit.

    (ii)   Selling prices can be minimised in states with high levels of irrecoverable VAT (and similar taxes).

    (iii)   The value imported into countries with high tariff levels can be minimised.

(b)   It can be used to **move profits to the home country** from states with restrictions on repatriation of profits or on currency exchange.

(c)   It can be used strategically:

    (i)   It can **disguise the attractiveness** of an operation to competitors by reducing profits.

    (ii)   It can enable a **low-price strategy aimed at driving out competition** without arousing the suspicions of the local tax authorities by declaring a very low level of profit. However, this course of action is likely to lead to accusations of dumping.

9.9.2 Centrally determined transfer prices and strategy

These considerations produce pressure for multinational companies to set their transfer prices centrally. However, this can have important considerations relating to **autonomy**.

Transfer prices which are determined centrally can seriously affect the ability of national managers to **influence the performance of their divisions**. This can affect their overall motivation, encourage them to seek ways around the restrictions imposed and make it more difficult to assess their overall performance.

9.10 The Eccles matrix

R J Eccles suggested that the method of setting transfer prices should reflect the organisation's **degree of diversification** and its **degree of vertical integration**.

(a)   Where both diversification and integration are low, as, for example, in the relationship between two shops in a retail chain, a transfer price may not even be required, but if it is, it can be set collaboratively.

(b)   Where diversification is low, but vertical integration is high, as in the relationship between two different stages of product assembly, co-operation is important, so the transfer price should be negotiated: it should probably be set at full cost so that resource allocation is appropriate and the supplying division's costs are covered.

(c)   Where diversification is high and integration is low, as in the now unfashionable diversified conglomerate, transfers are likely to be uncommon and should be at market price, as is the rest of each subsidiary's trade.

(d)   Nevertheless, where diversification and integration are both high, as may be the case when there is extensive trade along a supply chain combined with similarly extensive market-based exchanges, once again, the transfer price should be set collaboratively.

Section summary

Transfer prices are a way of promoting **divisional autonomy**, ideally without prejudging the measurement of **divisional performance** or discouraging overall **corporate profit maximisation**.

An ideal transfer price should reflect **opportunity cost**.

Cost-based approaches to transfer pricing are often used in practice, where there is no external market for the product being transferred, or the external market is imperfect due to limited external demand.

10   Divisional performance and control

Introduction

Many organisations are split into different business units, with authority and responsibility being devolved to managers with specific areas of responsibility. However, this raises potential problems as to how to appraise the performance of these managers, if aspects of the performance of their business units depend on factors which they cannot control.

When measuring the performance of a business unit or a division, one of the key issues is distinguishing which items the manager of that business unit can control (and therefore they should be held accountable for) and those items over which they have no control (and therefore they should not be held accountable for).

10.1 Controllability

The principle of **controllability** dictates that **managers should only be made accountable for those aspects of performance they can control**. In this respect, the controllability principle suggests that uncontrollable items (such as, for example, reapportioned head office costs) should either be eliminated from any reports which are used to measure manager's performance, or that the effects of these uncontrollable items are calculated and then the relevant reports should distinguish between controllable and uncontrollable items.

In practice, the controllability principle can be very difficult to apply, because many **areas do not fit neatly into controllable and uncontrollable categories**. For example, if a competitor lowers their prices, this may be seen as an uncontrollable action. However, a manager could respond to the competitor's action by changing the company's own prices, which could then reduce the adverse effect of the competitor's actions. So, in effect, there are both controllable and uncontrollable actions here.

Similarly, if a supplier increases the price of their product, this may be seen as an uncontrollable action. However, a manager could respond by looking to change supplier or by using a different product in order to reduce the adverse impact of the supplier's actions. Again, there are potentially both controllable and uncontrollable actions here.

Accordingly, any analysis of performance would need to consider the impact of the competitor or supplier's actions as one element, and then the impact of manager's response as a second element.

10.2 Controllable costs

Controllability can also be a particular issue when looking at costs within companies.

Consider the following example.

A company has three operating divisions and a head office. The divisional managers think it is unfair that a share of indirect costs – such as central Finance, HR, Legal and Administration costs – are included in their divisional results because the divisional managers cannot control these costs.

Importantly, however, there is a distinction here between considering the divisional **manager's** performance and the **division's performance** as a whole.

Horngren provides a good illustration of this.

'The most **skilful divisional manager is often put in charge of the sickest division in an attempt to change its fortunes**. Such an attempt may take years, not months. Furthermore the manager's efforts may merely result in bringing the division up to a minimum acceptable ROI. The division may continue to be a poor profit performer in comparison with other divisions. If top management relied solely on the absolute ROI to judge management, the skilful manager would be foolish to accept such a trouble-shooting assignment.'

In order to evaluate the **performance of the divisional manager**, then only those items which are directly controllable by the manager should be included in the performance measures. So, in our mini example, the share of indirect costs reapportioned from the head office should not be included. These costs can only be controlled where they are incurred. Therefore the relevant head office managers should be held accountable for them. As the divisional managers have suggested, it would be unfair to judge them for this aspect of performance.

However, in order for the head office to evaluate the **division's overall performance** for decision-making purposes (for example, in relation to growth, or divestment) it is appropriate to include a share of the head office costs. If divisional performance is measured only on those amounts the divisional manager can control, this will overstate the economic performance of the division. If the divisions were independent companies, they would have to incur the costs of those services which are currently provided by the head office (for example, finance and HR costs). Therefore, in order to measure the economic performance of the division these central costs, plus any interest expenses and taxes, should be included within the measure of the division's performance.

10.2.1 Impact on information requirements

The potential requirements to measure different aspects of performance (eg manager's performance; divisional performance) could have important implications for a management accounting system. The system will need to be able to produce the different types of report required, or distinguish between controllable and non-controllable costs as necessary. If the management accountant cannot produce the reports required, then any performance measurement based on those reports also cannot be undertaken.

10.3 Rewarding managers

Rewarding managers for their performance is a method of **control**, although money is not the only type of reward they may seek. Managers may also look for power, status and responsibility.

Rewarding managers for their performance is a method of control in the sense that it is **assumed that attempts will be made to achieve the organisation's objectives in return for rewards**. This, in turn, **derives from motivation theory**, which suggests that people have wants or desired outcomes and modify their behaviour accordingly.

10.3.1 How to link performance and rewards

As we noted in the previous chapter, monetary reward may not be the only type of reward that managers might seek.

However, a good reward system should have the following characteristics:

(a)   It should **offer real incentives**, sufficiently high after tax to make extraordinary effort worthwhile.

(b)   It should **relate payments to criteria over which the individual has control** (otherwise they will feel helpless to ensure their reward, and the expectancy element in motivation will be lacking).

(c)   It should **make clear the basis on which payments are calculated**, and all the conditions that apply, so that individuals can make the calculation of whether the reward is worth the extra level of effort.

(d)   It should be **flexible** enough to reward different levels of achievement in proportion, and with provision for regular review and adaptation to the changing needs of the organisation.

(e)   It should be **cost effective** for the organisation.

10.4 Problems with incentive schemes

One of the major dangers of incentive schemes is that they may lead to sub-optimisation, particularly in relation to incentive schemes for divisional managers. Sub-optimisation refers to actions or strategies that appear to be beneficial but aren't. Examples of sub-optimisation might be:

Short-termism – actions taken to achieve short-run performance targets at the expense of the long-run performance.

Dysfunctionality – actions taken because they benefit one division although they may not benefit the organisation overall.

Risk of manipulation – excessive pressure to hit results (in order to qualify for an incentive) may result in a culture where it is considered acceptable to use 'creative accounting' to improve the reported figures.

10.4.1 Short-termism

Although the usual argument is that strategic decisions should look at the long term and should avoid short-termism, there are still some problems associated with performance measures and incentives specifically designed to avoid short-termism.

(a)   The link between current expenditure or savings and long-term effect may not be clear.

(b)   There is a danger that investment for the future may have such an adverse impact on present performance that the future envisaged is impossible to achieve. In the worst case, if current performance deteriorates too far, an organisation may not actually have a future.

(c)   Incentive schemes for long-term achievements may not motivate, since effort and reward are too distant in time from each other (or managers may not think that they will be around that long!).

A short-term approach may be appropriate in certain circumstances:

*   In **highly uncertain and changeable situations**, for example in the fashion industry

*   When a short-term approach is **consistent with long-term goals** (for instance a business may make do with old, inefficient plant, awaiting the availability of a new technology)

*   When **stakeholders also take a short-term view**

*   When **competitors** do likewise

*   Under **financial constraints** or difficulties such as workflow problems or insolvency

*   Some organisations have **duties to maintain a certain financial position**

Section summary

Results measures work most effectively when the individuals whose performance is being measured are able to control and influence the results. **Managerial performance** should be assessed on those items that are directly controlled by the manager in question.

If **controllable factors** cannot be separated from **uncontrollable factors** then the results control measures are unlikely to provide any useful information for evaluating the actions taken by individuals.

11   Strategic management styles

Introduction

Goold and Campbell identified three major approaches to running divisionalised conglomerates: **strategic planning**, **strategic control** and **financial control**.

The **role of the corporate centre** in a divisionalised company has been the subject of much theory and research. Indeed, the diversified conglomerate has itself been challenged as a form of economic organisation. There are **three generally accepted possible roles for the centre**:

- Determination of overall strategy and the allocation of resources
- Controlling divisional performance
- Provision of central services

All three of these roles have been subject to debate.

Centralised determination of strategy has been challenged as inappropriate in a diversified conglomerate. Similarly, **resource allocation**, it has been suggested, is the proper role of **capital markets**; and the rigour of the vetting carried out by central staff has been questioned.

Controlling divisional performance is subject to all the arguments for and against decentralisation already discussed. The ability of the centre to prevent **strategic drift** has been questioned, though the radical market alternative can only work in drastic ways, such as takeover.

Centralised provision of certain **services**, such as legal and HR departments, is promoted as enhancing efficiency through the attainment of economies of scale. However, it is also suggested that many of these services can be contracted for locally at no greater cost and with the advantage of precluding any tendency to empire-building at the centre.

11.1 Research

Goold and Campbell researched the role of the centre in 16 UK-based conglomerates. They concentrated on the first two roles summarised above, which they referred to as **planning influence** and **control influence**. The variation in these roles allowed the identification of eight distinct **strategic management styles**.

Planning influence was exercised in a variety of ways, but a fairly smooth spectrum of styles was observable, ranging from minimal, where the centre is little more than a holding company, to highly centralised, where the managers in the business units have responsibility only for operational decisions.

Control influence was exercised by the agreement of **objectives**, the monitoring of **results** and the deployment of **pressures and incentives**. This gave rise to three distinct categories of control influence: **flexible strategic**, **tight strategic** and **tight financial**.

Of the eight strategic management styles they defined, Goold and Campbell found that three of them were particularly common; each was associated with one of the three **control influence** categories mentioned above and with a different degree of **planning influence**.

11.2 Strategic management styles

11.2.1 Strategic planning

The strategic planning management style is associated with a fairly high degree of central planning influence, but less control influence. The centre does not impose rigid targets and constraints over the divisions. The strategic planning process is the main mechanism for the corporate centre's control over the divisions.

The **centre establishes extensive planning processes** through which it works with business unit managers to make substantial contributions to strategic thinking, often with a unifying overall corporate strategy. The strategic planning process involves a lot of dialogue between the corporate centre and each division. Performance targets are set in broad terms, with an **emphasis on longer-term strategic objectives**, which arise from the planning process. The corporate centre also allocates resources to different divisions according to its view of the Group's need to secure competitive advantage in certain divisions.

Business units tend to follow bold strategies and often achieve above industry average **growth** and **profitability**.

11.2.2 Strategic control

The strategic control management style involves a **fairly low degree of planning influence** but uses **tight strategic control**. The centre prefers to leave the planning initiative to the business unit managers, though it will **review** their plans for acceptability. **Firm targets are set** for a range of performance indicators and performance is judged against them. However, within this framework of Group objectives and goals (laid down by the corporate centre) divisions are allowed to pursue their own business strategies. The centre allocates resources to the divisions according to long-term strategic considerations, but it only does so in response to requests from the divisions for resources.

The centre concentrates on rationalising the portfolio. Such companies achieve **good profits** but are **less successful at achieving growth**.

11.2.3 Financial control

The centre exercises influence almost entirely through the budget process. It takes little interest in business unit strategy, and divisions make their own strategic decisions. Financial control companies do not have formal long-term strategies; instead any strategic decisions revolve around the annual budgeting process.

The centre exercises control through financial targets (eg ROCE, profit). Careers are at stake if budgets are missed, and managerial rewards and progression are based on meeting budget targets. Strategies are **cautious** and rarely global. Business unit managers tend to sacrifice market share to achieve high profits. As a result, these companies produce **excellent profits**, but **growth comes mainly from acquisitions**.

In general, the corporate centre allocates resources and funds requested by the divisions, provided that the centre is convinced by the competence of divisional management. However, the centre will manage the acquisition or disposal of any subsidiaries or major assets.

Section summary

Goold and Campbell identified three different strategic management styles which the corporate centre uses when dealing with its business units. These styles (strategic planning, strategic control and financial control) reflect differences in the level of planning influence and control influence the centre has over its divisions.

Chapter Summary

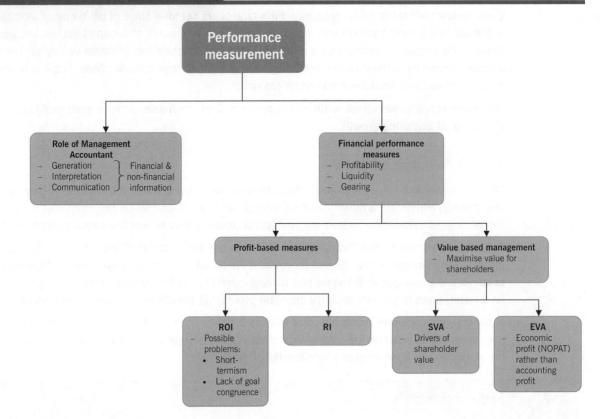

Quick Quiz

1 What is the main problem associated with ROI as a performance measure?

2 Residual income (RI) is a measure of the centre's profits after deducting a notional or imputed .... cost.

3 A shareholder value approach takes a longer-term view of value creation than profit-based approaches to performance measurement.

 True or false?

4 A company's operating profit for the last year was $168.0 million. Tax paid in the year was $8.0 million.

 Included within its operating costs, the company spent $7.4 million on marketing and promotions, and $4.3 million on research and development. The research and development has not been capitalised. The operating profit is also stated after an accounting depreciation charge of $5.0 million.

 Economic depreciation for the year was estimated to be $6.8 million.

 In the context of Economic Value Added (EVA), what was the company's net operating profit after tax (NOPAT) for the year?

 $........................... million

5 What do you understand by the term 'divisional autonomy'?

Answers to Quick Quiz

1   The main problem relates to the difficulty of accurately measuring the value of the assets used to produce the return. For example, it is probably most common to use return on net assets. Inflation and technological change alter the cost of fixed assets, so that it becomes difficult to compare the performance of different divisions.

2   Interest

3   True

    A shareholder value approach to performance measurement involves moving the focus away from short-term profits to a longer-term view of value creation.

4   $169.9 million

	$
Operating profit	168.0
Less tax	(8.0)
Net profit	160.0
Add back:	
Marketing	7.4
R&D	4.3
Depreciation	5.0
	176.7
Less economic depreciation	(6.8)
NOPAT	**169.9**

5   The term refers to the right of a division to govern itself; that is, the freedom to make decisions without consulting a higher authority first and without interference from a higher body.

Answers to Questions

12.1 Manipulation

(a)   Keep gross assets to a minimum

   (i)   Avoid capital expenditure
   (ii)   Acquire all assets on operating leases

(b)   Manipulate current assets

   (i)   Factor debtors (ie sell the debts).

   (ii)   Introduce over-generous settlement discounts, set not by the prevailing interest rate (the true cost) but by divisional ROI targets to encourage early payment.

   (iii) Sell all inventories before the balance sheet date and repurchase them immediately after.

   (iv)   Refuse credit.

(c)   Manipulate the return by investing in projects with higher long-term risk even if they offered better short-term profits.

Compare these measures to the balanced scorecard: clearly they cause dysfunctional behaviour in customer relations and in internal processes (eg inventory management). Too much effort is devoted to manipulating the figures, not improving the business.

(**Note**. This exercise is based on an example cited by Ward in *Strategic Management Accounting*.)

12.2 Head office

Decentralisation recognises that those closest to a job are the best equipped to say how it should be done and that people tend to perform to a higher standard if they are given responsibility. Centrally imposed decisions are likely to make managers feel that they do not really have any authority and therefore that they cannot be held responsible for performance. They will therefore make less effort to perform well.

12.3 Strategic significance

(a)   The firm is using capital efficiently – or is operating at high capacity.

(b)   The firm has to reach a high profit level to pay its lenders – it might have less flexibility in pricing than competitors.

(c)   This might imply that the firm is more capital intensive; in other words, that perhaps it has invested in technology rather than labour. Given the high level of fixed costs which can be deduced from this, the firm might have to price aggressively to maintain market share.

12.4 Subsidiaries

	A Ltd £	B Ltd £
ROI	$\dfrac{£60,000}{£300,000} \times 100\% = 20\%$	$\dfrac{£120,000}{£800,000} \times 100\% = 20\%$
Asset turnover	$\dfrac{£1,250,000}{£300,000} = 4.17$ times	$\dfrac{£2,400,000}{£800,000} = 3$ times
Profit/sales ratio	$\dfrac{£60,000}{£1,250,000} \times 100\% = 4.8\%$	$\dfrac{£120,000}{£2,400,000} \times 100\% = 5\%$

A Ltd has a higher ROI than B Ltd. This is because, although it earned a lower net profit per £1 of sales (4.8p compared with 5p) its capital employed generated more sales turnover, and its asset turnover was nearly 40% higher, at 4.17 times compared with 3 times for B Ltd.

12.5 Calculating EVA

NOPAT	$'000	$'000
Net profit		90
Add back:		
Non-cash expenses	8	
Amortisation of goodwill	5	
Interest (net of 30% tax) 15 × 0.7	10.5	23.5
		113.5
Assets		
At start of period		450
Non-capitalised leases		20
Amortised goodwill		40
		510
WACC		
Equity 15% × 75%		0.1125
Debt (10% × 0.7) × 25%		0.0175
WACC		0.13
EVA: NOPAT	113.5	
Capital charge		
13% × $510	(66.3)	
EVA:	47.2	

12.6 Overcapacity

(a) (i) Pflatte sources from the UK (£1 = 20 ZAR)

		£	*Pflatte* ZAR	Yen equivalent
Selling price		–	2,000	28,000
Sourcing cost from UK	75 × 20		(1,500)	(21,000)
Transport from UK	10 × 20		(200)	(2,800)
Gross profit margin			300	4,200
Margin				15%

(ii) Pflatte sourcing from the UK (£1 = 15 ZAR)

		£	ZAR	Yen
Selling price (ZAR)		–	2,000	28,000
Sourcing cost from UK	75 × 15		(1,125)	(15,750)
Transport from UK	10 × 15		(150)	(2,100)
Gross profit margin			725	10,150
Margin				36.2%

(b)

	£	ZAR	Yen
Revenue	–	2,000	28,000
Cost (UK)	(75)	–	15,000
Transport	(10)	–	2,000
Profit/(loss)	(85)	2,000	11,200

Tutorial note

Further permutations can be tried. For example, the relative exchange rates between £ and Yen, and ZAR and Yen would also affect the decision. So, even though greater Yen profit is made by Pflatte, the differences in production costs can, at **some** rates of exchange, make it easier for Pflatte merely to sell Andantes imported from Sharp. In option (b), no currency changes hands between Pflatte and Sharp, but at prevailing rates of exchange, it is still better for Pflatte to sell Andantes made at Sharp than to make them itself.

Now try these questions from the Practice Question Bank

Number	Level	Marks	Time
12.1–12.5	Intermediate	n/a	10 mins
12.6	Examination	25	45 mins
12.7	Examination	50	90 mins

Question 12.7 does not relate exclusively to Chapter 12. Instead it is a longer case study question to revisit some of the ideas we have covered in this Study Text as a whole.

PRACTICE QUESTION AND ANSWER BANK

What the examiner means

The table below has been prepared by CIMA to help you interpret case study exam questions.

Learning objectives	Verbs used	Definition
1 Knowledge What you are expected to know	• List • State • Define	• Make a list of • Express, fully or clearly, the details of/facts of • Give the exact meaning of
2 Comprehension What you are expected to understand	• Describe • Distinguish • Explain • Identify • Illustrate	• Communicate the key features of • Highlight the differences between • Make clear or intelligible/state the meaning of • Recognise, establish or select after consideration • Use an example to describe or explain something
3 Application How you are expected to apply your knowledge	• Apply • Calculate/ compute • Demonstrate • Prepare • Reconcile • Solve • Tabulate	• Put to practical use • Ascertain or reckon mathematically • Prove with certainty or to exhibit by practical means • Make or get ready for use • Make or prove consistent/compatible • Find an answer to • Arrange in a table
4 Analysis How you are expected to analyse the detail of what you have learned	• Analyse • Categorise • Compare and contrast • Construct • Discuss • Interpret • Prioritise • Produce	• Examine in detail the structure of • Place into a defined class or division • Show the similarities and/or differences between • Build up or compile • Examine in detail by argument • Translate into intelligible or familiar terms • Place in order of priority or sequence for action • Create or bring into existence
5 Evaluation How you are expected to use your learning to evaluate, make decisions or recommendations	• Advise • Evaluate • Recommend	• Counsel, inform or notify • Appraise or assess the value of • Propose a course of action

1.1 – 1.5 Objective Test questions

1.1 Which one of the following best describes the purpose of formulating strategies?

A To understand the organisation's environment
B To control the behaviour of employees
C To achieve the organisation's objectives
D To assess the internal resources available to the organisation

1.2 Approaches to strategic planning can be described in terms of resource-based approaches and position-based approaches. Which one of the following is an advantage of a resource-based approach?

A It exploits the organisation's distinctive competences.
B It allows the organisation to exploit opportunities.
C It takes account of the distinctive competences of competitors.
D It ensures extensive market research is undertaken when developing new products.

1.3 HAN plc uses the rational model to guide its strategic planning process. HAN's management team are currently undertaking a PEST analysis and a five forces analysis.

Which stage of the planning process has HAN reached?

A Position audit
B Corporate appraisal
C Gap analysis
D Environmental analysis

1.4 When it began, BPP was a training company, and lecturers had to prepare their course material. These materials were offered for sale in a bookshop in BPP's training centre.

Due to unanticipated demand, BPP began offering its material to other colleges, in the UK and internationally. BPP Learning Media, which began as a small offshoot of BPP's training activities, is now a leading publisher in the market for targeted study materials for the examinations of several professional bodies.

The growth of BPP Learning Media is an example of which approach to strategy?

A Rational model
B Incremental
C Emergent
D Planned

1.5 Which one of the following is NOT a feature of poor corporate governance?

A Lack of dialogue with shareholders
B Boards composed of relatively elderly directors
C Lack of involvement of the board in strategic decisions taken by a company
D The board is dominated by one person

1.6 AB Electronics   36 mins

AB Co manufactures, markets and distributes a large range of electronic components, and it has established a significant market share across Europe and the US.

AB has three different divisions: the Domestic Electronic Components (DEC) division, the Industrial Electronic Components (IEC) division, and the Specialist Components (SC) division. The DEC division and the IEC division supply standard electronic components for domestic and industrial use, while the SC division supplies specialist components which are often unique and made to specific customer requirements. Each division has its own factory, with DEC and IEC's factories based in the same Eastern European country and SC's factory based in a Western European country.

All three divisions have been profitable over the past five years, although the board has traditionally taken a relatively cautious approach to providing strategic direction for the company. However, AB's institutional shareholders are now looking for increased growth and profitability. In the past, the institutional shareholders have been critical of AB's board for being overly cautious in their attitude to risk.

In AB's most recent annual report, published in March 20Y0, the board stated that AB's overall strategic aim is to: 'Achieve growth and increase shareholder returns by continuing to produce and distribute high quality electronic components, and develop our international presence through expansion into new overseas markets'.

Two years earlier, in 20X8, AB established a separate trading company with a local partner in Asia to sell the IEC division's products. The ownership of the company is shared: 50% by AB and 50% with a local entrepreneur. AB chose this structure because of local legal requirements. A further legal requirement is that, in the case of the company ceasing to trade, AB will be required to reimburse the local entrepreneur the full amount of his original investment (which was $500,000).

This expansion was initially very successful, with good levels of demand being experienced for IEC's products. Recently, however, a number of environmental factors have rapidly changed. These include a forecast of declining demand for IEC's products in Asia due to adverse world economic factors (which have slowed the growth in demand for electronic components in total) and a move towards protectionism in some Asian countries. The trading company had originally been forecast to make a profit of $2 million in 20Y1, but this figure has now been re-forecast to $1.6 million.

IEC has also been unfortunate in that its direct labour costs in Asia have increased by more than the planned level. Economic intelligence suggests that this inflation will continue increasing for the next two years.

However, analysis by AB's management accountant shows that the trading company's costs (and in particular its wage costs) are proportionally much higher than its competitors.

Required

(a) Advise the board of AB how strategic management accounting could help it manage the performance of the trading company in Asia. **(8 marks)**

(b) Discuss the factors which AB should consider before withdrawing from the trading company it has established with its partner in Asia. **(12 marks)**

(Total = 20 marks)

2.1 – 2.5 Objective Test questions

2.1 The courier company Federal Express used to have the very brief mission statement 'Absolutely, positively overnight'. FedEx's mission statement was then expanded to highlight that the company remains 'absolutely, positively focused on safety, customers and communities'.

In general terms, which of the following elements should organisations include in their mission statements?

(i) Policies and standards of behaviour
(ii) Profitability
(iii) The organisation's fundamental objectives and the nature of its business

A (i) and (ii)
B (i) and (iii)
C (ii) and (iii)
D (i), (ii) and (iii)

2.2 Zeus Co is a small private limited company with two directors (who are also its shareholders) and three staff. Zeus Co has a relatively high level of financial gearing due to an overdraft facility and a loan granted by Pluto Bank.

Zeus is looking to expand, but will need to take out an additional loan to achieve this.

In terms of stakeholder mapping, what is Pluto Bank's level of interest and power in relation to the proposed expansion?

A   Low interest and low power
B   Low interest and high power
C   High interest and low power
D   High interest and high power

2.3 CIMA's Code of Ethics identifies five categories of threat which could compromise an accountant's ability to comply with the fundamental ethical principles.

Which one of the three threats occurs if an accountant is promoting a client's position, to such an extent that the accountant's subsequent objectivity is compromised?

A   Advocacy threat
B   Intimidation threat
C   Self-interest threat
D   Self-review threat

2.4 Large companies often include a reference to social responsibility in their mission statements.

Which of the aspirations below reflect a genuine concern for socially responsible behaviour?

(i)   To support the local community and preserve the environment
(ii)   To keep employees informed of policy, progress and problems
(iii)   To pay at least the minimum wage to all employees

A   (i) and (ii)
B   (i) and (iii)
C   (ii) and (iii)
D   (i), (ii) and (iii)

2.5 One of an organisation's objectives for the past year was to increase operating profit by 5% compared to the prior year.

The organisation operates a profit-related pay scheme for its staff, but staff only become eligible for profit-related pay if the organisation exceeds its profit target for the year.

Staff motivation has been low during the last year, because they cannot understand why the operating profit target has been increased for the year when there has been a general slowdown in their industry.

Which aspect of 'SMART' objectives has the organisation failed to meet in relation to its operating profit target?

A   Specific
B   Measurable
C   Achievable
D   Time-related

2.6 WRL gold mining company   45 mins

WRL is a multinational gold mining company. Its mission statement explains that 'WRL exists to make the maximum possible profit for its shareholders whilst causing the least damage to the environment. WRL will, at all times, be a good corporate citizen'.

Three years ago, in 20X7, WRL was granted a licence to mine for gold by the national Government of Stravia, a small country whose economy is mainly based on agriculture. The national Government of Stravia was very keen to develop its economy and saw gold mining as an important aspect of this. The area where WRL was granted the licence is very remote and has no towns or cities nearby. There are small villages near the site of the gold mine. One of the conditions of the licence is that WRL would employ local people wherever possible, which it has done. WRL is entitled under the terms of the licence to dispose of the waste from the gold mining wherever is convenient for it.

The terms of the licence granted a payment by WRL to the national Government of Stravia, payable in US dollars, which in 20X9 totalled $50 million. This is a significant amount of foreign exchange for Stravia's economy. Similar levels of payment by WRL to the national Government are likely to continue annually for the foreseeable future. The mine has operated profitably since it began.

WRL's mine is in an area controlled by the Eastern State Government. The Eastern State Government was not involved in the negotiations to bring WRL to Stravia and is not entitled to any payment from WRL. However, Stravia's national Government granted the Eastern State Government $1 million in 20X9 from the payments which it received from WRL.

The Eastern State Government discovered that WRL's proposed mining techniques use a great deal of water which becomes polluted. The cheapest way for WRL to dispose of this polluted water is to dispose of it in a lake near the mine and it intends to do this.

The Eastern State Government feared that if the polluted water was disposed of in the lake this would kill all the aquatic life in the lake and have a long-lasting adverse effect on the lake and the surrounding area. Therefore, the Eastern State Government took legal action against WRL in the Eastern state courts to prevent the disposal of the polluted water in the lake.

During the court action, WRL argued that if it was not allowed to dispose of the polluted water in the lake its mining operations in Stravia would become uneconomic and the mine would have to close. A small number of WRL's shareholders argued that it was better to close the mine than to pollute the lake.

The state courts granted the Eastern State Government's request to prevent WRL disposing of the polluted water in the lake. However, upon appeal to the National Supreme Court, WRL has been granted permission to pump the polluted water into the lake as its licence imposes no restrictions.

Required

(a) (i) **Categorise**, according to Mendelow's matrix, any **three** of the stakeholder groups of WRL with respect to the decision about the disposal of the polluted water. You should explain what the power and interests of the three stakeholder groups you have categorised are likely to be.

Note. You are not required to draw the Mendelow matrix.   **(9 marks)**

(ii) **Advise** the board of WRL on the actions it should take to resolve the problem of its stakeholders' competing objectives.   **(7 marks)**

(b) **Discuss** the extent to which WRL's mission statement is consistent with its plan to put the polluted water in the lake.   **(9 marks)**

(Total = 25 marks)

3.1 – 3.5 Objective Test questions

3.1 An organisation has been assessing the potential opportunities in its external environment, and has identified one particular strategic uncertainty that it wants to investigate in more detail.

The organisation's managers believe that if the uncertainty were to materialise it would affect virtually all of the organisation's business units. However, the managers believe that the likelihood of the uncertainty occurring is very unlikely.

How should the uncertainty be classified in terms of Aaker and McLoughlin's strategic importance / urgency matrix?

A High strategic importance; high urgency
B High strategic importance; low urgency
C Low strategic importance; high urgency
D Low strategic importance; low urgency

3.2 Which one of the following would result in a company's customers having a low bargaining power?

A Information is readily available about alternative products, and switching costs are relatively low.

B The company's product is a luxury item rather than a necessity.

C The company is suffering financial difficulties.

D The company is the sole supplier of a product with no apparent substitutes.

3.3 Which one of the following is NOT a benefit of scenario planning?

A It identifies the key uncertainties to which an organisation could be exposed.

B It forces management to look externally at wider business issues, rather than only looking internally at their own organisation.

C It allows management to forecast what is going to happen.

D It can provide managers with useful insights into the future of their industry which can help shape their strategy.

3.4 Which of the following theories or techniques is most useful in highlighting to management that an important part of an organisation's strategy is how it interacts with the other players in its industry?

A Foresight
B Game theory
C Real options
D Scenario planning

3.5 Which technique for gaining insights into the future is described below?

A number of experts are asked to independently and anonymously give their opinions and insights on a particular trend and how it may develop. These initial results are summarised and the summary is returned to the experts who are then asked to respond again once they have seen the responses of the group. This process is repeated until a consensus is achieved.

A Delphi method
B Cross-impact analysis
C Morphological analysis
D Visioning

3.6 BBB international bank   36 mins

BBB is an international bank with retail banking operations in many countries. BBB's retail banking is geared primarily towards individual customers and is provided through branches as well as the internet. BBB offers a wide variety of retail banking products including savings and cheque accounts, debit and credit cards, insurances, mortgages and personal loans. BBB has a strong international brand image and a long record of success, particularly in Western countries.

BBB has offered retail banking services in country R for the last three years (since 20X8). BBB decided to invest in R because, at the time, R had a rapidly growing economy, and in 20X8 BBB considered there were good retail banking opportunities as only 50% of the population of R had a bank account. BBB initially invested $200 million entering R and establishing its own branch network there. It also purchased a local bank in R for $150 million just after the start of the global financial crisis in 20X7.

R liberalised its economy 20 years ago which means it now allows the free flow of capital into and out of the country. The banking sector contains some state-owned institutions that compete strongly for retail banking business. The largest state-owned bank, SB, has half of R's retail banking business and has a strong position of dominance. This has been strengthened recently due to a reorganisation in its senior management and the launch of some successful new retail banking products. These new products have proved to be very popular with customers and are very profitable.

One banking analyst has recently commented that 'R's government has chosen to energise the banking sector through SB. It is less keen on foreign competition. The potential rewards for retail banking in R are great. There is plenty of growth left in this market and the margins are excellent. However, R's population is very conservative, they don't like change.' Within R, mortgage and consumer lending has grown at 20% per year compound from 20X7 to the present day. BBB's economic intelligence unit has forecast that this growth will continue for the foreseeable future because this reflects the policy of R's government.

There are a number of foreign banks which have been established in R for over 15 years and these are all profitable. They have 35% of R's retail banking market. Since the beginning of the current year, BBB has identified two foreign banks which entered R at the same time as BBB, but which have withdrawn from R. One of the foreign banks has stated its reason for withdrawal as being 'Our operations in R have reduced group profitability.'

Required

(a)   **Evaluate**, using Porter's Five Forces model, BBB's future potential for a profitable retail banking business within country R.   **(15 marks)**

(b)   **Advise** BBB, using your analysis from part (a) of your answer, whether it should continue its retail banking business in country R.   **(5 marks)**

(Total = 20 marks)

4.1 – 4.5 Objective Test questions

4.1 Which one of the following is NOT an aim of strategic supply chain management?

  A Reliability of deliveries in terms of timeliness, quality and quantity
  B Reducing the number of suppliers
  C Closing relationships between companies in the supply chain
  D Frequently changing suppliers

4.2 One of the strategic business units in the FGL Group is the G&L chain of gyms and leisure centres.

  G&L's share of the total market in its country is 11%, but the market is quite fragmented and its largest competitor only has a market share of 9.5%.

  In the last year, the overall gym and leisure market grew by 1%, but G&L's revenue increased by 12% as a result of a successful marketing campaign and opening 2 new gyms.

  According to the classifications of the BCG matrix, G&L is a:

  A Star
  B Question mark
  C Cash cow
  D Dog

4.3 Which of the following statements about the product life cycle is/are correct?

  (i)   Competition is stronger in the growth phase than the introduction phase.
  (ii) Sales volumes are higher in the growth phase than in the maturity phase.

  A Neither of them
  B (i) only
  C (ii) only
  D Both of them

4.4 Some of the cashiers at DEF Bank have become concerned about the length of the queues which have been forming as customers wait to be served. They have mentioned their concerns to their managers, and the managers have suggested that DEF should try to gather information about the way other companies control the length of their queues to see if DEF can learn from this.

  Currently, DEF has compared its performance with a supermarket, a railway station, and an airport – all of which are regarded as having very efficient queuing processes.

  What type of benchmarking has DEF been undertaking?

  A Historical
  B Competitive
  C Internal
  D Process

4.5 Which one of the following is a primary activity in Porter's value chain?

  A Service
  B Technology development
  C Procurement
  D Human resource management

4.6 BBB fashion retailer   30 mins

BBB is a fashion retailer with a chain of 20 shops, each with its own manager. BBB believes it can best compete by offering a wide selection of high-quality products sold at a reasonable price. BBB has trained all its staff in customer care and prefers to employ staff who have worked for other fashion retailers.

As a large proportion of BBB's products are clothes which only remain fashionable for a short period, it is important that good inventory control is maintained. BBB has recently invested in a robotic system to improve materials handling in its warehouse.

As a service to its customers, BBB will deliver to their home, within 24 hours, any items bought from one of its shops. BBB's competitors do not offer such a service. BBB knows that it has demanding customers who appreciate the retail experience and after-sales service which BBB offers. If a customer has any dissatisfaction with a purchase, BBB will make a refund without question. BBB frequently sends its regular customers special offers and invites them to fashion shows held in its shops.

BBB's head office is organised into departments which are responsible for the procurement of products, setting of personnel policies, investigating innovations in fashion retailing and general corporate administration.

BBB's management accountant has been investigating the acquisition of high-tech 'Smart Tills' which would provide the following information for each shop:

- Sales transactions and analysis
- Staff statistics (sales per staff member)
- Gross profit
- Inventory turnover and balances
- Audit information (a database recording all transactions)

If BBB replaces its existing tills with Smart Tills, it will be able to better manage cash and inventory and optimise its sales due to accurate real-time information. This will have the benefits of identifying and controlling wastage and improve the accuracy of its forecasts.

The overall advantages offered by the Smart Tills are that BBB will be able to react more quickly to customer demand, ensure that it has sufficient stock in its shops, minimise wastage, reduce its investment in working capital and enable its head office to know, on a real-time basis, how well each of its shops is trading.

Required

(a)   **Explain** how BBB could use Porter's value chain to achieve competitive advantage. Your answer should give examples from BBB of the NINE activities in the value chain and explain how each one of them could add value for BBB.   **(13 marks)**

(b)   **Advise** BBB how it could improve its profits by use of Smart Tills.   **(4 marks)**

(Total = 17 marks)

5.1 – 5.7 Objective Test questions

5.1 PQR manufactures low-emission, hybrid cars and it is constantly looking at ways to improve the productivity of its manufacturing processes and to minimise its overhead costs so that it can afford to sell its cars at a lower price than competitors' low-emission cars.

PQR has recently relocated one of its factories, because this will enable it to make a significant reduction in its operating costs, including wage costs.

Which of Porter's generic strategies best describes PQR's strategy?

A   Cost leadership
B   Differentiation
C   Cost leadership – focus
D   Differentiation – focus

5.2 Which one of the following would be an appropriate growth strategy for an entity which wishes to continue selling its current product range, but wants to expand into new markets?

A   Market development
B   Product development
C   Market penetration
D   Diversification

5.3 Which of the following factors could encourage a firm to establish a production facility in an emerging foreign market?

(i)   Closeness to customers
(ii)   Lower production costs
(iii) Avoiding import tariffs or quotas

A   (i) and (ii)
B   (i) and (iii)
C   (ii) and (iii)
D   (i), (ii) and (iii)

5.4 Which of the following statements about franchising is/are true?

(i)   Franchising allows a business to expand using less capital than if it grows organically.

(ii)   There is less scope for a company's reputation to be damaged if it grows by franchising than if it grows organically.

A   Neither of them
B   (i) only
C   (ii) only
D   Both of them

5.5 Which of the following are possible disadvantages of a joint venture arrangement?

(i)   Disagreements between the venture partners over management and marketing strategy.
(ii)   Profits have to be shared among the venture partners.
(iii) Confidential information about the partners could get shared between them.

A   (i) and (ii)
B   (i) and (iii)
C   (ii) and (iii)
D   (i), (ii) and (iii)

5.6 A company is evaluating a strategy to see whether it is appropriate for the company's current situation.

Which of the following issues relates to the suitability of the strategy (in the context of Johnson, Scholes and Whittington's model of suitability, feasibility and acceptability)?

[*Select as many as you think are correct*]

A   Whether the company has enough resources to implement it

B   The amount of return on investment the strategy will generate

C   Whether the strategy suits the organisational culture of the company

D   Whether the strategy will help to generate or sustain a competitive advantage for the company

5.7 Fill in the gap.

A .... is the purchase of a business from its existing owners by members of the current management team, generally in association with a financial institution.

A   Management buy in
B   Demerger
C   Liquidation
D   Management buy out

5.8 GHK restaurants   18 mins

GHK is a restaurant chain consisting of eight restaurants in an attractive part of a European country which is popular with tourists. GHK has been owned by the same family for the previous 15 years and has always traded at a profit. However, a number of factors have meant that GHK is now in danger of making a trading loss. There has been a substantial drop in the number of tourists visiting the region whilst, at the same time, the prices of many of the foodstuffs and drinks used in its restaurants has increased. Added to this, the local economy has shrunk with several large employers reducing the size of their workforce.

The owners of GHK commissioned a restaurant consultant to give them an independent view of their business. The consultant observed that the eight restaurants were all very different in appearance. They also served menus that were very different; for example, one restaurant which was located on a barge in a coastal town specialised in fish dishes, whereas another restaurant 20 miles away had a good reputation as a steak house. The prices varied greatly amongst the restaurants; one restaurant in a historic country house offered 'fine dining' and was extremely expensive, yet another located near a busy railway station served mainly fast food and claimed that its prices were 'the cheapest in town'. Three of GHK's restaurants offered a 'middle of the road' dining experience with conventional menus and average prices. Some of the restaurants had licences which enabled them to serve alcohol with their meals but three restaurants did not have such licences. One restaurant had a good trade in children's birthday parties whereas the restaurant in the historic country house did not admit diners under the age of 18.

The consultant recommended that GHK should examine these differences but did not suggest how. The owners responded that the chain had grown organically over a number of years and that the location, style and pricing decisions made in each restaurant had all been made at different times and depended on trends current at that time.

Required

Advise the owners of GHK how the application of Porter's Three Generic Strategies Model could assist them in maintaining or improving the profitability of their restaurants.

Note. You are not required to suggest individual generic strategies for each of GHK's restaurants.

(10 marks)

5.9 Packit Co

27 mins

Len Wills, Managing Director of Packit Co, a medium-sized manufacturing company based in a European country, has been faced with an interesting dilemma.

Packit Co has produced a unique, easy opening packaging process which had found a ready market with large multinational food companies in Europe. Packit's packaging process had a significant competitive advantage over its rivals, and the company ensured its technological superiority was protected by patents.

However, as its dealings with global customers have increased, Packit has come under increasing pressure to become a global supplier with some form of presence in America and the Far East. Having a global presence would help secure its technological leadership, and its increased size would help prevent its American and Asian competitors moving into the European market.

Packit has been considering the various strategic options which are open to it. Acquiring a similar packaging company in an appropriate location seems unlikely, as few companies are for sale. Furthermore, Packit's technological advantage meant that a joint venture was not a realistic short-term possibility.

Eventually the decision was taken to pursue some form of internal or organic growth. Packit has looked at three alternative options. One is to achieve this growth by opening a company sales office in a number of key markets. The second is to establish foreign manufacturing operations handling the final stages of the manufacturing process and buying semi-finished material from the parent company. The third is to appoint agents or distributors to look after Packit's interests in the key American and Asian markets.

Len has asked for your assistance in evaluating the risk and benefits associated with these alternative ways of expanding its international operations.

Required

Analyse the advantages and disadvantages of the three stated organic options open to Packit Co in its move to become a global company. **(15 marks)**

5.10 Product market strategy

45 mins

It has been stated that an industry or a market segment within an industry goes through four basic phases of development. These four phases – introduction, growth, maturity and decline – each have an implication for an organisation's development of growth and divestment strategies.

The following brief profiles relate to four commercial organisations, each of which operate in different industries:

- **Company A.** Established in the last year and manufactures state of the art door locks which replace the need for a key with computer image recognition of fingerprint patterns.

- **Company B.** A biotechnological product manufacturer established for three years and engaged in the rapidly expanding animal feedstuffs market.

- **Company C.** A confectionery manufacturer which has been established for many years and is now experiencing low sales growth but high market share in a long-established industry.

- **Company D.** A retailing organisation which has been very profitable but is now experiencing a loss of market share with a consequent overall reduction in turnover.

Required

(a) Explain:

    (i) The concept of the industry life cycle; and

    (ii) The phase of development in which each of the industries served by the four companies is positioned. **(7 marks)**

(b) Discuss how Ansoff's product market growth vector matrix may be applied by the firms in developing their growth and divestment strategies. **(18 marks)**

(Total = 25 marks)

6.1 – 6.5 Objective Test questions

6.1 Which of the following are valid reasons why an organisation needs an IT strategy?

    (i) IT could provide the organisation with the competitive advantage needed for commercial success.

    (ii) The quality of the information available within an organisation could affect the success of the organisation.

    (iii) IT is best left to the technical department.

    A   (i) and (ii)
    B   (i) and (iii)
    C   (ii) and (iii)
    D   (i), (ii) and (iii)

6.2 Velma plc is a large car manufacturer that regularly has to source large numbers of component parts for input into its range of vehicles. The aim of a project led jointly by Velma's finance director and its IT director is to reduce the bargaining power of Velma's key suppliers and thereby to get the best price for the inputs to the business. Several options surrounding the use of IT have been suggested.

Which of the following would be expected to reduce the bargaining power of suppliers?

    (i) EDI linking with the major suppliers that Velma has dealt with over the last three years to allow online ordering and payment

    (ii) Velma joining an online marketplace, set up as a joint venture with other large vehicle manufacturers

    (iii) An extranet link to provide key suppliers with access to future production schedules at Velma

    A   (i) and (ii)
    B   (ii) only
    C   (i) and (iii)
    D   (ii) and (iii)

6.3 Which one of the following activities is part of information management (IM) strategy?

    A   Identifying the systems which will best enable the use of information to support the overall business strategy

    B   Analysing an organisation's data storage requirements

    C   Identifying the technical solutions required to enable an organisation to implement its information systems strategy

    D   Ensuring that information can be accessed by people who need it

6.4 According to Rockart's work on the general sources of CSFs, which one of the following is NOT a general source of CSFs?

    A   The industry that an organisation is in
    B   An organisation's situation within its industry and market
    C   The external environment
    D   Internal departments

6.5 In Peppard's applications portfolio, applications which have high strategic importance in the current competitive environment but are expected to have low strategic importance in the predicted future competitive environment are .... applications:

    A   High potential
    B   Strategic
    C   Key operational
    D   Support

6.6 GHK restaurants   27 mins

> **Note**. Part (a) of this question forms Question 5.8 of this Question Bank. Part (b) of this question should be attempted now as Question 6.6 of this Question Bank. However, if you have not already answered Question 5.8, you should answer both parts of the question now.

GHK is a restaurant chain consisting of eight restaurants in an attractive part of a European country which is popular with tourists. GHK has been owned by the same family for the previous 15 years and has always traded at a profit. However, a number of factors have meant that GHK is now in danger of making a trading loss. There has been a substantial drop in the number of tourists visiting the region whilst, at the same time, the prices of many of the foodstuffs and drinks used in its restaurants has increased. Added to this, the local economy has shrunk with several large employers reducing the size of their workforce.

The owners of GHK commissioned a restaurant consultant to give them an independent view of their business. The consultant observed that the eight restaurants were all very different in appearance. They also served menus that were very different; for example, one restaurant which was located on a barge in a coastal town specialised in fish dishes, whereas another restaurant 20 miles away had a good reputation as a steak house. The prices varied greatly amongst the restaurants; one restaurant in a historic country house offered 'fine dining' and was extremely expensive, yet another located near a busy railway station served mainly fast food and claimed that its prices were 'the cheapest in town'. Three of GHK's restaurants offered a 'middle of the road' dining experience with conventional menus and average prices. Some of the restaurants had licences which enabled them to serve alcohol with their meals but three restaurants did not have such licences. One restaurant had a good trade in children's birthday parties whereas the restaurant in the historic country house did not admit diners under the age of 18.

The consultant recommended that GHK should examine these differences but did not suggest how. The owners responded that the chain had grown organically over a number of years and that the location, style and pricing decisions made in each restaurant had all been made at different times and depended on trends current at that time.

Required

(a) Advise the owners of GHK how the application of Porter's Three Generic Strategies Model could assist them in maintaining or improving the profitability of their restaurants.

Note. You are not required to suggest individual generic strategies for each of GHK's restaurants.

         (10 marks)

(b) Advise how GHK could employ a range of organisational information systems to support whichever generic strategy it chooses to adopt.   **(15 marks)**

         (Total = 25 marks)

7.1 – 7.5 Objective Test questions

7.1   Knowledge management activities aim to capture and organise knowledge of an organisation's processes and make it more widely available. However, staff within an organisation might not always want to share their knowledge.

Which of the following are reasons why staff might NOT want to share knowledge?

(i)   Possession of knowledge can provide power and status.

(ii)   Staff might be reluctant to express opinions which do not comply with managerial perspectives.

(iii)   They enjoy the process of discussing new ideas and sharing their thoughts.

A   (i) and (ii)
B   (i) and (iii)
C   (ii) and (iii)
D   (i), (ii) and (iii)

7.2   Which one of the following is NOT a feature of a learning organisation?

A   Employees' workloads are managed so that they have time to try out new ideas and/or reflect on their experiences.

B   Employees are not blamed for taking calculated risks, even if they turn out to be unsuccessful.

C   Individual performance is linked with organisational performance.

D   The HR department is solely responsible for learning and development.

7.3   Fill in the gap with the word or words which most accurately complete the passage below.

'Big Data analytics is likely to be very important in making use of the potential value of Big Data. It relates to the ability to analyse and reveal insights in data which had previously been too difficult to analyse due to the .... of the data involved.'

A   Volume
B   Variability and velocity
C   Variability and volume
D   Velocity and volume

7.4   The internet can have a significant impact on elements of the five forces. Which of the following statements about the impact of the internet on the five forces is/are true?

(i)   The ability to compare prices directly between different online retailers reduces the bargaining power of customers.

(ii)   By removing the need for a physical presence (for example, shop space for a retailer) the internet removes some of the barriers to entry to an industry.

A   Neither of them
B   (i) only
C   (ii) only
D   Both of them

7.5   Match the following Web 2.0 marketing activities (1–3) with the definitions (A–C) below.

    1   Blog
    2   Podcast
    3   Social network

    A   A site that facilitates peer to peer communication
    B   An online diary or news source
    C   Delivery of audio, or video, content

7.6 AAP estate agents   45 mins

AAP operates an estate agency business in a northern European country, M. An estate agency business arranges the selling, renting or management of houses or other properties.

AAP has been in business for the last 30 years and has 10 offices located throughout Country M. It specialises in marketing and selling high value, exclusive residential properties in Country M. AAP has seen the number of its property sales decline steadily in the last five years. AAP's board believes that this is due to the current economic downturn and its impact on residential housing sales rather than as a result of any underlying problems within AAP itself.

AAP uses a standard estate agency software package to manage its buyer enquiries, property viewings and marketing. AAP also uses the estate agency software package to automatically match buyer enquiry details against its database of properties. AAP does not have a customer database to record customer information.

AAP has a website on which it advertises all of its properties located throughout Country M. However, this website allows customers to view the basic property details such as internal photographs and floor layout. In order to obtain more detailed information on each property, customers must visit one of AAP's offices or telephone one of the agents in order to be sent a printed version of the property details. AAP has an email system which allows customers to contact its offices. The email system is also the main form of internal communication between employees and is often used to transfer files from one office to another. The estate agency software package and the website are not linked. Therefore, if any changes are made to the information held on the estate agency software, this change has to be duplicated on the website. This has, in the past, led to incorrect information being viewed by customers on the website, as the information was not completely up to date.

Until now, investment in information technology has been minimal and the board of AAP has not considered information technology to be a critical aspect of its business. AAP's board has never considered developing an e-business strategy as it believes that its main strategic priority is enhancing AAP's reputation of high-quality, face to face direct customer service. The Managing Director stated at a recent board meeting that 'we must retain our focus upon keeping our customers happy. Developing our website to sell our properties is merely a distraction from what we do and what our customers want'.

The Marketing Director is concerned that AAP is not keeping up to date with technological developments and that AAP should use its information systems more strategically. Having researched a wide range of websites, the Marketing Director has identified a range of Web 2.0 technologies that AAP could use to improve its own website. He is also aware of a new technology development which enables potential home buyers to receive property details whilst viewing a property, by using location-based applications on their mobile phones.

The Marketing Director intends to write a report to the board of directors outlining his research and his belief that AAP could benefit significantly from developing an e-business strategy.

Required

The Marketing Director has asked you to provide him with a report in which you:

(a) **Explain**

    (i)   The criticality of information systems to AAP, using McFarlan's strategic grid   **(4 marks)**

    (ii)   Why the investment in information systems by AAP should be a strategic decision

                                                                                  (5 marks)

(b) **Advise** on the benefits AND problems of developing an e-business strategy for AAP   **(8 marks)**

(c) **Recommend**, with reasons, TWO different applications of Web 2.0 technology that AAP could adopt   **(8 marks)**

                                                            (Total = 25 marks)

8.1 – 8.5 Objective Test questions

8.1   Which of the following would be valid reasons for segmenting a market?

    [Select as many as you think are correct]

    A   Demand for your product is greater than supply.
    B   The level of competitiveness within the market is high.
    C   Your company has limited resources.
    D   Your product is unique and difficult for competitors to imitate.

8.2   Which of the following are benefits of branding for an organisation?

    (i)   It reduces the importance of price as a source of competitive advantage.
    (ii)   Branding acts as a barrier to entry to potential new entrants into a market.
    (iii) Brands can have much longer life cycles than products.

    A   (i) and (ii)
    B   (i) and (iii)
    C   (ii) and (iii)
    D   (i), (ii) and (iii)

8.3   Which of the following are features of relationship marketing?

    (i)   It devotes marketing resources to maintaining and exploiting an organisation's existing customer base.

    (ii)   It focuses on establishing loyalty among customers.

    (iii) It encourages only low to moderate contact with customers.

    A   (i) and (ii)
    B   (i) and (iii)
    C   (ii) and (iii)
    D   (i), (ii) and (iii)

8.4   A company has been analysing the expected customer lifetime value of a cohort of customers and has made a number of assumptions about the churn rate in future periods.

    If the actual churn rates turn out to be lower than the company has anticipated, the customer lifetime value of the cohort will be lower than expected.

    True or false?

8.5 The internet and online marketing techniques can play an important role in relationship marketing.

Which one of the following is most useful for customer extension rather than customer acquisition?

A   Affiliate marketing
B   Comparison sites
C   Recommendations
D   Search engines

8.6 CFE coffee shops   **30 mins**

CFE was established in 20X1, and operates a chain of 40 coffee shops across Teeland. It is a privately owned company.

The number of coffee shops in Teeland has increased rapidly over the last decade, and there are now thousands of branded coffee shops operating across the country. Their total turnover now exceeds $1 billion. Although the majority of the branded shops are run by internationally recognised multinational companies, CFE only operates in Teeland.

The range of products offered by the shops has increased over the last few years, in response to customer demand for a larger range of foods and better-quality products. The branded coffee shops have been able to command higher than average prices for their products by using quality and service as differentiators. Price appears not to be a particularly sensitive factor, although CFE's prices are largely the same as those charged by the branded shops run by the multinational companies.

In 20X1, when CFE first opened, most other coffee shops only served a selection of hot and cold drinks and a small range of snacks and cakes. However, right from the outset, CFE also sold a range of freshly made sandwiches and other food items, all made from high-quality ingredients.

All CFE's shops operate from rented premises, but before opening they are fitted out to ensure they have the same high standard of shop design and fittings. Having a high quality of shop design creates a good atmosphere, and makes the coffee shops a popular place for people to meet.

CFE's shops generate a high turnover. However, profitability has been lower than some of its competitors. Reasons for this include: high rental costs for some of its city centre shops; high staff costs (as high-quality customer service remains a priority for CFE so it pays above the industry average); and lower than average gross margins on some products (due to the high procurement cost of the quality ingredients chosen).

CFE also earns lower margins than some of its rivals on its coffee products because over 80% of its coffee beans are procured from suppliers who deal only with 'Fair Trade' coffee producers. Some of the regional managers have argued that their shops would be more profitable if they stopped using 'Fair Trade' coffee, but CFE's directors remain adamant that the company will continue to buy coffee from Fair Trade suppliers wherever possible, because it is a socially responsible company.

At a recent board meeting, the Marketing Director said he thought CFE should introduce a loyalty card scheme, and for every six hot drinks loyalty card holders buy, they get their next one free. He argued the card scheme will help CFE's profitability by improving customer loyalty and strengthening the brand.

The Finance Director said that CFE should also consider whether it could increase the prices of its coffee products in order to increase the margins it earns on them.

A summary of CFE's trading results for the last year is shown below:

($'000)	Coffee	Other drinks	Food & snacks	Total
Revenue	19,517	5,541	32,322	57,380
Cost of sales	(3,767)	(2,638)	(13,975)	(20,380)
Gross margin	15,750	2,903	18,347	37,000
Operating profit				5,606

The largest branded coffee shop in Teeland (which has 130 shops) generated revenues of $180m in the last year, with a gross margin of $124m and operating profit of $22.5m.

Required

(a) With reference to the Marketing Director's proposal to introduce a loyalty card scheme, evaluate the importance of brand awareness on CFE's business performance. **(12 marks)**

(b) Discuss the importance of external information in relation to the Finance Director's suggestion for CFE to increase the prices of its coffee products. **(5 marks)**

(Total = 17 marks)

9.1 – 9.5 Objective Test questions

9.1 The management team at MLK Co has realised that a 'Big Bang' approach to change is required to help them deal with the current crisis the company is facing.

The extent of the changes required at MLK mean that changes will have to be wide ranging, and are likely to fundamentally alter the way the company operates.

Which of the following types of change is MLK most likely to experience?

A Adaptation
B Evolution
C Reconstruction
D Revolution

9.2 You are the manager of a department which is moving to a new shift system. There has been some resistance to this change from the staff within the department.

Which one of the following is likely to be the most effective way of changing staff attitudes to the change and of gaining acceptance for the change?

A Pay the employees to accept the change

B Get team leaders to instruct members of their teams about the benefits of change

C Present the change to staff as 'a done deal' and emphasise that there is nothing you can do to change it

D Tell staff the change is for a 'trial period' and hope they get used to it

9.3 An organisation has introduced a new bonus scheme, and staff's ability to earn a bonus is dependent on them adopting the introduction of a new methodology.

The new methodology has been introduced in a change process which followed Lewin's stage model of change.

Introducing the new bonus scheme is part of the .... stage, as described by Lewin's model.

A Unfreeze
B Change
C Refreeze
D Move

9.4 In recent months, the directors of LMP Co have become concerned that the company's net profits have fallen behind target. Two separate initiatives have been proposed to try to help improve LMP's profit:

(i) Senior management have identified a number of potential staff redundancies across the company which would be made to help reduce costs.

(ii) Managers have been encouraging their staff to suggest improvements and to share knowledge, to ensure that LMP makes best use of ideas from staff throughout the company.

Which of the proposed initiatives is consistent with a Theory O approach to change management?

A Neither of them
B (i) only
C (ii) only
D Both of them

9.5 Which one of the following is NOT one of the aspects of the cultural web?

A Capability
B Control systems
C Organisational structure
D Symbols

9.6 Steyn Steel Co   27 mins

Steyn Steel Co has recently appointed a new Chief Executive Officer (CEO), and the new CEO is intent on making the company more competitive.

The CEO has made it clear than he considers the current operational performance to be below acceptable levels. He feels that a number of managers who have worked for Steyn Steel for a long time have become complacent about the company's performance, and this is having a detrimental effect on its competitiveness. The CEO has publicly stated, 'Costs are too high and productivity is too low.'

Global demand for steel is still growing, particularly in countries in the Pacific Rim which Steyn Steel exports to. The CEO believes Steyn should capitalise on this. However, to do so, he believes some changes in the working conditions at Steyn will be necessary. A reduction in import duty in some of the proposed export markets will also be necessary for Steyn to trade profitably with them.

The majority of the steel workers at Steyn belong to a trade union. Their union is well organised and has promised the workers it will defend their wages levels and working conditions in the face of any changes.

Required

(a) Analyse the forces for change and the causes of resistance in the Steyn Steel company.

(10 marks)

(b) Using an appropriate stage model of change, recommend how the newly appointed CEO at Steyn might manage the process of change he wants to implement in the company.   **(5 marks)**

(Total = 15 marks)

10.1 – 10.5 Objective Test questions

10.1 As a result of the changes affecting an organisation, a manager has had to communicate a number of messages to her team. Due to time pressure, the communication has been predominantly one-way, with the team getting little opportunity to ask questions or give feedback on any plans.

Although a number of the team are unhappy about the lack of opportunity to ask questions, many of them are reassured by their manager's commitment to the plans which was clear from the way she spoke about their benefits for the future of the organisation.

What style does the manager appear to have used when communicating with her team?

A Consults
B Joins
C Sells
D Tells

10.2 You are responsible for communicating a change to your team, and your aim is to convince the individuals in your team to accept that change.

What key message should you emphasise?

A The expertise that has gone into making the decision
B The authority of the change agent to enforce the change
C The speed with which the change needs to be implemented
D The problem or threat which has caused the change to be necessary

10.3 Which one of the approaches listed is most likely to be an effective way for a manager to deal with conflict?

A Dominance – using their own power or influence to settle the conflict

B Compromise – bargaining, negotiation and conciliation

C Denial – ignoring it, in the hope it will resolve itself

D Suppression – smoothing over the issues in order to preserve working relationships, despite minor conflicts remaining

10.4 A change agent can best be described as:

A An external consultant who analyses an organisation and recommends the changes that need to take place in it

B A senior manager who knows all the parts of the organisation and therefore understands what needs to change

C A senior manager who proposes a strategic change in an organisation

D A person, or group of people, who takes on the role of promoting strategic change within an organisation

10.5 In the G-plas factory, a project team has been assembled by management to solve a problem with workflow on the factory floor. The team is starting to put forward some really innovative ideas; they get quite animated in brainstorming sessions, and are uninhibited in putting forward their views and suggestions.

However, two factions are beginning to emerge, with each thinking their overall approach to solving the problem is better than the other's.

What stage of team development has the team reached?

A Forming
B Norming
C Performing
D Storming

10.6 Simon Clark   36 mins

Simon Clark is Head of the Department of Business at a local public sector college which provides professional training on a part-time basis for students who are already in employment. The students are mainly studying for professional qualifications in either accountancy, marketing or personnel. A number of students are also studying for general management qualifications. Increasingly this college is experiencing competition from a newly established private sector organisation. This private sector organisation is able to deliver programmes more efficiently and effectively than the older established college because of its more flexible work contracts and working practices. The traditional method of tuition has been on a part-time day release basis (one day or one half-day a week) away from work, studying within the college. With local companies becoming more reluctant to give their staff time off on a regular basis to study, Simon is proposing that more of the training should be carried out on a distance-learning basis, often being supplemented by taught weekend programmes. This will involve the staff in writing study materials and working weekends.

Simon's college has a teaching staff who, in recent years, have had to adapt to new situations including organisational structure changes and syllabus changes. However, they are most unhappy about the current proposals which could result in their conditions of service worsening. They are reluctant to work on a weekend basis without additional payments. This would make the college uncompetitive. The private sector college, although it employs high-quality staff, is able to absorb the high costs by employing lecturers on a freelance basis and by having larger class sizes, the students being drawn from a larger catchment area. Simon is becoming frustrated by his staff's apparent opposition to accept the proposed changes, and he is contemplating what to do next.

Required

Simon has arranged a meeting with his staff to discuss weekend working and study material production.

(a)   Identify and discuss the different tactics which Simon could make use of in dealing with this
        conflict.   **(10 marks)**

(b)   Discuss how Simon might encourage his staff to be more supportive of the proposed change in
        work practice.   **(10 marks)**

(Total = 20 marks)

10.7 Auto Direct   22 mins

Mark Howe, Managing Director of Auto Direct, is a victim of his own success. Mark has created an innovative way of selling cars to the public which takes advantage of the greater freedom given to independent car distributors to market cars more aggressively within the European Union. This reduces the traditional control and interference of the automobile manufacturers, some of whom own their distributors. He has opened a number of showrooms in the London region and by 2004 Auto Direct had 20 outlets in and around London. The concept is deceptively simple; Mark buys cars from wherever he can source them most cheaply and has access to all of the leading volume car models. He then concentrates on selling the cars to the public, leaving servicing and repair work to other specialist garages. He offers a classic high volume/low margin business model.

Mark now wants to develop this business model on a national and eventually an international basis. His immediate plans are to grow the number of outlets by 50% each year for the next 3 years. Such growth will place considerable strain on the existing organisation and staff. Each showroom has its own management team, sales personnel and administration. Currently the 20 showrooms are grouped into a Northern and Southern Sales Division with a small head office team for each division. Auto Direct now employs 250 people.

Required

Produce a brief report for Mark describing how he should pursue his proposed growth plans, using appropriate strategies for managing change.   **(12 marks)**

11.1 – 11.5 Objective Test questions

11.1 The four statements below represent a selection of objectives, CSFs, and KPIs. Which one of them is a CSF?

A   To ensure prices are at least 1% lower than the average prices of rival companies

B   Percentage of customers who would recommend the company to friends

C   Using economies of scale to procure high-quality goods as cheaply as possible

D   Number of products which are more expensive than equivalent products sold by competitors

11.2 Which of the following statements is/are true?

(i)   Financial indicators tend to be leading indicators, which can point to future performance problems or successes.

(ii) A problem with financial performance measurement systems is that they often focus on annual (short-term) performance, and so may not be directly linked to longer-term organisational objectives.

A   Both of them
B   (i) only
C   (ii) only
D   Neither of them

11.3 The strategy map which Kaplan and Norton developed as an extension to the balanced scorecard illustrates that there is a hierarchy among the four perspectives of the scorecard.

According to the strategy map, which is the highest level perspective?

A   Customer
B   Financial
C   Innovation and learning
D   Internal business process

11.4 Which of the following statements about the performance pyramid are true?

(i)   The pyramid focuses on a range of objectives for external effectiveness and internal efficiency.

(ii) The pyramid encourages organisations to look at performance measures in relation to a wide range of stakeholder groups, such as customers, employees and suppliers.

(iii) The hierarchical levels of the pyramid encourage operational performance measures to be linked to strategic goals.

A   (i) and (ii)
B   (i) and (iii)
C   (ii) and (iii)
D   (i), (ii) and (iii)

11.5 A hotel has noticed that its financial performance has been declining in recent years, and it has identified that one of the reasons for this has been its inability to cope with fluctuations in demand (for example, by adjusting the price of its rooms to reflect seasonal changes in demand).

In relation to Fitzgerald and Moon's building block model (results and determinants analysis), which determinant appears to be having most impact on the hotel's performance?

A   Flexibility
B   Market share
C   Quality of service
D   Profitability

11.6 CCC Car insurance   **45 mins**

T is the Chief Executive Officer of a motor car insurance company, CCC. T, together with the board of directors, developed a mission statement last year (20X1) following a detailed analysis of the company's operations and marketplace. The mission statement states that 'CCC wants to continually grow through its commitment to quality and delivering value to its customers'. CCC has developed a complementary vision statement which aspires to:

- Provide superior returns to our shareholders
- Continually improve our business processes
- Delight our customers
- Learn from our mistakes and work smarter in the future

CCC's overriding objective, also developed last year, is to double the size of its revenue by the end of 20X5.

T has identified the following areas of concern:

- Poor customer service has led to CCC losing 15% of its customers in 20X1/20X2. The customer sales manager had sponsored an initiative to reward customers with a discount if they renewed their motor insurance. However, most of the sales executives were not familiar with the details of this scheme and did not mention it to customers considering renewing their insurance. The discount scheme had not affected the rate of loss of customers.

- The average age of CCC's personal computers (PCs) was five years. There have been many complaints from CCC's staff that their PCs are not adequate for their current demands. The last time an initiative had been undertaken to bring PCs up to date was three years ago.

- CCC's internal auditors had conducted performance reviews in three departments during 20X1. They found a common pattern in all three departments: many of the staff had only minimal educational qualifications which were inadequate for the jobs they were doing. This resulted in an unacceptable level of errors being made. No initiatives had been undertaken to address this problem.

- Investors have been critical of the low dividend yield on their CCC shares.

T is worried because, despite the time and effort put into the development of the mission and vision statements and the overriding objective, CCC is not making sufficient progress towards achieving its revenue target. Its revenue growth rate in 20X1 was 10%.

CCC's shortfall against its revenue target was discussed at a recent board meeting. The Corporate Affairs Director stated that 'the board is 100% behind our strategy and vision but it's just not happening. I have experience in my previous company of working with an integrated model, the balanced scorecard. Could the balanced scorecard help CCC?'

Required

(a)   **Advise** T how a balanced scorecard could assist in delivering CCC's vision and strategy. **(5 marks)**

(b)   Assume that CCC has adopted a balanced scorecard approach to help it achieve its vision.

      Recommend FOUR perspectives, and for each perspective show:

      - An objective
      - A measure
      - A target
      - An initiative   **(16 marks)**

(c)   **Discuss** briefly TWO drawbacks of the balanced scorecard.   **(4 marks)**

                                                              (Total = 25 marks)

12.1 – 12.5 Objective Test questions

12.1 Using the four words (A–D) below, fill in the gaps in the four phrases (i)–(iv) which describe the role of a charted management accountant.

A   Benchmarks
B   Information
C   Control
D   Decisions

(i)   Generation, communication and interpretation of financial and non-financial .... for management and other stakeholders

(ii)   Provision of specific information and analysis on which .... are based

(iii)   Monitoring of outcomes against plans and other .... and the initiation of responsive action for performance improvement

(iv)   Derivation of performance measures and benchmarks, financial and non-financial, quantitative and qualitative for monitoring and ....

12.2 The figures shown below are an extract from the accounts of Ridgeway Co, which has capital employed of $1.5 million.

What is Ridgeway's return on capital employed (ROCE)? ....

Revenue	$1,000,000
Cost of sales	($400,000)
Gross profit	$600,000
Distribution expenses and administration cost	($340,000)
Profit before interest and tax	$260,000
Finance cost	($50,000)
Profit before tax	$210,000
Tax	($45,000)

12.3 Rappaport proposed that the value of a business can be calculated by reference to seven 'value drivers'. According to Rappaport's model, what impact will an increase in fixed capital investment rate have on the value of a business?

A   Increase
B   No change
C   Decrease
D   Could either increase or decrease

12.4 In the calculation of economic value added (EVA), which one of the following will NOT be added back to operating profit in order to determine NOPAT?

A   Economic depreciation
B   Marketing and promotions expenditure
C   Operating lease charges
D   Provisions and allowances for doubtful debts

12.5 At 1 January 20X4, a company's share price was $5.00.

At 31 December 20X4, the company's share price had risen to $5.60, and the company paid a dividend of 20 cents per share in 20X4.

What was the company's total shareholder return for 20X4?

A   10.7%
B   12%
C   14.3%
D   16%

12.6 Management accounting information   45 mins

It has been said that management accounting has traditionally been concerned with providing information for decision making and controlling costs. It has often been criticised for not providing sufficient relevant information to management because it tends to impose general techniques as a solution in situations which demand custom-designed (directly applicable) methods and specific information.

Required

(a)   Discuss the validity of this criticism of management accounting.   **(13 marks)**

        To be relevant to the needs of the organisation, management accounting systems need to be designed to accommodate its specific requirements taking account of the circumstances of its particular business environment. One such circumstance may be the change in traditional working patterns. For example, it can no longer be assumed that all employees will be located on the organisation's premises in carrying out their duties. Some are likely to provide their services from remote locations.

(b)   Compare the approach to providing relevant management accounting information for strategic decision-making purposes in:

        (i)   A manufacturing organisation which employs staff on site; with

        (ii)   A service organisation which employs contractors. The contractors mainly work from home to provide technical solutions for customers engaged in large-scale building projects.

                                                                                (12 marks)

                                                                        (Total = 25 marks)

12.7 The S group   90 mins

Company development

The headquarters of the S Group is located in K, a country which has experienced rapid economic growth in recent years.

S itself has been established for over 100 years. Two brothers first started trading in K and developed the group, which is now a highly profitable international conglomerate company. Its diverse business activities range from capital goods manufacture, through materials handling to operation of airlines and banking. Some of its activities involve the transfer of partly completed goods between manufacturing and assembly plants located in different countries. The group operates a divisional structure.

Economic circumstances

Over the last three years the region of the world in which K is located has been subject to serious economic difficulties. K itself has not been affected as much as some of its neighbours, owing to the fact that its independent currency is pegged to the US dollar.

There has been much activity and intervention by the monetary authorities in K to protect the value of the currency, and this has proved to be largely successful, despite the intense pressure exerted by foreign speculators. Nevertheless, the effects of the regional economic difficulties are being felt. This is exemplified by the recent emergence of unemployment after a period of 30 years of full employment and a dramatic fall in property prices.

Organisational economic objectives

Fifty five per cent of S's holding company shares are held within the families of the original founders. The remaining forty five per cent of the shares are mainly held by international banks and other financial institutions located all over the world. These institutional shareholders maintain constant pressure on the directors to improve earnings per share and increase dividend payments. The directors have stated that their main objective is to increase shareholder value. In satisfying the requirements of the shareholders

the directors are conscious of the need for improved efficiency in the group's operations. Consequently, the holding company's board of directors carefully scrutinises the activities of the constituent subsidiary companies within the group.

Divisional performance measurement

S has always applied a traditional form of measurement to assess the performance of the group's subsidiaries. It uses return on capital employed (ROCE) and defines this as:

$$\frac{\text{Profit before interest and tax}}{\text{Average capital employed}} \times 100$$

(The capital employed value is the average of that shown at the beginning and end of the year.)

The performance of the divisional managers is strictly monitored on this basis and their remuneration increases if they achieve growth in their ROCE, which is measured annually. Inevitably, the divisional managers strive to improve their performance as measured by this method.

The Agricultural Equipment (AE) division

The AE division, which is not located in K, assembles components into a single product. It receives the components from other subsidiaries in the group which are situated in other countries. The group as a whole has been able to benefit from economies of scale, as a result of other subsidiary divisions, which have long experience in manufacturing, supplying AE. Following assembly, AE ships the product to various customers throughout the world. The geographical location of the country in which AE is situated enables the product to be easily exported, but the division is subject to high levels of corporation tax.

The transfer prices of the components transferred to AE are set centrally by group head office located in K. The divisional manager of AE has no influence over them at all. The group head office may vary the transfer prices during the financial year.

Comparative results for the AE division over the last two years (translated into K's currency) are as follows:

	Last year		Previous year	
	K$m	K$m	K$m	K$m
Sales		800		750
Components	600		400	
Assembly costs	100		75	
		700		475
Gross profit		100		275
AE Division Head Office (all fixed)		75		75
Net profit before interest and tax		25		200
Average capital employed		2,020		2,000

Selling prices over the two years remained stable.

It may be assumed that the variable costs of the supplying division, relating to the transferred components, were neutral in respect of AE division's profitability over the two years.

The budgeted and actual selling price per unit was K$50,000 in each of the 2 years. The budgeted production and sales level for each year was 18,000 units. It can be assumed that there were no opening and closing inventories of finished goods or work in progress in either of the years.

The budgeted cost per unit for each of the last two years was as follows:

	Last year	Previous year
	K$	K$
Assembly	6,000	5,000
Components transferred	35,000	25,000
	41,000	30,000

It can be assumed that there was no change in the currency exchange rate between the AE division's host country and K$ in the last two years. There have been discussions at S Group headquarters regarding the

deteriorating performance of AE and there is growing pressure to close it down. The AE divisional manager believes there is little he can do in the circumstances, where he only controls a small proportion of the total costs of the division.

Potential for growth in AE division

Despite the reduced profitability in the last financial year, the divisional manager of AE believes there is potential for growth. He has put forward plans to group headquarters to take over a competitor company in the country in which the division is situated. This would result in an increase for the division in worldwide market share and provide the capacity to increase the range of agricultural equipment supplied in accordance with the divisional manager's perception of demand. To do this AE will need to obtain funds which will be secured against group assets.

Required

(a)   Identify the sources from which the board of directors of S may obtain information relating to the group's business environment and how it might use that information for strategic management purposes. Explain how the board of directors might assure itself of the quality of that information for strategic management purposes. (You are not required to consider the ecological environment in answering this question.) **(12 marks)**

(b)   Making use of the information contained in the case, produce a critical appraisal of the method applied by S Group's directors to assess the performance of the AE division. **(16 marks)**

(c)   Discuss the factors which should be taken into consideration by the directors of S in deciding whether the strategic development proposals put forward by AE's divisional manager should be pursued. **(10 marks)**

(d)   Assume that the AE division makes the acquisition as proposed by its divisional manager. Recommend how S Group's directors should improve the methods of measuring the performance of the AE division in order to assess its contribution to the group's strategic requirement to increase shareholder value. **(12 marks)**

(Total = 50 marks)

1.1 – 1.5 Objective Test questions

1.1   C   To achieve the organisation's objectives

Objectives must be identified first, then a suitable strategy can be developed to try to achieve them.

Understanding the organisation's environment and assessing its internal resources are important elements of strategic planning, but they are not the purpose of it. Controlling employee behaviour will also assist in achieving objectives but, again, is not the purpose of strategic planning.

1.2   A   It exploits the organisation's distinctive competences.

A resource-based approach identifies distinctive competences within the company and then exploits these strengths to create sustainable competitive advantage that is difficult to imitate.

However, looking at internal factors alone is not enough to guarantee success. An organisation should also consider environmental factors, adjusting its strategies to the opportunities and threats it perceives around it. (This is the basis of the position-based approach to strategic planning.)

1.3   D   Environmental analysis

PEST analysis and Porter's five forces analysis are both tools which are used for analysing the external environment (ie environmental analysis).

A position audit looks internally at an organisation's strengths and weaknesses. Corporate appraisal then combines the opportunities and threats identified through environmental analysis with the strengths and weaknesses identified by a position audit, to generate a SWOT analysis.

1.4   C   Emergent

The key point here is that the level of demand was unanticipated, and therefore the move into selling material to colleges was a response to outside influences rather than being a planned strategy.

It is important to remember that emergent strategies are not necessarily planned, and do not necessarily come from ideas generated by people at the top of an organisation. They could equally arise in response to suggestions or observations made by more junior members of staff, or in response to external influences.

1.5   B   Board composed of relatively elderly directors

The age of the directors, in itself, is not an issue for corporate governance. The UK Corporate Governance Code (as an example) identifies that boards should have an appropriate balance of skills, experience ... and knowledge – which are all attributes that older directors could possess.

1.6 AB Electronics

Top tips.

For part (a), think about the features of strategic management accounting which distinguish it from 'traditional' management accounting: for example, a focus on external factors, and on non-financial information as well as on internally generated financial information. How could these features be useful to AB for managing the performance of the trading company?

Part (b). Although there are likely to be financial implications of withdrawing from Asia (eg the liability to the local entrepreneur) you should not have focused solely on this in your answer. There are also likely to be non-financial implications: for example, what will be the impact on AB's reputation?

Moreover, if AB withdraws from Asia, are there any alternative markets it can move into to generate replacement sales and growth? Remember, the shareholders want increased growth and profitability, and the company has declared a strategic aim to expand internationally.

In this respect, it is important for AB to consider both the short-term cost implications and the longer-term organisational issues, and the discussion in your answer should reflect this.

(a) **Strategic management accounting** – Unlike 'traditional' management accounting which looks primarily at internally generated financial information, strategic management accounting looks at information which relates to **external factors**, and it looks at **non-financial** as well as financial information.

Competitors' costs – For example, as well as looking at the trading company's own operating costs and margins, strategic management accounting would also encourage AB to look at competitors' costs. This will help focus attention on the need to control the trading company's costs if it is going to compete successfully with its competitors. For example, why are the trading company's wage costs proportionally so much higher than its competitors' costs?

Given the nature of IEC's product (standardised electrical components) cost efficiency is likely to be an important factor in the trading company's competitiveness. There is likely to be little scope for differentiation as a competitive strategy.

Market growth – Strategic management accounting will also encourage AB to look at market size and growth, and the trading company's share of the market. The scenario highlights that the downturn in economic conditions has slowed the growth demand for electronic components as a whole, which could intensify competition in the market. Instead of market growth being a source of increased sales, the trading company will now have to increase its market share in order to increase its sales.

Although the scenario mentions the presence of competitors, it does not give any indication of the number of competitors or their size relative to the trading company. However, these factors could both affect the trading company's ability to compete successfully in the market.

In this respect, strategic management accounting's **external focus** is very important: AB needs to understand the market environment in Asia in order to analyse the trading company's current performance, and then to evaluate future strategies for the company.

Analysis of current performance – Strategic management accounting can contribute to the trading company's success by **monitoring its performance** and results compared to its competitors, and then assessing whether its current strategy appears to be working successfully or not.

For example, the trading company's revised forecast suggests that its profit for 20Y1 is now expected to be 20% lower than had originally been expected. Some of this shortfall may be due to an over-optimistic budget, since the trading company is still a relatively new entrant to the Asian market. However, it could also be an indication that the trading company has not been able to sustain its initial success and break into the market as successfully as it had hoped. Therefore it

will be useful to compare the company's performance against its competitors, for example to see the extent to which their revenues and profits are growing or falling.

If it appears the trading company is performing relatively worse than its competitors, then AB should consider how it could revise its strategy to help improve the company's performance.

Forecasting – Strategic management accounting can also be used to help forecast performance.

AB's forecasts should not look solely at the trading company's own performance but should also look at competitors' performance and market trends in general. For example, how realistic is the level of forecast sales growth in the context of a slowdown in the market?

Equally, economic intelligence suggests that wage inflation is going to continue increasing over the next two years. However, the reason the trading company's wage costs are currently much higher than its competitors' may be that it is paying above the market rates. In which case, it may be able to offer lower annual wage increases than many of its competitors who are currently paying lower wage rates. If not, the trading company will need to review its staffing model and its labour productivity, and try to reduce its wage costs relative to its competitors.

(b)   **Sales potential** – Despite the trading company not seeming to be as profitable as had been hoped, it is still generating a profit for AB (with its 50% share of the company's profit expected to be around $800,000 in 20Y1). It is not clear how much AB has invested in the company is, or what its target rate of return is on any investments.

Although the local entrepreneur has invested $500,000, it is likely that AB has invested more, given the level of profit the company is generating.

Therefore, before deciding whether to withdraw, AB needs to consider how profitable it expects the trading company to be in the future, and equally whether it feels it could invest its capital more profitably elsewhere.

Impact of environmental factors – The trading company's performance appears to have been adversely affected by **economic factors** (economic slowdown) and **political factors** (protectionism) in the external environment. However, it is not clear the respective impact that these two factors have had on the trading company's performance, nor the impact that other factors have had on its performance.

Long-term or short-term impact – Although economic conditions have worsened at the moment, they should improve again in the future, at which point AB might expect demand to increase again. Therefore the protectionist policies introduced by some of the Asian countries may be a more significant factor, if they are expected to remain in place for the longer term.

Alternative business structures – Although AB is considering withdrawing from the trading company, this need not mean it withdraws from Asia completely. Although the trading company does not seem to have been as profitable as it had hoped, AB should consider whether it stops selling its products in Asia altogether or whether it needs to find an alternative channel. For example, if there is still a market for IEC's products in Asia, it could consider using Asian sales agents to act on its behalf.

Strength of competition – However, AB should also consider the strength of **competitive rivalry** within the Asian markets, because this will affect its profitability, both in the short term and the longer term. Alongside this, AB could also consider factors such as the **threat of new entrants**, and the **bargaining power of customers** which could also affect its profitability.

Exit barriers – AB and the local entrepreneur both have 50% shares in the trading company. If AB withdraws, the local entrepreneur will have to decide whether he wants to acquire AB's share and try to maintain the trading company himself, or whether the company should cease trading. If the company ceases trading, AB will be liable to pay the entrepreneur $500,000. This exit payment could affect AB's decision of whether to withdraw or not.

Wider implications – The trading company seems to have been AB's first significant venture into Asia. If AB withdraws from the venture within about three years of establishing it, this could be damaging for its reputation. This could be problematic either if AB wants to continue selling its products through sales agents or if, in future, it wants to re-establish a joint venture company.

(As we have noted earlier, although market conditions have worsened at the moment, they should improve again in future at which point AB might look to expand into Asia again. But if AB has a poor reputation in Asia, local businesses will be reluctant to become venture partners with it.)

Business portfolio – Moreover, before withdrawing from the Asian company, AB should critically assess the growth prospects of its current European and American markets. If there are limited growth opportunities in these markets (for example, because they are **more mature** than the overseas markets), the board might be advised to persevere with looking at expansion into new overseas markets.

Fit with strategic aims – AB has stated in its annual report that it wants to develop its international presence by expanding into overseas markets. Establishing the trading company in Asia is a way of helping to achieve this aim. By contrast, withdrawing from the Asian market would seem contradictory to this aim, and to the shareholders' wishes for increased growth and profitability.

2.1 – 2.5 Objective Test questions

2.1   B   (i) and (iii)

A mission statement should identify an organisation's fundamental purpose and objectives, and the nature of its business. A mission statement should also identify the organisation's values and culture.

Profitability will be an objective for a business, rather than an element of the mission statement.

2.2   D   High interest and high power

The bank will want to be sure that Zeus Co is able to meet its interest payments and repay any loan capital outstanding in due course. Given that Zeus already has a relatively high level of gearing, the bank will have a high level of interest in a proposal which will increase the gearing level further.

As Pluto Bank appears to be the main source of the company's financing, it will also have a high degree of power over Zeus, and therefore may be able to influence the company's strategic decision making.

2.3   A   Advocacy threat

An advocacy threat occurs if a professional accountant is promoting a client or employer's position or opinion to the extent that the accountant's subsequent objectivity is compromised.

An intimidation threat arises when the accountant is deterred from acting objectively by an actual or perceived threat.

A self-interest threat occurs if a financial or other interest inappropriately influences the accountant's judgement or behaviour.

A self-review threat is the danger that the accountant will not properly evaluate the results of a previous judgement (by themselves or another member of their organisation) but they will then rely on that judgement as part of a current service they are providing.

2.4   A   (i) and (ii)

Social responsibility relates to an organisation's obligation to maximise positive stakeholder benefits while minimising the negative effects of its actions. It reflects the whole range of stakeholders who have an interest in an organisation.

However, social responsibility entails more than simply conforming with legislation, which is what option (iii) is describing. By paying a minimum wage to its employees, an organisation is fulfilling its legal obligations, not its social responsibilities.

2.5   C   Achievable

The organisation's employees do not believe that increasing annual operating profit by 5% is achievable, given that there has been a slowdown across the whole industry.

As a result, the staff will not bother to try to achieve the target – which is inevitably the consequence of setting objectives which either **are**, or at least are **perceived to be**, unachievable.

2.6 WRL gold mining company

(a)

> **Top tips:** This should have been a relatively straightforward question, in which you identified and categorised the stakeholder groups mentioned in the scenario and then categorised their levels of power and interest.
>
> Note that you are only required to categorise **three** stakeholder groups. However, there are seven stakeholder groups identified in, or inferred by, the case study: (i) the board of WRL; (ii) local people; (iii) employees working in the mine; (iv) shareholders in general; (v) the minority shareholders who oppose the decision; (vi) the Eastern State Government; and (vii) the Stravia national Government.
>
> For tutorial purposes, all seven have been categorised here, and their interest and power explained. However, **you should only have included three in your answer**.
>
> Note also that the question asks about stakeholders' power and interests specifically in relation to the decision about the disposal of the water, not about WRL's operations in general. Make sure your answers relate specifically to the decision. And make sure you only consider stakeholders identified in the scenario; do not introduce additional stakeholder groups of your own.

   (i)   <u>High interest; High power</u>

     1.   **Board of WRL**: If WRL is not allowed to dispose its water in the lake, its mining operations in Stravia would become uneconomic and the mine would have to close.

       The board's **interest** is therefore high, because the decision is crucial to WRL's continued operation in Stravia.

       As the board makes the decision about where to dispose of the water (and is given free rein in this decision by the licence) its **power** is also high.

     2.   **Stravian national Government**: The licence fee which WRL pays the Government ($50m in 20X9) represents a significant amount of income for the Government.

       Given the Government's desire to develop its economy, and the role it sees for gold mining in this development, the national Government has a high **interest** in the outcome of the decision.

       Power: The Government granted WRL its licence to mine for gold, which shows the Government has a degree of power over WRL's operations. The Government's licensing power means it is also likely to have the power to revoke the licence if it is unhappy with the way WRL is operating (for example, if the Government feels the

environmental cost of disposing the polluted water in the lake outweighs the economic benefits of WRL's operations in Stravia).

High interest; Low power

3. **Employees working in the mine**: WRL's mine is in a very remote area, so if it were to close there are likely to be very few alternative job opportunities for the local people currently working for WRL. Therefore they have a high **interest** in the continued operation of WRL's mine.

    However, the local employees are only likely to have low **power** over the decision because it is unlikely that they have senior or high-profit jobs within WRL. Equally, it is unlikely they will have any significant influence over the governments (either the Eastern State Government or the national Government).

Alternative stakeholder groups you could have included:

High interest; Low power

Local people: The local people are likely to be interested for two reasons: first, the mine offers jobs for local people; but second, disposing the polluted water in the lake will have a long-lasting adverse effect on the lake and the surrounding area. This second factor could be a particular concern if the people use the lake as a source of drinking water or for catching fish for food.

These two reasons together mean that the local people could have a **conflict of interests** about the decision, although their level of interest in it is likely to be high. Nonetheless, they are likely to only have low **power** over the decision because they are unlikely to be able to exert any influence over the Government or WRL.

Eastern State Government: The State Government's **interest** is such that it took legal action against WRL to try to prevent the polluted water being disposed of in the lake.

However, the local Government's decision has been overruled by the National Supreme Court, suggesting that ultimately the local Government only has relatively low **power**.

Minority shareholders: A small number of shareholders feel sufficiently concerned about the impact of the polluted water on the lake that they would rather close the mine than pollute the lake. In this respect, they have a high **interest** in the decision.

However, the fact that their number is only a small minority of shareholders means they will have little **power** to affect any decisions.

Low interest; High power

There are no stakeholder groups in this category.

Low interest; Low power

WRL's shareholders: WRL is a multinational company which exists to make the maximum profit for its shareholders. Although the shareholder's level of interest will be influenced by the contribution the Stravian mine makes to WRL's profits overall, it is likely that Stravia is just one among many countries in which WRL operates, and so the shareholders' **interest** in decisions affecting any one specific mine are likely to be low.

The shareholders could exert significant power if they all joined together and voted to force WRL to stop polluting the lake. However, this seems very unlikely as the shareholders are likely to be more interested in the profits from the mine. Consequently, if they are not willing to act collectively to vote against the pollution, their **power** to influence the decision can be categorised as low.

(ii)

> **Tutorial note.** In (a) (i) we have organised stakeholders in relation to the four quadrants in Mendelow's matrix.
>
> The requirement for (a) (ii) asks for advice about how WRL's board should deal with stakeholders, so Mendelow's matrix is again a good framework here because it provides suggestions for how to deal with stakeholders with different levels of power and interest.
>
> However, note three points:
>
> - There is no indication in the requirement that you should only look at the three stakeholder groups you categorised in (a) (i); instead, you should look at how the board should aim to deal with conflicting interests across all stakeholder groups.
>
> - You are advising the board of WRL (not the Government).
>
> - You should try to make your advice specific to the scenario, and not let it become generic advice based on Mendelow's matrix (eg don't just say: 'Make the strategy acceptable to them'. This will **not** be sufficient to earn a good proportion of the seven marks available here).

High interest; high power

(Stravian national Government)

Because the national Government has both high interest in the decision and high power over it, it is a key player. Therefore, WRL needs to make sure its **actions and strategy are acceptable** to the Government.

However, as the Government views gold mining as an important way of developing the economy, and it has given WRL the licence to dispose of waste water wherever is convenient, it seems likely that a strategy based on economic benefits rather than environmental costs will be acceptable to the Government. Therefore, there doesn't appear to be any reason that WRL will need to change its plans to make them acceptable to the Government.

High interest; low power

(Local employees working in the mines; Local people; Eastern State Government; Minority shareholders)

Although these groups have a high interest in the decision, they only have relatively low power to influence it. Therefore, the board should make sure these groups are **kept informed** about its plans, but it does not need to be concerned with making sure its plans are acceptable to them. Their lack of power makes it difficult for these groups to disrupt WRL's plans.

Low interest; low power

(Shareholders in general)

As this group only has a low interest in the decision, as well as low power over it, the board should only spend minimal effort considering the shareholders' position in respect of the decision.

Mission statement – As well as categorising the stakeholders according to their power and interest, the board should try to relate the stakeholders' objectives to its own mission statement, and ensure that it acts in the way that best follows its mission statement.

In this respect, WRL's primary objective is to make the maximum possible profit for its shareholders. Although WRL has also expressed an aim to minimise the damage it causes to the environment, this is likely to be a secondary objective behind the need to be profitable. The board's dealings with the different stakeholder groups should reflect this prioritisation.

(b)

> **Top tips:** This is another question which requires a high level of application rather than simply a demonstration of knowledge. You were not asked to discuss the role of mission statements in developing a strategic plan, or to discuss the merits of having a mission statement. Instead you should have identified, and discussed, those areas of the plan to pollute the lake which were consistent with the mission statement identified in the scenario, and those areas of it which were not consistent.

WRL's mission statement highlights both the economic and environmental aspects of mining, and the potential conflict between profit and pollution which it is facing in relation to its operations in Stravia.

Areas of consistency with the plan

'Make the maximum possible profit for its shareholders' – The mine has **operated profitably** since it began. However, if WRL were not able to dispose of the polluted water in the lake, it would become uneconomic and would **have to close**. So to the extent that the plan enables WRL to continue with a profitable operation, it is consistent with the mission statement.

'WRL will ... be a good corporate citizen' – In line with the condition in its mining licence, WRL **employs local people** wherever possible and so brings jobs and incomes to the local economy.

WRL has generated a significant amount of foreign exchange for Stravia's economy, and mining is playing an important part in developing the economy. So, in this respect, WRL has been acting as a good corporate citizen – but WRL would no longer be able to make its positive contribution to Stravia's economy if it had to close the mine because it had become uneconomic.

Moreover, WRL is **acting lawfully** in accordance with its licence, which is why the National Supreme Court upheld its right to dispose of the polluted water in the lake. Again, by acting lawfully, WRL is being a good corporate citizen.

Areas of inconsistency with the plan

'Causing the least damage to the environment' – The decision to dispose the polluted water in the lake has been taken because this is the **cheapest option**, not the one which causes the least environmental damage.

'WRL will, at all times, be a good corporate citizen' – Disposing of the polluted water in the lake will kill all the aquatic life in the lake, and have a long-lasting adverse effect on the lake and the surrounding area. In this respect, the decision does not portray WRL as a good corporate citizen.

It could also be argued that acting against the wishes of the local State Government and proceeding with the plan is also not the behaviour of a good corporate citizen.

Stakeholder wishes – The mission statement focuses on achieving profit for shareholders and suggests shareholders' interests are solely economic. However, there are a minority of shareholders who would rather close the mine than pollute the lake. So, if WRL proceeds with the plan it will be acting against the interests of these shareholders.

Extent of consistency

WRL's decision to dispose of the polluted water in the lake is consistent with the economic aspects of the mission statement (to maximise profit) but it is not consistent with some aspects of being a good corporate citizen or with minimising damage to the environment.

However, part of the problem here is that there appears to be a degree of incompatibility in the mission statement. WRL seems faced with a choice of **either** maximising profits **or** causing the least damage to the environment. It cannot do both, although the mission statement seems to suggest it should try to.

3.1 – 3.5 Objective Test questions

3.1   B   High strategic importance; low urgency

If it materialises, the uncertainty is likely to have a significant impact (high strategic importance) on the business – because it would affect virtually all of its business units.

However, the likelihood of the event occurring – and therefore its immediacy or urgency – is low, which may mean the uncertainty may not yet be worth acting upon.

3.2   D   The company is the sole supplier of a product with no apparent substitutes.

As such, a customer cannot easily take its business to an alternative supplier meaning the customer has a low bargaining power.

The other options would create a high bargaining power for customers.

3.3   C   It allows management to forecast what is going to happen.

Scenario planning is not designed to create a forecast or an accurate prediction of what is actually going to happen, but rather to create some insights into what **might** happen, and the uncertainties which an organisation might face in the future.

3.4   B   Game theory

Game theory highlights that competition and co-operation can both exist in an industry, and therefore an important part of an organisation's strategy is how it interacts with the other participants in its industry.

Scenario planning and foresight both aim to assist an organisation in designing its future strategies, but they do not focus specifically on an organisation's interactions with the other participants in the industry.

3.5   A   Delphi method

The Delphi method (or Delphi technique) involves a number of experts being asked to independently and anonymously give their opinions and insights on a particular trend and how it may develop.

3.6 BBB international bank

Top tips:

Part (a): It is important to remember that Porter's five forces model looks at the profitability of an **industry** rather than a single firm. However, just because an industry is profitable doesn't mean that all of the companies in it will be equally profitable. This appears to be the case with the banking industry in R.

In part (a) you should work through the five forces in turn and evaluate their strength in relation to the banking industry in R. This will then give you an indication of the likely profitability of the banking industry as a whole.

However, remember the requirement asked you specifically to evaluate BBB's future potential to make a profit, not the potential for the industry as a whole to make a profit.

Planning this question is vital, to ensure you avoid repeating points between parts (a) and (b).

Part (b): A number of the features that will influence BBB's decision relate to the five forces (eg competitive rivalry). The question requirement highlights this by asking you to 'use your analysis from part (a)'.

However, in part (b) you need to focus specifically on BBB's ability to sustain a profit in country R. In this respect, it is important to consider whether BBB has any resources or competences which will allow it to establish a sustainable competitive advantage in R. If it doesn't, then it is unlikely to be able to sustain a profit there, and so should leave the market.

Remember that the question requirements asked you to 'Advise ...' so you need to give clear advice to BBB at the end of your answer as to whether it should continue in country R or not.

(a) <u>Threat of new entrants</u>

The threat of new entrants is limited by **barriers to entry**.

Capital investment – The main barrier to entry to the banking market in R is the **capital investment** required to enter that market. In total, BBB spent $350 million to enter the market ($200 million to establish its own branch network, and $150 million to acquire a local bank).

Dominance of SB – In addition, **SB's dominant position** in the market (being a state-owned organisation, accounting for half of R's retail banking business) might act as a potential disincentive to potential new entrants thinking about investing in R.

Recent withdrawals – The fact that two foreign banks have recently withdrawn from R may also discourage potential new entrants from investing there. The banks' claims that their operations in R served to reduce group profitability suggest that R may not be a very profitable market to invest in.

<u>Competitive rivalry</u>

Strong competition – The state-owned institutions provide tough competition for retail banking business in R. Within this context, SH has established a position of dominance, accounting for half of this business. In addition, a number of well-established foreign banks account for a further 35% of R's retail banking market.

Although the well-established foreign banks are all profitable, it appears the more recent entrants have been less successful. Two of the banks which entered R at the same time as BBB have withdrawn due to the poor levels of profitability their operations in R have generated. Therefore, although there appear to be high margins in the banking industry in R, it appears that banks need to have reached a certain size (a critical mass) before they can begin to earn those margins.

Market growth – Nonetheless, the banking analyst's report indicates there is plenty of growth left in the banking market in R, and the margins are excellent. This suggests the competitive rivalry may not be as intense as it might otherwise be, but the dominant position of the established banks still suggests there is a **high level of rivalry** in the banking market in R.

<u>Bargaining power of consumers</u>

The banking market in R is geared primarily towards personal banking, but individually, customers will only have a low degree of bargaining power.

Choice of bank accounts – However, the degree of choice customers have in relation to which bank to use increases their bargaining power. For example, people in R could choose to bank with SB; one of the other state-owned institutions; BBB; or one of the other foreign-owned banks.

It is likely to be relatively easy for customers to switch from one bank to another, which again could increase customers' bargaining power.

Conservatism – R's population doesn't like change, which means they are naturally more likely to use one of the established banks than a relatively new foreign entrant such as BBB. In effect, this could reduce the bargaining power of customers on the existing banks. By contrast, though, it could increase their bargaining power over new entrants such as BBB. BBB is likely to have to offer the customers significantly better deals than existing domestic banks in the short term to attract new customers.

Threat of substitute products

Although there are a number of different banks which consumers could use, these reflect the level of competitive rivalry in the industry, rather than the threat of substitute products.

Similarly, although there is scope for consumers to switch to internet banking services rather than using the branch network, this again represents a switch within the industry rather than a substitute product.

In this respect, there don't appear to be any substitutes for banking products as a whole, so the threat here is low.

Bargaining power of suppliers

Liberalised market – R has a liberalised economy which allows the free movement of capital in and out of the country. This suggests that BBB (and the other banks in the industry) should easily be able to supply their capital requirements in R under normal market conditions, although the global financial crisis could have an impact on these market conditions overall.

The scenario does not indicate any other key suppliers who could influence BBB's operations in R, so we cannot make any judgement about the strength of their bargaining power.

Potential for future profits

Overall, it appears there is a relatively high level of competitive rivalry in the industry and customers also have a moderate level of bargaining power. However, the threat of new entrants and the threat of substitute products appears to be reasonably weak.

Looking at these forces together suggests that the market should be a profitable one, and this corroborates the analyst's view.

However, the market is not necessarily equally profitable for all the banks in it. Consequently, the potential profitability for BBB's banking business within R is likely to be lower than that of SB's.

(b) **Market profitability and growth** – The analysis in part (a) suggests that the retail banking market in R should remain a profitable one. There is plenty of growth left in the market, not least because a high proportion of the population do not currently have bank accounts (this figure was 50% 3 years ago in 20X8). As more of the population open bank accounts, the size of the banking market in the country will necessarily increase.

Competitive rivalry – However, although the market overall is profitable and growing, there is still likely to be a high degree of competitive rivalry in it.

SB presents the strongest competitive threat to BBB. SB already accounts for half of the retail banking business in R, and its position has been strengthened by its recent reorganisation, and the launch of some successful (and profitable) new products.

Consumer preference – Consumers' attitudes to change should also be a concern to BBB. The customers' dislike of change means they are likely to continue using SB and established banks rather than switching to BBB. Even though BBB has a strong brand image and a long record of success, this may not be sufficient to convince customers to switch to BBB.

Profit levels – The fact that BBB is already successful in a number of other countries means that it should only continue in R if it can sustain an acceptable level of profit there. It appears that the two foreign banks which entered the market at the same time were not able to do this, and so they left.

BBB does not appear to have any sources of sustainable competitive advantage which will enable it to be more successful than these banks, or to reduce SB's dominance in the market.

Advice: Therefore BBB should be advised not to continue its retail banking business in country R.

4.1 – 4.5 Objective Test questions

4.1 D Frequently changing suppliers

Supply chain management involves the organisations in the supply chain working together to deliver goods and services to customers.

Responsiveness and reliability are two key themes in supply chain management, and they encourage the members of a supply chain to develop a mutual understanding and trust of each other. As such, supply chain management tends to encourage long-term relationships between organisations – rather than changing suppliers frequently.

4.2 C Cash cow

Although G&L's market share is only 11%, it is still the largest player in the market since its largest competitor only has a market share of 9.5%. G&L's relative market share is 1.16 (ie greater than 1) which constitutes a high relative market share.

Similarly, although G&L's revenue increased quite rapidly, the market is only growing slowly (1% in the last year). The BCG matrix measures market growth rates, rather than a company's growth.

G&L has a high relative market share in a market with low growth, meaning it should be classified as a cash cow.

4.3 B (i) only

Competition is low in the introduction phase of the life cycle, but increases thereafter.

Sales **volumes** are at their highest in the maturity phase, although the rate of sales **growth** is higher during the growth phase than the maturity phase.

4.4 D Process benchmarking

Process benchmarking involves comparing an organisation's processes to similar processes (ie queuing and customer handling) in other organisations which are not competitors but which use innovative or best practice processes. The aim is to improve an organisation's processes by incorporating aspects of the best practice demonstrated in the other organisations.

If DEF was comparing its performance to other banks, it would be undertaking competitive benchmarking, but it is comparing its performance with companies in very different industries.

4.5 A Service

The primary activities (in sequence) in Porter's value chain are: inbound logistics, operations, outbound logistics, marketing and sales; service.

The support activities (which support those primary activities) are: firm infrastructure, human resource management, technology development and procurement.

4.6 BBB fashion retailer

Top tips:

Part (a)

The scenario provides a range of information about the different activities in BBB's value chain, and so you should have been able to use this to explain how the value chain could be applied by BBB.

However, note that the question requirement asks you to explain how BBB could use the value chain **to achieve competitive advantage**, not merely to explain what the value chain is, or to give examples of the different value activities at BBB.

The question requirement clearly asks you to give examples, from BBB, of all nine activities in the value chain so a sensible way to structure your answer would be to use each of the activities as headings and then explain how each of them could add value for BBB.

But remember you need to explain how the activities add value and generate competitive advantage for BBB, not simply to explain what they are, or how they could add value to an organisation in general terms.

(a) **Competitive advantage** – Porter argues that firms achieve competitive advantage through the way they organise and perform activities. Businesses are made up of value-creating activities, which create value for their customers.

The value chain helps firms identify how they are deploying their resources to satisfy customers, and how they are adding value for their customers. Therefore, by using the value chain, BBB should ensure that its activities are adding value for its customers, and this in turn could help it achieve competitive advantage.

Primary activities

Inbound logistics – BBB has invested in a **robotic system** to improve materials handling in its warehouse. This should improve the speed and efficiency with which items coming into the warehouse can be processed and then, in turn, distributed on to BBB's shops. This should help BBB improve the service it provides to its customers by making new items available for them as quickly as possible. This is important because BBB's clothes only remain fashionable for a short period.

The improvements in materials handling in the warehouse should also reduce wastage, which will contribute to a greater margin.

Operations – BBB has trained all its staff in customer care, and tries to employ staff who already have experience of working in fashion retailers. By using staff who already have experience of working in other shops, BBB should ensure that the service it offers customers is at least as good as those other shops. And providing its staff with additional training in customer care may help BBB's performance exceed that of its competitors in this area of operations.

This is likely to be important given that BBB has demanding customers, but ones who appreciate the retail experience which BBB offers.

Outbound logistics – BBB will deliver any items bought in its shops to customers' homes within 24 hours. BBB's competitors do not offer this service, and so this delivery activity is a feature which explicitly differentiates BBB from its competitors. Even if not all customers take advantage of this service, BBB knows that customers appreciate the after-sales service which it offers.

Marketing and sales – BBB frequently sends its regular customers special offers and invites them to fashion shows held in its shops. By doing so, BBB keeps its customers informed about new products which have come into stock, and hopefully also encourages them to keep buying products from BBB.

In addition, by inviting its customers to fashion shows, BBB may help to make its customers feel valued, which should encourage them to continue buying products from it.

Service – If a customer is dissatisfied with any purchase, BBB will make a refund without any question. This is also likely to be one of the features which contributes to customers' appreciation of BBB's after-sales service. By offering a refund without any question, BBB should be able to appease any dissatisfied customers which, in turn, should help improve BBB's customer retention rates.

Support activities

Firm infrastructure – BBB's general corporate administration and infrastructure is unlikely to generate any competitive advantage in its own right. However, BBB needs a suitable departmental structure, management structure and management information to support its primary activities.

Moreover, planning, finance and quality control will all be important to BBB's strategic capability in its primary activities. So if BBB is able to organise these aspects of its infrastructure better than its competitors, this could provide a potential source of competitive advantage.

Human resource management – We have already identified that, when recruiting new staff, BBB prefers to employ people with previous experience at other fashion retailers. BBB also trains all of its staff in customer care.

This suggests that BBB's human resource management policies are geared towards providing customers with a good retail experience, which is something they appreciate. If BBB can provide its customers with a more favourable retail experience than its competitors, this should help it achieve competitive advantage over them.

Technology development – One of the head office departments investigates innovations in fashion retailing, and it seems likely that this has prompted BBB to investigate the introduction of 'Smart Tills' into its shops. By allowing BBB to manage inventory better and respond to customer demand more quickly, amongst other things, the 'Smart Tills' should help improve BBB's overall performance and competitiveness. Being able to respond quickly to changing customer demand is likely to be particularly important in fashion retailing because of the short periods of time for which clothes remain fashionable.

Procurement – BBB's competitive strategy is to offer a wide selection of high-quality products at reasonable prices. Therefore its procurement function needs to be able to acquire an appropriate selection of products. Moreover, BBB needs to be able to procure its clothes quickly given the short period of time for which they will be in fashion. As a result, BBB's procurement activities play a vital part in underpinning its competitive advantage.

(b)

> **Top tips.**
>
> **Part (b).** Make sure you read the requirement carefully here. The question does not ask you how BBB could benefit from using the Smart Tills in general, but it asks specifically how using the Smart Tills could help BBB improve its profits.
>
> Make sure you explain clearly how any benefits you identify will help BBB improve its profits.

Real time information – The Smart Tills will provide BBB with accurate, real-time information about sales.

Inventory management – On the one hand this will allow BBB to manage its inventory more effectively. For example, it will have an up to date record of the inventory levels for any product, which will help managers know when to reorder. In this way, BBB should be able to reduce the risk of stock-outs (and therefore lost sales) but also over-ordering and having too much working capital tied up in inventory. Both of these aspects should improve profit.

Responsiveness to customer demand – Perhaps more importantly, the real-time information should also increase BBB's responsiveness to customer demand. For example, the tills can provide

an analysis of all the sales transactions, which should help BBB identify which products are selling well, and in which shops. This knowledge should be able to help BBB meet its customers' requirements better; for example, by increasing stocks of popular products, and possibly also by increasing stocks of similar, or complementary, products.

The more effectively BBB can meet its customers' requirements, the greater the revenue it should be able to generate. Increased revenues, in turn, should help improve profits.

Staff performance – The Tills will also provide BBB with information about the sales for each staff member, which could be used to help manage their performance. For example, staff could be given **incentive schemes** under which they qualify for a bonus if they achieve a sales target.

Equally, however, the Tills could identify if there are significant variations in the levels of income staff members generate. For example, some staff members may need additional training to improve their customer service skills and therefore make more sales. Alternatively, the level of sales staff members are generating in certain shops may be low because the shop is overstaffed. Either way, the sales statistics which the Tills provide should alert BBB to the potential issues, such that BBB can take action which could then lead to improved profitability.

5.1 – 5.7 Objective Test questions

5.1   C   Cost leadership – focus

PQR's desire to minimise costs at every opportunity indicates that it is trying to be the lowest-cost producer. So it is pursuing a cost leadership strategy.

However, PQR is only interested in being able to sell its cars more cheaply than other low-emission cars (rather than being the lowest-cost producer across the car industry as a whole). This indicates that PQR is pursuing a 'focus' strategy.

5.2   A   Market development

Market development involves selling an existing product into a new market.

Product development involves selling new products into an existing market; market penetration involves existing products and existing markets only; while diversification involves new products and new markets.

5.3   D   (i), (ii) and (iii)

All of the factors may be reasons for establishing a production facility in the foreign market.

If a firm makes a lot of sales to the market, it might be advantageous for the firm to move production closer to that market – particularly if transport costs are high for the finished good, or the good is perishable.

The firm may also be able to increase sales by producing in the foreign market and thereby not being subject to import tariffs or quotas.

5.4   B   (i) only

Franchising allows a business to expand using less capital than if it grows organically.

Businesses often franchise because they cannot readily raise the capital required to set up company-owned branches.

However, one of the potential risks of franchising is that poor performance by individual franchisees could harm the overall brand.

5.5   D   (i), (ii) and (iii)

A major disadvantage of joint ventures is that there can be conflicts of interest between the venture partners. These may arise over profit shares, amounts invested, management of the joint venture, or marketing strategy.

Profits from the venture have to be shared among the partners, reducing the amount each earns.

Partners can gain confidential information about each other, which one partner subsequently uses competitively against another.

5.6   C   Whether the strategy suits the organisational culture of the company; **and**

        D   Whether the strategy will help to generate or sustain a competitive advantage for the company

These two options relate to the strategic logic of the strategy, and therefore relate to its suitability.

Whether the strategy will generate a high enough return to satisfy stakeholders relates to its acceptability. Whether the company has enough resources to implement the strategy relates to its feasibility.

5.7   D   Management buy out

A management buy out is the purchase of a business from its existing owners by members of the existing management team, generally in association with a financial institution.

A management buy in is similar to a management buy out, but the new management team comes from outside the current business, rather than being the current management team.

5.8 GHK restaurants

> **Top tips.** The scenario identifies that the restaurants in the GHK group seem to have a variety of different generic strategies: some are cost leaders, some are following differentiation strategies, some have focus strategies, but some are stuck in the middle. So make sure you link the ideas of Porter's model directly to the scenario. How can they help GHK's owners maintain or improve profitability?
>
> At an individual restaurant level, Porter's generic strategies could be used to help achieve a competitive advantage for the restaurants stuck in the middle. However, it is also worth considering whether this variety in strategies between the restaurants means that the group overall risks being stuck in the middle if it tries to use a single brand across the different restaurants.

Choosing a competitive strategy – Porter's logic behind his Three Generic Strategies Model is that a firm should follow only one of the strategies in order to achieve **competitive advantage**. If firms try to combine more than one of the strategies they risk becoming '**stuck in the middle**' and losing their competitive advantage.

Applying these ideas could help the owners of GHK assess whether their restaurants are following a coherent competitive strategy – either individually or as a group – or whether they are becoming 'stuck in the middle'. If they are becoming 'stuck' in this way, the lack of a clear strategy might be contributing to the **decline in GHK's profits**.

Generic strategies – Porter suggests firms should choose between three generic strategies: cost leadership, differentiation and focus.

Cost leadership – If GHK chooses to become a cost leader, it must ensure it has the lowest costs in the industry as a whole. By having a lower cost base than its competitors, GHK could achieve a greater profit than them, even if its prices were the same as theirs.

Although this aspect of Porter's strategy focuses primarily on cost rather than price, it appears that GHK's **restaurant near the railway** is pursuing this kind of strategy, since it claims to be 'the cheapest in town'. However, to maintain its profitability, it must ensure it can continue to keep its cost base lower than any of its competitors' cost bases.

Differentiation – If GHK chooses a strategy of differentiation, it must deliver a product or service which the industry as a whole believes to be unique. As a result of this uniqueness, GHK will be able to charge its customers a **premium price**.

It appears that the extremely expensive '**fine dining' restaurant** in the historic country house is charging a premium price in this way. However, to maintain its profitability, the restaurant must ensure it maintains its distinguishing features – be they the quality of the menu, the service, or the ambience. These features are what differentiate the restaurant from others in the industry and they make it attractive to customers, even though it is charging a premium price.

Focus – A focus strategy will involve segmenting the industry, such that GHK would then pursue a strategy of cost leadership or differentiation within a single segment of the restaurant industry.

Three of GHK's restaurants seem to be following this type of strategy and tailoring their offering to a specific **market niche**: the barge restaurant specialising in **fish dishes**; the **steak house**; and the restaurant catering for **children's birthday parties**.

Stuck in the middle – GHK has eight restaurants in total. We have identified five of them as following one or other of Porter's generic strategies, but this means the other three – with conventional menus and average prices – are stuck in the middle.

In this respect, GHK needs to look urgently at finding a way of establishing a competitive advantage for these three restaurants. This should allow them to improve their profitability.

Strategy and marketing – We do not know whether all the restaurants in the chain are branded unilaterally as GHK restaurants, or whether they have retained their own names as well as their own styles and prices. If GHK is trying to run the restaurants as a single group, under a single brand name, then the analysis of the restaurants' current position indicates that the **group as a whole is at risk of being 'stuck in the middle'** due to the diversity of its strategies.

In this respect, Porter's generic strategies model suggests that GHK would be best advised to run the restaurants as separate business units, and to develop marketing strategies which support their individual characteristics.

However, if GHK chooses to do this, it still needs to consider whether the restaurants' current strategies can deliver a **sustainable competitive advantage**. For example, the prices of foodstuffs and drinks are rising in GHK's country, which will increase its cost base. So, how sustainable is a cost leadership strategy, particularly as there is little evidence of specific technologies or processes which will allow GHK to sustain a lower cost base than any of its competitors?

Given the overall economic context in which GHK is operating, GHK's owners might decide that Porter's **focus strategies** (either cost-focus, or differentiation-focus) offer them the most practical way of maintaining or improving the profitability of their restaurants.

5.9 Packit Co

> **Top tips.** Do not ignore the explicit reference in both the scenario and the question to organic options. The firm has ruled out global expansion using either merger and acquisition or joint venture. Therefore answers which set out to describe the advantages and disadvantages of merger/acquisition and joint ventures would not score any marks.

Part (a)

Companies can grow **organically** (via internal development), building up their own products and developing their own market. This is the primary method of growth for many companies. Some form of organic growth needs to be chosen by Packit Co: the choice will depend upon the prevailing attitude to **risk**, the **timescale** available, and the **opportunities** for growth that each option creates. The preferred strategy should reflect the **long-term goals** of the company. Furthermore, each option will affect the

structure and processes within the company, and will have its own implications for staffing and management control.

Overseas sales office

Advantages

Setting up a sales office in an international location probably involves **low risk** and **low cost** with respect to changing manufacturing and technological processes.

The company is already based in Europe and so already has operations in Europe. Its experience of selling to the European market (outside its home country) may be transferable to other markets.

Packit Co will need to consider whether it sells to its customers directly, or through a local distributor, after developing its brand sufficiently. Having a localised sales office will allow Packit to get a better understanding of customer requirements in those markets.

Disadvantages

Opening an overseas sales office will not prevent Packit being subject to any tariff barriers.

Local sales staff could act independently from head office. Management at head office will have to devote time to controlling the sales office.

Packit may find it difficult to recruit suitable local staff.

Manufacturing operation

Advantages

A manufacturing plant may be the only option in some countries, where governments might be looking for **inward investment and job creation**. Governments may impose **prohibitive tariffs** on imported products to protect local products and jobs.

Producing overseas may also **lower production costs** if resource costs (especially wages) are cheaper than in Packit's home country.

Disadvantages

A manufacturing facility involves **more commitment of finance and other resources**, and a significant alteration to the **value chain**. The required investment may in some cases be prohibitively expensive, and it may be difficult to find enough suitable local staff if there is no local partner in the operation.

In Packit's case, the **logistics** of getting the semi-finished product to the overseas manufacturing base will also need some thought. The plant may actually end up acting independently, which will affect the **level of control** that can be exercised by Packit, and may end up increasing the **business risk**.

Quality control will be of importance. Involving another plant may add considerably to quality risks.

Agents and distributors

Advantages

Agents will have already **established business networks** and local expertise which Packit can take advantage of.

There will be no capital costs incurred for setting up overseas manufacturing bases, and there will be no changes to the current manufacturing process.

Disadvantages

Gaining the **motivation** and **full commitment** of local agents and distributors could be a major problem. They might be carrying the products of several firms, and will be tempted to commit themselves to those products that earn the best return. The question of **exclusivity** therefore becomes important, and this may be able to be negotiated by Packit Co.

The provision of attractive **commission and other financial incentives** will help the relationship. However, if the commissions the agents demand become too high, the operation will not be economic for Packit.

Controlling agents and distributors can be difficult, so it is important for Packit to set out realistic performance expectations, and contracts should be clear to all parties involved.

5.10 Product market strategy

Top tips. This question requires practical application of two syllabus models to various companies in different industries, and as such it is typical of questions at this level. You must be able to analyse the information presented, in this case identifying the phase of development reached by each industry, then applying Ansoff's matrix. You may have been distracted by the phrase 'industry' life cycle, but this is no different in principle to the product life cycle with which you should be familiar. Being able to tie the industries in question to the respective life cycle phases in part (a) should cause few problems, and indeed is not worth too many marks.

Part (b) is more challenging. We have opened our answer with a diagram to link the narrative to, as it makes the answer easier to follow. You may have done the same, as it helps to focus the mind!

In summary, our conclusions for part (b) were broadly as follows:

Key feature	Option	
• Company A	Innovation	Product development
• Company B	Growing market	Product development and/or market penetration
• Company C	Mature market	Market development
• Company D	Weak position, with sales down	Divestment to free resources before fighting on where possible

(a) (i) The **industry life cycle** reflects the fact that the profitability and sales of an industry can be expected to change over time. It is an attempt to recognise distinct stages in an industry's sales history. The classic **life cycle pattern** is commonly described by a curve as follows.

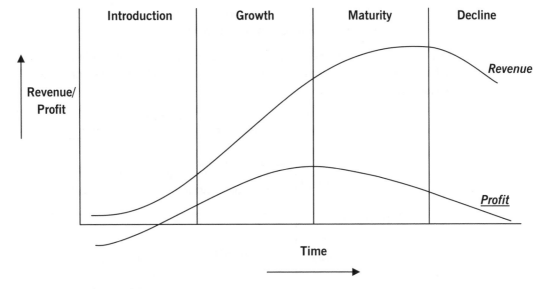

Introduction

(1) A new industry product takes time to find acceptance by would-be purchasers and there is a slow growth in sales. Unit costs are high because of low output and expensive sales promotion.

(2) There may be early teething troubles with technology.

(3) The industry for the time being is a loss-maker.

Growth

(1) With market acceptance, sales will eventually rise more sharply, and profits will rise.

(2) Competitors are attracted. As sales and production rise, unit costs fall.

Maturity

(1) The rate of sales growth slows down and the industry reaches a period of maturity which is probably the longest period of a successful industry's life. Innovation may have slowed down by this stage.

(2) Most products on the market will be at the mature stage of their life. Profits are good.

Decline

(1) Sales will begin to decline so that there is overcapacity of production in the industry. Severe competition occurs, profits fall and some producers leave the market.

(2) The remaining producers seek means of prolonging product life by modification and searching for new market segments. Many producers are reluctant to leave the market, although some inevitably do because of market fragmentation and falling profits.

(ii) The industries in which each of the companies appear to be operating are as follows:

(1) **Company A**. This is operating in the introductory phase of what is a very new innovation, but this innovation is located within a very old industry.

(2) **Company B**. This is positioned in a rapidly expanding and relatively young industry, experiencing a growth phase.

(3) **Company C**. This company is in a mature industry, as witnessed by the low growth but high market share. Profits are likely to be good.

(4) **Company D**. While the retailing industry itself is not in decline, this company appears to be, as it is losing ground to competitors in what is a highly competitive industry. The competitors may be larger companies able to compete more effectively on marketing mix issues such as price.

(b) **Ansoff** drew up a **growth vector matrix**, describing a combination of a firm's activities in current and new markets, with existing and new products. The matrix can be represented diagrammatically as follows.

Market \ *Product*	*Present*	*New*
Present	Market penetration; (for growth) or consolidation (to maintain position)	Product development
New	Market development	Diversification

Company A is involved with launching a very **innovative** product to revolutionise an existing market (home security). Such product development forces competitors to innovate and may provide initial barriers to entry, with newcomers to the industry being discouraged. This will give Company A the chance to build up rapid **market penetration**, but as competitors enter the market it must make sure that it keeps household and commercial customers interested via constant innovation. The drawback to this is the related **expense and risk**. Company A must also make sure that it has enough resources to satisfy demand so that competitors cannot poach market share.

Product improvements will be necessary to sustain the market, so Company A must make sure that enough resources are given to **research and development** of new technologies (and hence new products) in its field, as well as to maintaining sufficient production capacity to satisfy current demand.

Company B is engaged in a rapidly expanding market that is likely to attract many **competitors** keen for their own share of the market and profits. The growth strategy is limited to the current agricultural market, so referring to the Ansoff matrix above, the company is going to be mainly concerned with **market penetration** and **product development**, with an emphasis on the latter to make life more difficult for new competitors. By investing in product development, the company will see a necessary expansion in its R&D facility. To keep the new products and the company itself in the public eye, it may need to invest more in **marketing** and **promotion**.

With **market penetration**, the company will aim to achieve the following:

- Maintain or increase its **share** of the current market with its current products, for example through competitive pricing, advertising, sales promotion and quality control.

- Secure **dominance** of the market and drive out competitors.

- Increase **usage by existing and new customers**. The customer base is likely to be expanding.

Company C is in the **mature phase** of its life cycle. As the current market is mature, the company can achieve growth via the investigation of **new markets**. Referring to the Ansoff matrix, this means pursuing a strategy of **market development**. Seeing as the current market is mature, with satisfied customers and little innovation, there is small scope for market development, unless it is via short-term aggressive tactics such as cuts in prices.

Selling current products to new markets is likely to be more successful, and may include one or more of the following strategies.

- New **geographical areas** and export markets

- **Different package sizes** for food and other domestic items

- **New distribution channels** to attract new customers

- **Differential pricing policies** to attract different types of customer and create new market segments

- **Mass marketing techniques** that encourage customers to switch brands

The company may also investigate the possibility of developing **new products** to make up for those that are in the **decline phase** of the life cycle. This may lead to the creation of more **cash cows**.

Company D is in a difficult position, with a weak position in a well-established market. It needs to undertake some rigorous **analysis of costs**. A strategy of **divestment** may be advised to enable it to reduce costs and concentrate on more profitable areas of activity. **Resource limitations** mean that less profitable outlets or products may have to be abandoned. This could involve analysis of individual contributions, perhaps using **direct product profitability** techniques.

The market has become less attractive and Company D needs to assess its image and profitability. It is likely that customers have become more discerning on price, as has happened in the UK retailing sector in the past few years. When some product areas have been divested, the company may find that it has the **resources** to pursue strategies of **market penetration** for some products and **new product development** to improve its image with customers.

A strategy of **total withdrawal**, and **diversification** into wholly new industries is not seen as appropriate for any of the companies described in the question. It could not be recommended because of the attendant **risks**.

Company D does need to be careful, and it is facing the most difficult situation of all the companies that have been described. It is one thing to eliminate unprofitable products, but will there be sufficient growth potential among the products that remain in the product range?

In addition, new products require some initial **capital expenditure**. Retained profits are by far the most significant source of new funds for companies. A company investing in the medium to long term which does not have enough **current income from existing products** will go into liquidation, in spite of its future prospects.

6.1 – 6.5 Objective Test questions

6.1   A   (i) and (ii)

An organisation needs an IT strategy because IT could provide the competitive advantage need for commercial success (for example, through new e-business opportunities).

The organisation's success (in particular, management's ability to make effective decisions and to control the organisation effectively) depends on the quality of the information available; and IT systems are likely to be crucial in providing this information.

However, if IT is left to the technical department alone, the decisions made may not be business-led and so may not be appropriate.

6.2   B   (ii) only

Joining the online marketplace will mean that Velma has access to a large number of suppliers who will then have to compete on price and other terms to win each contract.

Options (i) and (iii) will strengthen the relationships between Velma and its suppliers. While this may lead to better service from the suppliers, it could also increase their bargaining power because Velma is committed to trading with them, and it could be more convenient for Velma to trade with those suppliers than ones with which it doesn't have any equivalent linkages.

6.3   D   Ensuring that information can be accessed by people who need it

IM strategy plays an important part in ensuring that information can be accessed by all the people who need it, but also ensuring that access to information is restricted to those people with a genuine need to access it.

Identifying the systems which will best enable the use of information to support the overall business strategy is part of an organisation's information systems (IS) strategy.

Analysing an organisation's data storage requirements and identifying the technical solutions required to enable an organisation to implement its IS strategy are both part of an organisation's information technology (IT) strategy.

6.4   D   Internal departments

The four general sources of CSFs are: the industry that an organisation is in; the organisation itself and its position in the industry; the external environment (for example, customer trends and economic trends); and temporal organisational factors (for example, new laws or regulations).

6.5   C   Key operational

Key operational applications have high strategic importance in the current competitive environment but are expected to have low strategic importance in the predicted future competitive environment.

Strategic applications have high strategic importance in the current competitive environment and are expected to remain strategically important in the future.

High potential applications have low strategic importance in the current competitive environment but are expected to become strategically important in the future.

Support applications currently have low strategic importance, and are expected to remain strategically unimportant in the future.

6.6 GHK restaurants

(a)

The answer for part (a) is shown as Question 5.8 above.

(b)

Top tips. Although the question refers to 'a range of organisational information systems' you could usefully consider these systems at two different levels: systems which provide strategic information, and systems which provide operational information.

Also, try to think of the range of information which it would be useful for GHK's owners to find out about: the external competitive environment and market information; customer details and marketing information; and restaurant usage, costs and revenues.

Make sure you show how the systems can directly help GHK rather than simply talking about information systems in general, though.

Market research – In order to decide look at the suitability of any potential strategies for its restaurants; GHK needs to have detailed **market** and **demographic information** to see whether the proposed strategies are suitable. For example, if GHK wants to pursue a strategy of differentiation, it will need to assess whether there are sufficient people who are willing to pay premium prices to eat in the restaurant in order for the restaurant to be profitable.

Market research could also identify **new opportunities**, especially if there is market demand which is currently not being met. This could allow GHK to adapt its strategy (particularly in the restaurants which are currently 'stuck in the middle') to cater for this latent demand. For example, market research might identify that customers want a restaurant which serves locally sourced, organic food, and they would be prepared to pay a premium for this food. In this way, the findings from the market research could support a focus differentiation strategy.

Market share analysis – GHK should also try to get overall market revenue figures for the various market segments in which it operates, and compare its own performance against these overall market figures. This will indicate whether its market share is increasing or decreasing, and therefore will give some indication of how successful GHK's strategies are proving.

Customer information – We do not know whether customers need to book in advance to eat at GHK's restaurants, but it is likely they do for the 'fine dining' restaurant and for the birthday parties, at least.

Website – If GHK develops a website which customers can use for booking this will allow GHK to build up a **database of contacts**. If customers give an email address when they book, GHK can use these addresses for future e-marketing campaigns.

GHK could also introduce a **loyalty card programme** as a way of getting a database of customers, finding out which of its restaurants they use, and how frequently they use them.

Such information could have two different uses:

- **Customer relationship management** – On the one hand, it can be useful for customer relationship management – for example, GHK could send reminder emails to lapsed customers who have not been to one of its restaurants recently, or it could inform customers of any special offers they might be interested in at restaurants they have visited recently. Given that the local economy has shrunk recently, **maintaining customer numbers** is likely to be an important issue for GHK.

- **Trend analysis** – On the other hand, the database could be analysed to highlight patterns and trends in customer usage at the different restaurants. Understanding these trends could, in turn, be useful for marketing campaigns or operational decisions, for example working out staffing levels.

Management information systems – GHK's owners are clearly concerned about the performance of their business. Therefore it will be important that they have timely and reliable management information which they can use to see how the restaurants are performing. For example, the owners might find it useful to have summary reports which provide them with daily or weekly snapshots of restaurant revenues and customer numbers, and the gross profit margins at each of the restaurants.

Operational information systems – In order to provide this summary information, GHK will need a way of capturing detailed operational information. If the waiters and waitresses in all the restaurants recorded customer orders on **hand-held personal digital assistants** (PDAs) the information from these could be captured, and ultimately transmitted back to a **central data warehouse**. The PDAs could capture, for example, customer numbers, the days and times of orders, and the dishes being ordered. Analysing this information could highlight, for example, whether some items on the menu are more popular than others, or whether some times of day are busier than others.

This information could then be used to help the owners make decisions such as whether the **menus need changing**, or whether the opening hours need revising. For example, if there are some items on the menu which do not sell well, they should be removed or replaced. If they were removed, and the menus were shortened, this would mean that GHK needed to hold fewer ingredients in stock, which would be beneficial in a period of rising food prices. Equally, if there are times of day where customer numbers are low, the owners may decide not to open all day, or to introduce some **special offers** to attract customers during those off-peak periods.

In addition to the hand-held PDAs, the **tills in the restaurants** should also be linked to the central data warehouse, so that the management information system can update figures for **sales receipts** and **cash takings** on a real-time basis. Given that GHK is now in danger of making a loss for the first time, it will be important to be able to monitor sales figures closely, to see what impact any new strategies have on sales.

Performance information – There is no indication that GHK has any key performance indicators (KPIs) for its restaurants. However, the information available from the operational information systems could be used in **KPIs**. The management accountant could report how well the restaurants are performing in certain key areas; for example, spend per customer head, or spend per waiter. These again can provide useful headline information to the owners to enable them to see how the business is performing in areas which are critical to its success.

7.1 – 7.5 Objective Test questions

7.1   A   (i) and (ii)

Possessing knowledge can provide power and status, so staff may feel that if they hold personal knowledge they are more valuable to an organisation. Staff from one department may also not want to share knowledge with another department if there are inter-departmental rivalries.

Staff may feel uncomfortable in expressing opinions which are different to management's opinions, particularly if they are concerned that these opinions might adversely affect their career progression in the organisation. However, being able to express conflicting opinions and ideas in this way is an important part of organisational learning.

If staff enjoy discussing new ideas and sharing their thoughts with colleagues, this should help, rather than hinder, knowledge sharing.

7.2   D   The HR department is solely responsible for learning and development.

In learning organisations, learning and development is not seen as the preserve of a single organisational function (such as the HR department) but is regarded as the responsibility of all departments.

7.3   C   Variability and volume

Big Data analytics refers to the ability to analyse and reveal insights in data which had previously been too difficult or costly to analyse due to the variability and volume of the data involved. The aim of Big Data analytics is to extract insights from unstructured data or from large volumes of data.

7.4   C   (ii) only

The ability to compare prices directly between online retailers creates price transparency, which increases, not decreases, the bargaining power of customers.

7.5   1 – B

2 – C

3 – A

Blog: an online diary or news source

Podcast: delivery of audio, or video, content

Social network: a site that facilitates peer to peer communication

7.6 AAP estate agents

Top tips:

Part (a) (i):

In the past, examiners have noted that candidates appear not to have sufficient knowledge of the IS/IT areas of the syllabus. This question highlights the importance of ensuring you cover all areas of the syllabus in your revision, as any aspect of it can, and will, be examined.

Part (a) (ii):

This part of the question relates to Earl's points why IS/IT is strategically important. However, note that the question asks you to explain specifically why investing in information systems should be a strategic decision for AAP; not why investing in information systems should be a strategic decision in general terms.

Part (b):

Note the requirement here is to advise on the benefits **and** problems. Of the eight marks available for this part of the question, you should assume that there are a maximum of four available for either benefits or problems.

When approaching this question, think about what e-business actually is – the transformation of key business processes through the use of internet technologies. With this in mind, ask yourself how can IS/IT transform AAP's key business processes?

(a)　(i)　**Strategic grid**

Current vs planned importance – McFarlan and McKenney's strategic grid evaluates the strategic importance of the information systems to an organisation currently, against their expected strategic importance in the future.

Strategic importance of **planned** information systems		Strategic importance of **current** information systems	
High		*Turnaround*	*Strategic*
Low		*Support*	*Factory*
		Low	High

It appears that, until now, AAP has not considered its information systems (IS) as being strategically important to the business. Moreover, the absence of an e-business strategy and the fact that the Managing Director sees developing the website as a distraction from 'what we do' suggests that the company will continue to view IS as having low strategic importance in the future. In this respect, AAP's IS appear to be 'Support' systems in terms of the grid: having low strategic importance both currently and in the future.

However, it appears that the marketing director **has** realised the strategic importance of AAP's information systems and is going to try to convince the organisation of this. Web 2.0 technologies and the mobile phone applications which the marketing director has researched suggest that IS could become increasingly important to AAP in the future.

Moreover, the lack of integration between the estate agency software package and the website, and the problems which arise from this, suggest that AAP's IS could already be vital for the effective running of the business. In this case, despite AAP seeming to treat IS

as a 'Support' function, we could argue that it should actually be treated as a 'Strategic' function, since it is already strategically important, and is likely to become more so in the future:

		Low	High
Strategic importance of **planned** information systems	High	*Turnaround* Mobile phone applications; customer database; basic website	*Strategic* E-business (website for advertising and sales); Web 2.0 developments
	Low	*Support* Current property database; generic estate agency software	*Factory* Improved property database; linked to website

Strategic importance of **current** information systems

(ii) **Importance to competitive position** – Despite the board thinking that the decline in the number of AAP's property sales is due to the current economic downturn, it seems likely that AAP's lack of investment in information systems has also contributed to this decline. If AAP continues not to invest in its information systems, this could have a long-term detrimental impact on the business, in terms of customer numbers and property sales and, in turn, revenue and profits.

If the number of property sales AAP achieves continues to decline (because house buyers and sellers are using estate agents which are more up to date technologically) this could ultimately threaten the survival of the business.

IS as a basis of competitive advantage – It appears that some aspects of the IS investment at AAP will be required simply to remove current inefficiencies and to enable it to offer customers which other estate agencies are already offering them (for example, up to date property information on the website).

In effect, these elements of the investment will provide AAP with a threshold level of competence. However, AAP also needs to find a way of differentiating itself from its competitors, in order to develop a competitive advantage over them. (For example, if AAP introduces the mobile phone application and no other estate agents offer customers a similar app, this could be a source of differentiation for AAP.)

The potential ability of information systems to be a source of competitive advantage means that decisions surrounding investment in IS should be an important part of the strategic decision-making process rather than, for example, being taken as ad hoc decisions.

Technological developments – The introduction of mobile phone apps and the range of Web 2.0 technologies which the Marketing Director has identified indicates that there are a range of technological developments which could affect the estate agency market. Therefore it is important for AAP to monitor its own information systems in relation to the systems available so that it remains competitive.

Home buyers are increasingly using information systems to help in their property search, which reinforces the need for AAP to consider investment in such systems as a strategic decision.

Levels of investment – The investment in IS/IT required is likely to involve significant expenditure for AAP. In itself, the level of expenditure suggests that the investment decision should be a strategic decision. For example, AAP will need to assess whether it has sufficient funding available to support any proposed expenditure.

However, the potential risk attached to IS/IT projects reinforces this point. It will be important for AAP to select its IS/IT carefully so that it meets customers' needs effectively, rather than becoming a costly mistake.

Complexity – Any new information systems introduced at AAP are likely to be complex, and will affect many different areas of the business: estate agency software, customer and property databases, the website, and internal office communication. Therefore any new systems need to be carefully planned before they are introduced to ensure they are all compatible.

Equally, AAP will need to consider whether the managers and staff have the necessary expertise to manage any new systems and, for example, how much training they may require in using the new systems.

(b) **Benefits**

Strategic importance – Internet technologies are likely to become increasingly important to AAP's survival. Developing an e-business strategy will highlight the importance of e-business to the organisation, and will make staff and management realise how significant IS/IT are to the business.

Moreover, if AAP's competitors are already making use of e-business strategies, developing a similar strategy of its own should prevent AAP finding itself at a competitive disadvantage to its competitors. As the absence of an e-business strategy appears to be contributing to the decline in the number of property sales AAP has made, introducing an e-business strategy could help to reverse that decline.

Customer needs – AAP's Managing Director has correctly recognised the importance of meeting customer needs and requirements. However, he would seem to be mistaken in his argument that developing a website will be detrimental to customer requirements.

By contrast, developing an e-business strategy should enable AAP to be more responsive to customer needs. For example, having a more sophisticated website would enable customers to view the detailed property information online as and when they want to, rather than having to request AAP to send them a printed version each time they want to look at the details of a property.

Customer database – Equally, an e-business strategy could help AAP understand its customers and their requirements better; particularly through developing a customer database, based on the property searches customers have made on the website. This kind of database would enable AAP to be proactive and send customers details of similar properties they might be interested in, rather than relying on customers to search for properties themselves. In this respect, the e-business strategy should help AAP in its customer relationship management.

Social media – E-business would enable greater interaction between AAP and its customers – for example, through emails, blogs, and social networking sites. Interactivity between suppliers and customers is a key feature of e-business and Web 2.0 technologies, and the feedback which AAP could gain from its customers could be useful in helping it know how to market the properties it has for sale more effectively.

Geographical expansion – E-business could offer AAP opportunities to expand into new geographical markets; for example, advertising and selling properties in foreign countries. For example, potential customers from foreign countries who are looking to buy a house in M could look at the details of possible properties on the website; but this kind of expansion is unlikely to be possible if AAP continues to focus only on face to face customer service.

Problems

Loss of personal contact – The board believes that AAP's main source of competitive advantage comes from the high-quality, face to face customer service it offers its customers. If all of the other

estate agents focus increasingly on e-business and online media, then offering personal service in this way could actually be a source of differentiation for AAP. In particular, this could be valued by AAP's customers because it is dealing with 'high value, exclusive' properties. Equally, it could be valued by more elderly customers who might prefer this face to face contact to the remote interactions which would be involved in e-business.

Technology focus rather than customer focus – Moreover, if AAP's management become focused on technology and technology developments, they may prioritise these at the expense of customer service, which could lead to AAP losing more customers as a result of its e-business strategy rather than gaining them.

Resistance to change – If AAP's staff feel that the business's focus should be on direct customer service, they are likely to resist a change which they will feel is sacrificing that customer service for technology. This resistance to change could also be increased if the staff don't have experience of using e-business.

Lack of experience – It is not clear how many of AAP's management team or staff have previous experience of e-business, but from the board's attitude it appears that there is little e-business experience or expertise within AAP.

This lack of experience could also introduce the risks associated with developing an e-business strategy; for example, if the IS/IT implemented is poorly designed and doesn't prove attractive or reliable for potential customers to use. In addition, the 'look and feel' of AAP's online services will need to be consistent with its niche position as a specialist estate agent dealing in high value, exclusive properties. If AAP fails to achieve this, there is a danger it will incur the cost of developing its e-business systems, without gaining the intended benefits of increased customers and property sales.

AAP's internal lack of experience is also likely to increase the cost of developing its e-business strategy because it will need to use external consultants to advise it; for example, in relation to designing and installing new IT systems.

> **Cost** – There will inevitably be costs involved in the IS/IT infrastructure need to implement e-business. However, since AAP already has a website, and uses some technology with its estate agency software and email system, it is not clear how far AAP's existing systems can be upgraded to support its e-business strategy, or whether new systems will be required.

(c)
> **Top tips:** The requirement here was specifically for **two** different applications of Web 2.0 technologies. Therefore you should have limited your answer to **two** as no additional credit will be given for providing additional examples and your time will have been wasted.
>
> We have recommended mash-ups and blogs; however, there are other possible options which you may have chosen instead that are equally valid and as such would gain the same number of marks. Examples of other Web 2.0 technologies you could have discussed are shown in the box below our answer.

Web 2.0 technologies – Web 2.0 technologies enable internet users no longer to be simply recipients of information, but to participate in the creation, sharing and evaluation of content. Web 2.0 technologies can help marketers and sales staff develop better insights into markets and customers, and also develop greater interaction with their customers.

Mash-ups

A 'mash-up' is a web publication that combines data from more than one source into a single web page to increase the amount of information available to people using that page.

'Mash-ups' could be particularly useful for AAP by enabling the details of individual properties to be combined with a map of the surrounding area, as well as information about the local area – for

example, links to local facilities and amenities (eg schools, restaurants, healthcare services), local crime statistics, or local planning portals.

Moreover, because 'mash-ups' would enable AAP to make use of links to existing websites or information sources, rather than having to create and embed information on its own web pages, they would provide it with a cost-effective way of providing valuable information to potential customers.

Blogs

Blogs provide an easy way for users to publish content, and they could be useful to AAP in both an internal and external context.

Internal blogs – Internal blogs can only be viewed by the employees of an organisation, and can provide an effective means of sharing information within that organisation. At AAP internal blogs could be used by senior management to share information with staff across the ten different offices, thereby reducing the need for meetings or numerous emails. For example, the Marketing Director could publish a blog describing any new marketing initiatives which AAP's office should be following; or outlining how well sales figures are performing against target, and any steps which are being taken to improve performance.

External blogs – External blogs are publicly available, and would provide AAP's staff an opportunity to share information with customers. For example, AAP could post blogs on its website describing new properties when they come on to the market; or to announce new sales incentives or promotional campaigns which it may be running. Equally, it could use its blog to comment on wider issues, such as perceived changes in the socio-economic environment in M and the impact they could have on the market for exclusive residential properties.

In effect, AAP could use its blogs in the way that companies have traditionally used press releases. Moreover, if more people are attracted to AAP's website to read a blog posting, the hope will be that they also view some of the properties listed for sale on it.

Microblogs – In addition to full blogs, AAP could use the microblogging site, Twitter, as a medium for publishing short messages. This could be particularly useful for alerting potential customers to a new property coming on to the market, especially if customers 'follow' AAP on Twitter.

There are a number of other suitable applications of Web 2.0 technologies you could have recommended:

Social media – AAP might be able to use **social media** (such as Facebook) to advertise its properties and its services. For example, it could set up a Facebook page which it could use to promote sales events or particularly exciting new properties becoming available. In addition, potential customers could leave messages for AAP through its Facebook page.

Although we have included Twitter (micro-blogging) in our recommendation for blogging, the marking guide indicated that you could have recommended Twitter as a social media application.

Instant messaging (such as Skype or Facetime) could also be appropriate here: for example, if a customer sees property details, they could then 'talk' to one of AAP's sales agents through an instant messaging service.

Syndication – AAP could allow companies which offer property-related services (eg architects, interior designers, solicitors, builders, or removal companies) to advertise on its website.

In this way, AAP can earn additional revenue from the advertising links. Equally, however, the ease of being able to find the majority of services they need to move house via a single source (AAP's website) could be appealing to customers, and could encourage additional users to visit the website.

8.1 – 8.5 Objective Test questions

8.1   B   The level of competitiveness within the market is high.

       C   Your company has limited resources.

          If demand for your product is greater than supply, or if the product is unique, then the product is likely to succeed whether a company segments the market or not.

          By contrast, if the market is competitive, then it is advisable for a company to segment the market so that the company can target its marketing activities to the customers most likely to buy its products.

8.2   D   (i), (ii) and (iii)

          Branding reduces the importance of price differentials between products, and so makes price less important as a source of competitive advantage between products.

          Strong brands can form barriers to entry into a market.

          Brands can have much longer life cycles than products, especially when technology is developing rapidly and reducing product life cycles.

8.3   A   (i) and (ii)

          Relationship marketing focuses on developing relationships with customers, to promote customer retention and customer loyalty.

          As such, relationship marketing encourages high levels of contact with customers, with each contact being used to improve information about the customer and build the relationship further. By contrast, transactions marketing encourages only low or moderate contact with customers.

8.4   False   The churn rate is the percentage of customers that end their relationship with an organisation in any given period.

If the company's churn rate is lower than anticipated, this means the proportion of customers being retained is higher than anticipated, and therefore we would expect customer lifetime value to be higher than anticipated.

8.5   C   Recommendations

Affiliate marketing, comparison sites and search engines can all be methods for acquiring customers.

However, recommendations are useful for customer extension. For example, when an existing customer logs back into an online store, the customer is given recommendations for additional products they might like to buy, based on their previous purchasing history.

8.6 CFE coffee shops

Top tips.

Part (a). The marketing director's proposal is that CFE should introduce a loyalty card scheme in order to improve customer loyalty and strengthen CFE's brand. The key question, however, is what impact this customer loyalty or brand awareness will actually have on CFE's performance.

Notice that you are asked to 'evaluate' the importance of brand awareness so you need to think of its potential benefits for CFE's business performance, but you should also think whether there are any potential limitations on its impact.

Part (b). The success (or failure) of the Finance Director's plan is likely to depend on customers' reactions to it. So it is important that CFE understands its customers and their buying decisions. This highlights the importance of looking at CFE as an open system, and how its activities and decisions are affected by the external environment.

(a)   **Competitive market** – The high number of branded coffee shops in Teeland suggests that the market there is likely to be competitive, because customers will have a high degree of choice about where to buy their coffee. In this respect, branding, and the loyalty card scheme, could be valuable to CFE if it encourages customers to keep returning to CFE shops to buy their coffee rather than going to rival shops.

Customer loyalty – By creating customer loyalty a strong brand identity is a way of increasing or maintaining sales; for example, by improving customer retention rates and encouraging repeat purchases. This is the logic behind the loyalty cards being proposed by the marketing director.

However, whilst increasing sales will allow CFE to increase its profits overall, it may not, by itself, have as much impact as the Marketing Director might hope.

Importantly, CFE currently generates more revenue per shop than the market leader, although its profit margins are significantly lower.

Comparison of financial performance

	CFE	Market leader
Revenue per shop ($'000)	1,434.5	1,384.6
Gross margin (%)	64.5%	68.9%
Gross margin per shop ($'000)	925.0	953.8
Operating profit margin (%)	9.77%	12.50%

In this respect, it seems that CFE's cost structure and its product mix may have a greater impact on performance than brand awareness. For example, CFE makes the highest profit margins on coffee sales, so if it could sell relatively more coffee drinks compared to food and snacks this would

improve its profit margins. The loyalty card scheme could help here, by encouraging customers to buy hot drinks so that they qualify for their free drink. (Obviously, though, margins will then be reduced by the 'free' seventh drink.)

Product mix

	Coffee	Other drinks	Food & snacks
% of total revenue	34.0%	9.7%	56.3%
Gross margin (%) earned per product	80.7%	52.4%	56.8%

However, although there appear to be more important factors affecting CFE's performance than its company profile, branding could still have a positive impact on its performance.

Brand awareness – Brand awareness would be an indicator of CFE's position in the coffee shop market, and would indicate whether customers or potential customers do actually differentiate CFE from its customers, for example as offering higher-quality products and service. If customers don't associate CFE's products as being higher quality than the competitors, then the money spent on higher-quality ingredients and service staff is effectively being wasted.

Quality and trust – One of the key attributes of a successful brand is that it conveys a sense of quality and trust to potential customers, thereby encouraging them to buy the product or service in question in preference to a rival product.

Quality seems to be very important to CFE: it uses high-quality ingredients for its food and drinks, and seeks to ensure customers receive a high standard of service (by paying its staff wages above the industry average).

Differentiation – In this respect, CFE appears to be trying to differentiate itself from its competitors on grounds of quality. If it can ensure that its brand becomes synonymous with quality, then this will help CFE compete successfully with other branded coffee shops.

Premium price – Branding messages are usually qualitative rather than focusing, and therefore reduce the importance of price differentials between a product and its rivals. This could be very important for CFE. Customers do not appear to be price sensitive, yet CFE is charging broadly the same prices as its competitors.

If CFE is able to strengthen its brand, by focusing on quality and service, this may in turn allow it to charge a higher price for its products. This could be crucial for CFE's profitability, because it could allow CFE to reverse the current situation in which its gross margin percentages are lower than its competitors'.

(b) **Demand for the product** – When deciding whether or not to increase the price of its coffee products, CFE needs to consider what impact the changes in price are likely to have on customer demand for them. Therefore market research will be important to assess how demand (and consequently revenue) will be affected by any change in price.

It seems that CFE's customers are not particularly price sensitive, which should increase the chances of the Finance Director's proposal. However, CFE should still research their reaction to any change before implementing it.

In this respect, it would also be useful for CFE to gauge the strength of any brand loyalty towards it.

Amount of increase – Equally, market research will give CFE an insight into what price customers are willing to pay for their coffee. CFE's competitive strategy (of differentiation based around quality) might enable it to charge higher prices than its customers to an extent and still retain its customers. However, if CFE increases its prices too much, it is unlikely that the customers will remain loyal to it, even if it offers higher-quality coffee and service than its competitors.

Competitors' pricing policies – Currently, CFE's are largely the same as those charged by the multinational competitors. However, these competitors might also be planning to change their prices. For example, if CFE's competitors increase their prices, that could give CFE greater scope to increase its prices.

Competitors' plans – Currently, CFE seems to serve a higher proportion of 'Fair Trade' products than its competitors, and this might help it justify its higher prices. However, if its competitors are also planning to use more 'Fair Trade' coffee, or increase the quality of other ingredients, this would reduce the basis of differentiation between CFE and its competitors. In this respect, any insights which CFE could gain into its competitors' plans before it changed its prices would be useful.

Input prices – The Finance Director's suggestion is designed to help CFE increase margins. However, if the price of coffee beans rises, it might need to increase prices in order to maintain its current margins.

Equally, if costs such as the rents CFE has to pay for its premises rise, these may also increase the pressure on CFE to increase its prices in order to maintain its profit margins.

9.1 – 9.5 Objective Test questions

9.1   D   Revolution

Types of change can be classified in a matrix according to their nature (speed) and scope (extent).

'Big Bang' changes are rapid changes. Rapid change which is transformational in scope is classified in the matrix as 'Revolution'.

Adaptation and evolution both relate to changes in which the nature of change is incremental rather than 'Big Bang'. Reconstruction represents a rapid change, but the scope of change is less extensive than in Revolution.

9.2   B   Get team leaders to instruct members of their teams about the benefits of change

People who instruct others on a new viewpoint usually change their own ideas faster than those who just listen. Getting the team leaders to support the change will improve the chances of the rest of the team shifting in favour of the change.

Paying the employees to change might ensure compliance with the change; however, it is very unlikely to change their attitude, and there is also the risk that it could be seen as bribery. This would further reduce respect for the change.

The presentation of the change as a 'done deal' may strengthen resistance to it, due to staff's resentment over the lack of information and consultation during the change process.

Lying to staff is never a good idea (ie telling them the change is for a 'trial period' when it is in fact intended to be permanent). It is very likely that staff will find out the truth about the plans, and this will increase resentment to the change as well as leading to a lack of respect for you as their manager.

9.3   C   Refreeze

The refreeze stage of the change process is required to consolidate and reinforce the new patterns of behaviour adapted during the change (or move) stage.

The bonus scheme is designed so that staff will only earn a bonus if they use the new methodology, rather than lapsing back into using old methodologies.

9.4   C   (ii) only

> Theory O changes are concerned with developing an organisation's human capability to implement strategy. A key element in Theory O is that change is participative and emergent, rather than being top-down and planned. Encouraging the staff to make suggestions and share ideas (as in Option ii) suggests a participative approach.
>
> By contrast, in Theory E, change is viewed as a top-down process, and changes are planned and programmatic. Therefore, Option i is more characteristic of a Theory E approach than a Theory O approach.

9.5   A   Capability

> The capability to manage and implement change is one of the contexts of change highlighted by the change kaleidoscope, rather than one of the aspects of the culture web.
>
> The six manifestations of culture in the cultural web are: stories, symbols, routines and rituals, power structures, control systems and organisational structure; and collectively these manifestations underpin the organisation's paradigm.

9.6 Steyn Steel Co

> **Top tips:**
>
> (a)   In effect, this question is asking you to work out the forces which need to be considered in a force field analysis at Steyn Steel. However, the question asks you to analyse them, so you need to discuss them. Do not be tempted to draw a force field analysis diagram.
>
> (b)   Although the question does not specify any specific model, Lewin's three stage model is a useful model to use here. The CEO will need to unfreeze existing behaviours, make the changes he believes are necessary, and then refreeze the new behaviours he wants to establish.

Part (a)

Forces for change

Internal

New CEO – A new CEO has recently joined Steyn Steel and he has identified areas where the company's performance needs to be improved. More importantly, he has also made it clear he intends to address these directly in order to improve Steyn's competitiveness.

As an 'outsider' joining the company, the CEO is likely to look more objectively at performance issues than managers and staff who have worked for the company for a long time.

Poor operational performance – The CEO is only having to act because Steyn's current operational performance does not appear to be competitive. These performance issues are characterised by costs being too high and productivity being too low, and may reflect the perceived complacency among the staff.

External

High export demand – It seems that the scope to increase sales is greater in export markets than in Steyn's domestic market. However, the CEO has suggested that Steyn will need to change some of its working practices in order to capitalise on these export opportunities.

The fact that the CEO is clearly focusing on exports as the main source of revenue opportunities suggests that he doesn't see any real growth opportunities in Steyn's domestic market. This again reinforces the need to change working practices in order to be competitive in the international market.

Forces resisting change

Internal

Long-serving managers – The managers who have worked at Steyn for a long time do not appear to be worried about the company's performance and so may not appreciate the company need for change. In this case, they are unlikely to support any proposals for change.

Alternatively, it may be that the long-standing staff members have become familiar and comfortable with the current practices and so do not want these to change. Change will bring uncertainty into their routines, and may involve them having to learn new skills or adapt to less favourable working practices.

Trade union – The trade union has promised the workers it will defend their wage levels and working conditions, and so this could lead them into direct conflict with the CEO if he tries to make changes.

If the pay and conditions which the workers (particularly the long-serving workers) receive are more favourable than the industry standard, this may be another reason for them to resist changes. If the CEO's proposals are aimed at bringing them more in line with industry standards, this may be disadvantageous to the workers.

External

Import duties – Steyn's ability to increase its sales into export markets appears constrained by the high import duties it has to pay in some of these markets. Given the strategic importance of increasing export sales, the ongoing presence of these duties could be a significant problem for the company.

Part (b)

In his work on force field analysis and stage models of change, Lewin suggested that, after the forces for change and the forces resisting change have been established, efforts need to be made to break down the forces resisting change and also to reinforce the influence of those supporting it.

Unfreeze – 'Unfreezing' current working practices and attitudes is the first phase of Lewin's stage model of change.

The CEO will have to set up a programme of education and support for the complacent managers and enter into negotiations with the trade union. Given his concern's about Steyn's performance, the CEO may well be advised to emphasise the financial problems which the company could face if action is not taken to improve its competitiveness.

Communication will be vital here, and the CEO needs to explain to the staff not only what his plans for the future are, but why they are required.

Change –The second phase of the change programme will require action to change employees' behaviours: establishing new patterns of behaviour and reinforcing them.

Communication will again be important, but staff may also need training and development programmes to help them adapt to the new behaviours required.

Refreeze – For the change programme to be successful, the CEO will need to ensure that staff continue to embrace the new culture and behaviours rather than slipping back into their old ways. It is likely there will need to be a mixture of rewards to recognise good performance and also sanctions against staff who lapse back into their old habits. In extreme cases, staff who persistently refuse to adapt to the change may even be made redundant, although Steyn will be aware of the union presence and so will have to handle any such decisions with great care.

10.1 – 10.5 Objective Test questions

10.1   C   Sells

The nature of the communication as a largely one-way process, with little opportunity for feedback, means that the manager has used either a 'tells' or a 'sells' style.

The fact that the manager has attempted to gain staff's commitment to the plans (by emphasising their benefits to the organisation) highlights that she has used a 'selling' style.

10.2   D   The problem or threat which has caused the change to be necessary

Individuals will often resist a change if they think they are being asked to change 'for change's sake'. By focusing on the problem which has prompted the change, you are selling the change to your team by demonstrating that there is a rational basis for it. This approach could also engage the team's self-interest and show how the change will help them (ie by enabling the organisation to respond more effectively to the threat than it would otherwise be able to).

10.3   B   Compromise – bargaining, negotiation and conciliation

Handling conflict is never easy, but the compromise approach will have the best chance of being effective. In particular, negotiation might help to bring about a mutually acceptable solution because it gives the parties to the conflict the chance to try to resolve their differences through discussion together.

The other three responses are unlikely to provide a permanent solution to the conflict. They are likely to leave lingering resentment which, over time, will perpetuate the conflict.

10.4   D   A person, or group of people, who takes on the role of promoting strategic change within an organisation

A change agent is an individual, or group, that helps to bring about strategic change in an organisation. A change agent can be either internal or external to an organisation. Crucially, the change agent's role relates to bringing about change, rather than identifying or recommending the need for change in an organisation.

A senior manager who proposes a strategic change in an organisation is a change advocate rather than a change agent.

10.5   D   Storming

The team has moved beyond the initial 'forming' stage, in which members are likely to be wary about introducing new ideas. They are now assured enough to put forward ideas, but the different approaches are leading to conflict between team members.

The existence of different ideas and approaches competing for ascendancy is a key feature of teams at the 'storming' stage of their development.

10.6 Simon Clark

Part (a)

> **Top tips**. It is important to stress that knowing the theory will not be enough for success in the case study exam. You must relate your knowledge to the setting, as we relate it in our answer below.
>
> You could use Lewin's models to approach this question and you would be awarded appropriate marks so long as you demonstrated the pressures and influences on Simon Clark and integrated your answers with the case scenario.

Simon has a range of possible responses to his problem of potential conflict with his staff.

Deny problem exists

Some essentially trivial problems blow over without particular management effort. This type of problem can be ignored. If Simon feels that this is the case here, he can effectively deny that a problem exists and withdraw from considering it further. However, the proposed changes would require very important changes to working practices at the college and conditions of service and the staff are 'most unhappy'. It seems unlikely that denial and withdrawal would be a satisfactory response, since teaching as an occupation is particularly demanding of individual motivation.

Smoothing over disputes

A more active policy would be to suppress the problem by smoothing over any overt disputes, if possible, in order to preserve working relationships. This approach is unlikely to produce the changes evidently required at the college, so Simon may have to combine it with a certain amount of coercion, imposing necessary changes unilaterally. This is a recipe for continuing dispute and the lingering hostility of 'win-lose' situations. The effect on motivation is likely to be even more dire than a policy of denial and withdrawal. Indeed, the teaching staff may retaliate by withdrawing their co-operation and working to rule.

Compromise and negotiation

A more positive approach for Simon to take would involve a willingness to make compromises via a process of bargaining, negotiation and conciliation. It is likely that there is some room for manoeuvre in the matter of weekend working, perhaps by offering time off *in lieu*. The staff are no doubt well aware of the potential threat to their interests from the private college and may be prepared to adjust their initial position.

Integration and collaboration

This approach may, perhaps, be extended into a more sophisticated process of integration and collaboration, in which a continuing dialogue can establish both common ground and general agreement as to what is necessary for the achievement of the overall task. To achieve this, Simon must overcome his frustration and attempt to bring the staff into full participation in the changes that affect them.

Part (b)

> **Top tips**. Generating support is an important aspect of change management generally. This question is about one department in quite a small organisation, so more complex change management strategies, such as the Gemini 4Rs, are probably too complex. We are concerned here with management techniques that would be useful to the head of a single department in such an organisation.
>
> This is essentially a problem of practical leadership. Some aspects of the solution, such as providing resources, are easy both to specify and to implement. Other, less concrete, measures related to human behaviour, such as the importance of communication, are less easy to describe and, indeed, to perform. Do not shy away from these less material things and do cover them in as precise a way as you can. It is very easy to be vague and woolly about such matters. Try to be definite. For example, don't just say 'communicate'; say 'hold a meeting' as well.

It seems likely from the staff's initial reaction to Simon's proposals that he has not given sufficient thought to enlisting their support. This may reflect his managerial technique, or lack of it. If he is to succeed with his plan to change the way things are done, he will have to improve the way he deals with his staff in both material and intangible ways.

Improve communications

The highest priority is to improve his overall relations with the staff. He must make more effective communication a continuing personal target in order to improve motivation and mutual understanding. He must ensure that the staff see him as approachable and sympathetic to their concerns, within the limitations set by reality.

Improve understanding

Simon Clark should ensure that his staff understand that his proposals are a response to a serious commercial threat that affects them all and not an arbitrary decision. He should point out the potential effects upon them of failing to respond to the commercial competition and the opportunities and rewards that success will bring. He should encourage the staff to think for themselves about the situation the college is in, invite them to debate it among themselves and make alternative proposals if they can. Such participation, even if it does not produce any feasible new ideas, will make whatever solution is eventually decided upon more acceptable.

However, Simon must not abdicate responsibility. It is his role to make the final decision and to implement it. There are several measures he can take to promote acceptance of change.

Promote acceptance of change

He may be able to **enlist the support of more senior staff** who have the respect of their peers as change agents. Their role would be to lend their credibility to the new arrangements, to assist with its planning and implementation and to provide practical day to day leadership in the context of change.

He should **support positive responses** to change with praise and reward and deal firmly with negative behaviour such as murmuring and absenteeism.

The need for change has been forced upon the college and the department and it may be that time and resources are limited. However, Simon's aim should be to introduce change at a measured pace and avoid the rush and panic that is sure to upset the staff and provoke hostility.

Similarly, he should make a case for the provision of resources to the change process so that, for instance, some promotions might result, or working conditions be improved. Quite small enhancements such as decorating the staff common room or providing a new photocopier would help to present the change in a positive light.

10.7 Auto Direct

> **Top tip**. You must think hard about the wording of this question. Superficially, it asks you for a summary of change management strategies in a particular context, which would be a large job to do properly, but offers only 12 marks. The implication is that you must not descend into too much detail about any particular model or approach.

Managing Director, Auto Direct

Date

Report: Change management strategies and methods

The change that you are contemplating, while extensive, is incremental and does not involve the transformation of your organisation. It therefore falls into the category of **adaptation**, which implies that you may proceed step by step and leave your basic assumptions and approach unchanged.

It would be a very worthwhile exercise to consider some of the factors that might affect the success of your programme of change. Chief among these are likely to be the various human factors present in your staff.

Presumably you will include some element of promotion and cross-posting of your existing workforce in order to provide a basis of experience at your new sites, so you should consider the degree of **readiness** (or willingness) of your staff to undertake the development you plan.

You should also consider your company's managerial **capability** and **capacity** in terms of resources to undertake change. The former depends largely on past experience.

While good **project management** of a programme of change is very important, it is the **human aspects of the change management process** that are crucial. This is because change will not happen unless people make it happen. A number of strategies are proposed for dealing with this aspect of change management.

Participation in decision making is sometimes recommended as a way of improving motivation generally and may be useful in the context of change. It is probably advantageous to involve staff in decisions affecting them, their conditions and their work processes and at least hear what they have to say. However, participation is not a universal panacea and can be very **time consuming**. Also, the normal **management style and culture** of the organisation must be considered. It is probably inappropriate to promote participation exclusively in the context of change if staff are not used to it: their main reaction may be one of suspicious cynicism.

An **autocratic** approach, imposing change by means of **coercion**, can work reasonably well in some circumstances, especially where the staff expect nothing else. It has the benefit of saving time and is probably the **best approach in times of crisis**. However, it does have the weakness of ignoring the experience and knowledge that staff may be able to offer.

In any event, **communication** with staff about the proposed change is commonly regarded as an essential process. Ideally, information will be provided as early as possible, explaining why change is necessary and the course that will be followed. Anxiety, particularly over job security, is common during change and a programme of communication and education can go a long way to allay it.

Sometimes neither participation nor coercion can resolve all problems and **negotiation** may be required. This is often the case when the labour force is strongly organised and when there is disagreement between management factions as to the best course to follow.

This has been a brief overview of some approaches to change management. You will no doubt be in a position to decide which are most appropriate to the circumstances of Auto Direct.

11.1 – 11.5 Objective Test questions

11.1 C   Using economies of scale to procure high-quality goods as cheaply as possible

Critical success factors (CSFs) identify what an organisation needs to do well in order to be successful and to achieve its objectives. An organisation can then use key performance indicators (KPIs) to measure whether or not it is achieving its CSFs.

Option A is an example of an objective, and Option C (the CSF) identifies one of the ways by which the organisation could achieve that objective. Options B and D are examples of KPIs.

11.2 C   (ii) only

Option (i) is incorrect: Non-financial indicators which allow an organisation to assess how well it is performing against its critical success factors can often act as leading indicators, whereas most traditional financial performance indicators tend to be **lagging** indicators, reporting on past performance and past events.

11.3 B   Financial

The financial perspective is the highest level perspective, meaning that the measures and goals an organisation seeks to achieve in relation to the other three (non-financial) perspectives should, in turn, help the organisation to achieve its financial goals.

11.4 B   (i) and (iii)

The pyramid focuses on a range of objectives for both external effectiveness (related to customer satisfaction) and internal efficiency (related to flexibility and productivity).

The fact that the hierarchical nature of the pyramid encourages individual departments to link their operational goals to overall strategic goals is seen as one of the main strengths of the model.

However, one of the criticisms of the pyramid is that it tends to concentrate on two main groups of stakeholders only: shareholders and customers. It does not look at measures which relate to other stakeholders, such as employees or suppliers.

11.5 A Flexibility

In results and determinants analysis, the four determinants which are perceived to underpin the competitive and financial performance (the 'results') of an organisation are: quality of service, flexibility, resource utilisation, and innovation.

Flexibility relates to an organisation's ability to deliver goods and service at the right speed and at the right time to meet customer requirements, and to cope with fluctuations in demand.

Quality of service looks at matters such as reliability, responsiveness to customers' needs, and courtesy.

Market share is one of the factors which could be measured when analysing competitive performance, while profitability is a factor which could be measured when analysing financial performance.

11.6 CCC car insurance

(a)

> **Top tips**. The requirement here does not ask you to advise what the balanced scorecard is, nor to describe what the four perspectives of it are. Instead, you are asked how using the scorecard could help CCC deliver its value and strategy.
>
> Did you notice that the four points in CCC's vision statement correspond very closely to the four perspectives of the scorecard?
>
> Spotting this was crucial here, because it means that if CCC introduces the scorecard and then introduces performance measures for each perspective of the scorecard, by doing so it should also address each aspect of the vision statement.

Strategic implementation – Although CCC has developed a vision statement and its overriding objective, it appears that it has been unable to implement its strategy successfully.

This highlights the importance of recognising strategic management as a process, involving strategic analysis, strategic choice and strategy implementation.

In order to develop its mission statement, vision statement and overriding objective, it seems likely that CCC has undertaken strategic analysis and made strategic choices. Therefore, the weakness in its strategic management process appears to be in its implementation.

Balanced scorecard – Kaplan and Norton (who developed the scorecard) suggested that one of its main uses is in enabling organisations to improve their strategic performance.

The scorecard seeks to translate mission and strategy into objectives and measures, in relation to the four perspectives in the scorecard; for example by setting measures and targets relating to each perspective. The scorecard can also be used to communicate standards and targets to staff, and it can be used as a control mechanism. By providing the directors with information on how CCC is performing against key measures, the scorecard will enable them to assess how well CCC's strategy is being implemented, and what corrective action is required to improve its performance.

Scorecard perspectives – The four aspects of CCC's vision statement can be aligned to the four perspectives of the scorecard:

Provide superior returns to our shareholders – This relates to the **financial perspective** of the scorecard: how CCC should create value for its shareholders to succeed financially.

Delight our customers – This reflects the **customer perspective** of the scorecard: how does CCC need to appear to its customers in order to achieve its vision.

Continually improve our business processes – This relates to the **internal business perspective** of the scorecard: what business processes CCC must excel at to achieve financial and customer objectives.

Learn from our mistakes and work smarter in the future – This illustrates the **innovation and learning perspective** of the scorecard: how can CCC continue to create value and maintain its competitive position through improvement and change.

If key performance measures were identified, and then monitored, for each of these perspectives, this should provide the directors with more information with which to manage CCC's performance. In turn, this should help CCC implement its strategy more successfully.

(b)

> **Top tips:**
>
> The key to this question is to define exactly what each of the aspects required is:
>
> *Objective* – what CCC wants to achieve
>
> *Measure* – a means of expressing the progress CCC is making towards an objective
>
> *Target* – a specific value or deadline for achieving a measure
>
> *Initiative* – the actions taken to achieve a target
>
> Importantly, notice the distinction between measures and targets. Measures identify what is to be measured; targets are the specific values which CCC is aiming to achieve.
>
> Note also that you are only asked to recommend suitable examples for each of the aspects; you do not have to give reasons to support your recommendation. Therefore your answers can be kept very brief.
>
> The examples given in the answer below are not the only possible examples you could have given, and you would have earned marks if you recommended different examples, provided they were relevant and were attributed to the correct aspect (ie that what you recommended as a 'Measure' was indeed a measure and not a target.

The four perspectives which CCC should use are the four perspectives identified in the balanced scorecard.

Financial perspective

Objective – To increase dividend yield on investors' shares

Measure – Dividend yield

Target – 8% dividend yield by the end of 20X3

Initiative – Improved customer retention to increase profits

> **Initiative** – Cost cutting exercises or business process improvements designed to increase profits

Customer perspective

Objective – To increase customer satisfaction

Measure – Number of customer complaints

Target – Reduce the number of customer complaints to 1 per 100 transactions by the end of 20X3

Initiative – Increased staff training for sales executives

> **Measure** – Number of customers renewing/not renewing their policies
>
> **Target** – 95% of existing customers renew their policies in 20X2/20X3 (or less than 5% of customers do not renew their policies)
>
> **Initiative** – Properly promoted discount schemes linked to insurance renewals

Internal business perspective

Objective – Use up to date hardware and software

Measure – Age of PCs/Frequency with which PCs are replaced

Target – All PCs to be less than 2 years old by the end of 20X3

Initiative – Look to negotiate a deal with PC suppliers to provide new PCs at a competitive rate on an ongoing basis

Innovation and learning perspective

Objective – Raise the level of educational qualifications of CCC's staff

Measure – Number of staff with a higher education qualification (or number of graduates employed)

Target – 50% of staff to have a higher education qualification by the end of 20X4

Initiative – Sponsor staff to attend part-time/evening higher education courses

(c)

Top tips:

This question is essentially a test of knowledge, because there is no requirement to identify the drawbacks which CCC could face from using the scorecard. Instead you are simply asked to discuss two drawbacks of the balanced scorecard itself.

However, it is important that the drawbacks you discuss relate specifically to the balanced scorecard, rather than being drawbacks of performance measurement in more general terms.

In our answer below we have suggested a number of potential drawbacks you could have discussed. However, you should only have discussed **two**, as instructed by the question requirement.

Difficulty in choosing measures – Some measures in the scorecard may conflict with each other. For example, the cost of training programmes (innovation and learning) may affect profits (financial). Sometimes it can be difficult to determine which combinations of measures will achieve the best results for a company overall.

Selecting measures – Companies may select measures because they are easy to measure, rather than selecting those which add value to the organisation. However, companies should measure those aspects of performance which are crucial in achieving their critical success factors, and in delivering value to their customers.

Appropriate measures – Measurement is only useful if it initiates appropriate action. Therefore measures should be developed by someone who understands the business processes concerned. If the measures are decided by senior managers or directors who do not understand the processes sufficiently, this could lead to inappropriate measures being chosen.

Time and cost taken to implement – It will take time for managers to decide what aspects of performance should be included in the scorecard. Time could also be required for training managers (and staff) how to use the scorecard.

The scorecard may also require investment in new software (for example, in order to measure additional aspects of performance). However, the benefits an organisation could gain from using the scorecard may not justify the time and cost which will be incurred to introduce it.

> **Cultural change** – For companies which have not used the scorecard before, introducing it can require a significant cultural change. For example, if an organisation's current performance management system focuses solely on financial performance, the change to measuring (and managing) non-financial aspects of performance as well as financial ones could be difficult to achieve, particularly if it also affects reward schemes.
>
> Given that introducing the scorecard will be seen as a change, then there is also likely to be **resistance** to that change.

12.1 – 12.5 Objective Test questions

12.1 (i) – B

(ii) – D

(iii) – A

(iv) – C

(i) Generation, communication and interpretation of financial and non-financial **information** for management and other stakeholders

(ii) Provision of specific information and analysis on which **decisions** are based

(iii) Monitoring of outcomes against plans and other **benchmarks** and the initiation of responsive action for performance improvement

(iv) Derivation of performance measures and benchmarks, financial and non-financial, quantitative and qualitative for monitoring and **control**

12.2 17.3%

ROCE is calculated as profit before interest and tax (PBIT) divided by capital employed.

$260,000/$1,500,000 = 17.3%

12.3 C Decrease

Rappaport looked at the value drivers in terms of their ability to generate cash.

Cash invested in non-current assets reduces free cash flows (and therefore is deemed to reduce the value of a business) even though investing in the assets may lead to growth in the future.

12.4 A Economic depreciation

The adjustment between accounting operating profit and NOPAT requires accounting depreciation to be added back and replaced with a charge for economic depreciation (ie accounting depreciation is added back, not economic depreciation).

When calculating EVA, expenditure on marketing and promotions – and similar items which will generate value for a business in future – should be capitalised, and so need to be added back to profit.

12.5 D 16%

Total shareholder return (TSR) is calculated as:

$$\frac{\text{Dividend per share} + \text{Movement in share price}}{\text{Share price at the start of the period}}$$

TSR = ($0.2 + $0.6) / $5 = 16%

12.6 Management accounting information

> **Top tip.** The question is broken down into two parts. The first requires an analysis of the validity of the criticism that management accounting information is irrelevant for decision making. The second part asks you to think about the provision of management accounting information in two different types of organisation.
>
> Our answer to the first part takes the stance that while new techniques are available, many firms do not sufficiently tailor their information collection to specific decisions, and need to develop systems to make sure that they are able to undertake financial analysis, planning and control. No one solution will suit all businesses.
>
> Our answer to the second part considers issues of financial vs non-financial information, organisational structure and performance measurement. These will vary between the two organisations concerned.

(a)   In the 1980s and 1990s critics began to question management accounting's relevance to decision making. Seeing the challenge facing management accountants as being one of providing more relevant information for decision making, critics argued that traditional management accounting systems may not always provide this. Management accounting information is often biased towards the **past** rather than the future, and management accounting systems do not always detect **strategic issues**.

Decision making is a **forward** and **outward** looking process, and management accounting information has been too inward looking and directed largely towards **financial reporting**. Historical costs are necessary to report to shareholders, but the classifications of transactions for reporting purposes are not necessarily relevant to decision making.

Internal vs external focus

Much management accounting information is devised for **internal consumption**. However, strategic management involves looking at the **external environment**, and strategy is pursued in relation to **competitors**. Their actions need to be understood and quantified to be able to devise appropriate response activity.

Some management accounting techniques such as **variance analysis** are seen as too simplistic and largely irrelevant for decision making in a 21st century business. Modern business is embracing new ways of working, including **outsourcing** and **homeworking**, and there is constant pressure to improve quality and service and reduce costs. Some techniques such as **activity based costing** have been developed which are designed to take specific business processes and cost drivers into account when measuring profitability and performance. Techniques such as **customer account profitability and direct product profitability** attempt to replace general analysis with specifics, but in general many firms continue to use old costing systems which are too general in their application to be able to support specific strategic decisions.

It could be argued that the production of more relevant costs does not necessarily make the management accountant a strategic partner for the chief executive overnight. However, management accountants do need to tackle this issue of the relevance of the information they provide for **strategy formulation** and **control decisions** at higher levels in the organisation. Strategic plans may cover a long period into the future, and often involve big changes and new ventures. How can the management accountant support such developments?

CIMA has defined '**strategic management accounting**' as 'a form of management accounting in which emphasis is placed on information which relates to factors external to the firm, as well as to non-financial information and internally generated information'. Ward suggests that the role of the strategic management accountant can be analysed as being split between **financial analysis, financial planning** and **financial control**. These roles encompass the current **position** of the business, its **goals** and **objectives** and its **feedback** mechanisms, which compare planned with actual performance. They may involve obtaining information from other **functions** in the organisation, such as production, distribution or marketing.

Contingency theory is a theory that has been developed which states that there is no universally applicable best practice in the design of control systems such as management accounting systems. Specific **business** and **environmental** factors will influence the operation of the system, such as organisational structure, technology and the market. The management accountant needs to analyse and present information which takes these specifics into account.

(b) Both types of organisation are going to be interested in the provision of a range of both **financial** and **non-financial information**. On the financial side, both organisations will be interested in measures such as cost control, contribution, profits, return on investment, cash flow measures, liquidity, competitiveness and market share. Non-financial measures will include issues such as product or service quality, levels of innovation, customer satisfaction and flexibility in meeting customer needs quickly.

The main distinction between the two companies is in **organisational structure**. One of the companies operates from one site. Usual methods of cost collection, reporting and profitability analysis will be able to be employed. The other is highly fragmented and so information collection may require more detailed systems and closer monitoring of the operatives working from home.

Performance appraisal of staff will be easier for the manufacturing company, and it may be that the staff identify with the company more strongly and are more motivated to achieve **company objectives**, both because they are contracted employees in the traditional sense and because they work together at one site each day. The homeworking contractors may have less sense of such loyalty and could be motivated mainly by considerations such as adding to their own stock of experience and their hourly rate.

The homeworkers are also likely to be working on their own individual projects or tasks, and could all be facing different problems and issues in the effective performance of their work. The standard management accounting system will not necessarily recognise this. It is also possible that they are being paid at different rates according to their experience (this is less likely to be sustainable in a one-site company), making comparisons of individual profitability more complex.

Many organisations operate with off-site employees, and it is becoming increasingly common to employ **outworkers** as traditional working methods are replaced. Standard reports on activities and profitability, both historical and future, are still capable of being produced despite the fact that off-site employees are now more common. The **collection** of such information may be more complicated, but advances in **technology** and computer links should enable information to be logged from remote sites all over the world if necessary.

This scenario provides an example of how management accounting systems need to be **adapted** to organisational realities. Some techniques may be consistently applied in all organisations (measuring employee productivity, for example) while others will be adapted. The one-site company may find it easier than the fragmented one to establish, define (and therefore control) meaningful **cost centres**. Individual **contract profitability** should be easily measurable by both companies, regardless of staff location, although comparing the costs of off-site employees may need to take pay rate differentials into account, as mentioned above.

Measures such as **return on investment** will be more easily defined in the manufacturing company because it is likely to have significant investment in plant and equipment. For the service company, on the other hand, the chief asset is its body of professional staff, which may have a high turnover and which is less capable of being assessed in this way. As ROI is normally used to apply to investment centres or profit centres it generally reflects the **organisation structure** of the business. As mentioned previously, such centres are more likely to be a feature of the site-based company.

12.7 The S Group

(a) A key task in the strategic management of any company is a willingness and an ability to understand the environment and anticipate future trends. Information will be required at both strategic and operational level. This is known as strategic intelligence, which can be defined as what a company needs to know about its business environment in order to be able to anticipate change and come up with appropriate strategies for the future.

There are many sources of environmental information.

Internal sources, or sources relatively close to the company, may include the sales force. It deals with the customers and so is in a position to obtain customer and competitor information. Stakeholders in the business such as employees, management and shareholders will influence the business and so are also a good source of internal information. It will be appropriate to set up a **database** for this information, containing both financial and non-financial indicators.

The **management information system** may generate information about the environment as well as information on sales, costs, market share and profitability.

External sources of information are various. The media (newspapers, periodicals and television) offer many types of environmental information covering all kinds of environmental issues: social, political, economic and technological. Export consultants might specialise in dealing with particular countries (possibly relevant to a multinational like the S Group thinking about new markets), and academic or trade journals will give information about a wide variety of relevant issues to a particular industry. The S Group is likely to subscribe to some of these. As a large multinational, it may be represented on a trade body (an example is the British Retail Consortium in the UK) where it can meet competitors and discuss issues of interest. The **internet** is also a fruitful source of information.

The **Government** and public **databases** can be a source of statistical data, maybe relating to the money supply, the trade balance and so forth. Stockbrokers provide investment reports which often contain detailed analysis of industries and countries, and specialist consultancy firms can provide information. Universities and academic journals publish research results, with projects often being sponsored by large companies like the S Group.

Using the information

The information can be used in **devising appropriate strategies** for the future direction of the business environment. It is easy to be overwhelmed by the volume of relevant environmental information on offer and the variety of data that could be used, so S must make sure that the information it collects is collated and presented in a **coherent** fashion. This will enable the directors of S to assess the current position of the company and decide upon future strategies appropriate to the business environment.

Assuming that a company the size of S has some kind of **strategic planning function**, then it must make sure that the strategy planning process involves the divisional managers, who will be able to see that the business environment (of which they will be keenly aware) is being taken account of in strategy formulation.

Quality of the information

To be relevant and useful for decision making, the information gathered by S, both internal and external, must be **accurate** and **reliable**. A key priority is an understanding of **why** the information is being collected, and **what** it will be used for. This will indicate the level of detail required.

To be sure of the reliability and accuracy of internal information, **specialists** from the relevant company departments may be required to give assurances on the accuracy of information provided by their systems. Staff 'on the ground', such as the sales staff mentioned earlier, will have a far better knowledge of individual markets and competition activity than strategy setters higher up in the organisation.

Databases must be used with care as they can rapidly go out of date and must be regularly maintained. S should assure itself of the quality of data from both its internal and external databases. Comparing information from various sources can provide checks as to accuracy. As time goes on and S develops more and more **information sources**, it is likely that these sources will fluctuate in number as the less reliable sources are replaced with more accurate ones, and new methods of collecting information are devised.

(b) **ROCE**

By using return on capital employed (ROCE) as a performance measure, S is using an **historical measure** which is no guide to future performance and shows a lack of a forward looking perspective. **Past results** are not necessarily an indication of **future profitability**. Since the manager of AE is judged on this basis, he may be tempted into decisions which increase AE's short-term ROCE. An investment might be desirable from the group's point of view, but would not be in the individual manager's interest to undertake. Thus there is a lack of **goal congruence**. A desire to increase ROCE might lead to projects being taken on without due regard to their **risk**.

If we look at ROCE for the AE division for last year and the previous year, we can see that it has decreased from 10% to 1.24%. This has very little to do with an increase in average capital employed (which has only increased by 1.1% over the year) and everything to do with an erosion in gross profit from 36.7% to 12.5% (see below).

The tiny increase in capital employed probably reflects the fact that there is little incentive for the manager to invest (assuming the investment decision is his to take) because any decisions which reduce ROCE in the short term will reflect badly on his reported performance. It is difficult to comment further on this small increase in capital employed, as no information is given in the scenario.

A **fair comparison** between different divisions using ROCE is not easily achieved. Fixed assets may be of different ages or may be depreciated in different ways. If a division maintains the same annual profit, and keeps the same assets without a policy of replacement, its ROCE will increase year by year as the assets get older. This can give a false impression of improving 'real' performance over time.

Sales and profitability

AE has suffered a reduction in gross profit from $275m to $100m, a decrease of 64%. Head office fixed costs remained constant, but budgeted costs per unit increased from 63% of sales value to 87.5%. This can be attributed to **transfer pricing policy** (see below).

Despite this, it can be demonstrated that the performance of the division last year was an improvement on the previous year.

	Last year	Previous year
Budgeted sales	K$900m	K$900m
Actual sales	K$800m	K$750m
Increase on previous year	6.67%	–
Actual volumes	16,000 units	15,000 units
% short of revenue target	11.1%	16.7%
Contribution volume variance	K$18m (A)	K$60m (A)

Assembly costs increased by 33.3% across the year, which is surprising given the much smaller increase in sales revenue, and the fact that the budgeted increase was 20%. No more information is given on assembly costs to enable further comment, although the divisional manager should certainly examine these costs as they fall under his control.

The **contribution volume variance** is calculated by multiplying the shortfall in unit sales volume from budget by the budgeted contribution per unit. Performance by this measure appears to be much better than the previous year, but it is probably unwise to read too much into this figure as the unit cost structures in both years are so different, with the budgeted contribution being

dramatically reduced last year (from $20,000 to $9,000) after the rise in components transfer costs (which are in any case beyond the control of the divisional manager).

Transfer pricing policy

This is the area of prime concern as regards impact on AE division profitability. Transfer costs have risen to 75% of sales value last year, which compares with 53% in the previous year. They were budgeted at 70% of selling price (50% in the previous year). Total components costs have increased by 50% over the year, with sales up only around 7%.

Questions need to be asked about how the transfer price is being set. If the transferring division is inefficient, it is transferring those inefficiencies to AE, and AE's profitability is being severely affected. Alternatively the head office of S, under pressure to increase returns to its shareholders, may be deliberately imposing a large transfer price in order to cut AE division profits and **minimise its tax** bill in what is a high rate regime. This is likely to be investigated by tax authorities, especially since there has been a big year on year increase.

Either way, the performance of AE is being assessed on factors beyond its control. From the figures given in the question, the transfer pricing policy has contributed to 86% of the division's unit costs and is therefore a highly significant factor in assessing its performance. The board must consider AE's longer-term potential for adding to shareholder value. Assessing its performance using ROCE alone, especially when that return is rendered artificially low by high transfer prices, will be to ignore its future profit potential.

(c) The key objective of the board of S is to **increase shareholder value** and it must ensure that the AE divisional manager's plans fit in with the overall **strategic direction** of the group. Some acquisitions are driven by the personal goals of the acquiring company's managers. Again, the issue of **goal congruence** needs to be addressed. If it is true that the acquisition will enable AE division to increase market share then the board should give the proposal serious consideration.

It is important for the company to understand its reasons for acquisition, and that these reasons should be valid in terms of its strategic plan. The acquisition may give the AE division a new product range, heightened market presence and enable it to consolidate its distribution process, for example. However, the board of S must consider the level of **risk** involved. Acquiring companies in overseas markets is risky.

The divisional manager of AE is likely to believe, seeing as his division is under threat of closure, that the opportunities offered by the acquisition cannot be found within AE itself. However, acquisitions do have associated problems and the board of S may have to consider the following issues:

(i) **Cost**. The deal may be too expensive, or resisted by the target company. The necessary funds may have to be diverted from other group operations. Advice fees (bankers, corporate financiers) may be high.

(ii) The **customers** of the target company may go elsewhere and the promised market share fail to materialise. Has enough **market research** been carried out?

(iii) **Incompatibility**. In general, the problems of assimilating new products, customers, suppliers, markets, employees and different management systems might create problems of 'overload' for AE.

(iv) **Lack of information**. Will the improvements in market share really be achieved? How strong is the competition? Does the AE division have the skills and experience to see the plan through? It has failed to achieve its own turnover targets, so can it manage those of an entirely new company?

Following the analysis presented in part (b), it should be clear to the directors of S that the AE division is improving its performance, despite the transfer pricing policy. This profitability may be jeopardised by the acquisition.

Aside from financial factors such as **expected costs and revenues** (which S must be fully satisfied on if it is to commit funds which could, after all, be deployed elsewhere in the group), the group should bear in mind **non-financial factors** regarding the takeover.

Some major problems of **implementation** may arise relating to human resources and personnel issues, such as morale, performance assessment and culture. If key managers or personnel leave, the business will suffer and future development of the new entity (maybe into more new markets) may be compromised.

This acquisition may well be an opportunity not to be missed, but S must make sure that this is indeed the case and that **market development** is likely to flow from it.

(d)   **Performance measurement** should become more **forward looking** than merely placing a reliance on historical measures such as ROCE. In this way the future of the AE division can be planned with more clarity, and its contribution to increasing shareholder value will be considered over the longer term, although this may clash with some investors who are looking for a **short term return**.

As an increase in shareholder value is a key objective of the business, performance indicators will be required to assess whether or not the management team is fulfilling this duty. The use of what is known as a **shareholder value approach** to performance measurement involves moving the focus of attention away from simply looking at short-term profits to a longer-term view of **value creation**, the motivation being that it will help the business stay ahead in an increasingly competitive market. The success (or otherwise) of the new AE division will contribute to the determination of shareholder value.

Shareholder value analysis

This is defined as 'an approach to financial management which focuses on the creation of economic value for shareholders, as measured by share price performance and flow of dividends'. The main premise is that a business is worth the net present value of its **future cash flows**, and these are driven by the following factors: sales growth, operating margin, fixed capital investment, working capital investment, cash taxes, the planning period and the cost of capital.

It follows that these are therefore the factors that the directors of S need to focus on when measuring the performance of the AE division.

When looking at future sales growth and margin, the directors will want to see whether the divisional manager's forecasts of increased **market share** have been realised, but will also need to extrapolate **forecast trends** in the market. This may include a consideration of new products.

Investment in both fixed and working capital will be required if growth is to be **sustained**. Forecast cash flows may need to be revised if growth and return to shareholders is to be achieved. Additional funding may be required.

The level of **corporation tax** borne by the AE division has been high in the past. S has sought to mitigate its effects via its transfer pricing policy, but this may not be viable in the longer term (the policy is onerous, as we saw in part (b)) and S may need to look again at **tax planning** for the division.

The cost of funding the project is fundamental to its success in increasing shareholder value. If the **incremental value** of the acquisition is in excess of the **cost of capital**, then **shareholder value** will be added. The cost of capital should be minimised, and any changes to it reflected in revised NPV calculations.

Economic value management

This is another form of strategic value analysis and hinges on the calculation of **economic profit (EP)**. The calculation of EP requires several **adjustments** to be made to **traditionally reported accounting profits**. These are intended to produce a figure for capital employed which is a more accurate reflection of the base upon which shareholders except their returns to accrue, and to provide a figure which is a more realistic measure of the **actual cash generated** for shareholders from recurring business activities.

In the case of the AE division, adjustments could be made to take the transfer price items out of the calculation and apply a **notional cost of capital** to the adjusted profit. This would eliminate the somewhat artificial (and high) transfer price from the consideration of the **economic value added** by the division. The figures would read as follows:

		Last year K$m	*Previous year* K$m
Sales		800	750
Division costs	– assembly	(100)	(75)
	– head office	(75)	(75)
Cost of capital (say 12%)		(242)	(240)
EVA		383	360

This analysis can be carried further and presented in terms of future expectations for the new division. This will enable future performance to be planned and any action taken that may be necessary to ensure that the acquisition continues to deliver acceptable results.

712 | Practice answer bank

INDEX

Note: **Key Terms** and their references are given in **bold**.

Review Form – Paper E3 Strategic Management (01/18)

Please help us to ensure that the CIMA learning materials we produce remain as accurate and user-friendly as possible. We cannot promise to answer every submission we receive, but we do promise that it will be read and taken into account when we update this Study Text.

Name: _____ **Address:** _____

_____

_____

How have you used this Study Text?
(Tick one box only)

☐ Home study (book only)

☐ On a course: college _____

☐ With 'correspondence' package

☐ Other _____

Why did you decide to purchase this Study Text? *(Tick one box only)*

☐ Have used BPP Texts in the past

☐ Recommendation by friend/colleague

☐ Recommendation by a lecturer at college

☐ Saw information on BPP website

☐ Saw advertising

☐ Other _____

During the past six months do you recall seeing/receiving any of the following?
(Tick as many boxes as are relevant)

☐ Our advertisement in *Financial Management*

☐ Our advertisement in *Pass*

☐ Our advertisement in *PQ*

☐ Our brochure with a letter through the post

☐ Our website www.bpp.com

Which (if any) aspects of our advertising do you find useful?
(Tick as many boxes as are relevant)

☐ Prices and publication dates of new editions

☐ Information on Text content

☐ Facility to order books off-the-page

☐ None of the above

Which BPP products have you used?

Text	☑	Passcard	☐
Kit	☐	i-Pass	☐

Your ratings, comments and suggestions would be appreciated on the following areas.

	Very useful	Useful	Not useful
Introductory section	☐	☐	☐
Chapter introductions	☐	☐	☐
Key terms	☐	☐	☐
Quality of explanations	☐	☐	☐
Case studies and other examples	☐	☐	☐
Exam skills and alerts	☐	☐	☐
Questions and answers in each chapter	☐	☐	☐
Chapter overview and summary diagrams	☐	☐	☐
Quick quizzes	☐	☐	☐
Question Bank	☐	☐	☐
Answer Bank	☐	☐	☐
OT Bank	☐	☐	☐
Index	☐	☐	☐

Overall opinion of this Study Text	Excellent ☐	Good ☐	Adeqate ☐	Poor ☐

Do you intend to continue using BPP products? Yes ☐   No ☐

On the reverse of this page is space for you to write your comments about our Study Text. We welcome your feedback.

The BPP Learning Media author team can be emailed at: cimaqueries@bpp.com

TELL US WHAT YOU THINK

Please note any further comments and suggestions/errors below. For example, was the text accurate, readable, concise, user-friendly and comprehensive?